Love
Can Build
a Bridge

Love Can Build a Bridge

Naomi Judd

VILLARD BOOKS
NEW YORK 1993

Since we're all much wiser and more together now, I've changed the names of a few characters in this book. Doctors respect patients' confidentiality, so I've likewise protected them by not using their real names.

All rights reserved under International and Pan-American Copyright Conventions. Published in the United States by Villard Books, a division of Random House, Inc., New York, and simultaneously in Canada by Random House of Canada Limited, Toronto.

Villard Books is a registered trademark of Random House, Inc.

Library in Congress Cataloging-in-Publication Data

Judd, Naomi.
    Love can build a bridge/by Naomi Judd—1st ed.
        p.   cm.
    ISBN 0-679-41247-6
    1. Judd, Naomi.   2. Judds (Musical group)   3. Country musicians—
United States—Biography.
    I. Title
    ML420.J87A3   1992b   782.42164'2'0922—dc20   92-53656
    [B]   CIP
                                          MN

Design by ROBERT BULL DESIGN

Manufactured in the United States of America on acid-free paper

9 8 7 6 5 4 3 2

First edition

This book is lovingly dedicated to my future grandchildren and their descendants. This is who we are and how we lived.

The written word may be man's greatest invention. It allows us to converse with the dead, the absent, and the unborn.

—Abraham Lincoln

ACKNOWLEDGMENTS

I'VE NEVER EVEN read a book on how to write a book. One night when I was praying about whether I could do this or not I got a message: The Judds' lives had a voice of their own—just sit perfectly still, be silent, and listen to it.

That's what I've done for the last two years secluded at my farm, Peaceful Valley. I got so far into it I walked through a hole in time and really got out in the cosmic lost and found. Larry, Wynonna, and Ashley claimed me and pulled me back in.

When I'd begin to feel as if my own life was like pages of a novel torn out and scattered by shifting gusts of fortune, my confidante, whom I'll call The North Star, helped me put them back in order.

I thank you, my dear family, for your trust in allowing me to share my version, my perception of our private lives, and for rooting me in dynastic awareness of our shared history. You pulled back the curtain and allowed me to see the little girl who grew up to be me, and to understand all of us as human beings.

Diane Reverand, you're a class act! I thought editors were supposed to be ogres! In fact I've enjoyed working with everyone at Villard Books, and this may be the smoothest collaboration ever.

Once again I've come to appreciate our symbiotic relationship with the media, as I had excellent documentation of our career at my disposal.

Gee thanks, Bud Schaetzle, for assistance with some of the preliminary research, "grunt work" as you put it, to help me get organized so I could concentrate on writing this book, and to Deborah, Sloan, Peggy, and Dorthey for great office help.

Ken Stilts, Martha Taylor, and Chuck Thompson, as usual you've made me use the left side of my brain. Nobody said this would be easy!

I am so grateful to the everyday folks out there who offer words of encouragement as we pass on the street and to the dear fans who surround us like a circle of light.

Our lives and music are audience participation. So is this book.

CONTENTS

And if You Look Real Close You'll See Our Eyes Are Just the Same

*C*HRISTINA CLAIRE CIMINELLA en-
tered this world screaming on key and searching for harmony.
She was thrust into the eye of the Judd family hurricane on
May 30, 1964, attended by the same nurse who had overseen my own
birth in the very same room, only eighteen years before. Christina
arrived at King's Daughters Hospital, a block from our house, in
sleepy Ashland, Kentucky, just as I had when my own eighteen-year-
old mother had me. It was a quiet moment of personal joy for humble
parents hardly prepared for the greatest job on earth. At Christina's
birth, I crossed the threshold to adulthood, ready or not, and took
the first baby step on a giant adventure.

Christina and I plunged headlong into an epic, lifelong search
for harmony that would alternately unite and divide us a thousand
times. A journey that would see us grow up together, scale impossible
heights as partners, and embrace the elusive rhythms of a unique
mother-daughter relationship. Some say we helped to reshape the
history of country music in the process, but for us the experience was
deeply intimate and richly private—even though we lived it in the
public eye. It's been quite a modern fairy tale, what this infant
brought into my life and the lives of millions of other people, but in
1964 there were other, more pressing matters on my mind.

All I knew right then was that I had given birth to a healthy,
beautiful little girl. I had somehow known my child would be a girl;
I had had a powerfully instinctive feeling months before and had

already picked her name. She would be called Christina Claire, and it would fit her perfectly. Much later, of course, she would become "Wynonna," and that too would fit her perfectly. We are not born with our destinies stamped on our foreheads.

When the nurse brought my baby in, I looked into her face and saw myself—her eyes, her skin, her expressions, her spirit. She looked up at me and smiled her first hello. A broad and mischievous grin lit up her face, a sign that told me in no uncertain terms that this was a child to be reckoned with, a child who would be worthy of great things. From that moment on my heart was all hers. I was terrified, elated, proud, and complete . . . all at once. We began our lifelong search for harmony with slow and halting steps, a teenage mother and an unplanned child on a journey that would lead to magic and milestones that neither of us had dreamed possible. Wynonna and I were instantly one, a partnership, a team—just the two of us against a frightening and unknown world. On that spring day in 1964, we began our wonderful duet, a blend of heart, mind, and soul that continues to this day.

This is our story.

NAOMI JUDD
Peaceful Valley
Franklin, Tennessee
October 1993

Love
Can Build
a Bridge

Grandpa, Tell Me 'Bout the Good Old Days

*A*S FAR BACK as I can remember, people would pat me on the head and say, "My goodness, what a pretty little girl. You look like a perfect little China doll." I assumed they were telling the truth, because adults told me so and I never questioned grown-ups. It seemed I was special, and this was the way the world was meant to be. Then, it was all very simple to me, Diana Ellen Judd, the first child of Polly and Glen Judd of Ashland, Kentucky . . . the center of the universe.

I've realized in the forty-seven years since my birth that your reality comes from the way you see things—or rather from the way you need to see them. As a child, my reality was radiance, warmth, and light: bright morning sunshine when Mommy came in to wake me, the blinding glare of high noon when I went to the filling station to bring Daddy his lunch, and the hazy summer afternoon glow at the old Judd family farm in the country with my grandparents and all my aunts and uncles. I knew my family, like that light, existed simply because of me, and it followed that their only purpose in life was to bring me joy. I knew in my heart I was the reason they lived and breathed, the pride of their lives and the core of their substance. Light was everywhere and life was good. The darkness that would creep in around the edges was a long way off when I was a little girl in Ashland.

I grew up in the northeast corner of the Bluegrass State along the Ohio–West Virginia border, just a stone's throw from the coal mining towns of West Virginia, near the fertile horse country of central Kentucky in the lush Ohio Valley. Surrounded by rolling green hills and awash in the scent of goldenrod, the Judd roots were firmly planted in this rich Kentucky soil on the rim of the Appalachians. We all knew the state motto: United we stand, divided we fall. In retrospect, it's a piece of advice we all might have taken closer to heart, but in the late 1940s and early 1950s my idyllic small town on the Ohio River was perfectly beautiful. I was born in an era when promises were kept, doors went unlocked, and God was as real as our house.

During my childhood, my family was—and to this day remains—quite a cast of colorful characters. I suppose we, like all Appalachian clans, did the best we could, handling, with a minimum of fuss, life's challenges as they presented themselves. What I took for strength and character as a child, I would much later mourn as something entirely different.

My Daddy was quiet, proud, and rarely showed much affection, but I knew he loved me beyond any shadow of a doubt. He was what some would call a simple man, a hardworking native son who put food on the table for his family and ran a reputable small business. From my child's perspective, he had every answer I would ever need. My memories of him are cast in specifics, snapshots of a man I wish I had known more and understood better.

I would play outside our house with Trouble, our beloved beagle, and hear the distinctive sound of Daddy's old black truck coming up Twenty-third Street. Running as fast as my little legs would carry me, I'd fly to our front gate, Trouble yapping behind me, and would greet him at the top of the steps. Daddy carried with him manly scents that I can recall to this day: the essence of gasoline, oil, and sweat—the staples of his day at work. I'd hug and kiss him and tell him that I loved him, but Daddy never reached out to me and kissed me back in quite the same way. He kept his feelings to himself, but I knew that he loved me back. I knew it because Daddy always had our school pictures cellophane-taped to the cash register at work. What I couldn't get from him firsthand came down indirectly. It was always a quiet source of pride to see my picture there in his mysterious father-world. Once in a while I even overheard him bragging about me to other people.

Daddy owned an old-fashioned gas station with a red-tiled roof and a big sign that read, JUDD'S ASHLAND SERVICE. In front of the station stood a big blue soda cooler where I could get a bottle of pop anytime I wanted. Inside was a shiny glass case filled with every kind of candy bar. Air fresheners in clear plastic coverings hung on the wall; the skunk and Christmas tree air fresheners were down low. The girls in bikinis were hung much higher so that little kids couldn't see them, but my brothers and I stared at them every chance we got. The cardboard girls looked glamorous and grown-up and happy to be that way. Was it possible that someday I could grow up to look like that?

To the left of the counter was a pinball machine. Lester Cassidy, Luther Cassell, and Baldy Baldwin would swagger into Daddy's station on their lunch break to play a game. They'd look down and pat my head and smile at me. I'd smile back as cute as I could, so they would reach into their jangling pockets with their big hands and give me nickels. I'd get up on the pop case and play pinball like crazy. The men would watch, smoking unfiltered cigarettes and laughing loudly between snippits of conversation that sounded far too foreign and adult ever to comprehend.

Sometimes I could look out in the back and see Hicks washing cars. Hicks was an aging black man with four teeth and the yellowest eyes I'd ever seen. Every now and then, he'd drop by the station, strike up a conversation with Daddy, and wind up washing cars for wine money. He was gentle and quick to laugh, but my affections were reserved for another of my Daddy's helpers.

I would squeal with delight if Slick McGloan would stop and wink at me. Slick was Daddy's regular helper at the station, a country guy with black hair and sideburns just like Elvis, and I thought that he was the most handsome man in the whole world. He had crinkles around his eyes, he was older and mysterious, and I knew his wife had to look just like the girls-in-bikinis air fresheners above the candy counter. I was completely and totally in love with him.

When Daddy got tired of me hanging around the station and jumping on the rubber cable that signaled a customer, he'd send me on home. Mom would be in the kitchen . . . it seemed as if she was always in the kitchen. There was so much to do and so little time that her days were filled to the brim with domesticity. To my dying day I'll be able to close my eyes and feel the warmth of that room; summon the aromas of her cooking; and hear the sounds of silver clinking, water running, and the tinny radio playing over in the cupboard by the pencil sharpener.

The kitchen was the hub of our world, and it was always Mom's domain, subject to her rules and operating on a schedule that she set. When she finally got a washer and dryer, she put them right next to the sink and the stove so she wouldn't have to move to another part of the house to use them. Sometimes she'd sit at the table and share a cup of coffee and some gossip with our neighbor, Ruth Puffen-berger, a loquacious woman who loved to visit and chain-smoke cigarettes. They talked about grown-up things in hushed voices, things that always seemed to happen to other people. It was exotic to me . . . adult and mysterious. Sometimes they would shake their heads and cluck sadly over some poor acquaintance who'd fallen on hard times, but most of the time I would hear them laughing.

The best thing about Mom was that she was always there. Over the two decades I lived in Ashland, I came home only four times and didn't find her there. I vividly remember the occasions, because it was so unusual for her not to be home. Mom was a full-time homemaker twenty-four hours a day, seven days a week, three hundred and sixty-five days a year. It was her lot in life, and for years she bore it well. She had the attitude of many mothers: "Let the men run around trying to change the world. I just want to improve my family."

My Daddy subscribed to the tightfistedness that is often a hallmark of hardscrabble country origins. He wasn't raised to spend money blithely on fancy things, or "unnecessary extravagances," as he put it. Daddy's only pleasures were Camel cigarettes, Mickey Spillane novels, and sometimes, if he had time, squirrel hunting. Mom's only luxuries were her two rose bushes in our backyard, and reading. She never went to the beauty parlor and never had any good makeup or perfume. A bottle of Jergen's hand lotion was the nicest thing I can remember her having, but that never stopped her from laughing.

In true Appalachian stoic fashion, Mom never complained. Everybody adored her because she possessed a sharp wit and a lively sense of humor, taking energetic delight in having fun. While other mothers were out shopping for hats and new dresses, or playing bridge, Mom cheerfully turned our house into the center of activity for the kids on our block. She'd always dream up something inventive for us to do. If it was raining she'd set up card tables on the front porch so we could play Monopoly. In the wintertime, we used the card tables with blankets for tents in the living room. She made us popcorn in the evening while we listened to the radio. She told us riddles and jokes and kidded us about anything and everything. Even though we were on a woefully tight budget, Mom would save her pennies for special treats like the small sacks of warm cashews we would get at the dime store. When she spontaneously bought me the shiny red scooter I was admiring at Ben Williamson's Hardware Store, she had to negotiate with Daddy like the secretary general of the United Nations!

Before we were old enough to start school, Mom instilled in us a love for books. She believed the church and the library were two of the most important places in the world, so we got library cards the day we learned to read. Mom would get us kids to read the cereal boxes out loud during breakfast. One of her greatest accomplishments was talking penny-pinching Daddy into buying us a set of encyclopedias. She often reminded us that "reading is to the mind what exercise is to the body." One of the first words a mother teaches her kids is *look*. My Mom taught us how to look and see.

I had a girlfriend whose father ran the hotel in town. Barbara Parmalee lived in the Ventura Hotel and got to eat every meal in its restaurant, The Dinner Bell. I thought she had it made in the shade, but Barbara used to beg to spend the night at my house. Mom was the best cook around and our house was always hectic and messy, completely different from the quiet and proper hotel full of strangers. Our attic was full of favorite old toys and long-forgotten objects. The basement was dark and creepy, and smelled dank and musty. And there was my mother in the middle of it all, always smiling down on us and always up to her own brand of mischief. One night my brother's best friend, Jimmie Fannin, came over to spend the night and Mom expertly short-sheeted his bed.

My brother Glenn Brian was two years younger and my best buddy. He had red hair and bore a strong resemblance to Opie on the old *Andy Griffith Show,* which made him the object of considerable ribbing. He was in fact a charismatic child, the kind of little boy you really did see only in the movies. Full of tricks and jokes, possessed of a wicked temper, Brian was a source of much amusement around the Judd home. I was utterly devoted to him. We would fight like cats and dogs, always prodding each other, needling, and teasing. Once he got so mad, he chased me with a brick and threatened to crack my skull. I gulped and insisted, "Seriously now, Brian, you need to put that brick down. You know you'd miss me something awful if you killed me."

He shrugged in agreement, half-smiled at me, and good-naturedly dropped it. I felt lucky to have such a warm and clever little brother and was convinced he was special. I always wanted to protect him, a feeling that was so strong I must have sensed our lives together wouldn't last forever.

After saving our allowances, we walked downtown one Saturday to the Capitol Theater to see *Fiend Without a Face.* It was a black-and-white B movie about aliens that looked like disembodied brains with long stems that could somehow enter your skull. As we watched the movie in the empty theater we became petrified; Brian and I held our hands over our eyes and shrieked whenever a brain monster appeared. We couldn't wait to get out of that theater, but we hung in there until the film ended. As we stepped outside we were horrified to discover it was turning dark. It was fall and daylight had grown shorter. This presented an interesting dilemma: how to get home without being accosted by lurking alien brain monsters. We took a deep breath and decided to run all the way home holding hands. We took off down Winchester Avenue, which for the first time in my life seemed ominous and threatening. We crossed through Central Park and it was so shadowy and spooky that Brian began to cry. It just broke my heart, that little boy crying as it kept getting darker and colder. I tried to hold him and comfort him, but he wouldn't let me, because after all I was a girl, so I just held tightly on to his hand. The brain monsters never got into our skulls, and we made it home in one piece. Although we never spoke about it again, that night on our way to bed I caught a sparkle in his eyes that told me he knew I would be there for him no matter what . . . for life.

The little guy was unusually sensitive. I guess that was why I felt close to him. When we'd watch television together and someone was dying on *Dr. Kildare,* Brian would bawl his eyes out. That made him very special to me; he was somehow different from all the other children I knew. Even though he was as rambunctious and lively as any kid our age, when he contracted the usual childhood diseases he seemed to be hit harder than the rest of us. He would fall very ill, whether it was measles, chicken pox, or whatever. I gradually became aware that his health was his Achilles' heel.

Christopher Mark was born when I was four. I thought he was the neatest thing that ever happened. It was great to have a real live baby in the house. I knew that my Mom and Daddy must have had him for me and me alone. I laid aside my dollies and played at motherhood with the real thing. He beamed whenever he saw me, and when Mark spoke his first word it was *Diana.* Because he was such a beautiful baby, I told people he'd won lots of baby contests.

From the beginning Mark was a quiet child, probably because of his placement in the family. He always had to follow in Brian's shadow. When Mark moved out of his baby bed, he and Brian shared a room together, and from that day on they became a team. They were inseparable.

Mark was a collector of things. He collected baseball cards and money. He'd hoard his allowance like a miniature Ebenezer Scrooge and was constantly on the lookout for secret places to hide it. He set up elaborate booby traps for me because I liked to sneak into his room, mess up his baseball cards, and find his money and count it. I would then announce the amount at the supper table in front of everyone so he couldn't hit me. Mark never fought with anyone and was well liked, but Brian and I delighted in putting him up to pranks. Mark always got the blame for things, for instance, when James McDonald and Brian put cherry bombs under our neighbor's metal garbage cans. Mark evolved into a thoughtful and somewhat pensive boy, sensitive and caring, but revealing many of our father's reticent traits.

The final spoke in the family wheel came when I was six: Margaret Victoria was the last of Glen and Polly Judd's children. I remember with clarity the day they brought her home. The six of us slept in the same room for a long time. From the very beginning it was clear she would be a source of excitement and challenge. There was healthy friction between us as she grew older, the type of competition that can only exist between two siblings cut from the same cloth. She was always streaking around with her grubby, noisy little friends and showering an inexhaustible amount of energy on all of us. Margaret was a genuine nuisance to me as I self-consciously strove toward adolescence. Still, I was glad to have a sister. I saw a lot of myself in her from the beginning, and we would eventually become very close, during a crucial period in our adult lives.

Surviving the awkward trials of being a budding teenager was sometimes made even harder by the irritating presence of a pesky little sister. When I began to date, she'd bolt for the door, throw it open, and proudly inform the poor unsuspecting boy that I was still in my housecoat and big pink curlers. She'd describe with glee how ugly I was without makeup and how long I spent in the bathroom getting ready. Now, don't get me wrong, Margaret was a heart stealer. With her soft blond curls and beautiful face, she was angelic looking. Everyone commented on how well behaved she was. Still, none of this stopped me from nicknaming her "Maggot."

Squabble as we did, like all brothers and sisters, there was always the absolute conviction that we were a family. This was the ultimate, immutable core of our world; it was a given. Daddy worked like a brute at the station to support us and keep our world safe and secure. Mom was at home to soothe us when we were hurt, to put hot meals in front of us when we were hungry, and to have clean clothes for us to put on each morning. They shaped us with a steady but subtle force, like drops of water carving stone. This sameness of family ritual and response gave us our security. Our universe was 2237 Montgomery Avenue, and in its benign, unchanging cradle we each in his or her own way flourished.

. . .

Daddy was raised in the country, and I do mean in the country. My favorite part of childhood was when Daddy drove us out to the original Judd homestead, which his great-grandparents, Fanny and Elijah, had bought with Elijah's pension at the end of the Civil War. It was a nice, white, two-story frame house with a porch all the way across the front, situated on more than one hundred acres of fertile soil.

Elijah Judd was a Yankee sergeant in the mounted infantry, and in 1865 he settled down in Louisa, Kentucky's wilderness to become a farmer. He also gained a reputation as a formidable frontier adjudicator and was a greatly respected man. People came from far and near to have him settle disputes. Elijah hadn't gone to law school but was apparently so wise and fair that everyone respected his opinion. From what we know, he was a good and gentle man whose work ethic was proudly handed down to his descendants.

Elijah and Fanny Judd had seven children. The first daughter, Mary Jane, would suffer a bleak destiny. From her love affair with the area's only doctor she gave birth to a son, but her father, Elijah, refused to allow her to marry the baby's father. Her son, Roy Ogden, would one day become my grandfather. My Granddaddy told me his first memory was sitting at his mother's bedside when she died; she was only in her twenties. Ogden was then raised by his grandparents, Fanny and Elijah, and can be seen at their knee in the Judd family portrait taken in the 1890s. Coincidentally, both Elijah and Fanny lost an eye in separate accidents.

One of their other daughters, Margaret Ann, lived to a ripe old age and eventually took over the original Judd homeplace. Great-Aunt Margie was tall, gaunt, and quite homely. She never married and was privately thought of as an old maid. Margie was very genteel, proper, and correct. She was well educated, and each time we'd visit her she'd always ask me about my grades. Aunt Margie looked forward to our coming, because Mom brought her stacks of our old magazines. When I hugged her, she smelled musty, and she always wore a hair net and long skirts or dresses that almost touched the floor. I never saw her in anything but long sleeves—even on the hottest, most humid Kentucky summer days. I asked her once, "Why

don't you wear shorts or halter tops and go barefooted like me?"
Daddy quickly suggested I go look for crawdads in the creek.

Aunt Margie lived in the big house with Zora, her distant
cousin. I loved Aunt Margie, but I was just plain crazy about Zora.
I remember Daddy telling me that Zora showed up on Aunt Margie's
doorstep, because they were both alone and complemented each
other. They needed to combine their survival skills to make it. Zora
fell right into place beside Aunt Margie and became the de facto
handyman. Zora built the fences, planted the garden, and did all the
"man's work" around the place. She had shiny coal black hair, which
was pulled back into a tight bun, and her skin was very dark from
working in the fields. She was quite a beautiful woman. In the winter,
Zora would layer on clothes as the temperature dropped, all sorts of
mismatched crazy things. She was a very curious sight. During our
drive to Louisa, Brian and I would have a contest to see who could
come closest to guessing how many articles of clothing Zora would
have on.

As she grew older and her eyesight began to fail, Zora just kept
layering on eyeglasses too. She'd take the wire frames from one pair
and wrap them around the frames of another until she was looking
through two or three lenses at a time to get the magnification she
needed. I even saw her once with two hats on! To us youngsters, she
seemed a kindred, childlike spirit whose disdain for rules and the
expectations of others rang true. I adored everything about her, and
in retrospect, I learned a lot from her about being my own person.

Together with Zora, Aunt Margie ran the Judd General Store,
right down the road from the big house. Zora couldn't divide or
multiply; all she could do was add and subtract, which must have
made for some fairly interesting accounting at the store. I remember
the one-room building as a miniature variety store offering locals
everything from farm implements to articles of clothing, from feed to
food. Zora delighted in taking us to the store and handing out
Zagnut candy bars.

Daddy told me about the first time Zora had ridden in a car. He
had taken her into town to see Margie, who was sick and in Louisa's
tiny country hospital. Daddy turned on the radio, and quick as a flash,
Zora jumped out of the slow-moving vehicle and ran around to the

rear bumper. My Daddy, puzzled, asked her what she was doing, and Zora told him, "I'm a lookin' for the cord!"

She thought Daddy had forgotten to unplug the radio before they started off. The streetlights were the most amazing thing she'd ever seen in her life. Zora was quite a character.

The ancestral homeplace couldn't have had more opposite but perfect tenants. Zora kept the grass mowed and Margie planted wild roses around the porch and added a swing. The farmhouse was primitive but clean. Later there was electricity for some lights, but never any indoor plumbing. It had a little coal-grate fireplace in the living room and a wood cookstove in the teeny kitchen. Pots and pans hung from nails pounded into the walls. The table was covered with a square of oil cloth. I never missed a chance to threaten to throw my sister, Margaret, down the deep, dark well out by the back porch.

We still talk about one time when we were there for Sunday dinner. The grown-ups talked on the front porch while Zora went for a chicken in the barnyard. She grabbed up her hatchet and whacked its head off in the blink of an eye. The bloody chicken dropped to the ground then jumped up and flopped around as if it were furious about losing its head. We kids shrieked at the top of our lungs and ran wildly into the woods. Zora stood there speechless, thoroughly perplexed that we didn't perform this ritual for our own chicken dinners.

The dappled woods bordering the house, shot through with enchanting summer sunlight and cool, dark green shadows, were magic to me. I never liked to be dirty, but it was a small sacrifice to make for being turned loose in those marvelous hills. I felt the most incredible sense of freedom there, and my rich imagination soared. I roamed and prowled like a wild animal. In the living shelter of the forest I was free to become my alter egos: the Indian Princess Skydancer, or an alien from a far galaxy named Zeeper, who was visiting Earth for the first time.

Louisa is not just one of my fondest childhood memories, but one of the most influential experiences of my life. It's been said the only two lasting bequests parents can give their children are roots and wings. It was here I saw land that wasn't just held in place by roots from trees, wildflowers, and crops, but by people.

Daddy would sit in the shade by the fields our ancestors had plowed and tell me stories about them that made them real people to me. He'd pick a potato from the garden or an apple from a tree and slice it with his pocket knife. As he lifted the piece to his mouth on the blade of his knife, I sometimes saw him as an aging boy. It was here I came to feel a spiritual connection to the land and was molded into becoming our family historian.

When I stood in the Judd family cemetery, just up the dirt road from the house, those committed to the silent memory of God sang to me in the voice of yesterday. You can't see peace, but you can feel it.

Daddy and most of his five sisters were born in a cabin on a hill directly across from the main house. Aunts Pauline, Evelyn Watseka, Mariolive, Ramona, and Faith would take me to the remains of the one-room school and log church they had attended. I saw that they too could walk to the cornerstones of their little world. One of my favorite stories they told about my Daddy was that he would hide when time came to go into town. Although usually an obedient child, I took to doing the same thing when my parents would start "yooo-hooing" for us to return to the city.

Later, there was a second farm, not far from the original homestead, bought by Grandmommy and Granddaddy Judd while I was young. We called it Little Catt, because Little Catt Creek flowed through it. Daddy's oldest sister, dear Aunt Pauline, lived there.

Shy, tenderhearted, and introverted, she remains one of my all-time favorite people. Slightly plump, she wore her short gray hair pulled to the side with a barrette, and rolled her thick stockings down below her knees. Because she was missing a few front teeth, she always raised her hand to cover her mouth when she laughed—and Aunt Pauline laughed a lot. She'd declare, "Well I swanee!" or "They lands!" I watched her talking to animals in her own secret language. She helped me understand that we are related to all living things. I never remember her having fewer than six dogs, and there were more like a dozen dogs at Little Catt Farm. She named every animal on the place, usually after presidents and other politicians. And Aunt Pauline taught me to make her delicious applesauce cake on her wood-burning stove. Once I asked her if she'd ever thought about getting indoor plumbing and she just looked at me and asked, "What for?"

Her barebones farmhouse could best be described as "decorating takes a holiday." For there were no pictures on the walls, only a calendar from the feed store and a few nails for her plain clothes. No need for a living room either, since she never entertained guests. Instead, we all sat on the screened-in back porch. She chose a simple life close to the land to escape the confusion and roar of modern life.

As Aunt Pauline handed me an extra quilt one night, she advised, "You'll be needing this. We'll have snow by morning."

I awoke in the middle of the night and peeked out the small window in the upstairs bedroom. There was a bright splash of moonlight on the meadow beside the farmhouse, and large fluffy snowflakes were beginning to fall toward earth. I decided to find out just how Aunt Pauline could predict such amazing things without the aid of any meteorological equipment.

"Well, Di honey, I just smell it in the air," she answered casually at breakfast.

"Now please be more specific," I insisted.

"Take a look at the hubcaps I've hung out on the fence posts," she began. "I put bird seed in 'em and cardinals were feedin' right heavy. And the cows came across the ridge early last night and headed straight for the barn. I figure we're in for a right smart snappy winter this year 'cause the animals have unusually thick fur and the well water's frigid."

Aunt Pauline would remind me, "Diana Ellen, you be sure and start home when it's two fingers and no later."

She had shown me to close my fingers and hold them horizontally between the bottom of the sun and the top of the tallest ridge. When those two fingers filled up the space between the bottom of the sun and the top of the ridge, I knew it was time to start back to the farmhouse. Each finger at that time worked out to be about ten minutes, so if there were two fingers' worth of sunlight left, I had twenty minutes to get on home.

These were full-on country people with a natural, endemic Appalachian wisdom. Every piece of information, every snippit of advice, every down-home do-it-yourself shortcut, every herbal remedy conveyed a feeling of common sense that was refreshing. They leaned heavily on their intuition. It just flowed out of them in fascinating bits and pieces, as second nature to them as tying my shoes was to me. While others search their whole lives for it, they knew where they fit in the scheme of things. When I was a girl, I assumed everybody had eccentric relatives like this who knew such wonderful things.

I attended Crabbe Grade School in Ashland, a foreboding cut-rock building that looked medieval, set on the perimeter of Central Park. The radiators clanged and hissed in the winter and sometimes stopped working altogether, driving us out to the cloakroom to fetch our coats to wear during class. I can still remember the disinfectant odor of the washroom and the unpleasant smells of the cafeteria. Lunches then were thirty cents and an extra carton of milk three cents. The food was awful, but Mom made me tasty lunches with sandwiches wrapped in wax paper. I would ask to eat outside because it upset me that classmates from poor families had to work in the kitchen, serving food or washing off messy tables to get free lunches. It seemed humiliating and unfair for children and disturbed me greatly.

My brothers and sister and I were good students and we made the honor roll. Daddy wouldn't have it any other way and gave us a dime for each A. When I was fourteen, our seventh-grade homeroom teacher, in a snit, gave the entire class "whispers too much" on our report cards. I had all A's but nonetheless got a spanking for this bad behavior mark. Daddy had just stripped wallpaper in the front hall. While he ate dinner, I painted a huge mural on the bare space of a villainous man beating a helpless haloed little girl. She was bleeding profusely and holding a perfect report card. It made Daddy madder than a beaver with a toothache and got me a second spanking. I decided to give up painting forever. I did however appeal to the principal and got the mark reversed. In silent protest, I didn't speak to Daddy for a week.

Daddy didn't have to use the belt on me very often, because I loved to learn. Mom said learning was high-energy brain food to fuel me for my journeys through life. I also wanted the teachers to like me.

For that matter, I wanted everyone to like me. I genuinely loved people and hoped they knew it. It was extremely important to me.

My Daddy's way of showing he loved us was to work those extra hours at the station so I could have braces on my teeth or take those piano lessons I wanted. And he worked so very hard. All I ever saw him dressed in were his work clothes. His station was the cleanest gas station in town, with the fastest service and the best prices. The cans of motor oil were lined up with the labels facing forward, the tires were lined up like shiny soldiers, the countertops sparkled. Daddy was Ashland Oil's Filling Station Operator of the Year every year. When we'd be out around town, he'd drive by other stations to check them out. And that was his life.

He rarely had time to eat meals with us. Mom would put leftovers in a brown paper sack, and then we'd all jump in the car and run them over to Daddy for his lunch. Once in a while, when he got good help and felt he could leave the gas station, he'd come home to eat an evening meal with us, but not too often. Usually, it was just me, Mom, my two brothers, and my sister around the dinner table and sometimes our friends. Daddy would come home at 9:00 P.M., lather up with Lava soap, and eat a warmed-up plate on a TV tray in the living room. He'd chain-smoke a few Camels in his favorite chair, read Mickey Spillane, and go up to bed. On Friday night we watched *Gillette Cavalcade of Sports Boxing.* I was the only eight-year-old girl in town who knew the rules of the World Boxing Association and could name the reigning champ in each division. I'll never forget the night I won fifty cents on Chico Bejar.

Showing affection to each other never came easy for my parents; in fact, it hardly came at all. I realize now one of the greatest things a father can do for his children is to love their mother. I never once in my whole life saw my mother and father hug or kiss. Nope, not even one time. Robert Mitchum was my favorite movie star because he reminded me of my Daddy. I'd go to the movies on Saturday afternoons and pretend it was Daddy and Mommy when Robert Mitchum was kissing Ava Gardner. My folks very rarely went out to a movie or did anything social together, and they never had another couple over to our house. Daddy seldom ever gave Mom anything for Christmas or her birthday.

One occasion he did give her a blue nylon nightgown, and I exclaimed in shocked surprise, "Mommy, look what Daddy got you!"

She looked the nightgown over sadly and said something that broke my heart. "Well, he didn't buy it till Christmas Eve when I guess he thought he had to."

Looking closer I saw then that the nightgown was sort of cheap and wasn't the right size, but she accepted it just the same. There was something passing between them in those days that didn't make sense to me until much later.

But Mom wasn't much of a complainer; she was so self-sacrificing. She never demanded anything from Daddy and never stuck up for what she thought she might deserve. If she wanted more, who could she ask? I pondered this long and hard, because what I was witnessing at home bore little resemblance to how the parents of my friends treated each other. When I learned more about Mom's family background I began to understand what made her so long-suffering.

Cora Lee Burton, my mother's grandmother, had been abandoned to the care of another family when she was eleven or so. Her father was an itinerant carpenter who couldn't make enough money to keep her, so Cora Lee was taken in by a good-hearted childless couple on Tygart Creek in Greenup County, Kentucky. Her new father was the country doctor, and at a very early age, Cora Lee became his assistant. She only went to seventh grade but she was plenty smart.

Her life must have been very hard, and she must have received little affection, for Cora Lee never showed emotion. I realize now she hid her feelings to shield herself from pain of future abandonment. She wasn't like my Judd grandparents at all. She never once hugged me, never once gave me a gift, never even told me she loved me. Everyone called her "Miss Cora Lee," but I never really called her "Grandmother" or "Great-Granny" or anything for that matter. She was a rigid, controlled woman whose only passion in life seemed to be playing bingo. She played it with a vengeance.

Her husband, Edward Burton, was even more withdrawn. Whenever we would visit them, he would sit in his rocking chair, staring out the front window with his mouth set in a hard line. I was an affectionate child, but I never went anywhere near Great-Grandfather Burton, never even touched him. I can't remember ever wanting to. He seemed cold as marble. For a man who at one time had enjoyed some measure of success as a local politician in Portsmouth, Ohio, he seemed remarkably devoid of people skills.

It must not have been chilly all the time, though, because Miss Cora Lee and Edward produced nine children. Besides a set of triplets who died at birth, Cora Lee birthed six children all at home.

Edie Mae, the oldest daughter, eventually became my grandmother. She married my grandfather, Howard Oliver, a poor soul whose family history made Edie Mae's look like a Walt Disney movie.

Howard and his younger brother, Norman, had been the offspring of the tragic union between Tillie Weichmann and David Oliver. Tillie had been only fourteen when she fell in love with David, a stone mason, who boarded in the Weichmanns' home. Later, she became fed up with rumors of her husband's womanizing and confronted him. Tillie packed up and told David she was going into town to stay with her parents and think things over. "You take care of the boys!" she shouted, as she slammed the door behind her, leaving the children, ages seven and five, alone with their father.

Whatever demons take possession of a man's soul were surely at work in David that night. He sat his two young sons down and commanded them to be still. He closed all the windows and locked the doors, then turned on the gas. As his terrified little boys watched, David threw a rope over a rafter and hung himself.

Howard was only about seven but he was able to break out a window and save himself and Norman, but he wasn't big enough to pull his father down. Outside, through the broken window the horrified children watched their tortured father hanging from the rafter, realizing he had just tried to murder them as well.

The younger boy, Norman, was never really the same after that. He didn't talk for years and he grew up withdrawn with what is called a "dull affect." He found a modest job and spent the rest of his life working in a shoe factory. Having seen his father, David, commit suicide in front of his eyes and living with the realization his dad had also tried to kill him and his brother, Norman was psychologically damaged for life.

I wince now as I remember how we children made fun of Great-Uncle Norman because he was so peculiar. Once he got a new car and asked my cousins and me proudly, "You want to see my big trunk?" We laughed with the cruelty of insensitive youth, but he brushed it aside and even managed to join in the laughter himself.

My Grandpa, Howard Oliver, lived through his tragedies and seemed to come out the other side a reasonably well-adjusted man until he met up with my grandmother. She, too, was a redhead, with porcelain skin, dancing eyes, an easy laugh, and a fondness for partying. When they married it surprised no one that their union quickly turned tumultuous. They brought three innocent young lives into their highly unstable home. Howard named his only son after his own unfortunate brother, Norman; second was my Mom, Polly; and their third child was Martha Lee.

One spring day when my Mom was only nine years old, Howard, her father, was found dead in the bathroom at home, shot through the head. His death was officially ruled a suicide like his father's, but there's a very real possibility that my grandma Edie Mae (and her lover at the time) killed him. Things were very confusing around the time of the shooting, and there were a lot of whispers, murmurs, and unanswered questions. One thing that brought Edie Mae's guilt into sharper question within the family was the way she high-tailed it out of town after the shooting. She had earlier dumped my Mom with her brother and sister at their grandmother Cora Lee's house. I'll never know whether my grandpa Oliver was a suicide victim like his own father, David, or whether my grandmother Edie Mae and her lover murdered him, and I guess we'll never know, because my Mom is the only survivor of her entire family.

Edie Mae was a dreadful parent who gave little, if any, attention to her children. From an early age, my mother was the hero of the family and literally raised herself along with her brother and sister. Edie Mae couldn't be bothered. She was always out running around town, doing her makeup or painting her nails. It understandably left deep emotional scars on the children.

The rumors never did die down, so Miss Cora Lee and her husband picked up and moved to Ashland from Portsmouth, dragging their own brood of misfit adult children and abandoned grandchildren with them. Miss Cora Lee purchased the Hamburger Inn and turned it into the best restaurant in town. She ran it herself, every day, and carried a pearl-handled Smith & Wesson revolver for protection against the local riffraff she was sure would show up. As far as I know she never had to put it to use, and the gun was eventually handed down to me. I still have the pink satin money belt that Miss Cora Lee fastened around her leg to carry her bingo winnings in and a jar full of her buttons. I think it's safe to say that beginning with Miss Cora Lee, strong women began to leave their mark on the Judd lineage, a pattern that continues to this day.

My mother lived with Miss Cora Lee in the same house with her own brother and sister and her aunt and uncles, who worked at the family restaurant. What sounds like a large, close-knit family actually was anything but that. Edie Mae's sister, Great-Aunt Ruth, lived at home because she was bisexual and felt unwelcome in the outside world, which was no doubt the case at that time. Great-Uncle Leroy, a homosexual, operated a beauty salon, had bleached-blond hair, and a poodle with a rhinestone collar. Great-Uncle George lived at home and was an alcoholic and a gambler. Great-Uncle Carl retired from the air force and bought a small bar in Dayton. He got drunk and fell down during Christmas, then died before anybody could find him. Oh yes, worthless Uncle Howard was an alcoholic too. Even their errant sister, Edie Mae, eventually returned to live at home after her lover was accidentally electrocuted. As I was growing up, I would accompany Mom as she'd stop by to check on them. I remember the plain house was always clean, but the shades would be drawn and the air was filled with the haze of cigarette smoke. They'd be sitting around drinking, reading, or discussing current events. These misfits never stood a chance. Miss Cora Lee was a cold, overly independent woman, who along with her weak husband failed to provide the children any example or paradigm. My memories indicate that the Burton menagerie was a tangled web of secret lives and hushed truths.

How do you like our family so far?

Following the Burton family tradition, my mother went to work at the Hamburger Inn as a cashier. Miss Cora Lee was always aware that her granddaughter was the only normal one. Hardworking and ambitious, Polly was her grandmother's favorite. Norman and Martha sensed that Cora Lee favored Polly and turned against their sister, becoming jealous and spiteful. My mother felt very alone, rejected by her lazy brother and selfish sister, ignored by her deviant aunt and uncles. The only affection she received was from gay Uncle Leroy, who stood ready to help her fix her hair and share her excitement when she saved up enough money to buy a new dress. Mother always had a tender spot in her heart for her Uncle Leroy, who by today's standards was a caricature of a flamboyant homosexual. Besides Miss Cora Lee, he was the only family member who ever showed her kindness.

Soon a light began to shine in my mother's workaday life. There was a gas station down the block from the Hamburger Inn where a quiet young man named Glen Judd worked. He would come in on his dinner break when Polly was behind the cash register. Pretty soon the shy glances turned into eager smiles. It wasn't long before Glen Judd worked up enough nerve to ask pretty Polly out on a date.

Mother must have thought she'd died and gone to heaven when Glen asked her out. Glen Judd was an honor student in high school, and everyone thought of him as an intelligent and conscientious young man sure to go places. My mother yearned desperately to have a normal existence, filled with the sort of homey routines that everyone else took for granted. She had never been exposed to a stable home herself. She'd been on her own all her life and deserved someone who would appreciate her. Her well-worn dream of a warm family life with a good man who stayed at home and provided for her had always seemed implausibly far away. Now, all of a sudden, in the twinkle of Glen Judd's eyes, it was so very close.

Daddy was eighteen and Mom fifteen when they were married by the justice of the peace. I was born at King's Daughters Hospital two years later on January 11, 1946. Daddy bought the gas station that August of 1946, cleaned it up, and renamed it Judd's Ashland

Service. Shortly after that, he also managed to buy our first home, a modest two-story brick house on Hilton Avenue.

My Judd grandparents and aunts and uncles lived only a block away from us. As far as I am concerned, they were the only real grandparents I ever had. I loved to go over to Grandmommy and Granddaddy Judd's house, because as the firstborn grandchild, I was automatically the cat's meow. I got presents on my birthday, at Christmastime, and sometimes for no reason at all. I felt loved, adored, and very special.

When I was barely four years old, I walked out of my house on Hilton Avenue, crossed one busy street, and toddled on over to my grandparents' house on the corner of Montgomery Avenue. Granddaddy was working in the yard and seemed shocked to see me.

"Hi, Granddaddy!" I chirped.

He stared at me and looked confused. "Where's your Mommy and Daddy, Di honey?"

And I remember replying, cool as a cucumber, "Daddy workin' and Mama's in the kitchen."

Granddaddy Judd bent down to pick me up and hugged me real tight, relieved that I was safe after my unsupervised journey. He was a great old guy, very religious and soft spoken, with a quiet grace and a wonderful ease with children and animals. I recall his well-worn Bible on the table, a landmark of his faith. Mom and Dad bought the house at 2237 Montgomery from my grandparents a week later for $20,000. After Grandmommy and Granddaddy Judd moved to a farm in South Shore, Kentucky, my brothers, sister, and I would take over the very rooms I remembered my Judd aunts and uncles living in. My roots ran very deep.

Grandmommy Judd was *the voice* of the Judds, the matriarch who ran the family, similar in that way to my Great-Grandmother Cora Lee. Miss Cora Lee Burton and Sally Ellen Judd had their names in the phone book, which was very unusual at that time. Their husbands deferred to them. Of course, my Daddy had his name in the phone book because he was the owner of Judd's Ashland Service. I was very proud of that.

It's easy for me to understand now why Mom accepted her

life, such as it was, with Daddy. She had her family close at hand, her man provided for her well-being, and she had her house. She had respectability and decency—everything she had always wished for, all the elements of her private dream. If it somehow didn't match up to the rosy pictures she painted in her head while growing up in Miss Cora Lee's funny farm, well then, she thought, that's just the way life is. So let's get on with it; things could always be worse, don't you know?

All these grown-up issues seemed a million miles away to a four-year-old girl who stood supremely at the center of her comfortable world. I had created a myth of familial stability based on the love of my mother and father and the special attentions from Judd grandparents and relatives. Why, I had dinner on the table every night at five, I had clean sheets on my bed in a big, warm house, and I knew every kid on the block. What could be better?

The friendly camaraderie that all the children in our neighborhood shared in those early years remains fresh in my memory, intimate and dear. We loved to play hide-and-seek during the long summer evenings, darting to and fro, our foreheads glazed with sweat. The light would fade and the trees would turn dark, but for a while the air remained warm, and we could squeeze a precious few extra moments of joy out of our day.

When it began to chill, there was always the beautiful beacon of home, my sanctuary and safety net, where the people I loved with all my heart anxiously awaited my nightly return: 2237 Montgomery Avenue was the center of my universe. I could walk to our two movie theaters, to the downtown shops, and to Daddy's station. The old folks' home was down at the other end of our block and every Fourth of July after dark, they'd have an ice cream social. As we sat out on the lawn under Chinese lanterns licking our homemade ice cream, I'd gaze at these elderly people, certain they'd been born and contentedly spent their entire lives right there on our block, too.

The kids on my street were my playmates. I could walk to Sunday school and see them there; I could walk to school and they were there, too. I needed them to be there, and they never let me down. Such was the constancy of my robust childhood days . . . days that were woven in the textures of family and friendship.

I used to tell everybody I'd never leave Ashland, I was going to stay forever and live next door to all these wonderful, loving souls. Why would anyone ever want to leave?

The whole world was right there.

Don't Tell Me I Was Born to Be Blue

*A*S I WAS nearing my teens, more and more of that childhood light began to fade away, no matter how hard I tried to save the brightness. When I was in the fifth grade, Mom contracted a serious kidney disease and came close to dying. My Daddy took her away to a clinic in Ohio in the dead of winter; we kids were farmed out to relatives and neighbors.

I was the one sent to stay at the farm at South Shore for a couple of weeks, but it seemed like an eternity. I wondered why all the good things rush by but the bad things seem to take forever. I stayed upset over Mom, worried about Daddy and the other kids, and grew concerned about getting behind in school. Ice and snow were on the ground, and it was bitterly cold. I couldn't play barefoot in the woods, and was so lonely I would even have welcomed my ornery cousin, Timothy, and that's saying something because he was untamed as a wild Indian and scared me to pieces!

When I needed to go to the outhouse now I had to put on my coat and boots. I'd never been confined inside the farmhouse like this before. Of course we didn't have television. Granddaddy said, "It allowed folks inside your home you wouldn't really want inside your home."

The old farmhouse was so drafty I took sick. Grandmommy Judd would rub Cloverine salve on my chest and bandage me with clean rags. I couldn't stop thinking, "I want to be buried next to

Mommy." This was the first time it ever occurred to me that something bad could happen in my family.

Mom slowly recovered, but something changed in me after that. I began to see things I hadn't noticed before. I'd never seen Mom stand up to Daddy until the furnace incident. Living in the northern part of Kentucky, the winters got really cold, and we didn't get a furnace until I was sixteen years old. Until then, my brothers would haul coal up from the basement to burn in the living room fireplace, and in addition, there were a few small gas heaters. My seven bedroom windows would be frosted over when I woke up, so I dressed either under my covers or huddled in front of the tiny electric space heater in the bathroom.

Truth was, Daddy made a decent living but was just plain tight. When Mom complained about the cold, he was on his way out the door to collect free plastic from the dry cleaners to tack over all our windows. Mom wasn't about to have us looking like the Beverly Hillbillies. As we say back home, she pitched a fit!

Daddy worked hard, but there never seemed to be any money for Mom. Penny Webb, my best girlfriend when I was growing up, came from a family with money. She spent a good deal of time at my house and casually mentioned one night while her parents were attending a ball, "I bet it's nice that you don't ever have to worry about your parents going out."

I wasn't too sure how to take this. From my humble Judd perspective it seemed as if going out every once in a while, enjoying social activities, and seeking new friendships were all part of the spice of life.

A fuzzy picture was beginning to come into sharp focus. The more I watched television and the more movies I saw down at the Capitol or Paramount theaters, the more I realized that my mother and father did not have a "normal relationship," if such a thing actually does exist. Our home was not really the cozy Walton-esque existence I had constructed in my mind, although I knew movies and television exaggerated reality. The more time spent at my friends' homes, the more I realized something was conspicuously absent. I'd see my friends' parents touching each other, smiling, giving each other little caresses or pecks on the cheek. You know, just normal marital shorthand, an arm around a waist here, a wink or a pat there. Because my parents never went anywhere, you'd figure there'd be a good chance of walking in occasionally and catching Mom sitting in Dad's lap. Nope, it never happened.

It began to hurt me in a selfish way that my mother didn't have clothes like other mothers. She always seemed to be in a plain dress in a cluttered station wagon dragging a bunch of noisy kids to the swimming pool. Lord knows, she didn't even have nice attire for church, and we went to church every Sunday morning. If there was ever a setting for me to feel awkward about her lack of style, church was definitely it.

Church has always been a part of my life in varying degrees. During my childhood it was a routine that was expected to be recognized and respected. You got up on the Lord's day and went to Sunday school and church automatically as a demonstration of deference and gratitude to God and as balm and inspiration for the soul. Church provided us all with a sense of spiritual identity. Although I briefly strayed from attending regularly in later years, I always knew God existed, had created me, and loved me.

The ritual was very comforting. Our Sunday school lesson books were lined up underneath our Bibles next to the boxes of envelopes bearing our names for our tithes and offerings. As we came downstairs dressed in the best outfits we had, Mom would be in the kitchen putting a roast or such in the oven so when we returned home we had a hot, delicious meal ready. Mom helped out in the church nursery during services, thus enabling her to complete a full seven days of selfless service for the week. What she did every day for six days, she repeated on the seventh: managing a roomful of screaming kids, changing diapers, and wiping runny noses. But to her, it was important to give something of value to her community and to put her natural talents to work in the service of others. She drew a quiet satisfaction for her volunteer efforts, and I believe it helped keep her foundering self-esteem somewhat balanced.

Church presented some difficulties for me: I often sensed that other people weren't feeling God the same joyous way I was, and I didn't think our preacher was telling us all we needed and wanted so badly to hear. The Reverend Mr. Morton would stroll up to the pulpit with his Bible on his hip and give us both barrels from the King James version! Then it was "Open to Hymn 36. . . . Stand up. . . . Bow your heads. . . . Pass the plate."

I resolved at an early age to seek out a church when I grew up that would allow more freedom of expression. It would take the better part of four decades before I would find my true spiritual home.

Despite these iconoclastic notions, worship in the halls of faith at First Baptist educated me and served to expand my horizons. I was curious and fascinated with Bible stories, life's blueprint for successful living handed down through the millenia, and I soaked it up. Church also served as a rallying point for my family, a place where we could meet individual needs that couldn't be expressed anywhere else.

Mother believed in the rewards of Proverbs 22:6: "Train up a child in the way he should go: and when he is old, he will not depart from it." She'd experienced its truth already in her own life. The greatest thing Miss Cora Lee ever did for Mom was take her to church. Her grandmother's own kids wouldn't go, and Mom had seen them wind up with crippled lives, but it taught my mother the deepest source of her identity was God. She developed a personal accountability to Him. She learned that beliefs have consequences.

Although she crawled out of a cruel, fractured background, Mom not only survived but ultimately triumphed in her life. Not having love or acceptance while growing up, she discovered how much God loved her and was able to garner the strength to see her through and to find meaning for her life. After I found out about how hideous her early life had been, I sincerely came to appreciate Mom as a true-life heroine.

I believe the fact that she was so painfully neglected made Mom almost uncannily aware of children's needs. She tried hard and succeeded in being the antithesis of her own self-absorbed vain mother. I learned so much about compassion from Mom's example.

I watched Mom perform as the care provider for everyone, an example I find worthy of emulating. When her sister, Martha, seemed to be copying their Mom's self-centeredness and gave away her illegitimate son, Mom brought the boy into our overflowing home until there was a decent environment for him elsewhere. Sometimes I was mean to Eddy. I warned him I kept an alligator named Gillette (because he had razor-sharp teeth) in the basement. I threatened to throw Eddy down to Gillette unless he did whatever I asked, until Mom caught on. She saw to it that we treated Eddy as an equal, taking him on family vacations, and so on. Eddy is now a minister in Dayton, Ohio, with a happy family. He attributes his time living with us as his only model for a happy, normal home and credits these events as one of the primary reasons he's in the ministry today.

Mom's brother, Norman, was a lazy alcoholic who deserted his wife, Roberta, and their three small kids. Mom helped them every way she could. We had them over for meals and gave them toys and clothes. On Christmas and their birthdays, Mom paid special attention to Becky, Howard, and Chuck. We were very close and grew up together and Aunt Roberta became one of Mom's closest friends.

Although mistreated by her brother and sister, Mom forgave them and continued to clean up the messes they made of their lives. Looking back on all this, I've come to the conclusion that mothers give us our consciences.

Mom's curiosity rubbed off on me at a very early age. She prompted us to listen to the radio in the kitchen while she cooked. *Big John and Sparky* was one of our favorite programs. When there was a word that we heard or read but didn't understand, Mom would get an index card out of her recipe box and write the word down, propping it up against the sugar bowl in the middle of the table. By dinnertime the next day, we needed to know how to spell the word, define it, and how to use it correctly in a sentence.

And so began my lifelong love affair with words, and with Mom's encouragement I devoured English. She'd say, "Words are the clothes our thoughts wear, and I know you love to be well dressed!" It was my favorite subject in school. I had no interest in science, and I hated math so much it felt like a mental enema. I'd cram and make decent scores on tests and then ask myself, "Who needs this nonsense?" But English! It was a pure pleasure for me to diagram a sentence, I loved the coherent structure and organization of language. The wonder and power of all those marvelous words! Why? Because they empowered me to communicate.

I loved to organize things, and became a natural leader. Daddy would bring me cigar boxes home from his station for dividing, sorting, and storing my various treasures. I was the one who suggested, "Let's all meet at my house at one o'clock after lunch. We'll walk to the park and play on the swings. Then why don't we come back home and play kick the can, after supper perhaps we can . . ." Everybody let me get away with it, because I always seemed to come up with the best idea and plan. Today people needle me about my take-charge ways, but back then there was never any question about it. It's just the way things were.

What a little perfectionist I was! While I baby-sat for our neighbors, the Parks, I also cleaned their house for only fifty cents an hour. I'd rearrange Jean's kitchen cabinets and bathroom shelves and linen closets into perfect order. I'd wander their empty houses after the children were in bed and imagine what it would be like to have a perfect home: It would be spotless, exquisite, and everything would match. It would be much more like the television shows I was watching than my own real life. I longed for order and symmetry and began to realize that finding such a mix might actually mean choosing a different path—and separating myself from everyone I knew.

Being a natural pretender from the get-go, I was in demand at slumber parties for my terrifying ghost stories. My imagination often got the better of me, but I delighted in trying to make wildly improbable scenarios stick. When I was in the second grade, I looked forward to reading *Your Hit Parade* magazine with all the words to the popular songs. I bragged to the kids at school that I was a famous singer who had records out and had appeared on the *Your Hit Parade* television show. Russell Powell and a few junior skeptics asked me to bring my record in because they needed proof. They kept after me for weeks, and I worried about how I was going to get myself out of this ridiculous fantasy I'd created.

In desperation I told them that my song was recorded on a German record label and I was waiting for the next shipment from abroad to come in. They responded, "Well then, just sing it live for us." So at recess I stood up with all the kids sitting around me on the roots of my favorite tree on the playground. I confidently began singing absolute gibberish, just making up what I figured were German-sounding words and nonsense syllables. To my delight and astonishment, they bought it! I remember thinking, "Ah-ha! I've got something here. I'm pretty darn good at this!" Even Russell Powell applauded and cheered.

This, of course, just egged me on. I must have been terribly convincing, because I would exaggerate like crazy, and my playmates would buy it nine times out of ten! I'm sure their confidence helped give me the courage to chase after some mighty big dreams that were to present themselves much later.

In my baby book, the first entry Mom made was "Diana Ellen has a very vivid imagination." How she knew this when I was so small, she's never said, but there it is, my own mother's first observation and self-fulfilling prophecy!

We didn't get a television until I was about eight. I had this feeling when I listened to the radio or watched TV that I wasn't listening or watching so much for entertainment, but because I wanted to *do* it too. I wanted to make sounds people would listen to and do things people would watch. I wondered if I could do it. Brian, Mark, and Margaret were my first audience. All along, people had been telling me I could do anything I really set my mind to, and I figured that this was one of the big requirements for getting on TV.

When I was eight years old and in the third grade, I had my first public performance. Mom's not-so-secret fantasy was to be a tap dancer. She would do the Shuffle Off to Buffalo around the kitchen in her apron for all the neighbor kids. I'd begged for tap dancing lessons and was so excited about our recital at the Paramount Theater.

All went well during the program, then one fortuituous moment occurred during the finale. Our kiddie chorus line returned to close the evening with a cancan number. At the end of the routine we held up our ruffled skirts and bent down on one knee in a straight line across the stage. I was dead in the middle and slightly out front, so that when the curtain came down it fell behind me and Mary Rush, separating us from all the others. She and I were left stranded out on stage together in front of the curtain, absolutely horrified. The parents began tittering, "Isn't that just darling!" But all I could think about was how Mrs. Nancy D. Holmes, our tap dance teacher, was going to kick my little butt.

Then suddenly I began to realize that the audience perceived it to be cute. When Mary abruptly ducked underneath the curtain and left me out there alone, I didn't follow immediately. Something swept over me to stay out there in the limelight a beat longer. I milked a few more laughs, and then skipped offstage to a round of healthy applause. Totally out of breath with exhilaration, I felt a tingle of excitement I'd never known and recognized something important for the first time: I had held an audience's attention. And you know what? I liked it. No, I genuinely *loved* it.

Mom kept those black patent leather tap dancing shoes preserved in a box labeled, "Diana's Tap Shoes. Eight Years Old. 1954." A souvenir from my show biz debut. A ham was born!

In the fourth grade, I played the lead role of Priscilla in *The Pilgrim's Progress*. My all-time favorite teacher, Mrs. Mildred Rigsby, supervised the play. She used to tell me that I could do anything, and oh, how I loved to hear that. She was everything you always wanted a teacher to be, kind and supportive. Mrs. Rigsby actually listened to our questions, arbitrated our disagreements, and encouraged us to enjoy and treasure our time in school. I looked forward to her having us sing at the end of our school day. "Put your heads down on your desk," she'd instruct in her gentle voice, then she'd lead us in singing: "Now the day is o-over, night is drawing nigh-igh, Shadows of the evening steal across the sky." It felt so comforting and complete. I liked closure.

The only teacher I didn't care for was my third-grade teacher. She was a dreadful old spinster who didn't appear even to like children. She never smiled, instigated any fun, organized any games, or encouraged the personality of a single kid. Still, this teacher unwittingly taught me a valuable lesson.

When my Mom explained to me she was a lonely, unhappy woman, it dawned on me that my teacher was a real person and had a life outside of our classroom. I decided it wasn't that my classmates and I were bad—she was already unhappy with herself. I found as the years rolled by that this knowledge might have been one of the most important tools in my psychological box. This experience taught me not to hate anyone and to look deeper into behavior. Perhaps it was all because of something Mom was forever telling us four kids: "Be kind to everyone, because you can't know what it's like for them at home."

There was a program for retarded children in the basement at our school and one tall, thin, hollowed-eyed girl haunted me. She would stop when she saw me and just stand there, staring at me. I felt so sorry for her it sometimes made me cry. I wanted to give her my clothes, my lunch, my brain. Describing her to Mom one night after supper, I said, "Even her name is strange. It's Naomi."

"Why that's not strange," Mom corrected me, "it's from the Bible." Mom encouraged me to think of the Golden Rule everytime I smiled at Naomi. "Do unto others as you would have them do unto you."

But teenagers! Now they can be unkind, unthinking, and self-centered. I went through a phase of caring too much about what people thought. For instance, when the mother of a boy I liked came by to meet me, I was so embarrassed that I wouldn't invite her into our house. I knew how messy it was inside and Mom had piles of Daddy's work uniforms all over the kitchen floor. I suggested, "Let's sit out on the porch," and somehow threaded my way through a very stilted conversation. It hurt Mom's feelings.

In response to Mom's lack of a nice wardrobe, I began to be very clothes conscious myself, as if my dressing better would somehow compensate for her lack of style and maybe in the process just blind everyone to the real situation in my family.

I worked out a nifty deal with Daddy that he would match whatever I made as a baby-sitter to augment my regular allowance. I had just three or four dresses, blouses, and skirts, but I took enormous pride in how I looked. My socks matched perfectly, my blouses were always freshly ironed, and I coordinated colors to get the maximum effect.

A selfish demand for a new party dress backfired on me one evening. I was already in hot water for not doing my chores but then was actually stupid enough to storm into the kitchen whining about not having anything new for a pool party I was all dressed up for. Just as my date rang the doorbell, Mom calmly looked up from the potato salad she was making and poured the contents of a large jar of sweet pickles on top of my foot-high, teased and sprayed hairdo.

I started scheming to get something nice for Mom at Christmas, because nobody else ever seemed to care. Mom, whom I loved so much and who was the most important person in my life besides Daddy, was simply not getting from the world what I knew she so deserved. I badgered my brothers and sister to chip in their allowances to buy her a pair of Daniel Greene house slippers for Christmas. It became an annual tradition for us after that first year.

I longed desperately for our holidays to be more than they were. I thought they should be like the happy family celebrations I saw in the movies and on television, where attractive people laughed and hugged each other a lot. On Christmas morning I would beg Mom to run down and put Christmas music on our phonograph before we all came downstairs. I did my level best to foster what was my impression of genuine yuletide cheer. On her birthday, Mom's cake had to be just right, with the exact number of candles and presentation. It was the beginning of my flair for the dramatic, and everyone recognized how I loved staging special events and organizing celebrations. I could make a production out of anything!

Each time neighborhood pets died, I officiated at the funerals in our backyards. When Tweety, my parakeet, died, I wrapped him in my favorite turquoise chiffon scarf from Kresge's. I conducted a solemn ceremony as he lay claws up in an open Tipparello cigar box. There were touching words about him soaring in a realm higher than eagles fly, enough so to make Barbie Hinton weep. Pokey, my turtle, however, failed to illicit such a response. Swathed in a toilet paper shroud within a Quaker Oats box tomb, his eulogy was cut short when I was unable to come up with a poetic rhyme for turtle.

Eventually, I became Mom's vicarious social contact with the outside world. Believe it or not I was very quiet. Still, I managed to know just about everybody and get along with kids and grown-ups from every level of society. I genuinely liked people! Mom's contacts with our community came largely through us children. We gave her incentive to become more visible and more actively involved. She baked cookies for the PTA bake sale and was there for all our talent contests and recitals. She cheered us on when we got into scouts and Little League.

It even worked out that way for my Daddy. Baseball actually brought him out of his shell from time to time. He and my brothers were huge Cincinnati Reds fans and never missed a game on the radio or TV. Since Cincinnati isn't too far from Ashland, we adopted the Reds as sort of our family team. Daddy began managing my brothers' Little League one summer, and stayed with it for fifteen years.

The lack of healthy give and take between my parents affected me in those formative years.

I know now why I'm such a demonstrative person, why I've spent my adult life making such a conscious effort to communicate with people. That's all entertainment really is, communication, and I never had enough of it when I was a young girl. I wanted it so badly.

I walked around like a great big piñata, wishing someone would break me open so I could spill out my emotions, secrets, and feelings. I now know that all families are dysfunctional to a degree. "Normal people" are just folks we don't know well enough.

Just after I entered junior high, something sinister and unspeakable happened in Ashland. It sent out warning signs that my wonderful, perfect little town wasn't so safe after all. It was late fall and the days were getting dreary. Two boys that sat right next to me in study hall were convicted of killing a young couple parked on lovers' lane. It was a violent, senseless double murder, and the guilty pair confessed in court that they had done it for kicks, just for the sheer hell of it. That warm, all-embracing cocoon that was Ashland, Kentucky, turned brittle in the winter air and shattered. Montgomery Avenue never felt quite the same to me after that. I had an eerie feeling that danger lay coiled and out of sight. We decided we'd better start locking our doors.

I had to get out of that study hall where the two empty seats beside me chanted "murder" every time I looked at them. These boys had often made lewd remarks to me and the whole thing had been just too close for comfort. The murder weapon had been found under the floor of the house where one of them lived, right behind my Aunt Roberta's house, which I visited often. In my elective period I transferred to become one of the dean of girls's "office girls." We answered phones, ran errands, and acted as Mrs. Pope's assistants. Since you had to be on the honor roll and be recommended by your teachers, it was considered a prestigious position.

One afternoon I overheard Mrs. Pope talking to a man whose daughter was a new student and didn't know the way home. Since this was her first day and because I knew the area like the back of my hand, I volunteered to show my new classmate the best route.

Mari Tanner was one of the most beautiful girls I'd ever seen. It was obvious she was not from Ashland because she dressed differently. She even wore a scarf around her head. I'd never seen anyone our age wear a scarf that way. Just women like my Aunt Ramona when she rode in her convertible. As we walked home together, I asked Mari where she'd come from. Her tragic story made me aware of what a lucky little girl I was. After seeing the evil visited on the innocent murdered couple, I had to ask myself, "Why not me," for the second time that week.

Mari told me she'd actually been born in Ashland but that her mother died when she was very small and she and her sister, Jackie, had been sent to an orphanage far away. Wait a minute! I couldn't believe my ears! I stopped dead in my tracks and blurted out: "You lived on Hilton Avenue and your Mom had multiple sclerosis! Why, you were my first playmate! I remember walking into your darkened living room and seeing your mother lying on a table in the center of it, paralyzed, and wearing only a diaper!" We were only three years old, and it had registered as my first memory. Seeing someone's Mommy in diapers when you're just getting out of them yourself will make a lasting impression on you!

"One day I came down to get you and your house was empty and you had vanished. Someone said your Mommy died and they put you in an orphanage. Your memory has followed me around like a shadow all these years."

We were both crying over our discovery and reunion and instantly became each other's new oldest best friends. It dawned on me that nothing is more perfect than a circle.

There were actually two junior high schools in Ashland, and when we finished the sixth grade it had been disconcerting to see half my friends go one way and half another. I liked things predictable, cozy, and defined, and this separation meant more unsettling changes. I always had a lot of girlfriends, who were very important to me, but I sometimes had the feeling that I felt things differently, perceived things more intensely. I often felt older than a lot of my friends. Things that were so immediate and important to other girls my age sometimes seemed frivolous to me.

At the same time, I sometimes made mountains out of molehills. Leslie Hagans lived next door, and she and I were then the best of buddies. I'd never had a bad argument with a friend before, but one afternoon I dropped a brick on her pet turtle. Leslie screamed like a banshee, calling me a cold-blooded (no pun intended) murderer. I felt sick to my stomach when I realized what a senseless, cruel thing I'd done. I had symbolic nightmares about my house caving in and pianos falling on top of me. I still feel bad about it thirty-eight years later.

I went through a stage of throwing myself into solitary pursuits and becoming a bit of a loner. I didn't miss the popular activities and felt the introspection I gained was worth it. I enjoyed rainy days because I would gather walnuts from our backyard tree and crack them as I read Nancy Drew mysteries in my bedroom. One time I even turned down an invitation to a homecoming dance so I could learn to play "Autumn Leaves" on the piano. I dressed up, turned out the lights, and lit a candle on top of the piano. It was fall and I was filled with all kinds of yearnings: *Wuthering Heights,* Heathcliff-and-Cathy feelings. I can never remember feeling lonely, because I always had my imagination to keep me company.

I was only fourteen years old when I met Michael Ciminella. My special girlfriend, Linda Ann McDonald, who lived across the street, was going steady with a boy from Fork Union Military Academy in Virginia. Linda's boyfriend, Wendell, was looking for a date for a friend of his. Linda tried to convince me to go, but I was reluctant. Boys were not at the top of my agenda at that time. My first real date was at thirteen with Herschel Gardener, for the Y-Teens dance, unless you count going to a few Saturday matinee movies with Sammy McCalvin in the third grade (okay, if you must know, Sammy *did* kiss me). Most of the boys I knew my age were gland-driven creatures who talked about uninteresting things like sports. Jimmy Keeton, my good pal, was always my comfortable escort to social functions.

Linda, who was a year ahead in school, was like a big sister, and had a lot of influence on me. Her younger brother, James, was the only person who could make me do what we called the bent-over-double-belly laugh. The McDonald family possessed a fine, proud spirit. Her daddy, Earl, worked at the hardware store, but they made polite rituals out of all the things my family was lacking. They valued heirlooms, traditions, and propriety in a way that fascinated me.

Linda had perfumes, powders, and all kinds of prissy decorations in her room. I sensed she avoided coming over to my house because it was so unkempt. After her Daddy passed away, her Mom married a well-to-do respected businessman and Linda only dated rich kids from the country club. Linda McDonald was considered one of the classiest girls in Ashland, and as her "little sister," I couldn't turn her down when she started turning the screws. She was determined to fix me up with her boyfriend's dateless buddy.

"He's already sixteen years old and drives a brand new car," Linda gushed. "He's high-diving champion at the Bellfont Country Club, and he's la-di-da something-or-other at the military academy. You should go out with this guy because you'll get to come with me to all the country club dances!"

"What's the big, fat, hairy deal about the country club dances?" I queried. I would have much rather stayed at home and watched *The Twilight Zone* or played with my brothers and sister. But Linda Ann won out, and for a minute, I actually allowed myself to get excited.

Michael drove up in a shiny Chrysler Imperial wearing his military school uniform and smelling of Old Spice. In spite of myself, I admit I was impressed, not about the guy himself, necessarily, but with all his rich-kid accouterments. He looked like the kind of young man who was already familiar with some of the social ins and outs that were beginning to dawn on me. And having been raised around a gas station, I was crazy over his fins!

My parents were stern when it came to dating. They had to meet every boy and know a few things about him. They imposed a strict curfew. Michael passed their initial scrutiny and off we went. He was smooth and chatty, and he seemed quite taken with me. That was his greatest attribute. I loved attention. There was a popular Steve Lawrence song playing on his car radio, "Portrait of My Love," and he promised me that before the night was over it would become our song. I thought, "Give me a break. I'm fourteen stinkin' years old!" It was your basic first date, full of butterflies and overeager clumsy attempts to seem cool and detached.

Unaware as I was, Michael Ciminella was arriving in my teenage life at exactly the right time and in the right form. He was the perfect screen for my fantasies and a wonderful vehicle for my imagination. I was infatuated with the image of a handsome, dashing young man in uniform going to a romantic prep school. The fantasy fed on itself and blossomed, and I embraced it for all the wrong reasons.

No one in our family had ever set foot inside the gates of the Bellfont Country Club. I decided I liked having options. Michael held the keys to a kingdom that I had only just heard about. Once I got a taste of it, it seemed foolish not to enjoy myself. The country club was where privileged and worldly people went about the business of socializing on a plane that no Judd had ever reached. There was curiosity in our house about what exactly went on in such a place. I felt like I had somehow gone up a rung on the ladder. Mom and Dad would always wait up until I arrived home safely from a date. Daddy would go on up to bed, but Mom got a kick out of hearing who was there, what they wore, and what they had to eat. I was beginning to feel like a princess for the first time.

I had never heard of fried shrimp before. It seemed like such a special treat when Michael took me out to nice restaurants that I ordered fried shrimp every single time. It became a running joke between us. Since Daddy didn't like fish, the only kind we'd ever had growing up was salmon patties with catsup on Friday night before the fights on TV. I felt as if a whole new world of exotica was opening up before me.

I started subscribing to *Seventeen* and *American Girl* magazines and became intrigued with style and glamour. I just loved magazines; they opened doors into new realms. I cut out the glitzy covers of high-fashion models, who reminded me of those forbidden girls-in-bikinis air fresheners at Daddy's filling station. I tried to copy hairdos from the Vargas girls on the cover of *Cosmopolitan,* and began spending my allowance on perfumes, powders, and nail polish. I felt myself on the threshold of the wonderfully improbable mysterious portal to womanhood. Michael Ciminella was the catalyst.

With Michael away at military school most of the time, I found new ways to devote my time and energy. Every night I listened to the *Sandman Serenade* radio program up in my room . . . to the strains of popular songs like "Mister Blue" and "Where the Boys Are." I concocted teen movie plots in my head starring Michael and me. (Move over Sandra Dee and Frankie Avalon!) I bought pretty parchment stationery at Parsons and a fountain pen with colored inks to match the paper. I wrote him long love letters scented with dime store perfume, filled with romantic fluff that I'd learned from movies and TV. I'd dash home after school every day and rifle our mailbox eager for letters from him. We wrote dozens and dozens of letters, oozing with adolescent glop. Linda confided he was so proud of my letters and pictures he passed them around all over his military academy. I loved all the fuss being made over me and I loved the notion of being in love.

The only hitch was that I never really felt as if I was in love. I was going through the motions, but in the back of my head something major was missing. I wasn't yet old enough to understand what was lacking. After all, Michael was my first real suitor and I had nothing with which to compare my feelings. Or I guess I should say, lack of feelings. I spent hours trying to convince myself that as usual I wanted too much or that my standards were too high. I realized I was too young to know what love is and just enjoyed the attention and status of being escorted by "Cassanova" as my girlfriends called him. I had caught an extremely desirable fish in the sea of Ashland society and until the real thing came along, why throw him back?

As I walked to classes at Coles Junior High, I'd look around at the boys my own age. They were sweet, awkward boys who smelled faintly like Noxema. Guys like Petey Gayheart, who made me giggle over the funny faces he was constantly making. He got me in trouble in Mrs. Ori's journalism class. "That's enough," she'd holler, "Becky Stamper you trade seats with Diana Judd again so the rest of us can get some work done in here!"

Later someone would begin whispering and pointing excitedly, causing us to rush to the window. There it was, a sleek Imperial stretched out almost a block long, with an older, mysterious driver at the wheel, waiting to take me places I'd never been.

The more time Michael and I had to get to know each other over the next few years, the more I saw how different our lives were. He was an only child and had begged to go away to school. This was hard for me to grasp because I got homesick being away at scout or church camp for a week. He just didn't seem close to his parents. His mom couldn't have been more the opposite of mine. Billie (short for Bernadine) Ciminella played golf at the country club, and got her hair done every Thursday at the beauty parlor. She had a cleaning woman and her quiet well-appointed house was in perfect order. Her dishes were china and she kept her embroidered hankies neatly folded in a drawer scented with lavender sachet. Meanwhile, on the other side of town, our house was filled with laughter or arguing, someone was always eating, watching TV, or producing healthy chaos. The differences could not have been more striking.

Billie was always worried or upset about something. For Christmas I saved up my allowance and bought her a bed jacket from the nicest store in town. I'd never heard of a bed jacket until I met Billie, but it seemed the appropriate gift to give a woman who took to her bed so much.

Michael was also a loner, an outsider without any real friends in Ashland. Although I required short spurts of solitude myself, I was an extrovert. I'd be late getting home from school every day because Carolyn Murphy and Mary Martha and I paused so long visiting on every corner. I had to talk to Pat Bailey and Diane Sinnette every night on the phone, and Michael would be angry because our line was busy. In the days before dial telephones, our number was Grand 709. I always enjoyed hearing the operator pleasantly inquiring, "Number please?"

Distance was one of the main reasons that our relationship teetered along as it did. If Michael had gone to Coles Junior High, and I had seen him on a daily basis, there wouldn't have been anything out of the ordinary to recommend him to me. As it was Fork Union, Virginia, was a long ways from Ashland, so Michael would rarely come home. His parents took me to dances and graduation at the academy, but I never asked him to my school events. I never really considered that we were going steady, although in a typically duplicitous teenaged sort of way I saw nothing wrong with letting him think we were. The separation made it easy for me to go out with other boys. After junior high, I began dating other boys in Ashland who were more interesting. They may not have had Michael's style or his money, but I decided that Michael was lacking in some other key areas.

In fact, I was genuinely trying to cool it with Michael, who now had flunked out of Georgia Tech in Atlanta, but had somehow gotten into Transylvania College in Lexington, Kentucky. I told him I needed some time to think things through and decide what to do with myself. He knew that my feelings for him were nowhere as strong as his for me. Michael had first asked me to marry him when I was fifteen. I assured him that absolutely nothing could be further from my mind every time the subject came up over the course of the next two years. He admitted I was a challenge, and he wouldn't take no for an answer. Michael seemed determined to win me over. He was very forceful.

Life was becoming so complicated! All the daydreams and illusions I had created were stumbling over each other and mixing everything up; my fantasies were threatening to smother me.

Ashland's only high school, a dinosaur building a couple of blocks from home, where I had spent my sophomore and junior years, was being abandoned. We were being shuffled to a brand new high school constructed on the outskirts of town. The older I got, the more things changed, and these unfamiliar variations unsettled me deeply. Things didn't seem cozy and close anymore; now high school was unknown, distant and unreal. Throughout my elementary, junior high, and high school years, I had consistently maintained good grades, and thoughts of college and a career were beginning to swim in my mind. I felt ready to look out into the world. Even though I wasn't sure what the future would bring, I was filled with a strange mixture of apprehension and exhilaration as womanhood now approached. I wanted to make something of myself and make my family proud.

As the days of summer 1963 began to fade, I was sitting next to Brian at the dinner table one night and noticed a lump on his shoulder. He was convinced that it was caused by the shoulder strap on his paper bag from his daily paper route, but Mom looked frightened. She went straight to the phone and called Dr. Wayne Franz, our family doctor. His initial exam indicated the lump represented some form of leukemia and he recommended Mom take Brian to Dr. Charles Doan, a leading hematologist at Ohio State. Stunned and shaken, Mom and Daddy drove Brian to Columbus.

It was the very first time in my sheltered life that I'd ever been left alone at home. It was also the night before I was to start my senior year in high school: My best clothes were laid out in an assembly line ready for the next morning, the brand new notebooks and sharpened pencils were poised on my dresser, ready for service in what I was positive would be the most exciting year yet. Little did I know it would go down in my personal history as the worst year of my life. I did not act like much of an adult that first night on my own in our empty house. No, I didn't even act like a responsible teenager. Instead, I messed up big time. Lots of my girlfriends were sexually active, but I had successfully held on to my virginity. Oh, I suppose you could say I was taken advantage of because of the circumstances. I was worried about Brian and too emotionally spent to put up my usual defense, but I wasn't physically forced into having sex.

It wasn't what I'd expected and dreamed about; there was no tenderness, mystery, or romance. When I awakened the next morning to begin that first day of high school, I felt ashamed, guilty, and cheated. I could barely smile or be myself. I covered up by telling my friends I was worried about Brian, which I truly was.

Mom and Dad returned home from the hospital with heart-breaking news. The diagnosis was Hodgkin's disease, specifically reticulum cell sarcoma. They were too worn out and down to talk much so I grabbed my library card and headed toward the library through Central Park. I'd never been out alone walking this late before, but I was in a panic to find out what was happening with Brian. As I ran through the park, I remembered our escaping the lurking brain aliens. This time there was a real monster after us.

The librarian helped me find what I was after. I recall the definition and description of reticulum cell sarcoma hit me like a hammer. The medical terms were like a foreign language, and I could not believe that this had anything to do with my little brother. I couldn't comprehend what I was reading.

I flipped the pages frantically as words like *radiation, chemotherapy, cancer, terminal,* and *fatal* shot up and hit me between the eyes. Was Brian actually dying? Could this unspeakable thing actually be happening? My first instinct was to scream at the top of my lungs: "We're going to show you. Nothing can happen to Brian Judd. He's my brother! Don't you see, he's special!" But I walked home devastated.

In the months that followed, it was hard for me to keep everything in perspective; to focus totally on Brian's illness. I had been missing my menstrual periods, and I was real nervous. I thought to myself accusingly, "Okay, I did the 'dirty deed.' It is now within the realm of scientific possibility that I could be pregnant." I was petrified—not just for myself, but for my entire family, who were about to be put to a terrible test. A nightmare of doctors and disease was about to hit the Judds in gale-force proportions, and I had no business adding to our woes. I imagined that Mom and Dad could see through me and knew what a stupid, cheap thing I'd done. I expected bells, whistles, and alarms to go off any minute announcing I'd been caught.

One night when my parents were away at the hospital for one of Brian's chemo treatments, I broke into my pink poodle piggybank for cab fare. I'd never been in a taxicab before, but I couldn't drive. There were only a couple of cabdrivers in Ashland, and I was so relieved that they didn't send Chet Bytell, my Daddy's buddy. It was fall, sometime after Halloween, and the nights were beginning to get chilly as I rode out to see Dr. Franz. When I told him I thought I might be pregnant, he just sat there behind his desk stunned and silent. The look of disappointment in that good man's eyes has never left me. He didn't have a cure for Brian, and now he didn't have any answers for me either. I got up and walked around behind his desk and laid my hand on his shoulder. That was the night I grew up. I told him I was going to go ahead and marry Michael Ciminella and give my baby the best chance possible.

As I left the office I knew something had been lost forever. I wasn't a child anymore. No more magic woods, tap shoes, and contracts with German record labels. I was grown up now, like one of the air-freshener girls in their bikinis. And I felt so all alone riding home in the cab that night, as if I were on a one-way, dead-end street.

Brian had always been like sunshine in our house, and that light was fading now. Everything had changed. The mood became somber and oppressive. We seemed afraid to talk out loud for fear our words might somehow make Brian's sickness even worse. The simple routines of daily life became exhausting. Mom didn't have anyone to help her, and the sheer logistics of house cleaning, washing, ironing loads of laundry, and cooking three meals a day for six people suddenly seemed too much for her.

I just couldn't burden my parents with the lab report that had come back confirming what I already knew. It would've been too much. An abortion was absolutely unthinkable. I also knew I could never let them send my baby to Mari Tanner's orphanage. The only solution my tortured seventeen-year-old mind could summon was to kill myself.

I wrote a poetic suicide note and was particularly nice to everyone that day. I selected a knife from the kitchen and locked myself in the bathroom. I sat on the toilet so I wouldn't make another mess for Mom and held the blade against my belly, pushing the dull point deep into the folds of flesh on my abdomen. I kept pushing and the blade went a little deeper, but it wasn't puncturing the skin. "Hari

Kari never looked this difficult in the movies," I grumbled. We'd been too preoccupied to sharpen knives in a while and I took this as a sign. Stabbing oneself seemed so gory anyway.

Instead, one night when Mom and Dad were finally asleep, I sneaked the keys to our old blue station wagon. I would drive myself to a high precipice on water tower hill and throw myself into the void. At midnight, just as I was slipping out the front door, our stately, old grandfather clock in the hallway sent its resounding gong throughout the house. It struck twelve times like a death knell. But, in the typical style of my unfolding melodrama, I realized I didn't know how to drive. Shivering and cursing, I kicked at the tire, returned the keys to Mom's purse, and crept back into bed, ashamed and frustrated.

Well, obviously, I didn't really want to kill myself. I just thought on behalf of everybody else it seemed like the right thing to do given the situation. I was in such torment, such guilt. I may have been secretly envious of the loving attention that Brian was receiving. At least suicide would make everybody feel sorry for me.

I had strong feelings toward my baby since the moment I realized it was there. I loved this unborn child. I understood that it was part of me. I loved it on some primal, unquestioning, unconditional level. It was mine. I didn't feel like it belonged to anyone else. No one even knew about it but me. We were attached and already sharing our first secret.

Sound was our first communication and it occurred to me my baby couldn't see, taste, smell, or feel in the womb. I sang and talked to it. I told it life was surely a heck of a lot better in there than it was on the outside. This baby became my little partner. It was the only confidante I could cry to about Brian, about how ashamed I felt, and how scared I was for both of us. We were a strange team.

That first semester Mom was often away at the hospital with Brian, and Daddy was either with them or at the station working. I was left alone sometimes with Mark and Margaret. Margaret was content staying with Cecil and Mary Agnes next door. They were the kindest folks in town, and sent over food and checked on us. Mom's oldest friends, Kitty and Joe Southers, brought over casseroles and called to make sure the three of us were actually going to school.

I couldn't keep my mind on my schoolwork and quit practicing the piano. I even stopped playing piano at Sunday school out of shame. I blamed my behavior on having to do laundry and dishes and taking care of Mark and Margaret. I'd walk to Park View Grocery down our block for necessities and old Mrs. Hankess would say, "If there's anything I can do, just let me know."

I felt like yelling at her, "Okay, sell me a magic wand!"

Outside my bedroom window was the family tree. No, not the kind that charts your lineage, this was a magnificent, living being that stood guard at our front gate. It watched over us and saw everyone that came and went. I'd spent some of the happiest summer days of my life in its sheltering shade. Now it was autumn and as I stared out my window that night, I felt like one of those fallen leaves that would never return to its sacred source.

I decided to tell Linda McDonald I was going to have a baby. She'd been demanding to know why I refused to communicate with Michael. She didn't understand why I wouldn't take his calls or answer his letters. Linda swore my secret would be safe with her, and then wasted no time in running right out and telling both Michael and her mother. Mary Francis McDonald surprised me by generously opening her heart and offering to help me. I have never forgotten her kindness. She knew that my own home was hardly the environment for a newborn baby.

Michael immediately wrote insisting that we get married. There seemed to be no choice in the matter. I glumly realized it was the only thing to do. I folded his letter up and stuffed it under my mattress. Bad move.

When I came home from school the very next day, the moment I saw Mother waiting for me I knew she had found the letter. She knew me better than anyone, of course; saw that I had been acting strangely; and sensed that something was wrong. Mom had gone through everything in my room until she found the answer. And now she was hysterical! She was so out of her mind with Brian's illness that this seemed more than she could handle. She cried and screamed at me and said awful things, and I just sat there listening patiently, because I deserved it all.

It was a living nightmare. You just can't do this, I told myself! It's 1963, I'm still in high school and I'm not married, I get $1.50

allowance per week! Brian is downstairs on the sofa throwing up, his hair falling out because of his chemotherapy treatments, and I'm pregnant. Mom's losing her mind and our family's falling apart. Pinch me! Hit me! Wake me up! Someone get me out of this!

Absolutely the worst thing Mom could possibly have said was, "I told your father." I knew that Daddy wouldn't come home until after nine o'clock that night when he closed up the station, and all I could do was sit in my room and wait. Frozen with fear, I was sitting on my hands at the edge of my bed staring at the doorway. As it always did at this exact time, a train whistle blew as it rumbled by on its tracks just two blocks from our house. Listening to it tonight, I wished I was on it. How I dreaded having to face Daddy as I kept shuffling his possible reactions over and over again in my mind. I went downstairs and checked to see if his hunting rifle was still in its place. I was so humiliated.

When he finally came home it would be the first time I had ever seen Daddy drinking. I was almost as shocked as he probably had been when Mom told him his little girl was going to have a baby. He was such a hardworking do-right kind of guy and he never kept liquor in our house. After closing time on Saturday night, sometimes Daddy would lock up, total his receipts, stand around inside the station, and sip from the bottle with his buddies. It was his night out with the boys. Our town was dry and there were no bars.

I always thought it odd that some Sunday mornings when I came downstairs dressed for church, Daddy would be sitting slumped over the kitchen table with no shirt on, barefoot, his head in his hands, sipping a Pepsi. I assumed he was so tired from working all week that by Sunday he was just ready to collapse. But innocence be gone, I was a grown-up seventeen now and there were weighty issues ahead.

This time the sound of his old truck bathed me in dread. He clumped slowly up the stairs and came straight down the hall. I finally looked up and acknowledged him standing in the doorway in his stained work clothes. His hands were hanging loosely at his side and his eyes were glassy and heavy from fatigue and booze. The faint aroma of grease wafted through the room. Daddy didn't shout at me, he didn't assign any blame. He just stood there crushed, a beaten down man. And he only asked me one thing, "Do you love him?" I made myself get up off the end of my bed, walk over, and stand in front of him.

I lowered my eyes and muttered, "No."

The silence that immediately followed that statement was so wrong that I quickly changed it to, "Uh, yes. Yes, I do."

Daddy thought about it a second, then sighed. "Well, Di, I guess you're going to have to marry him then."

As usual, he never entered my room, but he wrapped his arms around me and briefly hugged me before turning to leave. As I watched him walk away down the hall I realized for the first time that my Daddy was small. Just a little guy. I had always seen him as a giant, now he just looked bent and slight. He turned into his bedroom and closed the door. Mom and Dad closed the door to their room a lot these days, but time was when it remained open and we could just walk right in. Now it seemed to be shut all the time, as if to shut the problems of the world out and to prevent us from asking questions for which they had no answers.

If Daddy had beat me, yelled, or thrown me out of the house, it would have been more than I deserved and I would have accepted it, because I knew I was the reason our family was gone. We had fallen completely apart. Brian's cancer was terminal. Mark was like a mute witness to a crime, and no one paid much attention to him or little Margaret anymore. Mom and Dad had long stopped talking; they passed each other in our kitchen now like ghosts.

My Daddy just hugged me loosely and then disappeared into his bedroom, as I had seen him do a thousand times before.

This time when he closed that door, my childhood ended forever.

I'll Go Home and Cry Myself to Sleep

*B*RIAN LOST A lot of hair from his chemotherapy treatments, so he went up to Heck's Department Store to find a hat. He returned with one of those bright orange hunting caps with ear flaps, the kind that glows in the dark. I was mortified and begged him to get something more stylish, but he wouldn't hear of it. At school I could see him coming a mile away. It was his problem, and he wanted to find his own solutions.

He was now thin and wan. Of course, he'd always been fair-skinned, but now he'd taken on an unhealthy pallor. Everyone could see that Brian Judd had a very serious health problem. I realized that people's stares and whispers were gnawing at him. He so wanted to get on with it, lick this stupid problem and just get back to being a normal high school kid again.

Mark and Brian shared a room. Sometimes late at night after everyone else had gone to sleep, from my bed I could hear them whispering across the hall. Mark knew something terrible was happening, but no one was helping him deal with it. He grew quieter and more worried as he tried to grapple with this invisible, menacing invader in our home. Mark had always turned to Brian with his fears, questions, and problems. We never talked about it. It was just another example of country pride and stoicism, coupled with an unhealthy lack of psychology. The Judds just didn't know any other way.

I think Brian knew he was dying. I guess I knew it, too, but it was one of the few subjects he and I failed to dissect in our usual way. Mortality was far too heavy for us to contemplate. It seemed as if our wits and sanity were simultaneously deserting us. Brian would reminisce about how only yesterday we were full of energy and fun with dreams and plans.

He went back and forth to Columbus for his treatments. Mom would put pillows and blankets in the backseat of our station wagon for him to lie on, because the long drive was hard on him. She usually drove Brian up for his treatments alone because Daddy had to stay home and work. The medical bills were piling up fast.

Sometimes I went with them to the big hospital. It was stark, institutional, and smelled antiseptic. It felt the way I thought a prison would feel. Brian would lie in his bed full of nausea and pain from his treatments, and confide in me as he had always done, but with a desperation I had never seen in him before.

"I don't want to go to the hospital anymore," he'd whisper. "I just want to be at home. Why can't I lie on the couch in the living room?" It was agonizing for both of us, but we tried to find familiar ground in grappling with his misery. We would hatch elaborate, hilarious plots on how to break him out of there and spirit him away to Montgomery Avenue. We contemplated ropes made of sheets, the ol' laundry-cart getaway, and taking his least favorite nurse hostage Jimmy Cagney–style. At that time, *Dr. Kildare* and *Ben Casey* were popular shows on television, and we'd compare his real doctors and nurses to their dramatic counterparts and create our own fantasy hospital. It would be a warm, happy place with brilliant, comical doctors and no pain, a place where everyone gets better and has a great time in the process. It was just our way of getting him through another day, another treatment, another bout with fear. Brian's remarkable courage impressed everyone with whom he dealt.

One weekend our family drove out to visit Aunt Pauline on Little Catt farm. Always very close to Brian, she'd been writing to him in the hospital constantly, passing on news of everyday rural life to comfort him and letting him know she was thinking of him: ". . . a calf was born this morning," she'd write, or ". . . the creek swelled up last night during the bad storm." How Brian adored the farm! It was such a special place for us, our touchstone for our Kentucky heritage and a fantastic playground all rolled up into one. He was eager to see it for what we all feared would be the last time, which was ironic, because the farm was always a place where time had no meaning. Mom took a picture of him standing in the dirt road in front of the farmhouse petting Lady Bird—one of Aunt Pauline's twelve dogs. He looked skinny and sick, a mere shadow of the vibrant young man of a few months before. When we were getting ready to leave, I could tell by the look of sorrow on Aunt Pauline's face that she knew this was probably the last time she'd see Brian. I looked back over my shoulder and saw her standing in the yard crying as we drove off.

With Brian's cancer, my pregnancy definitely took a back burner in the family's list of priorities. It was like, "Oops, Diana's pregnant, but wonder if Mom will be home tonight to make supper." When Mom told Mark and Margaret I was the big "PG," it made about the same impression as if she'd told them we were having macaroni and cheese instead of meat loaf that night. It just didn't register as it might have under ordinary circumstances. We were too emotionally bankrupt to muster anything that passed for empathy for each other. Our job was to get through Brian's treatments, nothing more.

There were never any alternative options discussed about my pregnancy because it was simply assumed that I would marry Michael Ciminella. You just got hitched, that's what you did in those days. We didn't even discuss my health or the progress of the baby. I don't think any of us were quite ready to address a key issue, which was that none of us cared for Michael Ciminella anymore. Mom didn't like him, Dad didn't like him, and I didn't love him, but I still had to marry him because that's the way it was in Ashland, Kentucky, in 1963.

Christmas came and went without causing a ripple in the swamp of depression at our house. I was about four months along at this time and starting to show, and I knew word had gotten out at school; I thought people were starting to stare at me on the street. Now, I was born and raised in this town, lived in the same house almost all my life; went through the public school system; was active in the First Baptist Church, Girl Scouts, Y-Teens, and student council; was a volunteer candy striper, etc., etc. Everybody knew me and everyone knew I was going to have a baby, because everybody knew everything about everybody else. Being a pregnant senior in high school with no husband was about as scandalous as could be. I had no experience in scandal; Elwanda Boggs was the only girl I knew whose parents were even divorced. It was like being in the eye of the storm. All the gossip and rumors swirled around me, but no one ever talked to me directly about it. The Bluegrass Drive-In was the mecca for teen socialization and I had to find out what was being said about me. I called my trusted friend, Bev Lambert, who was characteristically candid. "The buzz is that you're the last person anyone expected this to happen to, and you got a raw deal."

I knew I couldn't go back to school. I didn't want to walk the halls following this big pregnant belly around. I also hated the prospect of sending the wrong signals out to other young girls. I had this awful fantasy that the school board would call me in, stand me up in front of them, and scream in unison: "We're kicking you out of school because you are knocked up, and we can't allow the message to go out that we condone this wicked lascivious behavior. Shame on you! You tricked us by dressing so nicely in your Pendleton pleated skirt and being a favorite with our teachers. You pretended to be quiet and respectful and wore your hair like a Breck girl. We can't stand the sinful sight of you. Put this scarlet *P* on for pregnant, step over to be fingerprinted, and have your mug shots taken. We are canceling your subscriptions to *American Girl* and *Seventeen.*"

All the while, the doleful lyrics of "A Town Without Pity" was playing in the background. What if there were no choice but to leave town? Except that all my friends, family, and neighbors were here, I didn't even know anybody who lived anywhere else. Plus, I had no money, no job, no husband, and I didn't own a suitcase.

There were many times that I'd slump against the door of my room and look around at all the things that were so familiar to me. My eyes would burn with hot tears and I'd think, "I don't want to leave this room. I'd give anything to go back to school! I love my books and my classes, and I love my friends. Can't anybody see that I'm still just a kid?"

Gradually, I had to accept the inevitable, but it wasn't easy. Our house, which had once been alive with friends and relatives, phones ringing, and kids running in and out, had grown as silent as the grave. I got wind of a slumber party that my girlfriends were having, and I was stung when I realized I wasn't invited. Now it seems like such an insignificant thing, but at the time it was crushing. I had become an outsider, the same kind of person I had privately criticized Michael for being. My poor girlfriends didn't know what to do about me. At least Michael's parents were supportive. They loved me, were willing to accept the situation and pay the hospital bills.

After Christmas, Michael and I casually remarked to my parents we were going out to see a movie. We knew a couple, Nina and Bob Yancy, who had crossed our state line into Tennessee to elope. We were planning to follow in their footsteps, because in Kentucky you have to have a parent or guardian sign for you if you're under eighteen. I definitely didn't want my parents involved in this awful mess. I had been responsible for enough misery in my family and I was determined to do something to ease the predicament.

We sneaked out and drove down to the historic courthouse in Jericho, Tennessee. Inside it was dark, polished mahogony and looming, shadowy hallways. While they were drawing blood for the tests, we discovered no one could marry us. I was younger than Nina, and at I was only seventeen, my parents still had to sign for me. I just sat there in the bewildered clerk's office crying. It seemed as if nothing would ever work out right again. By now it was late afternoon, so we stayed in a cheap motel and slunk home the next morning. Perhaps it was only my guilty conscience, but I sensed my parents were disappointed to see me again. I suspect they had been expecting us to elope and take care of some unpleasant business.

A few days later Mom and Dad got together with Mr. and Mrs. Ciminella. The gist of the conversation was short and to the point: "We've got to get these kids married and we've got to do it fast. We're going to accompany them to grant permission." On January 3, my parents and I, along with Michael and his folks, drove to Parisburg, Virginia, to put it all to rest. We never once considered getting married in Ashland in the First Baptist Church where we were members. The idea was sacrilegious and would simply have been too disgraceful for our families. On the way to Parisburg, everyone in the car made an effort to make polite conversation, but it was awkward and uncomfortable.

I wore my mother's best royal blue wool suit because I was starting to show and couldn't fit into my little eighteen-inch waist skirts anymore. My father bought me a corsage, which was very sweet and sad at the same time. All I could think of was that matronly suit, and dinky corsage, looked like I was playing dress-up. I'd often felt so much older than my years, but now it was a feeling that I suddenly didn't like anymore.

The six of us stood before the preacher in the town's Baptist church. He gave a brief generic talk, then the ceremony itself was mercifully short. I'm sure he was wise to the situation, no guests, no children, no smiles. Just the six of us, standing there stoop shouldered with long, glum faces. It was so far removed from what I had dreamed my wedding would be like that I felt as if I wasn't even there. I was some Diana Ellen Judd puppet mouthing wedding words while the real Diana was back in school laughing with her girlfriends. I vividly remember thinking, "I can't believe I have to say what I'm saying! This is preposterous! Am I the only one here who sees this is insane?" I stood there and repeated in a low voice, ". . . till death do us part," and "I do."

What I meant was: "I'm sorry, God, here I am standing here in your house with a genuine preacher in front of me exchanging vows like some kind of sincere, adult married person and it's pure bunk. See, I even have my fingers crossed."

Daddy took some 8mm home movies of the wedding, pitiful stuff to say the least. Poor Daddy looked as if his heart was going to break. I felt so bad for Mom and Dad. They were experiencing catastrophes with their two oldest children at the same time. Billie and Mike were heartbroken too. This wasn't exactly the sort of future they'd dreamed of for their only child either!

After the ceremony we stopped to eat. The six of us chewed our food slowly and didn't say much before driving back to Ashland. I saw my picture in the paper for the first time that following Sunday morning. It was for the wedding announcement in the *Ashland Daily Independent*'s society page. They had to use my school photo.

And then, presto change-o, it was time to be a wife. I begrudgingly ambled up to my room and packed up some of my stuff and
moved it to Michael's bedroom in his parents' house across town on
a quiet cul-de-sac. His bedroom was an attic loft with a sloping ceiling
so you could only stand up in the very center of the room. There were
two tiny windows and as I was to discover, that room got very hot
in the summertime. Let's just say it's not my idea of a happenin'
honeymoon pad. It was so ironic: moving out of one kid's bedroom
and into another. I wound up bargaining with Michael to take down
some of his diving trophies so I could put Margo and Nanette, my
favorite dolls, on his chest of drawers. It was oddly similar to a
brother and sister rooming together, saying, "Hey, move over, you
gotta share."

Ashland's homebound tutor, Ada Brown, came out to the
Ciminella house so I could finish out my senior classes and graduate
from high school. For my English term paper, I chose the theme
having a baby. I got an A. After we finished with my lessons, she'd
go over to tutor Brian, who had now become too ill to attend school.
Brian and I used Ada to send notes back and forth to each other. It
was as if we were both hostages and this was the only way we could
communicate. I identified myself as a stick figure with a belly that
grew larger with each note. Brian sketched himself wearing his orange
hunting cap. Whenever I went back to our house—the house I knew
inside and out—I felt estranged. I realized I didn't belong there
anymore. I'd slip up to my room and close the door, and for a few
precious moments I'd pretend that this was still the safest place on
earth. Then it was time to go back to Michael's cramped room across
town with the diving trophies and military school photos.

I had a small bridal shower when I was seven months pregnant.
There weren't very many people there, but I received a few pieces of
china, which I put in Mom's attic and which are still there to this day.
I suppose I was trying to keep my umbilical cord attached. Mom gave
me an iron for a wedding present. In my mind I could hear the gavel
come banging down, sentencing me to a life of drudgery.

When Mom started moving things out of my room, throwing
them away or storing them in the attic, I felt as if she were erasing
parts of my childhood that I couldn't redraw. To her, all my old stuff

was just junk, reminders of the unfortunate turn my once-promising young life had taken. It was difficult for me to admit that these simple objects had no value for her, but to me they were all I had. As long as these things remained in their place, there was a chance Michael would evaporate.

Anytime I had to go somewhere, I tried to find an excuse to ride by Montgomery Avenue. Michael would tersely say, "You don't live there anymore—just call them on the phone." One bitterly cold day, I begged him to let me stop there to get my gloves—but I just wanted to see Brian. As I reached out to turn our front door knob, it wouldn't budge. The door was locked so I knocked at first, then began pounding loudly with both fists. I called out for Mom and Brian, but got only silence. Michael was hollering out the car window at me that they must be away at the hospital for Brian's treatment, as I was running around trying to find an unlocked window. I became almost hysterical as I rattled the back door handle in vain. "Please let me back in!" I had *never* been locked out before. I wanted back inside my world . . . but I didn't even have a key.

It was February 1964 and the Beatles had just released "I Want to Hold Your Hand." I remember hearing it on WTCR and getting excited and thinking, "Man, I need to call Cathy Napier and Marsha Fields to check this out!" Then I caught myself and began feeling like an imposter. I wasn't just a carefree teenage girl anymore. The dreary reality was beginning to sink in. Stuck, stuck, stuck! When I met other classmates on the street they would be embarrassed, feel sorry for me, and wouldn't know how to act, like ignorant people do when they see someone in a wheelchair. At our worst moments, we turn away and don't acknowledge them except for a silent and guilt-ridden "There, but for the grace of God, go I." I was beginning to understand the feeling of being on the other side of the fence. I resented seeing girls I knew that slept around but didn't get pregnant. I was a *good* girl with some real bad luck.

I began my marital internship and dutifully took on wifely tasks. Michael's mother, Billie, was patient with me as she taught me all the tricks of the trade, like the exact procedure for ironing a man's shirt and the correct order for washing dishes. I took notes, bored, but ultimately resigned to my fate.

She instructed me how to dust and wait to vacuum until after the dust settled. This woman had made an absolute science out of housekeeping, with rules and laws as immutable as those governing the heavenly bodies. Heloise, jump back! Billie gave me Dear Abby and magazine articles on recipes for a happy marriage and home.

Michael seemed happy being married to the girl to whom he wanted to be married. At this point he'd gotten what he wanted out of life, which was something. But Michael was essentially a lonely person. As a child, he had had rheumatic fever and missed a lot of school. He had been sickly and unable to take part in sports like the other young boys. His mother, who was so generously taking me under her wing, had been so smothering with Michael that he wasn't allowed to play outside, scrape his knees, or get his clothes dirty and as a result he had few friends. A product of a sterile environment, he became a loner. But now, all of a sudden, he had me—his own built-in wife and best friend.

In a benevolent attempt to save my sanity, Linda McDonald invited me to spend a weekend at her dormitory at University of Kentucky in Lexington. She was trying to get me out with people my own age and probably thought this was as close as I would ever get to college. That weekend I felt like a kid with a sugar addiction and no money in a Godiva chocolate store.

Meanwhile, I was completing a normal pregnancy, and playing the role quite well. My fashion consciousness had slipped a bit, due to my changing physical dimensions and the fact that we had no money. I had to adapt with a complement of three maternity dresses. The days passed by slowly and I grew increasingly anxious to see my baby. My term paper stated that the optimum suggested weight gain was twenty-three pounds, so I gained twenty-three pounds. Somehow I had no fears. It all felt very natural, and I knew my instincts would guide me through it all. I prayed every night for three things: for Brian to live, to be forgiven of my sin, and that my baby be okay. It came as a complete surprise to me when I learned I had to have a cesarian section.

On my due date as I was lying on the table in my obstetrician's office, Dr. Williamson exclaimed, "Whoops!" Just the thing patients love to hear when their doctor is examining them. He peered up over the drape and informed me, "I'm afraid you have CPD." I figured he meant syphillis or gonorrhea and I thought, "Boy, this is not my year." He went on to explain that CPD meant cephalopelvic dispro-portionment; *cephalo* means "head" in Latin. The baby was going to be too big to come through the birth canal, or in plain language, I was too small. As he went to schedule the operating room, my immediate response was, "Nothing in my life is ever going to be easy or normal again."

Our house was on the next block behind the hospital and I ran straight over to tell Mom. She was sitting at the kitchen table with our pastor's wife, and looked embarrassed to see me right at that moment. It broke my heart; I felt terrible shame. I announced, "Mom, I have to have a c-section," but what I really wanted to say was, "Mommy, I have to go in the hospital and have an operation and I've never been before so I'm scared and the doctor told me I have to have a c-section and I don't even know what that is and I'm afraid that I might die and something will go wrong with the baby and I want you to take me in your arms and say you'll stop all this madness and fix everything right now, please, hurry."

My mother half-listened and was blasé about the whole thing. With the weight of the world on her shoulders, my c-section and my baby didn't rate very high on the big life-or-death drama scale. Our pastor's wife was there confiding to Mom that she and the Reverend Mr. Reid were getting a divorce. I decided Ashland must now rank as the sin capital of America!

I gave birth when I was eighteen, during graduation week, on May 30, 1964, in the same room of the same hospital, attended by the same nurse who was there with my mom when she had me at age eighteen. Daddy came over from the station and stood around in his everyday work clothes, a sketchy version of a grandfather-to-be. It was obvious he hadn't quite gotten used to the idea of being a grandparent and was even less ready for his own teenager to be a mother.

When the nurse brought my newborn to me I cried—tears of joy at beholding the child of my body and tears of fear that I might not be able to be a good mother to her. As I pressed her up against me I realized I was witnessing my first miracle. I felt an instant camaraderie with this perfectly formed miniature human. She had been my only confidante during the last nine months. We were already a team. I had felt like a victim of life's circumstances, but when I looked down at this helpless infant less than one hour old, I became her protector for all time. Perhaps because lately I had been needing my own mother so desperately, my mothering instincts began in gigantic proportions. Mom and Daddy had always been the most important figures in the universe, and I was now aware of the importance of their acceptance, example, and love. I vowed to try to be there always for this baby. I'd carefully chosen the name Christina Claire for her months before. Christina was born in the eye of a hurricane and I looked down into her precious, tiny face and whispered, "Hello my little partner. It's you and me against the world."

When I woke up, my mind was cloudy with painkillers. I looked around at sweet familiar faces dressed in white standing over me and thought, "Okay, so now I've died. It figures!" It was a group of my girlfriends who had come to see my new baby. One friend's mom, Mary Lou Irie's mother, had just had a baby in the room next to mine. It was wonderful to see them freshly scrubbed and virginal, full of excitement over the rites of passage of graduation from high school. I, on the other hand, had graduated into motherhood. I petitioned Penny Webb to see to it they sent my diploma in the mail.

As soon as I got out of the hospital the first thing I did was take Christina to meet Brian, Mark, and Margaret. Mom and Dad were home, and their reaction was, "Oh well, Diana's okay and this new baby's okay so everything's fine." It didn't seem like a real big deal to them, but to me, my new daughter was *everything*.

The Ciminellas had what we called a "little room" off the kitchen, which became the baby's nursery. We had furnished it with a bassinet, a layette, and a small rocking chair. When I brought Christina home, I was surprised to find something new had been added. It was now equipped with industrial-size cans of Lysol spray and surgical face masks. I summoned up the courage to tell Billie that

I was not going to have my father and mother putting on a mask and being covered in a fog of disinfectant when they came to visit their own grandchild. It was hard to stand up to her, especially as it was her house.

When Christina started crawling, Billie put thermometers down on the living room floor to check the temperature before she'd allow anyone to sit her down. We tried to be patient with her eccentricities, but even Michael was beginning to snap.

I will always be indebted to the Ciminellas for taking me in. I truly believe they did the best they knew how and I certainly appreciate that they never made me feel guilty. I guess they knew in their hearts I really was a sad little girl, who wanted to be home with her own family. I would escape when I could and take Christina down to Montgomery Avenue, where I would watch Mom trying to be a grandmother. She had been a great mother and she wanted to be a grandmother so badly, but taking care of Brian was taking its toll. She'd come home from every hospital visit with heavy suitcases filled with dirty laundry. Then she still had the rest of the house to take care of and two younger children who needed attention, too. It would have been nice to say, "Hey Mom, watch Chris for a second while I go sit on the swing again like I used to," but when I looked into my mother's face, her eyes dark with fatigue and worry, there was no way I could have asked her the favor. While feeding my new baby I'd look over at Mom and realize the only way children can come to appreciate how much their parents love them is when they either have to bury them or have children of their own. Becoming a parent myself took my sympathy for Mom and Dad to an even deeper level of love and understanding.

That fall we moved a couple hours away to Lexington, Kentucky, so Michael could continue to go to college. It was a relief finally to get away from Michael's parents, after almost a year of living with them. But the projectlike apartment we moved into was almost as small as the bedroom we had been staying in, and the Ciminellas drove down almost every other weekend to see us.

Michael's father, Mike, quickly pegged with the nickname "Papaw," tried hard to balance out his wife's idiosyncrasies. He was always there for us, and he absolutely doted on Christina. To this day they are extremely close, and he draws great pride from her successes.

Billie and Mike helped us out financially in a big way. Michael arrogantly accepted it as his due, and I always wound up saying the thank-yous. Michael's parents would leave and he'd grumble, "More ground beef. Why couldn't they bring us a few steaks?"

I knew we wouldn't have had anything without their help. I remember thinking "You bring me a sack of Cut-Rite green beans and what I really want to do is grab Chris and run out of here and join the Peace Corps."

I unfairly directed lot of anger toward them, when it was really my own self-made predicament about which I was frustrated.

I hated apartment life! Thin walls separated us from weirdos and zombies. We had no money to spend on ourselves, and a film of desperation coated everything. Going to the dingy Laundromat was a drag, so I got an old-fashioned washboard and did Chris's cloth diapers by hand in the bathtub. When our neighbors set their pop bottles out in the hallway before taking them back to the store, Michael would steal them at night to cash in the deposit. We were cutting coupons, recycling everything we could, and tightening our belts in ways we never imagined before.

I was only eighteen and going stir-crazy in our tiny roach-infested apartment, so I learned how to drive so I could take Chris for a spin out to the countryside around the big horse farms. It was my only treat. I told Michael I needed to go to college, too, but he shot me down by humpting that the notion was ridiculous. What in God's name did I need to go to college for, anyway? We were having enough trouble getting one person through school.

I wouldn't take no for an answer. Signing myself up at the University of Kentucky, I made a trade-off deal with the nice lady across the hall. Kay baby-sat for me during the day and I took care of her daughter, Lisa, at night so she and her husband, Doug, could go out to a movie now and then. I took English, home economics, art, and psychology classes. After a couple of semesters, I saw that going to school with a baby at home was too much; Christina needed constant attention, and she was definitely my priority. Plus, quiet studying was impossible in our cramped apartment. I believe a mother should spend as much time as possible with a child, especially during the formative preschool years. I promised myself that someday I would get a college degree.

During all this Michael belonged to the Kappa Alpha fraternity, a rather dubious distinction given the organization's *Animal House* reputation. It began to bother me that my parents—who had enormous medical bills and two children still at home—paid our rent and the Ciminellas laid out money every month to support us, while Michael spent most of his time out of class drinking and partying with his frat buddies.

My Dad agreed to pay for the $75-a-month apartment while Michael was in college. Michael promised that when he graduated and landed a good job, he would repay Daddy. I watched them shake hands on it. Daddy used up all his savings on Brian. Years later, my father would fully understand what kind of man Michael was when Michael flatly refused to honor his debt.

Michael sometimes changed diapers or fed Christina, but something important was missing. I felt he was never really there for the baby or for me. As undemonstrative as my own father was, I still knew that he was always there for us. Daddy was the caretaker of his family and that was his single, driving purpose in life. I had always felt safe with my father that way. With Michael, there was none of that feeling.

When I would try to talk to him about my fears he would listen condescendingly, eyes hooded, offering nothing in the way of reassurance. I knew nothing would come of my concerns, and there wasn't so much open strife between us as there was general apathy. He had begun to feel tied down, saddled with a wife and a baby at the exact moment he wanted to be out chasing cheerleaders and attending keg parties and poker games.

I badgered him about his not working until finally he got a job at a men's clothing store. It lasted a few months, until he came home complaining about his boss. I could only imagine what had really happened.

The days and weeks and months dragged on. I busied myself with mundane domestic matters, I cut out recipes from magazines and organized them in a little box, I'd scrub and wax the linoleum floors once a week. My grocery budget for the week was $11, so shopping demanded constant creativity. I lived for Top Value stamps and S & H green stamps. I'd paste them in their books. When Michael would come home, we'd sit in front of the little black-and-white TV and eat ground beef cooked a thousand different ways. Christina's favorite gourmet meal was wieners sliced with a strip of Velveeta cheese down the middle, wrapped with a piece of bacon and cooked under the broiler.

There were six colorful families in our building. I figured they'd find the guy who lived behind us someday sitting naked up in a tower with a high-powered rifle. A lady who lived in the back was forever being beaten by her husband. You could hear the shouting and screaming through the thin walls. I'd be out in the front yard wearing my two-piece bathing suit, watching Christina in her plastic wading pool, and the woman's husband would lean over and flirt with me. I would stare at this poor woman in the hallways and wonder how anybody in her right mind could live with this man. Maybe she was wondering how I could live with Michael Ciminella.

Meanwhile, Brian kept getting worse. Mom and Dad had heard of an experimental drug being used down at Bowman Gray Medical Center in Winston-Salem, North Carolina.

I went to Ashland to see him off when the ambulance came to transport him to North Carolina. The neighbors were all watching from their porches and windows as Brian was loaded into the back on the gurney.

As they strapped him down in the back of the ambulance, I felt a hollowness down inside that I'd never experienced before. Brian had tumors throughout his body and was constantly wracked with pain. It seemed horribly unfair that his suffering could be so severe and prolonged; I ached for him and wished with all my heart I could take his pain myself. He'd done nothing to deserve all this and struggled courageously. I thought back to the day we first learned of his illness and I had naively vowed, "We'll beat this thing! He's a Judd and he's my brother!" It all seemed so far away. I was a nineteen-year-old grown-up now and discovered life sometimes was incredibly unfair.

I hoisted Chris and our beagle, Trouble, into the back of the ambulance to say good-bye to Brian. Children can pick up the vibrations from people around them and she sensed that the strange vehicle was filled with sadness. We both began to cry as I took her and our family dog out and Daddy closed up the doors.

I left Christina with the Ciminellas and drove down to the hospital in North Carolina with the rest of our family. It was a typical southern fall, chilly and somber; the skies were leaden and the sharp winds had blown most of the leaves from the trees. The almost-frozen ground crunched under our feet as we checked into a ratty tourist home. We had a silent meal in a cafeteria before going to see Brian at the medical center. It depressed me to see him there, even farther from home and getting worse. Small talk idled on for a bit, his doctor came in and checked a few things, and we all tried hard to swallow the lumps in our throats.

There was a point in our visit when everyone had left the room but me. For a moment, it was as it had been when we were children. Brian and I talked vaguely about what Chris was doing, then his eyes lit up when he recalled how we used to watch *The Rat Patrol* on TV. He floated off in memory, chuckling as he reminded me how we used to climb the chain-link fence and play on the huge tanks in the National Guard Armory—the armory was just a couple of blocks from our house and provided a real-life setting for our pretend war games.

We relived the afternoon Randy Memmer had shown up with his father's dog tags. In a mock wedding ceremony, Randy placed the tags around my neck, proclaiming me his sweetheart as he went off to war. Then he and Brian and our other comrades climbed down into their tanks to go forth and stop Hitler's Nazi invasion.

Brian came sharply out of his reverie and looked up at me. "Get me out! I gotta get out of here. Please make them take me home. I miss Aunt Pauline's farm." The helpless tone in his voice stabbed me to the core, and I was mute. He wasn't just asking me to get him out of this hospital; he wanted out of the illness, out of the painful procession of days that had sapped his soul, out of this institutionalized life that had betrayed him. I turned away so he wouldn't see me cry.

The doctors felt it best for him to stay in the hospital so they

Growing Up

The Judds at their homestead in Louisa, Kentucky, at the turn of the century. This photo inspired Naomi to write "Guardian Angels" for the *River of Time* album. The lyrics refer to Fanny and Elijah Judd (Naomi's great-great-grandparents), who are seated on the far right. Her grandfather, Ogden Judd, is the small boy at Elijah's knee. Naomi now considers friends and fans as guardian angels too, because they watch over her, Wy, and Ashley with love and support.

Naomi's mom, Pauline Oliver Judd, seventeen years old.

Judd's Friendly
Ashland Service at
Twenty-first Street
and Winchester
Avenue, Ashland,
Kentucky,
about 1970.
(POLLY RIDEOUT)

Charles Glen Judd
next to his gas
station's cash
register, where he
taped his children's
school pictures.
(POLLY RIDEOUT)

Naomi Ellen Judd (age two, about 1948) was a very happy, sweet-natured child, according to relatives.

(RAMONA JUDD SEXTON)

Brother Glenn Brian, and Naomi Ellen: best buddies, about 1951.

(RAMONA JUDD SEXTON)

Cousin Becky shields her face from the sun, Brian is to her left, Mom is holding baby Margaret, Daddy, Mark not wanting to stand still, and Naomi, posing—as usual. (POLLY RIDEOUT)

Left to right: great-aunts Margie and Zora, Naomi, Daddy (*rear*), Mark, Brian, and Margaret (*front*), at the Judd homeplace, Louisa, Kentucky, about 1959. (POLLY RIDEOUT)

From left: Naomi, Billie Ciminella (Michael's mom), and Linda McDonald attending a dance at Fork Union Military Academy, Virginia. Naomi, age sixteen and wearing braces, had already been dating Michael for two years.

Grandparents Glen and Polly Judd (*rear*), and Mike and Billie Ciminella, holding seven-month-old Wy, at the Judds' house, Ashland, Kentucky, Christmas 1964.

Glenn Brian Judd pets Lady Bird, on last
visit to Aunt Pauline's Little Catt Farm. The
last photo taken of Brian, Naomi's brother,
shortly before he died of Hodgkin's disease.
(POLLY RIDEOUT)

Wy, age three, in Lexington, Kentucky.

A glimpse into the future: Wy, three years
old in 1967, with Naomi, playing friend
Penny Webb's guitar. (PENNY WEBB)

Michael, Wy, Naomi, and Ashley in Sylmar, California, about 1969, just before Naomi made the move to Hollywood and asked for a divorce.

Wy, eight, in the third grade (*left*), and pal Astrid Santic. Naomi was their Brownie leader, "trying to give the kids a normal life in Hollywood."

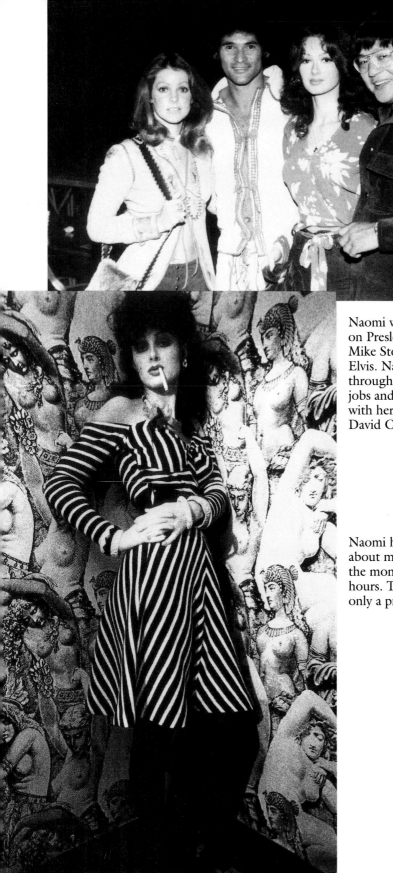

Naomi with Priscilla Presley on Presley's first date, with Mike Stone, after leaving Elvis. Naomi was going through a variety of colorful jobs and was on duty here with her boss, kung-fu champ David Chow (*far right*).

Naomi hated everything about modeling—except the money and the hours. The cigarette's only a prop.

could keep an eye on him. We really didn't have the presence of mind or the togetherness as a family to argue. It never even occurred to anyone that it would be possible or best to keep him at home. I still felt like a traitor because he had asked me point-blank to rescue him. We all trudged back to Ashland: Dad to his station, Mark and Margaret to school, and I to Christina. Everyone had his or her own routine to get on with. Only Mom remained behind to stay with Brian.

On the long trip home, Daddy asked me to drive a while. He was exhausted and badly needed to rest. I was still learning to drive and made him so nervous that we had to pull over and change places. I recall thinking, "I let my Dad down *again*. Just like I always do, time after time."

I felt utterly ineffectual: I couldn't fix Brian, I couldn't fix Mom and Dad, and I couldn't fix my own marriage. Helpless and hopeless.

Not long after we arrived home, Dad got word that it was time. He and dear Aunt Roberta flew back down to North Carolina in a plane the Ashland Oil Company had graciously provided for their perennial Station Operator of the Year. Shortly afterward, I received the call saying they were coming back to get me; I ran upstairs to get my things together, but when I came down I saw Mom's friend Ruth Puffenberger coming up the sidewalk. She quietly said, "Di, come in and sit down. I have something to tell you."

I knew by the look on her face what she was going to say, but I abruptly snapped, "I don't have time. I'm going to see my brother. I'm going to get him out of there and bring him home like he asked me to."

Very gently, she stated, "He's gone, honey."

"Where's Mom? Where's my Dad? Why aren't they telling me this?" I demanded.

"They thought it best I tell you," Ruth offered. I felt a terrible isolation. They were right there at Brian's side when his life slipped away, but they couldn't even tell me themselves. They were too grief-stricken and overwhelmed. Ruth stayed a while, but she couldn't help, it was all too late.

As Mom and Dad had prearranged, our neighbors, Mary Agnes and Cecil Hinton, drove to school to pick up Mark and Margaret and break it to them. Waiting alone at the kitchen table in my parents' house, I stared at Brian's empty chair. It seemed so impossible that he could be dead! How can someone I love so much be gone forever? Can someone have so much life, personality, memory, and emotion and then simply be invisible? I'd heard somewhere that death is a thin veil that separates our worlds like walls separate rooms of a house. I wondered if Brian's spirit might have immediately left that hospital room and come home before going to heaven. I hoped he was beside me there in the heart of our home. Since Brian and I were so close, I began talking out loud to him even though I couldn't see him. I pleaded that he show me a sign by making the glass in front of me move. I could not come to grips with the finality of death. I was never to see Brian again. He died on November 6, 1965. He was barely seventeen years old.

Mom and Dad and Aunt Roberta flew home in the oil company plane. When they walked in our front door, nobody could speak. Nobody cried or hugged; everybody just went into his or her own room and closed the doors. Words couldn't come, tears wouldn't come. Dr. Franz came over later and gave us all little red pills so we could sleep.

It was cold on the day of Brian's funeral. The sky was heavy and dark and it began to sprinkle rain. My parents had decided to have an open casket funeral and I was furious. All his friends from high school were there and I knew they were probably looking at a corpse for the first time. But that dead person was my brother, and I could barely stop myself from running up and slamming the lid shut on the coffin. I wanted to walk up and slap everybody, knock them to the ground, and scream, "Hey, this is my little brother! Leave him alone! Get out of here! Get out!" But I didn't do any of those things. I sat there like a statue and let the events unfold. Daddy looked strange wearing a suit and it was the first time I had ever seen him cry.

Six of Brian's friends carried the casket to the hearse and everyone followed in their cars to Rose Hill Cemetery outside of town. The funeral procession looked like it stretched for miles. It seemed the whole town had turned out to pay their respects to Glen and Polly Judd's son. I kept thinking this was some kind of cruel hoax and that

Brian would be hiding under my bed waiting to jump out and scare me when I walked into my room.

After Brian had been laid to rest we went on home. People brought over the flowers from the funeral parlor, and neighbors carried in covered dishes. Years ago, Mom had assigned each of us kids a drawer in the big wooden kitchen cupboard to stash our personal junk. That night before I went to bed, I opened Brian's. There in his familiar handwriting on a folded sheet of notebook paper was a poem he'd memorized for school, "Thanatopsis" by William Cullen Bryant:

> So live, that when thy summons comes to join
> The innumerable caravan, which moves
> To that mysterious realm, where each shall take
> His chamber in the silent halls of death,
> Thou go not, like the quarry-slave at night,
> Scourged to his dungeon, but, sustained and soothed
> By an unfaltering trust, approach thy grave,
> Like one who wraps the drapery of his couch
> About him, and lies down to pleasant dreams.

There was no fantasy in Brian's death, no vestige of dreams, no fable, no noble conquests. The tumors, the tubes and bandages, the dingy hospital room, the cold and rainy funeral were all too frighteningly real. Too close to home to be made up or imagined. An injustice had been visited on the Judd clan, so tragic that no one could find the words even to talk about it. The impending possibility of Brian's death and how we might have felt about it was always ignored, pushed out of mind. We just didn't talk about things like that. We simply kept it all inside and tried to lock the gates of our hearts. We turned away from each other and suffered alone. It wasn't right, it wasn't wrong. It was just the Judd way.

I returned to my other life in Lexington. I was reading nursery rhymes to Chris at bedtime when I finally broke down. Frightened, she looked up and asked, "Mommy, what's wrong?" I replied, "Oh honey, everything's broken now. All the king's horses and all the king's men could never put us back together again."

Maybe Your Baby's Got the Blues

THE TERRIBLE SENSE of loss we all felt at Brian's death, heart wrenching and far reaching as it was, was eased somewhat by the wonder of Christina. Children have a way of filling voids, and watching my beautiful child sail headlong into life was a constant delight. We spent two years in the apartment in Lexington, and Christina grew up right on schedule, a happy, healthy, and eager kid thrilled by everything she saw. Easing comfortably into my role as proud mother, I ran for the phone to announce to the grandparents when she uttered her first words, when she sprouted her first tooth, and when she wobbled her first step. Before I knew it she was three years old.

Chris usually awakened before I did, and in a funny glimpse of what was to come, she'd pound on the wall with her glass bottle until she gained my full attention to jump-start her day. As I fixed breakfast, she'd bang away on her toy xylophone at my feet. She'd use the long stick with the red ball on its end to sing into like a microphone. She belted out songs that only she knew the words to. I would push our coffee table against the front window for her to stand on like a stage. She'd hide poised behind the closed curtains, while I introduced her to an invisible adoring audience. Then I'd dramatically pull the curtains open to reveal her. Jumping out with her xylophone stick microphone, she'd throw back her blond curly locks and wail "Old McDonald Had a Farm." I'd applaud and whistle hysterically after every song until I finally gave out. It was her favorite game with her favorite playmate.

Later I'd ask her, "Christina, do you want to go to Der Wienerschnitzel?" and she would look up at me and grinning and nodding, pronouncing *Wienerschnitzel* in her own butchered way. We'd both get dressed up and then, as if I were handing the queen of England her scepter, I would hand Christina her tiny, red patent leather purse just as we'd walk out the door. This small hot dog diner was the only place we could afford but for some strange reason was kind of like going to an amusement park for her. We'd order our hot dogs and field compliments from the other patrons who'd say, "My goodness, what a cute child!"

It was always a big treat for us to go out together, because we'd create our own fun. Christina was wickedly funny in her own way, and she'd often provide a running, garbled commentary on what we were doing and who we were watching. I felt as if I had been given a remarkable gift from God, this bright little one who had not a care in the world and an indomitable disposition. I was instilling a love for ritual, production, and ceremony in her way back then.

Chris loved the *Batman* television series, and she'd grab a towel from the bathroom and tie it about her shoulders to make her own cape. It was the only time that she was allowed to get up on the back of the sofa. My caped crusader would stand poised with knees slightly bent and grubby hands against the wall singing along with the theme song. At the right moment she'd scream, "Batman!" and jump down to the floor and race through the apartment. It was raucous, and earsplitting, and with the exception of a few bad dreams incited by actor Frank Gorshin's portrayal of the Riddler in the show, Batman was one of her favorite games. To this day she smiles when the subject comes up.

Michael hated going back to Ashland for any reason, so if I wanted to visit Montgomery Avenue, Chris and I would usually go alone. Mark and Margaret were crazy about Chris and were wonderful with her. "I love Uncle Mark!" Chris would chirp, "'cause he takes me to the swimming pool and buys me snowcones at the park!"

I was proud to see him this enthused about being an uncle.

Margaret, now a budding teenager, was bringing a much-needed spark into the house again.

Mom was much quieter these days, still grappling with the death of Brian. She didn't seem to care about leaving the house and slept a lot. Sometimes she'd offer to take care of Chris so I could walk around the park and be by myself for a bit. She and I spent time together just sitting at our kitchen table making chitchat. There were unspoken secrets between Mom and myself now. We could only acknowledge them with our eyes, but it wasn't my place to speak them aloud. I knew she and Dad were at last falling apart, and she knew I wasn't happy with Michael. We were two generations of unhappy women.

My life had slipped away from me; I had no control over anything anymore. Fate had switched me from being Glen and Polly's daughter to being Mr. and Mrs. Ciminella's daughter. *The Twilight Zone* was one of my favorite shows and I now felt as if I was living in it. I just couldn't shake the eerie feeling that I was still a kid pretending to be a housewife and mother.

Things were getting stranger across the board. Instead of my Daddy giving me a dollar-and-a-half allowance every Saturday morning, I was regularly swallowing my pride and accepting money from Mike Ciminella. Billie was now buying me clothes, instead of my own Mom. I knew she worried about us and loved Christina very much, but Billie felt as if financial support entitled her to a larger say in how we did things. One day she announced that she'd chosen Christina's godparents. I shrugged my shoulders, wondering silently if I should have some say in the matter. Michael and I were just two hapless kids barely getting by on the generosity of our folks, and it struck me as ungrateful to hurt Billie's feelings.

Michael barely graduated from college and found a job as a salesman for Amphenol, a company that manufactured components for the aeronautics industry. We were sent to Broadview, Illinois, a suburb of Chicago, for his training course. Although I was hoping Michael might wind up tackling something a bit meatier, a parts salesman seemed better than an unemployed frat boy. I was intrigued by the idea of living somewhere else for a while. Anything sounded better than another year of ennui and frozen dinners in that dreadful apartment.

I'd barely gotten unpacked in our new apartment in Illinois when I discovered that I was pregnant again. I was surprised, but very excited. I instantly felt the same love toward this baby that I had toward Christina. I was determined to make it a happy experience this time around.

Soon Michael came home announcing that he had completed his training with Amphenol and was being sent to Los Angeles. My immediate reaction was, "Thank God, we're finally going to be on our own!" Then I realized how far away from Mom, Dad, Mark, and Margaret I'd be; I couldn't imagine being so far from home. Los Angeles might well have been in outer space for all I knew. Although it was a place I had never even contemplated visiting, I vowed to myself, "I'll go anywhere as long as it's forward."

September 1967 we arrived in California, and in spite of some trepidations, I found it exciting. When we landed at Los Angeles International Airport, I'd never seen so much hustle and bustle and felt as if I had my nose pressed up against the window to the world. It was the "Summer of Love," and hippies were everywhere, robed in outlandish, garish colors. This was the other end of the spectrum from Ashland, Kentucky. We rented a tiny three-bedroom tract house in Sylmar out in the San Fernando Valley.

On April 19, 1968, I checked into Holy Cross Hospital in Granada Hills, went through another straightforward c-section delivery, and gave birth to the most beautiful baby girl. I named her Ashley Tyler, and she was absolutely radiant—dark hair and skin, dark eyes, very different looking from Chris and clearly in full possession of Ciminella genes. When I cradled her in my arms for the first time I cooed that she was "my sunshine" and told her she was my child of the light! It was one of the happiest moments of my life.

Suddenly, I was taking care of an infant and a very lively four-year-old. I found myself trapped in the house all day, without any friends or family to talk to, and it was quite an occasion when Michael informed me he'd invited his boss and wife home for dinner. I cleaned the house from top to bottom, cooked a great meal, and got all dressed up for the big event. The boss man and his rather plain wife sat down at our table, but after just a few minutes of small talk I realized that these were the most horrendously uninteresting, tedious people I had yet met in my short life. I wasn't expecting Henry Kissinger or Robin Williams, just someone with some brain cells and a sense of humor. The banal conversation dribbled and droned on until I wanted to shriek, "Someone throw a pie! Tell a joke! Break wind! Cluck like a chicken! Someone do *something!*" Was this what being a married adult meant? Could I continue to exist in a life so inane? The evening left its mark; I had the itch.

The only joy, wonder, or laughter in my life came from the kids. Chris was almost five and showing signs of becoming a highly independent child; she was always busy, playing some boisterous game, and she absolutely adored her new, cute baby sister. Ashley was a perfect baby. She slept through the night and rarely cried. So quick to smile, she made sweet noises and was unbelievably lovable. We called her "Chipmunk" because of her fat cheeks, and I was constantly smacking strangers' hands as they impulsively reached to pinch her face. Watching them grow into little people was constantly amazing. There were moments when I would just sit on the couch and watch them carry on, completely oblivious to me and the rest of the world. A marvelous, warm feeling would wash over me. Tears would spring to my eyes, my heart would flutter, and I realized that what I was experiencing was love in its purest form. Unconditional love, the mortar between the bricks of life, the prize we spend our whole loves trying to win, the gift we can only pray we are generous enough to give. I felt so lucky to have been shown this at such a young age; I was twenty-two now but I had learned one of the greatest lessons of my life. A bond was being woven between Christina, Ashley, and me, and I realized even then that it was my life's treasure.

Every bit as amazing was the mischief those two could get into. Chris was unpredictable, the kind of kid who inquires loudly in front of company, "Why does that lady have a mustache?" One afternoon I was busy in the kitchen with the front door open, when I heard Christina's wood-soled sandals clopping down our sidewalk at breakneck speed. She raced inside and slammed the door shut, leaning her back against it like a fugitive. With her face flushed and breathing hard, she insisted, "Mommy, no matter who knocks on this door, or what lies they tell you, don't open it." This desperate plea was immediately punctuated by Sue Heller, our neighbor, pounding on the door.

"You won't believe what Christina just did," Sue huffed. "She was smacking my Stevie up the side of his head with her doll!" I calmed Sue down, but something about these recurring incidents made me uneasy, because Chris was developing into a crafty and somewhat ornery little cuss. Next year she was to start kindergarten—for which I was more than ready—but I was already starting to hold my breath. Visions appeared in my head of her refusing to obey her teachers, getting in fistfights at recess, being sent to the principal's office, starting grade school riots! I reckoned that only time would tell how she'd channel her energy.

The longer we stayed on DeGarmo Avenue, the more I disliked the neighborhood. I came home one night and found our baby-sitter in an embarrassing situation on the sofa with her boyfriend. It was the last time she ever baby-sat in our house, and I assumed it was the last I'd hear from her. A month later we were burglarized and the thief turned out to be her brother, who had been initiated to where everything in the house was.

It was at this time Michael started chumming around with a playboy salesman named Stan. Stan lived in a typical bachelor pad at the beach and ran around with stewardesses and regularly called in sick with hangovers. Michael was running around with Stan, and Stan was dating stewardesses. It didn't take a rocket scientist to figure out what was going on. Something had struck me funny about Michael's "sales meetings" and the late hours he "had to work." There was also another recreational vice.

Michael was fiddling around with marijuana. I'd never had any experience with mind-altering substances before. At Michael's frat parties, I'd sipped a few mixed drinks but that was the extent of my participation with alcohol. I'd never been drunk, or had a hangover. There was never so much as a beer in our house when I was growing up and drinking has never been a temptation for me. Liquor tastes like floor wax and brought back reminders of my Mom's family's downfall and that awful night when my Daddy wobbled in my bedroom door and acknowledged my pregnancy. Drinking seemed not only unnecessary but downright stupid. Unfortunately, pot became quite another matter.

The first time Michael brought it home, I thought he was out of his mind! I ranted on and on about his being a family man with a job and responsibilities. He couldn't afford to be sent off to Sing Sing! Michael was persuasive and eager to share his new discovery with me. I think he saw it as a way of bridging the ever-widening gulf between us. The first time he pulled out his sandwich bag full of grass, I was repelled and horror-struck. I expected our door to be kicked in by a SWAT team and hauled off to some hell-hole prison for one hundred years. He just laughed at me and kept demonstrating how to hold a joint, and inhale it. This went on for months. I didn't speak to Michael at first, but I was gradually observing how mellow it made him and I grew to prefer his pot-smoking mood over his drinking.

Then it happened. One night when the girls were asleep, he handed me a joint and I took my first hit. After I almost coughed to death, I finally got the hang of it.

I liked the sensation it provided. It seemed to smooth things over. All the lost, empty years. All the sorrowful memories of Brian's death and the destruction of our family, the loss of my childhood, and the plans I had for my future. Magically, all the guilt and negativity seemed to go up in smoke. Or so I thought at the time. So easy, so simple, so wonderful.

It was 1970, the dawn of a revolutionary new decade. The world was in chaos, the hippies were trying to install a new order, and all bets were off. Every red-blooded American under the age of thirty had a responsibility to question and experiment with society's standards, to push the boundaries even farther in the search for enlightenment, awareness. I was more than ready to buy into it since the norms hadn't served me too well up to this point. I was young, eager, feeling very frisky, and desperate for change. I wanted pot to help me escape the suburbs mentally. This superficial mind-set proved temporary and unfulfilling. They call it a mind-altering substance, because that's all it does. When the blue haze evaporated, the dirty dishes were still sitting in the sink, Michael was still there, and my life was as big a lie as the pot. I guess that's why they call it dope.

Sometimes people in pain or crisis search recklessly for relief in the wrong places. I know now that dabbling in pot was just an immature diversion. It seemed like harmless recreation, just a plaything, and I took to it much like a child attaches itself to a bright shiny new toy; I didn't once give any thought to the basic health implications of putting smoke into my lungs, although I would never have smoked cigarettes. That's how shortsighted my thinking was at the time. It was my own mind-set that needed changing, my hunger to break out of the persistent monotony that was suffocating me. I felt cut off from and so far away from family and friends. There was no one watching me anymore. Everyone here in L.A. seemed to be from somewhere else. I had no inkling that pot could be psychologically addictive or harmful, and never thought about it being against the law!

I'm terribly ashamed and regretful now that I tried it. Most people I know will admit to having smoked it at least once, but I nonetheless wince at what I did. I make this confession in the hope it might cause someone to wake up, come to their senses, and do something constructive about their situation. At the least, pot causes you to waste your precious life. At its worst, it can lead you to try other addictive substances, destroy relationships, harm your health, cost you your job, and oh yes, land you in the slammer!

I began going out on my own, exploring Los Angeles in an effort to find something meaningful. I became curious about astrology and went to meetings at the Theosophical Society. It only took one glance at people in the class to know they were different from my humdrum dinner guests in Sylmar. Pretty soon I was casting and delineating horoscopes. Imbued with an insatiable curiosity about anything and everything, I loved discovering things for myself. I opened myself to new experiences while maintaining my inner reserve. In this case I quickly arrived at the informed conclusion that astrology is arcane flapdoodle. Pure myth and folklore with absolutely no basis in science or truth. But I began making friends; the conversations I had with these free-thinking people nudged open the doors in my narrow life.

I'd taken the girls to a nearby Baptist church, but was intrigued by Los Angeles's plethora of religious choices. Thus began my zealous scrutiny of Eastern religions. The study was revitalizing as well as educational. I came full circle, returning to my Christian beliefs, satisfied and better informed.

At one of my stopovers, the Unitarian church, I developed a political awareness, and in no time I was canvassing door to door for Eugene McCarthy. Frustrated by the inept way the U.S. government was handling the Vietnam War, I attended peace rallies. I was behind our soldiers 100 percent and resented the obscene way America treated our returning vets. My quarrel was with Jane Fonda and what she was doing to undermine our troops. Michael's chief customers were Lockheed, Boeing, and North American Rockwell, and there I was on the six o'clock news protesting them. Michael's fury and my pacifism created interesting dialogue!

In July 1969, as we landed a man on the moon the first time, our neighbors Jerry and Sue Heller came over to watch it on television. Jerry, a nonpracticing Jew and an agnostic, had a Ph.D. from MIT and worked for Jet Propulsion Laboratories, which developed technology that helped put the astronauts in space. He was very well read and extremely knowledgeable about the space program and its implications for our future. This led to a lengthy discussion about the existence of God. Because of his background, I began arguing for God's existence based on the law of probabilities. As he and I tossed our personal theories back and forth, it dawned on me that he was taking me seriously. "News flash: What do you know, I have a brain." It felt indescribably good to be taken seriously by an intelligent human being, to be, for just a moment, something more than Glen and Polly's daughter, Michael's wife, or Christina and Ashley's mother.

The time for change was at hand. First, I had to escape from Sylmar. I covered our old blue Dodge with huge flower decals and began calling it "the getaway car." I was antsy to get out of the valley into Hollywood, where people were more interesting and exciting things were happening and I thought I might find a job.

I knew I couldn't stand living in an apartment again, so I found a two-story house in West Hollywood at 1124 North Larrabee, right off Sunset Strip, smack-dab in the middle of all the action. The house was in terrible condition and hadn't had a coat of paint in thirty years, but it was love at first sight. I saw the possibilities. My future was in the hands of an elderly widow.

As she looked down at my two girls they smiled at her. She said Ashley reminded her of her granddaughter. I was so grateful, I gave her an antique piece of cut-glass Billie had given me when we left Kentucky.

When I signed the lease for $350 a month, I felt as if I was getting a new lease of life itself. It was Easter of 1970, a sign I might also be resurrected from the dead!

Now each day I waited for Michael to come home at six o'clock at the house in Sylmar. After putting the girls to bed, I loaded the car with cleaning supplies, tools, and paint and drove over the hill into Hollywood where I'd work all night. I painted the kitchen mustard yellow and navy blue and put up some orange posters for accent color. I picked up a wood soda pop crate like the one I used to stand on to play pinball at Daddy's station, painted it mustard, and nailed it up on the navy blue wall to put spices in. I painted all my kitchen utensils and hung them up like pieces of art. It was a Peter Max, pop-art feel, something completely different from anything I'd ever known. My landlady almost fainted.

Each wall of the patriotic bathroom was painted either red, white, or blue lacquer. I put a mattress on my bedroom floor and covered it with an Indian batik spread. The lampshades were draped in sheer scarves giving them a sexy, bordello look. I loved fringe and sewed it on lampshades all around the house. There were plants everywhere. The best part was that the place was now mine.

We all moved in, but Michael just didn't fit into the picture. This was my idea, I had searched it out, scrubbed and scoured, polished, wallpapered, and painted it. I had breathed life into it, and he just didn't belong. He was like a bad guest who wouldn't leave.

One night I finally worked up the courage to sit him down and declare, "Michael, I'm dying inside. I don't want you here anymore and I have to start over."

I never thought I'd be getting a divorce, but then again I never expected to have to marry under the circumstances under which we got married. Michael knew it had been building to this. He'd been sleeping on the couch for a long time, and I couldn't remember when we had last said a nice word to each other.

We fought like cats and dogs for the next few weeks. He screamed at me because I didn't love him and warned I'd never find a job, that the kids would starve to death, and that he wouldn't let me have the car.

I was fighting for both my own life and my children's future. I didn't want them growing up in an environment where their mother and father didn't love or respect each other. I blamed myself for taking so long to come to this juncture, because the situation was now taking its toll. Christina developed asthma and started sleepwalking. She sometimes woke up screaming with nightmares.

I phoned the Ciminellas back in Ashland and declared, "I'm calling you because I know Michael won't. You've been good to me and I'm sorry to have to tell you, but you deserve to know what's going on. I'm filing for divorce."

Mike flew out immediately to try to patch things up between us, but even he realized it was hopeless and inevitable.

Mired in traditional macho southern thinking, it was difficult for Michael to conceive of a single uneducated mother being able to support a family. He just couldn't grasp the fact that I was actually going through with this. It *would* be tough. I'd been trying to put away a dollar in my underwear drawer now and then, but it had proved futile. At the end of the week, there was never anything left.

I'd never had a job before and didn't have any skills, but I longed to be independent. I knew I could do something meaningful if somebody would just give me half a chance. Michael was so alarmed and frustrated with my newfound attitude that he beat me down with the only weapons he had: fear and money.

On the morning of September 19, 1971, I was standing over

him as he awoke on the living room couch. "Everything has a sooner or later, Michael! Pack up and move on—you'll never spend another night in the same house with me."

Startled, he grabbed his things and moved in with his friend Harry down at Manhattan Beach.

We had two cars at the time: our personal car, the aged blue Dodge with flower decals, displaying hippie-style protest of the mundane, and his company car. Michael and his friend took them both and left the kids and me stranded in Hollywood. It was so selfish and cruel that I was stunned at first, but this was typical of him.

"You can't leave me and the children without a car," I protested.

"You should have thought about that before you threw me out, bitch," he charmingly replied.

For the next few months I hitched a lift to the grocery store on payday with my dear friend Nancy Balazs from across the street. She had a little red Mustang and we always had to be careful what we bought so we could be sure that everything would fit in the car. When Nancy wasn't around, I walked down to the Alpha-Beta on San Vicente, bypassing all the more convenient little specialty markets on the way, because they charged seven cents more for a can of tuna and ten cents more for a loaf of bread.

Things were really rough for a while. The kids begged for a pet, but I certainly didn't have money for pet food. When they were invited to birthday parties they had to go without a gift and invent some excuse to cover it like: "I forgot it at home" and "I'll bring it tomorrow." I lived in guilt because I couldn't provide for Chris and Ashley as they deserved.

Those were scary times. No car, no money, no job, no skills, no connections. On the way to the supermarket I would stand on the corner at Sunset waiting for the light to change. The hot sun was burning like a fuzzy lemon drop through the smog as I watched all the Mercedes and Rolls Royces pass by, air-conditioners on and windows rolled tight. My eyes would sting from the fumes and I'd wonder, "Seriously now, what am I going to do?"

Yet somehow, at that particular moment, I knew I would come

up with something. My wheels were turning, ideas were flowing. My mind turned to the astronauts floating in freefall thousands of miles from the earth. It must have been a terrifying yet ecstatic feeling.

Beaming a wide smile to dozens of anonymous passing motorists as I strolled to the grocery store, I glowed like the California sunset. The world was a menu and I was starved! I began chanting a new mantra over and over again: "Free at last, free at last! Thank God Almighty, I'm free at last!"

Don't Be Cruel

THE BEST PLACE to find a helping hand is at the end of your own arm. Looking through the want ads became a daily ritual. I got my hopes up on one opening for a receptionist at Mark Gordon Enterprises on Palm Avenue in West Hollywood. The office was just a couple of blocks from my house, so it didn't matter that I didn't have a car. As Mark introduced me to his wife, Florence LaRue, it dawned on me that they were the Fifth Dimension, who were in their heyday right then.

I was really nervous because I already felt as if this were the only available job I could handle and my life were on the line. They were simply looking for a person to answer their phones and didn't know how hard I was praying for the chance to join the ranks of the employed. It didn't faze me that their song "Age of Aquarius" was number one on the charts and the anthem of the popular musical *Hair.* I put on my happy face and had no idea how I came across, considering it was the first job interview I had ever been to in my entire life.

Mark thanked me for coming in and said he'd give me a call, in a few days. When that call came he informed me he'd decided to hire a black girl for political reasons. Their entire office staff was white, and many of their black business associates didn't like it. My heart sank, but then Mark offered me a secretarial position with his agent. I had had only one semester of typing in high school, had no clue what shorthand was, and had never touched a filing cabinet, but I thought,

I'll try anything! I was ecstatic: My first job! I started singing "Age of Aquarius" and danced around the room with Chris and Ashley.

Even though I worked for his booking agent, Mark Gordon kept me busy whenever I was available. He asked me to find a bigger house for his family. I was informed of what they had in mind and introduced to his real estate agent. Together we drove all over Beverly Hills and looked at dream houses. I'd never seen anything like it before. I looked at all these showy mansions and thought of something my Daddy might say, "It ain't home, but it's much!" I couldn't believe that someone would pay me to visit one celebrity home after another and judge if they were acceptable or not. It was beyond the map to the stars' homes! Paul Newman and his wife, Joanne Woodward, had just moved to Connecticut and had their estate for sale. I remember wandering through it and trying to stay nonchalant. When we reached the master bath, I excused myself, shut the door, and sat down on the john. "I'm sitting on Cool Hand Luke's throne!" I squealed, under my breath. I would tour Anthony Quinn's and Cher's homes and then go back to my own, sleep on my mattress on the floor, and eat beans and weenies.

Nancy from across the street agreed to help out with the babysitting. There were few kids in the neighborhood, and Nancy was looking for a playmate for her daughter, sweet Gabrielle, who was the same age as Ashley. By this time Christina was in the first grade, and went straight to Nancy's after school. Nancy had been a beautiful blond model: Ten years older, she was now resigned to being one of the throng of struggling single moms working as salespeople. She made me realize how short lived a modeling career is.

Ashley was two and a half when we moved to Hollywood and was developing into quite a different child from Christina. I felt a lot of it had to do with the fact that the Ciminella grandparents weren't around telling me how to raise Ashley. Chris had been born to high drama and had adopted some of its characteristics, while Ashley appeared like the sunshine after a hard storm. I was more relaxed and confident when she came along, and Ashley responded to the change in atmosphere. She was a thoughtful, quiet child with a special glow and a loving, open personality. Ashley had a whole coterie of imaginary playmates, a creative exercise Chris never went through. Full of curiosity and always smiling, Ashley would crawl up into a stranger's lap and make herself right at home. The recipient of these spontaneous affections would invariably pronounce her a most charming child. She began to read at a very early age, and to this day is the most voracious reader I've ever known. She and I were inseparable from the moment of her birth.

Chris and Ashley grew up very close because there were so few other children around. There was one little boy, Kurt, whose mother, Brandi, was the featured exotic stripper at the Classic Cat Club down on the corner of Sunset Strip. Many mornings he'd show up on our doorstep with dirty clothes and messy hair, hungry and alone. We always made him breakfast, because his mother danced all night and he couldn't wake her.

I suppose I was imitating something good old Mom would do when I became Chris's third-grade Brownie leader. However, the girls in my own troop back in Ashland had mothers who were ordinary housewives and whose fathers worked at Armco Steel Mill. Chris's troop members were more in line with Mariska Hargitay. Her mom was Jayne Mansfield and her dad was Mickey Hargitay, the Hungarian muscleman, à la Arnold Schwarzenegger. Chris's best friend was Angelique L'Amour. Her famous dad, Louis, was the best-selling western author. He and his elegant and gracious wife, Kathy, helped out at Brownie events and gave us our first interesting peek behind the veneer of fame and wealth. Chris often spent the night at their lovely home and couldn't get over their having a live-in maid. The L'Amours were genuinely nice folks who never looked down their noses at us.

My first job with the Fifth Dimension was interesting. I got to meet fledgling songwriters like Kim Carnes and Paul Williams, as they came in to pitch their songs. I'd talk on the phone with Tony Orlando and his two female partners, setting up their tours.

My secretarial career was not without its nerve-wracking moments. I soon discovered that my boss was having an extramarital affair, and it dawned on me that it was only a matter of time before he replaced me with his new girlfriend. Lo and behold, it happened sooner than I thought, and before I could line up another job, I was back out on the street.

After a week or so of out-and-out panic, I took a job in the secretarial pool at a large insurance company downtown. I was shuffling papers one day when my boss invited me into his office for a "chat about my future." His desk was decorated with loads of family pictures, but without wasting any time he invited me to come away with him for a ski weekend. My heart sank. I wondered . . . is it always going to be like this? It was only my second job, and I desperately needed the money. "Gee thanks," I apologized, "but I promised to take my kids to the beach Saturday, and we've got church on Sunday. Besides I don't ski."

I worked a few more days, decided I hated the tedious job and riding the bus. I just didn't want to do battle with this guy.

Of course, if this kind of sexual harassment were to happen today there would be so many avenues open to fight it. Thanks to courageous women like Anita Hill, a woman can expose the man and help protect the workplace for others. Twenty years ago it was tough: A woman could either endure his inappropriate behavior or get herself another job. It was my first taste of sexual harassment and the incident added to my sense of helplessness and anonymity.

I often took Chris and Ashley to the park on San Vicente in West Hollywood after work and weekends. That's where I met a well-known photographer, Ron Wood. I observed him taking photos of me playing with the kids. As we chatted, he suggested I try modeling and offered to use me in his night class at the Art Center School of Design. Because it was evening work, it was a perfect way for me to pick up an extra $5 an hour. Since I'd never done any modeling before, I was taken aback at the first question the school receptionist asked me. She needed to know if I had done life modeling.

"What's that?" I wondered.

"Nudes," was her blunt answer.

I responded as politely as I could muster, "No, and I hope I'm never that desperate." The idea of standing up stark naked in front of a room of total strangers staring at me and drawing me for an hour gave me the willies.

"Very well," the woman continued with a sly smile. "We'll wait and see how desperate you get then."

I didn't know quite how to take that statement, but before I had time to dwell on it I was hired as a model—a clothed model, thank you very much.

I was dressing in quite an eccentric fashion at the time, and enjoying the freedom of style in Hollywood. While furnishing my house on Larrabee I had discovered flea markets, and the vintage pieces I bought so cheaply became the entire basis for my eclectic wardrobe. I dressed like Rita Hayworth in shoulder pads and tight-waisted peplums and wore my hair 1940s style. I accessorized with big authentic clip earrings, and I even bought used high heels to wear with seamed nylons. Whenever I arrived for art class, the students chimed, "What a great costume!" assuming I had dressed in charac-ter especially for them.

The agent who booked models for the school took a shine to me and scheduled me whenever she could. During the holidays, the Art Center wanted to create some Christmas tableaux, so I brought Christina and Ashley in with me. We wore cozy flannel granny gowns and posed on a chaise lounge while I read to the children. While Chris was absorbed in my bedtime story, Ashley fell asleep with her thumb in her mouth. It was a comforting moment: My little ones at peace while admiring art students sketched silently at their easels. And I was getting paid! "Where there's a will, there's a way," I surmised. "We're going to make it in this town. We're going to survive!"

I took on all sorts of extra modeling work. The Doors were shooting some kind of musical film—probably a form of early music video—and I was hired as a woman who aged a century. The makeup man, Ralph Gulko, who did *Planet of the Apes,* layered me with spirit gum and latex, and using time-lapse photography they aged me through twenty, thirty, forty, fifty years—all the way to one hundred. I didn't recognize the old crone in the mirror when he was done and thought, "Wow! I wonder if this is what I'll look like when I'm one hundred. But now, how do I get this stuff off?"

They used acetone, and for days my face was pink and sensitive.

One morning as I was scouring the want ads, I spotted an ad for models for a bicycle layout at the beach. It seemed kind of strange, because usually companies call agencies to get their models. I didn't have an agent, so I brushed aside my qualms, accepted the assignment over the phone, and went down to Marina Del Rey. I had accumulated my modeling portfolio by asking for copies of photographs from the Art Center and from various photographer friends. I presented my book to two weird men who immediately announced that I was hired. Two other young female models and myself went down to the docks and were told to board a large cabin cruiser. One of the guys started the motor and I obviously wondered, "Wait a minute, this is a bicycle ad. What are we doing on a boat?"

As we headed out to sea I became more and more uneasy and questioned myself, "Okay, what's wrong with this picture? Here I am with two big guys and two other models in bikinis, no photographic equipment in sight, sailing out to sea and nobody knows where I am."

The breeze was cold on the open water, but I was so nervous, I was sweating. I spoke up and informed one of the guys that I had to get home, that I had to relieve the baby-sitter. He looked me over and inquired in a suave way if I had noticed what a beautiful day it was. "Why don't you just relax?" he murmured.

I demanded that he turn the boat around and let me off on shore. He tried to dissuade me, but I refused to shut up or back down. They eventually turned around and took us back to shore. The two other timid girls were terrified.

Back on land we hightailed it out of there. I promptly called the Better Business Bureau and learned they had the police after them. The two were small-time con artists. I called the phone number from the ad the next day, but, of course, it was disconnected. I couldn't stop trembling as it dawned on me that this was California, Crack Pot Headquarters. I suddenly realized I had probably just narrowly escaped some horrible incident. I wondered if I might have a guardian angel watching over me.

Actually, for me, modeling never had any of the allure and appeal it holds for some young women. I found it vacuous and unchallenging. Being told I was attractive had never registered as having anything to do with who and what I really am. Genetics gets credit or blame for outward appearance. What I consider "attractive" is kindness, a sense of humor, and intelligence. Modeling was merely a matter of dollars and time to me. I found I could make more in one afternoon "shoot" than I made working a full week, because being unskilled, I could only make minimum wage in any normal workplace. It also freed me to be with my growing girls, who needed more attention than a single working mom could give. I had to keep a constant eye on Chris to make sure she didn't get into trouble.

The trouble with trouble is it starts out as fun! I met an avant garde lady named Roxy Wallace at our next door neighbor's party. She was a hip folk singer/songwriter who had just released an album on a major label. Roxy's personal story was intriguing, because she left her husband and gave up custody of her child to devote her life to being an artist. I was absolutely flabbergasted at the thought of a woman giving up her family to find fulfillment on her own. Needless to say, this was a foreign concept to someone from my background, where family and home life dominated virtually every aspect of an individual's existence. I was never able to feel particularly close to her because of our differences in values.

I'd go to see Roxy perform at funky nightclubs and cafés around LA. She had an artsy image and a cult following. Roxy stayed up all night and seemed to be the center of a lot of fun. She lived in a great Hollywood pad up in the hills under the *D* in the Hollywood sign and made extra money by renting rooms out to musicians. It fascinated me to see a living room that didn't have a television set, a La-Z-Boy, and a *TV Guide* on the coffee table. Instead, there was a drum set, a piano, and a lot of rehearsal equipment lying around. The messy house was often filled with eccentric musicians or other bohemian artist types. It didn't take long for me to discover I liked being around musical things and people, and some of Roxy's ways of doing things were filed away in my subconscious for future use. Her life seemed like such a different world. Here was a single female going after a career in music against great odds.

Roxy was distraught over the breakup with her live-in boyfriend of the past few months, James Dean, Jr. James was new in town, and after leaving Roxy, he moved in temporarily with our mutual friends, the gay next door neighbors. James was working as an actor on one of the daytime soaps. Although he had no training as an actor, the guy had charisma and unaffected natural appeal. Knowing that Michael and I would be separating, he'd been flirting heavily with me, and we both figured it was only a matter of time.

In 1972, James was country when country wasn't cool. He wore cowboy boots and tight, faded jeans and had the aura of a man with a checkered past—just the kind of guy that could spark my interest. Blond haired, he strongly resembled James Dean and acted recalcitrant as Clint Eastwood. I'd been instantly attracted to him.

Friday night after work, several friends and I decided to go dancing at one of our favorite honky-tonks in Sherman Oaks, The Brass Ring, where Delaney and Bonnie were performing. James followed in his blue Corvette convertible and hung out with us. We wound up as partners because he was a killer dancer and very funny. We had a few glasses of wine and a lot of laughs, and I was delighted to discover that he was interesting, intelligent, and possessed a great deal of personal charm. And boy did I love those tight jeans!

By the end of the evening I was totally infatuated: gone, gone, gone. I later found out James had come from Oklahoma City, where at the age of only fourteen he had an experience that ruined his life. He left junior high school one afternoon with a stomachache, walked into his house, and found his mother having sex with one of the biggest political leaders in the state. James's mom was the man's secretary at the time, and had been having an affair with this guy for a long time. James ran down the street to the fire station where his father was on duty and described in explicit detail in front of all the other firemen what his mother and this other man were doing. His father's macho ego was wounded, and in his embarrassment and fury he turned on his son. James was only in the seventh grade, but he never went home again.

He dropped out of school, too, and lived on the streets in abandoned cars, gradually becoming a full-fledged juvenile delinquent. James collected pop bottles at first, got clothes and food from friends, then moved up to hustling pool for money before graduating to rackets and robbery. His first brush with the law came when he was caught stealing air-conditioners out of new homes and selling them back to the crooked contractor who had originally installed them. Eventually James did jail time in Oklahoma for possession of marijuana. After his release from the penitentiary, he hitchhiked to California, carried on his brief affair with Roxy, and waltzed right into my life. I was a sitting duck.

It was time. The next morning after our fun group party at the club, he came straight over to the house as soon as Christina and Ashley left for school. The instant I saw him at the back door I could see the heat in his eyes. Without even knocking, he came straight in at me and lowered me to the floor. He whispered urgently, "I've never been as attracted to anyone in my life as I am to you." I couldn't breathe or move. After a lifetime of being defined by men on their terms—first as Glen Judd's daughter, then as Michael Ciminella's wife—my head was swimming as I considered this nakedly passionate creature. On the heels of eight lonely years of being a devoted mother to my children, struggling to make ends meet, and denying myself a whole array of simple human pleasures, I didn't stand a chance. Not a chance. I was swept away.

James was the most intense and passionate man I had ever met. He loved to laugh and was one of the most talented people I knew. He wrote poetry and music, painted pictures, and cooked wonderful meals, each with equal flair. He played exuberantly with my daughters, made their school lunches and stuck notes with riddles or jokes inside. At first Christina and Ashley seemed to accept him, and he loved them back. What could be more perfect? Because he was new in town and without a home I invited him to move in. He pitched in with household chores and took care of the kids while I was at work.

James and I were in sync on many levels. We decided to try a business venture together, so after he scraped up some capital, we formed a video production company that we dubbed Nomad Video in honor of our peripatetic lifestyles. James somehow purchased some expensive video equipment, including a huge mobile truck, which sat in my driveway.

It never occurred to me at the time to question where all the money was coming from. I assumed you just went down to the neighborhood bank and got a loan, that's how incredibly naive I was. I dreamed of making classy educational National Geographic–style documentaries, but in the mean time we paid the bills by recording home videos for people like Berry Gordy, the creator of Motown

Records. Occasionally a tasty project would wander in the door. We videotaped Diana Ross as she worked on *The Billie Holiday Story*. She revealed to us that she was nervous about her acting debut, and she seemed to benefit greatly by evaluating her performance on our instant replays of scenes. We had a lot of fun videotaping Chris and Ashley and our friends. James got Ashley's visit to *Romper Room* as well as vignettes of our daily life, like me cutting the girls' hair on the back porch.

There was a darker side to my infatuation with James Dean, Jr. He was the quintessential outlaw, a lusty boyfriend whose past was spiced with hints of the reckless. I was like a moth drawn to a flame. The outlaw image turned out to be better-founded than I would have liked, however. He had a buddy named Jack who lived in a hippie pad in Topanga Canyon and was one of the biggest pot dealers in southern California. Jack showed us a room without furniture, stacked with large garbage-size bags of marijuana. I tried to keep my eyes in their sockets and was thankful I hadn't brought the girls along.

There were often strange men and women at Jack's house, and James told me later the parties often turned into orgies. The last thing I heard about Jack was that he smoked too much THC one night and stole a cop car. After a scary high-speed chase he was captured and did time.

Sometimes we'd ride in James's blue Corvette convertible out to the ranch of an Indian named Henry Medicine Hat. We'd ride horses and sit around taking in the beautiful scenery. Dean Stockwell used to hang out there along with Flo and Eddie of the Turtles. Sometimes Dennis Hopper would drift in, but I got such weird vibes from him, I didn't make any attempt to talk with him.

As unorthodox as some of these people were, I was somewhat comfortable in these places. I felt like Ma Barker, out partying with dangerous and colorful fringe dwellers. There was one aspect to all this running around that I loved. The bucolic canyon hideaways reminded me a little of Aunt Pauline's farm. The old-fashioned houses were tucked away in pockets of rough natural land. It harkened me back to a time when I would visit our farms in Kentucky. There was a sense of timelessness to that kind of existence. Sitting on a peaceful canyon hillside visiting with a few convivial friends seemed familiar and comforting to me.

These echoes of rural Kentucky life brought to mind the wonderful light of my childhood. Jack and Henry Medicine Hat and his wife had long hair and went barefoot. Jack wore his long hair braided, went around without a shirt, and wore leather pants and turquoise jewelry. The roads to their houses were so untraveled, we'd all stop what we were doing and look up when we heard a vehicle in the distance. There were horses, dogs and cats, and wild creatures in the woods. They raised herbs in their gardens and hung them to dry in bunches from rafters in their kitchens.

Henry's house had lace curtains and doilies on the furniture. There were antique oak buffets against the walls and Navajo rugs on wood floors that evoked warm, communal feelings. There was always a big jug of sangria in the fridge and a pot of soup ready on the stove. Everyone was welcome and shared with everyone else.

I wanted these offbeat uninhibited characters to be like distant cousins of my colorful Kentucky relatives. It was the home place, brought forward twenty years and transplanted to the West Coast. I was home again . . . sort of. In reality these were not people I would have been with if it hadn't been for James.

I was just beginning to see that the years of humdrum existence contributed to my attraction to James. He was as demonstrative as my father had been undemonstrative and was so different from any man I'd ever known. Initially, I found his jealousy flattering, since I wasn't accustomed to compliments and overt affection. He was so aggressive and unbridled in his display of emotions that I had been spellbound at first. Passion persuades.

Now he'd turned possessive and was showing a side of himself that worried and frightened me. He'd look at my grocery list and set a time limit for me to do shopping and errands. James had a short fuse and I walked around on pins and needles. Things were getting way out of hand.

As we were leaving a movie theater one evening, an extremely handsome guy stopped to flirt with me as I was waiting in the lobby while James was in the rest room. "Beat it, buddy!" James warned the guy menacingly. We walked stiffly in silence to his Corvette and as soon as I shut my door, he suddenly slapped me hard across my mouth. When I raised my arm to ward off more blows, I saw blood smeared on the back of my hand. "You filthy little tramp!" he screamed. "You whores are all alike! I should have known, you're just like my mother."

My heart raced as I suddenly realized how much James was still affected by that awful incident from his childhood. He was equating all women with his mother, after catching her in the act of unfaithfulness. It was an episode that not only ruined his image of her but drove a wedge between him and his father and instantly shattered their home. It orphaned him and scarred him for life, and no one had ever tried to help him. I knew better than to stand up to James's jealous rage and apologized in spite of my innocence.

I had never in real life seen a man hit a woman. Michael's abuse was verbal, although he did shove me several times. As we drove on home I felt a hideous sense of entrapment once again. The next day James wrote me a beautiful love poem and apologized for my swollen lip and black eye. From that moment on, I began figuring out a way to get rid of him.

I told him I was confused due to the recent divorce and just needed a little time by myself. "One hurt deserves another," he snickered. He protested but moved out of my house. A few days later he phoned and told me to look out my front doorway after I hung up. As I looked across the street, I saw him standing in the window of the once-empty apartment above Nancy's. He was just standing there, smoking his cigarette, and staring back at me, an ominous sign to say the least. He had taken a job as a night clerk at a 7-Eleven market and was now devoting all his time to monitoring my activities from his perfect vantage point in his new apartment.

After a while I grew more and more restless to date other men but knew better than to expose myself or a potential suitor to James's wrath. I could not figure out how James knew what time I was getting home while he was away at work. One morning I found a cheap smashed watch in my driveway. He'd been placing one under my back tire when he left for his job in the evening. If I backed out of the drive, I ran over the watch, stopping it at that precise moment.

James had learned a lot of tricks in prison! Every time I went from the house to my car I felt open to danger. I was being stalked. This went on for months.

Minutes after a male friend stopped by to visit me, James came flying through the unlocked front door, fuming something about "killing him with his bare hands." Before my startled friend even had time to realize he should defend himself, James landed a brutal punch squarely in the middle of the poor guy's face. He broke my friend's nose and in doing so badly broke his own hand. Weaponless and wincing in pain, James disappeared just as abruptly as he'd appeared.

I met an interesting man, explained why he shouldn't pick me up and agreed to meet him at a nice restaurant for dinner. After our date, I returned home well before midnight. I'd taken a job as receptionist in a law office on Avenue of the Stars in Century City and my Dad bought me a used car. Driving my usual route to work the next morning, I casually glanced up into my rearview mirror at a stoplight to put on my lipstick. There was a blue Corvette convertible behind me. I didn't know whether James knew where I worked or not, but I knew I couldn't let him follow me and cause a scene. Picking up speed, I began racing through alleys and taking side streets. He stayed right on my tail. I got so mad I finally threw my clumsy Impala into reverse and slammed backward into his sports car. It stopped him, while I sped off to my office.

About an hour later I looked up from my desk as an enraged James came bursting through the door. As James was approaching, I had buzzed the attorney to come rescue me. There were several clients in the waiting room, who watched in shock as he marched straight over and tried to pick me up.

James and my boss knew each other, because the attorney and his family lived next door to us on Larrabee. Wade had just left the legal department of one of the networks to form his own private practice and recruited me to help him set up his office. Wade was able to calm James down by reminding him this was a respectable law office and he had no business being there. Wade also indicated that he thought it would be unfortunate to have to call the authorities and nodded toward the witnesses, who sat dumbstruck observing all this commotion. Cursing under his breath, James split. Wade warned me

I hadn't seen the last of James and suggested I get a restraining order.

On my way home I stopped at the West Hollywood Sheriff's Department on San Vicente. I'd seen it many times as I took the kids to the small park across the street. I was uncomfortable being inside a police station for the first time. I did my business with a handsome officer, who was divorced. Al began stopping by in the evenings with his partner. I'd offer them a cup of coffee and dessert or just chat a few minutes. The deterrent effect of their patrol car sitting in my driveway was working. As an added bonus, the officer and I really enjoyed each other's company!

The uneasy calm was broken by one bizarre incident. I was awakened from a dead sleep at 3:00 A.M. by the telephone. I recognized James's voice instantly, and I was hanging up when I heard him insisting, "I have Christina." I was alarmed and screamed at him as he tried to report to me that he was watching the house when she suddenly walked out the front door. He described the pajamas Chris was wearing as she headed straight for Sunset Boulevard, alone! In the middle of the night! He'd chased after her, and after he grabbed her, he asked her what on earth she was doing. "I'm going to the store for Scotch tape for my Brownie meeting," was her monotone reply. She was sleepwalking again. I retrieved Chris and was not amused when James asked if I wasn't even going to say thank you for the surveillance. He sat on the front porch all night, whimpering like a cow dog to be let in.

The next day I called our pediatrician to consult with him about Christina's sleepwalking. I had locks installed at the tops of the doors and kept an ear out for Chris at night from then on.

Some months later I returned home one night from modeling and stopped to drop off my things at the house before stepping across the street to get Chris and Ashley from Nancy's. I set my satchel down inside the hallway, and as I looked up, I noticed something in our living room that caused me to freeze in fear. A window pane in the French doors leading to the patio was broken, and the door was ajar. I was paralyzed with terror as I realized that someone was inside my house.

Before I could reach for the telephone, someone grabbed me from behind and slammed me up against him. "Who've you been with, bitch?" James had completely snapped. He grabbed my hair and jerked my head back forcefully causing me to wince with pain. He smelled my neck for traces of men's cologne. Then he shoved me to the floor and rifled through my cosmetic case and wardrobe bags looking for evidence. I knew to keep silent while he was in such a blind rage. My things were strewn all over the hallway, and I spied my work assignment sheet. "There's your documentation on where I've been tonight," I offered in as calm a voice as I could muster. For the next seven hours he paced and ranted, hitting me and cursing me, his mother, and all womankind. My natural inclination to help him and to "fix it" was blown to hell by the rather pressing issue that he just might kill me. As he ripped my clothes off and was raping me, it never even occurred to me this was the same man I once thought I was in love with.

This was just some sick, violently out-of-control stranger. My lip stung and bled from the slap, and I could feel my eye swelling and pounding from his punches. I held up a lamp to shield myself from further blows. Angry and desperate, I kept thinking I didn't want any broken bones or injuries serious enough to put me in the hospital. I needed to work every day to keep food on our table, and I prayed he wouldn't kill me because my kids needed me.

At one point he dragged me into the kitchen and began to fix something on the counter, and it wasn't a bologna sandwich . . . he was fixing heroin to shoot up. I stood by in horror as he prepared and drew up the substance, tied off his arm, and injected himself. In my mind I saw the DEA officers bursting through the door and shackling both of us. James ran to the bathroom to heave, a requisite part of a heroin high. It was my first exposure to heroin, and I was now in terror of how this evil drug would exaggerate James's insanity. I kept thanking God over and over that Chris and Ashley were safe in bed across the street at Nancy's.

Finally, around 6:00 A.M., he fell asleep, and I escaped. I grabbed the kids and drove to the Holloway Motel near Barney's Beanery. As I rushed up to the reception desk, I realized I had no money. The older man could see my busted-up face and my two bewildered kids and gave us a small room free. I called Al, my knight in shining patrol car. When he and his partners arrived at the house, there was no sign of James. Just the debris from my night of terror. James knew he was still on parole and would go back to prison. For now he was guilty of breaking and entering, assault and battery, rape, and possession of heroin. I never saw him again.

James came into my life at the worst possible time. We'd both just been released from our prisons. My whole existence had felt stifled for so long. My yearnings and desires had been locked up inside me. James represented everything I'd never been allowed to be: reckless, lusty, footloose, and impetuous. He was a free-spirited daredevil, sucking the juice out of life. We had been uncontrollably mad for each other.

But James was also just plain mad. Beware of handsome outlaws . . . they'll give you the "Rompin', Stompin', Bad News Blues." I see now that James was really a tragic figure. He was so emotionally damaged by the traumatic events of his youth that he was doomed to act out his confused rage. I felt lucky to have escaped, because I know he could have killed me. I thanked God and my guardian angel. I was a victim but I wasn't going to be a volunteer.

I wish there had been a shelter for battered women in West Hollywood in 1973. My heart goes out to battered women, especially those with children and poor finances. There's no place scarier than home.

Baby, Baby, Have Mercy on Me

M Y   B O S S ,   T H E attorney, had helped me file divorce papers against Michael and had rescued me from James, but now, things had changed. It now seemed like without bad luck, I'd have no luck at all! The longer I worked for Wade, the more sleazy stuff seemed to ooze up around him. He was like a character you'd meet hanging out at Santa Anita racetrack, something right out of central casting. A true wheeler-dealer, he was always working the angles. His wife was a college professor; they'd adopted two darling children and set up a seemingly happy home together, but I soon discovered Wade led a secret life. He was involved with a number of women at the same time, did amazing amounts of cocaine, and hung out with pimps and hookers. He'd laid out every dime he could borrow to set up his posh new offices. I came across some correspondence indicating he'd been fired from his previous position with the network, so it was no wonder the clients weren't materializing.

When he started paying me with bad checks and then refused to honor them, I grabbed a stack of his confidential files, took them home, and hid them in my basement. I phoned him that night, gave him the teller's number at the bank we both used, and promised to return the files the minute he made good on what he owed me. I admonished him, "Hey, you can't get away with this! I have two kids that need to eat breakfast every morning. I've worked my butt off for you and been a darn good kid. I'm your next door neighbor, whatever happened to 'love your neighbor as thyself'?"

He evidently got the picture. My money was deposited in the bank the next day. I immediately returned his incriminating files and quit.

I must have been nuts to have done what I did! That character could have had me taken care of in a hundred scary ways. Yet he apologized and begged me to stay. I forgave him and we remained neighbors, but alas, I was out scrambling for work again. While I was looking through the want ads, the girl who lived below Wade called me from work. Elaine asked if I'd look out my kitchen window and tell her whether her boyfriend's motorcycle was still there. When I reported yes, she sounded uneasy and confided he'd tried suicide before. Since he seemed despondent when she'd left that morning, Elaine asked me to climb her patio fence and go into her apartment and check on him. I found the guy unconscious on her living room floor and called 911. Screaming and trying to rouse him, I spotted an empty pill bottle on the coffee table. After the paramedics arrived it was the first time I'd ever seen CPR. Her boyfriend was in a coma for days, but did survive.

My job hunting was further interrupted by Chris's illness. Plagued by recurrent bladder infections, I'd been taking her to a urologist. With this particularly bad flareup her doctor advised she be checked into a hospital at once for further tests. The first question the hospital asked was if I had health insurance. The answer was, of course, no. It was time to swallow my pride.

Michael had gotten a better-paying job and had moved to Chicago. After getting his number from a mutual friend, I phoned and calmly inquired as to how he was doing. He reported that he was great and preparing to go snow skiing with his new girlfriend.

"Michael," I implored. "We're in trouble and need your help. I'm calling from the hospital with Chris and as you know we don't have any medical insurance. I don't have any money."

There was a moment of silence on the line. "Well," he sighed, repeating his now famous line, "You should have thought about that before you divorced me." With that, he hung up.

I stared into the pay phone receiver. I couldn't believe it. Not one word about, "How is she? What's the matter with her? Are you calling from the emergency room? Will she be okay?" Terrible feelings of helplessness flooded over me. What now?

The lady in the admitting office suggested I go to an organization called Aid to Families with Dependent Children, which essentially provided welfare benefits to people in my situation. Because their father was legally bound to pay child support as clearly demanded in the divorce papers, I first filed more papers notifying the state that he'd not been living up to his obligations. I petitioned the state to intervene and collect monthly on the children's behalf. The clerk grumbled about how they were backlogged with deadbeat dads and that we had the added snafu of Michael living out of state.

They put me on emergency medical assistance and I slogged through bureaucratic red tape for years, trying unsuccessfully to get Michael to honor his financial responsibility to the children.

Jobless, I was standing in the welfare line when a man approached me with a proposal. Introducing himself as a talent agent, he complimented my figure. Then he segued into offering me $5,000 to do a centerfold spread. I felt naked just standing there! "No thanks!" I answered tersely. "It's humiliating enough having to be on welfare, stripped of my pride. I'm not stripping off my clothes, too."

Later I realized these guys probably prowl the welfare agencies knowing the women are desperate for money.

Next I waltzed right into what would appear to be a glamorous job, working as a personal secretary to David Chow. David, a financial and investment consultant, was a wealthy man, who drove a Maserati and took part in a lot of philanthropic and social activities. The job itself was a bore. Alone in his mansion all day, I was in charge of writing checks; bookkeeping; and supervising the housekeeping, gardening, and pool service. The best part of my day was reading scripts for the popular David Carradine series *Kung Fu.* As the undefeated International Kung Fu Champion, Chow was the show's technical adviser. The studio sent me scripts to scour for portions pertaining to martial arts. Then I would spoon-feed David by highlighting them for his instant critique. Sometimes I followed him around his house reading aloud while he did other things. David lived on Blue Jay Way in the Hollywood Hills in the same house where former Beatle

George Harrison had once lived. It was not what you could call a stimulating job, but David was a nice guy, and it paid my bills.

As his secretary, I was assigned to assist him at a martial arts exhibition sponsored by an instructor named Mike Stone. Mike was waiting to greet us, and who should be standing beside him but Priscilla Presley! They had on custom-made matching leather outfits with bare midriffs and exposed navels, very 1970s looking. Priscilla and I struck up a conversation that uncovered several strange parallels in our lives. We were the same age; Priscilla had met Elvis when she was fourteen, the same age I was when I met Michael (although I was quick to point out that Michael was no Elvis); I lived with Michael's parents as Priscilla lived with Elvis's parents while he was in the army; and my Ashley and her daughter, Lisa Marie, were the same age. The more we gabbed the more coincidences popped up. It was an unusual, amusing evening. Priscilla was a spunky woman and confided to me, "I just left Elvis Presley for this man. Do you think I'm crazy?"

"Nope." I chuckled. "Believe me, I can relate."

Besides the rather pertinent fact that I possessed no marketable skills, another reason I kept seeking personal secretary jobs was the flexibility of the hours. Chris was in West Hollywood Elementary where Ashley had now begun kindergarten. Chris's medical problems had stabilized, but both girls required occasional trips to the pediatrician or dentist. This way I could also easily arrange to attend their school events, plus leave work in time to pick them up each afternoon.

If I were forced to punch a time clock in a rigid workplace, Ashley went to Nancy's, but Chris became a latchkey kid. This modern-day problem was becoming more dangerous as Sunset Strip was disintegrating into a mecca for riffraff. The police called me at work one day telling me something had happened to Chris.

A man sitting in a car parked outside the school playground had motioned her over to his window and exposed himself. She and her terrified playmate ran to the girl's house nearby where Gilda's mother phoned the authorities.

Sitting safely in my lap, Chris patiently described the pervert to the police sketch artist. The composite drawing confirmed what the detectives suspected. This guy was the child molester they'd been after for some time.

As the patrol cars pulled away, standing in our driveway we looked down at the garish lights of Sunset Boulevard and our deteriorating neighborhood. My children's everyday route to grade school took them past the Classic Cat Club, Turner's Liquor Store, Filthy McNasty's, and the Whiskey A Go-Go.

I talked my way into a job at the Golden Carrot Health Food Store, just about sixty yards from our house on the corner of Larrabee and Sunset. Now I could keep closer watch on my girls. It was considered hip to be a vegetarian around this time, and I was becoming more health conscious. Various celebrities would stop in for a smoothie at our juice bar. I conscientiously memorized what beverage each star preferred; sort of like a bartender setting up a regular customer's favorite drink without being told. I even began naming concoctions after them, deliberately contributing to their already oversize egos. One of the most popular male soap stars came in almost daily after his tennis game and tried unsuccessfully to bed me. Although dashing and insistent, the louse made no bones about being married. Assuming that all actors and actresses were vacuous and self-centered, I rationalized they needed to portray other people to compensate for their own lack of personal history or character. It was just one more opinion I would later reverse.

I learned a lot about health and nutrition at that job but was subsequently witnessing how the Strip was changing. One evening when I was working alone, a couple of funky black guys came in and asked for a pack of Marlboros. After I explained that the orientation of our store conflicted with cigarettes, they added they'd also come in for several pounds of lactose sugar. The next day the owner explained to me how lactose sugar is used to cut cocaine and heroin. From then on I decided to keep a gun under the cash register. Ironically, there was a popular song that kept playing on the store's radio, "The Times They Are a-Changin'."

I'd also begun to incorporate hippie fashions into my wardrobe: long flowing skirts, Mexican blouses, ponchos, halter tops, and handmade moccasins. I let my hair grow long and wild and sometimes stuck a fragrant flower over my ear. I refused to wear makeup except for a little lipstick. Protesting Hollywood's preoccupation with youth and beauty, I had already turned my back on modeling. One afternoon I became so disgusted and fed up with being treated like a sex object, I walked out of a Maybelline commercial cattle call.

Everywhere I turned there were "beautiful" people. It wasn't normal or real! When I took Chris and Ashley to the beach in Malibu, I thought I'd walked into the midst of Hitler's master race. Big-boned, broad-shouldered, blond-haired, blue-eyed Aryan storm troopers in bikinis marched on the beach.

I was getting more and more homesick for 2237 Montgomery and Aunt Pauline's farm, so I plotted an ingenious scheme to earn money for our airfare. I became a professional game show contestant. Making it through a full week on *Hollywood Squares,* I achieved "champion" status there but lasted only three days on *Password,* because an inebriated Peter Lawford became distracted and more interested in squeezing my knee than playing the game. Mom put an article in our hometown newspaper that I was on television. One afternoon when *Hollywood Squares* was on, Mark had an accident. While waiting for him to be treated at the doctor's office, Mom ran down to a nearby furniture store. She wrote me how all the store employees were sitting in La-Z-Boy recliners watching me on the wall of televisions. Only in Ashland! An interesting TV debut!

Meanwhile, back in Ashland, my younger sister, Margaret, had eloped with a boy who, shall we say, was "inappropriate." Actually, she was trying to escape the tension and hostility brewing at home between Mom and Dad. Margaret described how her new husband moved her into his little bedroom in the modest house he shared with his parents in Greenup, Kentucky. "Does Judd history repeat itself or what?" I asked jokingly. "Does he have any diving trophies?"

Margaret went on to explain that after she complained about the living arrangements, the guy admitted he had no intention of getting a job or moving out. Margaret realized what she'd done, quickly got a divorce, and she and her brand new redheaded baby girl moved back home to 2237 Montgomery. She wrote to me in California that things had gone from bad to worse between Mom and Dad and life at home had become unbearable.

Margaret's life had always been very different from mine because of timing. When I was forced to leave home at seventeen, all my happy, secure childhood years had already formed me and the memories were sealed away lovingly in my heart. That all-important first part of my early life was warm and cozy with Mom and Dad together and our family intact.

Margaret had been only eleven years old though and not even out of grade school when the Judds exploded into chaos. I had married and moved away. Brian was dying of cancer. Mark was withdrawing from reality and Mom and Dad had decided they didn't have anything left to say to each other anymore. Margaret and I grew up in the same house, but under very different circumstances.

Brian, Mark, and I had loved the two farms in Louisa, but Margaret hated even to go there. She was never interested in picking fresh vegetables straight from the garden and washing them in well water before eating them. The rooster chased her on the path to the outhouse, and she hated drinking warm milk with the "yellow stuff" floating on top. Margaret would be the first one in the car whenever it came time to go home.

I had been so wrapped up in my own Hollywood dramas for so long that I hadn't paid much attention to what was really going on back home. I wrote back to Margaret with this suggestion: "I've got a plenty big house out here and am also raising kids without help from their absent father. Why don't you come on out and we'll start a single mom's club?"

Margaret wasted no time packing up and heading west. I had offered her the perfect opportunity to escape. Three months later on March 4, 1972, the five of us celebrated little Erin's first birthday in California. Sister and I were two Ashlanders trying to make our way now on our own with nothing more than our wits.

Margaret quickly settled in and set up shop, earning a meager living by manufacturing hand-sewn false eyelashes. It was work she could do at the house while she took care of Erin. The Judd mothering instinct was in evidence once more and Margaret was great with her daughter.

It was wonderful being together again while watching our girls grow up together. Now there was laughter and fun in our busy household. Together we took the kids to the beach, the park and every free recreational place we could find.

Being feisty, single women, we'd leave the kids at Nancy's and head out on Friday night to kick up our heels. Margaret was very pretty and an amazing dancer, so we could always count on meeting guys at places like the Topanga Corral. We each had our dates and it worked out well. Margaret had good taste in men, but I was still picking them up out of the gutter . . . rogues with life's footprints all over them.

Margaret fell head over heels in love with California. It was the perfect place for her to escape. Feeling no strong emotional ties to her past, California rose up to embrace her. She was becoming a rebellious and liberated woman.

I, on the other hand, was always proud of being from Kentucky and looked for ways to make my heritage work for me. I had long ago noticed that everyone in Hollywood wanted to be someone else. Brandi, the black receptionist Mark Gordon hired instead of me, wanted to be a singer, the guys at the supermarket were really actors, and the fellows who pumped my gas were screenwriters waiting for their big break. Taking pride in letting people know I was not a Hollywood wanna-be, I underscored it any way I could. I could exaggerate my accent and my hillbilly mannerisms at the drop of a hat. Acting shocked and innocent at all the right moments, I indulged my genteel southern ways. I expected my dates to behave as gentlemen. There was never any doubt about where I was from and how I had grown up. Some people made fun of me, but most found it charming and refreshing.

When Margaret and I had friends and dates over, we'd make pitchers of sangria and play the Moody Blues, the Guess Who, and Cream for hours. Spinning tales of growing up in Ashland, I dutifully portrayed it as a Steinbeck-type small town and the best of all possible worlds. I'd describe the colorful characters, friendly neighbors, and schoolmates, whom I remembered being imbued with vast resources of country wit and charm. Our guests would giggle in all the right places until Margaret would interrupt with her different and exasperated, "Give me a break, Diana!" She'd blurt out, "The girl you're talking about is a walking land mass with a perm who works at Tipton's Bakery and eats brownies on the sly. She's not a character and she's certainly not funny. Just a pathetic, middle-aged woman who got exactly what she settled for in life." We had very different perspectives.

Margaret and I had been doing our best to create a cohesive home for our three fatherless little girls, all the while painfully aware that the childhood experiences they were logging in their early memory banks bore no resemblance to ones we cherished from 2237 Montgomery. They had no Cecil or Mary Agnes Hinton living next door for role models. Nowhere on our street could they observe even one example of a traditional family, daily fulfilling their complementary roles, to create a richly woven tapestry of domestic stability. Because there were no children, they never got to play kick the can and feel the comforting sensations of being part of a neighborhood. Such communal experiences and games help instill ethics like share and play fair, don't take what's not yours, and don't hurt others.

There was no familiar Aunt Roberta dropping by to ask how the kids were doing in school. Our neighbors were furtive characters with no visible means of support. There was just Nancy and Gabrielle across the street reflecting back at us a picture of a distressed mom and her puzzled child paddling for all they're worth, trying to keep their heads above water.

Margaret was an industrious, ambitious, disciplined fireball, who was itchy to get on with her own life. She got herself into a good job-training program and located a decent apartment over the hill in North Hollywood. Holding Erin with one hand and her suitcase in the other, she bade us good-bye. The house seemed quiet and lonesome for a long time. Pleased we'd reconnected after the void created by tumultuous years of family division, we had reclaimed our sisterhood and formed a lifelong bond of mutual understanding and respect. Being around brainy Margaret helped me take stock of myself. She had won science and math awards in school and made A's effortlessly. We shared the wacky Judd sense of humor, but she had sharper edges than I did. She was skeptical while I was naive and idealistic; she was logical and pragmatic while I was a daydreamer. I saw that Margaret wanted to work with her hands and intellect. I began to recognize I wanted to work with my imagination and with people. It was during this time that I realized our futures were set for very different courses.

I began to feel "like a John Deere Tractor in a half acre field trying to plow a furrow, where the soil's made of steel." I'd grown tired of being handmaiden to powerful men. Fed up with getting patted on the butt and paid in pennies. My job at the time helped me realize just how much I longed for something meaningful to which I could give myself. It was the proverbial last straw that broke the camel's back.

Mr. Adams had earned his millions creating the neon signs for Las Vegas. He was now retired with his wife and living in the Trousdale Estates in Beverly Hills. My comfortable office was in the cabana by their large swimming pool. There was a small refrigerator next to my desk with soft drinks and refreshments stocked by their full-time maid. I had flexible hours and no pressure and was close to the kids' school and home.

I paid his household bills and communicated with his stockbroker on maintaining his vast, impressive portfolio. The Adamses often spent weekends on their yacht or at their condo in Marina Del Rey and invited Margaret and the kids and me to use the pool in their absence. For a few blissful, heady hours we'd pretend their estate was ours.

Then some of the major investments took a nosedive. We let a couple of his cars go, and I had to sell the yacht to Elton John (Mr. Adams kept calling him "John Elton"). The condo at the beach was next. Even though they knew they had more than enough cash and sure investments for the rest of their lives, they were terribly upset about losing some of their toys . . . their "stuff."

Mr. and Mrs. Adams were in their seventies. I struggled to reason with them, attempting to discourage their obsession with materialism. I suggested they relax and enjoy each other and spend more time with their children and grandchildren. They weren't into counting blessings, just money. The situation saddened me so much I resigned. What they could not grasp turned out to be one of life's great lessons for me. Although I was barely able to pay monthly rent and keep peanut butter for my kids, I felt richer than the Adamses. On my last day I left this note for them:

Money will buy a bed, but not sleep; Books but not brains;
Food but not an appetite; Finery but not beauty;
A house but not a home; Medicine but not health;
Luxuries but not culture; Amusement but not happiness;
Religion but not salvation;
A passport to everywhere but heaven.

Chris, Ashley, and I had spent six interesting years in Hollywood. As I contemplated the colorful variety of minimum-wage jobs, the misadventures, all the near disasters, I had to admit to myself I was wasting my life. I was now twenty-eight and all I'd gained was my freedom and magna cum laude honors from the school of hard knocks.

The real bucket of ice water in my face was the matter of two innocent little girls. Christina was now eleven years old, bright, curious, energetic, and wickedly funny, but she had several bouts with serious asthma attacks. The LA smog was getting so bad there were days when she couldn't even play outside. We were reduced to living according to the daily smog alert. Ashley was seven and showing signs of being a remarkable child, if only some stability would come along to bolster her natural gifts.

My daughters were growing up in the wandering transient spirit that defined the 1970s. Too often they had to fend for themselves while I struggled to make a living for us. They thought Ashland and Louisa were merely quaint and peculiar places to visit briefly during the summer. I would not tolerate the realization that they thought LA was normal and Kentucky was not.

I had to get us out of this phony town! I'd been renting out the basement to a woman who taught Transcendental Meditation to the Beatles and who was dating Richard Beymer, who had played Tony in *West Side Story*. After deciding to turn the house over to her, I frantically packed up our clothes, our photo albums, and the kids' toys, and stored them in one room. It was the end of another school year and time again for the girls to go visit their grandparents.

Bright and early one June morning in 1974 our milkman knocked at the kitchen door to warn me there was a homeless man asleep in our backyard by the swing set. A homeless person . . . a human being in America with nowhere to sleep? It was such a radical concept to me then. As I followed the milkman to check him out, I shuddered in self-recognition. How frighteningly close the kids and I lived to being out on the streets ourselves! Always just one paycheck away from not being capable of paying our way in today's society. Hollywood was never meant to be our real home. Out here people were so busy falling for everything they didn't stand up for anything!

I put the girls on a plane, then loaded my bags into my old car and drove off into the night in search of our new home. In search of myself.

Destiny doesn't come with a map, but I surely could have used one. I was on a mission to find a place that was a cross between the only two homes I'd ever really had, small-town Kentucky and "Hollyweird," California. You can't go home again, but you can't escape it either.

A girlfriend from Austin, Texas, had told me intriguing stories about her hometown. Our perceptions are colored by our needs, but it sure sounded like my kind of lifestyle. Ginny swore they harkened back to the old-fashioned values and strong family ties, with a deep sense of history. Not to mention the cowboys! I was ready to see some real McCoys and replace all those egocentric actors, male models, fancy barflies, and smooth-talking hipper-than-thou ladies' men.

As soon as I arrived in Austin, I saw a truck just like my Daddy's carrying cowboys, whom I just knew did an honest day's work and had rough hands. They tipped their hats and nodded a "Howdy Ma'am," and it was love at first sight with the Lone Star State. My host and I instantly hit it off as well.

Ginny Vick had set it up for me to stay with her best buddy, David Swann. David was a mail carrier, who backpacked all over the world, loved foreign films, took night school classes in subjects he just happened to be curious about, and read a lot. I felt confident and safe he'd never put a move on me and turned out to be right for once. My heart was closed for repairs, and I'd begrudgingly come to grips with the now well-established fact I had just plain awful taste in men. Maybe the reason I wasn't attracted to David was because he was so intelligent, kind, responsible, and gallant!

Anyway, in exchange for his couch, I cleaned his house and learned to make fabulous Mexican dishes. David enjoyed coming home to wildflowers on the table, music on the stereo, and laughter. We were extremely compatible, and he began showing me around town.

It was 1974 and Willie and Waylon were cashing in on the "outlaw" rage. They were among the many musicians who lived in Austin, and owned clubs. David introduced me to Texas dance halls like the Broken Spoke, Soap Creek, and The Armadillo. We danced to indigenous acts like Alvin Crow, Marsha Ball and the Firedogs, and had a blast! There was more live music per square inch in that town then than any other city in America. It was my first exposure to country music, and it provided the perfect sound track for my odyssey. The lyrics, harmony, and sentiments struck a familiar chord within me. We got to know Asleep at the Wheel, which was one of the most popular local western swing bands. After their set they invited us to an after-hours jazz club, the Ace of Spades, to see Double Trouble with Lou Ann Barton. They in turn introduced us to local blues heroes, The Fabulous Thunderbirds. Every night was like a New Year's Eve party.

There was something forceful pushing me, like a ship moving with the wind. I was on a voyage of self-discovery. My life had always been so hectic, so crammed with demands on all my senses. As I explored miles and miles of Texas, I found that silence is refreshment for the soul. The wide-open spaces allowed me to relax, untangle my nerves, and listen to my innermost thoughts. It was so exhilarating to be standing alone on the rim of a canyon at dusk surrounded by mesquite trees, sagebrush, and cactus. The only thing on my mind was wondering how far it was to the horizon. The honking sea of cars and neon glitz of Sunset Strip seemed like an old, bad dream.

I interviewed for weather girl on Lyndon B. Johnson's TV station and found a rental house out on West Gibson. The girls had been in Ashland two weeks now and I had come out to the countryside to make a decision. The dark eyes of the caves seemed to be staring back at me probing, "Are you moving here to live forever? Is this the end of your rainbow?"

As darkness drained light from the valley, I listened to the soulful entreaties of a chorus of coyotes, and arrived at two conclusions. One was an epiphany as dramatic as a jagged bolt of lightning across a midnight sky. On that spot, I swore to myself and the kids I would never live in a city again the rest of my life. The second revelation was that this wasn't the end of my journey, but just the beginning.

I didn't want to be a TV weather girl who had to wear her hair and skirt length to suit the station manager's testosterone levels or the ratings. It seemed I was always more interested in learning human nature than a trade, in making a positive impact on lives than earning lots of money. There are two kinds of jobs: for one you shower before you go to work, for the other you shower after the work's done. Me, I may glisten if it's hot, but I don't like to sweat.

When I phoned Ashland to check on the kids they were having a ball! Because they hadn't seen either set of grandparents in a year, they were taking turns staying with the Judds and the Ciminellas. The Ciminellas took them swimming at the Bellefonte Country Club and out to restaurants and shopping. Nana and Papaw Judd took them fishing and to Aunt Pauline's farm. Explaining to my folks that I'd found neither location nor vocation as of yet, I asked if they'd baby-sit longer. Decisions like these were too important and far-reaching to rush.

On some occasions during summers past when I'd gone home to visit, Mom and Dad were baffled by my fashion statements and unconventional attitudes. Dad would have been content for me to work at the bank, but Mom wanted me in college. I tried to persuade them that it's with our heart and imagination that we see into the future. As we hung up, Daddy said at least this meant I had twenty-twenty vision.

Excavating my psyche, on the trip back to California, I dug up the answer. All these years I'd been haunted by my helplessness in Brian's suffering and death, and I acknowledged my deep desire to silence those lambs. Having always been unusually sensitive toward suffering and fear, I felt a calling to become a nurse.

Equipped with my few clothes, a couple hundred bucks, my list of smaller nursing schools and tales of northern California's beauty, I became a practicing dream chaser. Under heaven's bright blue smile, I offered my morning prayer for guidance and began one of my most memorable adventures.

As I traveled to interview with nursing recruiters, I also paused to chat with everyday sages on the street. I hung out at health food stores with locals who were also trying to avoid mind-numbing conformity and the crush of modern society. I found that everyone has a story, his or her own reality and level of depth. Some folks would sooner die than think. In fact, they often do.

I would stop by the side of the road to rest in the shade, eat my granola and nuts and was often joined by bikers or hikers. I felt unchained, unfettered, no particular sense of belonging, but somehow at home. In villages like Boulder Creek and Bonnie Doon, I sat around the campfires of gentle people and was invited for supper or to spend the night.

Up in Humboldt County, sitting on the hood of my car one night under a starry canopy, I suddenly realized this was the first time in my life I'd ever been really alone. Then I contentedly went right back to admiring how the stars resembled ice chips from a giant's ax. These were the days before serial rapists and mass murderers like the Green River killer who later prowled that area.

I'd gone as far as I could go, all the way up to the Oregon border. Following along the San Andreas fault after studying Edgar Cayce's predictions of a catastrophic earthquake, I came on a gathering of believers in Arcata. These folks thought their combined healing vibrations could reverse the prophesied cataclysmic event. Slightly amused but ever hopeful, I thanked them on behalf of the rest of the state's unaware inhabitants and drove on. There was one last possibility: the Santa Cruz area.

An older couple, Dorothy and Henry Wells, found me singing to myself in a meadow outside Soquel and invited me to be their house guest. Dorothy, a retired R.N. and in her seventies, immediately took me under her wing. She had a bright mind but had grown lonely on their secluded two-thousand-acre cattle ranch. I enticed her to go to yoga classes and stimulating lectures and revived her interest in the outside world. Their guest quarters were comfortable, and I helped out around the ranch. I got sidetracked there for almost a month until I felt the winds of change and realized it was time for the kids to begin another school year.

I Know Where I'm Going

J CALLED ASHLAND to check on the girls that night, and Chris wondered aloud, "Why don't you just come back to Kentucky, Mom? It's nice here." Out of the mouths of babes! Not having found an area or school that felt right, the only option was to return to square one. Home is where one starts from, so I would go back where I started.

Working through the night, I loaded up the U-Haul hitched on the back of my car. The first things packed were the backpack I'd just finished for Ashley and the handmade quilt I'd sewn for Chris. Creating them had allowed me to make something tangible and useful for my girls while we were so far apart. First thing next morning I began calling colleges back in Kentucky.

Through researching nursing schools long distance, I learned that the R.N. program at Eastern Kentucky University in Richmond boasted graduates who consistently scored the highest on state boards. Richmond happened to be less than one hour from where the kids were presently visiting their long-lost dad.

Michael had earlier dropped out of society and tuned in to bucolic life in the forests of Oregon. Also searching for an alternative lifestyle, he had apprenticed there as a leather craftsman but had just recently relocated to Lexington, Kentucky. Michael usually slept in the quarters behind the leather shop where he worked but also was renting a summer fishing house at the end of Daniel Boone Road right outside town. It was a rough-frame retreat on the Kentucky

River, called Camp Wig. Chris and Ashley were enjoying their visit there.

Hmm . . . it was time to make a deal. Because Michael had not been paying child support, I decided to persuade him to let the kids and me stay at Camp Wig until we got our bearings and could locate a place of our own near my nursing school. I was determined to deprogram Chris and Ashley from the false myths, overstimulation, and materialism of their previous Hollywood environment. If I couldn't give my children all the things in life I hadn't had, at least I was going to try to give them the things I did have. I suspected it might take a little doing to find the right spot in which to settle. For the moment, we just needed a place to land.

A trip becomes a journey when there's a destination. Feeling a bit like a runaway slinking back home, I sent the dust boiling up around my tires as I struck out from Northern California on the long cross-country journey back to the Bluegrass State. It was to be my introduction to America the Beautiful. The potentially lonesome, monotonous drive was redeemed by the constantly changing scenery. I willingly allowed myself to be drawn into nature's moods. Even the dullest landscape can be transformed by the appearance of a wondrous neon sunset.

The days burned on, revealing everything in startling clarity as I became more and more anxious to see the sight my eyes really longed for—Chris and Ashley. Over the phone I had arranged for Michael to take them to my brother's house near the University of Kentucky campus in Lexington, where Mark was now a student. I needed the kids all to myself and certainly didn't want the homecoming spoiled by having to deal with Michael. Bursting in on my unsuspecting girls, the three of us had an ecstatic reunion.

And then, the culture shock began. Camp Wig was much more primitive than I expected, but I cheerfully set about unloading the U-Haul trailer and making the rustic house comfortable. No welcome wagon here. No indoor plumbing in some of the neighboring houses either.

On our dirt road lived a poor family with a bunch of kids with whom Chris and Ashley began riding the school bus. Chris came running to me one afternoon describing with wide-eyed astonishment how she had just witnessed Mr. Shanks eating a carrot without any teeth. It was far better than tricks she'd seen at the circus. Ashley made a startling discovery when she uncovered the slop jar, used as a substitute toilet and set out on their rickety front porch. One of the Shanks' girls stayed over one night and Chris discovered firsthand that the girl had never seen a shower. "Mommy come quick! She's standing under the running water with all her clothes on!"

We were still vegetarians. Chris, who longed for an occasional cheeseburger, implored, "Mama, can I just be a vegetarian in between meals?"

I raised all kinds of sprouts in large mason jars with pieces of screen and cheesecloth for lids. We hung herbs to dry upside down in the kitchen—out of direct sunlight, which zaps their potency. There were always wildflowers in a jelly jar on Miss Cora Lee's antique kitchen table.

My great-grandmother had dropped dead from a heart attack right on the main street in Ashland one hot summer day, and Mama had given me the family dining set. I'd also been heir to the quilt top Miss Cora Lee had last been working on, along with her two big galvanized wash tubs.

Now all I needed was a handy-dandy wringer washer to go with the rinse tubs. On our way to buy fresh butter from the Butter Lady, I spied a utilitarian beauty sitting out on a front porch. I parted with $75 and returned with a neighbor's truck to take our new, used Maytag home.

Each Saturday night the three of us made doing the week's laundry an enjoyable event. Chris fed their filthy overalls, flannel shirts, and granny gowns into the old-fashioned washer and I pulled them through the wringer into the first rinse tub. Ashley was in charge of sloshing clothes around in the second rinse, then I put them through the wringer the last time. We hung everything outside until the temperature started dropping. When the first frost came and our clothes froze as hard as sheet metal, I resorted to hanging clotheslines around the kitchen.

We serendipitously discovered the *Grand Ole Opry* on the radio one Saturday night and soon were singing the popular tunes and talking along with the commercials. Each of us quickly established our favorite performers and songs. Little Ashley would sing it the way she heard it. "Martha White self-writing flower. The one all purple flower. Martha White self-writing flower has gaudy eyes." Ashley was the princess of malapropisms. She would inform us that Samuel Morse invented the code of telepathy, called the Pacific Ocean the "specific" ocean, complained of the humanity (humidity) in the air, and declared after grace one evening that God was a sparerib (spirit). Ashley thought the world revolves on its "taxes."

The girls played outdoors like wild animals, coming in only to eat and when it got dark. They made a thick black ring around the bathtub. They got their first cat, Grits, and an assortment of dogs. In no time, they learned to identify birds and had a pet squirrel. Chasing each other with lizards and green snakes, they also learned that tomato juice gets out skunk spray.

Parts of my plan were already working. They were becoming resourceful, imaginative, and close. The sisters played together endlessly, although Christina constantly threatened to put Ashley's head through the wringer. "Feed the dogs for me so I can take a swim in the river, or I'll flatten you like a pancake," she'd threaten ominously through squinty eyes.

Ashley was genuinely afraid of being the only girl in her class with a pancake-shaped head, but she was also a sweet child with a generous nature, so she gladly fed our dogs.

As winter approached I found out the hard way why the rent was dirt cheap. Camp Wig was just a summerhouse to be used for fishing forays. Because no one was ever there during the winter, there had never been any need for heat in the house. As the saying goes, Necessity is the mother of invention. I purchased a pot-bellied stove and found myself in a serious discussion with a coal miner about the benefits of and differences between anthracite and bituminous coal. Ordering a few loads short of sixteen tons, I dumped it by our back door. The pot-bellied stove wound up in the corner of the kitchen next to the Maytag. So much for modern appliances! As the temperature dipped we layered on more clothes and stoked the fire-breathing stove monster. Ashley saw her first white Christmas. It seemed everything in our lives had changed as dramatically as the climate.

After the holidays it was back to school, but this time for all three of us. The kids had blended in well with their new classmates that first fall semester, and I'd spent my busy days getting us settled in at the camp. Now on that cold January day of 1975, I excitedly packed three school lunches, and my clunker fell in line right behind their big yellow school bus. I would get to my school every day by blowing my horn, at Mr. Horn. Being right on the Kentucky River, I simply drove down to a landing at the water's edge and tooted my car horn in the early morning stillness. Old man Odus Horn would come running out his front door, putting on his ball cap, and ferry me across to the other side.

As I wound past the vast stretches of woods, meadows, and farms, my spirit expanded and soared. The abandoned barns, reminders of forgotten human activity, seemed to be murmuring, "Where in the world have you been girl, and what took you so long?" I began to cheer in recognition at everything familiar—from wells with tin roofs at the back of a house to the muddy cow paths along the hillsides.

It had begun to snow steadily on that eventful first day, and I noticed I was the only vehicle on these lonely backroads. As I began descending a steep hill, I completely lost control of the car and began sliding down sideways across the middle of the road and off the other side. As my big car bounced into a ditch it flipped over on its side.

"Oh no! I'm going to be late my first day of school!" I protested loudly as I lay smashed up against the passenger's side door. It took every ounce of strength I could muster to open the driver's side door from underneath it. Cows coated with a light dusting of snow looked up nonchalantly to check out this rude disturbance. "Well howdy girls!" I sarcastically acknowledged as I began to plot. Where there're cows, there's got to be a farmer with a tractor.

Trespassing through white fields past the silent, suspicious animals, I spied the lights of a ne'er-do-well house in the distance. I began calling out as I approached the back porch, catching the yard dogs off guard. I reasoned with a cantankerous farmer that he and his cows could quickly be rid of me and the unsightly wreck if he would just pull my car out of his ditch. Almost an hour later, I thanked him profusely, trying in vain to explain to him the rewarding law of karma. Eventually arriving at campus in my now badly dented car, I felt drained yet exuberantly victorious! Neither Michael Ciminella, James Dean, Jr., the temptations of Hollywood, nor blows from Mother Nature had succeeded in keeping me out of these halls of higher education.

As I began registering for classes, I had the sensation of being scrutinized once again, but this time, by a different sort of herd. It was clusters of tietering nineteen-year-old girls wearing the latest coordinated fashions from the mall. As I glanced down at myself it dawned on me how much I resembled a frontier woman, who perhaps had just come to town for supplies. I was indeed a curious-looking stranger among such civilized young townsfolk. I was wearing a tall, thick fur hat, which from a distance must have surely looked as if I'd strapped some small dead animal onto my head. The sleeve of my old secondhand woolly coat was torn from my accident, and instead of hose and high heels, I clomped conspicuously from desk to desk in knee-high rubber milking boots. There was no driveway or sidewalk at Camp Wig, we lived down a dirt road, and besides, for crying out loud, it was snowing!

The only fashion concession I would later begrudgingly make was to keep my noiseless handmade moccasins in the trunk to change into once I arrived safely on campus. I was happy, warm, and comfortable in my long skirts and flannel shirts and instead of spending my precious time applying makeup or perusing glamour magazines, I dove headfirst into my studies—a decision that paid off with excellent grades.

Monday, Wednesday, and Friday were classroom lecture days, but Tuesdays and Thursdays we slipped proudly into our student nurse uniforms and were sent out to area hospitals under the watchful eye of our teaching supervisors. I was always odd man out. No one ever dared pick me for a lab partner. Once after observing a shy Nazarene girl mistake a urinal for a water pitcher, I recruited her for my buddy. I figured she could use some help, and I could use a challenge. We made a wonderfully wacky team until her many hilarious booboos piled up and got her kicked out. Then it was me and a hefty farm girl with B.O.!

I was perplexed one day when she asked me if I ever kissed Elvis. After I admitted regrettably no, I inquired as to why she would even ask. She confided that I was the source of spicy rumors and wildly improbable speculations. These sheltered small-town, recent high school graduates had heard bits and pieces of my modeling days and my living on Sunset Strip and were attributing far more preposterous escapades to me than I could rightfully take credit for. Oh well, a little mystique never hurt anyone. I'll never forget the day I became somewhat of a folk hero.

We had an instructor who had watched too many *Mr. Rogers* episodes. Using elementary words, she enunciated slowly and distinctly. In our pharmacology section, she lectured for hours on the five R's: the Right time, the Right patient, the Right pill, the Right dosage, and the Right route. Feeling so bored and frustrated I had to squelch the urge to scream, "Yeah, the right route is especially important when administering enemas!"

Then she painstakingly demonstrated the correct procedure for partial dosages. Carefully washing her hands, she took the cap off a bottle of aspirin, shook out one pill into the cap, jiggled the pill from the cap onto a clean surface and then meticulously placed a single-edged razor blade along the groove in the tablet. She pressed down until the pill popped neatly in two. Looking around at us with her smug smile, she then ordered us to practice the procedure of pill dividing. A ridiculous amount of time ticked by as we individually duplicated her example.

Meanwhile, we were all thinking the same thing. "This is kindergarten stuff!" We wanted to learn how to start an IV, do a major dressing change, remove stitches, or tackle a debridement on a burn patient. Always last, I tapped the pill into the cap, set it onto the sterile surface and then hesitated. The instructor gave me a sideways glance. "Now Miss Judd, let's see your version of how to divide a pill in half!"

I picked up the pill and bit it clean in two. The girls fell out in shocked, uncontrollable laughter. Such irreverent behavior would never have been tolerated if my grades hadn't been so good. As the weather got colder, our studies got harder. I loved anatomy, physiology, and microbiology but chemistry almost made me throw in the towel.

I cooked a big dinner every night and then straightened the

house, chatting all the while with Chris and Ashley. There was no TV and I could just see their imaginations blossoming. Each had her chores, and they were becoming quite self-sufficient. When I finally flopped into bed (a mattress on the bare floor with lots of quilts), I was bone weary. In too few hours I was up at 5:30 A.M. to start all over again. Instead of reaching for a bathrobe, I put on my thick fake fur coat, funny hat, and gloves to step out into the freezing predawn air to bust up chunks of coal small enough to fit into the ravenous mouth of the fire-breathing stove monster. Its appetite was insatiable and I begrudged its never-ending hunger. One frosty-cold morning I clomped sleepily into the kitchen to find the entire room covered with a fine layer of soot. The stovepipe had worked itself loose and the midnight black powder coated our all freshly laundered clothes. It clung to every square inch of surface. I raced out the back porch, and standing on the riverbank, I clenched my fists and screamed.

During the following weeks it took to clean up the horrendous mess, I'd sit in class and daydream about the clean, warm dormitories my classmates were going back to every evening. Perhaps they'd order a big hot pizza and have it delivered to their well-lit cozy room . . . then pay for it with their parents' money.

I hadn't been to a restaurant or anywhere socially in almost a year. Feeling like a good scout, who'd earned all my badges, I decided to treat myself to a night out. I'd grown very fond of my fellow students but had nothing in common with them outside of nursing class. Mark had driven the two hours home to Ashland for the weekend and I had no friends or suitors. I began to realize just how isolated I'd become when I didn't even know where to go or what I wanted to do. On my way into Lexington I stopped for a newspaper and saw that a bluegrass group called J. D. Crowe's New South was playing live music at the Holiday Inn. Accustomed to being stared at because of my pioneer woman garb, this time I now had the added stigma of being a single woman going into a lounge on a Saturday night.

Feeling quite conspicuous, I sat at a tiny table for one in the back and ordered my Coke. When the down-home–looking band started I was suddenly transported. It no longer mattered what I was wearing or that I was alone and couldn't even afford a second Coke.

The music filled me with such rapture, it was like a religious experience! A stooped-over man named J. D. Crowe made his old fiddle sing, while Tony Rice performed the greatest guitar finger picking my ears had ever heard. An intense guy with a funny haircut named Ricky Skaggs mesmerized me with his mandolin. When they introduced him as being from Cordell near Louisa, I adopted him as a distant cousin.

The music struck a familiar chord deep inside. The hairs on the back of my neck stood up when they sang . . . it was as if I'd suddenly died and gone straight to heaven.

The intimacy and magic of that strange night made an indelible impression on me. It was my first experience with bluegrass. I enjoyed it far more than all the rock and roll concerts I'd ever been to in LA. I went around singing their songs for weeks.

Meanwhile back at Camp Siberia . . . temperatures were setting all-time records. We pretty much lived in the kitchen as it was the only room with a stove. You could see your breath in the bedrooms, so the three of us began sleeping together in the same bed in an inner room with no windows or outside walls, which was next to the kitchen. One night we were curled up like a mother cat and her kittens until we awoke feeling cold and wet. One of the girls (I won't name names) had wet the bed, and to make matters even worse we were wearing our last clean long johns under our granny gowns. As I went into the bathroom, I saw an ominous sign. The water in the commode had a thin sheet of ice on it. Immediately grabbing the sink faucet, my worst fear was realized: The pipes were frozen. All three of us had hacking coughs and I knew enough by then to diagnose bronchitis. I had to get us out of there before we caught pneumonia and died.

Humiliated and depressed, I bundled up my grumpy little ones and drove all night to Mom's house. It tore at my heartstrings to see them with runny noses and chattering teeth huddled in the backseat. I was feverish myself, and we stayed in bed for days. I was also sick with guilt over not being able to take care of my babies. Mom took care of us, Dad gave me some money, and I felt that once again I'd let them down. I was more determined than ever to pay them back someday by making them proud of me.

Michael began to drop by more and more often down at the river. My heart would sink when I'd come home from college in the evenings and see his car there. He seemed to enjoy getting to know the girls. Who wouldn't, they were great kids! I don't know whether he was genuinely trying to do the right thing or attending an inner need to assuage the emptiness in his life. He brought rabbits he'd killed in the woods across from the camp, and I learned to make rabbit stew. When Ashley was asked to say grace over our meal, she spoke up with childlike sincerity. "Hello God and Jesus. Tell Mr. Bunny Rabbit we're sorry we're gonna eat him. And I sure hope it doesn't make me choke and die, 'cause I'm too young to go. Amen."

Heavy rains came that spring of 1975, and the old-timers remarked that it was the wettest season Fayette County had seen in years. Sometimes my car would get mired up to the hubcaps in the soggy yard and I'd have to trudge over to a neighbor who had a tractor to pull me out. When the river started rising, Odus Horn couldn't operate the ferry, so I learned to go park the car immediately on a high spot across on the other side of the river. The next morning I would row myself over the muddy waterway in a small canoe, get into my car then drive to school. My uniform and textbooks had to be neatly wrapped in a plastic bag to keep them dry in the canoe. Some days I'd arrive at school late, my own clothes splattered and caked with mud from battling the elements at Camp Wig; just one more reason for everybody to stare at me.

This time the storm went on for days, lashing our little house with icy rain and frightening gusts of winds. In the middle of the night I was awakened by a man's frantic voice accompanied by banging at our door. Buddy, the engineer who tended the lock and dam up the river, yelled that the water was rising fast and we had just a few minutes to clear out. I layered clothes on the girls, threw crammed backpacks on them, grabbed my purse and a couple of nursing books, and piled everybody into the car. It was black as coal outside, and the water was already churning up from the river to our doorway at the back of the house. The mighty Kentucky River seemed a formidable adversary as the starter of my old car ground away. I desperately chanted, "Start, start, start, start!" until finally the engine turned over and we sloshed up and out of the muddy drive-way.

When we came to a low spot in the flooded out road for a moment I thought we would be marooned. The girls were crying with fright as I gunned the motor. Water splashed over the wind-shield, came up through the floorboards, and seeped in under the bottom of the doors, but we eventually made it up to the main highway.

The only place we could go at four o'clock in the morning was to Mark's place in nearby Lexington. The kids and I bunked down on the living room floor of the house he shared with a fellow student, named "Tree" because of his height. While we were having breakfast the next morning, Mark and I realized this period was our chance to reunite. Mark is quiet (of course I love a good listener), has the patience of Job, and is a terrific uncle. We share a love of country life and the same off center sense of humor! He loves Monty Python, Spam sandwiches, knows the names of plants and trees, and can point out the stars and constellations. I love him dearly.

When I went back down to the river the next week to salvage what I could from Camp Wig, I had to row my canoe to get to the front door. We didn't have many belongings, but when I saw the mud and debris inside covering the floors I was heartbroken. The skies were gray, and the air was cold and damp; never had things seemed so hopeless. These harsh blows from Mother Nature felt like biblical punishments. As if raising a couple of kids alone and trying to educate myself so I could someday make a decent living weren't enough, daily survival was wearing me out. All this left me with no energy or patience to put up with Michael.

Along with Mark and his roommate "Tree," Michael had been helping us move furniture and clean up after the disaster. When he decided to stay in one of the other bedrooms, there was absolutely nothing I could do about it. The lease was in his name and I certainly didn't have any money to buy him out. Having him around caused disagreements, which escalated into arguments and then into battles. Soon the old bitterness drove me to flee again. I insisted the kids finish the last month at their school, so I rented a cottage for myself in the small town of nearby Berea until I could locate a house for the three of us. I had been looking for rental property all along but the physical demands of my everyday activities left little spare time, and I hadn't any leads.

I stayed in that one-room cabin for only that month of May, but it was my first experience at living all alone. I had a lumpy bed, a small chest, one chair, a gas heater, a kitchen sink, a two-burner stove, and a small cupboard. The "bathroom" was in the corner of the room: an old-fashioned tub with claw feet, a toilet, and a sink closed off from the rest of the room by a curtain. I called Chris and Ashley at Camp Wig every night from the phone down at the gas station and had them with me on weekends. We'd comb the backroads stopping to inquire about vacant farms from local folks at mom-and-pop grocery stores. We'd talk to farmers out plowing their fields and stop postmen on their route, but with no luck.

I was growing more uneasy about the girls being at the camp with just Michael, although they were at school all day and had established routines at night. On weekends they'd sing bizarre songs with adult lyrics, like Frank Zappa's "Hot Rats." Michael was into rock music and had keg parties. As they're known to do, the children sometimes let things slip. I found out he let Chris drive although she was only twelve, and he allowed Ashley to float out in the deep river unsupervised on an inner tube. It was all great fun for them; a lot like visiting a permissive uncle who lets them get away with murder while the parent was away.

The redbud tree in the side yard next to my cottage had begun to bloom and I spread out a blanket on the ground beside it to study. Lying there listening to the radio through the open window, I discovered the wonderful world of the Stanley Brothers' bluegrass. It was so comforting and soothing. I said a little prayer and asked God to help us find our spot soon.

The next night while driving past the hotel in Berea, the girls and I witnessed an elderly woman slip on the wet pavement, obviously hurting her ankle. Doing an immediate U-turn, we went back to help her. She introduced herself as Caroline Hovey, wife of a professor at Berea College. After taking her to the emergency room, we helped her into her house. The grateful family invited us in, and as we chatted I told them of our search for a home.

The very next day there was a cryptic letter in my box at school, from someone introducing herself as a professor of music at Berea College and a friend of Mrs. Hovey. She wrote that she had some interesting properties she'd like to show me. A hand-drawn map was enclosed, along with a time and place for us to meet. I could hardly wait until that next weekend!

The kids and I followed directions to a location on the map in a rural area called Morrill, outside of Berea. As we turned down the narrow gravel road off Big Hill Road we came to a red wood gate at the foot of a knoll. Passing through this entrance and starting up the paved drive the girls and I ceased our excited banter and held our breath at the sight before us. I could hardly believe my eyes. To my right on the crest of the hill stood the most wonderful house! It was a two-story, dark wood house with shutters, storm cellar, garage, and big front porch. Just as I was counting the apple trees in the front yard, a tiny old lady came tottering out. The kids and I had been frozen in our seats, our mouths open. "Well, jump out, girls, and *please* behave!" I whispered insistently.

In a thin scratchy voice that crackled like a severed power line, she began to introduce herself as Margaret Allen, the music professor who had written me. She continued on to tell us that she was widowed and her daughter was married to Norman Vincent Peale's son and that her own son was editor of *Reader's Digest*. We learned that Mrs. Allen taught at Berea College for a self-imposed salary of $1 a year, and that she sponsored a music camp for gifted children every summer here on this location for one week. She talked about living in Windswept from September through May to teach at Berea and then spending the summer at her estate in Vermont. She tried to explain that when it was time for the summer camp to convene, the music instructors resided for that one week in Chanticleer, then mentioned that there were additional cabins farther down the hillside for the camp children. My head was swimming and I just couldn't keep up. "Excuse me! Wait! What are Windswept and Chanticleer?" I interrupted.

"Why, Windswept is the name of my home at the top of the hill farther on up this road overlooking the valley, and Chanticleer is your new home," she proclaimed rather matter of factly. She nodded down at the wood plaque on which her left hand was resting. It read, "Chanticleer." Time skipped a beat, then suddenly I realized she was speaking to me again.

"Why you do want the place, don't you dear? It's a perfectly lovely house. It's completely furnished, you know, linens, dishes, silverware . . . everything you need. Come, I'll show you."

The three of us fell in obediently behind her and marched up the stepping-stones to the porch. When we entered the living room, I realized the place was indeed ready to live in. I mean walk right in and unpack your bags! In fact, it was like an Appalachian museum. Furnished with hand-carved Vermont maple furniture, it was filled with antiques, large hand-braided rugs, heirloom quilts, a stone fireplace, and glory of glories, a Steinway grand piano! Just as I was staring at it, Ashley squealed out from the next room, "Oh, could this be my bedroom, please?" Margaret Allen stated that since there were four, we could all have our pick. The thought of having their very own bedroom was beyond the girls' comprehension and suddenly brought me back to reality.

"Mrs. Allen, we couldn't possibly afford to rent this place. It must cost a bloody fortune!"

"Could you afford one hundred dollars per month?" she inquired with a sly smile. "It has been empty such a long time. I certainly don't need the money, I just want the right people to have it. Someone who believes in the Golden Rule. I've waited quite long enough for you."

I stammered some thanks, and the kids said good-bye to her. As we waved and pulled away, it all seemed very dreamlike. Driving home in a daze, it was the first time in my life I felt like I were in a fairy tale. Could Margaret Allen be my fairy godmother or a guardian angel? It was perfect timing; school was out in two weeks, and as we moved into Chanticleer that June, I had the strangest sense my life would be different from then on.

Our busy summer days vibrated with happiness. In the vast woodlands we picked blackberries and searched for sassafras and ginseng. Because there were eight apple trees in the yard, I got an apple press and learned to make apple cider, apple butter, and applesauce. I sliced the apples, too, and spread them out on window screens up on the roof to dry. As I was hanging the wash on the line one afternoon, one of those sudden summer thunderstorms came up, and the apples got soggy and ruined before I could get to them. Then I had a brainstorm! It was always so hot in the car, why not put them in there where neither rain nor bugs could get to them? The apples not only dried in half the time, our car now smelled great. Hey, I was beginning to get the hang of this country life! Having reinvented myself in the tradition of my beloved Aunt Pauline, I was the most content I'd ever been in my life.

Carl Jung believed, "People who know nothing about nature are of course neurotic, for they are not adapted to reality." And it was Jung who reminded us that when we discover the natural world for ourselves, we are engaging in a second creation.

The kids lived in their own magical world. Ashley built a miniature village in the root system of the big oak tree out by the front porch. Fairies and elves lived there. While she slept, I created their tiny footprints with match sticks and left notes and trinkets. She and Chris romped the surrounding countryside with their many dogs and cats. The favorite dog was a tan hound named Mule, our favorite cat was named Hovey after our benefactor, who told Mrs. Allen about her encounter with us.

I taught Chris and Ashley to bake homemade bread and make yogurt. We made everything from scratch and had a fear of frying. We put in a large vegetable garden and met there each evening to weed and care for it. Ashley was my finicky eater, so I hit on a scheme: I assigned her her own garden patch, and as she planted and tended the vegetables, she felt they were indeed hers. Chris and I applauded as she began to eat tomatoes and squash for the first time. At summer's end we invested in canning equipment and a hundred mason jars. For days we put up vegetables; enough to stock our storm cellar for the oncoming winter.

When we first moved into Chanticleer, I noticed Ashley and Chris running from room to room. "Hey Mom! We can't find the telephone or TV."

It turned out that Margaret Allen had no use for either. Neither did I. This was precisely what I had in mind! Without a TV or telephone to distract us, we became quite resourceful at entertaining ourselves. Although the days were full of useful activity, it got awfully quiet and still after the sun went down. We'd sit out on the front porch and listen to the bobwhites, crickets, and frogs or lie on a blanket on the hillside and count the stars. Sometimes we'd dance around waving our arms, pretending to be elves in *A Midsummer Night's Dream*. I'd fix popcorn or some dessert and make up stories. Once in a while I'd come up with a ghost story or a preposterous tall tale. Chris would beg, "Tell us the one about hillbilly vampires," and Ashley loved hearing about animals that talked and took on human characteristics while we slept. It was here I came to realize that I've always been a storyteller. A tale spinner.

Then something happened that would forever change our lives. It happened gradually and without fanfare.

Someone had given me an old guitar right before I left California, and I brought it out one night just for fun. During our stay at Camp Wig, Michael played a lot, and Chris watched him make chords. He would let her hold his guitar and showed her how to make chords by herself.

"Why, if only we could play that thing, we could all sing and entertain ourselves for hours," I mused. Christina normally had a very short attention span, but the guitar was somehow different. I noticed it right off. She'd set her jaw firmly as she embraced the huge instrument and sit hunkered over it for hours. It was just noise at first, then she figured out three chords: C, F, and G.

Something in me knew to encourage her newfound interest. I was growing concerned at her rebellious streak, which was coming out more and more often. I sensed it stemmed from the rather volatile situation between her dad and me. She was eight when he left and the whole ugly mess still disturbed her greatly. I found her a used, but nice, guitar at a joint at the foot of Big Hill where men traded knives and guns. It was a right pretty thing with pearl inlay. She was ecstatic when she laid eyes on it! "Gosh, Mom, that's the most beautiful thing I've ever seen!" Grabbing it from me, she sat right down and began to play. As I watched, it dawned on me how quickly she was improving.

There was a small music store in Berea that had a bin of used albums that sold for $1 each. I couldn't afford to buy the latest releases, but I often flipped through this bin and discovered a lot of great stuff. One day I found an album with a grainy black-and-white photograph of a farm on the front. It was a bluegrass record by a duo called Hazel and Alice, recorded on Rounder Records. What a concept, I thought, a record with two women singing together! I brought it home, and Christina and I listened to it on our record player. As we listened, we became absolutely transfixed. The women's voices were singing songs we'd never heard, but the blending of the voices, the harmony, and the intonation were as familiar as our own faces in the mirror. It was the sound of the Kentucky hills where I grew up, of Aunt Margie and Zora, Aunt Pauline and the magic woods, Slick McGloan and my Daddy's gas station. We were hooked.

Together Christina and I began to learn these songs, our voices accompanied by Chris plunking away on her new-used guitar and me on my old one. That wonderful summer of 1975 we learned every single song on the Hazel and Alice album: "Custom-Made Woman Blues," "Mining Camp Blues," and "Fly Away Pretty Bird." But one particular number stood out as our favorite. It was an old-timey Appalachian story about a mother's love, written back in 1936 by J. B. Coates. "A Mother's Smile" was the very first song Chris and I learned all the way through.

We knew nothing about singing, harmonizing, or music theory. The musical sound we began to create together was an audio representation of the mother/child bond already existing between us. We offered our version as a Mother's Day gift to my Mom. As Chris and I sat under the big fairy tree, we sang it so sweetly that Mom proclaimed we sounded like the angels. It was the first time she'd ever heard me sing. She was always taking care of the nursery while I sang in Sunday school and church, and we never even listened to music in our house when I was growing up. I noticed Mom crying and felt very close to her at that moment. It was touching how a simple song could unite our three generations. This was the moment I discovered that music helps us communicate and release our emotions.

. . .

We fell in love with remarkable Berea. It was absolutely alive with music, arts, crafts, and the creative spirit. The heartbeat of the small town is a unique college, and I mean unique for many reasons. Most obvious is the fact that you can't enroll there if your parents have much money. Instead, to pay tuition and earn board while preparing their minds for the future, the students work daily with their hands at producing time-honored crafts. They make guitars, violins, and dulcimers that are world famous. The Churchill Weavers, renowned for producing the finest authentic handwoven cloth items anywhere, is student operated. They not only create their own furniture, brooms, ceramics, wrought iron, and crafts but even run the shops that sell them. The gracious old inn, Daniel Boone Tavern, is a student-staffed and -run hotel, and its dining room features gracious hospitality and southern dining at its best.

Outside of Berea up at Morrill, the center of activity was the post office operated by the Sparks family. At one time they'd lived in the back of the white frame general store/post office, but now resided in a small home beside it on the main road known as Big Hill. Mary and Jack were quiet country folk who knew everyone in our rural area. They let me use their telephone, because we were without one, and seemed surprised and impressed that I never asked for credit at their store. Their friendly greeting to the kids each afternoon when we'd stop by to check our mail or get staples reminded me of my own after-school welcome from Mom.

Jack and Mary laconically inquired from time to time whether we'd run into Craig and the Yanceys, and I began to sense that there were other country bohemians on the loose here in the wilds. Then one evening an old truck with a New York license plate pulled in as we were leaving. The tall, lanky stranger wore a colorful hand-knit cap, a denim jacket, and silver jewelry; I knew he had to be Craig. He leaned against the kerosene pump in front of the post office and related how he had wound up "noplace in the middle of nowhere." He had come out of Vietnam emotionally wounded and also was searching for the black box in the wreckage of his life. Craig nodded in mutual understanding of my cynical assessment of modern society, and we knew instantly we were to become good friends.

Although we never had a single romantic encounter, Craig and I became very close. Living in a primitive one-room cabin back in the woods without water or electricity, he enjoyed full home-cooked meals and hot showers at our house. I also laundered and mended his clothes. At the other end of our symbiotic relationship, he took care of all our necessary household repairs, diagnosed any car problems, and brought us news from the outside world.

The first night Craig came to Chanticleer, we made a wonderfully fortuitous discovery. He'd been in a rock and roll band and immediately set about teaching Chris more guitar chords and technique. Soon she was picking out "Stairway to Heaven" along with the bluegrass standards. I asked Chris how she could play so well and she informed me: "Why it's just easy if you know how!" The three of us would play and sing for hours on end.

I don't remember exactly how we met the Yanceys. It was all so natural, so meant to be. Ten years older and quite stout, Minnie cut an imposing figure in her long frontier-woman's dress, cape, and heavy combat boots. She wore her midnight black hair pulled back in an old-fashioned bun and could set folks scurrying from her path when she squinted her eyes and set her jaw. There was an unpredictable air about her. You never knew whether she was going to curse and go for a rifle or slap her palms on her knees and cut loose with melodic laughter. Minnie and I hit it off at once.

Years ago her husband had left her and their four small children in a cabin in a holler in Hazard, Kentucky, with empty cupboards. She'd learned how to survive by using her wits and developing a multitude of talents. Minnie remains one of the most amazing people I've ever known. If I had to describe her in one word it would be *natural.* Minnie described herself as feral, meaning untamed and living in an uncivilized manner. This self-styled pioneer woman, who knew so much about so many things, taught me that artists must feel free. Being around her reminded Chris, Ashley, and me that we were connected to all things in the universe.

All by herself, Minnie built and then upholstered her living room couch. She also painted the portrait of Don Quixote hanging over their fireplace. She said to me, "A mind is like a home, you should furnish it carefully yourself." Being self-sufficient, she sewed all her own clothes and was a deft wood-carver.

She taught me how to make lye soap and about herbs and home remedies. Minnie has what mountain folks call "the Sight." Strangers would show up at her house by word of mouth for healings. I once saw her "talk the fire" out of a burn. Minnie supported her family of four by her foremost talent, weaving. At home she created fabrics on the enormous handmade loom in her living room and then worked in the weaving exhibit at Fort Boonesboro in Berea in view of tourists. Minnie was a natural-born teacher and a firm believer that everyone should learn survival skills. School is wherever you can learn, and I learned as many valuable lessons being around Minnie as I did in my college classes. At one of our get-togethers I gave everyone American Indian names. I dubbed Minnie Yancey "Keeper of Legends."

Minnie's daughter, Sonya, ten years younger than I, existed on an ethereal plane far removed from the one most of us are currently inhabiting. Everyday occurences were filled with signs, portents, prophecies, and revelations for her. She was a lovely fair-skinned girl with waist-length blond hair, and we called her "Songbird." She was a singer/songwriter who'd recorded Appalachian folk songs on an esoteric label. I remember Sonya playing her dulcimer by the fire singing "Simple Gifts":

> 'Tis a gift to be simple,
> 'Tis a gift to be free,
> 'Tis a gift to come round
> Where we ought to be.

Like her Mom, she also handcrafted items, such as homemade brooms, and was responsible for most of the household chores and cooking. Chris and Ashley treated the two younger Yancey boys like brothers and we all became one big alternative, extended, happy family. Convening up at Chanticleer, we'd get up a huge pot of beans or vegetable soup and spread out a buffet of vegetables contributed from all our gardens cooked a dozen different ways. I'd bake up skillets of thick yellow corn bread and slather on our freshly churned butter. Sometimes I'd bake sheets of hot biscuits and cover them with fried green apples or my homemade apple butter. From the blueberry bushes in the backyard or the blackberry patches all over our two-hundred-acre farm, we'd make cobblers and pies and homemade ice cream for dessert. One time Ashley lay down on the floor, and announced she'd eaten too much and couldn't move. The rest of the day Toddy and Butchie Yancey dragged or carried her around as she moaned and groaned, threatening to explode.

Friends who brought instruments would take them out after we ate, and our music fest would commence. The hills would ring with bluegrass tunes we'd learned from the Louvin Brothers, Rabon and Alton Delmore, Larry Sparks, and the Carter Family. We sat there surrounded by loving souls, the grass between our toes, our voices intertwined like fingers folded in prayer.

It was a magical summer of uninhibited laughter and play, music, nature, and friendship. It was in this marvelous setting that I felt inspired to write my first songs, stitching my vision of how life could be into melodies and lyrics. The titles are revealing: "Simple, Peaceful, and Good," "Dynamo," "Child of the Light," "Renegade's Song," "Grits," "Soup Beans and Cornbread," and "Daddy Are You Coming Home Tonight?"

On Saturday nights the sounds of another type of music foreign to our ears wafted on the air with the fragrance of the wild crabapple blossom. The one-room Holy Roller Pentecostal Church down on the main road was holding its unorthodox service. The door stood wide open, partially because there was no air-conditioning but probably as a symbolic beckoning for sinners and passersby. We'd been intrigued by the sounds and invited by the locals. Entering under a rough hand-painted sign that implored "Jesus died for your sins. What have you done for him lately?" we were assured there would be no snake handling. "Man! Would you look at that!" Chris whispered in amazement. "They've got an electric guitar, bass, and tambourine in a church!"

Ashley was enthralled when women, slain in the spirit, began dancing and jerking as if they had epileptic seizures. None of us knew what speaking in tongues was, so we were really baffled when an elderly man we knew well, Robert Chasteen, began hollering in a language we couldn't begin to comprehend.

Robert was the unofficial mayor of Morrill, and helped take care of the grounds at Chanticleer. When we were included in his family reunion picnic it was an honor. Chris said it felt like European colonialists being invited to witness secret American Indian ceremonies. The Chasteens and the Van Winkles populated the area and were musical. In their yard we learned a number of old-timey gospel songs. Ramona Van Winkle quickly became Chris's best friend and taught us two of our favorite songs: "City of Gold" and "Jerusalem Moan." Her Dad, Shorty, was a banjo picker in a bluegrass gospel group. By now music permeated our lives.

Chris seemed to have a short attention span and working up a song was the longest she ever devoted to doing anything. Her feisty personality was beginning to show its true power.

The girls were growing up without a responsible father, and Chris seemed troubled and angry. I suspect she resented me for throwing her father out of our house and out of her life. She was also watching me struggle to find my place in the world and seemed to be blazing her own trail in the same headlong fashion. When I asked her to do chores she'd groan out her standard dramatic plea: "Don't make me suffer." This hurt because there was already so much for me to do, and we all needed to pitch in.

One day I'd stripped the beds and was hanging Chris's sheets on the clothesline when she stuck her head out her upstairs bedroom window and began screaming, "Fire!" My heart stopped as I realized we were a half hour from the nearest fire department down in Berea and our wood house could be ashes before they even arrived. Then I remembered—we didn't even have a phone to call them in the first place!

I dashed into the house and started up the narrow staircase to Chris's room. Standing at the top of the steps, she just kept shrieking over and over: "It's on fire! It's on fire!"

As I pushed her aside and ran into her room, I saw where she'd lit a stick of incense and stuck it down in the cloth strap used for turning the mattress. My first reaction was to ask her how could anyone stick lit incense down in a mattress, but the ugly smoking black hole let me know I had to act fast. It was going to burst into flames any minute.

Heaving it off the bed, I got underneath and put the three-quarters-size mattress on my back and headed down the stairway. Chris had fled the room and was standing near the front door at the bottom of the steps. I was yelling at her to hold the door open for me as I staggered under the weight of the heavy mattress.

"No way!" she yelled up at me. "That thing's on fire, and I'm not coming near it. I'm not stupid!" Alternately threatening and pleading with her, I couldn't believe it when she ran out into the yard. Kicking open the door by myself, I dragged the smoking mattress out onto the lawn just as short flames began leaping out of it. I saturated it with water and then, furious, chased Chris deep into the woods. She slipped back into the house after dark, but I was lying in wait for her. We went at it tooth and nail.

Soon our golden summer days shortened, and it was back to a rigid schedule dictated by our schools. Arising at 5:30 A.M., I'd prepare a big breakfast, pack three lunches, slip into my student nurse's uniform and round the girls up to pull away from Chanticleer by 6:30 A.M. I dropped Chris and Ashley off at 7:00 at the Yancey's house, so they could go on to school with Toddy and Butchie. Then I'd drive to East Kentucky University's campus for my 8:00 A.M. class.

As the school year got under way, I had to meet with all Chris's teachers. She wasn't paying attention in class or turning in home-work, and there were absences I knew nothing about.

She shouted defensively, "They all hate me! All my teachers have it in for me!"

I'd explain how important an education is until I was blue in the face. "Look at me!" I'd insist, "I'm struggling against all odds to improve and educate myself! If you ever want to amount to anything you've got to go to school!"

Walking down Main Street in Berea one afternoon with Chris, I discovered the reason for her unexplained absences from class. A couple of passing, snarling college students called her a "pint-size pool shark" and vowed to win their money back. I stopped dead in my tracks, turned, and chased after them, while Chris protested loudly. Eagerly seizing their opportunity to get even, they proceeded to enlighten me. Chris and Toddy had been skipping school to hang out at the student activity center on campus. What a clever racket they'd devised! A cute little girl in overalls comes up and asks if you'll shoot a game of pool and offers to go "five bucks a game" if you'll only let her play. Then the amateur hustler bags the balls and cleans you out. I had to give them an A+ for originality.

A great row ensued, and we fought all the way home. Poor little Ashley would sit stoop shouldered, horrified as Chris threatened to kill me while I slept and "put me out of her misery." My princess of malapropisms would admonish Chris: "Don't look at Mom in that tone of voice!"

Meanwhile Ashley worked quietly and diligently in school making A's and capturing all her teachers' hearts. She was popular and well rounded. After school, she went to Brownies or a pottery class given by students at Berea College. At home she willingly completed her chores and read voraciously. While Chris and I began our love affair with music, Ashley became enamored of books. Playing school was her favorite game. It disturbed me that Chris was mean to her, and that Chris's tantrums often monopolized my time and drained my energy.

Some aspects of nursing were also beginning to bother me. The emphasis seemed to be on technology. We were treating the disease with little or no attention to the person who had the disease. We were being trained in surgery, administering pills, technique, and so on, but there wasn't enough education in the areas of prevention, stress reduction, and nutrition. I was still reading outside information on holistic medicine on my own, and every time I learned something new, I discovered how little I really knew. I was becoming a thorn in my professors' sides. Waving my hand at the back of the room, I questioned long-standing practices and pointed out gaps in our training. My instructors were becoming nervous and evasive. I'm sure they feared my radical ideas might be contagious. My books were losing their text appeal. One day I commented how I had thought we were supposed to be in the business of taking care of people, but I had now come to see why it's called the health care "industry."

According to folk legend, if you count the number of times a cricket chirps in a fifteen-second period then add thirty-seven, you'll get the temperature. The cricket only chirped once or twice at our farm, so we called for a wood-chopping party. Minnie noted the muskrats had really thick fur and predicted severe temperatures. While the women cooked, the men went out into our woodlands and got up enough firewood to see us through the winter. Craig remarked, "A man who chops his own wood gets warm twice."

That fall we frequently became ill with gastrointestinal problems and low-grade fevers. Because of what I'd learned in microbiology class, I began to suspect our cistern. It was a holding tank for our water supply made of concrete blocks and was located under our back porch. The blocks act as a rough filter, but there's no water purification system. Rain falling on the roof of the house simply collects there to be pumped in through our house faucets by an electric pump. Checking on the water level, I found it to be very low. I also discovered a very large snake, which I can only theorize had fallen out of a tree onto the roof and been washed down the gutter into the cistern.

Checking a water sample in my lab, the *E. coli* bacteria count showed up high, indicating ground contamination. We had to do without water for weeks. I packed water home from town for cooking and doing dishes. One early dawn we awoke to a deep snowfall. Grumpy and staggering, the girls and I threw on our boots and coats over our pajamas to trudge up the hill to the outhouse. It was so freezing outside I grabbed the quilt off my bed to bundle around us too.

What a sight we were! The three of us huddled together, racing in tandem as our bladders were about to pop. As the sun began rising gloriously behind the barn, Chris hollered up at the winter sky, "Good morning God! The family that pees together laughs together."

We were so looking forward to Christmas that year. We never had much money for presents, but we made up for it by making occasions special in other ways. For instance, on Ashley's birthday, Minnie baked a lavish multitiered "southern belle" ball gown cake around Ashley's Barbie doll.

Because we couldn't afford to buy a Christmas tree, we set off out into the woods to cut our own. Craig hooked up the rack used for hauling firewood on the back of his horse, Baba. The temperature was in the twenties and the skies were leaden as we struck out. The girls were so excited, and I'd been praying for snow to cast a spell on our ceremony. After almost an hour of futile searching, we were becoming cold and discouraged. As we were sitting down in a small clearing to rest, fat white flakes magically began to drift down from the sky. We were spellbound and no one spoke for the longest time. The pristine woods were hushed and we dared not break the delicate silence.

Then Craig began to explain how every snowflake is different—no two are exactly alike, sort of like fingerprints of the sky. By now everything was beginning to turn white and I observed how snowflakes are like people: fragile, but look what happens when they stick together!

It was little Ashley who led us to our tree. Following behind Baba, back to Chanticleer, the four of us sang every carol we knew. The fragrant pine certainly appeared smaller out in the open spaces, and Craig wound up having to cut several feet off to get it into our house. I cooked up plenty of hearty food, and the Yanceys came over for the tree-trimming party.

The ornaments and decorations weren't the only things made by hand that year: Most of our presents were, too. The only store-bought items were long underwear for all, books and a game for Ashley, and a cheap microphone and amp for Chris. Sonya sewed a suede Indian squaw outfit for Ashley's doll and wrote Chris and me a poignant song called "Home." Using a large cardboard box, Minnie constructed a dollhouse for Ashley. She decorated the rooms by pasting magazine cutouts of curtains, rugs, and furniture. Sonya's husband, Greer, gave me his used hammer. Toddie carved me a tiny miniature fiddle with its own red-velvet–lined case, and Minnie sewed me a fashionable sunbonnet for working in the garden. I loved the vase Ashley made me in her pottery class, and it immediately became our kitchen table centerpiece. She put a lot of thought and effort into her presents. Starting with small lumps of clay, she shaped them into designs, baked them on a cookie sheet in our oven, painted them, then glued fasteners on the back to create decorative pins for everyone.

Chris had been working on her present to me for many weeks, and I'd been enthusiastically guessing and begging for hints to demonstrate my appreciation for her endeavor. With Minnie's expert guidance, Chris had sheared sheep, carded and spun the wool, colored it with natural dyes, then woven it on the loom to produce a splendid satchel for me to carry my medical books in. The girls' handmade gifts of love remain priceless treasures and tangible symbols of our favorite Christmas.

Mother and Daddy spent Christmas in Morrill with us that year. Chris and I sang them an old mountain carol Sonya and Minnie taught us called, "Beautiful Star of Bethlehem." We sat around the fire and read aloud from the Book of Luke about the birth of baby Jesus.

We had no way of knowing this time would never be again. I was never to see my parents celebrate another holiday together.

Margaret Allen would say "all work comes from rest." After the holidays, as we returned to our daily routines, I always seemed to have a textbook in my hand. Two periods in our day were strictly reserved for discussing the girls' activities: during the long drive from school in Berea through the Daniel Boone Forest up to Big Hill and at the supper table. I was probably cramming for a test one evening when I broke my own rule and spread out my big medical surgery book beside my plate. Suddenly Chris and Ashley began to shriek in disgust. I looked down, and saw I was eating catsup-covered fish sticks while staring at color blowups of open-heart surgery.

Indians reckon years by winters, and if you've ever lived close to nature in a cold climate you know why. But snug and cozy, Chris and I sang in the evening by the blazing hearth in our Garden of Eden. Ashley was glued to her Laura Ingalls Wilder books and C. S. Lewis's *Chronicles of Narnia.* I would tell her she had diamonds in her mind.

One winter's day, on January 11, Daddy showed up by himself to visit. Always indifferent to our musical displays, he went about tending the fire after supper as Chris and I settled down to practice. It was my thirtieth birthday and someone had given me a Dolly Parton album. Enthusiastically, we set about learning her new song "Coat of Many Colors." Daddy sat pensively staring at the fire as we raised our voices in harmony. Halfway into the song, I saw a tear rolling down his face. It was only the second time in my life I'd ever seen Daddy cry. The first and only other time was at Brian's funeral. After we finished, I asked if I'd done something wrong. He was silent for a few minutes and seemed far away. Then Daddy softly told us he had a coat of many colors when he was growing up. His Mama sewed dresses for his five sisters and had made him a winter coat for school from remnants of their old clothes.

The flickering firelight in the darkened room, the smell of burning wood, the hiss and crackle of the logs and the warmth they radiated . . . something timeless and inexpressible was passing between Daddy, Chris, Ashley, and me. I understood for the first time that although it is intangible, music is the most powerful art. Those moments are crystalline in my memory. That haunting ballad would become my favorite song for all time.

Some popular music tends to bypass the heart and mind and go straight for the libido. Such were the songs Chris's schoolmates were into. She, however, was enthralled with Joni Mitchell's polyphonic harmonies and lyrical prose. She absorbed Emmylou Harris and Linda Ronstadt. We exposed ourselves to a plurality of styles.

For relaxation, I'd sit at the grand piano by the picture window in the living room, playing romantic classical pieces as I watched the seasons change. We went into town only every two weeks for supplies. When Ashley made a good report card and Chris mastered a number or did her chores, I'd take them to the Berea skating rink for a reward. It had to close every spring, because the small population switched attendance to Little League.

On one trip, Ashley narrowly escaped falling out of our car on a bad curve on Big Hill, when the old rattletrap's door swung open. I was able to reach across the front seat and frantically grab hold of her left arm, and still maintain control of the wheel. It was a completely unnerving experience. From then on that door remained tied shut with ropes through the right side front and back windows. We entered and exited through the two left side doors. The brakes weren't too hot either, so Ashley's job was to wedge bricks behind the back wheels whenever we parked. Not only had the heater never worked but now a couple windows had to be left open a bit because of the ropes. It was the dead of winter so we kept old blankets inside the junker to cover up with.

Afraid the girls would catch pneumonia, I swallowed my pride and called Daddy. He said I could have Margaret's red Volkswagan, so we hastened over to Ashland to get it. Soon after we arrived home, Daddy left to go on a hunting trip. I kissed him good-bye, and told him I was glad to see him getting away, because he put in such long, hard days at the station.

I remember where I was when it happened. I was still standing at the front door watching Daddy get into his truck, as Mom sauntered up beside me. Without looking over at me, she said he wasn't really going hunting. In a very controlled voice, she told me my Daddy was going somewhere with his girlfriend. Calling her by name, Mom went on to tell me where this woman worked, how she and Daddy met, how long it had been going on, and that she was my age.

Emotionally, I couldn't accept what I was hearing. I just couldn't fathom my Daddy doing anything wrong, and I certainly couldn't imagine him with anyone but Mom. Intellectually, though, I knew it must be true. Mainly because Mom never lied, but also because she and Dad had been in a cold war for years.

It was an ominous revelation, like one of those scriptural prophesies of Armageddon. It heralded the end of the world as I had always known it.

Daddy moved out. How strange it was visiting him over at Granddaddy Judd's house in Ashland, where he used to take my brothers, sister, and me when we were growing up! Grandmommy had just passed away, in 1973, and Granddaddy was never the same after he lost his Sallie Ellen. He'd never learned to drive, so he'd walk the five miles into town almost every day to hang out in front of the Second National Bank. Ogden Judd was the most faithful member of Crum Chapel. At one service we attended with him, someone in the congregation suggested they sing Brother Judd's favorite hymn, "I'll Fly Away." "Mom, we should learn it to sing to Great-Granddaddy," Chris suggested.

My Aunt Evelyn Watseka, Daddy's older sister who never married, was now retired so she took care of the house and cooked. She was frugal, very private, straightlaced, and religious. Aunt Evelyn was always good to me, and I loved her. When I was little, I'd make her tell me over and over about the time she met Jimmy Durante. As an adult I drive her crazy asking for stories about our ancestors. I also take great delight in making her laugh.

The fourth resident at the Judd home was Great-Uncle Milt, Grandmommy's brother who was a paraplegic. Uncle Milt had told me he was struck in the back by a bullet from a jealous man's gun, while Milt was walking home from church down the dirt road in Louisa. He was only in his twenties when he lost the use of both legs. Uncle Milt's joy in life was listening to the Cincinnati Reds ball games on the radio from his old-fashioned rocking chair. He'd spit a plug of his Beech Nut chewing tobacco over the right arm of the rocker into the Maxwell House coffee can on the floor. I never knew him to miss.

As I watched Chris and Ashley questioning their great-great uncle about what chew tasted like, if he ever accidentally swallowed it, and so on or taking turns hobbling around on his crutches, I flashed back to doing the same things. Then it dawned on me that ever since I'd been out running around in the world, Uncle Milt had been right there in that same chair in that same room.

Upon returning home to Morrill in our VW, we found the back door standing open and discovered we'd been burglarized. Our cheap record player was missing, along with all my dime store/swap meet jewelry and lots of other small items. We really had nothing valuable to steal. Chris immediately remarked that it was fortunate we had taken our guitars with us on our trip.

I became frightened and ran to my room to fetch my Smith and Wesson from under my pillow. It was gone. So was the hand-tooled leather holster from my bedside table drawer. Sometimes I strapped it onto my belt during our forays into the woods, especially during snake season.

I hurried Chris and Ashley back out into the Volkswagon so we could report the robbery to the state police from the Sparks' house. When the Richmond trooper said they couldn't come out till morning, we went back into the woods to get Craig to come stay with us, since our busted door couldn't be locked.

The next day, locals and the trooper said it was probably the man who lived in the shack at the bottom of our hill who'd done it. This character had already done time and looked like something out of the movie *Deliverance*. Folks had been constantly warning us to steer clear of him, saying he "wasn't right."

The trooper searched the man's tiny place and shed but turned up no clues. When the trooper left, saying there was nothing more he could do, I felt uneasy as I realized the suspect now knew I had accused him of stealing.

As the three of us were leaving for school the next morning, we found our mama cat, Hovey, dead on the welcome mat. As the girls began to cry, I knelt down, puzzled at what might have killed her. Every bone in her body had been broken. I knew it was the fiendish deed of our unbalanced neighbor suspect, but I never let on to the kids.

We didn't know anyone with enough extra room for us to stay over and, of course, a motel was out of the question; besides I wasn't about to let anyone run me off! Before we returned home late that night, I stopped down at the trading post and got another gun.

About 6:30 the next morning the girls and I went out in the freezing cold to bury our family pet before we had to leave for our long day. My shovel only made "chink chunk" sounds on top of the frozen crystallized ground. My mind went back to Louisa to Aunt Zora's musings, how she had always prayed to die in the spring or summer so the elders could bury her in soft warm earth. At Ashley's suggestion, later that night we cremated Hovey on a funeral pyre like the Indians she'd been reading about in *Little House on the Prairie*. As the sparkly golden embers rose and ascended into the night sky, I looked over toward the house where we'd once felt so happy and safe. Suddenly a shiver went up my spine as I realized we had never been in the custom of drawing our curtains.

I couldn't find Mule anywhere. He was our favorite dog, a

smart hound who'd suddenly appear out of nowhere running along-side us at the first sound of our VW's engine chugging up the hill. When he didn't show up the second night, I knew Mule was probably dead. Disturbed and restless, I bundled up in the middle of the night and went out to check the garage. His bed was empty and his food and water bowls hadn't been touched. I set out in search of my devoted four-legged companion. I figured he might be injured, but perhaps still alive.

The quarter moon cast an eerie bluish sheen over the glistening fresh snow. It was exquisitely beautiful; it was as if I were the only human alive on earth. Suddenly I slipped into a deep snowdrift and tumbled down a bank, twisting my ankle badly. As I lay there in the woods hurting, I realized I could freeze to death before anyone found me the next day. Eventually, I was able painfully to hobble back to Chanticleer, where I stayed in bed the next forty-eight hours. We never saw Mule again. One of the locals swore he saw a dog nailed on the side of the suspect's toolshed.

I contacted my brother, Mark, to come lend his manly presence when he wasn't working on the riverboat. He'd gotten burned out with college and had signed on as a river rat on a barge on the Ohio.

As spring arrived, Margaret and Erin came to visit. We had glorious days swimming in the lake, putting Erin on her first pony, but Margaret yearned for some urban excitement. We took her and Erin into Berea for pizza at Little Mama's Pizza Kitchen, even plied them nickels for the pinball machine, but Margaret needed more.

Margaret firmly insisted I borrow her makeup and begged me not to dress like Calamity Jane. Leaving our three girls with Craig, we set out for the big city like a couple of giddy high-school teenagers. She commented on how weird it was to be riding in her old VW again. I pointed out that we were headed for a girls' night out together once again, but now it was Lexington, Kentucky, instead of Hollywood, California.

As we were entering a downtown restaurant, an unusual-look-ing group of guys struck up a conversation with us. They said they were The Band. I asked whose band they were in and if they by chance played bluegrass. Margaret suddenly had a horrified look on her face. She began laughing nervously, making excuses for her hermit sister's ignorance.

They invited us to eat with them and to attend their concert. By the end of dinner, we had paired off. She with Bruce, their record guy from Los Angeles, me with the drummer, Levon Helm. I thought Robbie Robertson was attractive, but his behavior was that of a married man, and Rick Danko acted right strange. During the show I whispered to Margaret I thought they were good enough to "make it." Exasperated, she informed me they were superstars who were breaking up and on their "farewell tour."

As we all sat eating again at a late-night restaurant after their show, Levon called me his "mountain madonna." He had some unaccountable glint of knowingness in his eyes that intrigued me. Although I hadn't been with a man in years, I turned down his request to return to the hotel and spend the night. Levon and the record guy were ticked off. I never saw Levon again, except in the movies when he played Loretta Lynn's daddy in *Coal Miner's Daughter*. I began to wonder if I'd ever find a man with all the qualities it would take to satisfy me? A combination country boy like Doolittle Lynn and worldly Levon Helm.

This strange encounter began to make me uncomfortably aware of my self-imposed isolation, and I started to crave worldly intelligent conversation. I wanted more than the standard three R's that comprised the range of topics for locals: rain, religion, and relatives.

Daddy had gotten an apartment of his own, so he could date his new girlfriend. I declined ever to see it so I could keep my memories of him at home intact. The rotting black growth of bitterness was threatening to destroy Mom. She filed for divorce and enlisted me to testify against Daddy. Since she'd never worked outside our home, we'd sit up all night with the coffee pot trying to figure out what she would do. As she bemoaned her fate, I'd gaze around at the four empty chairs at our once-happy kitchen table and silently wonder how we ended up this way. And now, how was I going to choose between my parents? This psychological damage left me naked to the awareness of life's unpredictability. I returned to Morrill less than I was.

The state police came to our house to report that their new jail inmate, convicted of some other crime, had also confessed to being an accomplice to our burglary suspect when we were robbed. The inmate not only described in detail all our stolen property but told of the suspect's particular joy in finding my great-grandmother's pearl handled Smith & Wesson under my pillow. The trial date was set and I went out around Big Hill soliciting testimony of other previous victims.

To my horror, these scared locals shrunk back in fear of possible retaliation. Confronting the last name on my list, I urged a tall, lanky farmer to come forward. He stiffened up as if I'd slapped him. "Everybody knows he's the biggest thief in Jackson and Rockcastle counties," he allowed. "But if'n he ain't convicted or whenever he gets out, he could take a match and set fire to my barn full of tobacco. Then my whole year's worth of income would be up in smoke!"

I glared at the farmer a full minute and hissed, "C'mon, little girls. Let's get out of here before I lose my cool and call someone a coward!"

That night before the trial, the three of us awoke to a barrage of gunshots outside my bedroom window. Absolutely terrified, I threw the kids in the VW, put blankets on top of them and sped down the hill. As we bunked down on the Yanceys' floor, it dawned on me that those gunshots, warning me not to show up at the courthouse in the morning, had probably been fired from Miss Cora Lee's gun.

The suspect was found not guilty due to lack of evidence. The credibility of our only witness was shattered when the district attorney announced our suspect was carrying on an affair with the witness's mother. The defense suggested that our tattletale inmate accomplice was only trying to get back at his former partner in crime for cuckolding his father.

Defeated, alone, and badly shaken, I stumbled out of the courtroom. The suspect and some of his backwoods thugs snickered wickedly as they "accidentally" brushed by me. A chill went up my spine as I drove past his cabin on the way up the hill to Chanticleer. My sweet dreams of life in Morrill had curdled.

It was the end of the summer of 1976 and I sent Chris and Ashley on the Greyhound bus to Ashland, where I knew they'd be safe. Still refusing to admit defeat by leaving, I strapped on my new gun, kept all the doors locked and my shades drawn at night. But without a telephone or TV, the only human contact I had during the following weeks was when I walked the mile or so up to the post office/general store for mail and supplies.

I'd been praying for a sign, and one hot day it appeared in the form of two letters. My ol' Austin buddy, David Swann, knew it was nearing fall college tuition time and surprised me with an "I-believe-in-you" letter and a $500 check. The second letter was from my childhood neighbor, Linda Ann McDonald. On the pages, she described her glorious new life in San Francisco that had prompted her to change her name to "Piper."

As I walked outside the post office with both letters in my hand, I stood silently looking westward toward the horizon and realized the sun was also setting on our days at Morrill. I ran back up the long hill to the house and began packing. I finished loading the car at midnight, and being too wound up to sleep, I set out for my last moonlit walk in the woods. Under the glow of the haunting full moon, the Kentucky hills looked like dirt waves flowing through eternity. John Milton's phrase from *Paradise Lost* Book IV came to mind: "Millions of spiritual creatures walk the earth / Unseen, both when we wake, and when we sleep."

Liminality is the state betwixt one thing and another, a time and place where the ordinary rules do not apply. Morrill had been that for the three of us. A place to shake off the dust of life and exorcise the demons of civilization. A place to delve into ourselves and cocoon. In the rich nourishing humus of solitude our imaginations had sprung forth. And I had revisited my childhood, often feeling as if I were sitting at the feet of my own life, being taught by it.

My loyalty was divided between Appalachian traditions and the lure of new experiences in the West Coast's intellectual stew pot. The craving for exploration seems inextricably woven into my character.

Big fat tears streaked down my cheeks as I pulled away from Chanticleer at dawn. I knew it would be forever remembered as one of the happiest times in our lives. It was the setting for Chris's and my discovery of music and for Ashley's dream of being an actress. Driving down Big Hill for the last time I mentally bade farewells to my friends sleeping unaware in their cabins back in the woods. Down in Berea at Boone Tavern's pay phone I called Mom and the girls. Mom was the only one up and I simply told her I was going on a "little trip" before school resumed. I knew I was lying to my mother, breaking two commandments in one breath. I couldn't burden her with the details of how the pieces of my life had been blown away like bits of dry dandelion. Nor could I admit I was running away so I didn't have to testify against Daddy.

I kissed my native ground good-bye and said my pledge of allegiance to the road. Time to turn another page in life's book of experience.

Change of Heart

T. S. ELIOT wrote "We shall not cease from exploration / And the end of all our exploring / Will be to arrive where we started / And know the place for the first time." I had experienced a personal transformation as a result of returning to my birthplace as an adult.

It was dawn of Saturday, August 4, 1976, when fueled by high hopes and guided by intuition, I set out looking for the land of understanding. At 4:30 P.M. I began to have car trouble out in the boonies of Indiana. The young gas station attendant seemed too impatient to spend much time on my car. I commented that I hoped it wasn't anything serious, because I was in a big hurry. I remarked there was a world of ideas out there waiting for me. He countered by stating he had a hot little number named Diane waiting for him.

I listened to stories in truck stops. Pausing to play the jukebox or winding around to the restroom I got a chance to size up whom I wanted to sit next to at the counter. Cherry pie, a cup of coffee, and conversation.

A semiattractive girl named Marie turned out to be a nonstop verbal volcano. When she finally paused long enough to come up for air and light another cigarette, she asked what I was doing. I answered that I was on a safari. Marie helpfully informed me there was no big game in Iowa. "I'm hunting adventure," I corrected her.

"Oh yeah, I get it!" she whooped. She barked a hearty cougher's laugh and slapped her arm full of bracelets down on the

Formica counter. The big bangles were like manacles, handcuffing her to her fate as a prisoner of tackiness. Marie had run away from home in Florida and didn't have the first clue what she was hunting. She'd casually stated that she "worked in the area." Only later down the road did it dawn on me she was referring to turning tricks in the sleeper cabs of the eighteen-wheelers out behind the truck stop.

Sometimes when I stopped, I'd sit alone in the middle of the restaurant, pretending to be reading a newspaper so I could eavesdrop on conversations around me. Many times I observed that the average man thinks he isn't.

Under the starlight, the old VW seemed to sprout wings and glide. Locked in the womblike security of the rattling car, I became absorbed in *Mystery Theater* hosted by E. G. Marshall and National Public Radio. Energized from the exhilaration of new beginnings, I drove straight through the night.

By 11:00 A.M. Sunday my attention span was shot and my ears were ringing. As I checked into a hotel in downtown Lincoln, Nebraska, I remember being too tired even to brush my hair. After sleeping soundly until 6:00 P.M., I ventured down to the restaurant. There was a sea of permed blue hair and polyester suits milling around the Sunday buffet. A chubby, cheerful woman at the salad bar struck up a conversation and inquired why I'd left home. "Oh, I didn't leave home," I informed her, "I carry it right here in my heart." I smiled to myself as I pictured Mom and the girls at church back in Ashland.

As I enjoyed my first full meal, I wrote in my journal. I signed off at the bottom of the page: "Homer on the Range." After running back to my room to brush my teeth and pack my suitcase, I went straight to the front desk to pay my bill. My billfold was missing from my purse! Racing back into the restaurant, an elderly waiter approached me with my wallet in his outstretched hand. "Looking for this?" he grinned. Thanking him, I took the episode as a good omen . . . another guardian angel!

As I started the car I had the sensation I was getting my life back as well as my wallet. It was as if I were also covering emotional geography on an inward journey, so every mile seemed to be taking me farther away from the problems back in Kentucky. Then suddenly I drove right into a terrible storm. Noticing there were no other vehicles on the interstate I quickly switched on the car radio to hear hail warnings. In minutes, hail the size of golf balls came smashing down on my little car in an ear-splitting fusillade. The VW engine itself had been making worrisome noises for hours, and I was losing compression fast.

I coasted down the next exit into a gas station just outside Oglala, Nebraska. A crippled young blond attendant in greasy over-halls ran up to the car window and began to yell at me that I was crazy for being out on the road. The barrage of hail was so deafening, we had to go inside the station office to hear each other. I said the VW would not even start, my beetle had bellied up. He said the two area motels had no vacancies because of the storm, which had escalated to tornado sightings. Feeling trapped, I sat motionless in the office staring over at a map of the United States on the wall. I was stuck exactly halfway between Morrill and San Francisco.

It was after midnight when the unassuming station attendant said he was closing and that I had to leave. As I stood up to go sit out the night in the tiny car crammed full of my belongings, he offered to let me sleep in his extra room and the next morning bring me back when he opened up. The nearest VW dealership was back two hours east in North Platte.

The attendant had said he lived nearby and cautioned it would be dangerous for me to be outside in the storm totally alone. At least I would be safe and dry inside near a phone and a bathroom at his place. We kept driving in the storm out in the Nebraska plains till we finally came to a small beat-up trailer. Once I laid eyes on it, I didn't want to go in, but I knew I couldn't freak out. It was filthy inside, with grimy work uniforms and empty beer cans everywhere. My heart was pounding and I began to hyperventilate. I went into the bath-room to get control of myself. When I finally came out he was shirtless and barefoot, wearing only a pair of jeans.

My God, I suddenly realized, *no one* knew where I was. I'd only been gone two days, but my friends probably weren't even aware I'd left Chanticleer. All I'd told Mom was I was going on a "little trip." How in the world did I end up in a funky trailer out in the middle of nowhere in a hailstorm on the Nebraska plains . . . alone with a total stranger holding a Budweiser in his hand? I've always considered myself a reasonably intelligent woman, but this was unquestionably the stupidest thing I'd ever done . . . and the most dangerous!

The attendant reached out and flipped my hair and said I was the most beautiful thing he'd ever seen. His shy passiveness was suddenly gone. He was in his own home now . . . his territory on his terms. I kept looking around for the phone, insisting I needed to call my husband. He laughed and replied, "Baby, you don't have no wedding ring and I don't have no phone!"

It was the most terrifying, trapped, and desperate situation a woman can face. I knew that talking him out of rape was probably hopeless and I sensed that he knew no one could trace me here. I flashed on registering at the hotel back in Lincoln. For some unknown reason, I had signed my name Kimberly Parks.

Fearing I might be raped and murdered, the worst part of this nightmare seemed to be that my children and family would *never know why I left or what happened to me.* When my would-be assailant said he was going to get us a couple of beers from the refrigerator, I grabbed my purse and dashed out into the storm. Running pell-mell through the hail, I turned and looked over my shoulder as he was screaming something at me from the doorway. There was no place to hide out in the open plains.

Soaking wet and freezing, I was pummeled by hailstones and slipped and fell in the mud twice. My heaving chest hurt from running and crying with my mouth open. When I finally got back to my car, the keys weren't in my purse. I became totally hysterical and started running in the direction of the nearest motel. I put my hand in my pocket in a futile attempt to warm it and discovered my car keys. I went back and retrieved my suitcase from the car, then trudged back up the road. I cleaned up and changed in the public restroom of the motel and slept sitting in a chair in the lobby in view of the night clerk.

Early the next morning I called for a wrecker at the VW dealership in North Platte and had the driver pick me up at the motel. Together we went over to the station to get my car. There were customers coming and going and the attendant could only glare at me. I stayed close to the guy from the wrecker service until we pulled out.

The VW dealership in Oglala said they couldn't get to me for at least a week. A week! My brain was on fire to make it to the West Coast and I was running out of money. I hung around till the mechanic offered me a deal. For time-and-a-half wages he would work on my car that evening at his home.

After checking into a cheap, but clean, motel, I set out walking all over town to let off steam. When darkness fell waves of despair came crashing down on me. Stranded again! Back at the motel, I took out Chris's guitar and wrote "Stuck in a Motel Blues."

> Gideon's in the drawer
> Van Gogh's on the wall
> Sounds like the couple next door
> Are havin' themselves a ball
> Guess I'll turn on the TV
> To catch some local news
> Jesus but I'm down
> Got the "stuck in a motel blues"

I never finished the tune because the mechanic called just after midnight. He'd pulled the engine, said it had a crack in the engine block, and repairs would run at least $500. Frantic, I phoned Daddy to seek his advice. It was after 2:00 A.M. back home so at first he was alarmed to hear my voice. He was shocked that I was calling from Nebraska and not at the pay phone at Sparks' Grocery in Morrill, but he stayed fairly calm. When I repeated the mechanics' description of what was going on, Daddy sighed, "They've got you, honey. Sell the car and get out of there!" Only weeks before, Daddy had checked out the VW and put four brand new tires on it to get me ready for another school year.

I called the mechanic back and told him to make me an offer. He brought over only $125 cash to my room. I knew the four tires were worth twice that much, but he had liquor on his breath and was inside my motel room. Declining his offer to take me to the Greyhound bus depot, I got rid of him and called a cab.

My stuff was all in boxes and sacks, so I had to bundle it up with tape and string as best I could. Looking like a down-and-out vagrant,

I rode the bus from North Platte to Denver. At 5:30 A.M. as I stood in the ticket line at Stapleton Airport, I had to set the guitar down behind me. When I turned around it was gone! My car and my guitar in one night! What next? I felt out of control.

When my plane arrived safely in San Francisco, I felt as if I'd just been delivered from *The Twilight Zone*. Squeezing past flawlessly elegant women in the terminal, there stood my childhood friend, waiting by the curb in her full-length mink, standing alongside her new expensive car. We joked about the fact that our very different paths had once again converged.

When she was an infant, Linda's family had rented out part of my family's home on Montgomery Avenue. Later she moved across the street and we grew up together, walking to school side by side every day. She had introduced me to Michael. It was symbolic that Linda Ann, now renamed Piper, had once again reappeared in my destiny, helping me begin another new life far removed from Montgomery Avenue.

I was anxious to confirm my previous impression of the pastoral beauty and creative atmosphere of Marin County, north of San Francisco, across the Golden Gate Bridge. Renting a car, I drove out there, past the College of Marin, whose nursing program I'd already checked out. Winding my way past the expensive areas of Ross, Kentfield, and San Anselmo, I followed Sir Francis Drake Boulevard into the sparsely populated rolling hills of the San Geronimo Valley. Then, half an hour's drive from my future campus, I stopped at the very last hamlet at the edge of the redwood forest known as Samuel P. Taylor State Park.

I happened along a workman by the side of the road named Eldon Halseth. After striking up a conversation with me, the friendly local took me home to meet his wife and family. His wife was involved in the San Geronimo Valley church, and he thought she or his kids might know of a house for rent. When they didn't, he showed me to the small two-story building next to the Laquintas post office that housed a real estate office. A grandmotherly woman named Grace informed me the only rental property under $500 per month was a one-bedroom apartment right upstairs over their office.

Having no choice, since school would be starting the following week, I took it for $295. On my way back to San Francisco to spend the night at Piper's, I stopped at the valley grade school to enroll Chris and Ashley.

Upon my returning to Kentucky, Daddy brought Chris and Ashley back to Morrill in the biggest U-haul his station had for rent. He and Mark helped us pack all our belongings, and in less than twenty-four hours the truck was loaded. As Mark, Chris, and Ashley and I piled into it, I still recall Daddy's parting words as we hugged good-bye, "I don't know about your common sense, but you sure got more guts than anybody I know!"

At the top of Big Hill, I made the first of two stops. At Sparks Grocery, I bade a quick farewell and phoned Mama in Ashland to break the news to her. It was not a pleasant conversation. We both knew I was abandoning her. The second stop was the administration building of EKU in Richmond to obtain my transcripts. It was fall enrollment day and my instructors attempted to reason with me to stay on and finish my last semester. "Dreams are more powerful than logic," I responded as I hurried out to our double-parked U-Haul.

Then like the crack of a whip, we were off on yet another midcourse lifestyle correction. We'd placed our mattress in the back of the truck for the girls to take naps on. We propped the back doors open several inches for light and ventilation. Late into the second day, a highway patrolman's lights and siren pulled us over demanding we open up the back. The officer reported a shirt being waved under the doors in what appeared to be a distress signal. Concerned now myself, I raced back to throw open the doors. Ashley jumped into my arms, near hysteria. Chris had been terrorizing and tickling her so hard she was about to vomit. While I soothed Ashley, with my permission, Uncle Mark took Chris behind the nearest tree and spanked her.

Stopping at an Indian reservation in eastern Arizona, I met with the Bureau of Indian Affairs to discuss working with the Indians as soon as I finished my RN degree. Desperate for medical help, they were eager to enlist me to ride circuit on several reservation hospitals and clinics. Since childhood I'd found myself drawn to the plight of the Native Americans and had long harbored a romantic notion of noble self-sacrifice. But the ugly truth about their grim existence was more than I could subject my kids to. Unable to consider putting Chris and Ashley in substandard housing and grossly inferior schools, we left White River. My heart went out to them and I felt angry and inadequate.

When we ran out of the food I'd packed from Chanticleer, we stopped at diners. First, the four of us chose what we wanted from the menu, then some quick arithmetic on a paper napkin determined what we could actually afford to order. The U-Haul was a gas guzzler, and we still had a long way to go. We only stopped overnight twice at cheap motels, making the cross-country trip in four days.

Chris and Ashley loved the pine-covered scenery of their new homesite, but were less than ecstatic about the two-room apartment. Ashley and I slept on a standard-size mattress on the living room floor, allowing Chris the twin bed in the only bedroom. As she was still given to talking and walking in her sleep, neither Ashley nor I were willing to share a room with her.

Miss Cora Lee's simple dining table, sideboard, and four mismatched chairs were the nicest furniture pieces we had. I threw a bedspread over a used couch, laid colorful rugs on top of the horrid avacado green carpet and made the apartment as cozy and homey as I could. Our incongruous old Maytag wringer washer sat by the door like a statue of pop art.

Mark took the kids for a hike in the state park while I set out job hunting. Having plunked down my last dollar on a used Dodge Valiant, I was now getting desperate. Needing to be in the classroom and hospital all day, I was looking for a nighttime waitressing position. My grades qualified me for college grants and as usual, I took out school loans. Since there was no sign of child support, I relied on Aid to Families with Dependent Children for medical coverage. However, there was never any money for auto insurance. I drove carefully and defensively.

Because there were no upscale restaurants in our rural valley, I headed into the bustling, tourist town of Sausalito on the harbor. While filling out an application at one of the most popular restaurants, the handsome new bartender struck up a conversation. When Buck inquired where else I'd worked, I confessed that for all my previous employments, I'd never waitressed. I assured him though that I'd been serving meals ever since I was seventeen and this didn't look like something that required a degree in physics. When he warned me the manager would request good references, Buck kindly offered to vouch for me and say we'd worked together at the places he'd given as his references. I had to go along with him.

I got the job, then discovered Buck was also a porn star and there was pretty juicy speculation on the extent of our "partnership." It turned out he lived out in our valley with his two kids and I ran into him at school functions.

Okay, I admit to being the world's worst waitress. I was too solicitous to be efficient. The first day, a table with several boisterous kids kept eating foods saturated with sugar and ordering Cokes like they were water. When their beleaguered Mom began inquiring about desserts, I suggested their diet might be causing hyperactivity. If lonely looking singles came in for a meal or just a cup of coffee, I served up what they really wanted, an ear for their conversation.

This place was famous for a rich dessert called a "mud pie," but every time I went to squeeze the whipped cream garnish on top, the Reddi Wip can would be flat. Then I observed the dishwasher guys behaving strangely. You guessed it! I slipped up on them and caught them sniffing the fumes. Confronting them with the health risks, I also warned them the manager might call the cops before throwing them out. The next day I walked into the kitchen to overhear the mystified waitresses still throwing out flat cans of Reddi Wip. The dishwashers were once again high as kites, so I informed the manager.

She came out front to thank me, and before she walked away, instructed me "to marry the coffee pots." As I stared blankly at the twin burners, she caught on that I had no idea what she meant. "You've never waitressed before in your life, have you, Diana?" she said more as a statement of fact than a question. "Hey, you're a good kid, but you're not fast enough as a waitress in a hectic place like this. I'll call my friend about you working at his small diner." Taking off my apron, I thanked her anyway, saying fisherman's tips wouldn't be enough. "And by the way," I added, "I lied to you about references. I'd never seen Buck before in my life!"

Work is the rent you pay for space on earth. As if raising two girls by myself, maintaining a home, and going to college full time weren't already enough, I always had to work at some minimum-wage job too. It seemed like such a senseless waste of time, but I tried to maintain a cheerful attitude. I realize that living with me must have been as tricky and suspenseful as driving on an icy road at times.

My consolation lay in my discovery that everything that happens to us is a teacher. When we use both sides of our brain, we get a real education. The left side of our brain is for clear, distinct ideas, such as the medical facts I was studying in college textbooks. The right side of the human brain is the creative part. My constant face-to-face interaction at work with an ever-changing cast of colorful personalities from diverse walks of life also was giving me an education.

I encountered Sally Stanford, the most well known madam in American history. Her thriving whorehouse had serviced politicians and big wigs as well as thousands of regular johns. After being busted for the last time, her bordello was torn down. An ever-enterprising Sally auctioned off the bricks as sentimental keepsakes to former patrons. Now she was respectably prominent in the restaurant business, with a popular tourist eatery called The Valhalla, overlooking the water in Sausalito.

I knew nothing of this when I first walked in off the street applying for a waitress position. Sally immediately struck me as a Sophie Tucker figure. Seated in a barber chair, just inside the front door, she was solicitously greeting customers as they entered The Valhalla. As I waited my turn, I overheard her introducing herself as the mayor of Sausalito, while she autographed a copy of her autobiography. A made-for-TV movie based on Sally's book, *A House Is Not a Home*, starring Dyan Cannon, was in the works.

This time, in the same breath, I told her I needed a job, but had no waitressing experience. She said something about her former clientele preferring girls with no experience and laughed, but I didn't get it till much later as I was driving home.

She hired me purely on the basis that she'd "taken a liking to me." Working for Madame Sally was a strange job. The rococo decor was done in lurid reds, very bordello-like. She required us to wear our own full-length skirts, which made it difficult running around on busy nights. The patronage was primarily tourists and leering businessmen, only a few locals. It was a long forty-five-minute drive from Lagunitas, but the tips were good.

Brother Mark took off home to Kentucky on his motorcycle, which he'd carted out to California in the back of our U-Haul. Without him to baby-sit, I soon became anxious about being so far away from the girls at night and quit Sally's place.

There were two other apartments besides ours above the real estate office. Next door a single mom with a girl Ashley's age began watching the kids. Nikki told me about the San Geronimo golf course's restaurant where she waitressed days. I hired on working there nights and weekends. While one of us worked, the other baby-sat. I thought golf was boring, rather like injecting novocaine directly into my forehead, but I felt much safer being just a few miles from home.

The neighbor on the other side of us was a sweet, old man named Skipper, who bartended at Spec McAullife's, the pub on the other side of the Lagunitas post office. He had a bad eye, walked with a cane, and became like an uncle to the girls.

In our tiny two-room apartment, the three of us lived as close as an undersize rubber glove. The gestalt of San Geronimo Valley's beauty and stillness was mystically laid back. There were lot of artists who had shucked the artifice of the city for nature. There were aging hippies who seemed frozen in time by their inertia. They ran a large health food store up the road with the unlikely name of House of Richard. Being lacto-ovo vegetarians, we shopped there every other day for bulgur wheat, soybeans, yogurt, kefir, sprouts, and seeds. You could also buy huarache sandals, patchouli oil, incense and candles, books on holistic medicine, and wares and crafts from local artisans. Chris and I discovered a natural root called henna that stained our hair red. She called it: "a pigment of our imagination." When I was growing up, I'd stop in our neighborhood's Parkview Grocery to buy a Popsicle or Snickers bar from Mrs. Hankess. Chris and Ashley stopped at House of Richard for an apricot roll or a Tiger's Milk bar.

As we immersed ourselves in this subculture, our musical consciousness expanded as well. Chris came home singing the current hits of Little River Band and Little Feat. At work I heard about local musicians like Huey Lewis, who fronted a group called Clover. Maria Muldaur had a hit on the radio called "Midnight at the Oasis." While we hung out at the Laundromat in Fairfax washing our clothes, we met musicians and residents like Van Morrison's mother, who ran a shop around the corner. We were thrilled and encouraged to discover there were eclectic performers all around us in Marin County.

I saved change in an old tin box to buy records. We learned a dozen Bob Wills and the Texas Playboys songs and lot of Delbert McClinton's Texas rock. To make it a real musical crazy quilt, I taught Chris "Cow Cow Boogie" from Ella Fitzgerald's Greatest Hits album. We learned a bunch of Andrews Sisters hits, but were much more intrigued by the Boswell Sisters. Their innovative, daring style truly fascinated and inspired us. The 1930s trio of sisters were our favorite group.

But the single most important discovery we made was a white chick named Bonnie Raitt, who sang blues tinged with rock. Tough, yet somehow vulnerable, you could feel true heartache in her believable voice. And she played a mean slide guitar!

Every time I listened to her anthems of "the no-good bum did me wrong / eternal quest for a good man" I felt like rising to my feet with my hand over my heart and saluting. Chris and Ashley and I would turn her up loud and dance uninhibitedly around the room.

Music became Chris's best friend. Oh, Chris still loved Joni Mitchell's poetic jazzy songs and our Appalachian-flavored favorites from Emmylou Harris, but I think Chris recognized herself in Bonnie Raitt's style. Soon, we had every record Bonnie had ever made and had worked up many tunes. Chris was only thirteen years old, and it was unnerving hearing her sing numbers like "Louise," a sad song about a prostitute who overdosed on drugs.

Her rapt affection for the guitar continued to grow. She otherwise had no attention span and was easily distracted. Our verbal skirmishes erupted everywhere and anywhere, at any time.

She started the eighth grade at Lagunitas school under Mary Anne Kolanski, a kind and intelligent woman who was to become her all-time favorite teacher. Miss Kolanski spotted her creative side and

Another glimpse into the future: Ashley, five, starred in a short film project called *Windows* by UCLA film students, shot in the family's house in Hollywood, June 1973. Ashley is holding her own pet cat.

Every summer they tried to go to the real world of Aunt Pauline and Uncle Landon's farm in Louisa, Kentucky, to escape Hollywood.

Divorced and alone—
on their own
in 1972.
(MICHAEL WARD)

Ashley and Wy
in 1972.

Morrill, Kentucky

Living in Morrill,
Kentucky, a time
of togetherness, nature,
music, and magic.

The Yancey clan:
Wy is on far left, talking
to Minnie; Sonya,
Greer, and Toddie are
on the step; Ashley is in
the chair, at shepherd
Dan's cabin in Morrill,
Kentucky.

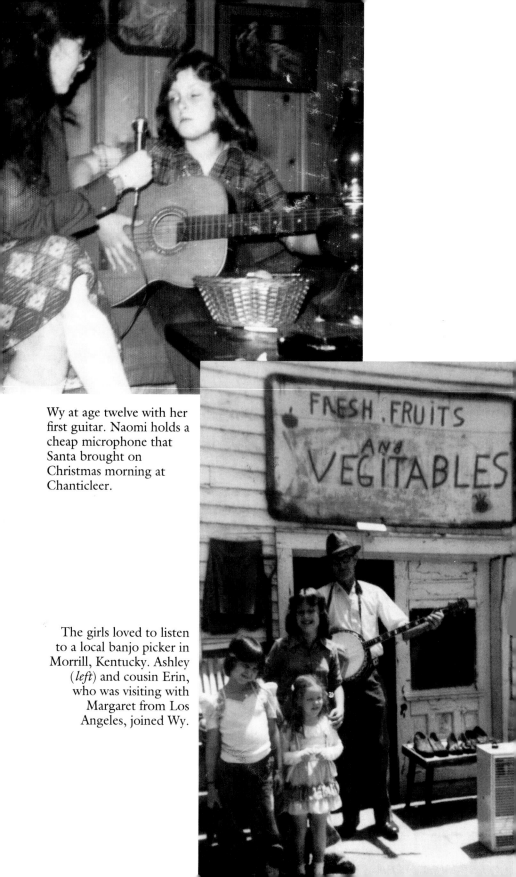

Wy at age twelve with her first guitar. Naomi holds a cheap microphone that Santa brought on Christmas morning at Chanticleer.

The girls loved to listen to a local banjo picker in Morrill, Kentucky. Ashley (*left*) and cousin Erin, who was visiting with Margaret from Los Angeles, joined Wy.

Lagunitas,
California, 1977:
Ashley helped Naomi
bake Wy a birthday
cake in their one-
bedroom apartment.
Cousin Erin has the
tambourine, and Wy
always had a guitar
in her hands by now.

Wy in Marin
County, California,
singing a Joni
Mitchell song at her
junior high school
graduation, 1977.

Onstage for the first time with Susie McKee and the Cowpokes at
Rancho Nicasio, Lucas Valley, California, 1978.

Best friends Asia Lee, sister Margaret, and Naomi the night of
Naomi and Wy's first performance.

Tres Virgos Studio,
Marin County,
California, 1978:
Wy and Naomi singing
for the first time in a
studio.

Marin County,
1979: Wy and
Naomi often
cruised the A&W
root-beer drive-ins
in their red
'57 Chevy.

Wy serenading a hitchhiker at a truck stop in Arizona while Naomi refuels Redhot on their way to Las Vegas.

February 22, 1979: at the Palomino Club with country singer Mickey Gilley, Naomi was wearing her Hillbilly Women jacket. This is where she first saw Larry Strickland, who became her husband ten years later.

was more understanding and supportive than any teacher had ever been or ever was to be.

Ashley, already a poised charmer, began the third grave in an experimental program held in a smaller building behind the regular school; it was an "open" classroom. There were no grades or report cards and students were allowed to work at their own pace. There were only four teachers and a coordinator; the alternative classes went only to the fifth grade. Each morning Ashley helped make her list of assignments and once completed, she'd have the rest of the day to herself. Since Ashley was so disciplined and bright, I was hopeful this program might be well suited for her. As it turned out, even the most strikingly self-sufficient and curious eight-year-old needs more guidance than was being offered. After just a few weeks, I switched her back into the standard curriculum.

Three things always impress people about Ashley: She's affectionate, unusually articulate, and has a vivid imagination. I began to notice both she and Chris had the ability to fit in with all types of people.

Marin County was the midwife that helped birth my new name. By now, so much had happened in my life I felt like a different version of Diana Ellen Judd. My family was scattered like pieces of a disassembled jigsaw puzzle. I wished sometimes I could lock little Diana up with all the good memories and put her away in a safe place.

The miles and experiences had brought me to a higher level of awareness, so that now I felt I needed a new label to attach to the metamorphosis. Names have always been unusually important to me, partly because I have a compulsion to organize and establish order. As a child I named dolls, toys, animals, events, and places. I even renamed classmates and neighbors. *Eke* means "extra" in Old English, and *ekename* when slurred over time came out to be "nickname." Giving someone an extra name personalizes your relationship even more, creating a special bond.

A name doesn't mean anything until you make it mean something. I had never forgotten the little retarded girl named Naomi who stared at me in grade school. Nor had I forgotten my mother's words about her. "Be kind to everyone, because you can't know what their life is like."

I'd never known anyone else with the name Naomi, but I loved the story about Naomi in the Bible. She was no great prophetess or saintly heroine, just a hardworking housewife, who cared for her two children and husband. They fell on hard times and Naomi lost her family. She was grieving and felt frightened and alone. As she was returning to her homeland of Judea so as not to be a burden on her two daughters-in-law, she kissed them both and asked the Lord's blessings on them. She convinced Orpah it was for the best, but Ruth was so devoted she refused to leave Naomi. Her declaration of love is one of the most touching passages in the Bible: "For whither thou goest, I will go; and where thou lodgest, I will lodge: thy people shall be my people, and thy God my God: Where thou diest I will die, and there will I be buried."

The sad saga has a beautiful ending. Ruth remarried and presented Naomi with a grandson named Obed, who grew up to be the father of Jesse. Jesse was the father of the great king David, who was the ancestor of Mary and Joseph, parents of Jesus Christ.

Quite a story! Perhaps I took the name Naomi because I identified with the pain of her loss and struggle. Maybe it was because she had a compassionate, devoted daughter (in-law) who stuck with her on the journey, presenting her with a wondrous gift at the end.

But I was in for a shock when I applied for a name change at the free legal clinic! I not only wanted to switch my first name from the original Diana to the new Naomi, but all these years I'd longed to drop my married name, Ciminella, and legally return to my family name of Judd.

To do so I petitioned the Los Angeles Superior Court where I'd gotten my divorce in 1972. The clerk wrote back immediately, informing me I'd failed to file the final dissolution papers. I was, therefore, still legally married! Eventually I succeeded in tracking Michael down to request that he sign the correct papers. So I went from my birth name of Diana Ellen Judd (Ellen is Grandmommy Judd's name), to Diana Ciminella, to Naomi Ellen Judd.

Since we were new to Marin, it was the perfect time to start off with a new name. That's how I enrolled at the College of Marin, and each time I met someone for the first time I began to introduce myself as Naomi Ellen Judd.

The nursing program offered more awareness of the patient's emotional needs, more emphasis on patient participation in his or her own care, and the role of nutrition in prevention and healing. Midwifery was of great interest to me, and I was delighted to discover it was commonplace out there. Participating in the miracle of birth is one of the greatest rewards of nursing. It's a glimpse into creation.

Prevention is my big thing, so nothing could have prepared me for that day at Kaiser Hospital in Oakland when a young black girl was wheeled in in full labor. Long a drug addict, she had medicated herself with a heavy dose of raw street drugs when her painful contractions began. The doctor in charge immediately instructed the staff to ascertain what she was using so we could treat her baby accordingly.

The head nurse wasn't making any progress. The belligerent girl wasn't about to admit her illegal drug habit to a white nurse. Just then, my best friend, Janet Greenwood, stepped forward and suggested they send me in alone to get it out of her. "Naomi has a way with people," she offered.

I poked Janet in the ribs and gave her a quick "I'll-get-even-with-you-later" look, just as the head nurse threw up her hands and said with a sigh, "Be my guest."

As I entered the room, I realized I felt more anger than pity for this girl. I got down in her face and assured her we were alone. Knowing sympathy and kindness hadn't gotten the head nurse anywhere, I tried a different approach. I had to relate to her on her level. "This is the deal!" I hissed. "Right now I don't care about what you're doing to yourself! You're a grown-up and that's your business. What I do care about is this innocent fragile new life that's fixin' to come out into this world. Your baby's going to die unless we treat it immediately. I'm not getting out of your face until you tell me what you've been using." Between contractions she told me everything I needed to know. I quickly prepared a bottle with liquid Valium in sterile water and gave it to the infant as soon as it was born.

If a female drug addict continues using drugs during her pregnancy the baby is born with the addiction also. An addicted baby is a horrible nightmare. As soon as he or she comes out of the womb and is unplugged from its mother's drug-rich bloodstream, the baby is in agony. Such babies shriek and scream, and their tiny bodies shiver and jerk spastically. They don't stop screaming until they're so exhausted they faint into sleep for short spells. They're not cute and cuddly. My heart went out to the nurses in the newborn addict section of the nursery.

The next eye-opening experience was VIPs. Believe it or not, that nice, prestigious-sounding title was what the hospital chose to call abortions: voluntarily interrupted pregnancy. As long as I live, I'll never forget the sight of a discarded dead fetus in the garbage bucket. I asked what would become of it and was told it would be burned in the incinerator with the rest of the "trash."

Beliefs have consequences.

Some very important concepts about healing were becoming clear to me. I had long suspected that feelings are chemicals that can kill or cure. Now I had proof. From my medical lectures and text-books, I got scientific data about the physical properties and functions of the body. I was learning about neurohormones, the chemicals in the brain that program the body. Then I'd put on my nursing uniform, walk into a real clinical setting to observe the patients' personalities and how their behavioral traits influenced their various bodily activities. Experience meets science.

People who have extreme fear, anxiety, or anger might tend to have ulcers or colitis. Constant tension can lead to high blood pressure, insomnia, and headaches and can precipitate asthma attacks and heart attacks. In fact, any negative emotion adversely affects the body. For every action there's a reaction. Stress takes an incredible toll. The normal body tries to maintain homeostasis or balance between all its systems, but stress can interfere to such an extent that it lowers the body's resistance to disease.

Once I got to know a patient and to see how he or she handled life in general, it was a powerful indicator of how the patient would handle his or her disease or injury. Those with positive, upbeat outlooks would likely require less pain medication, leave the hospital sooner, and experience better results in healing. I also began to appreciate the importance of faith and a support system from family and friends when dealing with problems. Confidence and a good rapport with the medical team is of great benefit to the patient.

I witnessed how important it is to inform and explain to patients everything that's going on with them and to include them in the recovery process. Information is our most valuable tool in dealing with reality and wards off fear of the unknown. If a patient told me he or she felt vulnerable and out of control, I discovered that making such a patient a participant in his or her own healing restored some measure of control. Personally, I believe one of the greatest things a nurse can do is listen. I saw how it not only calmed the patient, enabling the person to express his or her concerns, but created a bond of confidence between the patient and me and often gave me additional insight into the patient's problems.

Nurses are taught to be observant, and I guess I got an A + in that respect. In my personal ongoing research on how the mind affects the body, I was always trying to convince my instructors and fellow students. Once in class I used the blush as an example. When I embarrassed a student, she turned beet red! It was my simplest illustration of how something entering the mind instantly translates into a bodily reaction. By studying human nature, I was, of course, learning a lot about myself.

The patient's welfare was paramount to me. Back in Kentucky I'd almost gotten kicked out of the nursing program several times for doing what I knew was right. On one such occasion in the newborn nursery, a doctor who had lots of hair on the back of his hands and wore a large school ring failed to wash his hands as he entered. As he approached the first incubator, I stepped forward from my group of students to gently remind him he'd forgotten to wash up. The doctor's oversize ego and my instructor's embarrassment got me a stern admonishment, but I felt I'd done the right thing. A germ can spread like wildfire through a nursery and wreak havoc on its tiny, fragile victims. *Nosocomical* refers to infections acquired while in the hospital. One unexpected fact I'd learned is that a hospital can be a dangerous place.

College of Marin emphasized nutrition but not nearly enough for me. I often spent my breaks and lunch hours slipping back into a heart attack victim's room trying to explain to him or her the importance of improving the diet as well as quitting smoking and/or drinking, losing weight, and exercising. I felt as if I had to, since doctors would often neglect to tell patients about the side effects of their medications. I hated to think of them being surprised to discover some heart medicines cause impotency!

I was beginning to see that a little knowledge can be a dangerous thing—in any area. Marin County seemed to promote a climate of experimentation, so it follows that there were many good and bad ideas surfacing. There were various counterfeit religious sects waxing and waning in popularity all around us, and the girls would come home from their friends' houses confused. Sometimes it almost felt as if we were being offered religion du jour. It was tricky explaining to them how organized religion sometimes ruins spirituality.

Down the road from us were some sincere seekers who'd taken a turn down the dead-end New Age path. I'd get into conversations with followers of the humanist movement at the health food store who were being led to actually believe they were God.

Besides all these designer theologies, there was the omnipresent "anything goes" crowd—folks who act as if the Ten Commandments were multiple choice or the ten suggestions. They seem to want to see just how much they can get away with and still go to heaven. I call it "God Lite."

Because no one is perfect and we can always stand to learn from one another's mistakes, I tried to teach Chris and Ashley that it's useful to regard those with whom we disagree as teachers. That way they may challenge us to examine our beliefs, allowing us to gain a different perception of reality.

I'd try to encourage the girls to have respect for others' traditions and beliefs and to realize that spirituality is not the exclusive property of any religion or group. In fact, whenever we take "pride" in our spirituality, we have lost the essence of it. And actually, recognizing our ordinary humanness is grounds for authentic spirituality in any form.

I told Chris and Ashley, "The truth is the truth! It's God's domain and it will stand up to your questions. But never presume there's only one way to find the truth!" We read stories about

Buddha and Confucius and other important teachers and discussed their contributions. When Chris and Ashley wanted to know the difference between them and Jesus I replied, "These good men wanted to show the world the way, the truth, and the light. Jesus, however, *was* the way, truth, and light." The girls developed a curiosity and a heart for truth and understood at an early age that only the ignorant become fanatics. I reminded them, "After all, it was ignorance that killed Jesus."

Chris and Ashley and I would have discussions about taking responsibility for beliefs, values, and assumptions as issues popped up in their own lives. At this point in their lives, I was laying the groundwork for them to grasp that, as Frances Vaughn, Ph.D., says, spirituality is not a magical solution and is not for wishful thinking or abdication of their personal accountability.* The totality of life cannot be ignored.

Because spirituality is not merely personal and requires even more than personal integrity and self-knowledge, I took the girls to the only Christian church in the valley, the San Geronimo Presbyterian Church. In the secular, materialistic 1970s that so devalued the spiritual quest, we enjoyed the fellowship of other kindred seekers, learned to express gratitude in worshiping together, and witnessed examples of compassion and commitment to society. Ashley was ten and I began to see glimpses of idealism and humanitarianism in her.

In addition to the varied and different types of religious practices all around us, we began discovering unusual versions of families.

On an afternoon walk through the redwood forest, we came upon a mother and her eleven-year-old son living in their van, sharing a joint. After visiting with them, I tried to tell the mother it was harmful for the boy, but she was too stoned to comprehend. Man, did Chris and Ashley barrage me with questions on the way home!

Another occasion that prompted dialogue among the three of us was Ashley's new playmate. The first time I allowed Ashley to go home with the child after school, I picked her up there, to meet the family. The mother had recently divorced the father and alleged she

*Frances Vaughn. "The Search for Wholeness," *Journal of Transpersonal Psychology* 23, no. 2 (1991).

had to take in a boarder to help with the rent. Then I discovered the mother had switched to homosexuality and the woman now living with the family was her lesbian lover. Instead of the "birds and bees," I had to explain the "bees and the bees" that night.

Before giving my permission for Chris to baby-sit a local couple's small child, I drove over to their home to check them out also. They seemed nice enough. Later Chris told me they were nudists and wore no clothing when she was there and that they had an open marriage. Not much later I heard they'd gotten a divorce. Still more difficult questions for Mommy.

Because we were so far away from our family, that first Thanksgiving in Marin was depressing. It only took half an hour to eat our meal, then the three of us sat there staring at each other. We were thinking about Mom, alone and bitter. The divorce was final, and to keep the house she'd rented out the upstairs to strangers; she was living downstairs. Dad was probably eating with his girlfriend at his apartment. Mark was working on the riverboat. Margaret and Erin were fending for themselves in LA in their apartment.

To keep from being alone in our little apartment that Christmas, we accepted Piper's invitation to spend the day with her. Chris and I sang for the gathering of her friends, making it the brightest spot in our holiday. My girlfriend Nancy, who'd lived across from us in Hollywood, had asked for Chris and Ashley to come down for the week after Christmas since school was out. She and her daughter, Gabrielle, had missed the girls in the two years since we'd left Hollywood to go home to Morrill. We split the cheap airfare from San Francisco to Los Angeles and bingo . . . I was alone!

Piper gave me a tarot card reading for Christmas. I could have used food, clothing, or rent money, but she wanted me to meet her "reader." I knew messing around with tarot cards was inviting evil spirits and that no one can predict the future. So, like someone who invites Jehovah Witnesses in to attempt to change *their* minds, I set out on my mission to debunk her tarot card reader. I was ready with my proof about it being dangerous.

On the mountainous back road to Petaluma, a clumsy used station wagon I'd just bought fish-tailed out over the edge on a rain-slicked curve. Realizing I'd completely lost control, I thought I'd fall off the mountain and die in a fiery crash at the bottom of some secluded ravine. Then, suddenly, I crashed head-on into the opposite hillside! As my back end had spun out over the edge, the car turned around facing the opposite direction.

First I was forcefully slammed against the driver's door, then flung across the front seat down into the passenger-side floorboard. I felt a deep ache in my back and knew something was seriously wrong. I couldn't get up. Immediately I realized my car would be hit by the next unsuspecting motorist coming down the hill around the blind curve. It could cause such a collision that we might both get knocked off the edge. I knew I was a sitting duck in the middle of the road but I couldn't see from where I was down on the floor. I don't know how long I lay there until I heard men prying open the bashed car door. I remember nothing of the ambulance ride to the hospital in Petaluma.

I was in so much pain that it seemed as if I'd been lying on that table forever. The doctor's diagnosis was a compression fracture of my lumbar vertebrae. I held off taking any pain medication until I found out what was wrong with me. I could feel and move both legs, but was nonetheless concerned about permanent damage. And how long was I going to be unable to take care of my girls or go to school and work?

I phoned Nancy while I was on the gurney, calmly gave her a phone number where I was going to be for "a while," and told Chris and Ashley I'd had a mishap and was resting in a hospital. I told them I loved them, then lapsed into morphine oblivion. It was the only time I let them give me pain medication.

When I came to, I was overwhelmed with the feeling of helplessness and loneliness. Not knowing anyone in a town I'd never even set foot in, I called the pastor of our valley church, the Reverend Bill Fredrickson. The next evening, a strange woman with black hair and bangs dressed all in black entered my room. Claiming that Piper had called her, she introduced herself as the tarot card reader. I sensed an ominous presence, then suddenly Reverend Bill stepped through the door with his gray and white hair and wearing a white clerical collar. A smile broke across his face like a sunrise. He said our small congregation had taken up a love offering as he handed me the check. The psychic seemed uncomfortable and left. The occurence seemed terribly symbolic to me.

That night I told the orthopedic specialist I could only stay in the hospital a week, because I intended to go home to recuperate so I could be with my kids and study in quiet. He related how the nurses reported I'd refused any pain medication and asked why. I gave him several legitimate medical reasons; one was that narcotic analgesics decrease peristalsis (part of the digestive process). Since I was already immobile, flat on my back, and unable to get any exercise, there were too many conditions predisposing constipation. It's a common bother to patients with back injuries.

As soon as he left, my roommate flipped me a book of matches and told me not to be embarrassed about breaking wind. It was the beginning of a beautiful friendship.

Asia Lee was a UPS driver who'd injured her back unloading freight. She was a single mom of three children, and she was irreverent, wise, and funny. We hit it off immediately. Flat on our backs, side by side, staring at the ceiling or with heads turned sideways to each other, we talked and laughed all day and night. The staff often hung out in our room.

After my predicted week-long stay, I got fitted with a full back brace and checked myself out of the hospital against medical advice. I took over Chris's twin bed and had it moved against the window so I could look outside. From my tiny outpost I commanded the troops as my bones mended. Chris was now fourteen and Ashley, ten, and they were pretty self-sufficient.

Chris taunted me. Dangling the car keys just out of my reach, she'd threaten to take off. One instance she antagonized me so badly I painfully managed to get up on the side of the bed and slowly start after her. Shocked that I could move that much, she ran toward the front door. Continuing to follow her, I suddenly found myself outside in just my underwear and brace. Snapping at the air and pawing at the ground in frustration and anger, I watched as she disappeared down the road to her friend's house.

Time is a healer, and three months later I was back on the dance floor. Asia Lee and I became best friends. We visited often at her house in Petaluma where Chris and Ashley played with her three children. She introduced me to the area's live music scene. The first place Asia took me was a small club to hear a guitar/harmonica bluesman named John Hammond. It really inspired me to practice my harmonica. Norton Buffalo, one of the best blues harp players in the country, sometimes sat in on gigs out at Rancho Nicasio and had given me several lessons.

Frank, the mechanic at the Forrest Knolls garage, was a transplanted West Virginian and loaned Chris his 1934 Vega banjo. She mastered her first tune, "Banjo in the Holler," with me accompanying her on my guitar. When she played, she'd let out whoops and strange noises and stomp her foot. While she concentrated, a bizarre grin would creep in, looking like someone who was having a stomach cramp.

Then her Uncle Mark sent Chris a banjo. When the big box arrived, we were so excited you'd have thought we won the *Readers Digest* sweepstakes! Mark shared our love for bluegrass music and he'd recognized Chris's amazing penchant for musical instruments. Every day I drove by a music store that had a sign in the window offering lessons, and a fantasy began to develop.

Had a Dream

W HAT IF CHRIS, Ashley, and I became a trio? Chris on banjo, me on guitar and harmonica, and Ashley on fiddle! We would call ourselves "Hillbilly Women." I walked into the Amazing Grace Music Shop, signed Chris up for banjo lessons with Greg, and was introduced to the fiddle teacher, Pete Adams. Pete helped me find a three-quarter size used fiddle for Ashley for $50, and a friendship developed.

Always conscious that Ashley felt excluded when Chris and I sang, I hoped this would close the circle. Besides, she was so smart and disciplined, I knew Ashley had the perseverance to master an instrument. Feminine, sweet, and pure, the fiddle seemed perfect for her.

Together the three of us learned "Old Joe Clark" around the kitchen table. Every day I practiced my guitar. The steel strings of my huge blond Ibanez produced tough calluses on my fingertips. Ashley gave the fiddle a whirl, but soon it was apparent she would rather be outside riding horses with Juli Gensley and Elesha Wright.

Ashley was a happy-go-lucky child, who, in reality, simply didn't need music to communicate. Truth was music was the only avenue open to Chris and me. There was such bickering between us, music was often the only relief we got. In our harmonies was the sound of two souls longing to fuse but afraid to touch. As our voices glided through a duet, moving apart, then moving closer, and finally blending in sublime parallel, we felt peace. The feeling was still unspoken, but Chris and I were both beginning to feel a sense of destiny.

We were sitting on the mattress on the living room floor absorbed in working up a new tune, when we overheard Ashley and a friend as they came in from play to get a drink. Lisa had asked Ashley why we were always singing together. Nonchalantly Ashley shrugged, "Oh, they think they're going to be big stars someday." Chris and I stared at each other a few moments, then went back to practicing.

Through Pete Adams, we developed our musical family version of Morrill there in Marin. Soon we were entertaining fellow musicians around our kitchen table laden with soup beans, corn bread, and homemade pies. Out in the nearby redwood park, we'd spread out blankets by a stream and pick and sing all afternoon until nightfall.

Then one fortuitous day Pete took the three of us by a studio he and two friends had built in a garage over in Mill Valley. Chris and I walked in with our eyes big as saucers! Robin, the engineer, and Mike Stevens, the guitar player, had jobs like Pete, but all three dabbled in this recording studio as their hobby. Mike, a tall blond-haired volleyball enthusiast, seemed an unlikely CPA. But, quite the entrepreneur, he'd also started a local recording studio magazine titled *BAM* (for *Bay Area Music*) with some other friends. Mike was a guitar player, an outdoorsman, and an enterprising businessman. Hmmm . . .

Soon we began dating. Having very little personal time, I still liked to hear the phone ring and have an adult to talk to. I was always at college, work, the grocery, or the Laundromat. Not to mention slumped over the kitchen table buried in medical books! And when I did agree to see Mike, I suggested we meet at his studio, Tres Virgos, for two reasons. I could bring both the girls, and Chris and I could be around music. Too shy to speak up, we mainly watched other musicians practicing or cutting demos. We were enthralled.

This was such a new world, I decided to audit a course in studio engineering at College of Marin. I admit it was ridiculous, since I had trouble finding the power button on the cheap stereo at our apartment.

I'd wind up doing my nursing homework in the class, but my

purpose for showing up now and then was that the first day, the instructor had announced the culmination of the semester course was to go into a real studio in Sausalito and actually cut some tracks. I was determined Chris and I be the musicians. We could have a demo tape for free! In the meantime, we continued hanging out at Tres Virgos, until one day they let us sing into real microphones.

I met an unusual girl in that audio engineering class, who unknowingly planted a seed that grew into our first live performance. Susie McKee had a four-piece band called Susie and the Cowpokes.

I volunteered for Chris and me to sing backup harmony for her for free sometime and asked if we could come by her place and audition. I bet she took me up on my offer to see if I were crazy or kidding about my singing teenage daughter story.

When I explained to Chris I was picking her up after school to go sing backup for a person she'd never met, she was incredulous. "How the heck are we going to do parts with someone we don't know?"

Nervous and wary, as we walked in, Chris commented that Susie's small apartment in downtown San Rafael was similar to ours. When Chris discovered that Susie supported herself playing clubs, she started paying attention. As Susie pulled out her electric guitar and began doing a few tunes, Chris became fascinated. It was a hybrid of western swing and big band—kind of Roy Rogers meets the Andrews Sisters.

We jumped in when Susie began "Bei Mir Bist Du Schön," because we knew it backward and forward, and Chris instinctively knew to go tenor. I stayed with the familiar alto I'd been doing on her lead at home, and the three of us sounded great together!

Excitedly, Susie began taping the songs we didn't know, for us to take home and learn. As we said good-bye she stood on the sidewalk staring at us in disbelief as we walked out to our car.

We just had a couple get-togethers that entire semester because of my lack of time, but we sure had fun. I asked the engineering-class teacher if Chris and I could audition to be the talent for the class recording, but the news was discouraging. Almost every class member was a musician with the same hope as I for a free demo. Even Susie McKee.

But somehow we were chosen. I felt doubly bad, because I'd sat in on only three classes all semester, so I asked the disappointed classmates to be our backup band. It was a smart move, since unlike Susie and the others, we weren't part of an organized musical group.

We attended a couple of loose rehearsals in a guy's basement, where Chris impressed everyone with her singing and guitar playing. Then, in the studio, under the watchful eye of the instructor, we recorded "Hillbilly Boogie," an old favorite of ours by the Delmore Brothers. The rest of the class engineered, mixed, and mastered. Such a prize! We played our first amateur tape over and over and over again.

Exhilarated, Chris and I now had tangible proof of our secret dream! Our musical friends continued to encourage us and got a kick out of watching newcomers at Tres Virgos Studio or group get-togethers see us perform for the first time. Strangers expected that I'd take the lead and my thirteen-year-old would just chime in with harmony, so when Chris pulled out her big guitar and started off in that wonderful voice, the room would be filled with an instant buzz.

We'd lived in our cramped two-room apartment for more than a year when I heard of part of a house down the road at 6840 Sir Francis Drake Boulevard for rent. One side of it was a real estate office and we moved into the other half on October 15, 1977.

After school one afternoon, I was at the Laundromat with Ashley while Chris stayed home to take a nap. The burglar alarm went off in the real estate office next door after the agent locked up for the day. When sheriff's deputies responded, they were unaware anyone lived in a section of the house. When they spotted a back window open with the screen lying on the ground, they naturally suspected an intruder had gained entrance there. Actually, Chris kept the screen out so her cat could come and go.

Now a policeman, gun drawn, came creeping through the small window. Awakening, Chris could barely make out the silhouette of a large man with a pistol coming in on her. Jumping up out of bed in sheer terror, she made a run for the bathroom, the only room with a lock on it. The deputy chased after her, believing her to be the robber.

I pulled up with patrol car lights flashing in front of our house just as the deputy inside realized he had cornered a thirteen-year-old child in her underwear. He was almost as shaken as Chris and wouldn't stop apologizing.

From that evening on, everyone in the valley knew the three of us lived in Forest Knolls! When the upstairs of the white frame house right next to us came up for rent I called Margaret in LA immediately.

She and daughter Erin moved in lickety-split. Margaret was now an up-and-coming sales representative for a dental lab. She spent one day a week on the phone setting up her appointments for the rest of the week. We'd sit out in my totally secluded backyard, Margaret on the phone, me with my medical books, and sunbathe topless. We had great tans!

Chris, Ashley, and cousin Erin went to school and played together. Margaret and I felt happier and safer being side by side. One evening when she was baby-sitting, she had me paged at the market in Fairfax where I was shopping. Chris had gone into a severe asthma attack, and Margaret had called the rescue squad.

We seemed to live on the brink of disaster. Barely eking out a living from week to week, any unnecessary expense presented a serious threat. So it was, when the brakes went out on our old Dodge Valiant. While it sat broken down at the Forest Knolls Garage, I scoured the used-car section of the newspaper.

Responding to a one-owner ad for a 1957 Chevy in San Francisco, it was love at first sight. A Mexican mechanic kept the beauty in his small one-car garage while the family car sat on the street. He spoke lovingly of this vintage automobile as if it were a member of the family. A padlock bolted the hood and a toggle switch hidden under the dash had to be flipped for the engine to start. The rearview mirror wrapped from left to right all the way across the top of the front windshield. And it was white and lipstick red!

We cut a deal for $1800 and I drove the Chevy home. I bought a pair of baby shoes to dangle from the rearview mirror and put 1950s decals of Vargas girls on the two side vent windows.

The next day when I went to get the title changed at the Department of Motor Vehicles, I impulsively stepped into the personalized plates line. It was $25 and admittedly an extravagance, but

I decided to go without lunches. I loved this moving piece of art so much! I felt like I was in a parade when I drove it. Guess it also reminded me of Daddy and the gas station.

A fellow next to me in line struck up a flirtatious conversation. When I proudly described the '57 Chevy, he laughingly exclaimed I should name it "Redhot." Suddenly it was my turn at the window and I did just that.

The day I put the plate on, however, I realized I'd made a bad mistake. A trucker tugging eagerly away at his air horn almost ran me off the freeway in an effort to get me to pull off an exit with him. *Redhot* referred to my cool car, which was in mint condition, but males with high testosterone levels assumed *Redhot* was a description of the car's driver.

On December 15, 1977, I graduated from College of Marin's nursing program, a semester ahead of my class, and my classmates threw me a party. Every college's nursing program has its own special cap design. Janet Greenwood presented me with our school cap, spray painted with gold lamé, featuring my name in red sparkles. The girls dubbed me "the singing nurse" and chipped in to buy me another harmonica. Before I left, the women's studies program asked me to speak to their classes on a book they were reading called *Hillbilly Women* by Kathryn Kahn. I was flattered, but didn't have time.

Several months later I drove by myself up to Sacramento, where I suffered through the state boards with thousands of other nervous girls from all over California. At the midday break, we poured out from the examination hall to the coliseum's public restrooms. The recess was short, and there was a line as far as you could see for the ladies' room. I walked straight into the men's doorway and called out. Finding it empty, I used the restroom, came back out, and announced to the startled girls they should make use of it too.

It would be many months before the test results came in the mail telling me I'd passed every category with flying colors and was a registered nurse. Meanwhile, I'd taken a full-time job at a western-theme restaurant in Lucas Valley near our home.

Rancho Nicasio reminded me of a quaint lodge you'd find in

Colorado or Montana. The interior had dark wood, mounted animal heads, red-checked tablecloths, a small stage, and a dance floor. When I'd applied for the job as waitress, the bar manager relayed I'd also be doubling as a cocktail waitress. I informed him I had a problem with liquor. "Oh, are you a recovering alcoholic?" he inquired, surprised.

"Nope! Quite the opposite." I chortled. "I'd have a real hard time serving liquor to someone who was becoming intoxicated."

Bruce snapped his fingers in the air and announced, "By George, you just got yourself a job!" That week California had passed a law making a drinking establishment liable if a patron who'd gotten drunk there had an auto accident. Lucky for me—lucky for everyone!

How I enjoyed working at Rancho Nicasio! A local group called the Moonlighters was the house band on Friday night. Another big band group played on Saturday night for an older dance crowd. The patrons were cowboys and locals, and I got to know them by their first names. These guys didn't wink at me or pat me on the butt, and I could even wear my own clothes.

It felt so delicious being out from under the pressure of my studies, and after years of a relentlessly difficult schedule, I began to have somewhat more of a normal life.

Even though I was raising two children alone, working full-time and taking care of a home, I somehow saw this period as more of a breather. I knew when my nursing license arrived, I'd have to settle into working full-time in the intense position of an RN.

Driving out to Rancho Nicasio every day I passed by an Arabian Horse farm and hit on an idea. Chris had little discipline and, except for our music, no interests. Since she possessed an inexhaustible amount of energy and loved animals, I wondered if she might benefit from working outdoors at this stable after school.

Soon Chris was cleaning tack a couple of days a week after school. She loved being out in the open working with horses. A country music station played constantly, and it was her first exposure to country radio. She'd be singing the tunes when I picked her up.

I remember the afternoon it happened. As she climbed into the front seat of the Chevy, Chris immediately turned on the radio and flipped through the stations till she found KNEW. The station was sponsoring an upcoming Merle Haggard concert, and she was proposing a deal. If she used her stable money to buy us a pair of $6 tickets, would I take her to Oakland for the concert? Yes, yes!!

I was thrilled by her initiative. We began excitedly looking forward to our first country concert. Dressed in our usual 1940s outfits from St. Vincent De Paul's secondhand store in Fairfax, we parked out back of the Oakland Coliseum. I'd just put four $50 whitewalls on Redhot and was apprehensive about leaving it in the parking lot. We got in as close to the buses and trucks as we could for two reasons: security and because Chris asked to get a glimpse of the action.

As we strolled by Haggard's bus, he was stepping off to walk his dog. He acknowledged us, and Chris began petting his dog, Tuffy. When Haggard asked where we'd come from, I proudly told him about Chris using her own money for tickets. He asked Chris if she'd like to see the inside of his "home," and we couldn't believe it when Haggard began escorting us up onto his Silver Eagle bus. There sat his teenage son, Noel, with whom Chris began chatting.

Haggard's lawyer was on the bus discussing divorce papers Leona Haggard had just served the star. The singer disappeared into the back, came out dressed, announcing it was showtime. When I jumped up saying we needed to hurry out to our seats, Merle ushered us off the bus insisting we watch from the wings. Chris kept looking over at me to confirm what she was hearing, and we walked to the backstage of the coliseum surrounded by Merle and his entourage.

Marty Robbins was just finishing his opening set, and we probably acted like true yokels as we were introduced to him. In a daze, I had a recurring sense that this night was having an impact that couldn't be measured till much later in time. Boy was I right!

For slumber parties or get-togethers, Chris's buddies would tell everyone to bring her favorite records. Except for Chris. Her taste was far too eclectic. When she finished her last year of junior high, she sang Joni Mitchell's song "Both Sides Now" at the graduation. By then she was wearing my clothes and chose my long Victorian lace dress from a swap meet for the ceremony. I made a garland of flowers for her hair. My little flower child.

. . .

I called Ashley my "smart young lady" and enrolled her in
after-school Spanish classes. Returning from her lesson one day, we
were driving down Fourth Street in San Rafael in front of the movie
theater seen in George Lucas's film *American Graffiti.*

At that very stoplight two young guys on the curb leaned
forward and began hollering at me. "We work for George Lucas and
we'll pay you to use your Chevy in the sequel to *American Graffiti!*"

Dismissing this implausible coincidence as merely an ingenious
pickup attempt, I smiled a crooked grin and, shaking my head,
replied, "No thanks!"

As the light turned green, one of them pitched a folded piece
of paper in the open window, and yelled, "Call this number!"

Ashley read aloud the torn-off top of a receipt: "Industrial Light
and Magic Company" bearing a San Rafael address and telephone
number. Someone had once told me this was the name of George
Lucas's semisecret local movie company. Calling the number first
thing the next morning, I happily agreed to report to the set where
they were indeed beginning *More American Graffiti!*

As I signed the contract to rent my '57 Chevy for three weeks
at $400, I was aware of a lady staring at me. I was wearing my long
hair piled loosely on top of my head, and I had on a vintage sundress
and my cat's-eye sunglasses. The woman, who was with Ann
Brebner's Agency, offered me $30 a day to be an extra. I jumped at
the chance and reported to the wardrobe mistress, Aggie Rodgers.

Not surprisingly, I wound up wearing my own everyday clothes,
which fit right in with the movie costumes. I had been around the set
just a few days, when the associate directors, twin brothers Tom and
Steve Lofaro, noticed me and recruited me to join the crew as a
production secretary. From my outpost in a trailer, I manned the
phones and carried the messages out onto the set. Fellow crew
members assigned me the handle "Copperhead," for our walkie-
talkie transmissions.

I was very impressed with George Lucas, the visionary of Lucas-
film and the man who had at that time just made a major splash with
his masterpiece *Star Wars.* George was quiet and gentlemanly, not
brash or domineering as I'd halfway expected a great film director to

be. Wearing jeans and a trademark plaid shirt, he came off like a regular kind of guy. I observed him carefully to see if an extremely rich and powerful person was somehow intrinsically different from me, and was pleasantly surprised that the difference between us was only about $10 million. George was just a regular Joe, who was passionate about his work.

The first day Harrison Ford arrived on the set I thought he was kind of attractive. As our eyes met for the first time, he smiled at me. Harrison offered to take me for a ride on the motorcycle he'd ridden onto the set. I turned him down for several reasons. It just didn't seem professional for one thing, even though there were several romances going on during the filming of this movie, and dating an actor just didn't appeal to me.

For the country-western nightclub scene, I got Chris hired as an extra so she could witness what making a movie was like. When one of the stars, Scott Glenn, hurt himself jumping off the bar in the fight scene, I correctly diagnosed his injury as a hernia.

One of my duties was working hand in hand with transportation, headed by a husband-wife team, Henry and Jackie Travers. They teased me, saying I should be a movie star, and kept telling the director, Bill Norton, to put me in the film somehow. I ended up playing a convict riding on a prison bus across from Cindy Williams. As a result of this dubious debut, I got my Screen Actors Guild card.

It was sheer joy being in the center of that creative process! During the making of this movie, I realized how much I love being part of a team. Unfortunately, this movie was a lot more fun to make than watch. By the end of the filming, there was such a sense of family, the wrap party ended with sad farewells.

Speaking of good-byes, Mike Stevens dumped me. We'd worked up several tunes to perform with Susie McKee and the Cowpokes at a club called The Shadowbox in San Francisco. During their set, Susie called us up to sing harmony with her for a few songs. It was May 1978, and Chris looked older than fourteen. I'd let her use my makeup so we could get in the door, and we never let on we were mother and daughter. When we got such a good response, Susie let Chris and me do a number by ourselves with her band.

As we returned to our table out in the audience, I noticed that Mike wasn't smiling. At first, despite the great reaction from the crowd, I thought he hadn't liked our performance. He acted cold the rest of the evening, but finally admitted why he was upset. While we were onstage, he'd overheard some guys seated around him making predatory comments about me. Mike was a very intelligent man and I think he saw into the future that night. Having heard us sing at his studio and upon observing the public's acceptance of us, Mike sensed this was only the beginning.

He never called me again. Pete Adams said I scared Mike to death and he didn't know how to handle someone like me. I wasn't really in love with him, so it hurt my pride more than my heart. Mike was the only man ever to break up with me.

To cheer myself up I took Chris to an Emmylou Harris concert at the Great American Music Hall over in San Francisco. When Emmylou began introducing her band, I couldn't believe my ears as Ricky Skaggs from Cordell, Kentucky, stepped forward! This was the amazing musician in that first bluegrass group I'd heard back at the Holiday Inn in Kentucky. At the end of the concert, Chris and I rushed to the stage as the band began packing up their instruments. I hollered up at Ricky: "Say, when was the last time you got to eat at Hinkles?" Hinkles was the most popular restaurant in Louisa, Kentucky. Ricky's face lit up, and he came over to speak to us. When I expressed how much I'd enjoyed J. D. Crowe's New South, he motioned to a fellow standing in the wings to join us. It was Tony Rice, the guitar player in that bluegrass band. Tony had relocated to Marin County to play in a quasi-jazz group called the David Grisman Quintet. Being a flat picker myself, it was a thrill to meet the world's greatest, Tony Rice. Not to mention seeing homefolk!

Marin County was such rich topsoil for sowing musical seeds. Piper treated us to a Dolly Parton concert. Chris and I were mesmerized by her stage presence. One of our longtime heros, Doc Watson, opened for her; we couldn't believe we were listening to him live after devouring his records for years. These first concerts made lasting impressions.

Pete Adams took us to Point Reyes Station, a tiny town up on the coast where he and some buddies were performing in a festival.

Outside the town social center, the Dance Hall, a lad dressed in a kilt played away on a bagpipe. Inside, Chris and I sang several songs, including "Lazy Country Evening," a new soft-swing number I'd just written.

Then one night at Rancho Nicasio, I volunteered Chris and me to do backups on the Moonlighters' version of Merle Haggard's "Workin' Man Blues." Asia Lee and Margaret brought Erin, Ashley, and Chris. I took a three-minute break from my waitressing duties, ran over, and grabbed Chris out of the booth and jumped onstage.

It gave me an even better idea. I booked Susie McKee and the Cowpokes for a night at Rancho so Chris and I could sing half a dozen numbers. It was a blast! It came off well, and we got lots of familial applause, even though we didn't get a dime.

Sleeping in late the next morning, I happened to be waking just as the mailman was lifting the lid to our mailbox. I stepped outside in my flea market kimono and he blinked. "I'm used to seeking you up and at 'em much earlier than this!"

"Oh, we had a gig last night," I purred as nonchalantly as I could muster. It sounded so delicious saying it. "We had a *gig* last night!" I let the words roll off my tongue like precious stones.

How I relished this notion of being different! The demands of all my responsibilities had chained me to such a rigid schedule for so many years. Everyone I'd watched while growing up had such predictable routines. I loved feeling different! It was even a kick going back to waitressing that next night, because my coworkers and regular patrons would comment on our singing. The special sensation lingered several days.

I'd been pitching extra change into the sugar bowl for quite some time, saving for another demo. Our friends at Tres Virgos let us have a cut rate on studio time, and I borrowed the three musicians in Susie's band. We did "Kentucky," our old Bluegrass tune from Minnie and Sonya, and "Oatmeal Cookies," written by Roxie, the folk singer in LA. Subconsciously, we'd chosen songs by women who'd influenced us. Third, we chose a currently popular country single, "Let Me Be Your Baby."

Chris and I weren't studio savvy. Usually you lay down a lead melody vocal, then on a separate track put down the harmony. But the kid and I refused to do it that way. We always stood side by side at the same time, while looking into each other's faces. It was the joy of feeling the harmonies vibrate that inspired us. The technical concerns were of no importance to us, and it didn't even matter that we didn't know what we were doing.

Afterward we all went out together for Mexican food and had the best time! The camaraderie was so warm and convivial, we didn't want to go home. I wanted to pick up everybody's check, but could barely afford to pay for our two meals.

Money was such a drawback. Every month those envelopes with glassine windows were red flags warning me that danger was all around us. I always felt vulnerable and tentative.

One Saturday evening I didn't have a baby-sitter for ten-year-old Ashley. Knowing this was the busiest night at Rancho Nicasio, I nonetheless called to say I couldn't come in. Bruce, the manager, demanded I report to work.

The joint was jumping, still I was at the phone checking on Ashley every hour. About 11:00 P.M. there was no answer, although I let it ring twenty times. Nervously, I began running to the phone every fifteen minutes and got behind in my orders and couldn't concentrate. Bruce was giving me dirty looks and watching me closely. Finally, I said I had to run home and check on my child. Bruce sighed and informed me as I was leaving not to bother to come back.

When I burst into the apartment Ashley was sleeping peacefully in bed, but I was out of a job once again. I plopped down in a chair in that darkened room and stared out the window for hours.

No money, no job, no boyfriend . . . no prospects. I'd completed nursing school, I'd finished the movie. So many things in my life seemed to be drawing to a conclusion. There was really nothing to hold me in Marin anymore. I felt stuck. This was becoming a major word in my life's vocabulary: *Stuck, stuck, stuck!*

On top of it all, problems between Chris and me permeated everything. Acting out some deep-seated rebellion, she also fought with Ashley and was doing poorly in school. Teachers complained

Chris was a daydreamer, lacked discipline, and wasn't performing up to her ability. I took her to a therapist in Point Reyes Station, in hopes we could smooth out some of the friction between us. She clammed up and stared at me like I was imagining the whole thing.

When she and her best friend, Rachel, got into trouble, Chris would come up with elaborately illogical excuses. I could often tell when she was lying by the length of her story. "Truth is shorter than fiction," I would respond wearily.

Music and boys were the only things that concerned her. When I suggested we practice, she'd frown at me as if I'd asked her to have a root canal without anesthesia. Yet when we sang together, the line between reality and fantasy blurred. Blessed be the hope.

We all three needed some relief. Knowing it was time to get out of Marin, it also was evident that Chris and I must go onto the next stage of musical development. Ashley deserved to be settled where she could carry out day-to-day schooling.

Until I could decide where to land and get situated, I had to let Ashley go live with Michael. He had a real job back in Kentucky and it sounded as if he was finally getting a grip on life.

Using the Chevy as collateral, I took out a loan for our grub-stake. We went home to Ashland that Christmas of 1978. It was all very depressing. Having lost kidney function, Daddy had received a kidney transplant five months earlier on July 23, 1978. It was so sad seeing him ill and unable to work at the gas station where he'd devoted his life. My cousin Chuck Oliver had taken it over for Daddy, in turn becoming like a son to him. Granddaddy Judd had passed away shortly before we arrived in Ashland. Everything had changed.

Spending Christmas with Daddy and his young wife at their small house in Flatwoods, Kentucky, seemed unreal. Although she was polite to the three of us, we never felt at home around Daddy's new wife. I never brought this up to Daddy, since he wasn't well. I also wasn't willing to risk losing whatever affection I was able to coax from him.

On Christmas Eve I sat in the car outside our house on Montgomery and cried till no more tears would come. Every time I'd called Mom over the last couple of years since we left Morrill, I'd felt a shrug of her very cold shoulder. I didn't have the nerve to walk up and knock on the door. I knew I couldn't handle it if she slammed the door in my face.

I could feel her through the walls, sitting in there all alone. I wondered if she had a tree or any presents. It seemed so wrong for a woman who'd only said "Yes," "I will," and "Here, let me do that for you" to wind up this way. I felt I was to blame. I thought about that day I came home from school and found her waiting in my room with the letter about my being pregnant. It was as if I'd been convicted of stabbing her in the heart and was now serving out my sentence. I fought back the urge to burst in on the trespassing strangers who rented the upstairs and demand they get out of Our House.

Remembering Chris and Ashley were waiting up for me back at Daddy's, I took a deep breath, ran up to the porch, and dropped my small present onto the welcome mat, whispering, "Merry Christmas, Mom." I drove away wondering how many more tears and years would have to go by, until I'd be back inside our house again, back in Mom's good graces.

Painfully, we said good-bye to Ashley, then Chris and I returned to Forrest Knolls. We packed up household belongings into boxes, grabbed our few clothes, and locked the door behind us.

I had to find someone to help advise us how to start preparing for our musical career. With our demo tape in my purse, we headed for the country music mecca of Austin, Texas. I knew a few good people there, and Chris could hear live music like she'd never heard. I took her by Jimmy Vaughn's house, where blues brother Stevie Ray sat playing at the kitchen table. She was amazed at Lou Ann Barton with Double Trouble. "Mama, this lady sings like somebody's hurt her real bad!" We began to hang out with Asleep at the Wheel. One of our favorite songs in their lively show was "Route 66." Sitting at our table in the club, we'd sing along because we knew all the words by heart. Besides, we'd traveled Route 66 so many times and had been through all the cities!

> Flagstaff, Arizona
> Don't forget Winona
> Kingman, Barstow, San Bernardino

I loved the sound of *Winona*. It reminded me of the noise wind makes blowing on your face through an open car window. It made me think of travel, open spaces, and new destinations. Chris needed a new destination, a fresh start. Since we were changing surroundings, I wondered if she'd like to change her name.

We tried it out. The kid would always be the last one on Asleep at the Wheel's bus when it was time to go to a gig. As she tarried outside petting a stray dog, band leader Ray Benson would admonish the bus driver, "Don't forget Winona." Since she's such an original, we changed the spelling so it had more of a *why* sound. I liked the *y* hanging down. Kind of like Wynonna taking off on a bus that was going so fast she didn't even have quite enough time to pull her foot in the door.

But all that happened during our brief stopover in Austin was that Chris got a new name. When I thought of entertainment, all I could think of was Hollywood, and we had friends there, too.

Nancy in Los Angeles took us in. Wynonna slept with Gabrielle, while I bunked down on the couch. I took the first waitressing job I could find, at the Beverly Garland Howard Johnson's over in the San Fernando Valley. Then I hit the pavement.

Alone, I went to check out managers and agents. If they were okay, I'd take Wynonna so we could sing live. I didn't meet anyone I felt good about. One time we sang for a guy who just sat immobilized, exclaiming "Well I'll be damned!" I took Wy by the hand and left, explaining to her, "Never engage in a battle of wits with an unarmed person!" Most of these men were used to bottle blonds with that "buy-me-something" air about them. To help further differentiate us from them, I bought two inexpensive jackets and took them to the bowling alley to be monogrammed. They were navy and cream wool high school varsity jackets, with "Hillbilly Women" embroidered over our hearts, and our names written on the back. We loved them and wore them everywhere.

Wy and I longed to hear some live music, but it seemed in LA they think that originality is the art of concealing your sources.

I was constantly struggling to keep my soul intact. Missing Ashley, not knowing if I was doing the right thing, it was an unhappy period. Resilient and optimistic, Ashley sounded fine on the phone.

Just a few more weeks, I consoled her, and we'll be together again. I'd promised all three of us that we'd always live in the country, but I felt forced to hang out in the city long enough to make some connections first.

Depressed after talking to Ashley one night, I opened my Bible to Matthew 7:7–8: "Ask, and it shall be given unto you; seek, and ye shall find; knock, and it shall be opened unto you: For everyone that asketh receiveth; and he that seeketh findeth; and to him that knocketh it shall be opened."

On the way to work the next morning it was overcast, yet I decided they were clouds of promise. I worked at the Howard Johnson's every day. The brown plaid uniform was hideously ugly and I was embarrassed, but I figured no one would ever see me there.

There were some old-timers who hung out every afternoon at the fountain. Sunset Carson, from the old cowboy movies, could tell some colorful stories. It was the only bright spot in my shift. Tips were terrible, 'cause the menu prices were low. A couple of gay guys asked if I was an actress. "Oh no!" I answered for the umpteenth time. "I want to be a country singer!" Ceremoniously, one of them handed me a dollar bill and pronounced it my good luck piece, adding: "something tells me you'll make it!"

I realized it also was my tip as I stuffed it in my bra next to my heart. Later that night when I was making my bed on Nancy's couch, I folded the dollar bill in next to our demo tape. Not that I'm superstitious, I just never had anyone tell me anything encouraging and I was pretty down.

I rubbed my eyes in disbelief the next day when I walked up to a booth in my station to discover Mickey Gilley and his entourage! *Urban Cowboy*, now a box office hit, had been shot at his club Gilley's in Pasadena, Texas. Starring John Travolta and Debra Winger, the movie was responsible for a national rise in country music's popularity. Overnight, stockbrokers on Wall Street were sporting Stetsons and custom-made boots.

I was so nervous I messed up their order, but Mickey was very kind. It was late afternoon toward the end of my shift, so Nancy had dropped Wy off. Wy was having a milkshake while waiting for me to get off work. During small talk I mentioned to Mickey and his press agent, Sandy Brokaw, that my daughter and I sang country music. When I pointed to her sitting over at the counter, Mickey asked to meet her. Wy immediately began asking what John Travolta was like, and suddenly Mickey asked if she'd like to meet him! They were all on their way to do *The Merv Griffin Show* with Travolta and asked us to accompany them!

My first reaction was we didn't have nice enough clothes to be seen with them, but Wy turned to me and whispered, "If you don't let me do this, I will never again clean my room in your lifetime." We followed behind their limo in our Chevy to NBC Studios in nearby Burbank.

As Merv entered the greenroom to meet Mickey for the first time, he pointed out the large diamond "MG" initial necklace around Mickey's neck. "Hey, those are my initials too!" Merv exclaimed.

I was standing directly behind Merv's shoulder when I saw an expression of impulsive generosity flash across Mickey's face. Mickey was reaching up to hand over the piece when I began shaking my head no! I knew Merv was one of the richest men in Hollywood, and besides Mickey had just told me the necklace had sentimental value. When Merv departed, Mickey thanked me and said, "You're a smart lady! I'm gonna pay attention to what you say."

The leader for the show's house band stepped in the dressing room to check with Mickey on the song he would be performing. I didn't agree with their selection. Only a week earlier Mickey had won the Grammy for Country Song of the Year, and I felt he should perform it. I spoke up, and once again Mickey concurred. There was no way I could have known this quirk of fate would later almost cost me my life.

After the TV taping we all went out for Chinese food. As he was paying the bill, Mickey invited us to continue on with them to the Palamino Club to hear his favorite group. He raved on and on about J. D. Sumner and the Stamps Quartet, but I'd never heard of them. One of the premiere groups in gospel music, they'd backed Elvis for the last seven years of his life, on stage as well as on records. The kid and I tagged along wearing our Hillbilly Women jackets.

Seated beside Mickey at the front row center table, Wy and I agreed the Stamps were fabulous! They also were a fascinating collection of six personalities to watch. It was puzzling that J. D. Sumner got on stage to perform only two numbers, allowing a tall, dark, and handsome younger guy to sing bass the entire show. We decided J. D. must be only lending his name and reputation to the Stamps now.

This tanned younger bass singer had long straight black hair, and I remember wondering if perhaps he had some American Indian blood. Wy commented on his cool stage presence, but I could tell he was somewhat shy. They introduced him as Larry Strickland from Raleigh, North Carolina.

The only member of the Stamps I met that night was Richard Lee, the baritone singer. When I came out of the restroom during their break, Richard was standing by the cigarette machine pulling levers. After striking up a conversation with me, he admitted he didn't smoke. Brushing him off as the playboy type, I returned to our table. The memorable part of the encounter was hearing him report they'd all moved to Nashville to be in country music.

Mickey Gilley was a true gentleman and a genuinely nice guy. There was no heavy-duty come-on and when the night was over, Wy and I got in our Chevy and went back to Nancy's apartment.

While we had been enjoying our musical outing at the Palamino, the emcee announced talent night was held once a week with their house band. Wy and I exchanged raised eyebrows and plotted to return. With several friends in tow for support and protection, we returned the following night.

Nervously, and without any run-through whatsoever, we sang "Kentucky" with the Palamino house band. We didn't win, but a stranger approached us offering sincere-sounding compliments. Jeff Thornton said he was in town from Nashville, Tennessee, negotiating a TV special and had come out to the Palamino to unwind.

Jeff seemed quite down to earth, seemed nice, and produced his business card. It stated that he was also a manager and booking agent. When Jeff further handed me his wife's card showing she did graphic artwork for album covers, we felt comfortable answering a string of questions. Finally, when he dramatically proclaimed he believed we were "diamonds in the rough," I gave him Nancy's phone number.

The next day, as we sang for Jeff at Nancy's house, I explained our situation. I told him our household was packed, we were ready to relocate, and desperate to reunite with Ashley.

He offered a deal. He had just put together a TV special to be shot with Lola Falana in Las Vegas, so he said we should come with him to Vegas. He would use me to work in the production office in exchange for our room and board for the month's allocated shooting. He also promised to assign someone to assist us in putting a repertoire together, but the best part was that Jeff promised to help us move to Nashville! He agreed to hire me at his company and to help us find a place to live. My heart was beating so hard, I wondered if he could hear it!

I thanked dear Nancy, gladly turned in my Howard Johnson's uniform, and filled Redhot at the same gas station where we'd stopped before leaving Hollywood the first time for Morrill, Kentucky.

The phone calls back to Kentucky had been difficult. Little Ashley cried this time when I explained she had to stay with her Dad a little longer. It was important for her to remain in school until we landed in Nashville.

Speaking of school daze! It was March 1979 and Wy had now missed the first couple of months of the winter semester. Of course, she'd wanted to drop out of school for good and form a band, and this attitude greatly distressed me. Feeling as if I had no choice but to let her skip this semester, I warned her for the umpteenth time we would not get into music professionally until she graduated from high school. I ranted that once we got to Nashville, she'd have to put her bad habits behind her and become interested in school . . . or else!!

The Ciminellas and my folks were greatly disturbed by my bizarre scheme. Mamaw and Papaw Ciminella rightfully threatened to send a truant officer after Wy, and Daddy's trust in my judgment was shaky. His kidney transplant was successful and he was now back to working part-time at his station. Mom had gotten a job as a cook on a riverboat, but we still weren't communicating at all. She worked thirty days on the river, then was off for thirty. I was thankful she was getting away from the house of memories. The house of cards that had collapsed.

The drive through the Nevada desert to Las Vegas was ethereal. I'd really gone out on a limb this time! Wy was only fifteen, but a good driver. On the deserted straight stretches of road, I let her get behind the wheel. From the passenger side as I gazed over at her blowing huge bubbles with her Bazooka gum, driving and singing at the top of her lungs, I wondered if I was creating a monster. I began to have nightmares that she might run off with some shiftless musician when time came to register for school again. She was becoming more willful. It was during this period I had a premonition that our music would either save us or destroy us.

After singing Jesse Winchester's "How Far to the Horizon," we watched our first sunset in the desert, and I began writing a campy song. It was a cooperative tune requiring my call and Wy's response.

> I'd sing: "Mama sez."
> She'd answer: "Now don't you go downtown."
> Me: "Mama sez."
> Wy: "No, don't you mess around.
> I always do what my Mama sez and
> I say my prayers before I go to bed."

She smiled sarcastically, seeing through my thinly disguised sermonette, but she nonetheless liked my interesting new tune. Given the overall circumstances as well as that exact moment in our lives, "Mama Sez" remains symbolic of how the only way we could communicate at times was through music.

Wy's eyes were big as saucers as we drove through glitter gulch upon arriving in Las Vegas. The Alladin Hotel on the strip had given Jeff's crew an entire floor in exchange for his promise of plugging the hotel in the special. Being from Nashville, he hired the *Hee Haw* show crew. They taped all their *Hee Haw* shows in June, so they were free agents to travel and contract other work the remainder of the year.

Wy and I shared a room so I could know where she was every minute. She even accompanied me to the production office, which served as the nerve center for all the backstage elements of the project. A TV program appears deceptively simple when you see it on your set, but it's a highly complex undertaking. Hundreds of people are involved, from the director and assistants to an army of technicians who are responsible for setting up, maintaining, and operating the cameras along with sound recording equipment. The executive producer is like a general, commanding, coordinating, and instructing all aspects. Jeff's partner, Nick, was responsible for keeping the shoot within budget and on schedule.

The real work Wy and I had come for went on back in our hotel room. Still hoping desperately to instill in her some sense of professionalism, I wrote out schedules for our practice sessions. One of her homework assignments was to learn the songs on Linda Ronstadt's *Silver Threads and Golden Needles* album. A crew member involved with the show's music came to our room to supervise us. To set a tone for responsibilities, I demanded she be prepared for those appointments and punctual. I tried to make her feel she was on a work/study hiatus from school. Although there was maid service, I insisted she make up her own bed every day.

While in Vegas, I began to realize that Wy would never hold a nine-to-five job. She was cut from a different cloth. She wasn't thinking about college or even learning a trade. I prayed that somehow she'd want to sing badly enough that she'd come to understand that hard work and dedication are necessary for success.

Downstairs in the Alladin Hotel's showroom, Loretta Lynn was the headliner for an entire week. At first we simply sat back and enjoyed the performances. Then we began to study her show. We soon knew every note of every song and were singing some of them back in our room. We were being given a great opportunity to discover what a concert is all about. I made mental note that there was order to the set list by the way the songs flowed. The mood of the numbers caused emotional rise and fall. Loretta included a medley of her hits to please her fans. I observed her various costume changes and which ones worked best under the lights. Loretta was using video projected on a huge screen behind her while she sang. As she performed the elegant Elvis ballad "In the Ghetto," we saw footage of heart-wrenching slums. It was the first time I'd thought about theatrics underscoring and heightening the sentiment of a song.

On closing night, I managed to get us backstage to meet

Loretta. She was so warm and friendly as she invited us into her dressing room. Excitedly, she jumped right in telling us they were making a movie about her life called *Coal Miner's Daughter.* Loretta kept describing how the actress who would play her, Sissy Spacek, could sing just like her! Wy was unconvinced and said, "Loretta, nobody can sing like you!"

David Skepner, Loretta's manager, came in and described some dresses he'd bought her. Chris and I thought it was very odd. My observation was that Loretta seemed to have little control or say in her life.

We'd gotten to know her band from eating in the Alladin's coffee shop. More education à la "Roadlife 101." The first lesson they taught us was how much time a group spends away from home. They missed their wives and felt guilty about not being home to help out and see their kids grow up. The guys spent their days watching mindless TV, chain-smoking cigarettes, hanging out down in the coffee shop, reading the newspaper, or playing a little blackjack. This flip side to the glitz and glamour was a real eye-opener. I began to recognize the potential temptation for alcohol, drugs, and sex on the road.

I decided that Wy and I would have to be inventive with those other twenty-three hours in the day when we put our tour together. I started getting a fuzzy notion about someday creating a family atmosphere on the road to simulate the more normal daily routines of home. Meanwhile, I gathered Loretta's band together in the coffee shop and asked if anyone wanted to go to church together the Sunday morning after closing night. The black backup singer was dating a waitress in the coffee shop, who took us to a very happenin' church. We were the only whites there, but they were hospitable to us and the service and music were just what we all needed.

Lola Falana shut down a Vegas roller rink and threw a skating party at 4:00 A.M. so all the other strip performers could attend. Cher and I almost collided twice. Wynonna was having the time of her life! Her greatest wish had come true—she was out of school *and* roller skating with stars at 4:00 in the morning, eating in restaurants, and hanging out with musicians! We both recognized the wandering, random lifestyle of a touring musician fit Wy's personality like a glove.

Her musical gift was her greatest downfall and her saving grace at the same time.

The general outcry from the folks back in Kentucky was: "What in the world are you doing?" They called our room all the time and the fear and outrage in their voices jumped out through the receiver. I did appreciate their love and concern and recognized that sane voice of reason. Vegas is like Sodom and Gommorah and it was comforting to hear these familiar reminders of home. At the same time, I felt as if I were the only one who really knew what was going on. I didn't know where to begin to explain to them Wy's negative attitude toward school and how critical it was to try a different approach. Over and over again I assured them I had absolutely no intention of us getting into music until she completed high school. Then I promised we were moving to Nashville for good and I explained I was using music as the carrot dangling in front of the horse's nose to coax her into walking across that graduation stage.

Most of the time I could halfway convince myself and Wy that I knew what I was doing. Until I talked to little Ashley, that is. Then I fell apart and was overcome with guilt.

"When are you coming to get me?" she asked constantly. "What's Wy doing out of school? Is she reading books? Does she have any friends her own age?"

Ashley and Wy were so different it amazed me. Ashley enjoyed school and learning. She thrived on responsibility and was plugged into a vast social network. Ashley represented the respectable part of my own character. Wy brought out the other half of my personality. Mommy and Baby Outlaw.

Literally in the blink of an eye, the TV special disappeared. Based on Las Vegas performers, Lola Falana was to be the focus of the project. Then she scratched her eye while watering a cactus plant. We'd been at the Alladin going on three weeks now and the hotel bill for room and restaurant charges was astronomical. Time was up on the availibility of the *Hee Haw* crew and they had to go on back to Nashville. Jeff was in a terrible predicament, since he had no footage, and hadn't paid anyone a dime. We all wanted out of there in case the hotel decided to make each of us pay our own bill. And to top it off it was rumored the mafia owned the Alladin!

My buddy Gary Hood, the stage manager for *Hee Haw,* knew I had my Chevy and called our room frantic for a ride to the airport. We sneaked down a service entrance and ran for the car. He and a friend lay down in the backseat while Wy and I rushed for the airport. After dropping them off, we deadheaded back to Marin County, frequently checking the rearview mirror to see if we were being followed.

Jeff disappeared. Owing the hotel and other businesses in Vegas as well as the entire production crew, he hightailed it. Although he hadn't paid me a nickel, Jeff had promised that when we got back to our house in Forest Knolls there'd be two one-way tickets to Nashville. We stopped at a diner for supper and wrote a postcard to Ashley, telling her we were on our way to get her soon. We signed it Mommy, Big Sis, and Lord Helpus.

The moving van pulled away from Forest Knolls with our used furniture and sentimental keepsakes, filling up the leftover space from someone else's move. The mover had charged us a very small fee since the truck was already bound for Tennessee. The driver promised to come back and put Redhot in the next van with space headed that way, so I handed him the keys. I knew it was risky, but it would be way too rough on the Chevy driving it cross-country. Since the driver was doing this on the sly, there wasn't a contract.

I handed the man Jeff's office number in Nashville, and crossed my fingers that I'd see my beloved car again. Depending on the kindness of strangers had become routine in the day-to-day drama of my life.

As our plane ascended into the clouds, I had such an eerie feeling! We'd soon be landing in a new town with very little money, no place to live, no furniture, and no car. I suggested Wy pretend we were pioneers leaving everything we'd known behind, setting out in search of the promised land. She half-smiled as a worried look flashed across her young face. Drawing her close, I took her hand in mine and consoled her. "Stick with me, kid. Someday I'll buy you horse turds big as diamonds!"

Mama, He's Crazy

*L*IFE'S BIG MOMENTS should be accompanied by stirring swells of music. May 1, 1979, Wy and I set foot in Music City, USA. It was a rainy day and we were disappointed as we looked around. "Why, it's just another city!" I thought to myself. Jeff had sent someone from his office to pick us up, in an ugly army green Impala. This fellow said Jeff was lending it to me until my Chevy made it to Tennessee.

The old car wallowed around like a big-bottomed boat as it chugged down the road. Jeff's messenger drove us to a sleazy motel in a not-so-nice part of town. Once a Howard Johnson motel, the Music City Motor Inn on Murfreesboro Road was now run by a family from India.

"Welcome to your new home! Here's the address for our office and Jeff expects you to report for work at 9:00 A.M. tomorrow." With those parting words, the messenger disappeared.

Wy and I silently unpacked our bags in the small dumpy room. "Gee, I guess Tammy, Dolly, and Loretta must be on the road," I joked. "Otherwise they would have picked us up in their limo and settled us into their guest quarters!"

Wy began to cry. The only two cheerful things I could think of to say was that we were only five hours away from Ashley in Kentucky and there was a McDonalds next door. Our first meal in Nashville was a couple of Quarter Pounders.

Before I went to bed, it dawned on me I'd have to take Wy to work with me every day. I wasn't about to leave her in that awful motel by herself. We got up extra early to give us plenty of time to find the address of Jeff's office building in the music district.

We were in awe as we drove along Music Row for the first time! There were the big record corporations, the publishing companies, ASCAP, BMI, plus the Country Music Hall of Fame. It was as if we'd entered the pearly gates and were riding down streets of gold!

Jeff's office was in the Fender building just a few doors away from RCA on the main drag. As we opened the door and walked in, I realized Jeff and I were both dreamers and both a long way from the top.

His small office was sparsely furnished. The "staff" Jeff had referred to consisted of a bookkeeper and a guy who booked a couple of unknown lounge acts. I took Wy and Ashley's framed photo from my purse, set it on my desk, and handed Wy a book to read. But at least we'd made it to Music Row in Nashville!

On my lunch break we visited the Country Music Hall of Fame down the block. We were practically dumbstruck by the musical history staring us right in the face. The museum seemed almost like a cathedral filled with holy relics. Wy loved Elvis's convertible best.

Nobody knew or cared that the Judds had moved to town. We existed only in the parentheses of a few people's conversations. Every night as we drove back to our dreary motel room, the reality of how far removed we were from where we wanted to be saturated us.

We were existing from day to day. Jeff could only afford to pay me $150 a week. He had no income himself and all day at work I fended off bill collectors. In the evenings, Wy and I walked two blocks from our motel to a small deli and ate bologna and crackers, or fresh fruit from a market. One night Jeff and his wife invited us to dinner and it was such a treat to eat a hot, well-balanced meal in a real home. The next day, May 30, 1979, was Wy's fifteenth birthday and I felt sad not having a kitchen to bake her a cake, as I had for every year of her life. For her present I took her for a drive out in the country.

Ashley's school was letting out and we drove up to Kentucky to get her. Not having seen her for five months, we were very excited.

She was just getting over the chicken pox. When she walked into our motel room she commented, as we had, on the bad smell. Wy tried to brighten her up with news that we had a pet. She was referring to Fred, the roach in the bathroom.

At night while the girls watched TV, I sat in the tiny bathroom with Fred, working on an idea I'd come up with for a radio program. Knowing that many of America's earliest songs were based on real events, I composed a list of twenty. I wrote a half-hour show following the song's true story line, incorporating our singing the lyrics during the dramatization. I would visit the Country Music Foundation Library on my lunch hour and after work to do research on these old songs and the traditions of troubadours who traveled from town to town entertaining with them.

I encountered a bright young country music enthusiast named Robert Oermann working there. When I approached him for help, Robert was gracious and informative. We shared an obvious love for music and its history, but he didn't know I also considered him to be my first friend in Nashville. One evening I confided in him our juggernaut to become singers. I had no way of knowing Robert would rise to become one of the music industry's most venerable and formidable critics, one day reviewing our records, concerts, and achievements!

I also begged information from John Lomax III, another authority at the Country Music Foundation, and came up with my script for a pilot based on the folk song "Banks of the Ohio." Using Baptist Communications recording studio and coaxing unemployed actors into participating in the project, Wy and I portrayed the main characters. Still trying to get sponsorship for this idea as a radio series, I also took our professional audiotape to the local public TV station, WDCN.

They were intrigued with my futuristic concept of what would years later become music videos. I quickly discovered in our initial meeting that at the time there was no money to be made in public TV. I loved public TV, but I needed money badly!

Nothing ever came of my "Stories We Sing," and I put the tape in my box of souvenirs. I could only smile to myself when I later saw the first music videos. I wrote other TV scripts as well. One showbiz gossip program, "News of Nashville," was my 1979 version of the now-popular *Crook and Chase* program. I penned a script for a short informative feature called "You Just Might Learn Somethin'," in which I would teach old-time crafts (such as soap making), give natural folk remedies, homespun advice, and the like.

My favorite endeavor was a movie script I collaborated on: *The Kentucky Sweethearts.* Set in the late 1930s in a Kentucky coal-mining camp town, it tells of the struggle of a mother and daughter to reach the stage of the Grand Ole Opry. I even wrote the title soundtrack called "The Road to the Opry." My brain was always spilling over with ideas and my souvenir box was getting full!

Jeff Thornton encouraged my schemes but was in no position financially to back them. He'd quote Robert Schuller and tell Wy and me, "If you can conceive it and believe it, you *can* achieve it!"

I'd retort with: "Hey, I have no problem conceiving and believing. It's the achieving part I need someone to help me with!"

I had to get us out of that crummy motel. Needing a demo of us to start presenting on the Row, we'd set our little tape recorder in the tile bathroom. The window opened onto the parking lot, and just as we were finishing up a tune, a car would noisily interrupt. It was springtime and we longed to be out of the crowded concrete jungle.

The only constancy the girls and I really had in life was each other. When times got tough I'd remind them that the strongest structure is a triangle. We tried to keep each other's spirits up.

I had a phone number that a friend in Marin had given me to call in Nashville. When I rang up this friend of a friend, the stranger was very cordial and invited us to his home. Our mutual friend in Marin had already alerted him to expect a call from us.

Dressing the girls in their best outfits, I admonished them to be on their best behavior as well. Charles Bidderman opened the door with a broad smile. The modern, dark wood house at the end of a dead-end street was built with a lot of glass to show off the dense woods surrounding it.

We went there to gather suggestions about where the best schools were, what areas were the prettiest, where to live, and so forth. Charles, an entrepreneur from Wall Street in New York, had come to Nashville to start a magazine, and the overflow printing presses were in the basement of the house. He'd been robbed several times and admitted he was now afraid to leave the place unguarded.

Feeling a deep desire for spiritual renewal, he wanted to spend a month in a teepee in Colorado. In addition to feeling tied to his residence to thwart burglaries, his cat was ready to drop a litter any day.

After checking us over during lunch, he implored us to house-sit for him. I winked at the girls, whispered a thank you" toward the ceiling, and said, "A dead-end street's just a place to turn around!"

We moved our bags in as Charles was leaving for his sabbatical. The next morning, June 2, we were getting in our Impala to drive up to Kentucky to see Mark crossing the finish line. He'd met a sweet nurse named Middy and was getting married.

But that very morning the cat had her kittens, throwing Wy into a serious asthma attack. Hurriedly unpacking my stethoscope, I checked her chest and heart. Frantic, I laid her in the backseat and sped for the closest emergency room. The combination of spring pollen and the animals sent her into such an attack she was in Williamson County Hospital in nearby Franklin for several days. In the meantime I got a good, close look at that quaint town.

As I drove around the town square with its statue and cannon, down Main Street with the historic storefronts; Franklin looked and felt like an upscale version of Mayberry in *The Andy Griffith Show*. Steeped in Civil War history, there were landmarks of the infamous battle of Franklin. The turn-of-the-century stately homes and well-cared for lawns reminded me of the neighborhoods I grew up in at Ashland.

The surrounding farms were very similar to Morrill, Kentucky, and the crafts shops, health food store, and restaurant reminded me of Berea. There was even a parallel between Franklin and Marin County, in that quite a few music people spilled out from Nashville into the more inspiring atmosphere of the countryside.

If you follow the clues carefully, you'll find the prize. We'd found our prize. We began looking for a house to rent in the countryside around Franklin.

Meanwhile back at the office, I was now on a first-name basis on the phone with all the bill collectors. Having never even had a credit card in my life, it was a new and unpleasant experience dealing with creditors. Men in suits with serious faces started showing up in person too. Jeff seldom came in anymore.

So I was surprised to see Jeff saunter in one morning, but even more surprised when he announced he'd just signed another act. Betting it was someone obscure, I was wondering whether to fake recognition.

"Yep! I've snagged management and booking on J. D. Sumner and the Stamps!" he declared proudly. "Caught their show out at the Palamino the night before I met you gals. Gave J. D. my card and had a meeting." I commented Wy and I had seen them that same night when Mickey Gilley took us, and remarked at the coincidence.

It was mid-July and the Tennessee summer's heat was stifling, but we couldn't afford to run the air-conditioning. I was reading a magazine at my desk when a couple of guys from the Stamps walked through the door. I couldn't recall their names, but recognized them. The lead singer introduced himself as Ed Enoch and tilted his head sideways toward the man standing beside him as he acknowledged, "Brother Larry Strickland."

Since Larry was an amazing bass singer, I was waiting to hear that deep voice come out, but he just stared at me and took a long drag on his Marlboro. His jet black thick hair seemed even longer, and he had a bit of sideburns. He was even more tanned now and thin as a rail. Larry looked for all the world like a double order of trouble!

Ed talked a mile a minute, but I wasn't listening. In my peripheral vision I studied his mysterious pal for clues. Larry wore a nice watch, no wedding ring, slacks, and a red silk shirt that said "Daytona Speedway" over the heart.

Then Ed dragged the back of his forearm across his wet brow and sputtered, "Would you just look at this guy! No matter how hot it gets, that boy don't even break a sweat!"

"Oh yeah! I betcha I could make him sweat!" I blurted out. For the next few moments there was shocked silence in the room. I almost looked around behind me to see who'd made such a bold, brazen statement. What a totally out of character thing for me to say!

The only way I can rationalize it is that if you whack your thumb with a hammer, you let a cuss word fly.

Hastily excusing myself, I stepped into the supply closet and stayed there until Jeff called them into his office.

A week later, when I returned from my lunch-hour walk, Etta the bookkeeper said someone named Larry had called. The only calls I ever received were from Wy and Ashley, so I knew it had to be Larry Strickland. Each time my phone rang that afternoon I jumped out of my seat.

When it was finally he, I was fascinated by his sexy voice. It sent a rumble down inside me. Kind of like uneasy continents shifting on their subterranean plates.

He said very little and even that was separated by huge gaps. I was thinking if he had any intention of asking me out, it could tie up the office line all afternoon. After the usual questions about where I was from and how many brothers and sisters I had, he admitted he noticed me in the audience at the Palamino in Hollywood the night they performed. He had assumed I was Mrs. Mickey Gilley. He also thought Wy was my sister, and commented on our matching jackets.

Exasperated, I fibbed and declared I had to get back to work so he finally wondered out loud if he might "come by to see me" that evening.

From Charles's glass house set up on a hillside, I was watching the dead-end street when a low-slung sports car pulled slowly into the drive. Larry slid his lanky frame out of a silver Corvette. He was dressed in a khaki safari outfit. I watched him flick the stub of his cigarette on the pavement and rub it out with the pointed toe of his boot. He glanced up at the house and caught me watching him from the window. I froze and felt suddenly nervous as a high school girl.

We stood locked in silent paralysis, and the first few minutes were painfully awkward. When Larry did ask what I liked to do, I explained to him right off the bat I wasn't into night life. No clubs or bars for me, and I went to movies only if there was one that really interested me.

"What do you feel like doing tonight?" he wanted to know.

I drawled, "It's such a beautiful summer evening, I'd love to go for a drive in the country to check out a possible house to rent."

While scouring backroads the previous weekend, Wy, Ashley, and I had paused to chat with an old farmer named Boyce Rogers who was working his field. Boyce told us about an abandoned house that was in a state of disrepair. "Gosh, the windows are broken out and there's animals living inside, but it's the only house vacant in these parts." I remembered the directions he'd given me.

As we drove down the country backroads, black singer Al Downing's ballad "Touch Me" came on the radio. There were gorgeous low backup vocals on the record and I commented to Larry how great that bass singer sounded. "Thanks, that's me," he humbly murmured. I again felt that rumbling deep down inside.

As we pulled into the gravel drive alongside the house on Del Rio Pike, the little empty gingerbread house looked neglected and lonely in the moonlight. There was no sidewalk so we walked out in the tall grass of the front yard to look it over.

"Place'll take an awful lot of work!" Larry proclaimed. I'd begun to feel so comfortable, my mouth suddenly dropped open and words came flowing out like feed grain from a split burlap sack.

I revealed everything . . . about why it was essential to be in the country, about how my kids were central in everything I did, about our dream to be in country music.

Larry listened very attentively and there was something so accepting in his silence that made me think he understood. When my words dried up, he kissed me softly. It made my lips hum.

I suggested we drive to Main Street in Franklin for an ice cream cone at Baskin-Robbins. While licking away on our ice cream, I confessed this was the first date I'd had in a year. Then I asked to be taken home, because I had to work the next morning.

On my way to work the following day I had a sinking sensation. Why in the world had I come off like such a hillbilly to a man who sang with Elvis, traveled the world, and probably had girls in every town? All I had to look forward to was my two kids and that rundown house.

Larry called the next afternoon from the road. It was Friday afternoon and he gave me the number where they'd be staying that weekend in Denver, Colorado. I knew I was falling in love. I kept myself busy all weekend taking care of the girls and cleaning Charles's house. On Sunday we visited a church searching for a church home. Watching all the husbands and wives with their families leaving together, after the service, I went home to phone Larry.

He'd mentioned that he and Ed Enoch, the lead singer, roomed together, so I was caught off guard when a girl answered in his motel room.

"And who are you?" this possessive sounding woman wanted to know.

"My name's Naomi—I'm the manager's secretary," I answered truthfully.

Assuming I was calling regarding their gig, she volunteered more information than I was ready for.

"Oh! They're doing their sound check at the club. As soon as I finish packing I'm picking him up at the club and he's taking me to the airport to catch my flight. But I'll tell him you called."

Larry and I had only been on one date, but I'd already fallen in love and had my heart broken. I was terribly depressed. Would I ever find someone to love me? Would I ever have any of the things other people take for granted? Charles called that night saying he would be returning soon, so we needed to find a place quickly. The house on Del Rio would require a lot of elbow grease and backbreaking work. We barely had enough to eat, and my job at Jeff's office was a sham. Harsh and immediate realities of the most mundane sort were beating me down.

After the kids were in bed, I sat out on the porch and remembered something I'd heard in church that morning. Something about faith from Hebrews 11:1: "Now faith is the substance of things hoped for, the evidence of things not seen."

I thought about this idea for hours. It made so much sense, it became real to me. By now I'd been through enough that I'd learned a lot about survival. I'd always felt God was close, revealing His grace in one manner or another. I tried considering these threatening conditions as benevolent conspiracies to awaken me to God's presence. If all I had was God, it would be enough for me.

That night I resolved to step out in faith. Instead of feeling bogged down with my problems, insecurity, and fear, I looked beyond my temporary, immediate circumstances. As I visualized my future I switched my thought process to the positive.

I told myself someday I would own my own home. It would be clean and spacious and everything in it would work. We'd have a safe, big enough car that didn't clank, smoke, and break down. I'd be able to walk into a store and pick out new clothing for the girls and myself, buy them what they wished for on birthdays and Christmas. Someday I'd be able to afford medical insurance for all of us, even life insurance on myself. Maybe even a savings account!

One of the biggest challenges facing me was this dream of a career in music. It would really take an unbelievable amount of faith! This open-ended goal seemed so preposterous, I was almost embarrassed to pray for it. But I knew what Jesus said in Mark 11:24: "Therefore I say unto you, What things soever ye desire, when ye pray, believe that ye receive them, and ye shall have them."

The next day, Monday, Larry returned after his weekend in Denver and began calling. Hurt and disappointed, I wouldn't talk to him at first, but finally I met him at a restaurant. Larry sat me down and explained this groupie had been following him around the country for years, ever since he'd been on tour with Elvis. She had a lot of money and was very persistent. The trip to Denver had been planned long before he and I met.

As Larry confessed all this, my attitude began softening. Obviously, his relationship with the other girl was well established, and he and I barely knew each other. Why would I expect him to cancel their plans when he didn't even know whether he and I would ever want to have a second date? Larry said he'd never been in love with her and didn't care if he never saw her again. He tenderly took hold of my hand and asked me to be his "special lady." I melted.

On our second date Larry told me he was married. While serving in the army in Germany, he'd married a blond, Norwegian airline stewardess named Birgit who spoke six languages. After the army, they lived in his hometown, Raleigh, North Carolina, where he managed a computer operation. Larry maintained his own weekend gospel group, until one day he got the phone call to fly to the Las Vegas Hilton to join the Stamps on Elvis's tour. Life on the road 285 days a year took its toll on his marriage and they were separated. He and Birgit had no children, were on friendly terms, and he'd let her have their home. In fact, the road had broken up band members Ed Enoch's and Richard's marriages as well. All three were separated and sharing an apartment. It made me stop and wonder what was going on out there?

On our third date, Larry drove me over to his place at the Iroquois Apartments. We were sitting in his Corvette, parked next to the Dumpster out back. It was a balmy night in August and I had to ask him to move, due to the smell of rank garbage. After backing the car up, he turned off the ignition and stared at the dashboard. Words never came easy to this man and several silent minutes passed.

"I have something I must say," he began haltingly. My heart knew what was coming and my ears were ready to receive it. "I know this is just our third date and we've had a bumpy start. But Naomi, I'm in love with you. I knew I was starting to fall as we stood out in the grass under the moonlight the first night on Del Rio."

As he finished, so help me God, there were fireworks. Real ones! Kids were setting off leftover Fourth of July firecrackers and a few Roman candles in the parking lot. Larry and I stared over at them in disbelief. When we finished laughing, he looked at me imploringly and pulled me to him.

"I'm in love with you too," I responded. We kissed one of those week-long kisses as imaginary pop-bottle rockets whizzed over our heads.

Another interesting man came on the scene later that same week. A beleaguered-appearing songwriter sauntered into the office wanting to pitch songs. When I told him my boss wasn't in, he mumbled he'd stop back later.

Music Row is lined with buildings that house the offices of publishers, producers, managers, booking agents, and artists. It's a veritable shopping mall of music goods. Every day, hopefuls parade up and down the street.

There was a troubled sadness about this tune peddler. As he turned to leave, he asked for a drink of water. As I returned from the cooler with a glass, he was taking pills from bottles. He tossed a handful down and left.

The exact same thing happened again the next afternoon. As he sat down in the chair by my desk to take his prescriptions, I could read one of the labels, Lithium salts, the drug of choice for manic-depressive psychosis.

I knew enough from my psychiatric clinicals to know this poor guy had serious problems. Asking his name, I offered my hand and introduced myself. Smiling for the first time, he introduced himself as George Black. Alone in the office he began to tell me he'd written big hits for Elvis and Ricky Nelson.

Having fallen into a deep depression when his wife left him and took their daughter, he attempted suicide in California. George turned on the gas and sat down in the bathroom. Amazingly, he awoke, woozy and sick, and pulled out a cigarette to steady his nerves.

When he struck a match, it blew up the house and he was badly injured. George's family had him institutionalized in their home state of Alabama.

George had come to Nashville to do the only thing he knew how to do, write songs. But he had another sticky mental problem. Agorophobia.

It means fear of open or public places. George was petrified of crowds and unfamiliar surroundings. He'd gotten a small apartment near Music Row and traveled a very limited route.

He had no friends, and I can't stand to see anyone suffering. George was really a good man, but it was as if he lived in a fog. He was trapped alive in his body. Listening to him describe how difficult it was to be creative under the veil of all these powerful drugs, I questioned his dosage. I suggested he check with his doctor about the possibility of reducing the amount.

Trying to be of some encouragement, I gave George the phone number at Charles's and said he could call me at eight o'clock any night, if he needed to. He had good and bad days. I listened, praised, and comforted him. George was getting clearer and more alert.

Our friendship consisted strictly of this nightly ritual phone call and occasional drop-bys at the office. He'd stop in to play me tunes he was working on, and I'd give him honest critique. His songwriting was greatly improving.

I'd noticed he wore the same clothes all the time. George confessed he had no one to shop for him and there was no way he could go into a store because of his agorophobia.

Having witnessed a dramatic change for the better over the few weeks since that first day he'd walked in the office, I hit on an idea. I suggested we try an experimental outing. I wanted to take him to the Sears near Music Row to get him new clothes. George knew I was a nurse and trusted me. We prepared for it by talking him through it during the nightly phone calls.

On my lunch hour, I drove him to Sears. At first I didn't think he'd ever get out of the car. I knew not to push him and finally he took a deep breath as he opened the car door. There weren't many customers inside the store, but he panicked.

By the time I got him to the men's department George was starting to lose it. His eyes were bulging, he'd begun sweating and trembling, and was starting to hyperventilate. The salesman looked alarmed and asked me what was the matter. Feeling as if I'd bitten off a lot more than I could chew, I hurriedly ushered George out of there.

At five o'clock I rushed home to cook dinner. The Stamps had just returned home from several weeks on the road, and I'd invited Larry and Richard over for a home-cooked dinner at Charles's house. It was now the middle of August, and Wy and Ashley had gone up to Ashland to visit the grandparents before their schools started.

Larry, Richard, and I just finished eating and were settling into the living room. As the guys were telling me about their last trip out, the phone rang. When I heard George's voice I'd forgotten it was eight o'clock. He was elated about making it inside Sears earlier that day and he bragged about how brave he felt since he'd stopped taking his medication. Suddenly, he ceased talking and demanded to know who was talking in the background.

"I hear men's voices!" he shouted.

"Yeah, it's my boyfriend and his roommate," I stated innocently.

"Your boyfriend! *I'm* your boyfriend!" he yelled.

It felt like someone had knocked the wind out of me. I stammered and stuttered in shocked surprise.

"George, you're my friend. That's all!" My own voice began rising too.

"I'm going to have to kill him," he proclaimed matter of factly. Then I heard a click.

As I slowly set the phone back on the receiver, Richard and Larry were still laughing and talking.

I reassured myself that George not only didn't know where Charles's house was, but would never venture out into an unknown neighborhood.

We were just finishing desert when I heard a car come screaming into the drive. Jumping straight up out of my chair, knocking over my glass, I quickly commanded Richard to call 911, because "a disturbed man I'd befriended has arrived to kill us."

I raced through the kitchen for the open back door to lock it, just in time to see George stepping up to the porch! He was very agitated and had a look on his face I'd never seen before. George stopped two feet in front of the screen door when he saw me. I wanted desperately to reach out and hook the latch, but stood motionless.

"I got the address from the phone book!" he said proudly. "I knew I could make it out here after the trip to Sears today!" Then he switched gears.

"You're what's been keeping me alive. You've saved me, and you're mine now."

With his back flat up against the wall, Larry had been inching his way silently into the kitchen toward the screen door. He held a poker in his raised hand. Larry's eyes were fixed on me in his frozen pose.

Already absolutely terrified, my eyes then caught a glimpse of the butt of a gun sticking out of George's back pocket.

I couldn't let George know Larry was there because it might provoke him to begin shooting. Larry was anxiously watching me for some kind of cue, so I very slowly and discreetly lifted the fingers of my left hand as it hung at my side. The gesture meant "don't move yet."

Just then I saw Richard out of the corner of my eye with something in his hand, slip up alongside Larry. Larry raised his finger up to his lips in a gesture for Richard not to move or make a sound either.

I wanted to shriek, "He's got a gun . . . hit the floor!" But instead I stayed as calm as I could muster. I listened to George rant and rave.

"A few months ago, I was in a sanitarium in Alabama," he began crying. "They had me on so much medication I slept all the time. One day, in a stupor I sat in the recreation room watching daytime TV. It was *The Merv Griffin Show* and Mickey Gilley was singing a song. Somehow I began singing along! It was strangely familiar, but I had no idea why. I hid my pills that evening to try and figure it out. By the next day I was coherent enough to realize I wrote the damn song! In fact, I was able to remember winning a Grammy recently and even riding around in the limo with Mickey afterward!" George then plotted to get out of the institution and move to Nashville.

My mouth hung wide open in complete astonishment. Before I even realized what I was doing I interrupted George's revelation with one of my own.

"My God! I was there at *The Merv Griffin Show* and I was the one who convinced Mickey to perform that song!" I named the exact date and George was stunned at this unbelievable coincidence.

I began to talk soothingly like a kindergarten teacher. Slowly and distinctly I told him I'd continue to help him but he needed to go home now. I recounted he'd had enough for one day. Everything would be okay, I calmly assured him.

George seemed so blown away by this new discovery, he could only gaze at me through the screen as if I were an angel of God, sent to guide him. With all the authority and confidence I could muster, I firmly instructed him to go home to bed. Staring past my shoulder as if in a daze for a few minutes he began to turn and slowly walk back to his car, the butt of the gun now in full view.

Larry dropped the poker and lurched forward to grab me. Only then was I able to tell him and Richard about the gun.

In a minute, we heard sirens as the police cars arrived. I gave the cops a description of George, his car, and address. I found out what an "APB" is.

The cops staked out his apartment but warned me to leave Charles's house till George was apprehended.

Larry and Richard helped me grab some things and took me to their apartment. I couldn't stop shaking even after we got safely inside and bolted the door. Larry loaded his shotgun.

We sat around reliving the terrifying, bizarre experience, until we realized how drained we were. There was nowhere for me to sleep in the one-bedroom apartment and neither Larry nor I had money for a motel.

I had calmed down and felt so protected by Larry that I felt the need to return to Charles's house. After all, I'd promised to watch over things.

I drove, so Larry could hold the shotgun in his lap. Then Larry kept me pressed up directly behind him as we slowly crept through the house turning on lights, securing windows and doors.

The guest bedroom faced out over the cul de sac. Larry vowed to stand watch all night so I could sleep. As I lay in bed, he paced barefoot across the floor back and forth in front of the big windows. Wearing only his jeans, he hugged the shotgun. My protector, my hero.

That image of Larry, silhouetted against the moonlight through the window, is the stuff romance novels are made of.

Sometime later I was saddened to receive news that George had been reinstitutionalized and given a frontal lobotomy.

It was a night Larry and I will never forget. For many reasons.

Wy and Ashley returned from their annual visit in Ashland. After thanking Charles for his hospitality, we loaded up everything we had and headed for Franklin.

The house on Del Rio Pike was 120 years old. I guess it was my great imagination that allowed me to rent the dilapidated property for $350 per month. We replaced the busted-out windows and the rotted porch first, then we painted it inside and out. I splurged and put old-fashioned flowered wallpaper in my bedroom. You could see the dirt ground between the cracks in the floorboards in the kitchen, so we laid inexpensive linoleum. I scrubbed and varnished the rest of the house's hardwood floors, and covered them with throw rugs from Target.

The old farmhouse had no closets, except for a small niche in my bedroom. I had to put up a clothes rod along a short wall in a tiny room off the kitchen to hang all our clothes on. Initially, I could barely afford window shades from JCPenny. Later on, I added lace curtains.

As usual, I purchased three used mattresses from Goodwill to lay on the bare bedroom floors; I checked the seal to be sure they'd been deloused. Working feverishly, we had a modicum of creature comforts when the day arrived to enroll Wy and Ashley in their schools. The roof had a few leaks, but if we were expecting rain we learned exactly where to place pots and bowls to collect rainwater before we left every morning.

I made a point of being home from the office to greet the girls when the big yellow schoolbus dropped them off after their first day. Their classmates couldn't see inside our house, with its fresh white coat of paint, to see we had no furniture. In a week, a van, which filled its excess space with our stuff, dropped off our mismatched used furniture. Still no sign of the Chevy. Would I ever see Redhot again?

The generous Ciminellas had, as usual, bought the girls school clothes and I took them to Goodwill and Wal-Mart to fill in whatever else they needed. I hated the back-to-school ads because they served as a reminder that I couldn't provide the way other mothers did. We had no TV, telephone, or washer and dryer. But we made do, and held our heads high.

Ashley believed in magic. She laughed a lot, read every day, charmed her teachers, and jumped out of bed every morning.

Franklin High School where Wy began as a freshman had sixteen hundred students. Not your typical country school, it was mostly composed of middle- to upper-middle-class students. Williamson County is one of the wealthiest in the state. Since Franklin is the site of the largest rodeo east of the Mississippi, many students are into horses. Wy commented right away on how many kids drove trucks and wore western wear.

But she didn't own a pair of jeans or cowboy boots. Instead, she wore forties dresses and unusual hairdos, with hair combs or even a flower behind her ear. She also loved makeup. Because of her old-fashioned style, Wy was sometimes mistaken for a teacher. Initially, she tried joining some of the student body organizations. Funny and likeable, she made a few close friends, who tended also to be outside the "in crowd." Like Lance Jordon, who had an offbeat sense of humor and wrapped library books he'd checked out to give her as Christmas presents.

She didn't give a grunt about horses or saddles. She was interested in guitars and amps! Wy's life experiences at fifteen were so much richer and varied than her peers, she couldn't find other teenagers to relate to. Not when she'd been living around creative, free-spirited adults, who treated her as an equal!

Sometimes I'd drop by the high school to bring her lunch and eat with her. It didn't matter to us that no one else's parents ever did this. One day I couldn't locate her. Her pals kept sending me on a wild-goose chase from building to building saying, "You just missed her!" I found out later she'd snunk and worn my favorite dress to school and her friends had been running interference.

The first time Larry came in off the road I was out in the yard in my apron hanging clothes on the line. We kept the wringer washer on the small screened-in back porch when it wasn't in use. I'd fixed beef stew and a cherry pie for our first supper together. Sitting around Miss Cora Lee's dining room table with its lace tablecloth once again felt so good.

Larry, Wy, and Ashley were getting acquainted. Wy asked Larry if Elvis was really dead. "I'm afraid so," he said, sighing. He described to her how he stood right next to the open casket in the living room at Graceland and sang at the King's funeral.

"Wow! Those are some blue suede clues all right," Wy mumbled. "Too bad, 'cause me and him and Mama could have been pals and hung out together when we get famous, too."

We all looked over at Wy and saw that she was being very serious. She wasn't being irreverent at all. "I think Elvis coulda used some down-to-earth people around him to show him how to be happy."

Larry nodded his head as he smiled at me. Just then little Ashley did something that embarrassed me beyond description.

Being able to afford only a small amount of meat, I'd carefully put the most chunks of beef into Larry's bowl. Noticing this, Ashley held up her spoon with a piece of potato in it and offered: "Hey Larry, trade you some potatoes for a piece of meat!"

Catching on instantly, he quietly switched bowls with her. Next it was Larry's turn to turn red. After dessert, Larry rubbed his belly with exaggerated satisfaction then hooked his thumbs into his pants pockets and leaned back, tilting his chair back a little too far and fell out on the floor!

The girls and I screamed with laughter as we scrambled to help him up. And so it was with our first dinner together in our new home.

Larry knew we were poor. We felt lucky to have a clean house with electricity and running water. He offered to pay our phone bill, if I'd get a phone so he could call me at night from the road. I accepted.

As darkness came, we lit our kerosene lamps to save on the utility bill. The four of us moved out to the front porch to sit in the swing he'd hung for us that afternoon. I'd gotten a couple of rocking chairs, and decorated the porch with ceramic hoot owls and hanging plants.

Before bedtime I made an announcement. "Our U-Haul days are over, my children. We're finally home. We've found the Promised Land."

Why Not Me?

O N E O F T H E first things I noticed working on Music Row was that the receptionists were all women and the producers were all men. I made a couple of girlfriends. On our lunch hour, we gossiped about the music business and commiserated about our favorite topic—men! My best girlfriend Polly gave me quite a scare when she became terribly despondent after her boyfriend left her. Concerned when she didn't answer at her apartment all weekend, I went over and got the landlord to let me in in the middle of the night. Thank goodness Polly had just taken off to Florida to attempt to see the guy. Driving back home I began writing a song summing up these various men in my girlfriend's lives. His collective name was "Mr. Pain."

Carolyn, the secretary at Alabama's recording studio, the Music Mill, would occasionally meet me after work at a Music Row hangout, Maude's Courtyard, for a glass of wine. I was soaking up stories about what really went on behind the closed doors of those big offices. Pals like Bonnie Rasmussen gave me free promotional records and inside tips on which producers were good—in every sense of the word.

I'd wanted to find out all I could before leaving Music Row. My certification from the Board of Health to practice nursing in Tennessee had just arrived.

Even though he couldn't pay me, I felt sorry for Jeff. He'd resorted to kiting checks and had been officially subpoenaed. His wife had left him and taken the kids. When I requested to talk to him in person, he could only show up after five o'clock at the office and sneak in the back way.

First I thanked him for helping us get to Nashville, and for introducing me to Larry. Then I said I needed to get a real job.

Jeff squinted his eyes real tight and asked me to repeat myself. He'd heard me all right, but just couldn't stand to hear he was losing the last thing he had. I represented the proverbial last straw.

Suddenly Jeff began shouting and pounding his fist on the desk. Wheeling around to the wall display behind him, he grabbed Buford Pusser's walking stick down from its mounting, and declared he was going to kill me!

Instantly yanking off my heels, I ran from his office, grabbing my purse off my desk out front and flew down the back stairs. Speeding off into the night, I was as angry as I was scared. This was twice in a month that guys I'd tried to help threatened to kill me!

I never saw Jeff again. I parked his green Impala out back of the Fender building the next day. The next week I noticed a "Space for Rent" sign in the window of our old office.

We'd only lived in Nashville five months, and I'd had two bad incidents. I was now without a car, and Larry let us use his. He kept his shotgun propped up by my bed. "You drive men plumb crazy," he observed. "I'd better stay out here with ya'll."

Larry traded his Corvette for his wife's big Lincoln Town Car and drove the girls and me to Raleigh, North Carolina, to meet his family for Thanksgiving. I liked all the Stricklands the minute I met them. They're good, decent, hardworking folk.

Larry's from a family of six, same as me. His kind and humble father, Ralph, has been a preacher all his life. Therefore, Larry knew what it was to spend a lot of time in church and the importance of family life. Myrtie, Larry's strong but soft-spoken mother, was justly proud of her four children and grandchildren.

I could tell they were uneasy about Larry being in show business. Before the holiday was over, every member had taken me aside and mentioned how they'd love to see him settle down with me and the kids. I thought he was fortunate to have such a close-knit family, who cared so much about him.

They invited us back for Christmas so the next month we gladly returned. Larry is close to his older brother Don and sister-in-law Ann, so we stayed with them in their big farmhouse. His younger brother, Reggie, was in seminary and brought home Nancy, the girl he'd just asked to marry him. Larry's sister, Carole, and brother-in-law, Gene, had kids Wy's and Ashley's ages, and they all went to the movies and roller skating. After all this wonderful family time together, I unwittingly saw the other side of Larry's life.

The Stamps were playing a club in Kernersville, North Carolina, after Christmas so we drove over to meet up with them. Leaving Wy and Ashley in our nearby motel room, I watched their show for the first time since the Palamino Club in Hollywood. Afterward I pulled the Lincoln up beside the Stamps bus as Larry was coming out of the club. Out of nowhere, a cute, young blond leapt on Larry, throwing her arms around his neck and began kissing him. Unaware I was sitting there with the window down, she asked what his room number was and cooed that she'd missed not hearing from him over Christmas.

Larry looked trapped and nervous. Prying her off him, he glanced over at me with hooded eyes and jumped up onto the safety of the bus. I burned rubber getting out of that parking lot and sped back to the motel.

The desk clerk included a "while you were out" message as he handed me the room key.

It was from another girl, telling Larry that she longed to hear his voice and how much she was looking forward to "next weekend." Packing hastily and bundling the kids into the waiting car, I swallowed hard. This was the old girlfriend who'd answered his motel room phone in Denver months ago. He hadn't called it off with her after all!

I drove all night, sobbing and listening to sad country songs on the radio. I had to pull over when Hank Williams sang "Your Cheatin' Heart."

The following day, with dark circles under my eyes, I had to pull myself together. I signed up to work through a nurse's registry, for several reasons. Not knowing the Nashville-area hospitals yet, I wasn't ready to join a permanent full-time staff. Second, I needed flexibility in my schedule so I could check out music-related business.

On my first official day as an RN in Tennessee, I was sent to do a home visitation an hour away in Donelson. The parents ushered me back to the bedroom of their only child, Rodney. This wasn't a typical boy's room. It looked like a hospital room, with its hospital bed, supplies, and equipment. Although now almost twenty and growing a mustache, Rodney's development had been arrested at infancy after a tragic reaction to a routine measles vaccination. His parents never saw him take his first step or utter his first word. Rodney was retarded. After twenty years, they were still changing his diapers, feeding, and bathing him.

As the dreary winter day dragged on, I became more and more saddened at not being able to improve the boy's condition. After giving him total care and doing range-of-motion exercises on his atrophied muscles, I put his side rails back up and sat down beside him. I began singing and Rodney's eyes suddenly opened and he made gurgling sounds.

A wave of familiarity washed over me. I recognized Rodney from my very first clinical days up at EKU! He'd been a patient in a nursing home near Richmond, Kentucky, and I'd sat and played my harmonica at his bedside many years ago! When his folks returned they verified this. My life seemed riddled with coincidences.

It was dark and snowing again as I made the long drive home. My spirits were sinking dangerously low. A couple of miles from the house I had to abandon the car. The Little Harpeth River runs alongside the road before the turn for Del Rio Pike, and that stretch had frozen over. Walking home my feet were freezing and my toes felt sore and stiff. The plastic sole of my cheap nursing shoe came loose. I tried binding it up with dental floss, but nothing worked.

As I walked up to our screened-in back porch, my heart sank. There was no more wood. Our only heat in this house was the old woodstove in Wy's bedroom, and as I stepped inside, the temperature wasn't much warmer than it was ourside. Checking Wy's room I found the fire had gone out and she wasn't in her bed. Neither was Ashley in hers.

Throwing open the door to my bedroom I witnessed one of the

most pitiful sights I've ever seen. Wy and Ashley were lying next to each other with towels and throw rugs layered on top of them to keep from freezing.

Walking out into the kitchen I found a note on the table saying they'd eaten the last of our food. I opened the refrigerator and stared at the bare shelves. Swallowing my pride, I reached for the phone to call Larry for a loan. He'd been buying our groceries.

As soon as Ed answered at their apartment and heard my voice, his tone changed. His "I'm sorry Larry didn't come home on the bus with us after our last show," told me everything. Ed and I had become friends and I asked if there was someplace I could reach Larry. "He's visiting an old friend, but I don't think you want to call her house."

I was numb. Walking into the bathroom I noticed there was a thin sheet of ice in the toilet bowl. Turning on the faucet confirmed my suspicion: the pipes had frozen and we had no water.

Exhausted, scared, heartbroken, cold, and hungry, my knees went out from under me. I couldn't cry. I was too miserable. It was the most despondent I'd ever been in my life.

Curled up on the bathmat on the floor I thought about my great-grandfather and grandfather's suicides. Was it hereditary? There were pills and razors in the medicine chest. Was it destiny?

Light dispels darkness. I was awakened by sunlight shining on my face through the bathroom window. I listened for the sound of activity in the house, but there was only silence. Wy and Ashley were still asleep. I lay there listening so hard, my mind began hearing the refrain of an old song. A hymn from childhood. "Love lifted me. When nothing else could help, love lifted me."

I stood up slowly and walked stiffly over to the small window. The glaring brightness of the sun on the snow hurt my eyes. Looking out across the backyard my gaze stopped at the shed. Lying around inside were old broken chairs and a discarded bookcase.

Still completely dressed in my coat, hat, and gloves, I marched right out and began busting up the furniture into sticks of wood that would fit inside the woodstove, carefully pulling out all the nails and screws. More determined than ever, I felt like Vivien Leigh in her survival speech scene from *Gone with the Wind*. Wadding up every magazine and piece of paper in the house, I'd just gotten a fire started when the girls awoke.

I went straight to the phone and asked the head of the nurse's registry, Marsha Steakley, for an advance on my first paycheck. It was against company policy, so she loaned me cash right out of her own purse. Wy, Ashley, and I drove to Kroger for groceries and had a farmer with a load of wood follow us home. Out of the blue, the moving van arrived with the Chevy. I kissed Redhot's fender and parked Larry's Lincoln at his apartment in the same spot where he'd first said he loved me. I left a one-word note on the front seat: "Liar."

Larry began calling and when I just kept hanging up on him, he showed up at the back door. Begging to talk to me, he explained that these women were nothing but "old habits" who meant nothing to him. It was lonely and boring out there on the road, he confessed, and they showed up without invitation. He was miserable and unable to stop thinking of me.

And so it began. Ecstacy and torment, freedom and slavery. We were wildly, madly in love. We wanted to be together every possible second. He drove me to the grocery, or dried dishes just to be by my side. He'd cut the grass in the summer, raked the leaves in the fall, and now in the winter, kept the woodstove going and fixed the old electric water pump when it froze. Larry gave me every dime he made with the Stamps, which was very little. His only pair of dress shoes were worn-out black patent, pointed toe, short boots that I called "pimp shoes." He wouldn't buy anything for himself.

Larry brought the girls his tiny portable TV. Since Wy was open to any temptation not to do her homework, I was forced to put the TV in the trunk of Redhot when I went to work. I was a curious sight always toting my purse in one hand and a TV in the other. Not having any counter space in our old farmhouse kitchen, Wy and Ashley set the TV on the stove one night and melted it. "We fried your TV along with dinner, Larry," they confessed to him.

His Lincoln was the next thing to go. Larry was watching the kids while I went out in a rainstorm to the Laundromat. Caught in a flashflood, the huge car began to float. I lowered the driver's side electric window just before the car went dead. Climbing out the window up to safety, I sat on top of the car until rescuers came to my aid. Knowing this car was the only valuable possession Larry had, I pleaded with the fireman to accompany me home to explain what had happened. You should have seen the look on Larry's face as he opened the front door to find me soaking wet, wrapped in a blanket, flanked by a couple of guys in rain gear! All he cared about was that I was safe. The car was towed to the gas station, where they checked the wiring.

Several weeks later, Wy got off the schoolbus at the station to drive the "repaired" Lincoln home. Just as she was pulling into our drive, the car shorted out, caught fire, and burned to the ground. I was just starting a 3:00 to 11:00 P.M. shift at the hospital, when I got an emergency call saying there was a fire at my home. Racing toward Del Rio in the Chevy, I could see the rising smoke and smell the burning rubber from far away. We hadn't had enough money to keep up car insurance payments either so the car was a total loss. "First the TV, now we've cooked your car too, Larry!" I apologized as sweetly as I could.

Getting good at smooth-talking, I convinced Elmer Alley at WSM-TV into letting us sing one song on the early-morning *Ralph Emery Show*. I played Elmer our tape from California and implored him to give us a chance.

Then I had to talk Wy into it because except for *The Merv Griffin Show*, we'd never even been in a TV studio. I used to tell her, "The first step to making a dream come true is to *wake up!*" Little did we dream we'd have to wake up at 3:30 A.M.!

When our big day arrived, we had to get up while it was still dark and cold to get dressed, put our makeup on, and do our hair. Then it was almost an hour into the WSM studio. We were the first ones to arrive that morning on February 11, 1980, and a groggy security guard looked at us like we were out of our minds. We were as jazzed as if we were debuting at Carnegie Hall!

As the band the Waking Crew nonchalantly straggled in with coffee, doughnuts, and the morning paper, their leader, Jerry White-hurst, began inquiring about our performance. When I said we were planning to do a song I wrote, "Daddy, Are You Coming Home Tonight?" he asked for the charts.

"The whats?" I asked.

"You know, the *charts!*" he repeated.

Knowing we'd be on live TV soon, I knew to come clean and get it over with.

"I have no idea what a chart is," I admitted flatly. "It's a song I wrote in my head." Wy reached for her guitar as I grabbed my harmonica and we plowed through a rendition just before the cameras began rolling.

Ralph sat behind his desk, giving the weather report, the local news, and so on, and announced us as we stood terrified and rigid at our microphones.

"And now here's a couple of newcomers named Wynanoma and Neonmaha er ah . . . or something like that!"

After our performance, the TV cameraman Jim Yockey came up and introduced himself as he made a prediction. He informed us he'd taped our debut because we were destined for stardom. Jim became our first supporter and a smiling face to welcome us each time we did the show.

As we were leaving, Ralph walked over during the commercial break and apologized for crucifying our names. Repeating them over and over till he could say them correctly, he admitted he couldn't swear to get them right the next time, because they were too difficult to pronounce this early in the morning.

We flinched because he'd just unwittingly invited us to return another time! Ralph wrinkled his brow and studied us silently for a minute. "My cue card says you guys are mother and daughter. But come on now! We can't lie to our viewers!"

Quickly excusing myself, I pulled my driver's license from my billfold and proved we were. Ralph still looking at us in disbelief, reminded us not to forget to sign our vouchers to get paid, as he returned to his desk. Get paid? The notion hadn't even occurred to us!

One of the musicians, Norm Ray, had been observing all this and stepped over to tell us where to collect our $25. Twenty-five bucks apiece. Wow, our first paying gig!!

We were so thrilled, I took Wy to Shoney's for breakfast to celebrate. I was mindful to have her back at Franklin High School for her first class at 8:00 A.M.

A week later, Norm Ray had car trouble on Del Rio Pike, and as he walked up our driveway to use the phone, he recognized the '57 Chevy and automatically knew it was our house. The next morning, he reported to everyone on the set about our old Maytag wringer washer on the porch and how he actually found me in the kitchen making lye soap.

When Wy and I returned to Ralph's show later that month to sing, everyone was more friendly to us. When time came to introduce us again, just as Ralph had suspected, he forgot how to pronounce our names. In frustration he looked straight into the camera and announced, "and now, in their second appearance, here's the Soap Sisters!"

It stuck and we were never able to shake that label. Over the next years, we performed a wide variety of songs from quirky, folksy things I'd written, to popular hits of the day. Spider, the guitar player, told me everybody at the show got a kick out of us, because they never knew what to expect. Jerry Whitehurst never asked us for charts again, and just gathered his band around us as we ran it down for them cold.

Before long we knew everyone in the studio. Fred, in the control room, kept a running tape I'd brought in to record our performances. Killer, Keith Bilbrey, and the rest of the gang made it a pleasant learning experience. Although it was a live show open to the public, no one in their right mind showed up at that hour except the parents of the baton twirler or perhaps some good Samaritan promoting a chili cook-off for a worthy cause. The only regular audience members were two spinster sisters named Maude and Dorothy. Later in the year I dreamed up a goofy skit, talked them into donning ridiculous costumes and participating in it. They were good sports.

One morning as Ralph was chatting with us after our song, Wynonna asked if she could make an announcement. Ralph obliged, whereupon the kid asked farmers watching to call the station if any of them had a weaned piglet to give her! She added that she planned to name it Tammy Swinette, if it was a girl. I promptly cornered the station's receptionist instructing her quietly to give me those offers.

Wy waited in vain for weeks, while I pocketed the numerous messages.

Then there was the time I sprained my ankle and a huge furry bedroom slipper was all that would fit on my painfully swollen foot. Showing up at the studio in a nice church dress but wearing the slippers, I warned the cameraman not to shoot me below my knees. Unable to stand for long, I sat on a stool as we crooned a beautiful, heartfelt ballad.

When Wy came in from school later that same day, she said the kids and teachers who'd watched the show thought I was simply hilarious. "Why, she never even cracked a smile!" they had laughed. The cameraman had not only shown full-length shots but had actually gone to close-ups of the dowdy slippers as I sat there singing my heart out, totally unaware.

By now we were getting fan mail addressed to "The Soap Sisters c/o WSM." Regular viewers wrote in asking us to be on more often. Guys asked me for dates. People wanted to know more about us. We saved and reread every piece.

Ralph was always very gracious to us. Knowing he'd been doing this stuff since before Wy was born, we were tickled whenever he'd come over and take time to chat with us. He'd put his arm around Wy and give her a word of encouragement before I took her to school.

Intrigued with the notion that I made my own soap, Ralph insisted I do a demonstration on the show. Setting up a table with my actual utensils from home and wearing my faded apron, I demonstrated the step-by-step process with comical Norm Ray as my assistant. It was $99\frac{44}{100}$ percent pure corn pone!

Having no money for store-bought gifts, Wy, Ashley, and I would give away our homemade soap as presents. After a batch had cured, we'd set up a production line around the dining room table. Ashley cut squares from brown paper grocery bags. Wy wrapped each bar in the paper. Then I tied it up with a piece of colorful fabric and stuck a small floral seal on it. We kept some on hand in a basket lined with calico.

I enjoyed making soap for many reasons. It kept me in touch with my Appalachian heritage and allowed me a sense of self-sufficiency. I liked giving friends something useful I had a hand in creating for them. And I believe it's good for you!

My soap's PH is 4.5, the same as human skin, plus it contains no harmful ingredients, chemicals, or preservatives. I usually add ground oatmeal for its palliative, soothing effect. Sometimes I stir in ground pumice for scrubbing extra-dirty hands. And I put borax in our laundry soap. I experimented with natural scents and colors, eventually perfecting my system.

One of Wy's teachers called me about making soap for her small child, who had a severe dermatological problem. It worked like a charm! I put a patent on "Naomi's Homemade Soap" and tossed it in my souvenir box with all my other ideas.

Meanwhile, Wy was becoming a minicelebrity at high school. Classmates sitting next to her in the eight o'clock class would turn and say, "Hey, didn't I just see you on TV a few minutes ago, while I was eating my Cheerios?"

If she was a little late arriving for her first class, we eventually didn't even have to write an excuse note, because someone working in the front office would pipe up and verify, "Yep, just saw her and her Mom on the *Ralph Emery Show*!"

Seems the only person who never saw us was Larry. We tried to schedule our appearances while he was on the road, but if he was home, I'd delicately slip out of bed. I could do the show and be back home cooking breakfast in my robe by the time he awoke.

The Stamps opened for Jerry Lee Lewis in Europe that February of 1980, and when he returned home, Larry was miserable. Since Elvis's death, the former gospel group's repertoire and stage show had to be revamped. Knowing they needed to go in the direction of mainstream country, he realized he had to break away from his mentor, bass singer J. D. Sumner. The entire Stamps group enthusiastically followed Larry—singers, band, and all. All except for Ed Enoch, who at the time was married to J. D.'s daughter and couldn't leave for obvious reasons.

So Larry replaced Ed with another lead singer, got western stage suits for the new "country quartet," and bought a used bus. His brother, Don, helped back the group and functioned as business adviser. Larry named his repackaged group "Memphis" in honor of all the time spent at Graceland with the King. Baritone singer Richard moved to a bigger apartment at the same Iroquois Apartments, and with a new secretary named Joan, he began booking the group. Memphis hit the road playing clubs and lounges.

Pushing forward myself, I followed a lead from a man I'd met at my meeting at the public TV station, where I'd taken my *Stories We Sing* radio show script. Craig Deitschmann co-owned The Sound Shop, a top recording studio near Music Row. In a perfect example of how I often got my foot in the front door, I told the receptionist I'd had business dealings with Craig, whereupon he'd suggested I talk to one of their in-house producers. Bingo! Sitting in Jon Schulenberger's office, I handed him the two-page bio I'd written myself, to read as I played our most recent homemade tape for him.

Then I auditioned him! After inviting Jon and his daughter out to Del Rio for supper, I saw he was a nice guy . . . a family man. Ashley took his daughter into her room, where they wrote and recorded a radio soap opera, while Jon, Wy, and I sat and talked business around the dining room table. He phoned back the next day saying we were the most unusual people he'd met.

But we were too original for Jon. A jingle producer, he wanted to try his hand at producing records, but chose to play it safe. His shortsightedness was to stay within the current *Urban Cowboy* crossover pop phase. Jon allowed that my organic, imaginative tunes intrigued and amused him, but said "they" wouldn't grasp them. I kept asking who "they" were.

Jon claimed he was riveted by what he called our "crystalline duet harmony." The impact of the image of the two of us was what compelled enough interest to sign a production deal, but he copped out at the last minute. Deciding instead to go with a Tanya Tucker–Brenda Lee teenage wunderkind, he proposed a demo of Wy as a solo. This had *never* occurred to Wy and me! Agitated and turned off by the idea, Wy wanted to walk away from him.

After some serious soul-searching and an old-fashioned ego check, I decided to let Jon go ahead and see what became of Wy's solo attempt. I've always considered myself a mom first and wanted whatever's best for my children.

Now sixteen and wearing braces (thanks to Mamaw and Papaw Ciminella), Wy did not enjoy making the four-song demo. Nothing about it felt right. Especially the hired backup singers.

Jon shopped the tape to every label in town, but was turned down by every single one. He did manage to get us in to see Jimmy Bowen, even though Jimmy had passed on the tape. Jimmy was one of the biggest guys in town and once inside his office, I went over Jon's head and impulsively jumped in singing along with Wy. Since she was ill at ease singing without me, I couldn't help supporting her. (Also, I wanted to sing too!)

Jimmy suddenly perked up and leaned forward on his desk. "You two are very unusual! This puts things in a new light. You're still raw and need a lot of practice—let me just tell you this, my door's open."

Too nervous to listen fully, I didn't get what Jimmy meant. I stood up to help Wy pack her guitar and exit, since I thought he was telling us to get out. Jimmy actually was instructing us to come back when we had it together a little better!

Jon simply wasted his time and ours, because he didn't get it. He even tried to get me to change our name, stating Judd was too hillbilly. I know I was extra work for him, because Jon confided that men would call his office asking for my home number after our meetings with them. I wasn't about to let Wy go places without me along for a chaperone, but I didn't mean to be such a distraction.

Wy and I performed at celebrity golf tournaments, at our Sunday-morning church service, Baptist Convention prayer breakfasts, United Way luncheons—anywhere we could sing in front of live human beings. So we could not only improve ourselves but also pacify Wy.

We both wanted to be in country music so badly but had very different goals. Wy just wanted to live on a bus, stay in motels, eat in restaurants, and play smoky clubs with sawdust floors. She'd use Larry's bus, parked by our barn, as a clubhouse, sitting in it for hours practicing. She'd take her friends out there and describe to them just how she would decorate the one we'd own someday. She wanted out of that boring high school. Alas, the only bus I'd let her ride was the big yellow one that stopped down at our mailbox early mornings and after school!

One day when she was being particularly restless, I drove her down to Franklin's small radio station WIZO and talked station manager Judy Hays into letting us go on the air. During the course of a half-hour live interview we also sang several songs. I, in turn, invited the Franklin paper, *The Review Appeal,* out to Del Rio to do a feature-length story, complete with homey photos of me making soap.

Still practicing at Nashville-area hospitals through the nurse's registry, I picked up extra money any way I could. I even modeled clothes in fashion shows at area department stores. Patsy Bruce headed the modeling agency on Music Row and used me to hostess conventions. Dressed like Scarlett O'Hara in an antebellum hoop skirt, I served salesman mint juleps. Another time I dressed like a cowgirl and met arrivees at the airport to escort them on a Silver Eagle bus to Opryland. She said my "egoless capacity for hard work allowed me to take jobs other girls didn't want." Although kind and very supportive, there wasn't much Patsy could do for us. When she was casting a TV movie called *Living Proof,* the Hank Williams, Jr., story, she urged me to come down and read for a tiny part.

"Are you out of your cotton-pickin' mind?" I responded. "I can't act—and don't even want to!"

"Relax, honey! All you have to do is wear one of your tight dresses, high heels, put a flower in your hair and kiss the star. I know you can do that!" she laughed.

I got the part and realized I was portraying the very thing I hated—groupies. Being a *Waltons* TV show fan, it seemed almost sacrilegious to kiss the family-style show's star, Richard Thomas, who was now playing the role of Hank, Jr. But I made $630—a huge amount of money for me. I had only one easy line in my brief walk on. It wasn't acting. It was really more like modeling.

I did some rather interesting things on my days off from the hospital. I got to appear on Conway Twitty's *Lost in the Feeling* album cover after he spotted a picture of me at a photographer friend, Dennis Carney's studio.

Besides enjoying his music and the soulful growl of his voice, Conway had always been intriguing to me, because he seemed to be exactly the kind of man I like. He was a man's man, charismatic and deep, I found it interesting that despite his superstar status, he appeared to have no vanity, no posturing. I was so excited about getting to find out for myself if he was actually as humble and down to earth as he appeared. Was his nice guy image real?

I knew within the first ten minutes that it was indeed! We spent the day side by side, first posing for the cover, then sitting in his '53 white Cadillac convertible. I tried not to act like a fan or mention our musical aspirations, but I felt so comfortable with him I began asking his advice on being in the music business. Being a great businessman, he said a lot of performers fail to save or invest their money. As we talked on, I questioned him about why I never saw him doing interviews. Conway cherished his privacy. He confided, "I prefer to let my songs do my communicating." Conway's utmost urging to me if I ever got into country music was, "Never discuss your personal life with the public!"

I listened intently and thanked Conway graciously for sharing his practical words of wisdom. Yet I knew myself far too well ever to think for one minute that I could be as close-mouthed and discreet as he! Born wearing my heart on my sleeve, I was known for my honesty. "If you *really* want to know the truth, go ask Naomi!" my fellow nurses had recently told a coworker who was seeking opinions on her new perm.

I was a contestant on a country TV game show called *Fandango* hosted by Bill Anderson, and that led to being selected as a contestant on another country pilot.

I was the only white RN at the all-black Meharry Hospital for several months. I never bothered to ask whether I was sent there because I was the only registry RN experienced in working the intensive care and cardiac care units or whether I was the only one who volunteered to go. Eventually, I got my registry to get a "rent-a-nurse" contract with nearby Williamson County Hospital in Franklin, where Wy had been an asthma patient.

I loved the small, quality hospital and soon everyone who

worked there came to treat me as a regular staff member. Since I filled in wherever they were short handed, I got to work every department. As we sat eating in the cafeteria one night, a coworker who'd been there for many years pointed out that I seemed to know more employees than she did.

Known for my sense of humor, I sometimes got in trouble for laughing. As we were signing off charts at the nurse's station late one night, I was telling a hilarious story about something that had actually happened. It was so funny the girls began screaming with laughter and a couple of them dropped their metal clipboards on the Formica desk. From out of nowhere, the hospital supervisor appeared and sternly demanded to know what all the racket was about. The uproar was waking up patients and call lights began blinking. All the girls just stood around staring silently at their nursing shoes and not a one would rat on me. Stepping forward, I confessed to our supervisor and said although I was sorry, I couldn't guarantee it wouldn't happen again.

Fate assigned me to the room of a patient who held the key to unlock the door to our future. Dianna Maher, an angelically beautiful seventeen-year-old, had been badly injured in a car accident. Even though she was in a great deal of pain, she was never cross. Her mother, Janelle, and father, Brent, were glued to her bedside. My first impression of them was what a close-knit, loving family they were. Even younger brother Brian was concerned and solicitous. After a few days I'd grown very fond of Dianna.

I commented on the coincidence that my birth name was Diana and I had a brother who was also two years younger and named Brian! Suddenly, she recognized me from the *Ralph Emery Show*.

Dianna was a year ahead of Wy at Franklin High and said she and her Mom had often tried to get her Dad to watch us on Ralph Emery. "Dad co-owns Creative Recording Studio and is in the music business," she informed me. "We also raise Arabian horses so, unfortunately, he's always headed to the barn at that time of the morning. Mom and I told him how weird but how unusually good you were and that there wasn't anyone else quite like you. But since they never announce you ahead of time, Dad's never been able to watch you."

I drove home that night considering the relative roles that chance and personal determination play in anyone's life. Having always felt that "luck" is actually a matter of being prepared when an opportunity arises, I made my decision on how to follow up on this unlikely lead.

I never once mentioned my double life to Brent while taking care of Dianna in the hospital. Ethically, I felt I should wait until she was discharged to approach him. After she went home, on my very next day off, I summoned all the courage I could muster and walked into his recording studio with our demo tape in hand.

I was somewhat surprised when Molly, the friendly receptionist, took me to the back where Brent was working. No longer the capable in charge nurse gently explaining medical procedure to a worried father, I was out of my element and now on Brent's turf.

"Hi Brent! Remember me? I'm Ms. Judd, Dianna's nurse. You know, the one who always gave her pain shots on time?"

I was sort of laughing, jokingly insinuating that turnabout's fair play. He happily reported that his daughter was back at Franklin High and then I did the "Music Row handshake." That's when you extend your hand as if to shake hands but pass off a tape you're holding to your palm by your thumb.

I blurted out that I too had a daughter Dianna's age that I also loved very much. Politely, I asked for his consideration on our homemade tape made on our K mart $30 tape recorder. After pointing to our phone number on the tape, I turned to leave and asked him to give my regards to his family.

Every time the phone rang the next forty-eight hours, I'd almost break my stupid neck trying to get to it. Six weeks went by and I'd sadly resigned myself that our tape had wound up on Brent's scrap heap.

Sometimes it was hard to keep my spirits up. Still trudging from door to door on Music Row on my day off, I had nothing to show for our three years in Nashville, I'd met a lot of important rich men who were spiritually bankrupt, but this Brent Maher guy was different. Whenever I had doubts about whether we'd ever make it, I protected Wy from them. As far as she was concerned, it was just a matter of time.

. . .

We'd had a rough night in ICU at the hospital, and I was sleeping soundly the next morning when Wy began shaking my shoulder.

"Mommy, look outside! We gotta go get Ashley! My schoolbus just brought me home early 'cause they're predicting a huge snow-fall!"

The phone rang with Ashley letting us know she'd ridden her bus to Beth Inman's, her best friend. When they asked if Ashley could stay over to play in the snow, I said okay because our house wasn't comfortable in really cold weather.

As the white stuff piled deeper and deeper, Wy and I discourag-ingly knew what to expect. The pipes froze the first day and even the electric pump out in the little shed off the kitchen broke from the frigid temperature.

The rotting outhouse across from our barn was falling in, so we went out behind it. By the second day, Wy complained her buns were chapped from going out in the cold. The woodstove in her bedroom wasn't doing the job, so we wore sweaters over our long johns and flannel granny gowns. We had enough wood stacked on the porch, but by the third day we were running out of food.

I rationed it out to last several more days, because Del Rio was impassable. Wy was getting very cross and I too was suffering from cabin fever. Larry's group was playing at the Chisolm Trail Motel Lounge in Duncan, Oklahoma, and I was getting suspicious because he hadn't called in several nights. Then while I was checking on Ashley, our phone went dead.

Eventually, Wy and I got into such a horrendous fight, she locked herself in her room. Stuck in my bedroom feeling cut off from everyone, I was cold and miserable. The next morning I slipped into Wy's room to warm myself, while she'd gone outside to use the bathroom. I was stunned as I saw written on her wall in huge letters that she'd carved with a butcher knife, "I hate my mother." I hit rock bottom.

I'd been hoarding a can of salmon to make salmon patties and opened a can of green beans. I set her dinner on our tiny kitchen table that seated two. Across from her plate was my note. It read: "In this life, it's not what you get, but what you become. What are we becoming? What's happening to us??" I knocked at her door then hurried back into my room so she'd come out and eat.

On the fifth day, a man from church brought us some milk, eggs, and bread in his four-wheel-drive vehicle, and the phone service in our area was restored. Knowing our pipes had burst, we picked up Ashley and the three of us went to stay in Larry's empty apartment.

Reunited and comfortably warm, I was just luxuriating in my first bath in almost a week when the phone rang. It was a girl with a northern accent calling for Larry. It seems he'd left his shirt at her place and she also just wanted to tell him how much she missed him and loved him.

I immediately took care of getting our pipes fixed, and when we returned to Del Rio I hung Miss Cora Lee's quilt on the wall to cover Wy's blunt message to me and the world. I tore up every picture of Larry, stuffed his belongings in a Hefty bag and threw it out in the yard.

Every time the phone rang I expected it to be Larry, so when Brent Maher identified himself on the phone, I was caught off guard.

"Who are you guys—what are you?" he sounded puzzled.

Brent began to explain why we hadn't heard from him sooner. Living out in the country near us, he used his drive time to and from his studio in Nashville to listen to tapes. Ours had only just now reached the top of his stack.

"I almost ran off the road!" he exclaimed, still not telling me whether or not he liked what he heard.

"Well, do you think there's anything worth your time?" I wanted to know.

"My initial reaction is that it's wacky and different. How about me stopping by so we can talk?"

I felt shot through with electricity. When he came by on his way home from work the next evening, Wy and I were quite giddy. Informing him we had no living room, I pulled out a chair for him at our dining room table. The kerosene lamp in the middle of the table was lit and I observed Brent intently looking around the room at the framed Curtis photographs of Indians on the wall. A 1940s radio sat on a doily on a table beside a flea market floor lamp with a fringed shade. He was forming visual impressions of us.

We got right to it. Wy sat, guitar across her lap, anxiously waiting to commence. I was acutely aware we were in the presence of a blue ribbon music man, but she viewed Brent merely as another new person to play and sing with.

After plowing straight through several songs, Brent sat shaking his head and running his hands through his hair. Then came the barrage of questions: "Where'd those songs come from? Who came up with that arrangement? Wy, how long have you been singing and playing? Naomi, who taught you to do harmony that way?"

Brent offered that our voices were preternaturally sympathetic and genetically complimentary. Wy asked whether that was good or bad.

Then he asked to use our phone. We craned our necks as we strained to hear him out in the kitchen as he was informing Janelle that he was on his way home and couldn't wait to tell her what he'd discovered. Brent stepped back into the dining room, chuckling over our old-fashioned black phone, the kind where you hold the round ear piece up to your head, then speak into the mouthpiece on the top of the stationary stand.

He kept coming back. I'd make Wy finish her homework and I'd have supper dishes done, so we could devote several hours to our meetings before her school-night bedtime. One minute we'd be into bluegrass tunes, then switch abruptly to western swing, before going on to a gospel or country segment. Brent let us carry on uninterrupted, playing along or thumping his thumb on his guitar for rhythm.

The three of us felt so completely comfortable together. We liked Brent immensely. Boyishly handsome, he was casual and good humored. It also occurred to me since we were the same age and he was the father of two teenagers, he might understand our mother-daughter ticklish relationship.

It was so natural, the way it all began. Brent would suggest I lay out on a verse to set up the chorus better. He'd show Wy some cool guitar licks or get us to change a tempo. He'd stop Wy and point out when he couldn't understand her words, to make her aware of enunciating better. Brent encouraged us to sing from our diaphragms and gave us positive reinforcement when we used dynamics in the rise and fall of volume.

After Brent left one evening, Wy, motionless in her chair still staring at the door, proclaimed: "Mama, I do believe somebody *finally* understands us."

One Man Woman

RENT MAHER WAS like water after a drought. When we were scheduling our next practice session one night, he announced he'd be bringing someone special with him the next trip and wanted to spend the afternoon. Even at this early stage, our trust in Brent was so complete, Wy and I knew we'd like whoever it was, before we even laid eyes on him.

So when they pulled up that Saturday afternoon, Wy, Ashley, and I excitedly ran out to greet a prematurely gray-haired fellow with glasses. There was something very different about Don Potter, but I couldn't quite put my finger on it.

He was so soft spoken and unassuming. I kept looking over at him to be sure he was absorbing what Brent was telling us about him. Originally from Rochester, New York, Don had been playing guitar most of his life and had been Chuck Mangione's lead guitarist. Ah ha! This at least explained why we were already picking up on some jazz lingo in his conversation. When I asked what he was doing now in Nashville, Don grinned and said simply, "I'm a carpenter."

"One thing at a time!" Brent intervened. "Girls, let's go in and play something for Don."

Halfway through our first song, "John Deere Tractor," I glanced across the dining room table, and saw that Don had his eyes shut and was smiling to himself. Without a word, he picked up his Gallagher guitar and began playing along. There was some sort of instantaneous link between him and Wy. Her eyes followed his hands and you could see him pulling her along. Don Potter was a maestro. Every few songs we'd stop and chat, getting to know one another, weaving pieces of our life stories around music.

During a break, I did something embarrassingly shallow. Larry had been calling, begging me to give him another chance so I knew it was him when the phone rang. In an attempt to make Larry jealous, I tried to get Don to answer the phone. Instead, Don quietly asked me to take a walk with him down our country road.

In his kind and nonaccusing way, Don began talking to me about jealousy and guilt. He allowed that although guilt may force us to do the right thing, love naturally encourages us to do the right thing. He suggested I honestly consider how I really felt, what I truly wanted and get in touch with my feelings, instead of blindly lashing out and striking back. Before we stepped back into the house, Don looked straight at me with those understanding eyes and said, "To err is human, to forgive divine." As I lay in bed in the dark later that night, I couldn't stop thinking about this new person in our life. Don never once mentioned God, yet I felt like I'd been in church.

And so it was that a remarkable personal and professional relationship began. In the months that followed, as Brent, Don, Wy, and I gathered around the kerosene light in the sanctum of that darkened room, a bond was being formed. We'd laugh till our sides hurts. Our heads bobbing up and down in agreement, we'd slap our knees in approval. The most beautiful part was that finally, somebody was tuned into us. Brent and Don "got it." In spades!

From day one, Brent encouraged my songwriting. "You either got it or you don't, and girl, you were born with it!" I formed Kentucky Sweethearts Music Publishing for Wy and me. We laid down all eighteen songs I'd written and mailed it to ourselves. I pitched this "poor man's copyright" into my bulging souvenir box.

When Brent and Don asked to see our eclectic record collection, they said it looked like a vinyl Whitman Sampler! We'd been demonstrating how all the different subcultures we'd lived in had added to our repertoire. Don said an evening with us was "an audio mosaic."

Finally, at one session the three of us ganged up on "Brown" (as Don called Brent), demanding in mock, whiney voices to know what musical direction our "fearless leader" (as Wy called him), was going to take us. Rubbing his palms up and down over his face in pretend anguish, Brent responded in a dramatic wail, "It's just Judd music for cryin' out loud!" There was no conceit behind this label, since no one knew or cared who we were.

Wy was just a kooky minicelebrity at Franklin High because of our *Ralph Emery Show* appearances. She performed the Eagles hit "Desperado" in the school talent show and won. After she continued to win all the subsequent talent contests, they permitted her to enter but wouldn't let her be in the final judging. She also had a talent for driving me nuts!

While I was at work, Wy let underage Ashley drive the Chevy, whereupon they tore down a neighbor's fence. The cracked windows and dented fender demoted our car to the ranks of a beat-up wreck, instead of a cherished prize. I sadly covered Redhot with old blankets and parked it out beside the barn. There just wasn't any money to get it fixed.

Wy devised a nifty scheme to get her hands on easy bucks. Because our tiny refrigerator didn't have a freezer, we were constantly going to Kroger. She began returning canned goods for cash refunds. When I'd notice that sections of the cupboard were missing, she'd grin and claim, "Hey, I'm a growin' kid!"

If I was missing plates or pots, I'd march straight in and peek under Wy's bed. There among the huge dustballs were dishes covered with a funguslike growth that looked as if it could glow in the dark. When I confronted her the first time, she alleged it was for "a science project." I teased new visitors that they should have a tetanus shot before entering her messy room. She complained, "Just when I get it the way I like it, you make me clean it up!" And since objects taken through Wy's door tended to disappear forever, Ashley hung a sign on it which read, THE BERMUDA TRIANGLE.

I'd picked Ashley up from cheerleading practice after school one afternoon and we went shopping at Wal-Mart. While there, Ashley was attacked by a pedophile in broad daylight. We were talking and laughing while pushing the cart together. Not long after Ashley left to go to the back of the store to get an item on our list, I heard terrified screams. As I looked up, an unsavory-looking man ran past!

As I took off to find Ashley, she suddenly came running toward me with her face in her hands, sobbing. "That awful man!" was all I could understand.

At the top of my lungs I hollered, "Stop that guy!" as I bolted to chase after him. Racing down the aisles up toward the front of the store, I could see him way ahead of me going out the entrance. Male customers, cashiers, security, and the store manager were in pursuit headed toward the parking lot. A teenage boy leapt across the hood of a compact car and nabbed him.

By the time I got to the creep, they had him surrounded and in custody. Walking up to him, I made a tight fist and reared back to break his nose, but the security guard hastily reminded me he could press charges against me.

Thomas Gary Beard pled guilty and was convicted of aggravated sexual battery.

Dear, sweet Ashley! She surrounded herself with happy, well-rounded friends. At a school game, one of the mothers, Jeri Trimmer, told me she was thrilled her daughter, Paige, had someone like Ashley Judd to grow up with.

Ashley was so deserving, yet I always felt I was neglecting her. One time I was so late picking her up after cheerleading practice, the school parking lot was deserted and it was getting dark as she sat waiting alone on the curb. That sight is etched in my mind. She patiently waited in lobbies with a book while I did my Music Row shuffle. Ever delightful to visitors like Brent and Don, she'd politely excuse herself to her bedroom to do homework as Wy and I practiced. As we were singing on the early morning TV show, Wy and I could look out over our microphones into the nearly vacant studio, where Ashley sat wildly applauding and cheering us on.

She was our biggest fan, but music just wasn't her thing. Refusing to wear makeup and having little or no vanity, she investigated modeling for its travel opportunities and, as I had, for the money. She entered a competition in New York and won! Under the auspices of a reputable, prominent New York agency, she flew to Tokyo, for two months of modeling during her summer vacation.

Ashley scared me silly! I knew she was smart, mature beyond her years, and a good girl, but my fifteen-year-old child was on the other side of the world. Piper, Ashley's godmother in San Francisco, was involved in teaching her elementary Japanese and setting up Tokyo connections.

Upon her successful return, she put her earnings in a money market fund and subscribed to *Time* magazine. She was runner-up in the Williamson County Junior Miss Pageant. She was astonishingly self-motivated, and I always knew Ashley would be a huge success in life. With her shoulders pulled back, her head held high, and that megawatt smile, she charmed everyone and radiated the confidence of a natural-born winner.

I went to parent-teacher conferences that fall to check on how she was relating to her peers after her amazing foreign adventure. "Her grades are excellent, and she could be the first woman president!" one of her teachers told me.

"Yeah, yeah, I already know all that part," I'd explain. "What I want you to enlighten me on is how she's relating to her classmates." When they all agreed she was down to earth and treated everyone equally and kindly, I went home relieved and proud.

But Ashley resented Larry, because of what she saw him doing to us. The best way to put it is this: Larry and I were crazy over each other—making us do crazy things. It was a comedy of Eros.

When Larry was on Del Rio Pike, it was our Shangri-La. He came home off the road to a spotless, cozy little haven complete with home-cooked meals set on a lace tablecloth. We'd take an evening walk down our country road, then sit on the porch and listen to the nighttime serenades of crickets and bullfrogs. Before bed, I'd scrub his back and bathe him in the old-fashioned bathtub on claw legs.

Larry loved Wy and Ashley like they were his own and knew I was a one-man woman, so he felt secure with his ready-made family. We represented everything Larry had been raised to value and esteem. He called us every night from the road to get his daily dose of home. I'd recite the litany of everyday occurrences, the cat had kittens, report cards, the car broke down, and so on.

Our favorite pastime was driving around Williamson County looking for our dream farm. We'd pick out land and discuss houses, planning a life together. The problems came when we weren't together.

Since forming his group Memphis, Larry had nothing but head-aches. Unable to afford a bus driver and wary of entrusting the wheel to the guys in the group, Larry drove all night after singing on stage. The secondhand bus broke down frequently. He also functioned as the road manager, checking into cheap motels and taking care of all the problems, such as the guys charging incidentals to their room and sticking him with the tab. Larry had to handle equipment, sound checks, getting their money out of disreputable club owners . . . everything.

Playing clubs and lounges for several weeks at a stretch was dangerous. Word spread like wildfire among local girls that there were four handsome male entertainers in town doing two shows a night, with a half dozen musicians to boot. Starstruck girls threw their underwear and door keys onstage. They strutted in their bikinis out by the pool during the day and knocked on the motel room doors at night. All four of the singers had girls in every town, and these girls had girlfriends! There were also legions of groupies from the Elvis days, who followed them all over the country. It was another world out there.

Larry'd just come in off the road in the middle of the night and the next morning I spotted a handsome, new gold watch lying on the bedside table. Naturally curious, since he gave me every dime he had, I held it up to examine it. On the back was engraved "I love you." After fetching my hammer, I shook Larry's shoulder to awaken him. The watch lay only inches from his head, as I smashed it to smither-eens. "Your skull is next if this ever happens again!" I warned.

I turned into a bloodhound. I checked his clothes, his luggage, his bus. If I found a phone number on a cocktail napkin in feminine handwriting, I became uncannily adept at calling and obtaining infor-mation.

I swiped his post office box key and went through his mail. My jealousy bordered on pathological. All this was terribly intimidating and threatening. Here I was in my discount-store dresses and flea-market accessories, forever scrubbing away at our old house—not to mention, cleaning up vomit, emptying bedpans, and doing dressing changes at the hospital. I didn't feel very glamorous, but when Larry was home I always tried to look my best. I wore makeup and fixed myself up even when doing chores.

Larry presented me with a diamond ring and asked me to marry him. We were so deliriously happy at the time, and I told myself someday I could say yes. It was the "love-of-a-good-woman" theory. But soon thereafter, he left to spend three weeks in Fargo, North Dakota. I called his room in the middle of the night, and his sleepy roommate had no choice but to tell me Larry wasn't there. Larry sometimes used the alibi he was sleeping out on the bus, because, conveniently, there was no phone on it, but . . . this time it was below zero outside! I lost it. Unable to eat or sleep, I stayed up the better part of three days and nights and writing a song to release my anguish. In my delirium I imagined Larry singing "Change of Heart" to me.

By the time he returned home, I was really over the edge. I went for my .38 and shot over his head, breaking our dining room window and threw him out for the umpteenth time . . . until he came back swearing his undying love for me, perpetuating the same old vicious circle. I was so emotionally tangled I couldn't refuse him.

I felt myself being transformed into a monster before the girls' eyes. If my pride wasn't quite ready to take Larry's remorseful calls, I'd get Wy to answer the phone. I even got her to call one of those girls to tell her to leave our family alone.

Daily, I demanded respect from my children, although they saw I had no respect for myself. Through thin walls, they overheard dreadful scenes, followed by apologies, vows, and assurances. Finally, I began to realize my behavior was damaging my adolescent daughters, who might be forming patterns for their own future male-female relationships. Not to mention that a teenager already has more than enough confusion and inner wrestling without the added pressure of dealing with a neurotic parent in the house!

Wy's reaction to Larry was more complicated than Ashley's. Ashley witnessed how we existed on beans and corn bread, oatmeal and veggies until Larry's return. Then it was fried chicken and baked desserts. It was the ol' "trade you a potato for a piece of meat" story.

Ashley likened my on again–off again attachment to Larry with picking at a scab, which keeps the wound from healing.

Wy despised our domestic turmoil but had a vested interest in Larry's musical status. After all, he had a group, a band, stage wardrobe, equipment, and a bus! Besides being her clubhouse, his big Silver Eagle bus was a tangible reminder that she might have one someday herself. Wy arranged for Memphis to perform at a special program at high school so she could sing several numbers with them, thereby catching the attention of a certain football player. We'd go to Cajuns Wharf in Nashville to hear Memphis perform several times a year. Everyone in the group treated Wy as if she were one of them. She so admired Larry's smooth stage presence and amazing bass voice and was proud as a peacock to be seen with him. Pretty heady stuff for a seventeen-year-old aspiring entertainer!

I saw the gritty reality behind the scenes with Memphis and was learning from it. Not only was the group not progressing, but I wasn't about to put Wy through this lifestyle. Larry seemed willing to go through hell just to sing.

That, I could understand. But I wanted more . . . much more! I realized that having talent wasn't enough. It takes talent to have talent! Memphis was great but missed out on the big time because they didn't get a manager, producer, booking agency, or a record deal.

So I decided to profit from my association with Larry by doing just the opposite of him. As usual, I was determined to turn something negative into something positive. I'd find a manager and producer first, then secure a record label so I had help in putting all the rest together: learn from yesterday, live for today, hope for tomorrow.

On June 24, 1982, I drove out to Opryland to visit my *Hee Haw* crew buddies and trade war stories about our failed Las Vegas TV special fiasco. Ricky Skaggs was the guest star and remembered me from Emmylou's concert back in California; he came over to ask what I was doing in Nashville. "When my daughter graduates from high school, we want to get into country music too!" I chirped, pleased by his friendliness. "We're on the lookout for somebody who can help us."

As we chatted about the coincidences of being from eastern
Kentucky and bumping into each other all over the country, I became
aware of a bearded man chomping on an unlit cigar behind Ricky.
The fellow wore a tweed jacket with patches on the sleeves and
looked as if he'd been frightened by a callous at an early age, and
. . . he was definitely eavesdropping on us. As soon as Ricky left to
tape his number, the man introduced himself as Woody Bowles.

Woody stated he was in PR, and I interrupted to ask what that
might be. "Public Relations, but no, I don't have 'relations' in
public!" He snorted. This guy had a humorous streak a mile wide.

He questioned me regarding the daughter I sang with and asked
if I had a picture of her. I whipped out my proud mom assembly of
Wy's and Ashley's school pictures.

As he kept looking back and forth between my face and Wy's
photo, Woody asked how far along we were. I answered, "Mister, all
we've got is a demo of my original songs made on our cheap tape
recorder. Believe me, we've still got the bark on!"

Woody stuck his card under my nose and advised me to come
see him, adding "bring your daughter and everything you've got."

"She and her sister are all I've got, but we'll be there!" I
promised.

I'd set our apointment for 4:00 so I could pick Wy up after
school. I brought her best dress and excitedly she changed in the
girls' restroom for our Music Row audition. As we walked up to
Jan Rhees, who worked in Woody's office, it was a new and wonderful feeling to know we were expected, instead of having to talk
our way in.

Woody began by making polite chitchat, but I was more direct.
"It would mean a lot to us if you'd give us your professional opinion." I nodded over at Wy and we took off singing.

Woody only sat there, his feet propped up on his desk, chomping on his unlit cigar. He looked at us blankly after we'd done several
tunes.

"Well?" I asked softly as I leaned forward in anticipation. Slowly
taking his legs down from the desk, he settled down into his chair and
raised his hands back behind the top of his head.

"Please! Say *something*!" Wy and I were becoming uncomfortable.

"Gold mine," he uttered.

"What do you mean?" I pleaded.

"You're a gold mine," he repeated, his tone understating his glowing review of our performance.

"When do we start?" Wy wanted to know.

My mind flashed to a fantasy scene. Porter Wagoner was introducing us on the stage of the *Grand Ole Opry*. As Wy and I came out covered from head to toe in diamonds, the audience rose to greet us in thunderous applause. Larry, Ashley, Mom, and Dad were front row center, flanked by the president, Jack Nicholson, and Mildred Rigsby, my fourth grade teacher. They all wore sunglasses because of the glare from the brilliance of our outfits. Just then a farmer in overalls came waddling down the aisle carrying a pig under his arm, calling to Wy up on stage that she could finally have a pet swine. I was brought back to reality by Woody calling my name.

"Naomi, do you have any contacts at all?" I suggested he talk to Brent Maher, whereupon both men agreed to work with us on just a handshake, until we saw what we could come up with.

Woody flew out to Los Angeles to play our funky demo for Dick Whitehouse, the vice president of Curb Records, an independent label. Intrigued, Dick came to Nashville where we auditioned for him live in his hotel suite. Liking what he heard, he threw his hat in the ring too.

We did a four-song demo session at Brent's studio, to enable future listeners to obtain a perfectly clear idea of what we sounded like. This informal prerecording session with just Brent, Don, Wy, and me was effortless and fun. There was no band, just clean vocals bolstered by Don's cool guitar.

PR guys like Woody Bowles don't enter the picture until after a record's been cut and the act is polished and ready to present to the buying public. Then the PR person orchestrates the media exposure.

So what we really needed first was a manager. Someone with ethical business acumen; a sterling reputation; a smooth-running, well-staffed office; and loads of money to invest. Woody had a prospect.

Although Woody described Ken Stilts, Sr., as a prosperous, well-established, local businessman, I didn't get too excited. It almost sounded as if Ken had so much money he didn't know what to do with it, so he figured he'd dabble in the excitement of the music business. Ken had a small record label, Dimension, with Ray Price, Sonny James, and Eddy Raven on the roster.

While driving to Woody's office to meet Ken for the first time, it began to dawn on me the seriousness of the business side to being an artist. It's the flip side of the impulsive creativeness.

Ken rose as we walked in the room, causing me literally to stop dead in my tracks. He looked for all the world like a mafia don in his custom-tailored black suit; silk tie; expensive loafers; humongous gold, diamond-studded Rolex; and diamond pinky ring. While he firmly shook my hand and said, "Good evening, Miss Judd," in a deep voice, I glanced around the room halfway expecting to see bodyguards sporting sunglasses standing at attention.

Instead he was accompanied only by his secretary, Martha Taylor, an attractive, serious-looking woman slightly younger than myself. Wearing a gray tailored suit and sitting up perfectly straight in her chair, Martha balanced a burgundy leather briefcase across her lap.

Ken and Martha reeked of success and accomplishment, and they looked very, very serious. As Wy pulled out her guitar, we were so uptight we felt as if we were being asked to perform brain surgery in front of them.

Smiling weakly at them between numbers, I couldn't get so much as a twitch out of Ken. As we sang, I could feel Martha's eyes on me and was aware she was checking out my inexpensive dress and shoes. Why couldn't I be legitimate and normal like her? Oh well.

After we finished, Ken asked a couple of basic questions in a businesslike tone. I somehow didn't feel it was appropriate to be my usual lighthearted, talkative self, and I could only respond in stiff, short sentences.

As he thanked us for coming, Wy shot me an all-too-familiar look. Packing her guitar back inside its case she looked up at me with an expression that said, "Okay, they hate us and we wasted our time getting dressed up and driving all this way. You're going to have to take me to McDonald's to make up for this one!"

On the way home (as we chomped away on our Big Macs), I reminded her, "Honey, we've got to keep doing this until we meet somebody who wants us."

Surprisingly, Woody called the next morning to announce Ken and Martha liked what they'd heard. Ken requested we come out to his office complex, S & S Industries, in Mt. Juliet, for phase two. As we drove into the headquarters for the multimillion-dollar manufacturing company he'd taken over at the age of thirty, I realized Ken Stilts was indeed a man who could get things done.

Sitting behind his massive desk in his fancy office, Ken began to quiz us. Feeling at a disadvantage because I knew nothing yet about this reserved inscrutable man, I tried to extrapolate information from the surroundings. A huge oil painting of his pretty, teenage daughter, Tina, hung directly behind him. Family photos covered both the walls and his credenza.

We met his likeable son Ken Stilts, Jr., who worked down the hall and learned the other son, Steve, managed the Knoxville plant. As we walked down the corridors we were introduced to Ken's three brothers, five sisters, and six nephews, all of whom worked for him! I asked if the word *nepotism* meant anything to him.

Wy exclaimed, "Man, you believe in family in a big way!" Then something happened that confirmed my evaluation of Ken. We met his wife, Jo. She was probably the sweetest woman we'd ever met in our lives, and we would have signed a management contract right then and there because of her.

I suggested Ken go ahead and start drawing up a management agreement, in the event that they proved themselves by landing us a record deal, but he hollered, "Whoa! You got the cart before the horse! You need to sign the management deal with us first—then we'll worry about a recording contract!"

With an "I-ain't-budging" expression he stared me down until I declared, "Okay, begin the first draft." Ever the gentleman, he escorted us out of the building. At the door, I turned to him with this promise: "Ken, if you decide to work with Wynonna and me, I promise you'll find us infinitely more interesting and rewarding than all your previous business ventures."

I had never seen a contract of any kind before, so the one he presented to us looked like instructions on how to build a nuclear reactor! The first of many red flags went up when I found out we were expected to give Ken power of attorney to sign checks for us. I'd had to overcome great hardships to win my independence and I'd been on my own a long time now. It was thoroughly distasteful to me and terribly retro to have to answer to men again.

He sent revisions, but I was taking my sweet time, railing all the while against this specter of male dominance.

It seems Ken, Woody, and Brent believed so strongly in us, they'd decided to start at the top and had played our tape for the new head of RCA, Joe Galante. Boasting a roster that included Alabama, Dolly Parton, Kenny Rogers, and Ronnie Milsap, RCA was the number one label in country music and "Boy Wonder" Joe Galante was aggressive and innovative.

Based on our demo and Ken, Woody, and Brent's enthusiastic admonishment that Wy and I needed to be seen in the flesh to be fully appreciated, Joe agreed to an unprecedented live audition. Brent asked Joe to toss the conventional rules and expectations out the window and confessed that we had neither bio, photos, nor a band. This unusual meeting was scheduled at RCA. Ken and Woody had such high hopes for its outcome, they were frantic to lock us into management beforehand.

Feeling the pressure, I decided to get away from the kids and housework, to go on the road with Larry's group for a few days to concentrate on the contract. Memphis was playing in Lakeland, Florida. I was surprised to discover Ken had gone to his second home in nearby Tampa so he could invite all of us over.

When Memphis's bus pulled up in front of Ken's beautiful home, I was somewhat embarrassed as the scraggly band members and their groupie girlfriends poured out, but Ken welcomed us graciously and even had a buffet prepared. It was my first glimpse into his enormous capacity for hospitality and kindness. While the others partied around the pool, Ken and I sat hunkered over the final draft of that pesky contract.

Early the following morning, March 1, as Memphis was fueling up for the drive to their next gig in Dallas, I phoned Ken from a truckstop to let him know I had approved our compromise. To my surprise, Ken said he'd meet me in Dallas that evening, to do the signing. The RCA audition was the very next day, and I realize now he would have flown to Timbuktu!

We met up at a steakhouse for dinner before Larry's show. Ken sat across the table from Larry and me chain-smoking Marlboros, downing martinis, and pouring salt on a thick, bloodred steak. I observed that this busy man was also a classic Type A personality and was overweight. Having just spent the last month working the cardiac care unit at the hospital, I had a hard time keeping my mouth shut!

This is where a facet of our unique relationship began. Ken, the immovable mountain: hard, stationary, towering, and intimidating. Me, with my X-ray eyes, seeing the dangerous hot lava inside the mountain.

After dinner we retired to the lounge area of the restaurant, where I signed the contract. Patrons around us were glued to the TV, watching the final episode of *M*A*S*H*. Ken remarked that he too was looking forward to a long successful run, but stressed one thing: "I manage *both* of you. I will never manage one without the other."

As the ink dried, I handed the pen back to him and joked, "I hope you know what you're getting yourself into! You just became number one on my list of whom to call if anything breaks!"

We hurried over to the Belle Star Club, where Ken and I enjoyed Memphis's show. Shortly before the end of the set, Ken appeared tired and excused himself, saying he was going to bed. I assumed it was because he had to get up early and fly to Nashville for our big meeting at RCA. Alone back in his hotel room, Ken suffered a heart attack and called 911.

Oblivious to Ken's emergency, Memphis loaded up right after the show and Larry drove the bus all night. As he pulled into Del Rio, I crawled out of the bunk, fresh from eight hours sleep and walked into the house. Wy ran to meet me and blurted that Woody had just called with the shocking news that Ken was in the critical care unit in a Dallas hospital.

Reaching for the phone to call and find out Ken's condition, I thought of a line from an old song: "The Rockies may crumble, Gibraltor may tumble . . . ."

Ken was alive and had been stabilized. Relieved, I remembered our RCA audition was that very afternoon and hastily told Woody to postpone it.

Reciting Ken's phone instructions to Wy and me from his bed in the CCU, Woody repeated Ken's insistence we follow through with the plan. After hanging up, I sat at the kitchen table staring out at the field for a long time. Had I put too much pressure on Ken by not signing his management deal sooner? I felt guilty for not speaking out about his health risks back at the steakhouse the night before. What should I have done? Leapt across the table, snatched the cigarette from his mouth, ground it out in his steak and tossed the drink over my shoulder?

Then I noticed that my two cherished aloe vera plants' leaves were missing. I blinked my eyes at the bare branches sticking out of the pots. I'd lovingly transported the healing plants all the way across the country from Marin County so that I could make salve and ointments for skin irritations. It dawned on me that Wy and Ashley had let their rabbit loose in the house. Searching under everything, I found the big-eared culprit and chased it all over the house. Have you ever tried to catch a bunny when it didn't want to be caught?

Clutching Thumper tightly to my chest like a quarterback carrying a football, I raced out the back door headed toward my goal, the open field. Wy and Ashley were right on my heels in hot pursuit, screaming their protestations. I was angry about my plants, upset that the girls had disobeyed me (what else had they done while I was gone?), worried about Ken, scared and nervous about our audition.

When Brent came to pick up Wy and me to go to RCA at 5:30 P.M., she was still furious with me. Driving toward Music Row, I thought about how things couldn't have been in a bigger mess for this auspicious occasion: Ken had suffered a heart attack and Wynonna was barely speaking to me.

As Brent pulled into the narrow alley behind RCA, we had to pass right by the Fender Building's small parking lot. The way things were going I halfway expected my former boss, Jeff, to jump out and resume chasing after me. And there sat the big green Dumpster, where I'd hauled all our garbage. Such fond memories.

Stress is when your body shoots bullets and your mind shoots blanks. As we walked down the halls of RCA, past the gold and platinum albums lining the walls, Brent was jumpy, and Woody's lips were clamped so tightly around his cigar they were almost blue. As we turned to enter Joe Galante's board room, I reached over and grabbed Wy's hand. "Just remember, honey, these big guys are all naked under their suits!" She finally smiled back at me and squeezed my hand.

Mr. RCA was wearing a Hawaiian-type sport shirt and tennis shoes! And Joe and Randy Goodman, the vice president, were so young looking! Producers Tony Brown and Norro Wilson were also casually dressed and surprisingly friendly. Wy commented she expected to find them in sharkskin suits, wearing bags over their heads with just the eyes cut out.

Our nervousness was palpable. "We invited you for six tonight so everyone would be gone and we'd be undisturbed," Joe remarked, attempting to break the ice. Someone offered us Cokes, which I promptly spilled on my antique black velvet dress.

Mercifully, Joe suggested we play something for them. We suddenly felt as if they'd thrown a blinding spotlight on us. I noticed a fireplace in the room and instinctively took Wy's elbow and led her to it. Pulling up a footstool and chair, we settled down facing each other and I locked eyes with Wy. I vaguely heard Woody suggesting songs for us to perform, but I shut him out.

What I said next wasn't so much for the executives' benefit or to set up the song, but to ground Wy and me. I expressed how we gravitated to our own fireplace back at Morrill to sing together in the evenings after suppertime. To remind us who and what we are, we returned to our roots with the first song we learned, "A Mother's Smile."

As our voices glided through the air, the board room fell away and Wy and I were transported back to that mountaintop of years ago. When we finished, we looked over at the row of faces of the men who'd pulled their chairs up in a straight line beside us. Joe said nothing, just waved his hand sideways toward us motioning us to go on.

After several numbers, we remained perfectly still and looked to them for some sort of reaction. The listeners sat with arms on their chairs, heads bowed, glancing over at whoever was next to them out of the corner of their eyes.

Spontaneously, Wy did something that made me want to pop her. "Hey, Mom just wrote the coolest song! Ya'll want to hear it?" Of course the men politely said sure as I stammered a disclaimer, "Wait a minute—it's not a real song, 'cause I wrote it." Too late.

We'd barely finished singing when Norro Wilson finally spoke out. "Man, if that ain't a number one song, I'll quit this business!" The men rose to their feet, and Joe asked us to let them talk in private.

Assuming he meant "Go home and practice some more. Wy, clean your room and grow up. We'll get back to you," we thanked everyone and were shaking their hands as Joe finished by adding, "Go over to O'Charley's restaurant and wait on us. We'll join you there in a few minutes."

We looked to Brent as if to say "what's going on here?" and he headed us off to the restaurant. Wy and I babbled simultaneously or sat silently staring down at our plates. Although we rarely got to eat out in those days, we were too preoccupied to enjoy our dinner.

In walked the label men who held our fate in their hands. They stuck out their hands and loudly announced, "Congratulations, you're now RCA recording artists!"

Brent jumped up out of his seat and started hugging us. Wy and I faced off and began flapping our arms up and down at our sides like chimpanzees, oblivious that we were smack in the middle of a crowded restaurant. Bumming a couple of quarters from Brent, I made a beeline for the pay phone.

When Daddy accepted the collect long-distance call and I started off with my customary "It's Diana, guess what Daddy?" I could almost see his eyes rolling back in his head and hear him thinking, "Oh no, what in heavens name is she up to this time?"

"We just got a recording contract with RCA! We're going to be in country music, and I wanted you to be the first to know!"

There was a long silence on the line. Daddy came back with, "Gosh honey, surely you won't quit your job at the hospital, will you?" I flashed back to that afternoon I'd proudly handed him my honor roll report card, only to have him notice that one teacher had marked "whispers too much." Realizing he couldn't share my joy, I changed the subject. I asked if his kidney transplant was still giving him trouble, and he went on to fill me in about his dogs and the new jeep he'd bought to go to the farm.

Momentarily deflated, I looked back at our table where Wynonna was enjoying one of the happiest moments of her life. I dialed home where Ashley had been waiting by the phone. Our little cheerleader squealed with enthusiasm. Larry was happy but baffled.

On the drive back home, after Brent, Wy, and I settled down, I sat alone in the backseat considering how ironic it was that the two most important men in the world to me didn't understand our music. And yet, strangers did.

Turn It Loose

G OING STRAIGHT HOME right after hearing news that would change our lives seemed so anticlimatic! Wy and I didn't want to get out of Brent's car. We wanted to go stay at a hotel and order room service!

Once inside, Wy and Ashley and I threw back our heads, whooped, jumped up and down, then twirled round and round in the middle of the kitchen floor till we were dizzy and exhausted. I called Ken's house to be sure they got word to him in the hospital out in Dallas that we had gotten a contract with RCA.

I couldn't wait to tell the other nurses at work the next day, but I realized this might sound boastful so I kept it to myself. Everyone worked so hard, and we were all on the same level.

I waited till my Friday night off to celebrate and headed into town to meet my Music Row girlfriends. Wy was spending the night with Mindy Gentry, her best friend, and fifteen-year-old Ashley wanted to stay home alone. As I kissed her good-bye, Ashley nonchalantly asked me to call before starting on my way home.

Asking any parent to "call before you come home" is bound to raise suspicion. I didn't make it far from Del Rio before curiosity got the best of me and I turned around and headed back. Sure enough, a strange car was in the drive and as I approached the back porch I could hear boys' laughter intermingled with Ashley's. Bursting in, I surprised two hefty Franklin High School football players with beers in their hands standing in the kitchen. Ashley was just reaching to put their six-packs in the refrigerator.

Furious, I grabbed a butcher knife from the drawer and waved it wildly in the air, back and forth at the boys. Taking hold of one's varsity jacket, and getting right up in his face, I hissed at him through clenched teeth that I was half-crazy and suggested he warn his other beer-drinking friends not to ever come around again when I wasn't home.

His terrified partner fled out the door. I heard his car come roaring through the yard right up to the back. The boy I had hold of broke loose, bolted to safety and the pair sped off into the night. I began yelling at Ashley and she yelled back.

She was now a cheerleader at Franklin High, and to remind her of the rules, I went to the school office and pulled her from the squad. Ashley was petulant for several weeks.

Raising teenagers is always difficult, but it's even more so if they're pretty, resourceful, and willful females. When you're a single mom forced to work every night, leaving them alone out in the country can make you resort to desperate, drastic measures—such as feigning craziness.

My buddy who owned the Fifth Avenue Shell station thought I should know that Wy had a crush on his gas attendant, who was in his midthirties. As you might well imagine, I was not pleased to learn that an older man with worldly experience was coming by Del Rio in my absence to see Wynonna. Pulling in at the gas pump, I rolled the window down to ask him to fill up my car. As he reached in to hand me my change, I petted my .38 revolver lying beside me on the seat.

"Let's get something perfectly clear, Romeo," I calmly began. "My daughter's underage and I'm half-crazy. Therefore, I highly suggest you victimize someone your own age who's mother isn't an expert marksman."

Wy was solemn for the next few days so I knew my drama had been well received.

As I was leaving for work one afternoon, the local Fotomat called to inform me our pictures were ready to be picked up. "What pictures?" I inquired, puzzled. Overhearing my part of this conversa-

Harmonizing on the front porch right after moving to Franklin,
Tennessee, summer of 1979.

Ralph
Emery,
host of an
early-
morning
Nashville
television
show,
called
them
"The
Soap
Sisters,"
late
1981.

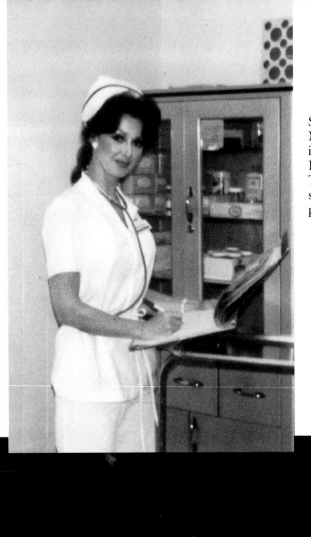

September 1982:
Naomi Judd, RN,
in Williamson County
Hospital, Franklin,
Tennessee, the week
she met record
producer Brent Maher.

Wy accompanied Larry
(*in background*) one
night on the road with
his country group
Memphis and per-
formed a song Naomi
had just written,
"Change of Heart."

Franklin, Tennessee, May 1983: Ashley was popular, smart, and well rounded. She went to her prom with producer Brent Maher's son Brian. Naomi helped her get ready.

At fifteen, Ashley went to Japan to model for two months in the summer; she already had the travel bug like Mom and Sis.

(COURTESY OF *GLOMESH*)

Franklin, Tennessee, 1984: Naomi, Wy, and Ashley in the backyard on Del Rio Pike.
(SLICK LAWSON)

Naomi always wore makeup and fixed herself up when Larry was home, even while doing chores.

With Brent and Don on Wy's twentieth birthday at the studio recording the *Why Not Me* album.

March 20, 1984: their first professional concert, in Omaha, Nebraska, opening for the Statler Brothers; they fought over who would get the sign off the door after the show. (JANEL MAHER)

Mike (Papaw) and Billie (Mamaw) Ciminella and godfather Clifford Weddle with Wy and Ashley backstage after the Judds opened for Ricky Skaggs at his home-coming, June 1984, in Louisa, Kentucky.

Combining business with pleasure. *Left to right:* Chuck Thompson, press agent; Martha Taylor, vice president, management; Earl Cox, hairdresser; Vanessa Ware, stylist, personal assistant; Wy and Naomi; and Nana (Polly Rideout, Naomi's mom). Wy's '57 Chevy, Redhot, has been restored. (PETER NASH)

Manager Ken Stilts and beloved wife, Jo, are the girls' extended family. They call Ken "Mr. Big."

At the American Music Awards in January 1991: Martha Taylor and Ken Stilts expertly handle all the business, leaving Wy and Naomi free to be themselves.

May 3, 1989: backstage at Bonnie Raitt concert with Raitt and Emmylou Harris—two of their musical influences who became their friends.

The wedding party. Naomi finally marries her Prince Charming, Larry Strickland, in a fairy-tale wedding, May 6, 1989. (PETER NASH)

There is a Judd family reunion every Thanksgiving at Nana's house in Ashland, Kentucky. *Left to right, back row*: Jamie Mandell, Margaret's husband; Larry; Wib, Naomi's stepdad; Tony King, Wy's friend; brother Mark holding Brian; and his wife, Middy Judd. *Center row*: Ashley; sister Margaret; Naomi holding Banjo; Margaret and Jamie's daughter Erin, holding Elvis and Little Bit; Nana; and Wy holding Loretta Lynn. *Bottom*: Allison and Joshua, children of Margaret and Jamie.

tion, Wy and Ashley began choking on their after-school snacks, sputtering for me not to concern myself with such a bothersome errand. They volunteered to ride their bikes into town to pick them up. It was pouring down rain.

Wild horses couldn't have kept me from that Fotomat. Those pictures were worth a thousand words! They showed bleary-eyed teenagers smashing beer cans on their foreheads, dancing throughout our house, jumping on my bed, and more.

Sitting in my car staring at this incriminating evidence, I immediately flashed back to one night when I came home from work at about 1:00 A.M. to find pieces of our furniture out in the front yard, the bushes trampled, and Miss Cora Lee's washtubs with water in them. Too exhausted to think straight at the time, I didn't put two and two together. But now I held in my hand a photo of our washtubs laden with iced down Budweisers.

Ashley was slick as snot on a doorknob, but Wy couldn't tell a good lie if her life depended on it (which it almost did sometimes!). Wy only skipped school once or twice but although she'd expertly forged my name on her note to the office, she got caught because of the pronoun: "Please excuse Wynonna Judd from school yesterday. I was sick."

Wy and I clashed constantly . . . over her grades, her refusal to help around the house, and her treatment of Ashley. Dramatic and overprotective, I was prone to overreacting.

Overworked and stressed to the max, I invited a friend to come over on my night off. That morning I painstakingly prepared my best recipe, left it in the refrigerator, and instructed the girls not to touch it. When I came in from running all the errands that had to be squeezed into my one afternoon off, the empty casserole dish sat in the stack of unwashed dishes.

Wy deliberately treated Dolly Gillespie, her friend from a well-to-do family, to our planned dinner. My friend was due in an hour and I had neither money nor time and energy to produce a replacement meal. I charged into Wy's room like a raging bull and chased her out of the house; she was in her slip.

Mamaw and Papaw had given her a car, and she swiped the

money from the sugar bowl and ran away for several weeks. She showed up at a club in Florida where Larry was performing, and he talked her into coming back home.

Wynonna was arm wrestling the universe. Sometimes violently angry, she seemed to resent me because I was all she had and she needed me so. It was an explosive mix for a teenager grappling with her need for independence. Crazy sounding as it may be, she loved me so much she hated me.

Wynonna and I had never needed a reason to sing, but boy we sure had a good one now! Scheduled for our first meeting at RCA, I remembered their Dumpster behind the conveniently windowless building. We sat in our car till no one was around the parking lot, then hurriedly slung the bags of smelly garbage in.

Back inside Joe's office, where we'd auditioned a week before, I had a comfortable, pleasant sensation wash over me this time. As Joe was informing Wy that at eighteen she and Elvis were the youngest artists ever to be signed to their label, I wandered over to the front window. Wy took notice and asked what I was staring at. As I leaned with my nose pressed against the glass gazing down on Music Row, I murmured, "All my life, I've been on the outside looking in. I want to savor and remember this new feeling of being on the inside."

Before I turned to rejoin the meeting, my heart went out to all the wanna-bes marching up and down on the street below. I wanted to throw open that window and shout, "Hey everybody—there's hope for you, too! If we can do it, so can *you*!"

It wasn't until some weeks later that Wy and I discovered what a rare opportunity our live audition had been. No one had ever done it that way before. In supreme naïveté we had just assumed that everybody did it that way. The kid and I got a kick out of breaking the rules and doing it all backward. Although large organizations can be dehumanizing, we proved there's hope for them too.

Continuing on with our do-it-backward trend, we decided to put an album out before anyone ever saw us, form a band, and *then* begin performing in public. Our intent was to create a demand, so we could get decent gigs when it came time to hit the road. I simply refused to allow Wy to be subjected to grungy clubs, where drunks hollered out pick-up lines above the music to girls wearing short skirts and cheap perfume.

The studio was booked to record our minialbum of six songs, a new RCA concept that had recently proven successful for several other artists. It's basically a shortened sampler of an album sold at the reduced price of $5.98 to introduce unproven talent.

We signed with BMI to monitor our publishing royalties. Frances Preston, Del Bryant, Joe Moscheo, and Roger Sovine treated us like we were "somebody" and pronounced our names correctly. We'd almost become known on the Row as "those two girls."

The first song to make our list was my self-penned "Change of Heart." Second was the sentimental bluegrass song "John Deere Tractor." We couldn't locate the songwriter, Lawrence Hammond, so BMI opened a bank account for his song royalties.

One night, Brent played us a Dennis Linde number called "Had a Dream (For the Heart)" at our dining room table. Larry, who'd come home in the middle of the night, woke up, and came out to ask about this midtempo song, puzzled that he somehow seemed to know it. Brent had to admit then that it was on an Elvis record called "For the Heart," the B side of "Hunka, Hunka Burning Love." For that reason, Brent was afraid we wouldn't touch it. He almost succeeded in keeping us in the dark, but Larry, who had played the song, blew it. Wy and I decided it was obscure enough, came up with a cool version, and kept it.

Brent knew only too well how difficult it would be to come up with good songs for an unknown act like us. He resorted to using the "live-and-in-person" approach with us again, this time to get songwriters interested. When he informed us he was bringing the great, legendary songwriter Harlan Howard out to Del Rio to meet us, we cooked up some soup beans and corn bread and made a big pitcher of iced tea.

Our big fear at the time was that the family of skunks living under our poorly insulated house would fire off while company was visiting. They'd set off in the middle of the night twice, sending us holding our breath, throwing open all the doors and windows. An old nag had wandered into the yard just as Brent arrived with Harlan and

I was running around trying to shoo it away. When we walked inside, my .38 revolver was still out on the buffet, and Ashley informed our guests I'd seen a copperhead earlier and had been trying to shoot it.

Rubes! The mask always gets jerked off, and we're exposed as rubes. Fortunately Harlan's one of the most unpretentious guys you'd ever want to meet. He quickly nicknamed Wy "Juvenile," honed in on us, and began writing songs for us with Brent. Their first effort was "The Blue Nun Cafe," inspired by Harlan's Nashville hangout the Bluebird Café.

When I questioned Brent later about exactly how he'd talked this man, who wrote classics like "I Fall to Pieces" for Patsy Cline, into coming to our house, Brent confessed he'd bribed Harlan by giving him some hand-tied fishing lures.

Songwriters submit their wares to the artists that they think will sell the most records, so when I went to publishing companies on Music Row, they played me "the cream of the crap." As an aspiring songwriter myself, I was interested in observing how the pros did it. It surprised me that some writers showed up daily at these offices for appointments to collaborate with other writers. It seemed so businesslike. I wrote songs out of my heart when I was out of my head—to keep from slashing my wrists.

At House of Gold, I ran into a staff writer named Kenny O'Dell, who casually played me his brand-new effort about a teenager confiding to her mother about her first love. The beautiful ballad, "Mama He's Crazy" hit home. When I told Kenny that Wy had just told me about her first serious boyfriend, he couldn't believe this coincidence. I explained how I'd discovered that coincidence is just the Lord's way of staying invisible!

So the last of the six songs for our first recording experience had been found, and Wy and I now counted the days down to the studio like kids looking forward to Christmas. When Ken recuperated from his heart attack and went back to work, the first thing he did was call us in to tell us his story of how the cow ate the cabbage. Assuming he was going to let us pick out a bus or something equally as fun, we couldn't have been more deflated when the meeting turned out to be about money. In Ken's absence I'd already made a costly mistake by signing a paltry record deal.

Ken started out by explaining that there was no way we could make any money for at least a year. As he laid out the financial realities, I was shocked when he conveyed the cold hard fact I wouldn't be able to quit my nursing job for some time. Wy yawned and glanced at Ken like "what time is recess?" until he suggested she get a paying job also.

Then the personal questions began and things livened up a bit. Requesting permission to run a credit check on me, I confessed to Ken I'd never bought anything on time in my life, had never owned a credit card, and therefore, had no credit rating. Needing to know how much alimony and child support I received so he could put together our starting budget, I surprised Ken yet again by reporting I'd never received a penny of alimony and only a few meager child support checks over the years. He and Martha looked at each other in disbelief. Before we left, Ken handed me $1,000, and I stopped on my way home and bought a washer and dryer. The kids and I were ecstatic about not having to trudge to the Wishy Washy Laundromat ever again. They proudly brought their friends in to see our new luxuries.

Springtime meant switching clothes. Wy, Ashley, and I had all the clothes we wore every day hung on one rod in the utility room, because our little house had no closets. We had to store the opposite season's wardrobe in a closet at Larry's apartment. It was time again for this ritual, so I stuffed our winter clothing into three garbage bags and laid them in the trunk. The following morning, Wy drove the car to school, and when she came home I went out to go do the clothes exchange. The trunk was empty! All the bags with our cold-weather clothes—hats, boots, and gloves—were missing. As I went running back toward the house to question Wy about their disappearance, a terrible thought flashed through my mind.

She'd been remiss about hauling our garbage to the dumpster behind some apartments on the way into town. Under the pretense of offering to do this chore only a week earlier just so she could have the car, she'd gone to see a friend instead. A few warm days later I noticed passersby sniffing as they walked by our car in a parking lot. Then from several car lengths away I too caught wiff of rank garbage.

Before I could finish my question about what happened to our wardrobe, the look on her face told me she'd unknowingly thrown away all our clothes thinking they were garbage bags. I sped into town but was too late: The Dumpster was empty.

Looking back I realize what an unusual sight I must have been in my vintage clothes, seamed hose, and cat-eyed glasses, driving the '57 Chevy. What folks couldn't see was Miss Cora Lee's money belt strapped around my thigh and the .38 under my seat!

Since we needed something to wear for our first album cover, Joe Galante volunteered to take us shopping with his wife. Wy picked out a purple top, and I chose a fuschia-and-purple cable-knit sweater that cost $175. Because I had never paid more than $60 for a dress, this felt so extravagant!

Never mentioning our "great Dumpster disaster" to RCA, Wy and I stopped at Wal-mart on our way home, where she got accessories and I bought some rose-colored slacks. To finish out our album cover wardrobe, we purchased boots at Payless Shoe Store.

The album photos were unusable. Rock-and-roll photographer Norman Seef had the most expensive camera and shot the most famous stars in the world, but he didn't "get it." Knowing he wasn't capturing us during the session, I found it hard to hold my tongue. Afterward in a "what-did-we-do-wrong" meeting at RCA, I did speak up.

"Imagine yourselves as explorers," I suggested, "and you've just discovered the lost Judd tribe. We're asking that you leave our culture as undisturbed as possible. Please just allow us to be our natural selves."

And that they did. We worked well with guys like Dave Wheeler, Bob Heatherly, Joe Galante, and appreciated their belief in us. We promised Joe we'd work hard to make him proud of us someday.

My Mom gave birth to me when she was eighteen, I had Wy when I turned eighteen, so on Wy's eighteenth birthday, my initial urge was to lock her in her room. But she never mentioned getting married, moving out, or even going to college. No-sirree-bob, she intended to stay right there at home until she drove me completely crazy!

That spring of 1983 was Wynonna's rite of passage: Her braces came off and she graduated from high school. We were in a hellacious fight and I did not attend her graduation ceremony. It was painful for both of us.

As I sat home alone crying, I remembered missing my own high school graduation while giving birth to her. It seemed only yesterday I held her in my arms for the first time. Where had all the years gone? Now I contemplated the reality of us becoming equal partners. The next day we would launch our recording career as a duo.

Because we felt slightly overwhelmed by the task before us, I took several small steps to protect our ability to remain focused on our music and be ourselves. Wy and I agreed on a dress code: no makeup; only sweats or comfortable cotton clothes; tennis shoes, thongs, or bare feet. I made a big sign for the studio door that warned: "Closed Session: Death to anyone who enters, and this means you, Bucko!" Wy drew an ominous skull and crossbones underneath.

As soon as Brent introduced us to the session players, he gathered us around and asked Don to start us off with a word of prayer. Don began by asking the Lord to place His hand on each of us, to bind us together, and to let our creative juices flow. Then he invited the Lord to guide Wy and me and for the music to touch lives.

Serenity filled the studio, and we all looked around at each other with a knowing, a sense of belonging, and an overwhelming sense something wonderful was happening. The players became enthused when Brent announced he was counting on their creativity. This time instead of telling them what to play, Brent played them our bare-bones demos of the six songs, featuring only our duet and Don's guitar, and encouraged the players to use their imaginations and decorate around what they heard. By the end of the first session, I'd instituted the "lick of the day award," given to the musician who came up with the most off-the-cuff performance.

During dinner breaks we'd all eat together at a home cookin' spot called Couser's, where the waitresses wore beehive hairdos and had two names, like Ida Lee. We were beginning to feel close to the guys and invited them to bring their families to have dinner with us the last session day. All six of them had distinct personalities but we were happily homogenous.

Eddie Bayers, the drummer, was the class clown. This irrepressible guy knew more jokes and had sampled all sorts of weird stuff to entertain us with. Bright and witty, Mark Casstevens, a guitar player, and I shared Monty Python bits and brought each other favorite "Far Side" cartoons. The bass player, Jack Williams, was the stodgy, lovable grouch of the group. Soft-spoken, amiable Sonny Garrish often won "lick of the day award" for his pedal steel and Dobro riffs. Keyboard great Bobby Ogdin was good humored and immensely encouraging to Wy and me. When he was available, we also used the talented Gene Sisk on piano.

As we were getting into our cars to leave the studio that first night, I overheard Eddie telling his fellow musicians: "Mark today on your calendars, boys. We're gonna be talking about these gals the rest of our lives!"

Wy and I glanced over at each other several times, basking in our reflected glory on the way home. We met out on the front porch swing before bedtime and confirmed our shared belief that this was the greatest thing that had ever happened in our entire lives. She was thrilled the songs were coming off so nearly perfect, and I couldn't get over what a closed system it was in that studio. Inside, we forgot if it was night or day, winter or summer. Supremely caught up in creating something from nothing, time stood still and the rest of the world just evaporated. I confided to Wy it felt as if we'd tapped into some cosmic pool of musical knowledge. The only way we were able to say good night to that incredible first day was knowing we got to go back the next one.

After cutting the music tracks in three days, Wy and I settled into laying down vocals with just Brent and Don present. Our singing came from instinct, deep and spontaneous. We responded to each song by the way it made us feel. Wy's voice is so powerfully evocative, and I wanted it to sound as clean and perfect as possible. My role with her in laying down harmony was the same as in life: to encourage, enhance, and support. Just as in life, very few people understood Wy; Brent observed that I was probably the only one who could match her unusual vocal phrasing and demanding melody treatment.

Brent is a genius producer and engineer. After observing his talent and hands-on meticulousness, I declared he put out handmade albums. He brought our album in at the unheard-of budget of $36,000. Don was the band leader and inspired us all with the most scintillating guitar licks. Together Brent and Don were helping us not only to crystallize and capture our first musical efforts but also to prepare mentally, emotionally, and spiritually for what lay ahead.

I was concerned about show business. It represents a microcosm of what's wrong with the world in general: ego, greed, materialism, the lust for power, selfishness, temptations, and excesses of every kind. Still working as an RN, I was plugged in to the everyday struggles of real people. I also was determined that what was left of my life count for something. What if I no longer felt as if I were doing something to help others? I was most worried about what the music business might do to Wy. At this point it really had hit me that Wynonna was not going to have a typical life. She literally had graduated from high school right into a recording contract.

There would be no chance to cut the apron string now, no living on her own. Wy was working for a temporary office service called Jane Jones, but everybody knew her own job was temporary. She'd turned nineteen while in the studio that May 1983, and as usual I'd baked her favorite cake. As Wynonna blew out the candles, surrounded by Brent and Don and the session musicians, I flashed back to her past birthday parties and wondered if she'd ever have normal friends her own age again.

Our family didn't know what to make of all this. When we finished in the studio, Daddy and his wife came to visit us and took the girls to Opryland. On one of the rides, Wy mused that someday she and I wouldn't be able to do this cause we'd be mobbed by autograph seekers. Daddy smiled and shook his head as if she were joking. He never said much about the tape we played him or acknowledged the album dedication to him because he just couldn't relate to show business. Daddy's kidney transplant was failing; he was on massive doses of medicine and having a difficult time.

After she divorced Dad, Mom had gotten a job as a cook on a riverboat and had fallen in love with the pilot. Wib Rideout had spent all his hardworking life on the river and was respected by everyone. They'd married in 1980, and I just sent flowers.

All these years, everytime I heard the word *Mother,* there were tears behind my eyes and unspoken words hanging in the air. Now we'd finally talked on the phone and broken the ice. She seemed happily getting her life back in order and was pleased and enthusiastic about our recording deal.

Mom had moved; I mean, she'd moved our house! The house was just a street away from the town hospital, and doctors' offices and parking lots were taking over Montgomery Avenue. My intrepid mother bought a lot on the opposite side of the block and moved our big three-story home down the alley to a new site. Neighbors and townsfolk turned out to witness the amazing feat, and of course, it was captured in the *Ashland Daily Independent.* "Come see our house's new home!" Mom suggested.

As Wy, Ashley, and I turned onto Bath Avenue, I saw it was the same residential street I'd ridden my bike down thousands of times. But as I looked up expecting to see Ms. Richardson's house, I saw instead our own house! It seemed like some illusionary magic trick—a huge house someplace it's not supposed to be!

There to greet us out on the front porch stood Mom with her new husband. Everyone stood back, quietly giving Mom and me space. After all the years of missing her, I didn't want to let go of hugging her. The big hole in my life was filled again.

We all took to Wib right off the bat. A native of West Virginia, he was quiet and solid, and we were just delighted to see Mom had such a dependable husband by her side.

We went out to visit Daddy at his modest home in Flatwoods, outside of Ashland, and I was growing increasingly alarmed over his failing kidneys. Years of prednisone had made his face round, which was a constant reminder of the life-threatening malfunction in his body.

Zora had passed away so Daddy took Wy, Ashley, and me back to Louisa to an empty farmhouse. As we walked together down the dirt road up to the family cemetery I impulsively reached over and took hold of my Daddy's hand. Time bends in the lazy summer heat and our awareness of the years gone by vanished. We were merely father and daughter again . . . aging boy and wise child.

"Do you believe in God?" I asked seriously, as cemetery hill was coming into view.

"Why sure I do!" Daddy answered matter of factly. His words were only temporarily comforting to my ears as I had a strange premonition this was our last time to be together at the ancestral homestead.

After we returned home, August 2, 1983, in yet another transitional milestone, Wy moved out. Woody Bowles had been trying to split us up because he couldn't control me. He smooth-talked naive Wy into moving in with him and his wife. He'd hoped having her under his roof would mean under his thumb, but his sabotage plan failed. When Ken realized what Woody was up to, he bought out his share of our management contract.

Instead of moving back in at Del Rio, we figured since we were now working together it might be wise for Wy to go ahead and have her own place. She rented a nice one-bedroom apartment, got a puppy she named Loretta Lynn, and called me every day.

"Had a Dream" was to be our first single. Before RCA sent it out to radio stations, they came up with a unique idea. Impressed with the way we came across in person, they organized an extensive tour of America's largest radio stations. They wanted disc jockeys to know who we were when they received our record.

Excited, Wy and I ran out and bought a complete set of sturdy luggage. I put my old cardboard snakeskin print suitcases with their red fabric lining under my bed. Unable to part with them because of all the memories from my travels, I decided I'd use them for collecting career souvenirs. Dolly Parton had the same luggage set in the movie *Best Little Whorehouse in Texas*. Brent and Janel stopped by to have a glass of wine and toast to "success" while I packed.

Why was I always so itchy to travel? Where had I gotten this wanderlust? I thought about this question while I drove to the airport and concluded I was ready to travel the world because of the strong sense of where I come from. I could remember my grandparents, aunts, and uncles living in the house we later bought from them . . . the deep-roots attachment to the Louisa homestead . . . a sense of nearness from being able to walk to school, church, downtown, and Daddy's gas station . . . the comforting assurance of being surrounded by neighbors and friends. Roots and wings! Ashland, Kentucky, was a great launching pad.

RCA has five promotion regions, so the game plan emerged for each area's representative to escort us around his or her territory. A big, warm-hearted bear of a guy named Jack Weston started us out. Scheduling us for practically a different city each day, he handed Wy and me our thick stack of tickets wrapped with a wide rubber band. Wy promptly lost hers. Jack straightened it out, then uttered these immortal words: "We're off like a herd of turtles!"

Walking into our first radio station of the tour bright and early, the kid and I were big-eyed and anxious. Jack was apprehensive too, wondering what we'd find to talk about, because there was no career to discuss yet and no one knew or cared who we were.

The first catchy words out of the DJ's mouth were "too bad this is radio, folks, cause you gotta see this mother/daughter duo to believe it! They look like sisters and have red hair." Those words were repeated everywhere we went. One of our favorite program directors, Bill Bradley, called us "the best looking duo you'll ever hear."

Soon we were clowning around and chiming in: "and we're wearing our teeny-weeny bikinis!" I impulsively asked if I could do the weather report, and the startled DJ enthusiastically pointed to the microphone and gave me a "be my guest!" "Today it will be cloudy with a chance of meatballs," I quipped. I then turned to a surprised and delighted Wy, who was sitting next to me, with the announcement that she would give us the traffic report. "All the pink cadillacs switch lanes with the red mustangs. Any yellow cars must take the next exit!" she stammered. Not to be outdone, I concluded by declaring, "The expressway will be closed for one hour so I can mop and wax it!" I noticed sweat had formed on the DJ's freshly shaved upper lip. More mischievous than ever, we had just discovered the thrill of being live . . . uncensored and unedited!

Halfway afraid to look back over my shoulder at Jack, who'd been sitting with his arms folded across his chest, I was relieved to see him was grinning from ear to ear, egging us on. We dragged out Wy's guitar and sang a couple of songs. It seemed hard to believe when the DJ told us no one else had ever done that. The phone lines lit up, and I excitedly requested to talk to the callers. By now the station manager and some secretaries were crowded into the tiny studio to check us out. Since Wy and I lived fully in the moment, there was a sense that no one ever knew what would happen next! Not even us!

We'd have the radio station folks over to our hotel suite every evening, serving them snacks, laughter, and live music. RCA also invited their main regional people and representatives from major chains like Sound Warehouse, Camelot Records, Roses, and Handleman. Wy and I were getting to know these people, making new friends. It seemed inconsequential that they held a life-or-death power over our fledgling career.

These often jaded guys perked up because there were so many unusual things about us. The daughter sang lead while the mother sang harmony. One of our favorite DJs, likeable Wade Jessen, commented that my "second part infiltrated Wy's truly amazing voice like it had been encoded," as he pointed to the goose bumps on his forearm. Wy would play guitar like nobody's business on a grab bag of quirky songs I'd written. I'd tell my jokes, and Wy obliged as straight man. If our guests asked where we came from, we'd entertain them with tales about living in Morrill and Hollywood, and our perilous experiences with fires, floods, and earthquakes. And of course, we talked about what it was like for a mother and daughter to be performing together. It was *everybody's* favorite question.

Wy and I felt as if we were in a whirlwind. Many of our get-togethers revolved around taking radio people out to eat, so I dubbed this stage of our career "the great American restaurant tour." Jack Weston, Tim McFadden, Dale Turner, and Gaylen Adams chaperoned us across the United States like proud uncles.

By the time RCA's Carson Schreiber picked us up in LA for the final southwestern leg, our schedule was like trying to take a drink out of a firehose! Our forty-eight hours in LA were jam-packed: In the morning we landed, dropped our bags at the posh Le Dufy Hotel, and were whisked off to an interview with Harry Newman from the Armed Forces Network. We met likeable Lon Helton, a big shot at *Radio and Records Magazine* at Butterfields on Sunset Strip for lunch. He remarked that Wy reminded him of a female Elvis. Then it was back to our room to freshen up for our performance/meet and greet in our hotel suite with Art Fein, Tisha Fine, and Tom Todd. The next morning it was an early breakfast meeting with Howard Benjamin, then a major interview with Neil Hailslop and Bob Kingsley of the "American Country Countdown" at their studio. Neil and I really hit it off.

Later the same day we landed in Oakland, California, in time to have dinner with the congenial radio program director from KNEW, Bobby Guerra. Wy told Bobby the story of how KNEW sponsored the first country concert we ever attended, with Merle Haggard performing, and that the KNEW bumper sticker was still on Redhot.

I was so exhausted by the time we got back to our room late that night I didn't finish the last sentence in my journal.

Wy and I tromped through record factories and wholesale warehouses. Employees, eager for a work break back in the bowels of the plant, would sit around in metal folding chairs while we serenaded them. Several observations were beginning to percolate, and I spoke up. "Okay, you guys. We're here because we recognize your importance and we want to acknowledge and thank you. Wynonna and I believe in teamwork and fully understand that you're only as strong as your weakest link."

I shared with them that we were still actively working as a nurse and a secretary and hadn't quit our day jobs either.

As we left, Wy suggested we bring along pizzas to the next such visit and hollered back to the smiling workers, "I think you should have the rest of the day off and get a fifty-dollar raise!"

Wynonna and I knew full well that we were off on an incredible journey. Everywhere we went, our enthusiastic attitude was "Come along with us!" We saw everyone as a potential friend and fan of our music.

For a week, Wynonna, Don, and I performed as a trio entertaining at rallies for presidential candidate Senator John Glenn from Ohio. Wy and I got to know Secret Service men personally and set our luggage out in the motel hall each morning to be sniffed by German shepherds. Wy always wanted to pet and play with them. Traveling in the same limo or plane as John and his wonderful wife Annie, we got accustomed to having our itinerary changed at a moment's notice for security purposes. Our favorite part of this unique week came late one night as the darkened plane carrying us and representatives from the major networks and media began singing "Amazing Grace." John told Wy astronaut stories as she fell asleep. A quip I once saw in *Reader's Digest* said, "Most politicians are like diapers: they should be changed often, and for the same reason!" But John Glenn is a rare exception and a true American hero in every sense of the word.

During these beginning months, Wy and I were getting our first taste of living in hotels—sometimes two different ones in a single day, and we loved it! One evening Wy answered a knock at our door to have a maid ask, "Would you like to be turned down?" Wy turned abruptly to catch my expression as I sat reading in bed. We howled with laughter as Wy reported to the woman we were just beginning to see some hope that our years of being turned down and rejected were over. As the maid patiently explained to Wy she was only offering to turn down our beds, Wy turned serious and replied, "Oh! But hey, can you come in and rub my feet a while?" Rubes.

Wy made me sit in the bathroom every night while she talked long distance to her boyfriend back in Franklin. To afford her some privacy, I'd get my pillow and climb into the empty bathtub and read or write. Although we were the consummate odd couple, we wanted to share a room so we could be together. She's messy and can't ever find her stuff, while I'm an organized neatnik. She loves TV and I don't. I'm punctual, while she's always running behind.

I had to start putting ear plugs in because Wy talks in her sleep. One night in the pitch black, I was shaken out of deep slumber by her terrifying screams of "Who are you and what do you want?" I stiffened up in bed and dove blindly for the lamp on the bedside table between us. Wy and I collided and almost knocked each other out. I had to use heavy makeup for a week to cover up the big bruise on my forehead.

As we were just fixing to walk out our door for another full day of important meetings, I stepped in the bathroom to rinse some dirt off the bottom of my high heel. Sticking my perfectly coiffed and hairsprayed head in the tub area, as soon as I turned on the faucet I was drenched with water from the overhead shower nozzle. Wy had forgotten to put the shower knob down again. Sometimes she was like a banana peel on a the floor.

Sure we got on each others' nerves and yes we fought, and yet I knew there was no way to hide this conflict between the two of us. We were now thrust out into the public eye. I still felt a strong parental responsibility toward her; if Wy did something inappropriate, I spoke up. I was her mother first, and after all, she was still growing up and I wasn't about to let her get away with wrongdoing. Conversely, if she caught me exaggerating, she'd bust me right on the spot. Things could get pretty explosive at any time and any place.

RCA was extremely nervous about this friction hurting our image and sent us to media-training classes. It was no use. Interviewers sometimes got caught in the crossfire. They became referees, psychologists, and mediators. It had to have been an unnerving experience for them. My candor was also unnerving for some people. I say what I mean and mean what I say.

There was never a shred of doubt in the mind of anyone who knew us that Wy and I loved each other. The parent/child relationship happens to be the most complex and intense of all relationships and has intrigued everyone throughout history. Wy and I were certainly contributing our share of drama to this mythic tradition!

During this first phase of our budding career, Ashley stayed with her best friend, Lisa Cicatellis, and her family. I arrived home from the radio tour in time to help her get ready for her tenth-grade homecoming. I'd started worrying about what to do about her when the time came to set out on a bus for long periods.

In the blink of an eye, I was back to work doing the bedpan boogie at the hospital, scrubbing floors at home, trying to make a pot roast last all week, pushing a grocery cart, and picking Ashley up at school. Then on November 16, 1983, our single shipped. Two weeks later Wy and I were on our way to do a WSM radio show with Charlie Douglas at the Opryland Hotel. It was exactly 7:50 P.M. in front of the Shoney's on Thompson Lane when we heard ourselves on the radio for the first time. At first we thought it was our tape playing, but then the DJ announced "And that was 'Had a Dream' by a brand new duo, the Judds!'' It's a darn good thing someone else was driving, cause we would have run off the road!

Out on a date a week later, Larry and I were leaving a restaurant and heard it again on WSIX. Larry's feelings were a mixture of happy for us and frustrated for himself. He'd given me a second diamond and asked me again to marry him that Christmas. Little had changed in his world, and he now shared a low-rent apartment with his keyboard player. So much was changing in my world and I was no longer sitting by the phone every night out on Del Rio hoping for his calls. We were still in love, but there was a wall going up between us.

Wy and I were spending a lot of time doing interviews at RCA. Ever eager for unusual and fresh stories, writers were perking up, and we were in great demand. Marching into the conference room one morning, I was thrilled to learn that Robert Oermann, my first friend from the Country Music Hall of Fame, was now music reporter for the morning newspaper, *The Tennessean.* The headline and first sentence of his story on us declared: "The Judds are the talk of Music Row.'' Robert assessed that our first single, "Had a Dream,'' was "an airy, haunting thing that sounds like nothing else on American radio. Its swing-style acoustic guitars and precise, pure, harmony vocals have made Naomi and Wynonna instant celebrities.'' More than anything, I was grateful that this man whose opinion I respected so much had liked our tune and understood our personalities and relationship. Wy was just excited we made the newspaper.

Cynthia Spencer, at RCA's publicity department, hired freelance writer, Bob Allen, to compose a bio on us. It was unsettling to be told a stranger was going to interpret our life for the American public, but Wy and I took to Bob immediately. Later, putting on a different hat, he was asked his personal opinion of our minialbum for the popular *Country Music Magazine,* and he concluded that "the two of them sing together with strong, flowing harmonies that bristle with energy, yet are so tight and precise they are almost seamless.''

We noticed a common thread running through the summaries of our sound. Serious observers, such as Bob Allen, were fed up with the "polyester, pretense and pop music pandering of the current

country music mainstream." Nashville had fallen into a slick overpro-
duced rut in the early to mid-1980s.

Our artistic vision and emotional authenticity were intregal parts
of our personalities, so it was sheer luck that we happened along at
this opportune time. I was beginning to appreciate the importance of
timing. As ardent country lovers, Wy and I longed to see our favorite
form of music stay honest and move forward.

Reviewers, like Douglas Browne, who praised our minialbum as
an "acoustic masterpiece," pointed out Brent's imaginative and sympathetic production and Don's rich guitar stylings. *Rolling Stone*
magazine expressed its view that the sampler album "had more soul
than a moccasin factory." Wynonna and I smilingly shrugged our
shoulders with a "Wow, can you believe it!" I told her they were
"just letting off esteem."

There was another public opinion surfacing. Our first mention
in the prestigious *Billboard* trade publication said, "If the Judds had
not occurred naturally, a marketing team might well have been called
in to create them. They are a publicist's dream. Not only does the
new RCA vocal act look good and harmonize superbly, it has a family
history that reads like a Judith Krantz novel."

After meeting us, *Nashville Banner* journalist Bob Millard
vowed our story was definitely "even stranger than publicity" and
was so fascinated he began writing an unauthorized book on us. Not
knowing the man and certain that a biography was premature, we
declined to be involved and asked everyone we knew not to cooperate
with him. The result was an inaccurate, but well-intentioned book.

This Week in Country Music's pretty cohost, Lorianne Crook,
came out to Del Rio on February 1, 1984, to shoot our first TV
interview. I had worked late at the hospital the night before and
hadn't had time to bring the wash in off the line. Wy and I thought
she was delightful, and appreciated that she treated us with dignity.
Lorianne and her crew commented on the quaintness of our little
house. When the episode of *This Week in Country Music* aired
February 18, Wy and I sat on the bed and watched it over and over,
squealing with delight at seeing ourselves on TV.

Just a few days later, I found myself driving down rural Highway
96 on my way back to work at the old Rutherford County Hospital

in Murfreesboro listening to the "American Country Countdown," which features the nation's top twenty country favorites. Driving past the countryside dotted with farmhouses, I was munching on my sandwich, when all of a sudden Bob Kingsley announced the eighteenth song on the chart: "Had a Dream." I almost choked. I pulled off into a pasture, slammed on the brakes, and turned up the volume. I sat there enthralled, beating on the steering wheel as I listened to our jazzy song with a herd of nonchalant cows.

Liminality strikes again. As I entered the hospital wearing my inexpensive uniform and support hose, no makeup and my hair pulled back in a ponytail, I felt very much in between two worlds. Althea Cimino, the three to eleven o'clock supervisor, assigned me to work the surgical C unit. She was a redheaded mother of five with a wonderfully sunny disposition; she was my favorite. I decided this would be my final shift as a nurse, but I just couldn't say good-bye.

When I walked onto the floor, Pansy, the sweet ward clerk, was beaming and gushed, "I've been hearing you and your daughter on the radio a lot!" A country music fan to the max, Pansy was bewildered that I was still working there. Mabel Thomas, one of the RNs, listened to the radio in her car on her way to work every day and dubbed me "the singing nurse."

That last night Ruby, a quiet LPN, was helping me bathe an elderly farmer. "What's the first things you're gonna buy when you get hold of some money?" she asked.

Thinking about it seriously for the first time, I responded, "A set of hot rollers and garbage pickup service!" Ruby said I was being uncharacteristically unimaginative.

Girls' Night Out

PROFESSOR AND ANTHROPOLOGIST Joseph Campbell admonished us to "follow our bliss!" and Yogi Bera suggested, "when you come to a fork in the road, take it!" Wy also cut her ties with the nine-to-five world.

The annual Country Radio Seminar came to the Opryland Hotel, and because we were RCA artists, the label had us sit in the booth to oblige disc jockeys' their station IDs. Bearing tape recorders and microphones, the radio people flocked to Alabama on one side of us and Kenny Rogers on the other. Embarrassed, Wy and I sat there in our cubicle self-consciously twiddling our thumbs. I remarked to Wy that we should have brought some lemonade and cookies to lure them to us.

At the reception that night, I found myself standing right next to Tammy Wynette. Not wanting to bother her, I was so tickled when she smiled and spoke to me first! We hit it off like gangbusters and I felt like I'd known her a long time. Tammy gave me advice on being a woman and mother on the road. I'd made my first female artist friend.

Finally Ken called with the exciting, much awaited news that we were going to get to perform at a real concert! Marshall Grant with the Statler Brothers organization heard "Had a Dream" on the radio and called RCA. "Is this some sort of trick?" he asked them. "We love their music but no one knows who these girls are! If this is for real, we'd like them to open for the Statlers out in Omaha in a couple of weeks for a week-long gig."

Knowing there wasn't enough time to audition and assemble a road band on such short notice, Brent called up some studio musicians and conducted a few quick rehearsals of the songs on our minialbum.

We all flew into snow-covered Omaha, and Wy and I, for the first time, asked for separate but adjoining rooms. We had seriously bad cases of the jitters that Tuesday night of March 20, 1984. Brent and Janel accompanied us and tried their best to calm us down. Janel snapped a "before" picture of us by our dressing room entrance just as we were walking to the stage to make our professional concert debut. Noticing the sign on the door bearing our name, we fought over ownership of it as we stood smiling for her camera.

Wy and I stood rigid and awkwardly nervous in front of our microphone stands behind the huge curtain. We'd been informed that on the other side of it was a sold-out crowd of Statler Brothers fans, waiting to see them. Wy and I looked back over our shoulders seeking some encouragement from Don in the band behind us. "You'll do just fine!" he whispered, nodding his head up and down in affirmation.

Unbeknownst to us, the Statlers always opened the evening's entertainment with a taped version of the Star Spangled Banner. Suddenly the grandiose national anthem began, and Wy and I about jumped out of our skins! Her eyes were wide with fear as she gulped and declared, "Mom, I want to go home. I'm dead serious. Take me home *now*!"

Panic-stricken, I looked over toward the wings for a way off the stage. I felt terror searing the pit of my stomach. What in God's name had I gotten us into this time? We don't have any business being here—we're not ready! We're going to make fools of ourselves and be an embarrassment.

Just then the national anthem ended, and a booming voice began announcing us. The two of us looked down to see the curtain in front of our feet rising. I instinctively lifted up my mike stand, moving it even closer to Wy, and grabbed her by the arm. She looked like a deer caught in the headlights.

"It's gonna be okay, Sweetheart, 'cause I'm right here beside you. We've got each other. This is what we've always wanted to do, so let's just try it one time. If you don't like it, I promise we'll never do it again!" Just as I finished these words, Don kicked up the band and we had to begin singing our opening song.

To tell you the truth, we don't remember anything about that first show. Brent, who was out in the house running sound, said we forgot to thank the audience after each song. Don laughingly described later what happened when I turned in a feeble attempt to acknowledge the band. He saw on my face that I was too preoccupied and scared to remember the musicians' last names. So, giving a grand gesture with a wave of my arm, the only introduction I could come up with was: "Ladies and gentlemen, uh, the Emergency Band!"

Wy and I ran off stage to deep rumbling applause. As soon as we cleared the wings, we faced off and jumped up and down, flapping our arms at our sides like chimpanzees again. Don and the band leapt on us for a group hug and we all paced around in the dressing room reliving the amazing half hour, talking excitedly at the same time. Brent and Janel came running in out of breath, raving like proud parents.

We hung around backstage the rest of the night soaking up the milieu. The Statler Brothers were wonderfully kind to us, and Wynonna and I must have thanked them and Marshall a dozen times for giving us our big break. When I finally hugged Wy good night in our adjoining doorway back at the motel, I reminded her, "We 'Had a Dream' and now we were being given a chance to make this dream come true!"

What a fabulous, luxurious feeling to wake up that next morning and realize "We're entertainers and we're on the road!" I put on full makeup hoping someone would recognize me and headed down to the coffee shop.

In the motel lobby I passed by the small gift shop newsstand where the little lady behind the register asked, "Good morning, are you the mother or the daughter? I read the review of your show."

My heart began thumping wildly and I dug in my purse for

change to buy the *Omaha World Herald*. I dared not even ask her if the review was good or bad and walked as fast as I could, without conspicuously running, back to my room. My mind was racing with horrible possibilities of what our review would say as I fumbled through the newspaper.

Roger Caitlin wrote:

> For the surprising opening act, believability was put to the test. The Judds are a new female vocal duo from Kentucky whose well blended harmonies owe as much to the Andrews Sisters as to country. They sing easy rocking songs with a gritty determination that matches that of Bonnie Raitt. The audience seemed to enjoy the fine music from the two, looking pretty as models in front of their five man band. But they were absolutely astonished when Naomi introduced herself as the mother and Wynonna as the daughter. Once the hubbub dies down about the youthfulness of the mother, folks will doubtless start talking about her songwriting ability, their musical appeal and the almost certain stardom in store for the Judds.

I sat motionless on the side of the bed staring into space. I wanted to write this man a thank you note, but wondered if it was improper. Slipping the review under Wy's door since she was still asleep, I went back and bought every paper at the newsstand.

Wy and I loved the camaraderie of hanging out with our band. We were a little clique, which went everywhere together. Every night, flushed with excitement, we sang all six songs from our minialbum plus the old 1950s rocker "Rip It Up" and a bluegrass gospel number, "Jerusalem," we learned while in Morrill, Kentucky.

Total strangers applauded us as if we were something special. We knew we weren't and felt instead that we were getting away with the biggest scam on earth. Wy and I each had only two outfits to our name. I'd carefully wash my album cover sweater in Woolite every other night. My backup outfit was a simple yellow cotton shirtwaist.

How we hated to see that first week come to an end! The last night my adrenaline rush would not subside. After my usual call home to Ashley, pausing to consider the role reversal of my being on the road, I phoned Larry at his apartment. Next door to us, Brent and his fishing buddy, Jeff Bullock from Wyoming, who had been observing Wy and me, were still up writing us a cool up-tempo song, appropriately called "Girls' Night Out."

RCA got word how well things had gone and booked Wy and me to open for established acts on their roster to give us exposure and experience. Sending the Emergency Band home, since we weren't making any money, the two of us and Don went to Cleveland, Ohio. When we arrived at the Front Row Theater to do a sound check, Wynonna and I freaked. Seating about two thousand, the venue has a circular stage in the middle that slowly revolves three hundred sixty degrees. Knowing that Wy and Don wouldn't open their mouths on stage to talk, I realized that, by default, I would be the emcee, and no one had ever given me any hints about how to do it.

So we felt duress for a different set of reasons here at our second concert. The auditorium in Omaha is so vast the audience looked like ants, an overwhelming feeling to be sure, but here we could reach out and touch the front row (hence the name of the theater) and see the whites of everybody's eyes. That made us very nervous too! We had no band to back us up either, so it would be just two crystal-clear voices and Don's ringing lead guitar and Wy on rhythm filling up this place. The three of us felt so small and insignificant on that large barren stage. The other two acts had full bands.

To assuage our fears and calm our nerves, I'd instructed Wy to join with me in pretending that this intimate setting was our living room and that these strangers were merely people we hadn't met yet but had invited over for an evening of music and conversation. Something magical happened that Saturday night, April 17, 1984. I fell in love with communicating with the audience.

The next morning someone slipped a review from the paper under my door.

Nancy Bigler Kersey wrote:

The Show's highlight came from the opening act, The Judds. The mother-daughter duo of Wynonna Judd, nineteen, and her mother Naomi, who just gave up her full time nursing job two months ago, is a powerhouse! With only the accompaniment of Wynonna's acoustic guitar and that of Don Potter, a Chuck Mangione dropout, they put out a robust sound, which gleams like a polished gemstone.

I came up with the idea that Wy and I could stop and visit children's wards at hospitals while we were out on the road. In the Oncology Ward at Rainbow Children's Hospital in Cleveland, nurses gathered children in the playroom to listen to us sing. We went to the bedsides of kids who were too fragile to be moved. It tore Wy all to pieces. She went in the nurses' lounge and threw up. So much for my good intentions!

Daddy was now in the hospital in Ashland because his kidney transplant had failed. We flew home to visit him. Sitting up with him one night, I encouraged him to hold on so he could experience our career with us. Things were really moving along, and I described meeting Johnny Cash when we were on the *Nashville Now* show. I shared our experiences of doing *Entertainment Tonight;* the *Bobby Bare Show; Music City, U.S.A., That Nashville Music;* and *Hee Haw.* Daddy asked me how in the world we were pulling this off, since he just couldn't conceive of his daughter and grandaughter being on TV or in a magazine.

The time came to do our first full-length album and RCA decided to put "Mama He's Crazy" on it and do a video. When the director from LA, David Hogan, described the white-frame ginger-bread house they were looking for to shoot the video at, I interrupted with, "I believe you're talking about Del Rio Pike! Besides we should shoot it where Wy told me she was in love for the first time on the front porch swing, and make it our real life! We want to wear our own clothes and use our car!"

Rushing home, I hosed down the porches, washed and ironed all the curtains and hung them back up, scrubbed the floors, and so on so it was absolutely spotless when the film crew of thirty guys with dirty workboots arrived with all their equipment to mess it up. Rubes again.

In the video, I get to kiss a young handsome guy on the lips, and I kept insisting I needed to rehearse the scene! The whole time I was thinking about Larry seeing it. It was the first time Ken had ever been out to Del Rio. Asking politely, "Is this where you really live?" I could tell he was getting the picture.

As soon as I got the house back to normal, the spring rains came and I sent Ashley to a friend's house so I could evacuate. The Little

Harpeth River didn't care that Wy and I had started to record our *Why Not Me* album. It was another reality check by Mother Nature.

I pulled on my knee-high milking boots and waded up the road to higher ground where I'd parked my car. Carrying a box containing some of our clothes and my purse above my head, the water began rising up over my boots, filling them and making them extremely heavy to walk in. Walking against the current was taking all my strength, but I eventually made it to the car and drove to Brent and Janel's to spend the night.

Wy, Ashley, and I drove up to Lexington, Kentucky, to be with Daddy again because his condition was worsening so much that he'd been moved to the University of Kentucky Medical Center. His wife and two of his sisters, Faith and Mariolive, were with him all the time now. It cheered him up to see the three of us, but his kidneys weren't filtering out the toxins in his bloodstream, and he felt wretched.

I showed Daddy the *People* magazine article that had just come out and our picture on the cover of *Cashbox* as I promised him I'd carry the Judd banner high. Wearing down now, he was slipping in and out of consciousness. Dozing in a chair in the corner of the room, I perked up to see Daddy squinting his eyes, struggling to sit up in bed as if he was trying to make out who I was.

He called out, "Is that you, Di?"

"Yes Daddy, I'm right here with you. It's Diana," I gently assured him.

"Oh, I thought you were an Indian princess on a white horse," he mumbled, half to himself as he closed his eyes again. Because I am an RN, I realized Daddy was hallucinating, but as his child, the symbolism penetrated my soul.

Under a cloud of sadness, we drove to Ashland the next day, June 29, for my twentieth high school reunion. The future was inevitable but the past was present! As I was leaving for the event, Ashley waltzed into Mom's kitchen with great élan wearing my high school prom dress. Next thing I knew, I was hugging old classmates or trying to recognize them through their graying hair or lack thereof.

In a twist of fate, the day after my high school reunion, we found ourselves at Ricky Skaggs Day in Louisa, as the opening act for his concert at the high school. Waving to people on the sidewalks along the parade route on Ricky Skaggs Boulevard from the back of the convertible, I flashed back to that night years before when I'd sat alone watching Ricky play in a bluegrass band at the Holiday Inn in Lexington. Wy and I had only just begun to sing together at that time.

Right before our show, I approached Ricky and asked if he'd join Wy and me on stage to sing the old song "Kentucky" with us during our set. Standing around the microphone not far from the cabin where Daddy had been born, as our three voices intertwined, I was singing to him lying in his hospital bed:

> Kentucky, you are the dearest land
> this side of heaven to me.
> Kentucky, your laurel and redbud tree
> When I die, I long to rest
> Upon some peaceful mountain so high,
> For that is where God will look for me.

Daddy died four days later, July 4, 1984. Mark, Margaret, and I gathered at our house. Mark had just graduated from the Baptist Theological Seminary and was now the pastor of a small, quaint church in Colesburg, Kentucky. Margaret had married James Mandell, a successful businessman from New York, and had two children with him. They lived in California. Mom went out to take care of young Joshua and baby Allison, so Margaret and Erin could come home for Daddy's funeral.

It was a strangely sad version of 1964 all over again. I, the oldest, left alone again with Mark and Margaret. Silence hung in the parlor at John Steen's Funeral Home, but the voices of our past resonated as the same dear souls who'd helped us bury Brian twenty years before filed by Daddy's casket. A man in his fifties stood in front of me waiting in vain to see if I would recognize him. "Diana, I'm Slick McGlone, from your Daddy's station years ago," he said.

Giving him a hug and thanking him for coming, my mind hearkened back to that simpler, more innocent world. Slick awkwardly attempted to have a conversation by announcing he had been hearing us on the radio. He wondered out loud, "How in the world did you do that?" What Slick meant was, "How can a little girl from Ashland, Kentucky, whose Daddy ran a gas station and who I watched grow up, become a star?"

"Dreams are more powerful than facts!" was all I could say in response.

Before I went to bed, I stared at the dish in the bathroom that every night of my life had been the repository of Daddy's pocket comb, tire gauge, Clove gum, and Camels. I closed my eyes to listen and thought I heard his footsteps coming down the hall. Now his illness had made him more open and demonstrative, but he was gone too soon. Now the unresolved conflict between Daddy and Margaret would never get straightened out. There would be no second chance for Daddy to validate or encourage Mark.

When the funeral was over, Wy and I had to rush to Memphis to open a show for Lee Greenwood. I struggled to gain control of my emotions and put on a happy face for the fans.

Onstage only hours after burying Daddy, I soaked up the smiles from the unaware audience and felt the summer night breeze blowing through my hair. I didn't come out of my bunk on the bus the next day. I decided to continue to use music to help change myself. Music was becoming my lifeline.

Ken had stood with us at the funeral and I felt as if he were becoming our ally in life's battlefield. I wasn't myself for a while, and he pitched in to help us check out personalities as we put our first road band together. Brent and Don auditioned them musically.

Mike Webber, the bass player, at six foot four and only 140 pounds, was a long, tall drink of water. On keyboards, Lee Carroll, also six foot four, walked over to Mike and said dryly, "Finally a band member I can dance with!" Charlie Whitten was picked for pedal steel and Dobro. Young Kip Raines was on drums.

Later that July, after opening a Friday night show for Earl Thomas Conley in Rome, Georgia, we arrived back home around midnight. As the bus dropped all of us off, Larry arrived straight from his gig at Nashville's Cajuns Wharf to pick me up. We'd seen each other infrequently over the summer, and I knew he was seeing someone locally. The tension between us was palpable and the ride out to Del Rio was awkward. Uncertainty clouded each carefully offered phrase of our small talk. I mentioned I'd bought steaks for us to grill the next day.

As we set my bags down inside, I noticed the blinking light on my brand-new answering machine. After Larry showed me how to play back messages, we were sitting side by side on the bed as RCA's Joe Galante jubilantly proclaimed: "Congratulations! 'Mama He's Crazy' just went to the top of the charts! It's the number one record in America and you're on your way!"

The machine clicked off and Larry and I just sat there staring at it. He didn't grab me and kiss me or twirl me around. Larry's face said it all. I was ecstatic and sad all at the same time. Without saying anything Larry slowly stood up and walked out. I heard the door shut and a car start. I ran out to the front porch and watched his taillights disappear. Our relationship was doomed. It was over.

The next day, all dressed up, I sat on the back porch stoop waiting, hoping against hope he'd come back to celebrate with me. The evening light faded and Larry never came.

When I phoned Wy, she and her beau were leaving to go celebrate. Desperate for company, I asked them to come get me. I danced all night at Chevy's with strangers and toasted to success, but in the corner of my mind was a broken heart.

Tennessee Williams said success and failure can be equally devastating. He didn't say anything about experiencing both at the same time! Our career was off like a rocket but I'd lost the two most important men in the world to me within weeks of each other.

In the studio, we'd been working on our first full-blown album, titled *Why Not Me.* Brent had co-written the soaring title song with Harlan Howard and Sonny Throckmorton. It had one of the strongest melodic hooks I'd ever heard, and when Don came up with his signature guitar licks it was a little slice of heaven!

"Mr. Pain," my song, co-written with Kent Robbins, that was a composite of all my girlfriends' bad-news beaus, made the list. Kent also contributed the gorgeous "Love Is Alive." "Girls' Night Out," the working-girls' party anthem; a chugging up-tempo tune named "Baby's Gone"; and "Drops of Water," with its underlying bounce, made the album. We dug up the shady "Endless Sleep," and Brent and Don collaborated on the sweetly sad "Sleeping Heart." Brent was turning into a real song meister, also coming up with a dreamy Texas waltz titled "Bye Bye Baby Blues." His talent for production was developing with inventiveness. Continuing to use accented, understated instrumentation in an acoustic setting, he adorned our vocal expressiveness. Brent liked to leave room for the listeners' imaginations.

We'd become a popular opening act. On August 3 at Louisville Gardens, we worked a show with George Jones. Onstage, after singing "John Deere Tractor," an enthusiast from the crowd hollered out, "Are y'all country gals?"

Without batting an eye, I leaned over into the microphone and loudly recited my response to his rhetorical question. "Honey, does a fat lady sweat at a dance?"

The crowd roared as my eyes fell on the front row—The Possum's fan club ladies sporting his T-shirts and none weighing in under two hundred pounds. Horrified, I smiled weakly at them as if to say, "It's only an expression! I wouldn't hurt anyone's feelings for the world!"

Coming off stage, Wy pounced on me, mock-scolding me all the way out to the bus. Our keyboardist, Lee Carroll, pointed to a notebook in which he claimed he'd begun documenting my bloopers. Ken rescued me by ushering us up onto George's bus, informing us "The Possum" was a fan of our music and had requested to meet us before he had to take the stage. George paternally told Wy she was his favorite female singer and admonished her to stay off booze. It was flattering and touching at the same time.

Wynonna and I often opened for Conway and he and I felt like old friends. While visiting with him and his secretary Dee on their bus one night after our show, I mentioned I was carless and would love someday to be in a position to buy one of his twenty-some antique cars. To my delight he offered to sell me a '53 turquoise Cadillac, because we'd appeared together in his similar '53 Caddy convertible on the back album cover shot.

I'd just received a check for $10,000 from my Daddy's will and Conway let me have the Caddy for that amount. "It's perfect!" I thanked him. "This big-moving piece of art reminds me of Dad's old-fashioned gas station. My Daddy believed a Cadillac was the essence of the hillbilly dream. "This beauty will be a tangible reminder of you and our first year on the road! I'll put 'Music' on the license."

One Saturday night after our show, Conway called me over to his bus to invite our gang to join him for Sunday dinner at the Carl Perkins restaurant in Jackson, Tennessee. It was on our route, and he wanted us to meet his legendary rockabilly pal.

At first, I thought Carl was very different from Conway. Conway's the kind of man one gets to know slowly. But when Carl met us out at our bus in his restaurant's parking lot and wrapped his big warm hand around mine, I was instantly taken with his openness and friendliness. Carl was almost pulling me inside as he graciously welcomed us all.

This pleasant afternoon has become one of my favorite road memories. Seated at a long table surrounded by Wy and the Judd Boys, Conway's group, and Carl's entire family we ate great catfish and laughed and we visited.

Carl regaled Wy with intimate stories about his good friend Elvis. "Wy, the reason he turned his shirt collar up was to hide the blemishes on his neck!"

Conway and Carl had both come from the rockabilly tradition and observing the two friends, I was beginning to see similarities between them. Both are deeply religious yet make no show of it, humble, family oriented, and scrupulously honest.

And neither got the recognition they deserve. They were never media darlings, never awarded, and never justly acknowledged for their amazing talents.

As we bade good-bye to Carl and his wife, Valda, and their clan, I knew our paths would cross again. What a special afternoon. Before we boarded our buses, I hugged Conway and told him, "You may not have won the prizes you deserve, but you *are* the prize."

The five band members, Wy, and I were slammed together on one bus, driving without brakes out there on life's highways, sometimes almost careening out of control. I bought Wy and myself spandex pants and had my alteration lady, Inous Wright, sew rhinestones on a couple of tops. I was later told that under the lights onstage, my golden pants paled out and made me look nude from the waist down. I never wore them again!

After shows, protectively surrounded by the band, Wy and I loved to go out to local clubs and dance to live music. As an attention-getter, we wore our stage outfits to attract cowboys. Lee Carroll, the official breath smeller, checked for liquor before giving his permission for guys to dance with us. Wildly independent, we kicked up our high heels until the house band announced, "You don't have to go home, but you can't stay here!"

We called our first leased bus the *Juddmobile* and it became our clubhouse on wheels. How Wy and I loved that crowded, noisy Silver Eagle, strewn with smelly socks and tennis shoes, food, clothing and personal effects! I'd been cooking, scrubbing, changing diapers, and out in the workplace since I was seventeen. This bus was my ticket to ride . . . my passport to freedom. The seven of us were a tight-knit family now . . . kindred spirits. We had no professional road manager, and no one out there watching over us. Bass player Mike Webber checked us into motels and collected the money each night. When we got our first T-shirts made, Lee sold them after the shows. It was very grassroots.

At our show at the Ponderosa Theme Park in Salem, Ohio, August 1984, I was feeling particularly ornery. I introduced the band as the "Fabulous Judd Boys," planting a hillbilly nickname on each one. Lee Carroll forever became "Cleon Leon," Charlie Whitten was "Odell," and Mike Webber was "Pops." Wy somehow became known as "Beautimus Maximus." Next week during a week-long Canadian tour, opening for rocker Neil Young, they, in turn, dubbed me "Mamaw."

And so began our infamous "road code." After memorizing portions of Pee Wee Herman's first comedy special, we joined his fan club and adopted the magician's "Mekka Lekka High, Mekka Lekka Hiney Ho" as the intro to our secret rituals. Paul Rubens (Pee Wee) got wind of it and called me on the road one night.

One such secret ceremony was Judd Court—conducted whenever there was a problem requiring disciplinary action. I presided as "Mamaw Judd Judge" with Wy and the Judd Boys as the jury.

Cleon, who collected fat pencils from all fifty states, was court sketch artist, and captured these events on paper.

We used pseudonyms to register into hotels, like Barb Wire, Patti O, Sue She, Bertha Dablues, Ilean Dover, Ben Dover, and Mike Rafone. Every night before retiring, they made me stand in the aisle of the bus and deliver a monologue. I'd come up with homilies such as, "Don't shower till the work's all done" or "Add more water to the soup Pa, there's better days a comin'."

During the Labor Day weekend at the Hee Haw Theater in Branson, Missouri, Wy and I purchased lawn statues of a concrete mama pig followed by two baby piglets. Each night we had Odell put the heavy pigs in front of our monitors onstage. As we sang, Wy and I watched people in the audience whispering, speculating about their significance.

We had a poster of the Road Warriors wrestlers on the bath- room door and followed the World Wrestling Federation for a while. Wrestling stars like Dusty Rhodes began showing up at our concerts. I had neon bumper stickers printed for all our cars declaring, "Raslin' Is Real!"

On our days off, we swam, went go-carting, or played miniature golf. Bowling was also a favorite pastime, and once we took over a bowling alley and each got our own lane for speed bowling. Judd rules were whoever finished bowling first and had the highest score won.

Throughout the giddy thrill of "there's no school tomorrow" first six months of touring, Don, now called "Doo-Don," was our anchor. Although he hated being out on the road away from his wife, Christine, and their church, he made this sacrifice for Wy and me. He was like a concerned parent, lovingly teaching us to take our first baby steps. Coming out of a painful childhood, Don had hit rock bottom with drugs and booze while on the road with Chuck Mangione in the 1970s. Jesus saved him. Now Don was one of the happiest people we knew, at peace with himself and the world. Wy said it best when she observed that "everybody who knew Don wanted some of what he had." We relied on him as our moral compass to point us in the right direction.

Time had come to let Doo-Don go back home, so we hired two

guitarists to fill his big shoes: Mark Thompson on rhythm and Steve Sheehan on lead guitar.

On the flight home in September, after six straight weeks out on tour, Ken informed me my house had been burglarized and insisted I move for my personal safety. Wy had her own secure place, and we'd decided to send Ashley to a private school, Sayre, in Lexington. Suddenly the house on Del Rio Pike was full of nobody.

I'd been calling Ashley from pay phones at truck stops all across the United States, and missing her was the only drawback. Autonomous and self-motivated, the "Can't Miss Kid" (as I now called her) settled into school.

Fearful of my being alone, Ken had Odell, our steel player, stay in Ashley's room when we were off the road. Odell was like my little brother and was mighty good company, because it was a letdown coming home now. He was a simple country boy from Lynette, Alabama, who preferred my big home-cooked meals and rocking on the front porch after supper to Nashville's night life.

Pops Webber kept the *Juddmobile* parked at his house near us out in the country and would pick up Odell and me and let us off down at the end of the driveway, where Wy and Ashley's old schoolbus had once stopped. Sitting on our suitcases at 6:00 A.M., waiting for our bus one day, I remarked to Odell we were going to stage school and becoming "Road's Scholars." After a while, I turned the little white-frame gingerbread farmhouse loose, stored my furniture, and moved into the Travelers Rest Motel on Franklin Road for several months till I could find a safe place to live.

I preferred being out on the road all the time with our surrogate family, because it was lonely living by myself in one rented room in my own town. Everyone else went home to their loved ones, and Wy was snug as a bug in a rug in her cute place. Through the grapevine I'd learned that Larry was living with a young girl. I wondered if he missed me or ever heard us on the radio. I'd lie awake at night performing an autopsy on our relationship.

Here I was surrounded by men, yet I didn't have one of my own. Ken held the reins, and I'd grown to completely trust this enigmatic man. In the year we'd been associated with him, he'd done everything he promised to do and more. Ken always seemed to be right and to have the answers.

It was a rare occasion when he and Martha showed up for our show in Denver, Colorado, September 24, but made even more special because Joe Galante and the RCA bigwigs had also flown in to see what we were like onstage.

Wy and I were fighting. The natural mother/daughter friction was increasing because we were now together twenty-four hours a day in close quarters, under extremely stressful circumstances. I was called on to be not only Supermom but also Superpartner. I needed all my energy to get myself ready, and it made me extra mad when she took my hot rollers just when they got heated or if she borrowed my things and didn't put them back.

We had visited two big Denver radio stations, and as we drove to the venue, my nerves were frayed. Wy and I sat on opposite sides of the backseat, refusing to look at each other, staring stubbornly out the windows. When we pulled up just in time to change into our stage outfits, Ken was waiting in the dressing room to remind us that the RCA VIPs were all assembled to critique us for the first time. I grew even more alarmed about taking the stage with Wy.

Our tempers were already big loaded guns, ready to go off, and now we were trigger happy. Ricky Skaggs now was a big name, and we felt lucky to be opening for him. Ken informed us that the place was sold out. Suddenly Wy, who'd begun rifling through her wardrobe bag, exclaimed, "Oh no! I can't believe it—I left my outfit back at the hotel!"

The hotel was too far away, and we were mere minutes from show time. I opened fire with both guns and began blazing.

"You stupid kid, aren't you ever going to grow up and get your act together? I cannot live like this any longer!" I screamed.

"I hate you, and I'm not singing with you tonight!" she shrieked back at me at the top of her lungs. We held nothing back, and our ranting echoed down the halls. Ernie Stuart, Ricky's road manager, had the announcer stall and everyone held his breath, wondering if there would even be a show. Facing each other, bent over at the waist, flailing our arms in the air, we were close to blows when Ken stepped in between us.

"Ladies," he intoned, giving us time to consider whether the label fit. "May I remind you of an important issue. There are several thousand people out there, who've paid their hard-earned money to hear you tonight. You must decide whether you're going to rise to professionalism or be a disappointment to everyone, including me."

If Ken had threatened us, or joined in the shouting match, the bickering would only have escalated. Instead, his calm, rational manner struck a nerve.

Martha abruptly appeared in the dressing room with our alternate stage outfits, suede dresses fresh from the dry cleaners in Nashville. She'd brought them with her on the plane and had run out to get them from their rental car when she realized what was going on. I could have sworn I saw wings on Martha's back as she turned to leave while Wy and I dressed in stoney silence.

Soon after taking the stage, pointing to Wy I began to announce to the crowd, "You're looking at the orneriest redheaded b-b-b-b-b—hillbilly singer in the business!" Wy almost dropped her guitar waiting to hear whether I would actually call her the B-word onstage.

Two significant things happened that night. Wy and I recognized that if we were going to avoid or at least survive future technicolor fight scenes and general disagreements, we would have to defer to Ken. Out on the bus after this show, we vowed to let him have the last word, the final say in all matters. We not only trusted his decision-making ability, but felt a tremendous sense of relief at having a mediator after years of butting heads. Wy brought out the protective fatherly instincts in Ken, and I saw her enjoying this new experience of a kind and authoritative male influence in her increasingly complicated life.

Second, not only had our growing respect for Ken drawn us out of our feuding, but we were starting to feel a sense of responsibility to the fans that extended beyond the musical aspect. For months we'd gone out and signed our eight-by-tens every night. After the show, the Judd Boys took out folding tables from the bin under the bus and set them up either out in the parking lot, or inside the clubs where Wy and I sat until we'd signed every last photo.

Since we were gone so much and I had completely stopped

nursing, Wy and I had lost touch with our friends at home. We enjoyed visiting with these folks on the road. I commiserated with other single parents and single women. Younger individuals came up to chat with Wy.

We had a ball playing dance halls in Amarillo, Nacagdoches, and Texarkana that week. At the Loadin' Chute, a guy gave me a sheer red negligee, and I passed it onto Pops to give to his wife. I stepped onto the bus after the show to find Pops (all six feet four inches and 140 pounds of him) modeling it, with his skinny, boney legs crossed, and my high heels dangling from his toes. He was calmly dragging on a cigarette. It was not a pretty sight!

Sometime during the night we stopped at a truck stop to fuel up, and everybody went in to eat. Shoving a couple of tables together, we laughed and carried on as we wolfed down our food. The heady sensation of being in a band, seeing our bus through the window, and such jovial company of our new family washed over us just as another patron punched "Mama He's Crazy" on the jukebox. Wy leaned across the table and asked me, "Did Texas invent country music?"

The next day, still spandexed out, we performed on the hip *Austin City Limits* TV program. We were becoming real road dogs, opening for Ricky Skaggs, Lee Greenwood, Ronnie Milsap, John Conlee, Roy Orbison, Eddie Rabbitt, Nitty Gritty Dirt Band, Earl Thomas Conley, and Conway Twitty. We earned in the low four-figure bracket and were booked through the Halsey Company by top agent Steve Pritchard.

After this six-week stint of being on tour, I was home shopping at Super-X in Franklin to replenish my makeup when a middle-aged couple pushing their cart toward me stopped. My heart fluttered, because I'd thought I'd been recognized and was about to be asked for my first non-postshow autograph. Instead, the man exclaimed, "Why Ms. Judd, don't you recognize me? I was your patient at the hospital!"

Quickly shifting gears, I innocently blurted out: "Oh! I just didn't recognize you with your clothes on and standing up!"

At my next stop at Kroger, the lady handing out free food samples did recognize me as she stuck a pizza roll on a toothpick in my face. "Why you're that singer, who looks like her daughter's sister!" she squealed. "I love your song and I hope you ride that 'which is which' riddle to stardom!"

If Wy and I were side by side, recognition was more likely. We got such a kick out of this new experience. Unaccustomed to being stared at, we'd assume that our slips were showing or that there was spinach between our teeth.

Our first industry recognition came as the Country Music Association (CMA) nominated us for three awards: Best Single for "Had a Dream," Group of the Year, and the prestigious Horizon Award, presented to the most promising new act. This triple nomination caused quite a stir, because we didn't even have a full-length album out yet.

When we discovered we were going to get to attend the awards show, Wy and I were elated! For years Wy, Ashley, and I had gathered side by side on my bed in our favorite old bathrobes to watch these annual TV specials, throwing popcorn at the screen if our picks didn't win.

A Colorado designer, Greg La Voi, submitted sketches offering to work with us, and I immediately called him insisting I design our dresses myself. Wy went along with me, as I promised her the most glamorous movie-star ball gown anyone ever laid eyes on! "We don't have a chance of winning," I confided, "but we'll look great!"

The day of the show, Greg arrived with the outfits we'd been working on for weeks over the phone and through the mail. Wy and I were so tickled about our fancy dresses and so excited about attending the awards show, we almost busted the seams! Ashley looked fabulous in a sky blue ball gown she bought with the money she'd made modeling in Japan.

Ken reserved us a dressing room out at Opryland where the show's televised, and I proudly showed our creations to Fay Sloan, the wardrobe supervisor, whom I knew from the Las Vegas fiasco. "Oh now Naomi, are you sure you want to wear these in public?" Fay tactfully asked.

I thought she was implying they were simply too fabulous to risk damaging.

Wy's was hot pink, and mine was turquoise satin. The dresses were full-length antebellum-style with huge skirts and puffy sleeves, bordered in black with billowy black net stoles, which wrapped around the shoulders. They were an outlandishly garish combination of Miss Kitty saloon girl and full-on *Hee Haw.*

Nashville hairdresser Earl Cox, who'd been cutting our hair at the salon where he worked, came out to Opryland to do us, so we felt totally pampered.

Ken hired a limo to take Wy, Ashley, Mom, and me to the theater. It was the first time in a limousine for all four of us and we oohed and ahed the entire short ride. Wy and I were nervous, but we tried not to hold hands. Surrounded by Nashville royalty, our tickets placed us right behind Alabama and on the aisle, just across from Earl Thomas Conley, whom we felt 100 percent sure would win the Horizon Award. Earl had just had all four of his singles go number one!

Sitting in our seats, we flinched every time a cameraman or any crew member passed by, thinking we'd been discovered and they'd come to evict us. We were so new, so inexperienced, we hardly felt worthy to even be there. Wy whispered it's how she felt when she slipped into clubs as a minor with a fake ID. I raised my eyebrows and assured her out of the corner of my mouth that we'd discuss that topic later at great length.

We were completely enjoying the show until they began to announce the nominees for the Horizon Award. When Tammy Wynette and Ray Stevens said, "And the winner is . . . the Judds!" Wy and I thought our imaginations were playing tricks on us! But everyone turned around in their seats and were smiling at us and applauding. Wy and I were immobilized with fear. We looked at each other wishing, "Don't make us come up there—you just mail the statues to us!"

Hoisting up our full-length skirts, our shaky legs, we made ourselves run down the aisle and up the steps. It was such a different perspective, standing on that fabled stage looking out over a sea of our heroes in country music. We were gasping for breath! "Well slap the dog and spit in the fire!" I cried out. This hillbilly colloquialism slipped out in my excitement. And that was our first introduction to the country audience on national television.

We related "how nervous and shocked we were and that we'd figured out a long time ago that's it's no use trying to act cool" and enthusiastically admitted that "this was the most exciting, thrilling moment of our lives." We thanked Ken, Brent, and RCA, the DJs, all the fans who'd supported us and Doo-Don "our spiritual mentor."

Frankly the only way we actually knew what we said in our first acceptance speech was from watching the videotape replay at home the next day. It was like being in a car accident. It all happened so fast, and we were so shocked. It was a big blur.

As the trophy girl steered us offstage, Earl, our hairdresser, and his partner, John Ferrari, were waiting in the wings. They grabbed us, and Wy and I bawled and smeared our makeup all over their white tuxedo shirts. I was vaguely aware of Tammy Wynette patting me on the shoulder declaring "It couldn't happen to nicer girls," stating that she was proud to be able to say she'd handed us our very first award. Ray Stevens offered congratulations as he walked by and said something, but I have no idea what. It was probably something pretty goofy.

The kid and I wanted to rush back out front to be with Ashley and Mom, but Chuck Thompson, whom Ken had just hired to handle publicity for us, instantly whisked us backstage to the media blitz. As soon as Chuck ushered us into the press room, pandemonium broke loose. People were grabbing at us, shoving microphones in our faces. Wy and I had never seen anything like it.

Kathie Lee Gifford was hosting the awards show coverage for *Good Morning America* and couldn't take her eyes off our dresses. "We all have a bet going that you girls made these gowns yourselves," she diplomatically professed.

"Why yes!" we simultaneously agreed. "How'd y'all know?"

"Well, er umm, it's just that we've never seen anything quite like them!" Kathie Lee was squirming. Just then I overheard a cameraman say we looked like "Scarlett O'Hara's worst nightmare." But Wy and I didn't give a hoot, we were the belles of the ball that night.

At the RCA after-show party at Arthur's, a swanky restaurant, everyone wanted his or her picture taken with us. We hung out celebrating with Alabama and felt comfortable with all those guys.

Randy Owen and I spent time talking privately at our table, and he reminded me of something nobody ever needed to tell me: how important the fans are.

We were the last to leave the party, and I squeezed Wy until she warned I might break her ribs. The limo took us to our cars, and as I watched her get into her boyfriend's car, I felt a pang of jealousy as I wondered if Larry and his girlfriend had been watching the show.

As I was driving home, silent from exhaustion, Mom spoke up with a weighty question, "Honey, why do you think all this is happening?"

Not even needing a moment to consider, since I'd already been asking myself the same question, I replied, "It must be the Lord's will."

"Good answer," Mom muttered as she reached over and gently patted my hand.

That night as I finally got under the covers, I thought about the fact that I'd never won anything in my life. I was thirty-eight years old now. Sometimes, life gives you a second chance.

Rockin' with the Rhythm

S SOON AS I awoke the next morning, I reached over to touch the award sitting on my bedside table to make sure it wasn't all just a beautiful dream. The title song from my favorite fairy tale, *Cinderella*, says: "A dream is a wish your heart makes when you're fast asleep."

Our picture was featured in the paper over the award show story and Chuck, our eager new press agent, called saying we'd been requested to come back out to Opryland and do more interviews. We were hot as a firecracker! Wy and I were ebullient and able to communicate a sense of awe that something so extraordinary could be happening to two ordinary women.

When the *Why Not Me* album came out shortly afterward, in October 1984, all four singles went straight to number one and the album was immediately certified gold and went platinum. Someone told us, "If at first you succeed, try not to act too surprised!" But we couldn't help it. I even said that we weren't an overnight success, we were an over-coffee-break success!

That Horizon Award kicked our career as hard as a strong mule! A very bright lady named Judi Pofsky, who was vice president of television for the Halsey Booking Agency, began obtaining lots of TV offers for us besides the standard country music programs. On December 4, 1984, they sent us to visit New York City to do *Good Morning America* for our very first time. Wy and I were dismayed by the noise, traffic, and smog. A small Coke at the hotel was $3.25 and everyone seemed to be in such a hurry! The noise from the street went on all night and kept us from sleeping, so we were puffy-eyed when David Hartman asked us our first on-air question: "So! How do you like New York?" Wy held her breath as I told him the truth.

Life magazine assigned one of its best writers, Jamie James, and *National Geographic* photographer William Allard to live on the *Juddmobile* with us for a week to capture our peripatetic adventures for a feature story. My proud Mom framed the entire spread and hung it in her kitchen.

NBC Nightly News correspondent Douglas Kikker's team traveled on the road with us for a "day in the life of" rags to riches story. It seemed unreal to hear famous anchorman Tom Brokaw saying our names on the six o'clock news.

We received an enthusiastic acceptance on our introductory Canadian tour that winter of 1984 and enjoyed making new friends north of the border. Wy and I made our debut on Canadian TV and met Hank Snow on the *Tommy Hunter Show*. We also ran into fellow Kentuckian Keith Whitley at the TV studio of *The Family Brown* show. As I bragged about Keith's marvelous voice I became aware of his humility and genuinely down-home personality.

Upon leaving Canada, we had to cancel a show for the first time in Santa Fe, New Mexico, in January. We'd been traveling in cold weather, doing a show almost every night, so Wy's throat was already sore when she went into an asthma attack just as we walked into the sold-out Line Camp Club. Wynonna's a real trouper but she was in serious trouble.

No sooner had we started our third song when she leaned over and said these words. "Take it Mom, I'm out of here." Finding myself suddenly alone onstage, a wave of panic came over me as I envisioned airborne beer bottles and rioting fans. Calmly I raised my hand for the band to cease playing, then I cleared my throat and addressed the standing-room-only crowd. I told them the truth.

It's a small world. One of my Ashland girlfriends, Carolyn Haywood, stepped out to the bus to tell me that she was living with one of the town doctors and could get Wy admitted to the hospital immediately. We rented a condo in Santa Fe to hole up for a few days while Wy recovered. In the meantime, we thought it would be nice having some private mother/daughter time together for a change.

The Grammys in February 1985 flipped us out! We were nominated for Best Duo or Group with Vocal, Best New Artist, and Song of the Year for "Mama He's Crazy." Not since 1968, when Jeannie C. Riley was nominated for "Harper Valley P.T.A.," had a country act been tapped for Best New Artist. We were also assigned to present an award. *Entertainment Tonight* sent a TV crew to film us during the entire event. At rehearsal, we bumped into was Huey Lewis, who exclaimed, "Wow . . . the Judds! Man, me and the boys have worn out your tape on our bus!" We would have gone home happy then and there!

Cindy Lauper came up to us saying she'd watched our "Mama He's Crazy" video on MTV and that now the three of us were going to have us a "Girls' Night Out!" Cindy beat us in the Best New Artist category with her "Girls Just Wanna Have Fun," but we won our first Grammy for Duo or Group with Vocal for "Mama He's Crazy." We'd gone from obscurity to stardom in less than a year. From the intimate shadows of the kerosene lamp to the glare of the brightest spotlight.

Now Pops Webber introduced us every night as "the CMA's Horizon Award winners, Grammy winners, and a couple of darn nice girls!" Since we'd been booked so far in advance, we were still an opening act working for a few thousand dollars a night. Wynonna and I opened a lot of shows for Ronnie Milsap and found him to be a true gentleman and a pure delight to be around. Wy was so impressed by the fact that Ronnie never sings off pitch. He's a singer's singer.

When we opened for Kenny Rogers, he was using a circular stage with a narrow runway around the orchestra pit. Wy and I were terrified we'd fall off the runway but chased each other around on it anyway. Kenny is immensely likeable; we joked and kidded a lot.

But it was nothing compared with what happened with the great Oak Ridge Boys! We first met them when we flew together out to the West Coast to do a string of dates. As Wy got comfortable and settled down to sleep on the long flight, she overheard Joe Bonsall telling Duane Allen he was going to take a picture of her drooling with her mouth open and send it to the tabloids. And so it began!

Our practical jokes and pranks even spilled over onto the stage. In Montecito, California, knowing Joe stepped to the edge of the stage every night to acknowledge us, Wy and I had made a huge sign that read "Applause!" As soon as he hollered: "And what do y'all think of our opening act, Wynonna and Naomi?" Wy and I ran out across the stage, behind Joe and out of his view, holding our applause banner high. Momentarily stunned by the onslaught of this provoked, thunderous applause, Joe turned to his fellow quartet members and caught them laughing and pointing at us skipping merrily out of sight into the darkness of the wings.

Wynonna and I had made a big mistake. We had one more show left on this particular tour, and we'd already learned that paybacks were hell. As we walked toward the stage that last night in Santa Rosa, the kid and I were jumpy and uneasy. Duane, Joe, Richard Sterban, and William Lee Golden were waiting for us by the steps with mischevious smiles. "Have a nice show, girls!" they recited in unison.

"Uh, oh!" Wy and I responded, also in unison.

We were down to our last song, "Girls' Night Out," when all of a sudden the crowd began laughing uproariously and pointing. Wy and I wheeled around to check it out and were startled by the hilarious spectacle. The Oaks, their road manager, and crew were gaudily dressed as women kicking up their ill-fitting high heels. You haven't really lived until you've seen William Lee Golden (Wy calls him "Rip Van Winkle") in a chenille bathrobe, big fuzzy slippers, and a hair net! We now refer to it as "Transvestites' Night Out."

Speaking of fashion, frustrated with not being able to find stage outfits at generic stores in ubiqutous malls, I sought out a Nashville stylist known for her hipness. Wy and I liked Vanessa Ware right away. Already familiar with our unique style of music, she guessed that we wouldn't be interested in fringe, sequins, gingham, or ruffles—the costume look of the traditional female country singers. Wy, Brent, Don, and I felt like musical quadruplets separated at birth, and Ken Stilts was the consummate personal manager for us; now we were excited that we'd found someone who shared our vision of how we wanted to look.

In our first get-together, I summed it up this way: "Vanessa, I feel like Cinderella going to the ball, so I want to look the part. I feel like we're living in a modern-day fairy tale and I'd like to look like a princess!"

Wy voiced her opinion adding, "We don't want to look like just any other girls living on your street. We believe if people go to all the trouble and expense of attending a concert, they want to be entertained with something to take them out of their own routine and allow them a fantasy."

We saw our wardrobe as yet another outlet for creativity, hoping to introduce a new sense of style, designed to reflect ourselves.

Vanessa, who was often hired by various record labels to do the wardrobe and create an image for album covers and videos, was a veritable 411 of information about where to find anything. She introduced us to Esben, an outrageous Danish designer living in New York who began to put together our first outfits.

Wy preferred hip, rockabilly-looking jackets, pants, and boots. Decidedly feminine, I wanted dresses and/or jackets to accent the waist, short skirts to reveal plenty of leg, and vibrant-colored petticoats to flash at the audience as I pranced and swished across the stage. We preferred interesting fabrics in jewel tones, and neither of us care for the color yellow. These first creations were approximately $2,000 each, and I was so proud of them I assigned each a name that either described its look or bore the name of the show on which it was debuted.

The "Ice Cream Suit" was a white lace beauty with tiny glittery rhinestones sprinkled all over it. The "Rita Hayworth" was a sexy, clingy full-length nude gown with black lace covering it that I wore for the Academy of Country Music (ACM) award show. "Mozart" was a hip faille turquoise jeweled jacket with pink toreador pants for the AMA's. The "Reagan" cream and gold pinafore was made for a daytime concert for the president. The "Peach Dream" was lightweight and short sleeved, designed for hot afternoon rodeos. I wore the stunning, dramatic black lace over the white "Change of Heart" dress in Europe. "The Dickens" was an emerald green faille three-quarter-length, Edwardian-style dress, featuring a fake mink collar for holiday shows. Everyone teased me about looking like "Snow White" in a sweetheart-style dress with black velvet bodice, white puff sleeves, long black gloves. When I debuted a purple snakeskin peplum jacket with a skirt that boasted standout bright green and fuschia crenolines on the *Joan Rivers Show,* the name stuck.

A reviewer wrote I looked like I was going to an "Alien Square Dance" in my neon yellow satin-topped original dress that suddenly burst into fancy ruffles at the bottom. By contrast, the "Valentine" was a rose red, romantic, dainty creation. Vanessa called me "Guinivere" whenever I wore a white textured dress decorated with antique gold beadwork trim. Every time I wore a white faille sundress and its bolero jacket with black soutache for outdoor summer night concerts I felt like a "Señorita." Vanessa and I copied versions of several elegant dresses from old glamour movie stars like the "Claudette Colbert" and "Merle Oberon." Wy took one look at my antique cream lace long gown and matching headpiece at the CMA and said I looked like a "Vestal Virgin."

Things were happening so fast now that we had difficulty squeezing in time for wardrobe fittings on the few days a month we were home. Wy and I felt like birds on a telephone wire, just lighting long enough to catch our breath, then off again!

March 1985, I moved into a brand spankin' new condominium located in Brentwood, fifteen minutes south of Nashville. Since I didn't have a credit rating, Ken had to co-sign for me to purchase my first home. It was a long awaited experience to be able to pick out new carpet, wallpaper, and drapes. I had to learn to operate my first dishwasher and finally was able to purchase dishes and silverware that matched! Ironically, after all those years of sharing one bathroom with two girls, I had two full baths and one half bath all to myself. Ashley, who was away at private school, came home often, and Wy was now renting a log house in the country outside Franklin. I wasn't used to having neighbors, but the condo was safe and convenient.

March 18, the very day I moved in, Wy and I were beginning work on our second album, *Rockin' with the Rhythm,* when Larry called at the studio. It was his birthday and although our brief conversation was tense and awkward, I could tell he still loved and missed me and the kids. I told him I'd moved, but he didn't ask for the condo phone number. I was dating someone exclusively, but was unable to forget Larry. The bigger the love the harder the fall.

Ken had suffered another heart attack while out on the road with us and was having triple bypass surgery. Sitting in the midst of his family in that hospital room, I fully came to realize how much I'd come to love and respect this man. A steady accumulation of shared milestones had formed a special bond among his family, Wy, and me. I fidgeted with the large diamond ring Ken had given me for Christmas as I let him know how much we loved and needed him. He not only recovered but was amazingly back out on the road with us just three weeks later. In keeping with my penchant for giving everyone a nickname, Ken now became "Mr. Big."

Mr. Big hired a golfing buddy to be our first bodyguard. At six foot five inches and 240 pounds, Bill "Snipper" Snyder became our constant sidekick. Wy and I teased good-natured Snipper unmercifully. She messed his hair up in public and taunted him by threatening to invite wild, drunken cowboys onstage. Snipper dreamed of inventing a "hormone detector" like the metal detector at airports to single out horny male fans. When some of his golfing and poker cronies showed up one night, I folded my arms across my chest and ordered the red-faced Snipper to "fluff my petticoats" in front of them. When he accompanied us to the mall, begging us to stay together because it was his responsibility to keep an eye on both of us, Wy and I laughingly split off and ran in opposite directions.

Every day was different. May 2, we were in the Kentucky Derby parade in Louisville with Rock Hudson. Pale and thin, Rock confided to us that he wasn't feeling well and was terribly exhausted. The following week it was publicly announced that he had AIDS.

From there we flew to Los Angeles for our third award show—the Academy of Country Music—where a charming Dick Clark greeted us. Filled with wonder, we still felt like fans instead of peers of the celebrities we now rubbed elbows with as we went backstage for the first time. Flabbergasted, we won Top Vocal Duo and Song of the Year for "Why Not Me." Our sincere acceptance speeches were zany and animated. It was chaotic as Chuck escorted us into the press area. Wy and I were beginning to sense the song title "Why Not Me" could be our theme song in life!

"Girls' Night Out," our fourth single, had just gone number one and a few days after the awards ceremony, we flew back to Los Angeles to film the video for our next release, the lushly romantic ballad by Kent Robbins, "Love Is Alive."

Arriving at a new, elegant European-style hotel in the middle of the night, Wy and I stumbled into our rooms. Because we'd been asleep in the car during the drive from the airport, I was wondering what part of our old Hollywood neighborhood we might be in as I stepped out onto my patio. I had to rub my eyes in disbelief as I looked out and saw our old house on Larrabee Street and the little health food store where I'd worked!

The hotel hadn't been built when we lived on Larrabee in the 1970s, and I couldn't believe the coincidence that I'd been assigned a room overlooking our past. I ran to the phone to tell Wy and she answered shouting, "Mommy! You won't believe where we are! I'm standing on my patio on the other side of this hotel from you looking down on my old grade school playground!"

The next day was May 12, Mother's Day, and she and I sat together in our jammies all day reliving and analyzing this amazing first year. I took advantage of the opportunity to remind Wy how crucial it is to stay grounded by remembering where we came from and what we'd been through. Wynonna understood all this and agreed when I suggested we request this hotel and these same rooms every time we stay in LA.

Only weeks later we found ourselves at the Music City News Awards show in Nashville, where we were slated to perform "Love Is Alive." It would mark our first performance at an awards show, and we were shaking in the dressing room backstage at the Opry. Dottie West had been watching us in the mirror as she finished her makeup and walked right up to me. Placing her hands on my shoulders, she sternly questioned, "Girl, is it true you were a nurse before all this?"

"That's correct," I admitted.

"Then decide right now what you want to do . . . give shots or sing songs!" Dottie watched me get things in proper perspective, then broke into that big wonderful smile of hers. I realized she'd just done to me what I did to Wynonna in Omaha at our first concert.

During the Music City News Awards show, we not only won

Star of Tomorrow but, ironically, Duo of the Year in the same show! This fan-voted awards program is part of an amazing annual phenomenon known as Fan Fair. It's exclusive to Nashville, because only in country music does such a mutually appreciative relationship exist between artist and fan. Booths are set up at the fairgrounds, where approximately thirty thousand fans from all over the world come to mingle with their favorite stars. Every night the record labels take turns hosting outdoor concerts at the grandstands.

Wy and I signed autographs for hours in RCA's Fan Fair booth, but we also set up our own fan club booth for an additional opportunity to meet even more fans and say thank you to them for coming out to hear us when we're in their hometown—and now welcome to ours! Wy and I had a major complaint with Fan Fair. It outraged us that Nashville couldn't provide a better facility with air-conditioning for all the fans. The summer heat was unbearable and we were especially concerned about the elderly, handicapped, and small children.

Months ago we'd met our first Judd fan at an outdoor show during a rainstorm in Florida. Linda Russell, three years younger than Wy, withstood the downpour, so we invited her on the *Juddmobile* to dry off. We were touched when she pulled a scrapbook out of her raincoat to show how she was documenting our fledgling career. We invited Linda to Nashville where she became president of our newly formed Judds Fan Club and a personal friend.

The end of Fan Fair week, Alabama invited us to perform at their monstrous outdoor all-day festival the June Jam in their hometown, Ft. Payne, Alabama. Sixty-five thousand folks showed up, and Wy and I had to be helicopered to the stage because of traffic. I'll never forget the sensation of looking down from that chopper onto a sea of faces looking up at us as if we were angels descending from heaven.

Alabama also invited us to be in their TV special, and we got to meet all their families at Randy Owen's mother's house. After the taping, Randy took us to his lovely home for a home-cooked meal with his wife, Kelly, and two kids. I liked Kelly's spunk. She confided in us how she handled the jealousy aspect of being married to a superstar like Randy.

That week something wonderful happened! Ken got us our very own customized Silver Eagle bus. Identical twin brothers, Jack and Jerry Calhoun, who make the best tour buses on the road, proudly showed us through our new home away from home. Up front was our "living room" with a couch and eating booth, three bunks, bath, microwave, TV, refrigerator, coffee maker, and more. In the middle of the bus were Wy's luxurious quarters, featuring a vanity with lighted makeup mirrors, closet, plenty of drawers, and two velveteen upholstered couches that folded out into a bed. Knowing I like my privacy, my room was at the rear of the bus with a full-size bed, chair, closet, vanity, windows on both sides and a sunroof. Both our rooms had televisions and stereos. I dove onto the dusty rose satin-and-velvet spread on my bed and screamed with delight!

I christened our $350,000 bus the *Dreamchaser* and proclaimed the jump seat across the aisle from the driver's seat as my throne. We hired a congenial fellow named Gaylon Moore as our driver and seasoned veteran of the road from Charlie Daniels Band, Wayne Smith, to be our first road manager. After we'd done a show and the five of us settled down to ride through the night to our next gig, I'd sit up on my throne pretending I was a pioneer woman in a Conestoga wagon setting out for unknown territory. Wy particularly loved the sensation of knowing that no one knew where we were.

It was indeed more difficult to keep up with us! When we played at Billy Bob's in Ft. Worth that summer, we felt a twinge of nostalgia knowing it was our last honky-tonk gig. When Wy and I were standing in between a couple of cowboys taking a photo after the show, we overheard them referring to each other as "Gristlehead" and "Brickbrain." The monikers became our CB handles.

Proud of our beautiful bus, I somehow talked Ernie Stuart, the new driver of the band bus, into racing Gaylon around a dirt track at the fairgrounds in Springfield, Missouri, after our show. Someone announced the impromptu race over the PA and the fans in the stands went crazy as the humongous buses lumbered around the racetrack churning up billowing clouds of dust. We won.

People around us knew that Wy and I had a terror of cracking up with laughter on stage and having to stop the show. We'd once gotten so tickled during a show at the Ponderosa Theme Park in

Salem, Ohio, we almost couldn't stop. At first the audience had giggled along with us, then grew silent and restless. At a show in Springfield someone, and we still don't know who, coerced a twelve-foot-tall Uncle Sam on stilts to come stalking down the runway toward our stage right in the middle of a tender ballad. Wy and I tried to ignore him, until all twelve feet of a towering Uncle Sam loomed in front of us. I leaned over, gave him a kiss, and whispered, "I'll pay you twice what the prankster offered, if you'll go away!"

We called these outdoor country and regional fairs the "Mud and Dust Tour." We stopped in St. Louis to pick up respected columnist Jack "Hawkeye" Hurst, a veteran reporter from the *Chicago Tribune* who was assigned to travel on *Dreamchaser* with us to chronicle our two shows with Ronnie McDowell that night at the Heart of Illinois Fair in Peoria. Jack understood the tour title when it was dusty for the first show but was raining and muddy for the second. In between sets, Jack watched us giving interviews, a photo session, wolfing down fair food, quarreling, and being loving. Jack's last observation in his long, well-written article about us was, "Why has neither complained even once today about this life that looks so easy from afar and so hard up close?"

Because we were happy! Happy to be together, happy to be singing, happy to be on the road. Happy to get to work with Mr. Good Guy, George Strait! Visiting with George out by the buses in the parking lot of the Indiana State Fair, I noticed his freshly pressed white shirt. The crisp crease in his tight jeans. The wedding ring on his left hand! I told George he even looked like his name—Strait.

During our show with him in Indianapolis, Wy was trying to cajole an unresponsive section to clap along and threatened, "If you don't, I'm gonna come out there and rip your lips off!" Observing that some folks weren't sure if she was teasing, I quickly bent over toward their direction and confided, "I think she's had too many corn dogs."

We ate corn dogs every day; collected tacky prizes in the game booths; watched taffy pulls, quilt displays, horse shows, and sheep shearing; and rode the rides on the midway. Wy held the record for going on the roller coaster the most times in a row but learned the hard way that she couldn't scream because she'd loose her voice.

At the state fair in Huron, South Dakota, Wy was leaving the stage in the middle of the show to change jackets while I introduced the band. As she turned to go, every head in the audience turned to watch her, and I could tell from the front row farmer's faces that they wondered where she was going. "Oh, she'll be right back," I assured them. "She's only going over to the livestock pen beside the stage here to deworm the cattle."

I could see them shrugging, "Oh! okay." The explanation seemed pretty natural to them. That same show, Pops Webber, wearing an Abe Lincoln stovepipe hat, asked all the women to meet him afterward out by the bus to exchange pumpkin pie recipes.

Four of the most unusual concerts we gave that summer were for prisoners, the Hells Angels, the FBI, and nuns.

Believe it or not there's a rodeo held by the prison in Huntsville, Texas, where inmates are the contestants. One of the officials told me the guys don't mind getting roughed up, cause they like being in the infirmary and getting pain medicine. We performed on a makeshift stage out in the center of the dirt rodeo arena. It wasn't large enough for all our band, so Odell (Charlie Whitten) had to play pedal steel on the low tailgate of a pickup truck parked next to us. Wy and I could hardly look in his direction because Odell made funny pitiful faces the entire set.

The maximum-security prisoners were cordoned off from regular inmates in a section of bleachers behind a wire screen in the grandstand. Someone once asked me if I believed in the electric chair and I responded: "I believe we should have electric *bleachers* for murderers and child molesters!" Each time our rotating stage passed in front of the section where the capital crime prisoners sat, Wy would lean over and whisper, "Now's your chance, Mom."

A minimum-security prisoner had been in charge of stocking our trailer dressing room with cold drinks, fresh towels, and such and came in to clean up as we were preparing to leave. Nervously trying to make small talk, Wy asked this hard-looking fellow what he was in for.

"Murdering my family," he replied offhandedly. "But I get

parolled next month. Where do you live?" He then began laughing uproariously, flashing a gold tooth.

When our bus pulled in at the backstage area for our outdoor concert in Pleasanton, California, Wy began hollering excitedly for me to look out my windows. On both sides was a sea of Harley-Davidson motorcycles. Milling around were hundreds of bikers.

"Oh great! Now we're playing a convention for serial killers!" I exclaimed, as I ran toward the front. Wayne, Gaylon, and Snipper looked out the window then back around at each other in disbelief.

"Quick, get out the contract for this show!" Wy suggested. Listed to appear were David Allan Coe, Johnny Paycheck, and our buddy Waylon Jennings. It was "outlaw day."

Fortunately, Ken and Martha had just flown in to see how things were going with all our new personnel. Ken looked serious and uneasy as he stepped up onto our bus. First question I asked him was if he had his nitroglycerine pills with him. He patted his coat pocket and flashed a quick fake smile. Ken informed us he'd been meeting with the show organizers for hours and assured us everything was under control.

"Listen to me, girls," he began. "You are the female entertainment they've chosen over everyone else in this business. This may sound strange, but right at this moment you are safer than any other women in America. They've put you up on a pedestal."

Wy wanted to know if there were any police around. "Yes, there's a very delicate truce between the Hell's Angels and the law right now. Sonny Barger, their leader and president of the largest California chapter, was killed just last week."

Speechless, Wynonna and I slowly sat down on the couch together and stared out at this amazing scene. Grizzled, wind-burned men, some bearded—most long haired—stood around drinking beer. Jeans, leather, and tattoos were the order of the day.

What got us were the women! Braless, many wearing tube tops or skimpy halters, bleached blonds with black roots showing, cigarettes hanging out of the corner of their mouths, tattoos on their shoulders and chest. Some of them were only in their teens; that's what got to me.

Mesmerized watching this biker cult activity, we'd almost forgotten to get ready for our concert. Gaylon came back to where I was putting on makeup and announced some of the leaders "had come to get me." The new president of the Hell's Angels wanted his picture taken with me on his motorcycle.

"We can't find Ken," Gaylon gulped. "And these dudes are insistent that you come with them right now!"

When I opened the bus door to step down, a massive bare-chested man with a shaved head and sunglasses reached up to help me. Introducing himself as "Deacon," he and my other leather-clad escort (I was too nervous to remember his nickname) led me to a canopied area where a large piece of red carpet had been spread out. On it were lined up the gleaming chromed-out prized Harley Hogs of the elite of the most famous motorcycle gang in the world. Smiling my purest Sunday school smile, I posed on the Leader of the Pack's chopper.

As Deacon returned me to the safety of our bus, he commented that this was an honor extended to very few outsiders. "Yeah, it's been swell." I thanked him.

Although skirmishes broke out in the audience, the stage was protected. Wy and I survived the entire episode unharmed and un-touched, just as Ken had promised.

Shortly thereafter we arrived in Missouri to sing at a small country fair with country crooner Gary Morris. When Wayne came back to awaken us, he declared in a serious tone that the director of the FBI was on his way. The Secret Service had just radioed ahead their requirements. I blurted out: "Wy, it's going to be all right, honey! Whatever you've done, Ken and I will get you the best lawyers. We'll beat the rap. Don't you worry about a thing." It took newcomer Wayne a minute to realize I was teasing.

Judge William Webster, the head of the FBI in 1985, was vacationing at his nearby family farm and simply wanted to attend our concert. Seated on a folding chair at the side of the stage, flanked by Secret Service bodyguards, he cheered and applauded. Judge Webster ate home-grown tomatoes, turnip greens, and barbecue with us at our crew meal. Wy and I had to keep reminding ourselves he wasn't just a typical fan.

Several weeks later when we played near FBI headquarters, he treated us to a VIP tour and invited us to spend time with him in his executive office. Judge Webster, an eligible widower, came to our shows when his schedule permitted, and gossip columnists had it there was a romance blossoming between us. Truth is he's a brilliant and wonderful man, and we simply enjoyed each other's company very much. Wy shuddered at the idea of my marrying the head of the FBI, lamenting: "My life will be over! I'll never be able to get away with anything ever again!"

August found us in the pastoral beauty of Amish country around Pennsylvania. It came as a pleasant surprise to learn hundreds of Amish folks were in the audience. Local police assigned to backstage security would report horse and buggies tied up near the concert site. A deputy observed, "There's not many artists they can relate to."

That's the same reason a convention of nuns gave for booking us in Maryland. Teasingly irreverent, Wy and I dedicated "Blue Nun Cafe" to them, noting the song had also been a favorite with the Hell's Angels. My mom was traveling on the road with us at the time and I introduced her to the sisters as the real "Mother Superior!"

Working our way through New England, opening for gentleman Don Williams, Cleon took us to a popular café in Boston on our night off. A couple of hours later back in my hotel room I realized I'd gotten food poisoning from the fried clams I ate. Desperately ill and throwing up for many hours, I was on the verge of passing out. Afraid that I was becoming seriously dehydrated, I called Wayne's room about 4:00 A.M.

"Get a car and directions to the nearest emergency room," I whispered cryptically and hung up.

I was laid out in the backseat on the way to the hospital as Wayne begged me not to die. "Mr. Big will fire me for sure if I have to call and tell him we lost Mamaw in Boston!"

When I woke up in the hospital and looked at the clock, I realized we had a show in Hampton Beach, New Hampshire, that night. The doctor kept insisting they needed to keep me another forty-eight hours as I sat up and began professionally unhooking my IV and removing the needle from my arm.

The reviewer of our show commented in the paper the next

morning that I leaned against the piano all night and was uncharacteristically subdued.

Now once again I had to play road nurse. I phoned Ken from a roadside rest area early that Sunday morning on September 1 to tell him I'd decided to cancel our scheduled show that night in Van Wert, Ohio. Wy, who refuses to complain of anything physical, had had her wisdom teeth pulled weeks earlier and now had "dry sockets." Every night I'd been shoving cotton packing saturated with oil of cloves into tender cavities and she was in misery. Ah motherhood, the second oldest profession!

Ashley had been hearing us on the radio, seeing us on TV, and reading about us in magazines just like everyone else in America. Any kid who was less secure, less sure of herself than Ashley would not have handled it so well. We talked about her ongoing adjustments constantly.

She and Wynonna are so different. Ashley has the discretion of a whisper; Wy, the urgency of a scream. Wy needs lot of attention and roars through life like some great steaming, hot, and noisy dynamo spinning at five thousand RPMs, requiring lots of work to keep it running. Ashley's the opposite. She's more like a smooth running, efficient waterwheel nestled in a quiet brook. Private and thoughtful, she has a fluid tranquility about her. Even at seventeen, she had the ability to go about her business, working her way through difficulties without undue melodrama.

Resilient and autonomous, Ashley had constructed an extended family at her school, Sayre in Lexington, the past year with Jennifer Simpkins, Lucy Backer, and Thomas Buckley, but she still needed her real family. Ashley traveled with us on the road that summer. She made $10 a day for cleaning the bus and devoted a couple of hours every afternoon to an algebra correspondence course. She always accompanied us to award shows and the major events, but this September it was time to settle down for her last year of school. Mom stepped forward and invited Ashley to live with her and Wib for her senior year.

"This is perfect!" I agreed. "Ashley can stay in my old bedroom and I'll know she's safe and sound. I can dial that phone number in my sleep."

Ashley had long lamented not having a normal family life. She craved structure and the trappings of domesticity. Now with Mom, she could count on a home-cooked meal on the table every night at about the same time and rest assured that her gym suit would be washed, folded, and sitting by the door with her lunch sack. Together Mom and Ashley read and discussed books and went on trips, like a weekend jaunt to Washington, D.C., to the art museums. School had just begun when Ashley became homecoming attendant. Her grades were excellent.

Meantime, Wy was growing up in public and making her mistakes in front of everyone. I often forgot my "partner" was still figuring things out. "The Traveling Teen" as I'd been calling her was now twenty-one. After we'd played Springfield, Missouri, with the Nitty Gritty Dirt Band, some guys we were signing autographs for invited her to their fraternity house party. It was all right with me, because one of our guys went with her. Besides, I thought, it may be her only chance to glimpse what most kids her age were doing. We agreed to change our departure to 2:00 A.M., thus allowing her several hours of "fraternization."

Gaylon took the bus to be refueled, Wayne collected our money and checked us all out of the hotel, while I got my bath and packed. At 2:00 A.M. the bellman escorted me to *Dreamchaser*, where Gaylon and Wayne sat looking over the map discussing the best route for our long drive that night. I saw that the band bus and our two eighteen wheelers were loaded and ready right behind us. We always try to run in a caravan in case of trouble. It's also much more enjoyable for all four of the drivers and helps them stay awake.

Wy wasn't in her room. "No big deal," I thought, as I got into my jammies and made some microwave popcorn. "So she's a few minutes late!"

An hour later, Gaylon, Wayne, and Ernie came back to my room where I was rearranging drawers to keep myself busy.

"Mamaw, we're running out of time to make it to the next gig. The crew needs to be there early in the morning to unload the trucks, set up the stage, install sound equipment and hang lighting. If we don't leave now we're not going to have a show tomorrow night!"

Of course, I'd been more aware of all this than anyone. I threw on my robe and ran over to the band bus to assure everyone my darling daughter would "be back just any second!" Then I positioned myself in the jump seat on *Dreamchaser*, where I could see the entrance to the street, and rehearsed what scathing recriminations might have the greatest effect on her. It dawned on me I no longer had any means of punishing Wynonna. What was I going to do, ground her from doing shows for a month and tell her she couldn't sign autographs?

By the time a carload of college students with beer breath pulled up to the bus door, I'd turned into a fire-breathing monster. "I just wanted to spend more time with kids my own age," she whined, believing a good excuse is better than none.

"First and foremost you have a responsibility to our fans and our guys," I shrieked, launching the worst road fight in Judd history.

Wayne and Snipper dove for the safety of their bunks and Velcroed their curtains shut. Gaylon put on his headset and turned up the volume on his tape recorder, as we rock and rolled the bus down the highway. Wy's road dog, Loretta Lynn, cowered in fright in a corner of the couch.

"I didn't ask to be born!" she reminded me.

"Well, if you asked me right now, the answer would be no!" I retaliated at full voice.

"The Battle of the Titans" (as it came to be known in Juddlore) waged all through the night. Finally, realizing we were losing our voices, I locked myself back in my room. Afraid to come out, I watched out my window as Wy followed the band and crew into a truckstop to eat breakfast about 6:30 A.M.

An hour later, I was lying in bed with one eye closed and one eye open, when there was a soft knock at my door. "What's on your mind—if you'll pardon the overstatement?" I sarcastically called out, struggling to rally for yet another round.

When there was only silence, I got out of bed cautiously to put an ear against the door between our rooms to check on what my worthy opponent might be up to now.

Barefooted, I stepped on something Wy had slipped under the door. It was only a small, pink satin heart pin cushion that she'd purchased at the truckstop. Bordered with white lace, it bore the words, "I love you, Mom."

I touched it gently to my cheek and wept. Wy and I slept all through the day and had one of the best shows ever that night opening for B. J. Thomas. She was usually the first to say, "I'm sorry."

Something began to change after this vicious battle. It began to dawn on Wy that I wasn't deliberately trying to ruin her fun or dominate her life. I only wanted to be her mentor, not her "tor-mentor." I tried to explain how she and I had volunteered to be the CEOs of the thirty guys on the road. It was such a huge operation, everyone needed to stay in tune and keep within the beat.

I always felt like a symphony conductor, as if everyone were looking to me to orchestrate things. Ready and willing to do that, I was beginning to see that I had to let go of feeling so responsible for Wynonna. I was trying to understand why it was so important to me that everyone love her. I thought she was the greatest kid and hoped desperately that everybody would feel that way. Also, when she screwed up, it reflected negatively on my parenting ability. Complicated stuff!

It was quite unnerving for our organization when Wy and I weren't getting along. They wondered sometimes whether there'd be a show or whether they'd even have a job the next day. I sat Wy down, describing to her that our relationship was like nuclear energy. It had the potential for enormous good or bad.

After this first year out on the road, Wy and I could see that fans were closely watching our mother/daughter situation when they began asking our advice. Baffled kids asked how she could spend so much time with me and confiding in person and in letters how they wished they were closer to their moms. Mothers sought advice on how I managed to garner respect from my daughter and keep her out of trouble. "A good spanking saves a month in detox!" I'd quip lightheartedly, feeling unworthy to give such advice.

Wy and I were starting to look at the tangled mess of our relationship and to analyze what went on between us with some degree of objectivity. Because of our strong desire to help the fans by at least setting a good example, we began to be kinder and more patient with each other.

In the middle of our next show at the Mid-South Fair in Memphis, Tennessee, I spontaneously confided to our audience for the first time that Wynonna and I wanted to be "hope sellers." Unable to explain exactly what this meant, I was now referring not only to the example of our rags to riches story, in encouraging people to pursue their own dreams, but to the healing that had begun between the two of us.

A limo picked us up as we came offstage and at midnight drove us to the legendary Sun Recording Studio in Memphis, where stars had gathered to record what was being called *The Reunion of '55 Album*. We walked into a room where Carl Perkins, Roy Orbison, Johnny Cash, Jerry Lee Lewis, and John Fogerty were already singing. A really cute guy with long, black, spikey hair came over and introduced himself as Marty Stuart. "Man, can't you just feel him here with all of us?" he whispered.

Wy and I knew he was referring to Elvis. We sang backup on these former Sun Record artists for the album and for the TV taping that captured the special event.

When we finally got back to our rooms about 3:00 A.M., I was too jazzed to sleep. I lay there remembering Larry taking me on the tour of Graceland. As soon as the lady who runs it spotted Larry in line, Patsy immediately closed the tour to the public and welcomed us in straight away. Taking down the roped-off barriers, she'd called all the tour guides together and asked Larry to lead us through Elvis's house. Characteristically modest and laconic, Larry relived fascinating private moments that happened in each room. I hadn't known before that Elvis was a prankster and that he had a craving for peanut butter and banana sandwiches! Larry described how they recorded "Moody Blues" around one mike in the Jungle Room. In the formal living room, he fell silent and seemed deep in thought. When I went over and stood beside him and asked what had taken place here, Larry could only mutter, "This is where I stood next to his casket and sang the day of his funeral."

Now tonight I couldn't stop thinking about Larry, how he'd

lived with Elvis and stood close to him on stage every night, singing harmony with the King as I did with Wynonna. The next morning I called Larry with a proposal.

I wanted to buy one of Elvis's stage outfits. Elvis and Larry were both about six feet and 175 pounds. After E. (as his entourage called him) had put on weight, he took Larry up to his bedroom at Grace-land and gave him some clothes. Elvis liked Larry and often told him he wished he could sing bass. Onstage, the King even referred to Larry as his alter ego.

After watching Ken enjoying the nostalgia in the Sun Studios the night before where Elvis recorded his early hits, and knowing he was a great admirer of the King, I came up with the idea of getting a stage outfit and having a wax figure look-alike created to give Ken for our upcoming second Christmas together.

My hand was shaking as Larry answered. During all our five years on Del Rio, Elvis's clothes had been stored under our bed. The bed collapsed a lot, so we'd carefully removed the bags of clothes to the safest place in the house. No matter how far behind we got in rent or how desperate for money we became, we never once considered selling any of these treasures. It had been a year now since that night "Mama He's Crazy" went number one and Larry walked out on me. Knowing Larry would never let Elvis's things out of the family, I'd know for sure he still dreamed of our getting back together if he agreed to sell them to me. This would be the acid test of whether he was still carrying the torch.

If he was surprised to hear my voice, Larry was even more surprised by my request! I encouraged him to take time to think it over, but just after a brief pause he agreed. Yes!

Trying to keep it businesslike, I asked to purchase Elvis's powder blue jumpsuit and scarf, plus two custom-made shirts. Larry agreed to the $2,000 price.

"I'd like you to sit down and write a description of the circumstances surrounding Elvis's handing you this particular outfit as documentation," I continued.

"It was during a break when we were recording 'Moody Blues' in the Jungle Room at Graceland," Larry distinctly remembered. "When can you come over to my apartment?" he asked.

"Oh goodness no! I'm too busy," I insisted. "I'll put Vanessa, my personal assistant, in charge of the project because I'm on my way to Portland, Oregon, to do a press conference with George Strait, Hank Williams, Jr., and Alabama."

A major event in country music was gearing up. Because cigarette sales were plummeting, Marlboro's marketing executives dreamed up a national tour boasting the biggest draws on one bill for a reasonable ticket price, in a state-of-the-art concert at major venues.

Ken was excited about the phenomenal exposure opportunities it would give us, but I refused to have any part of it because of my nursing knowledge that cigarette smoking causes cancer and was responsible for 390,000 deaths that year.* I was also aware that ad agencies, like the ones putting on the show, make more money than tobacco farmers. In the meeting, I was the only one in our organization who voted against it; thus I was outnumbered. Remember, Wy and I had *sworn* always to let Ken have the final say. He said the positive message we put out through our music and image would be received by a lot of folks, and he hated to see us turn down the tour.

Firmly, though, I warned everyone that I would never speak the word *Marlboro* or verbally acknowledge the tobacco industry. Instead, I would only allow that a percentage of a ticket dollar was going to the Second Harvest Food Bank and promised to visit these centers to give them publicity. Ever a champion of the underdog, I would also talk up the local country music act who won a talent contest in each market getting to open the show and take home the $5,000 prize. I was a thorn in Marlboro's side.

Marlboro only did the tour for publicity; they knew they would actually lose money on the concerts themselves, because of the sky-high production budgets involved in buying big-name talent, renting the largest venues, and paying for stage/lighting setups and video screens. In addition to enormous Marlboro banners in arenas and cigarette giveaways, contractually they required the acts to do a full press day to advance each concert date.

Meantime, Wy and I were so busy doing interviews, photo

---

*These figures come from the U.S. Surgeon General's Report, issued in 1989 from the U.S. Department of Health and Human Services, Office of Smoking or Health, Rockville, MD.

sessions, meetings, and videos as well as singing and traveling every night, we'd been carrying around shoe boxes of tapes to pick out ten songs for our second album. *Why Not Me* had been the only country album to go platinum besides Alabama's that year.

Brent got the idea for "Rockin' with the Rhythm of the Rain," the catchy title track for this second album, from watching us playing music on our front porch swing at Del Rio. Shortly after Daddy died, Brent played Wy and me a song by a new songwriter named Jamie O'Hara, called "Grandpa (Tell Me 'Bout the Good Old Days)." It took several takes to record it, because it made us cry. We were too preoccupied with its impact on our own emotions to realize the classic song would have such widespread appeal with its plea for traditional values. Brent said he cowrote the third song, a beautifully wistful ballad, "Dream Chaser" about us.

A tall British chap, Paul Kennerley, contributed two songs that were so cool they became singles: "Have Mercy" with its rockin' boogie groove and the sultry "Cry Myself to Sleep." Paul brought his wife, Emmylou Harris, to the studio to meet us. She was so sweet and down to earth. Wy and I were thrilled to get to tell Emmylou face to face how much we appreciated and learned from her artistic integrity, and we thanked her for forging the path we were now on. That night Larry and I took Emmylou and Paul out in our '53 Caddy to hear another one of our heroes, Ralph Stanley and the Clinch Mountain Boys, at a bluegrass joint, the Station Inn.

Wy and I had never stopped to think about any labels for our own music, so we found it interesting to read the critics' description of it. There were constant references that we were, in Robert Oermann's words, "hauntingly traditional, yet modern." *Stereo Review* decided we featured "high caliber material with essentially mountain voices and an amalgam of diverse styles."

Rolling Stone saw us as "heirs to the Everly Brothers' vocal kingdom" and voted us Critic's Choice for country album.

Ralph Novak, music critic for *People* magazine, started off his flattering review with "warm, ungussied, lilting and folksy. Mama Naomi and daughter Wynonna could rewrite the book on how to charm country music fans." I teasingly told Wy, "Flattery is when other people describe you as you see yourself!"

"Wow, gee whiz and unreal!" was our response when *Perform-ance Magazine* named us Stars of Tomorrow and gave us the Country Breakout Award. *Cashbox* magazine voted us Number One Country Duo—Singles, and Number One Country Duo—Albums. *Billboard* gave us four titles: Top Country Single Duo, Top Country Album Duo, Top Country Artist—Singles, and Top New Country Artist—Albums. Our walls were getting covered with plaques. Wy and I thanked them all, saying it that with every award it felt as if our career were sprouting an arm or a leg. Now we were off and running.

October is Country Music Month in Nashville, and it was time for the 1985 CMA show. We learned we'd been nominated for three awards: Vocal Group of the Year, Single of the Year, and Album of the Year. We also were asked to get the show off to a rousing start with "Have Mercy." As we won Group of the Year and Single of the Year, Wy and I held the awards up, encouraging other aspiring performers to persevere and ask "Why Not Me?" We admitted we'd almost backed out of coming because of nerves. We still weren't used to all this pressure.

It was the year of the "new traditionalists" and backstage that night we discussed how delighted we were to be a part of the movement to kick the recent pop-middle-of-the-road phase out the door. Ricky Skaggs was chosen Entertainer of the Year, Reba McEntire received the award for Female Vocalist, and George Strait won his first Male Vocalist award.

It was Reba's second CMA award, too. In our shared dressing room we congratulated each other and got along famously. We'd been on many shows with her and were so comfortable together.

After one concert with her and Conway in Shreveport, Louisiana, we were enjoying birthday cake with Reba on her bus. I had Charlie Battles, her husband at the time, take photos of the three of us wearing tiny, silly party hats and blowing party favors. I laughingly threatened, "Reba, maybe someday we'll all be real famous and I'll hold these ridiculous pictures over your head!"

I liked Reba's family; we held the same value system. She and I share a strong work ethic and Charlie called us "the go-getter girls."

By now our music had caught on like wildfire, and we started headlining some dates. It didn't matter to us about billing, we were just grateful for the opportunity to do a longer show.

Before we could catch our breath or really rest up from the excitement of the award show, we were back out on the road. We did an outdoor fair in Yakima, Washington, where it was so cold that fall you could see your breath. Wy and I had to borrow some of the band guys' heavy jackets to wear, hiding our beautiful stage dresses. Teeth chattering, I asked the crowd who sat bundled up on hay bales, "Are your buckets getting sore on the hales of bay?" Wy's lips wouldn't work properly either and the cold threw her into an asthma attack. Tennessee Ernie Ford, who was on the show, saw how exhausted we were and just as we'd hoped, he offered his famous, "Bless your pea-pickin' little hearts!" Then after our next televised Halloween concert at Walt Disney World in Orlando, Florida, we flew to Amsterdam, Holland.

It was our first time abroad and everything was, of course, "foreign" to us, including the currency, food, the accommodations, and language. But the canal district was by far the most unusual! We were out being tourists with the Judd Boys until we came across the sex shops. Prostitutes rent tiny store fronts and sit scantily clad in the picture windows baiting customers. Pot is sold and smoked openly in cafés. Since Wy hadn't really been into her studies during her school years, I'd been using our travel opportunities to teach her things, but this time she wasn't the only one getting an education! We quickly left the canal district to take in a tour of a castle instead. There's a large chain of stores in Holland named Winkles, and *winkling* became road code for "shopping."

We played at a theater in Amsterdam for KRO radio, then flew to London to introduce ourselves to Britain via interviews. Ken promised we'd get to actually sing on our next visit. Wy wanted to know why the English were incessantly polite, yet somewhat distant. As we were shopping in the very popular and crowded Harrods, I came up with my personal theory that the English have had to develop a civilized code of behavior to get along side by side in such a small country.

Switzerland was my favorite country, and Ken decided we should shoot a photo session for a Christmas album. Taking a train through the Alps, oohing and ahhing at some of the most breathtaking scenery in the world, we finally arrived at the Swiss village of Arosa.

Wy and I were seated across from each other in a large horse-drawn sleigh going up the Swiss Alps to the designated location for the photo shoot. Suddenly, the driver realized he'd taken the wrong narrow, icy road on the mountainside. The Swiss teenager began backing our sleigh out over the edge of the Alps in his attempt to turn around. Wy and I completely freaked out! Our terrified shrieks only frightened the horse more, and the driver began hollering the only English he knew, "No problem, no problem!" I frantically unsnapped the heavy sheepskin blanket they'd fastened us under, leapt out of the sleigh, grabbing hold of Wy's borrowed fur coat and pulling her to safety with me. Our hats askew and disheveled, we were trembling as we held onto each other and peeked down over the precipice. A headline flashed across my mind. "Judds' Frozen Remains Found at Bottom of Swiss Alps—Under Horse's Rump." To this day, everytime Wy and I look at that elegant picture on our Christmas album cover, we shudder at our close call with certain death.

Returning safely to the States, we taped a TV show every day that week in December. Dick Clark's *Rockin' New Year's Eve, Hour Magazine, Solid Gold,* and *The Tonight Show* with Johnny Carson.

The Tonight Show is live to tape at 5:00 P.M. so it can be shown at different times across the country to millions of viewers. While we did our sound check and rehearsal, *The Tonight Show* band members had been setting up too. After our run-through of "Grandpa," Doc Severinsen walked over to introduced himself.

"How'd you come up with that countermelody on your harmony, Naomi?" he quizzed me.

Not knowing if this was good or bad, I confessed to Doc I'd never had formal training and didn't even know what a countermelody was.

"Cool!" he responded. "Just dowatchado girl!"

Knowing how many people watch *The Tonight Show* and that it was rare for a country act to be on, Wy and I were unbelievably nervous. Judi Pofsky, our TV agent, explained that after our song,

Johnny would signal Fred De Cordova, the producer, that he either liked us or he didn't.

If Johnny liked an act, the performers would get invited over to the couch. If that conversation segment went well, you might get invited to perform a second number, so we rehearsed another song just in case. No one gets to meet Johnny until you're on the air with him. The tension was mounting.

Ed McMahon stopped by our tiny dressing room and cordially welcomed us. Wy had invited some of her girlfriends and they were gabbing like magpies. I fled to the quiet of the public ladies room to compose myself and bumped into Ken, who was nervously smoking a cigarette in the hallway. He was the most uptight I'd ever seen him in all the time I'd known him.

"You girls could bust your butts out on that hard road for a solid year and not be exposed to as many people as you'll reach on this one TV show!" Ken informed me unnecessairly. We acknowledged our shared fears and the toll such intense tension takes on the body. Out of nowhere, an old Ashland classmate, Bob Smith, appeared. Bob, *The Tonight Show*'s monologue writer, assured me that Johnny is a "kind and sweet man."

Not only did we get invited over to the couch after "Grandpa," but we got to sing a second song. While the credits were rolling at the close of the show, a charming Johnny came out from behind his desk and in a rare TV moment began to dance with me!

After TV tapings, Wynonna and I had a ritual. We'd return to our rooms and dive into the large, economy-size jar of Ponds cold cream and remove all our makeup. Then we'd get into our comfy robes, order room service in my room, and settle in to watch ourselves on the program when it aired. We would harshly critique our performance, cringe at our mistakes, and laugh at ourselves.

Doing *The Tonight Show* was such a big deal, we'd flown Ashley out to LA to be with us and ended up using her in our "Grandpa" video that same week. I had to write her a note to request an excused absence from school, and the dean of girls commented that most parents' excuse notes pertained simply to orthodontist appointments. The video director was extremely pleased with Ashley's performance.

She casually remarked for the first time she was considering taking some drama classes when she got to college. Hmmmm. . . .

Back home in Nashville, the husband of one of our secretaries had been paralyzed in a hunting accident, so we volunteered to do a benefit to help defray medical expenses. The day before our scheduled show, Larry called asking if he could attend. "I've never seen you and Wy perform." (As if he needed to remind me!)

I hesitantly agreed: "Okay, I guess." Then I panicked. Not knowing how Wy might react, I casually mentioned it during sound check, just hours before the benefit. "Oh my God!" she exclaimed with a look of "What'd you go and do that for?"

"Just don't freak out on me onstage," she warned.

My eyes trawled the audience as I was singing, but I never spotted Larry. I closed my eyes as we performed, "Change of Heart" in case I did see him.

Wy and I did "meet and greets" afterward, and I kept watching out the bus window for Larry in the line of folks still waiting to see us. Wy poked me and whispered, "Bet he chickened out," just as he was the last one to step up.

The instant Wy saw Larry, her arms went out to him. As they were hugging, he began telling her how proud he was of her—the show, the awards, all the hard work.

Standing back observing this reunion, I felt guilty about the mean thoughts I'd had during our year-and-a-half breakup. After Wy and I had a sold-out show, I used to imagine Larry playing to a handful of drunks in a lounge somewhere and feel a twinge of smug revenge, "You're getting what you deserve." I'd quickly reprimand myself that spitefulness is negative energy and would come back at me. Besides, I knew he deserved better and that I was still in love with him!

Larry didn't make a move toward me but just stood there with his hat-in-his-hands look. The moment was potent with irony. Wearing my first Esben-designed outfit, I stood regally in the aisle of our climate-controlled, customized Silver Eagle bus, safely surrounded by our manager, bodyguard, and road manager. After we'd exhausted the customary small talk, Larry looked down at his feet and wondered out loud, "What are you doing tomorrow?" Wy was standing in between us, her eyes darting back and forth watching our faces as if she were following a tennis match. Everyone knew the ball was in my court.

After I agreed he could take me to lunch and handed him my condo address and phone number, Wy shot Larry a stern "you better not hurt my Mom again!" look.

It was an updated version of our first date back in 1979, but instead of seeing the rundown house on Del Rio Pike for the first time, I showed him my upscale condo. It was Sunday, so we joined the after-church lunch crowd at the most popular "meat and three," home-cookin' restaurant in Franklin: Dotsons. Meat and three refers to selecting a meat dish from the entrée list and three items from the vegetable list.

Main Street in quaint Franklin was festively decorated for Christmas, and the shops were open, so Larry helped me pick out ornaments for the first Christmas at my sparsely furnished home. After hanging a wreath on my front door, he wondered if I cared to see a movie that night. "No thanks," I declined, trying to control my eagerness. "I really need to pack now to go back on the road tomorrow." He was too shy even to try to hug me. Larry just left.

That week before Christmas, Wy and I played Las Vegas for the first time. Imagine driving down the Strip and seeing your name in letters five feet tall under Merle Haggard's at Caesar's Palace!

Playing Vegas is *real* strange. For starters, you stay in one place all week, doing two shows very late at night. You sleep until noon or even later. There's no cable TV, because they don't want you to stay in your room—they want you down in the casino losing your money! Having worked too hard all my life for my money, I've never once gambled. It distresses me to see folks who can't just indulge in a game of chance for entertainment and stop, but wind up instead losing more than they can really afford. Because you have to go through the casinos to get anywhere, there was no escaping the ever-present slot machines and twenty-one tables. I immediately noticed there were no windows or clocks in the smoky casinos so you'll forget about time. Even the windows up in the rooms don't open, since distraught losers might jump to their death. The topic of conversation seemed to be the same everywhere you went, "Are you winning or losing?" For country girls used to fresh air and pastoral scenes, the Vegas atmosphere is hard on the morale.

Wy and I felt trapped in our suites. If we ventured out, we invariably would wind up standing near huge posters of ourselves advertising our show and would be mobbed by autograph seekers. We also had to look good all the time.

In Vegas, people traipse in to see whoever is playing at the big hotels on the Strip. Wy got discouraged because the Vegas audience wasn't responding like our regular crowds did when were out on the road. We were singing our hearts out to old men pawing young chicks, dazed conventioners with name tags on their lapels, and of course, drunks and dead-eyed gamblers. To keep our energy and spirits up, Wy and I decided to see the Vegas audience as the ultimate challenge and pulled out all the stops attempting to turn them into country music converts.

Opening night was nerve wracking, and all the Caesar's Palace VIPs were on hand to welcome us.

The critics loved us and once we got past opening night, Wy was building up her nerve to venture over to Merle's dressing room and tell him the story about how she cleaned stalls at the horse ranch to save up for tickets to his concert. She wondered whether he might even remember us?

Ken and I escorted Wy across the hall to his dressing room, and I knew at a glance Haggard was out of it. Wy had rehearsed what she wanted to say about him being her hero, but it just wasn't registering with him. Merle just looked past her and grunted.

Wy and I were lamenting this twist of fate when Ken came in to inform us the head of hotel entertainment was considering dropping Haggard from the bill because he'd been going onstage under the influence. This meant we'd become the headliner, since another big-name artist couldn't be brought in at the last minute.

Larry had been calling me, and it felt safe and comfortable getting reacquainted over the phone. He'd asked me to consider letting him fly to Vegas, and after thinking it over for a few days, I timidly agreed.

Larry and I got back together, and Haggard stayed just sober enough to finish out the week.

Back in Nashville for the holidays, Larry and I showed up together at Ken and Jo's annual Christmas bash, causing quite a stir. Everybody likes Larry because he's such a good guy and were genuinely glad to see him again.

Years before, I'd given the '57 Chevy to Wy, and as a surprise, Ken presented Redhot to her fully restored and drivable. Wy was elated! When she drove it I called her "Redhot Red." Ken presented me with something I'd never dreamed of owning, a full-length mink coat!

It was Mr. Big's turn to be surprised. Vanessa had commissioned a craftsman to make the handsome Elvis look-alike wax figure and dress him in the stage outfit I'd bought from Larry. Elvis was authentic, right down to his pinky ring, scarf, and boots. There was a hollowed-out place in his back equipped with a tape player containing the King's biggest hits.

As we ceremoniously unveiled this one-of-a-kind gift to Ken, we flipped a switch and Elvis began singing "Had A Dream" (our first single) into the microphone placed permanently in his hand. Larry loved Elvis the man, and was so respectful of him that he always cringed at any postmortem Elvis mania, but this look-alike was a first-class loving tribute to his friend.

Ken was thrilled as Larry handed him the costume's documentation and personally told him the story behind the clothes. It prompted Ken to size up Larry and me holding hands and declare, "So, Elvis is responsible for getting you two back together!"

The next day Larry drove to North Carolina to spend Christmas with his family and Ashley and I went to Mom's house. On Christmas Eve Wy flew in a private plane we'd been using occasionally. Ray Trotter, our pilot, had engine trouble and Wy was badly shaken and emotional when she finally came walking into Mom's safe, cozy kitchen.

Jumping up from our Trivial Pursuit game at the kitchen table, we all ran to hug her, but Wy threw up her hands to stop us. She was wearing her full-length, fake, cow-print coat with huge pockets. Suddenly, like a magician pulling a rabbit from a hat, she began producing tiny, real live puppies! There was a chihuahua for neigh-bors Alice and Nourvin, a miniature dachshund for a friend, and an adorable cocker spaniel for her Mamaw and Papaw! Wy, the animal lover, had done her last-minute Christmas Eve shopping at the pet store. Luckily, she gave me only a pair of pink house slippers!

Known for picking up strays, Mom said Wy's love of critters reminded her of Ellie Mae on *The Beverly Hillbillies,* and we added this new nickname to the list.

Old friends and neighbors dropped by during the holidays and let us know they'd formed a network of communication so they never missed anything we did. These dear souls made us feel like hometown celebrities. They called us Diana and Chris and recalled stories from our past, reminding us of who we really are. It was so meaningful to see them sharing in the joy of our success that it made us want to work even harder to make them proud. Wy assured them, "You all are one of the reasons I stay within the speed limit and out of that fast lane!"

As I tucked Ashley into bed in my old room that Christmas night, I recognized how wonderfully secure I felt. For the first time in my life, I had medical and life insurance, three burial plots, and a future.

Give a Little Love

*L*IFE—AT THE TOP—BEGINS at forty! I turned the Big Four-Oh that January of 1986 right where I wanted to be, in a motel on the road putting together the show for another new year. We picked up our second Grammy, threw a big celebration party and painted the town red. Then came another unexpected reward after I returned to my hotel room.

Larry called long distance to ask, "Guess what I did yesterday?" Knowing it must be something out of the ordinary for him, I gamely answered, "Went shopping?"

"Nope," he continued, "I went to that church you saw me do a gospel concert at with the Stamps back in 1979, just after we met."

A surge of elation knocked me back onto my bed as Larry began to convey that he wanted to completely change his life. "It was like I was on a hamster wheel when I met you. I was miserable but didn't know how to get off it. I always felt like I didn't deserve you and the girls." He confided that for the past year he'd been suffering panic attacks, once even while onstage and had to be taken to the nearest emergency room. Nothing could have prepared me for what came next.

"I've dissolved Memphis and I'm getting off the road. I've got to find some peace and happiness. I now know that I need you and the Lord in my life. What's your answer?"

"Whew!" I exclaimed. "I always said it would take an act of God to get us back together!"

Wy had gone out a few times with several musicians, like Barbara Mandrell's band leader, Gene Miller, and Ricky Skaggs's keyboard player, Gary Smith. Now she was dating Dwight Yoakam. Being from Pikeville, Kentucky, Dwight and Wy had things in common. He knew what a mirror ball was and she understood his song, "Readin', Writin' and Route 23."

We were really kickin' it! That February we were looking forward to playing the Houston Astrodome for the first time. Right before the concert we met a fan named David Brown, who was relating how he'd met his girlfriend, Susan Perot, at a club when he asked her to dance to "Mama He's Crazy." David said he'd been trying to get up the nerve to ask her to marry him that night and wondered if we'd sing the song. More than willing to play cupid, Wy and I stopped the show just before "Mama He's Crazy," pointed to the section of the grandstand where we knew they were sitting and announced to the crowd of twenty-six thousand, "Hey Susan Perot, David wants to know if you'll be his wife?"

Several days later, during our last song in front of a crowd of thirty-eight thousand at Ranger Stadium in Arlington, Texas, I playfully jerked my hand-held microphone from its stationary stand and impulsively jumped off the stage platform out in the center of the ballfield. Motioning Wy to follow, I headed for home plate and pointed my playful daughter in the direction of the pitcher's mound. Obligingly, Wy faked a dramatic wind up pitch to throw me an imaginary ball. Using my mike for a bat, I hit it over the scoreboard and ran the bases for a home run. Wy met me at home plate where we took our triumphant bows.

When we played the prestigious Radio City Music Hall in New York the following month, we didn't feel the freedom to be so playful, but Wy and I did feel free to go on a shopping spree, "winkling" at Saks Fifth Avenue the next day! Wy and I had never been in a store like it before. We walked in, looked around, and felt like two mosquitoes in a nudist colony. We knew what we wanted, but didn't know where to begin! It was our first binge and Ken, who so conscientiously managed our money, chastised us. I learned an important lesson: Never loan your credit card to someone you've given birth to.

Our favorite parts of the Big Apple were the shopping and the great restaurants. Wy observed that in New York, "You are where you eat!"

Every time we hit a major market like New York, there was a lot of press and TV to do. While there, we did the *Today Show* with Jane Pauley. The Marlboro people got so mad that I didn't mention them during our interview they refused to ride in the same car with me back to the hotel.

When we arrived at the studio to be on the *Phil Donahue* show later that same day, Wy, who lives very much in the present, hadn't brought anything to wear. She had on a shirt she'd recently worn bowling. Chagrined, I reminded myself how young she still was as I scoured the TV studio. My eyes landed on Martha's nice blouse. Once again, Aunt Martha (as Wy and Ashley affectionately call her) saved the day.

When sharp reporter Jon Bream of the *Minneapolis Star Tribune* came to my hotel room to do his first interview with us he unwittingly walked into one of our squabbles. Finding the barbs revelatory, he transcribed our conversation just as he'd captured it on his tape recorder and ran it as the actual piece, adding his own amusing running commentary. In "Judds: Precious Innocence Is Part of Their Charm," he began by comparing us with the then-popular Ivory Soap commercial, the which one's the mother, which one's the daughter ad. Then he insisted we were much bigger than a commercial, more like a TV sitcom!

It seems Wy had left her key in her room. Calling the front desk to have one sent up, she had to turn and ask me what her room number was. Of course I knew it off the top of my head, which made her zero for two. "Why you're just Miss Intelligent!" she retorted.

Jon watched as my eyes became lasers that could have burned the eyebrows off Wy's pretty little face. Wy immediately began ignoring me and told Jon, "There are days I want to tell Mom to get her own bus!"

Kurt Osslinger, Jr., of *Country Song Roundup* likewise got caught in the crossfire of the Cold War. The session was flowing along smoothly when I paused to reach up and fiddle with the air-conditioning. Wy, who likes the bus cold enough to hang meat, bellowed, "I hate room temperature! Turn it back down or you'll ruin my sinuses." We fought like third graders in a spat at recess over this ongoing issue.

Then I innocently referred to Wy as a teenager. Slapping the chair to protest, she pursed her lips and corrected, "Mom, I'm twenty-one now"—she held up her fingers to count in front of my face—"Remember? Twenty-one!"

Flustered, I tried to pick up where I'd left off describing our daily efforts to enjoy our gypsy lifestyle by using my favorite motto: "I believe that happiness is not at the end of the road, but—"

Wy pulled her hair, clutched her throat, and screamed in mock-agony, "Arrrgh! It's all along the way. It's all along the way!" Struggling to save face, I nervously allowed, "Well, Kurt's never heard it before."

The next night Wynonna and I got into it over some nude photos. After our show in Ada, Oklahoma, we had such a long ride ahead of us, we needed to clean up and leave straight from the venue. There was no shower curtain in our dressing room shower stall and no towels. I gathered some large garbage bags and hung them from a piece of pipe for a shower curtain. To protect my hair from getting wet, I put a big garbage bag over my head, tying it in a knot on top that made it stick up in a twelve-inch tall point.

As I was stepping out of the shower and began pulling back the makeshift shower curtain, the metal pipe fell onto the concrete floor in a great clatter, the bathroom door flew open and Wy began snapping Polaroids of me, naked as a jaybird, just as the floppy wet garbage bag collapsed down over my face.

She ran whooping and laughing as I chased her down the hallway wrapped in garbage bags frantic to retrieve those photos. I was able to stop her dead in her tracks with just two words: *Dwight Yoakam.* Everybody was dying to know the particulars of their relationship, and she knew that I could tell them anything and everything they wanted to know!

The truth is they enjoyed each other's company because for the first time Wynonna had someone who could fully understand the pressures of her strange lifestyle. Dwight and I got along famously, and Wy knew this was a prerequisite for any guy she ever brought home to the bus. But they were both much too independent and too into their separate careers to ever make a go of it. When Dwight called our bus for her, she'd be onstage. When she got around to returning his call, he'd be in the recording booth. They decided just to be good friends.

Wy quickly found another more accessible suitor and while we were being interviewed at her apartment for *US* magazine, John Reggers asked us what we were going to do about men. "Well, you can't live with 'em and you can't shoot 'em!" was my flip response. Knowing Wy was uncomfortable discussing the subject of romance, I tried to end it by teasing, "We could just have a double ceremony and both go on maternity leave at the same time!" The last line of the article was: "With that, Wynonna jumped up and ran screaming from the room."

Our first couple years there had been a plethora of basic questions about our rags to riches story. But now interviewers were curious about our private lives, our romantic lives.

"We prefer everyday men who aren't afraid to get their hands dirty," Wy elaborated. "It tickles us that some people assume we date movie stars, business tycoons, or international playboys, but nothing could be farther from the truth!"

Having witnessed the groupie phenomenon with Larry's group Memphis, Wy and I were curious to see what would transpire with us. Wy was often wide-eyed observing some of the ever-present groupies around all our male cohorts. One such star, whom I called "The Sultan" because of his veritable harem, infuriated Wy. After we'd see The Sultan's wife, I'd have to calm Wy down on the bus.

Guys sent us love poems and candy and proposed marriage; they also concocted many interesting date baits like Dave Scheibe. Dave promised his daughter Rhonda St. Marie a new Corvette if she could arrange him a date with me. She brought the press along to the Outagamie County Fair where I visited with her dad, but unfortunately I had to take a rain check because of our departure schedule.

Wy told Kathy Haight of the Knight-Ridder Newspapers in 1986 that she sometimes felt like her name was "Why-Doncha?" She alleged I was constantly calling out: "Why-Doncha clean your bus room," or "Why-Doncha learn to pack less?" And it struck a nerve with me. Did I sound like a warped record? It caused me to stop and acknowledge that I am a perfectionist. A daunting standard bearer. I considered how Wy often shriveled under my judgmental efforts to push her toward getting it together. I tried to put myself in her shoes.

There were many such times I found out what Wy was thinking while sitting next to her in a press conference or on a TV show. I remember settling into my hotel room on the road to read the new copy of *Country Music Magazine* over a tray of room service.

Our writer friend, Bob Allen, had interviewed us separately for an article titled "Two Down-Home Gals Ease into Their Cinderella Slippers."

Wy's words prompted Bob to point out a fact perhaps obvious to everyone but me. His psychological assessment was that despite her immense talent, she often displays the gum-smacking impulsiveness of a child. Wy seemed to rail against my quiet domination, but always sought my approval.

"Almost desperately seeks her approval" were his words. Hmmm . . . I needed to be sensitive to this. Being fifty-fifty partners, both still learning daily about the music business, tended to equalize our status. I am first and foremost her mom and she *was* always seeking my approval. I stopped to grasp that the way we see people either empowers or limits them.

I flashed back to a disagreement on the bus that very morning. When I chastised her, Wy's comeback was quite a vitriolic attack on me. I realized that her usual tactic had characteristically been "the best defense is a good offense." As psychologist Abraham Maslow stated: "When the only tool you have is a hammer, you tend to see everything as a nail!" We both needed new tools.

One of our best new tools were interviews. They became a form of therapy, often more immediate and revelatory than years of costly psychoanalysis. They not only brought us to an awareness of what the other was thinking but caused us to get in touch with our own feelings, verbalize our reactions to one another and the enormous changes going on in both our lives.

Our pace was so demanding, the events in our lives so monumental, interviews also were becoming a strange way of stopping to smell the roses. The immediacy of our daily schedule demanded dialogue such as "What are you wearing for today's magazine cover photo shoot?" "We have five minutes before showtime to make up tonight's song list," or "Luggage call's in ten minutes for the departure to the airport." Because the day ahead of us required so much of our energy, we'd learned to flush yesterday. Thanks to interviews, we got to slow down, pull off to the side of the road, and take out the map and check it to make sure we were going in the right direction.

One of the most beneficial insights came from the unanimous consensus that Wy and I are radically different. Although "joined at the lips," realizing the obvious fact of our differences helped us to begin seeing that our clashes came from our different realities.

We were the consummate odd couple! Robert Oermann pegged us by simply watching us before his interview even began. He began his piece by describing me as I sat waiting as "patient and sublimely professional, immaculately dressed, prompt and prepared, smiling calmly." Then Wy "rushed in late, clowning merrily, sporting a cascading tinted mane, and waving her arms in a rocker's flowing robes."

While I came off as inner directed and philosophical, "Wy was fidgety and blurted out answers impulsively." We corrected the other's anecdotes, cast critical glances, muttered beneath the other's speeches, and gently chided the other's shortcomings, but, as Bob knew, none of this evinced any malice, anger, or spite whatsoever. It was just part of being a family team.

Our music was bigger than both of us: The glue that bound us together, the motivation to be more patient, the inspiration to try to get along, and the reward for trancending our differences.

We'll never forget the night we acknowledged that our music has a mystical quality . . . a life of its own. Right in the middle of "Grandpa," I felt as if I'd been zapped. The best way I can describe it would be like a bolt of emotional, spiritual electricity. The stage felt like a charged force field. The look in Wy's eyes told me she'd felt it too. When we harmonized I often felt a floating sensation. As if I were walking around on paths of air.

As soon as this show was over, we hurried out to the privacy of the bus and asked each other at the same time: "What in the world was that?" Fans and reviewers would feel it all the way up to the bleachers of massive major coliseums like Lexington, Kentucky's Rupp Arena. Walter Tunis of the Lexington paper wrote: "Simply put, there is no finer country singer today than Wynonna Judd. But it was when the two sat together and harmonized that they created true magic. They created a mood that was both chilling in its intensity and so relaxed they could have been singing to you from their back porch."

Writers described how "sparks began to fly" when the tight strong harmonies soared. The consensus seemed to be that the blending of our voices was what gave our music its special appeal and made it, as James Tarbox of the *Pioneer Press Dispatch* claimed, "music of the spheres."

We began to feel ashamed when we fought. It seemed wrong to get upset after winning an award, having a single go to number one, or proselytizing the importance of family to a fan. I've always told Wy and Ashley that the family circle is sacred and that it represents creation, respect, tradition, and harmony. We all began attending church with Larry. The healing had now begun for the four of us.

One problem I had never had with Wy was conceitedness. Singer/producer Gail Davies said as early as August 12, 1985, in *Newsweek* that "Wynonna Judd will go down in history alongside Patsy Cline." Numerous music critics made comparisons of Wy and Patsy's talent and longevity. It became an interview topic that made Wy extremely uncomfortable.

Wy's unusual mix of immense talent and unpretentiousness make her as refreshing as a cold drink of water on a summer's day. My buddy Bill Littleton of *Performance Magazine* shared a story about some friends of his being impressed with her humility after observing Wy at a Nashville night spot. Upon learning she was standing in the rain waiting to hear Dan Fogelberg at the Bluebird Café, the manager came out to invite Wy inside. She politely declined, saying it "isn't fair to jump line." Determined not to ever let her get above her raisin', I'd point out daily that it was only by the grace of God; the hard work of Ken, Brent, Don and a lot of folks; plus the belief of the fans that was allowing us to be living out this dream.

Another element to which I felt we owed our acceptance was timing. The political, socioeconomic climate was such that America embraced the family-spiritual values we represented and espoused. Not since the Carter family wherein female relatives sang together, although not in duet form, had country music witnessed a mother-daughter team. In fact, aside from Girl Scout cookouts, I know of no other occasion wherein a mother and daughter sang together publicly.

The one thing that worried and disturbed me about Wy more than anything else was her asthma. After our show in Austin, she had such a bad attack we had to rush her to the nearest emergency room. I was always afraid she'd have one in the middle of Rooster Poot, Texas, or somewhere we couldn't get help. She took her Marax pills everyday and inhaled her bronchodilator, but sometimes nothing worked. As an RN, I know five thousand people die each year from asthma attacks and once the bronchus closes up, not even CPR helps, since oxygen can't reach the lungs or be expelled. A week earlier in the middle of our concert in Foust, Oklahoma, I had to signal the band to stall by doing their impromptu instrumental number so she could sit down and use her medihaler.

The next day, April 12, I canceled sound check for our show in McAllen, Texas, so Wy could stay in her room and rest. When Mom called long distance I knew instantly from the tone of her voice there was a crisis. Becky Thompson, my closest first cousin and also a redheaded RN, had just had her teenage daughter, Cynthia, die in her arms at their home from an asthma attack. We'd only recently visited their horse farm in Lexington, Kentucky, where Becky and I had caught up on the latest advances in asthma treatments. Badly shaken, I barely remember doing the show that night.

Scheduled to fly to the coast the following morning to appear on the ACM show, I called dear Becky who insisted I continue on to LA.

Ashley was waiting for us there when we won the award for Top Vocal Duo. Impulsively I grabbed her arm and pulled her to the podium with us. "Allow me to introduce my lovely daughter, Ashley, because I want you all to see that in real life the Judds are a trio!" At the press conference, I dubbed her "the unsung Judd."

Billboard singled out *Rockin' with the Rhythm* as the Top Country Album of the Year for 1986 and voted us the Number Three Top Country Artists of the Year. *Cashbox* magazine also voted us Number One Country Album for *Rockin' with the Rhythm* as well as Number One Country Duo for Singles and Number One Country Duo for Albums. We began to receive awards from overseas, too: the International Country Music Awards gave us the honors for Most Promising International Act, International CMA Most Popular Duo/Trio, and the International CMA Readers Choice Award. Whew! Wy's mantle at her home was sagging from all her awards and mine no longer would fit on my bedside table. I had a special lighted case built for them. Each had a special place in our hearts.

As we headed north of the border for our annual Canadian tour, we met up with our bodyguard Snipper at the Nashville airport. He'd just flown in from playing golf at Ken's second house down in balmy Tampa, Florida. Wearing white shorts, tennis shoes, a polo shirt, and sun visor, Snipper began rubbing his hands over his face moaning as we were preparing to land in Thunder Bay, Ontario, in a snowstorm. "It's okay, Snip. We've landed in worse weather than this!" I said soothingly, attempting to comfort him.

"No, Mamaw, I just remembered—all I have is what I'm wearing!" It was so cold I thought our blood would congeal.

Canadians in down parkas and fur coats stared at Snipper in the airport and Wy made him walk behind us. Soon as the stores opened the next day, he bought some appropriate clothes.

I am not funny enough even to make up the hilarious things Snipper did. He frequently forgot his luggage and would catch a cab in a strange city to a store to pick up necessities. Then he'd realize he'd forgotten what hotel we were staying at. (It happens when you're in a different hotel every day!) By now Snipper had a routine when this happened. He'd call the local country radio station and find out where the Judds were performing, then he'd phone that venue and ask our production manager the hotel address. Once Snipper flew into New York City to hook up with us. He came rushing into a posh restaurant, breathlessly asking for money to pay the irate waiting taxi driver. Only Snip would fly into the Big Apple without a dime in his pockets!

But this particular Canadian tour not only started off with a good laugh, our opening act, Vince Gill, helped keep up the fun the whole week. When I'd worked as an RN, the hospital staff was exasperated that no one could tell me jokes I hadn't heard. Vince, however, took great pride in being able to tell me new ones. Everyone liked Vince, 'cause he treated people with respect and kindness. Wy and I would stand in the wings and marvel at his beautiful voice. I got frustrated that the music industry and the public weren't giving him the credit he so deserved and became one of his biggest supporters. "Your day will come! Just be patient," I'd promise. Vince was also on RCA, so we got to do a bunch of gigs back home in the States with him.

We were performing a show every night and sometimes during the day we'd do "in-stores." That's an autograph party at a large record distributor or even a local Wal-Mart. Or we'd do other special extracurricular activities like riding in the Indianapolis 500 parade before the big race. Wy loved being in police escorts and hearing sirens. I don't know why, but that was one of her big deals.

On May 27, Ashley was graduating from Paul Blazer High School, my old alma mater, the only high school in Ashland. She'd finished up her senior year living with Mom and Wib in what she fondly recalls as one of the happiest years of her life. Mom threw her a party the night before graduation and most of her teachers attended. Each told me how satisfying it was having someone like Ashley who respected knowledge and exhibited such a passion for learning. Louise Curnutte shared some of the preconceived notions about the daughter/sister of the town's most famous natives. Louise said by the end of the first month, Ashley fit in with everyone and was one of the best liked students.

As our family walked up the steps to the high school auditorium, bystanders were staring at us. The last time I'd been there they'd stared at me in pity. "Look . . . there's that little pregnant Judd girl." Now they stared at me and that baby, turned star, every chance they got. The TV stations were even there. Cameras and lights flashed and microphones were being shoved at us. I told the TV crew we'd do a quick on-camera interview outside the auditorium and requested that they not be disruptive during the ceremony. After all, I wasn't the only proud parent there!

Onstage Ashley reached for her diploma and flashed a proud smile in our direction. My eyes filled with tears as the memories of her childhood flooded over me. My bright, beautiful little girl with the sunny disposition who was always playing some imaginary game or reading, used to ask me "Mommy, why don't bluebirds go south with the robins?"

Suddenly, someone was poking me in my back. Craning my neck to look behind me I saw another parent and old schoolmate, Chipper Miller. "Ain't seen you since 1963, when we were students!"

"Yeah, Chip, exactly twenty-two years ago this week!" I patted Wy's knee and realized she'd be having her twenty-second birthday in a couple of days. Standing to take pictures of Ashley as the graduates filed down the aisle to "Pomp and Circumstance," it dawned on me this was the first graduation I'd ever been to! Not only had I missed my own, but I missed Wy's because we'd been fighting.

Ashley finished eighth in her class, tied with her boyfriend, Bill McKinney. As we were driving home, we realized we'd forgotten to take home movies, but Mom reminded us we could stick a tape in her VCR and record Ashley's graduation off the ten o'clock news!

I found myself learning about both daughters through the press. While Wy and I had been singing at a fair in Kentucky, a reporter, Bob Dollar, from the *Kentucky New Era,* noticed Ashley and conducted an interview with her. I'd been surprised to read that she was interested in a film career. I wished she could be with us all the time and shuddered even to think of her going to Hollywood.

The next day after graduation, I returned to the high school principal's office where I presented the Brian Judd Scholarship to a deserving young graduate named Noel Quade, "for academic achievement under trying or adverse circumstances."

We high-tailed it back to Nashville where we were finishing up our third album. As usual Brent, Don, Wy, and I had chosen songs that drew on the influences we had long cherished: Appalachian harmony, the elegance of folk, the simplicity of classic country, the airiness of jazz, the boogie beat of rockabilly, and the sexy sultriness of R&B.

We asked if, for sentimental reasons, we couldn't put "The Sweetest Gift" on this album and have Emmylou Harris add a third high harmony. I'd always been flattered when reviewers compared my ability to harmonize with Emmylou's and it was a pleasure for the three of us to sing together.

Wy and I also pitched the old, campy Ella Fitzgerald "Cow Cow Boogie," since it had become our tradition to do a remake. The three singles from the album: "Turn It Loose," "Maybe Your Baby's Got the Blues," and "I Know Where I'm Goin' " all went number one! When two radio stations refused to play the fourth single, "Don't Be Cruel," because it had once been an Elvis tune, it became the first Judd song not to go number one. Personally, we were proud of our version and enjoyed working with the legendary Jordanaires, who sang on the Elvis original back in 1956. Gordon Stoker confided to Wy and me, after getting to know us in the studio, that we were the kind of folks Elvis would have liked to have as friends and it was a shame we'd never be able to hang out. "Oh man," Wy groaned, "we coulda gone bowling!"

Wy and I made it a policy to meet all the writers of our songs. A feisty lady named K. T. Oslin cowrote the beautiful country ballad "Old Pictures," which Wy and I especially loved to sing live every night in concert. My first impression of K. T. was that she has a clear vision of who and what she is.

How Wy and I looked forward to being in that studio! It was like a garden, where we grew, blossomed, and bore fruit. Brent and Don watered and weeded us. It was the opposite routine of being on the road. We wore no makeup and paid absolutely no attention to how we looked. We saw only each other, practically lived at the studio, forgetting all about the troubles of the world.

Every time we'd finish an album, Wy and I went into a funk, much like the postpartum blues a mother experiences after the birth of her baby. You never know what you've created, until you give it away. None of the ten song titles jumped out as a title for the still-unnamed album and RCA was getting frantic to release it.

We were performing at the Hilton Hotel on the Vegas Strip when the title popped into my head. Knowing I have a hard time with the atmosphere there, my Mom sent me Kentuckiana clippings from the *Courier Journal* and *The Big Sandy News* back home. At 5:00 A.M., unable to sleep, I was pacing in my penthouse suite looking out at the oceans of neon in the desert—the town that never sleeps. I began reading stories about mom-and-pop diners back home and old-fashioned general stores in the country; then happened upon a feature on small town Waddy, Kentucky, "where the Union 76 Truckstop played Loretta Lynn, Randy Travis, and the Judds."

I immediately fell in love with the town and began writing an open letter for its citizens to be posted on the post office bulletin board. "I'd rather be back in the heartland of America," I mumbled to myself as I signed it. When I called Brent the next morning from Vegas with my suggestion, our third album immediately became *Heartland*. In no time I began receiving cheery letters from the townsfolk of Waddy and souvenirs like a painting of a covered bridge and a ballcap from the truckstop.

We were soon gratified to discover that our audience was enjoying listening to *Heartland* as much as we enjoyed creating it.

Not soon enough for Wy and me, we were back out cruisin' life's highways out in the heartland on board the *Dreamchaser*. On any typical day, Wy and I would wake up about noon. I'd pull back the blackout curtains in my room and blink and yawn in the midday brightness. Usually, we'd be parked in a Holiday Inn parking lot next to our band bus. (The two trucks would already be over at the gig unloading the stage, lights and sound gear.)

But sometimes we'd awaken to find ourselves parked at the curb of some busy downtown street. Wy and I would bump into each other in our jammies on the way to the bathroom, amused that well-groomed businessmen and women were just on the outside of the bus rushing all around us. We'd comb our hair, brush our teeth, throw on some clothes and step off the bus into noisy throngs of hyper pedestrians. If you even can, imagine opening your own bedroom door and suddenly stepping into midtown Manhattan at lunch hour! Sometimes it couldn't be avoided, but Wy and I sure hated staying in inner-city hotels. We'd have to walk for blocks searching for grass for the dogs Loretta Lynn and Banjo and the din, traffic, and confusion is especially hard on the nerves when you've not even had your first cup of coffee!

Thank goodness though, we mostly stayed in outlying Holiday Inns! I could usually remember what town we'd arrived at and a quick survey of license plates in the parking lot verified the state. Occasionally, I resorted to checking the local paper in the racks as I entered the hotel lobby.

Wy would usually sleep later and linger on the bus, making instant oatmeal in the microwave or bagels in the toaster while watching daytime TV, talking on the phone, reading fan mail, or listening to music. Sometimes she even stayed on the bus until I came back out to get her around 4:00 P.M. for sound check.

Being the first one up and off, our road manager would draw us a map directing us from the bus door to our rooms and leave it beside our room keys on the front table. Stepping off the bus in a hat and dark glasses, (since we prolonged putting on makeup or doing our hair until showtime), we'd pause a moment to let our eyes get used to daylight, stretch and yawn to get our land legs. Often we'd be greeted by fans waiting curbside or in parked cars.

I admit Wy and I are not morning people and it was tricky being alert and coherent. The last thing we saw before we went to bed were fans with autograph requests, and that was the first sight to greet us each morning. I'd oblige them while I let Banjo take his morning constitutional, then run the labyrinth to find my room.

For me, having morning coffee is akin to taking holy communion. I'd play my special tapes and read a devotional or other interesting book. Silence is refreshment for the soul. I've always indulged in rituals because I believe they help us mark our days and give us a sense of security. This daily morning ceremony was usually the only quiet, self-controlled part of my day.

Then I'd check my messages, order lunch, and of course, unpack. Wy and I usually did "phoners" (telephone interviews to radio stations and newspapers) to promote upcoming shows.

If I had any time left over, I longed to get outside of town, to absorb the atmosphere of our locale. If we were downtown, I'd catch a cab to the outskirts. If we were already staying in the outer limits, I'd put Banjo on his leash and set out walking. I'd stop and talk to kids riding bicycles, smell freshly mowed grass, and chat with shop-keepers. I'd stroll down sidewalks in suburbs that seemed profoundly asleep. I'd imagine what life was like for housewives hibernating inside tract houses or meander through treeless new developments with pastoral names like "Woodland Meadows" or "Forest Acres," where the cozy bourgeoisie live. Pausing to allow Banjo to sniff their dogs' territorial markings, I'd stare at the front of a house and wonder what went on inside. I'd consider the possible variations of daily life's chilling redundancy. I'd imagine that I lived there and see myself checking the mailbox, looking through bills as I sauntered up the driveway and in through the carport to the cozy kitchen, where I'd make my famous meat loaf surprise for my salesman husband and our unruly brood.

I much preferred old residential neighborhoods with character. During a Sunday afternoon stroll in Van Wert, Ohio, before our show at their county fair, Banjo and I stepped out into the street to get around the back of a truck being hosed down by a middle-aged lady. She was bent down spraying the tires and accidently got my foot wet. As she was apologizing, I struck up a conversation.

"Getting spruced up to go see my girls at the fair tonight," she announced as she now began lathering up the bumper.

"What girls is that?" I innocently inquired.

"Naomi and Wynonna Judd!" she declared possessively. "Why me and my family just love them two girls to death!"

Tears sprang up in my eyes behind my dark glasses. I tugged at my hat brim to pull it even lower on my face.

"Well I think they're mighty fortunate to have someone like you supporting them!" I commented as I tugged at Banjo to hurry away.

Returning to the Holiday Inn, I walked right by a small rollaway marquee in front of a mom-and-pop restaurant that proclaimed: "Love Is Alive in Van Wert for the Judds." I ran straight to Wy's room to tell her of my wonderful, memorable afternoon.

Sound check over at the venue marked the beginning of our actual workday (not counting earlier interviews or public relations jaunts). Wy and I usually did four or five tunes so easygoing Brooks

Thomas, our monitor man, could make sure we could hear ourselves in individual monitors placed at our feet. I'd complain I needed to be turned up, then Wy would bellow that I was already too loud, causing Brooks to tear at his hair and throw up his hands. Besides Snipper, good-natured Brooks was our favorite person to aggravate.

John Cooper, our expert house audio engineer, worked the huge sound board out in the audience getting the complicated levels adjusted for each particular venue. Capable Han Henze ran our lights and supervised several assistants. Bruce Johnson, now stage manager, tuned and set up Wy's guitars and prepared the stage for all of us. A large, agreeable fellow named Scott Holloway was our electrician. "Punko," as he was affectionately known, looks a bit like Bluto of Popeye fame. Punko and I were close, and one night I teasingly grabbed him in the middle of the show, incorporating him into what went on to become a running sight gag.

While Loretta and Banjo chased each other around the stage, Wy and I stalked its borders, familiarizing ourselves with the layout of the room and getting into the mood. Wy bought a pair of Rollerblades during her brief fascination with roller derby and sometimes skated on the concrete floors after sound check.

We did our sound check first because we'd been headlining some now. The opening act checked their equipment last, so the stage and dials were set when they took the stage in a few hours after the doors opened. We were seldom booked with other females, but really enjoyed it when we were. At our show together in Hunter, New York, I invited pretty Lorrie Morgan onto the bus to spend the afternoon visiting. We mostly talked about men. Lorrie was divorced from George Jones's bass player so she and her daughter had been living with her mother. We shared stories about how tricky that is!

Wy and I always felt at home working with Patti Loveless, the Forester Sisters, Holly Dunn, Paulette Carlson of Highway 101, the Sweethearts of the Rodeo, Tanya Tucker, Marie Osmond, Sylvia, Lacy J. Dalton, K. T. Oslin, and Kathy Mattea. We also felt a special closeness to Sharon and Cheryl, the Whites. There were some women we never worked shows with and only got to see at TV tapings or backstage at award shows, for example, Crystal Gayle, Roseanne

Cash, k. d. lang, Amy Grant, and Barbara Mandrell. Trisha Year-wood, Mary Chapin Carpenter, Suzy Bogguss, Michelle Wright, and Pam Tillis were just starting out. Perhaps it was because Wy and I sort of had our own category, perhaps because I was slightly older, but whatever the reasons, we were relieved and proud of the feelings of sisterhood we enjoyed with all the other females.

After sound check, Wy and I would usually hang around to talk with the other band. Sawyer Brown's guys were always great fun! I'll never forget sitting on an amp at the side of the stage at the Sandstone Amphitheater in Kansas one pretty summer afternoon visiting with Willie Nelson. We talked about anything and everything, and he quickly became one of my favorite people. Willie's one of the best listeners I've ever known.

Crew dinner always follows sound check. A local catering service provides a hot meal in some large room backstage I referred to as "fellowship hall." Seated together, it's everyone's chance to mingle. Frequently Wy and I would sit with the other entertainers. If we ate with the Nitty Gritty Dirt Band, we'd laugh so hard we could barely eat, and we'd get so raucous, people at the other tables couldn't hear themselves talk. If we sat next to Randy Travis, conversation was subdued and laid back. Sometimes all he'd say was, "Pass the salt."

People would tell jokes, make personal announcements, get into discussions, gossip, and pull pranks. One running trick was that whoever was head of the buffet line would secretively point out Odell, telling the food servers to refuse to serve him any beans. He finally became so self-conscious, he quit stinking up the band bus.

Since Wy and I now lived in our own separate bus, I saw sound check and crew meal as important times to connect with our band and crew and to maintain a family atmosphere.

After our road family dinner, Wy and I would catch a ride back to the hotel with a runner, because Gaylon, our bus driver; Ernie, the band and crew driver; and Jim Baber and Rhett Evens, our two truck drivers, would sleep days so they could drive all night.

Once back at the hotel, Wy and I would begin putting on our Judd faces. Every day an itinerary was slipped under our door with a rooming list and schedule for sound check, show, list of folks to meet afterward, departure time, and number of miles to the next town. Occasionally, there would be a specific title for the day. For instance:

Profanity bothers me, so everyone demonstrated self-control around me. I appreciated it so much that to say thank-you for their gesture of respect, I began "Judd Annual Cuss Day." (The F-word and taking the Lord's name in vain were never permitted.) For twenty-four hours, I ignored cussing. Wy in particular got a kick out of this opportunity and worked hard at seeing just how many cuss words she could fit into a single sentence.

As we departed the hotel to do the show, usually around seven o'clock, Wy and I would really begin getting excited. We'd stop to walk our dogs and sign some autographs before we boarded the bus. The drive in the concert traffic, with fans honking and waving out car and truck windows, got us even more in the mood. Finally parked with all the other buses and semis back behind the venue, Wy would fix my hair back in my room where we'd talk about whatever was on our minds. Mark Thompson, our band leader, would come onto the bus to check out the set list one last time and let us know how much time we had before going on. I always asked whether the town we were in had anything significant going on so I could acknowledge it. Then, together, the three of us would do vocal warm-ups.

Cleon left our band to join his old friends in Exile as an equal member of their group. Wy and I hated to see him go. The night he told us he was resigning, I looked over at him onstage to see he'd taped a Help Wanted sign on the front of his piano. Cleon was the only person to ever resign from our organization. We found Larry Miller to replace him. We also hired a new drummer, George Honea, shortly thereafter.

After the show Wynonna and I would need a few minutes to calm down and freshen up on the *Dreamchaser*, then it was time to be hostesses. Personnel from the local radio stations and their contest winners ("the thirteenth caller gets four tickets and a limo ride to see the Judds!") would meet our road manager after the show and obtain backstage passes. There are two kinds of passes: "All Access" for members of the performers' organization so they can come and go freely to work and "After Show," which permits folks to have access only into the backstage area or out by the bus afterward. Because the crew is running around changing the stage equipment between acts and usually have just twenty minutes, the area must be clear for the huge cases and other stage necessities. Artists need a clear path to the stage, because we've got so much on our minds as we're mentally preparing ourselves.

Often there are friends or family to see afterward. Usually there are special requests, like the Make-a-Wish Foundation, an organization for children with terminal illnesses. Wy and I would frequently let fans up on the bus, too.

I was known to invite people I'd heard or read about to be our guests. For instance, after reading about a little girl from New Mexico who'd been severely burned, I called personally to invite brave Sage Volkmann and her family to visit with us on the bus.

This meet and greet portion had several road code labels: the Grip and Grin, the Shake N' Howdy, and if there were lots of people to see, the Human Sacrifice. If we had tour sponsorships, we'd go to receptions for anywhere from fifty to one hundred people and have our photo taken with each one. It was definitely tiring. Before pulling away from the venue around midnight, Wy and I (if time allowed) enjoyed walking out to chat and shake hands with "die-hard" fans.

We'd generally take about forty-five minutes back at the hotel to bathe, call home, and pack up. Then we'd walk Loretta Lynn and Banjo and talk to more hard-core fans who'd followed us back to the hotel. Their numbers were growing.

Once we loaded luggage down in the bins, I'd jump into my jammies and throw in a bag of microwave popcorn. If we had enough slack in the schedule or a reasonably short drive, Wy liked to go out to listen to live music with the Judd Boys. Often our guys would get up on stage to sit in with the local band, but not once did Wy ever join them. She had no interest in singing without me. They'd shoot pool, get a bite to eat, or dance. Occasionally, I'd be in my room already asleep before Wy returned and Gaylon began driving to the next town.

Usually, Wy and I would stay up, talk and laugh, and carry on. We'd go over things fans said and did and read their notes and letters. We'd discuss the show. We'd watch *Late Night with David Letter-*

man. Wy was trying to teach Loretta a stupid pet trick so we could be on his show. She successfully taught her to howl along with the theme to *The Love Boat*. If TV had gone off the air, we'd watch movies on the VCR. One time when we traded movies with the band bus, we accidentally got a XXX one, and I had to speak to the boys about it the next day in Mamaw Judd Judge Court! Sometimes band members rode with us so we could play games like Trivial Pursuit or Password.

When Ashley was on the road, she and Wy would lie in bed together while Ashley read to her big sister. Two of their favorite books were *A Prayer for Owen Meaney* by John Irving and *Victory Over Japan* by Ellen Gilchrist. They'd pick on each other good-naturedly and vie for my attention. With one on either side of me they'd lay their heads on my shoulder and revert to childlike behavior. We'd play Bonnie Raitt and the three of us would dance wildly and act crazy.

I loved to sit up in the jump seat for hours and think about our day or talk to Gaylon. Wy and I usually went to sleep around 2:00 or 3:00 A.M.

Things just seemed to keep getting bigger and better, and we were hiring more people. We hired a new road manager, Dwight Haldeman. Dwight has the weirdest sense of humor. Headed for a Fourth of July outdoor festival in Lake City, South Dakota, we were stir crazy from driving all day. "Didja ever see farther and see less?" he asked. Pointing out across flatlands strewn with big, brown rolled hay bales he informed us with his deadpan expression, "Look girls, it's a shredded wheat farm!"

As soon as we arrived onsite, I received tragic news that Wy and Ashley's Mamaw Ciminella had a stroke and was in serious condition back in Ashland. It had taken us a day and a half to get here, and we had thousands of people expecting a show in a matter of a couple of hours. I'd been told that a rancher had mortgaged his place to put on this concert, and I was trying my best to see to it he didn't lose it. We made the decision to do the show, and Ken lined up a private Lear jet to pick us up in Aberdeen immediately afterward to fly us home.

The big hurdle was to keep the news from Wy until after the

show, because I knew she'd go all to pieces. Dwight positioned a Judd Boy outside our trailer to warn people before coming to see us.

We were scheduled to close the festival that Fourth of July night with "America the Beautiful" and fireworks, but I went over to Tammy Wynette's bus and asked her to swap places so we could go on first and leave sooner. The South Dakota media were waiting in a trailer to do a press conference so Dwight and I crossed our fingers they didn't know about our family emergency.

During our long trek to South Dakota, we'd played games and Wy complained vociferously that I always seemed to win or know the answers. As we stepped up into the press trailer, the makeshift steps broke and I clumsily fell on my face into the entry. As people scampered to help me up, Wy sarcastically introduced me by my new title: "Ladies and gentlemen . . . my mother—the Queen of Everything!" Sometime later, I came up with her appropriately corresponding royal title: "The Princess of Quite a Lot."

As soon as we left the stage I gave a heartbroken Wy the news, and we flew home to join Papaw Ciminella and Ashley at Mamaw's bedside, where she was listed in serious condition. A week later when she was out of immediate danger we went back out on the road.

Emotionally exhausted, we were fortunate our next show happened to be in Nashville. We met the great Charlie Daniels when we were part of his Volunteer Jam before continuing our mud and dust tour out west. Our favorite rodeo was Cheyenne Frontier Days in Wyoming, called the "Grandaddy of All Rodeos." Wy and I also got to be spectators and made local friends who took us horseback riding on our day off.

On the afternoon of August 9, we flew to LA for our big debut at the Universal Amphitheater, opening for Merle Haggard for two days of sold-out concerts. It was such an important event, Ken and Martha were already there waiting. Haggard, however, wasn't. He'd been in a love spat with his girlfriend at a fair the night before and vanished. Ken was frantic. Popular artists are booked a year in advance and the summer months are the busiest with all the annual state fairs.

We sat in Ken's suite calling every big act we could think of until midnight that Saturday night. It was ridiculously impossible. Ken finally sighed: "Girls, you're going to have to headline tomorrow and we'll find you a local opener." I happened to have the private number of a new group, South Pacific, whose lead singer lived in Malibu. There wasn't time to inform the public of these changes.

While Wy and I dressed in nervous silence, we were each wondering how many unsuspecting concert goers were outside demanding their money back as they were informed Haggard was a no-show. "What if there's no one in the theater when we run out onstage? Isn't it nerve-wracking enough traveling, doing a show, without all this extra drama?" Wy moaned wringing her hands.

Well, no one asked for their money back and the press compared it with one of those Busby Berkley musicals in which the talented chorus girl is called on to substitute at the last minute for the star and then becomes a runaway success.

The following night at the Paso Robles, California, fair Wy and I had been keeping a nervous eye on a drunken, overzealous cowboy in the audience. The reveler kept making animal noises and tongue gestures, and screaming out things like "Marry me!" Wy and I knew something was bound to happen. The house security guards positioned across the front of the stage were just college boys who were watching us over their shoulders instead of keeping their attention focused forward on the crowd. Suddenly, as Wy and I were singing, we watched helplessly as the cowboy came bolting down the center aisle with his arms outstretched to seize us. Leaping onstage, he was headed straight for me when Snipper darted from the wings and tackled him. In their tussle, they knocked me to the ground, causing my skirt to fly up over my head. Bruised, I popped back up exclaiming "Who was that masked man?" so the crowd would know I was okay. Wy and I finished the song as police led the guy away.

Fans were actually very respectful of us. No one was ever rough or rude to Wy or me. They knew we were mother and daughter, and saw that we tried to act like ladies. I also think it was really obvious how much we appreciated and respected them.

I guess I heard "Which one's the mother, which one's the daughter?" and "You look more like sisters" a dozen times a day. Getting older has never seemed to bother me like it does some women—female entertainers in particular! I know that how you act

The family that prays together stays together. Reverend Mark Judd's one-room church in Colesburg, Kentucky, 1991. *Left to right:* Wy holds her cousin Brian Judd; Nana, Wy's grandmother; the Reverend Mark Judd; his wife, Middy; Naomi; and her husband, Larry. Wy calls Larry "Pops."

Nana is the Judds' number one fan and proudly attends all the awards shows. Shown here at the Academy of Country Music Awards in Los Angeles. (RON WOLFSON)

Naomi always told her girls, "A triangle is the strongest thing." They make time to be together on location during the filming of the 3-D video *Love Can Build a Bridge* in Sedona, Arizona. (PETER NASH)

June 1992: Wy has her own dream house down the road from "Mom and Pop." (JINNIE THOMAS)

When Ashley comes home from Hollywood, they ride horses, take walks and talk about everything, play with the animals, eat, and "laugh a *whole lot*."

The Judds have always
believed in getting close
to their fans. Typically,
they followed Ashley
Falks of San Antonio
through her illness and
death. Here they try to
cheer her up on their bus
after a rodeo.

Ashley as Swoosie
Kurtz's daughter Reed
on the NBC series
Sisters. Ashley was determined to make it on
her own, and has!
(NBC STUDIOS)

With Banjo, Naomi bedridden with chronic active hepatitis. "Alone at home, cards of support from family, friends, and fans keep me going." (*PEOPLE WEEKLY* ©1990, WILL AND DENI MCINTYRE)

On the bus during the Farewell Tour in 1991. Naomi as "Queen of Everything" passes crown and scepter to Wy, the "Princess of Quite a Lot." (CHRISTOPHER LITTLE)

Farewell Tour. Every night Naomi was saying good-bye to fans in each city, cherishing every moment, working through her grief, and struggling to prepare a distraught Wy for being without her. (CHRISTOPHER LITTLE)

The last road concert of the Farewell Tour was purposefully set in Lexington, Kentucky, so family and old neighbors could be there. Wy and Naomi tried hard to be brave for each other. Surrounded by the Judd Boys, Ashley, Ken, and Martha, they're on their way to the stage.

"Daddy Ken" manages all three Judds, shown here after Wy and Naomi won Duet of the Year for the last time at the Academy of Country Music Awards in 1991. They were also undefeated at the Country Music Association and the Music City News Awards for eight straight years. They won six Grammys, American Music Awards, as well as an array of other awards including many international honors. (RON WOLFSON)

Farewell Concert, December 4, 1991: on the last song Naomi tries to console Wy, admonishing her beloved partner to "Go Towards the Light." (S. RAY)

Stopping at Krystal where Naomi went after hospital shifts, this time after the Farewell Concert. With director/writer Bud Schaetzle. (ASHLEY JUDD)

Wib, Tony King, Wy, Nana, Vanessa Ware, Pops, and Ashley in 1992. Now Naomi's home, after all these years on the road, to bake birthday cakes herself again and take family photos.

Naomi fixes supper almost every night for manager-producer Larry,
after they take a twilight walk on their rural Peaceful Valley farm.
(CHRISTOPHER LITTLE)

is more important than how you look, plus being a nurse taught me how fortunate I am just to be healthy and alive.

I did comment, though, about the laugh lines around my mouth to my close friend, Norma Gerson, who did our makeup for special occasions. She teased it was my own fault for laughing so much, and then told me about collagen injections. Norma's a very intelligent cautious woman. She gave me the number of a respected doctor in Nashville who gives injections of collagen under the skin's surface to plump up lines. Collagen, normal skin's major component, is a protein that provides strength to the skin. The procedure is usually nonsurgical, safe, clean, and simple. I personally know many female celebrities who've had it done with satisfying results. It's not permanent and must be repeated yearly.

It was the week before the CMA awards of 1986, and Wy and I were nominated for five awards and chosen to open the show. I so wanted to look my best. I went to this doctor for the intradermal collagen skin test to check for allergic reaction. The test result showed no reaction, so the Thursday before the big Monday night award show extravaganza, I let him give me about ten shots on each side of my mouth (yes it stings!). By the time I drove home, I knew something was wrong. Each injection site swelled up like an angry bee sting. My face was a lumpy red mess!

When I returned to the doctor's office first thing the next morning, he was horrified! It was obviously a severe allergic reaction to collagen, so we were mystified as to why my skin test had been negative. When he sent my blood sample to the Collagen Institute in California, I registered the highest antibody count (allergic reaction) in collagen history. Now the doctor was afraid I would sue him for malpractice, and I was embarrassed to go out in public.

Of course, I didn't sue; it's not my kind of thing. Norma got DermaBlend, a heavy-duty makeup for problems like burns and scars, and the doctor came to my house the next night before the award show to give me an injection of hydracortisone (an anti-inflammatory) hoping to reduce the swelling.

At the Opry, I felt conspicuous as a chicken at a fox convention. The director, Walter Miller, asked Wy to begin singing "Rocking' with the Rhythm" from the front row of the audience. As she walked up onstage I was to come out from my position behind the stage curtain and begin singing after I joined her at center stage.

We'd never been separated like this before and it felt extra scary, on top of our award-show jitters. Willie Nelson and Kris Kristofferson, who where hosting the show, were watching Wy through a crack in the stage backdrop with me and I almost ran out to her. Willie and Kris tried to calm me, held onto my arm, and helped me wait until my cue.

We'll never forget winning the Vocal Group of the Year award because that year we really felt welcomed into the family of country music. It was our third CMA so Wy and I felt we'd bypassed the "flash in the pan" threat. We had a little more control over ourselves and were very serious when we made our acceptance speeches.

I said, "Each and every one of us needs to feel loved, needed, and accepted. Wynonna and I want to thank you from the bottom of our hearts for giving us this special feeling tonight. This is a magic moment that we'll remember the rest of our lives. So on behalf of all the Judd team, to everybody who makes, markets, or sells our records, to all the great folks at the radio stations across America who play Judd music, to everybody here at the CMA—everybody in the membership that voted for us tonight, my goodness, thank you. But especially, to all those dear and wonderful people, our favorite people in the world, the fans who listen to Judd music and come out to see us when we come to your towns. God bless you all. I wish that something as wonderful as this could happen to you in your lifetime!"

Wynonna stated, "It's a real blessing to wake up every day and realize that you're going to get to do something that you love. Judd music is from our hearts and it is our life. We want to thank you all for sharing it with us with smiles and a warm welcome. God bless you all!"

Although feeling like the Elephant Man because of my face, we did our photo session for the *Heartland* album cover that week, then flew to New York to do a shoot and interview for *Rolling Stone* magazine. People stared, but few had the nerve to say anything. In an effort to reduce the swelling, the doctor put me on a strong daily dose of the steroid prednisone. I continued to cover the miserable bumps with a makeup so thick and plastic that you could almost sculpt it.

Bad timing, because we couldn't have been any more visible. One of the networks had just proposed a weekly sitcom starring Wy, Ashley, and me loosely based on our lives. I said then that it should include high drama, comedy, virtual reality, and life-threatening situations, kind of a Brady Bunch on peyote feel!

When Ken first approached us about it, the thought of a TV show didn't interest me in the slightest, until I realized two things: Number one, Wy and I could finally include Ashley; and the possibility of working with both my children seemed too good to be true. I figured I'd either be the happiest woman in the world or on the waiting list for the Betty Ford Clinic. And number two, it would revolve around country values versus city values. I liked that.

As the meetings got under way, Wy and I began to realize what a major commitment this was and feared it might take us away from creating our albums and touring. Frankly, we couldn't stand the thought of spending much time in Hollywood either. In a meeting with the TV executives, I stood to announce: "We're terribly flattered and grateful for your interest, but you have more swimming pools out here than Bibles and, anyway, we belong on the road."

River of Time

Y NOW, WY and I had been on the road so long that when we came home, that standard-size bar of soap in our bathroom looked huge, and we'd catch ourselves reaching to call room service on our regular telephone. We were so road savvy, we'd learned to sleep on the side of the motel bed away from the phone because it isn't as lumpy. Wy told people we were on "The Judd Infinity Tour."

We zipped out to LA for the 1987 American Music Awards where we picked up two awards for Country Single of the Year and Best Country Video both for "Grandpa (Tell Me 'Bout the Good Old Days)." Afterward, awards still in hand, we raced from the Shrine Auditorium to the airport, where we changed in the public restroom from our stage clothes to street clothes for an eight-hour international flight. By now we had enough frequent flyer miles to go to Mars!

Instead, we flew to the south of France to be part of the Midem International Music Festival. The glamorous town of Cannes on the French Riviera was unlike anything we'd ever seen. "Why, there're dogs everywhere," Wynonna, the animal lover, exclaimed. "They're even in restaurants!" When we arrived at the Hotel Majestic, she whispered reverently at dinner, "I just know Meryl Streep stayed in my room when she was here for the Cannes Film Festival!"

Although Cannes was swarming with artists from all the European countries, the first person we met was Texan Lyle Lovett! He is humble, intelligent, and gentlemanly, and Wy and I appreciated

Lyle's esoteric style. A not so humble James Brown was on the show, but Wynonna and I were thoroughly entertained by the amazing "Godfather of Soul." Wy won a $5 bet with me that he could still do the splits. It was a pleasure sharing the bill with jazz vocal impresario, Al Jarreau.

Waiting backstage to make our European performance debut in front of a large, live audience, we learned this popular festival was also being sent out via satellite to three hundred million viewers in many countries. Wanting to acknowledge them in French, I quickly got a stagehand to teach me to say, "We are delighted to be with you tonight." Wy was terrified I'd mess it up by the time I got the chance to repeat it on stage. "Mom, you'll destroy our chances here in Europe before we even sing a note. You'll wind up telling all these people, 'You smell like my dog!' " But I memorized what sounded like nothing more than French nonsense syllables, *"Je suis ravi de vous voir,"* and pulled off the greeting as a frightened Wy and the Judd Boys held their collective breath!

On our day off we all trekked to Monte Carlo and acted like flat-out tourists. Wy and Ken got a kick out of playing a game of chemin de fare in the posh casino at Monaco. Then it was on to London where we appeared on their most popular TV shows: *Wogan* (their version of *The Tonight Show*) and *Whistle Test*. The kid and I were leery about our debut at the legendary, but sterile, London Palladium. Wynonna voiced her fears: "Mama, these Brits are extremely skeptical and their critics are said to have ice water in their veins."

But then another guardian angel appeared to help allay our fears and let us know we'd have a smiling friendly face in the audience. My girlfriend Polly, the one from Nashville's Music Row who'd gotten her heart stomped on, had moved back to her native London and was now married to Martin Satterwaite, the head of the Country Music Association in Europe. Considering the bleakness of our individual conditions when we'd last seen one another, we looked each other up and down declaring, "You've come a long way baby!"

We were not only relieved but thrilled by our overwhelming reception that opening night. They listened intently and reverently to ballads, then sang and clapped along to the rousing songs. They even gave us standing ovations. In our first European review in the *Record Mirror* the following morning, Stuart Baillie warned the United Kingdom to "prepare yourself for Juddmania on their next trip here."

The British not only are skeptical but as the other review from that night showed, have an unusual slant on matters. The Legendary Stud Brothers (their for real title!) called us the "Buffalo Gals" and referred to our "impeccable set of redneck credentials" and declared us the "new soul of Southern Comfort." Wy and I cackled at the blunt assessment that their "sensitive B—— S—— detectors registered none." When they went so far as to compare us with Kate Bush and the Supremes, Wy and I could only scratch our heads and shrug our shoulders.

I was struggling. Being on massive daily doses of prednisone was taking its toll. Prednisone causes insomnia, in addition to the difficult adjustment to the drastic time change between Europe and the States. I paced the floor all night and nodded during interviews the following day.

Our European album had been number one for many weeks and the demand for interviews in London was overwhelming. On several occasions, I went blank when asked questions because of sleep deprivation. It was definitely not like me.

Every morning when I looked in the mirror my cheeks just seemed to keep getting fatter. Extended prednisone use leads to Cushing's syndrome. I was beginning to look like a squirrel carrying around a jaw full of acorns. My mind suddenly flashed on a drawing I had of a beautiful woman seated at her vanity table. It's an optical illusion, so that when you stand back and look at it in it's entirety, it's also a skull. Little did I know, when my vanity prompted me to have collagen injections, that I would jeopardize my health.

One of the few things Wy and I enjoyed about Europe was that our faces meant nothing. We could sit together in sidewalk cafés drinking expresso and talk without being disturbed by a single autograph seeker. We ate our first uninterrupted meal in years. We could observe without being observed. This anonymity made us keenly aware of just how famous we'd become at home.

Fame is such a strange thing! People chase after it, then hide from it after they get it. It seems it's hard to achieve, but perhaps harder to handle. I'm aware the glamorous life can easily rob a country singer of the down-home integrity and charm that attracted fans in the first place.

We both felt like kissing the ground as we returned to the States after this European tour. Wynonna and I had gotten a bone-deep sense of America traveling on the *Dreamchaser* border to border and coast to coast every day for years. Our excursion through the United States was part travelogue, part work, and part family vacation. Aside from maps and constellations, we could chart our course by Holiday Inns, arenas, and truck stops!

As we played in all fifty states, I made a game of teaching Wy the state capitals. I took her to the San Diego Zoo, where she threatened to free the animals. In Dallas we drove past the book depository and discussed JFK's assassination. We sent postcards of the Liberty Bell from Philadelphia. In Alaska, we studied the Inuit culture.

From my perch on the jump seat I'd bask in timeless dream-scapes. Out west, I'd be indulging in black-and-white heroic imagery of how the west was won. Then suddenly come face to face with the stark reality of the squalid poverty of the American Indians on their reservations.

We'd be cruising down tree-lined streets in Norman Rockwell small towns, where American flags fly from clean white gingerbread porches. And the very next day drive through the grungy, threatening underworld of some inner city slum. Wy and I dislike big cities. We always seem to leave there drained of some measure of our humanity. I've decided the higher the buildings, the lower the morals.

I'd get strung out on these contradictions, furious and frustrated at what we're losing in America. Because we'd return to play the same towns every year, we'd see with our own eyes the changes. Shopping malls where family farms had been. Tract houses where beautiful open fields or lushly dense woods once stood. Every night Wy and I would look knowingly at each other as we harmonized on the chorus of "Grandpa." "They call it progress, but I just don't know. Grandpa, tell me 'bout the good old days."

Every time local politicians showed up to have their photos taken with us after our concert, I wanted to take them hostage on the bus for a few months to show them what was really going on. Plug them into real life by letting them hear some of the stories we were hearing about unemployment, crime, and lack of health care.

We performed at a California ranch for President and Mrs. Reagan, and while the president was standing next to me, I had resisted the urge to grab him by the shoulders and shake him, screaming "Wake up! Wake up! America's in danger!"

As you might imagine, there was tight security for our invitation-only concert. Yet, as Wy, Ashley, and I entered host David Murdock's ranch site, the Secret Service merely waved the three of us on through. We could only guess it was because of our image or because they knew of our friendship with Judge Webster, who was now head of the CIA. We were surprised to discover that there was a box under our stage where they'd stash the president in case of an attack. There was a suspended camouflage net to prevent him from being seen by snipers or enemy aircraft. Wy poked me and pointed to a man carrying around a suitcase. "Be nice to that guy," she warned. "He's got the phone in there that sends missiles."

As my older daughter stood shoulder to shoulder with the president of the United States, I felt an overwhelming sense of gratitude to country music for allowing the three of us such a behind-the-scenes look at the presidency.

Back home we rented a Nashville studio hall to put together our new 1987 show that January, but facing even an ordinary day was becoming increasingly difficult. I'd been popping prednisone pills like a junkie and another one of the side effects is irritability. Ken hired choreographer Chris Dunbar to help us construct stage placements and figure out moves. In the middle of rehearsal, I abruptly left . . . just took a powder. I went home, told Larry I wasn't to be disturbed, locked the door, drew the drapes, and went to bed. Because I am the heart and soul of responsibility, it freaked everyone out. They all knew the steroids caused my behavior, but it was disquieting nonetheless.

When the time came to debut the new show in Little Rock,

Arkansas, everyone had opening-night jitters. We'd hired an experienced new production manager, Kenny Rogers's nephew, Tim Rogers, designed a different stage, added more lights and such, and were debuting the *Heartland* album material. Newcomer heartthrob, Randy Travis, was our opening act and the tour was selling out everywhere.

The premiere Heartland Show was a tremendous success and I thanked the band and crew and went straight to bed. Ken and Wy were celebrating with them in the Holiday Inn lounge where they met a local with a '56 T-bird convertible just like the one in *American Graffiti*. Hoping to cheer me up, they decided to surprise me with the beauty. The deal was on if I noticed the T-bird parked up the street in the opposite direction from our bus the next day. Sure 'nuff, the minute I walked out of the motel, it not only caught my eye but I walked up the hill to drool over it. Ken, Wy, and the hopeful seller came running up exclaiming, "It's yours!" I put "Redheds" on the license and began alternating driving it and Conway's "Music." Ken later bought Wynonna a neat old '48 Ford truck. She painted it cream and put "Hilbily" on its license plate.

At the 1987 Grammys the following month I wasn't myself, and Wy, who'd never seen me even have a cold, kept asking, "Mom, you sleep so much and don't seem like your old self. What's wrong with you?" My throat stayed sore, and she found out I kept a humidifier in my motel room all the time because the mist often set off smoke detectors. We won a Grammy for Best Country Performance by Duo/Group with Vocal for "Grandpa." One of our favorite parts of the Grammys is getting to meet artists in other fields like Stevie Winwood, Michael Jackson, and Tina Turner. At the victory party, we hung out with talented Bruce Hornsby.

The following morning I was sternly admonished for my shocking low-cut gown and rock-'n'-roll hairstyle by Ken and RCA. The AP ran a photo of Wy and me, showing me screaming with delight over our win. This wire service picture showed up in a *Saturday Night Live* segment in which comedian Dennis Miller quipped, "And here's those nice Judds." My excuse is that this Ebsen-designed dress had arrived at our LA hotel room from New York only hours before showtime and the neckline was two inches lower than it was designed to be. I never wore this "Heavy Metal Bride" gown again and assured everyone I wasn't trying to be like Dolly, whom we were about to meet for the first time.

Scheduled to perform at Lincoln Center in New York City with Dolly and Alabama, Wy and I attended a press conference with them. Seated next to Dolly at the dias, I wasn't aware our microphones were on as I began to let her know I was one of her admirers.

"Dolly, you just scatter my acorns!" I offered by way of introduction. This quote made the *New York Post* the next afternoon under a photo of the three of us. Wy, who's also a Dolly fan, got a charge out of seeing Dolly and me together.

When we weren't fielding questions from reporters, Dolly and I carried on the soft-shoe patter of inside girl talk. Someone asked all the artists to recount the best advice their mothers had ever given them. Randy Owen and Dolly responded with something serious. Wy stated I'd advised her, "Always be on your best behavior because you may be the only Bible some folks ever read."

Having had enough profundity, my answer was, "Don't go in the water with boys' cause sperm swims." With that the newly slim Dolly poked me with her little elbow, and we began giggling all over again. "Hey," I warned her, "you get any smaller you'll have to use Chapstick for deodorant." That's when the moderator threatened to separate us.

One of my other favorite women is Minnie Pearl. Wynonna and I got to visit with her when we hosted (and won Duet of the Year) at the ACMs with Patrick Duffy that April. Minnie is absolutely one of the dearest ladies I know. In real life Sarah Cannon is as dignified, intelligent, and kind as she's naive, daffy, and gossipy in character. If we were scared, Wy and I often reminded each other of something Minnie once said to reassure a nervous new artist making their first appearance on the Grand Ole Opry: "Just love 'em honey and they'll love you back!" My favorite Minnie line is "We'll treat you so many ways—you're bound to like one of them!" I would always tell Minnie that I wanted to be just like her when I grew up and then she'd laugh and hug me.

.   .   .

Much was made of the fact that we broke the rules about women not selling as much as men. Historically, females don't sell records and concert tickets, because, ironically, women are the ones who purchase most of the music and seem to prefer to hear men. Women are likewise usually in charge of the Saturday night entertainment and want to see guys like Randy Travis and George Strait singing love songs to them. Yet somehow all the Judd albums except the new Christmas album went platinum and our concerts were sellouts.

I believe whatever appeal we have goes beyond the music. I think women see themselves in us. So many came up to us or wrote that it's as if we were "calling them by name and voicing their own thoughts." They knew I was a single mother who was struggling to raise my children on my own, working as a waitress, clerk, secretary, model, and nurse (the largest female work force in America). They knew we were from a small town and blue-collar background. They've seen Wy and me successfully working out our particularly difficult parent-child relationship.

I also hope women are vicariously enjoying our career with us! As Brent Northup, writing in *The Journal American,* saw it, "It's a story for every exhausted single mom who's ever collapsed into a big overstuffed chair and fantasized of the day she'd be swept away from the dishes, diapers, and bills into a world of stardom. And it's also a daydream for every teenage girl who's ever taken an old guitar out of the closet, turned on the radio, strummed and sang along, pretending the bare bedroom ceiling light was the spotlight at the Grand Ole Opry."

Musically, our qualities are clear. We sing about family, our belief in marriage, and the search for fidelity ("One Man Woman" went number one), but we also fiercely insist on equality in our songs and in our lives.

As early as January 1985, observers began noting how we try to avoid country's cliché roles for women. The image of women in country music has always been a problematic matter. Because it is a genre that thrives on the tension between traditional values (home, family, and marriage) and rebellious acts (infidelity, inebriation, and

lawlessness), country music places women in archetypal and, therefore, limiting roles. Female vocalists tend to present themselves as
either long-suffering spouses or guilty, loose women. Either way
you're a victim. We made a conscious effort to neatly avoid falling
into the usual female roles while representing a return to traditional
music, as Ken Tucker wrote in *The Philadelphia Inquirer.*

Mark Crawford of the *Reno Gazette* referred to us as the "next
generation of feminine feminists."

We took an aggressive approach to acoustic music not only
soundwise but also in content. Observing us, Jon Bream of the
Minneapolis Star Tribune saw that although we're "liberated and
independent, but hardly flag waving feminists, they refuse to sing
submissive songs. On such hits as 'Why Not Me' and 'Girls' Night
Out,' they wanted to be assertive and even aggressive without sacri-
ficing feminity or being threatening."

Like my friend Oprah Winfrey, who also declares it breaks her
heart to see women letting men tell them how to live, I encourage
women to take their lives out of men's hands. I, too, was once
overdomesticated, trapped, fearful, and uncreative! I'm willing to
share what happened to me when I allowed myself to be victimized
by men, then say "but look how I progressed after I figured out that
every successful victim in a codependent relationship is still a failure!"

We knew for sure we could trust Ken to manage our money,
and that he was always looking for ways to invest and grow. Since our
business was successful, Ken formed our own booking agency, "Pro
Tours," with our agent from the Halsey Company, Steve Pritchard.
This way we could book, promote, and be in control of Judd concerts, and Steve began handling endorsement offers as well.

Wy and I turned down just about all the products we were
pitched. As mother/daughter, we got offers to sell feminine hygiene
products. I recall one really lucrative, famous name-brand food,
which is loaded with dyes and preservatives. Wy said ruefully, "Can't
you just picture us in a commercial exclaiming, 'Mmm kiddies, if you
want clear skin, strong bones, and energy like us, eat this garbage!' "

There were many TV offers we nixed as well. Dr. Ruth got it
in her head I should be on her sex information show, explaining to

Wy about the birds and the bees. *Lifestyles of the Rich and Famous* called about every week. We couldn't imagine going on a show that implies, "Hey check us out—we're rich and famous. Don't you wish you were as cool as us!"

We did find a few products we actually used and were happy to endorse, like AT&T. Boy were we familiar with their service! Plus Kraft barbecue sauce (we're big on backyard barbecues), Target (Wy and Ashley claim they grew up there), and Oldsmobile.

The Oldsmobile agency hired Gordon Willis, who filmed *The Godfather*, to shoot the commercial in Franklin with Wy driving and me in the passenger seat. Wy was instructed to accelerate around a sharp curve on a one-lane country road where Gordon and his camera crew were set up. It was blistering hot, so Wy kept snatching brown glass bottles from a cooler. I was horrified that she was guzzling beer in the middle of the afternoon in front of cops as she drove a new car that wasn't ever hers.

Gordon placed a walkie-talkie in Wy's lap so he could broadcast the "Action!" cue, while all I could do was sit there nervously dreading the scene. Gordon's very intimidating and brusque, and as soon as he'd gotten positioned behind his expensive camera he began the countdown. Suddenly, Wy picked up the walkie-talkie and hissed, "Shut up you brick brain or I'll make you an offer you can't refuse!" Then she floored the pedal as we scratched off down the road headed for the curve.

"My God—you're drunk, you just insulted a famous director, and now you're going to miss this sharp turn and kill him and all six of the production crew!" I screeched as I grabbed hold of the steering wheel and ran us off the road.

"Are you nuts Mom?!" Wy began sputtering, as everyone came running toward our car. "Those were only *root* beers and I never even pushed the 'talk' button down on the walkie-talkie to be heard!" The two of us were laughing like hyenas by the time the crew reached us!

They gave both of us shiny Oldsmobiles, the first brand-new car I ever owned in my life. Everything on it actually worked and the primary coat wasn't "bondo." Being one of the most generous people I know, Wy presented hers to Martha Taylor. Wy had recently bought a BMW with our first royalty check. The license plate acknowledged the source: "YNOTME," and she bought Ashley one just like it, with a license plate indicating "FRMSIS." It gave me an idea to buy mom a new Cadillac and Wib a GMC truck. Everybody scored a new ride!

I was proud of the way both daughters were turning out. While they were growing up, every fall I dreaded the back-to-school commercial blitz, because I, along with a lot of mothers, could not afford to buy my children new clothes or even lunch boxes. Before Ashley started her first year of college at the University of Kentucky in Lexington, I flew her out to Los Angeles where Wy and I were doing TV. Better late than never, I hired a limo for a day to take the two of us shopping on Melrose Avenue and then to lunch at Chianti's. Neither of us will ever forget this milestone in our reversal of fortune.

Ashley loved her college experience and made the Dean's List, carrying a double major in French and history. During parents' weekend I visited her dorm, Instamatic camera in hand, and blended in with all the other moms and dads.

On Mother's Day 1987, Wy and I were doing a show in Chicago with Dolly Parton when Ashley surprised me by running out onstage in the middle of a song!

For her summer break, Larry, Wy, Ashley, and I rented a houseboat and went fishing on Lake Lanier after our annual show in Cummings, Georgia. Lanierland was always one of our favorite places to play. A sweet little woman named Mama Lois and her ladies serve up some great southern food and hospitality there for crew meal. We all sit together out on a big screened-in back porch and chow down.

It was culture shock as we flew from Georgia to Vegas to headline at the Desert Inn the next week as Wy turned twenty-three. On May 30 I wanted to surprise the birthday girl on stage. For "Cow Cow Boogie" I coerced Wy's girlfriend Lisa Ramsey and Wayne Smith to get into a life-size cow outfit together and come dancing out on stage, just as Larry offstage (in his lowest bass voice) let out a resounding cow bellow. Wy struggled to sing and keep a straight face but couldn't.

For the finale I'd asked Wayne to hire the famous chimpanzees who appear in one of the Vegas showrooms to come out and give her a kiss. Since the chimps were on stage the same time we were, unknown to me, Wayne had instead gotten a midget with a boxing kangaroo. As soon as the scared kangaroo wearing boxing gloves was brought out by the midget, Wy and I were totally horrified. Being animal lovers and compassionate women, we hastily apologized and ushered them offstage. We felt awful for weeks afterward.

Actually, I had been feeling physically awful for many months now, long enough to know I needed to see a doctor. Having been healthy as an eighteen-year-old cheerleader, I didn't have a regular doctor. When I looked up a congenial physician I'd worked with at Williamson County, I laid it on the line.

"I'm going to present a panoply of nonspecific symptomology, prodromal symptoms, but please don't patronize me by merely telling me I'm overworked and stressed out, 'cause I know my body and I'm telling you something's wrong! I feel lethargic and have a constant mild headache. There's omnipresent slight neuralgia, a low-grade temperature, and I'm having trouble sleeping. I also have a nascent sense of foreboding. Please do a urinalysis, complete blood count, an SMA12 and a monospot test for mononucleosis."

When he phoned that night with the results I could tell something was wrong by the tone in his voice.

"We've got a problem here. You have CMV—cytomegalovirus," he sounded serious.

It felt like my heart stopped for a moment, then I wondered out loud, "What in the world is that, am I contagious, and how did I get it?"

"It's similar to mono and should self-terminate in five to six months. There's nothing you can take for it. And no, you're not contagious. Anywhere from forty to one hundred percent of adults have been infected with CMV and have formed an antibody to it. In immunocompetent hosts, it remains latent and does not cause clinical diseases. In other words, just about everybody has been exposed to this virus, but if they're normally healthy they won't come down with it. Since you're out in public surrounded by people day and night, you've been exposed to CMV. The prednisone you've been on lowers the white blood cells, which fight off foreign invaders. Your white count is barely two thousand [the normal range is 4,500 to 11,000], and you're immunocompromised. It's a wonder you haven't gotten something else, 'cause right now you barely have any immune system!"

I verified all this in my *Luckman and Sorensen's Medical-Surgical Nursing* manual, and when I requested all my test results, I noticed my ALT (alanine aminotransferase—an enzyme indicating damage going on in the liver) was elevated. This doctor shrugged it off, saying it was probably "just a result of some muscle strain." Unfortunately, he failed to suspect hepatitis that spring of 1987.

I kept the diagnosis of CMV pretty much to myself. At least now I thought I knew what it was that had been making me feel so crummy for the past months. I set my jaw, prepared to wait it out.

When we arrived to play Lake Tahoe for the first time the next month, the ladies at the house I was staying at were talking about a strange new disease in nearby Incline Village, Nevada. The Centers for Disease Control in Atlanta had a team there investigating it. Similar to CMV, Epstein-Barr as it's called, can render its victim too tired to even brush his or her teeth. The bad news is it's chronic and incurable. (*Acute* refers to something short term, and *chronic* means ongoing.)

Realizing Wy and I had recently performed at Harrah's in Reno, which is also close to Incline Village, I naturally became suspicious about the similarities of symptoms between CMV and Epstein-Barr. I found out all I could about Epstein-Barr and taught my doctor in Franklin so I could have the blood test. Results indicated I'd had a brush with it but, thank God, didn't have it on top of CMV.

Several interesting things had happened while we'd played out our first week back at Harrah's in Reno. Wy met architect Bryce Edgar, a native Nevadian. Unlike some of the guys who followed her around, Bryce is no sycophant. He's his own man and everyone was glad to see their friendship last down through the years.

And on opening night, the exact moment we'd finished our last note of "Don't Be Cruel," all the electricity on Reno's Strip had gone out. The showroom went black and silent like some giant exclamation point! Wy exclaimed "Whew! If it had happened *during* the King's song, I'd never have sung it again!"

When Wy, Ken, and I arrived at Lake Tahoe the first time Wy chose to stay in the Star Suite penthouse atop Harrah's, saying "I prefer to be close to the action." I was assigned The Villa out on the lake and no description could have prepared us for it.

A rustically modern, sprawling 24,000-square-foot beauty, it's right on majestic Lake Tahoe. It has its own pier and boat, plus a royal blue Rolls-Royce and a silver Mercedes in the garage for the guests' personal use!

Dorothy Smith, Harrah's housekeeping supervisor whom we knew from Harrah's in Reno, met us at the front door and introduced me to my villa "staff." Holly was my cook; Helen, the housekeeper; and Manny, the groundskeeper. Unaccustomed to having "help," I immediately made friends with them and staying at The Villa (while doing two shows a night) became one of the highlights of our year. When they told me Bill Cosby brings his family to stay at The Villa while he's working, Larry and I flew in both sets of parents. On the last day of our week there I started an annual tradition, a huge all-day party with our entire group.

We stuffed ourselves, swam in the pool, went parasailing, and filled garbage cans with water balloons for outdoor fights. I'd gather everyone in a circle and ask each to express what they were thankful for. We'd play games in which we imitated someone we all knew or had to demonstrate some talent. When I discovered Odell does a great Randy Travis impersonation I began making him do it in our shows with Randy.

We were working with a lot of talented people that summer. Besides doing the star-studded Marlboro shows with Alabama, Dolly, George Strait, Merle Haggard, Hank Williams, Jr., and Randy Travis, we were packaging most our regular concerts with Randy. He is a sweetheart of a guy, quiet and humble. But boy he made the crowds go berserk!

Nice guys Dan Seals, Steve Wariner, Michael Martin Murphey, and John Anderson also worked a bunch of shows with us. We did a tour of Alaska with a great guy we'd been a fan of for years— Delbert McClinton. When "His T-Ness," T. Graham Brown, worked with us, we traded *Andy Griffith* tapes and I'd tell him he's only on country radio because he's too white to be on black R&B stations and has too much southern accent to go pop! There was great camaraderie between The Judds and Restless Heart and we had a blast going bowling on nights off.

Next month, when I saw we had a day off in northern California near Marin County where we lived in the 1970s, I rented a car for Wy and me to take a trip down memory lane. It made our usual bookends, bodyguard Snipper and road manager Dwight, nervous for us to go out unaccompanied, but I insisted on mother/daughter time.

We drove by College of Marin, where I'd gotten my RN degree, then down the road to Wy's school, Sir Francis Drake High. As the kid and I walked into the school office, the secretary looked up and declared matter of factly, "Well I'm glad to see you Wynonna Judd, 'cause you owe some money on school books!" I dashed out to get my billfold, while she walked the halls chatting with students.

Wynonna and I stood hand in hand in front of our old apartment in Lagunitas remembering how different our lives were there. Phyllis, the post mistress at the Lagunitas post office next door filled us in on what our old friends were doing. On up the road in tiny Point Reyes, we sauntered into the *Point Reyes Light* newspaper to comment on what a joyous relief it was to see that lovely, enlightened Marin County hasn't been raped by the commercialism of greedy developers. Of course, reporter Ken White grabbed his pad and began recording our comments. Marin County will always have a very special place in our hearts and is like a second home.

Wy made a new home in a nice condo complex in the Green Hills area of Nashville. We played a show for seventy-five thousand in Chattanooga, Tennessee, with Reba, that June 27, 1987, the very day Reba's divorce hit the papers. I slipped her my private number in case she needed someone to talk to. Soon Reba became Wy's neighbor in the same complex.

It was always so enjoyable being around Reba and Tammy Wynette. One night Larry walked into the bedroom wondering, "Who have you just been on the phone with for an hour and a half? You've discussed everything from men, raising kids, fans, hairdressers, gossip, the tabloids, decorating, wardrobe designers, to how to cook pork chops in cream of mushroom soup in a Crockpot on a bus!" Of course, it was my dear friend Tammy, with whom I can discuss anything.

That month Wy and I pressed our hands into wet concrete at Starwalk in Nashville with forty-nine other Grammy winners. When Lynn Anderson spied her ex-husband, Glenn Sutton, preparing to make an impression by sticking his nose in, Lynn sneaked up and kicked him from behind, shoving Glenn's entire face down in the wet concrete!

Our faces were on the cover of all the women's magazines. Unfortunately, they'd been cropping up on the front pages of the tabloids too.

Sounding upset, the lady who helped Wy called me one night. She'd just spotted us in the grocery checkout on the cover of one of the tabloids with an article called "The Battling Judds." "I work in Wy's home, travel with you two, see you in every possible situation, and I know this is nothing but a blatant lie! Why would someone do this, and how can they get away with it?" she demanded to know, reduced to tears.

Larry and I jumped in the car and drove straight over to Wy's house to tell her about it before someone else did. She cried and cried: "After all we'd been through together, having worked things out and being so close now, these false accusations are vicious and painfully cruel."

We were deeply upset and resentful of lies put into quotes to make it sound as if Wy and I, or "inside sources" or "close friends" had actually said them!

Even cynical Patrick Carr who had just finished researching us and spending a day observing us on the road for a six-page spread in the legitimate publication *Country Music Magazine* admitted we get along "beautifully," allowing that "the fabled Judd fights are a thing of the past." Typically, during his sit-down interview, Wy lay with her head in my lap. Patrick even questioned Ken, who added, "They really don't have the explosions they used to. They get along well!"

Like a lot of people, we once dismissed the "rags" as merely tacky adult comics about celebrities, read by uneducated gullible people. In reality, these shameful publications are no laughing matter. They're run by unethical, greedy people who make their dirty money by causing other people misery and promoting the moral disintegration of our nation. The only way to stop them is for people to refuse to buy these tabloids.

Wynonna pointed out that the ironic part is that she and I have always tried to treat the press with kindness and respect, we are naturally sincere and candid. In fact, I can think of no other entertainers who have been as open as the Judds. *Rolling Stone's* Laura Fissinger observed that "both women live with emotions naked enough to startle unsuspecting new acquaintances. Naomi speaks her mind before she has a chance to censor herself." We get memos and chastisements from our office about revealing so much to the public and have always been known for our brutally honest what-you-see-is-what-you-get personalities.

The media has been such an important part of our career, and we try to help them because we also understand that they're trying to do their job. All across the country, we actually consider most members of the media as friends. If we're in Los Angeles we look forward to seeing Robert Hilburn, in Oklahoma there's Ellis Widner, Dave Zimmerman in Washington, D.C., and Jim Bessman's up in New York.

With radio personalities there's a certain DJ who gets me in trouble. He and I are a dangerous combination, 'cause he has the ability to make me say and do really goofy things (okay, goofier than usual!). Gerry House in Nashville gave me his station's recording studio's private number so I go directly on the air. Wy warns me, "Now Mom! You could destroy our entire career in one single conversation with this nut!"

Gerry's one of the zaniest people I know, and I love and trust him because he knows how to be hilarious without hurting others. People who try to be funny at others expense aren't really funny, just petty and plain ol' mean spirited. Friends, Gerry brought me some cool earrings shaped like purses from his trip to Egypt, and I got him fancy underwear to wear under his tuxedo when he won Air Personality of the Year at the ACMs.

When we won Group of the Year at the 1987 CMA awards, Wy was given a chance to say, "I want to thank you for allowing a twenty-three-year-old to feel what I feel tonight and for allowing Mom to enjoy a second childhood!" My excited response was, "I'm not going to say music is the most important thing in our lives, but it's right up there with oxygen!"

That year we wore vinyl, and Wy promised, "If I spill anything on this black vinyl pant suit, you can hose me down!"

She looked like a record! Esben made the pants too tight, so she was unable to sit down in them. Scrunched together, Mom and Ashley and I roared with laughter as Wy rode stiffly at an angle across the back of the limo to the show. My fire engine red vinyl suit with its short stand-out full skirt and underlying red crinolines, was truly Esben's *pièce d'résistance*! After we performed "Turn It Loose" on the awards show, we turned these outfits loose to go on permanent display at the Country Music Hall of Fame. In the ceremony hosted by our girlfriend, vivacious radio and TV personality Kathy Martindale, Wynonna also contributed memorabilia from her high school days and I relinquished my well-worn nursing uniform and cap.

We had such fun playing dress up as we helped design our outfits through the years. When Esben moved back to Denmark, Vanessa found a classy seamstress from South Africa named Dez Zamek to make our clothes. The intricate hand beading and rhinestoning were so time-consuming, Wy used Mary Freeman while Lynn Kiracofe decorated my dresses. The two talented ladies also ornamented high heels and boots to match each costume. Vanessa and I had everything down to a science. We put rubber grips on the bottom of shoes so I didn't slip while dancing or jumping off stage risers. There were three sizes of shoulder pads with Velcro strips, and every single top I had (even PJs) had the matching Velcro strip to hold them. By now Vanessa knew us so well she could buy our underwear or shop for anything we needed. She was challenged by the contrast between Wy and me, and knew better than to try to dress us alike.

Wy would say: "The way we dress is an extension of our personalities, and I think it works onstage. It helps people delineate between mother and daughter. I like the differences, and it happens unconsciously."

Reviewers reviewed more than our music! Much attention was paid not only to our flamboyant clothes but also to these startling contrasts between our individual styles. Because of my size-six, figure-flattering dresses, I was called a "Barbie Doll." They'd compare Wy with Elvis because of her black pants, rhinestoned rock-and-roll jackets and matching boots. When I was reminiscent of the *Sweetheart of Sigma Chi* in an original design that somewhat resembled a prom dress, they decided Wy's black pants, black-lace blouse, and striped charcoal coat made her look like "the quiet but uninhibited girl out smoking with the bad boys behind the gym." I named her "The Countess of Hip" and she teasingly called me "Country Music's Miss America."

One night as we emerged from our respective bedrooms on our bus, we paused side by side for a last minute touch up in front of a mirror and began laughing at the obvious differences in how we were dressed. "You look like Davy Crockett from Rodeo Drive in that white fringed outfit!" I chuckled. She had a large diamond stud in one earlobe and pale crystal drop earrings in the other. There was a silver slave bracelet on her left hand.

She winced noticeably at my tangerine sherbert crinkled silk "Carmen Miranda" dress with its multicolored petticoats and delicate pastel roses set into huge puff sleeves.

"Oh my! And you're my little creampuff!" she retorted in a high-pitched voice with a sardonic grin. "If you were any cuter . . ."

I go for ultra-feminine, glamorous clothes that show off womanly curves. My trademark jewelry are beautiful earrings and bracelet sets and a dainty, sparkly anklet bracelet. Offstage, I like bright-colored, comfortable, casual clothes and tailored suits from the 1940s. I don't own a pair of jeans and never wear cowboy boots.

Describing her offstage style, Wy declares, "I'm a very animated dresser and have lots of moods. Sometimes, I'm conservative, sometimes I'm bizarre." She goes for tie-dyed outfits, wild shirts worn with cycling shorts, and cool decorated ball caps. For church, she wears velvet and Victorian lace. She has lots of custom-made cowboy boots, an enviable collection of gorgeous cross necklaces, and fabulous turquoise pieces.

Wynonna and I actually have the same taste. We buy things for each other all the time and have never been off on guessing what the other likes or dislikes. Too many times we've bought the same thing for our boyfriends. One year at an award show Larry and Bryce showed up in the exact same raw silk silver suits from the same store and then had to sit next to each other all night! On a day off in St. Louis, Wy and I met after an afternoon of shopping to share a cab ride back to our hotel. I grabbed up my store shopping bags after a quick peek into them. But when I got up to my room the clothing and shoes were all the wrong size. Wy and I had bought the same items and had each other's bags!

Since normally there's no concert held on Mondays, Wy and I have what we call our "beauty parties" with the "glamour team" in our homes. People have to come to us to be able to fit everything into one day. After wardrobe fittings with Vanessa and Dez, Gordon Robison would color my hair. Someone asked if I was prematurely gray, and I responded. "No, it's right on time!" "The Duke of Earl," Earl Cox, cuts and styles our hair. Patti Lively does my manicures, although Wy has short nails to play guitar. Adie Grey McKenzie uses her healing touch to give us massages. This congo line of workers streaming through our homes are also close, treasured friends who've been with us from the beginning. I call them our vitamins 'cause they supplement our minimum daily requirements.

When you have to be on the road so much, it's difficult to maintain normal friendships. We'd have several parties each year in Nashville for our organization and an annual summer picnic. I pulled an ornery trick at stage manager Bruce Johnson's wedding when I instructed everyone to wrap their toasters as well as their real gifts. We piled the toasters on a table where Bruce and his new wife, Kay, were opening presents and left their actual gifts in another room. Soon as they opened the first one, they exclaimed, "Well, every new household needs one of these!" With the second one, Kay replied, "Okay, we'll have a spare one for the last twenty-five years of our marriage!" After the third toaster appeared, we watched them glance down at the stack of remaining packages that were all exactly the same size. The newlyweds slowly looked at each other like, "Oh no! You don't suppose . . ."

Martha Taylor and Ken and Jo's family became like our own, sharing special occasions, holidays, and even coming on tour with us.

Traveling did have some advantages in that it afforded us the opportunity to visit with out-of-state relatives. If we were performing near where my sister, Margaret, lives in Pennsylvania, we'd drop in to spend a few precious days immersing ourselves in normalcy. When we happened to be there for my nephew Joshua's fifth birthday, I dressed him in the complete cowboy outfit I'd bought, then we all cheered and applauded as he serenaded us with the electric guitar and stand-up microphone cousin Wy gave him. While Margaret and I sat hunkered at the kitchen talking sister talk, Wy held a tea party with her little cousin Allison and took advantage of their washer and dryer to do her laundry.

The same was true for Mom and Wib and the Ciminellas anytime we were near Ashland. Wy and Ashley's Mamaw Ciminella passed away November 22, 1987. After a show in Binghamton, New York, I'd had to break the sad news to Wy and charter a plane to go to Ashland in the middle of the night. At her funeral, Ashley read scripture from John 14:2, "In my Father's house are many mansions," and Wy sang the old bluegrass song "Kentucky" as poor Papaw said good-bye to his dear wife of forty-three years.

Sometimes we'd awaken in our bus parked in the gravel parking lot next to my brother Mark's quaint white-frame church in rural Colesburg, Kentucky. Wy and I would slip into an old wooden pew alongside the thirty-member congregation, listening to Reverend Judd's Sunday morning sermon. I'd smile proudly up at him, realizing my little brother is a for-real preacher. Sometimes Mark reminds me, he too is surprised that his sister and niece have become entertainers! His wife, Middy, teaches Sunday School and plays the old upright piano during church service. Wy and I would inevitably be called to the front to sing duets of old Appalachian hymns.

That Veterans Day of 1987 Wynonna and I sang "God Bless America" at the Vietnam Memorial in Washington, D.C., during a blinding blizzard. It was truly an unforgettable experience looking out at the veterans and their families standing solemnly in the falling snow. I couldn't help wondering why the "invisible veterans," the nurses who served so selflessly in Vietnam, were never acknowledged. That night, along with Alabama and emcee Bob Hope, we gave a concert in Constitution Hall to raise money to engrave even more names on the wall. *Billboard*'s Nashville columnist Gerry Wood described the show as "electric."

The following week Wy, Ashley, and I found ourselves on our way to do a USO Tour by spending Thanksgiving at Guantanamo Naval Base in Cuba. When Ken informed us we were going over in a navy transport plane, I told him I preferred turquoise.

As my girls and I toured the only U.S. base inside a communist country, it just seemed unreal being there in Castro's stronghold in the middle of the Caribbean. Visiting marines stationed at outposts along the demarcation line, the three of us put on our brightest smiles as we tried to cheer up the men and women. After asking permission to address a battalion standing stiffly at attention, I commanded them to "Put your right foot in," and they immediately responded in perfect precision. "Now, put your right foot out. You do the hokey pokey and turn yourself around—that's what it's all about!" As Wy and Ashley groaned some apologies, I caught some corners of the soldiers' mouths turning upward.

I paused for a moment and stared across the low rusty barbed-wire border to the other side. I bent down and reached across it to touch the earth on the communist side. It was just like the soil I was standing on. I could see Castro's bunker and felt unseen eyes watching me.

Next thing I knew I was being lowered down to have a firsthand look inside a tank. Wy and Ashley laughed at the "what's wrong with this picture" scene, as I paused in my chic Norma Kamali outfit, smelling like rose water and talcum, to adjust the army green helmet. All day and night we shook every hand in sight and were able to tell many of the men and women we'd been in their hometowns.

As we were going through the chow line in the galley of the navy destroyer USS *Ponce* for Thanksgiving dinner, all I could think about was how much these freedom defenders missed their homes and loved ones. Suddenly, the navy chaplain approached, requesting that I offer the blessing. He handed me a microphone so those who were still manning their posts throughout the battleship could hear.

Flanked by Wy and Ashley, choking back my own emotions, I began, "Our heavenly Father, *You* are the supreme ruler of all men, of all nations . . ." After the meal Wy, Ashley, and I insisted on walking throughout the ship to chat with all those who'd been unable to leave their stations. Seamen Bret Tepe of Spearville, Kansas, and Darrin Ream of Winter Haven, Florida, were among those who thanked us for being there, saying, "Having you here helps keep our minds off not being home with our own families."

That night we performed our music in a concert for the base at "Gitmo" while TNN filmed it for a USO TV special. "Back home in the States, we're on our Heartland Tour, and since you're over here defending the Heartland we've come to bring you a slice of it." Closing with everyone joining in singing "America the Beautiful," there wasn't a dry eye in the crowd—or on the stage. Patriotic to our core, countless reviewers had long noted that Judd music celebrates American values of God and family through country music (Marie Ziomek, in the *Knickerbocker News*).

Then it was our turn to be entertained. Back home in Nashville the next night, international rock superstars U2 were performing. Ashley, who listens to all kinds of music, from classical and opera to rock, had turned us on to this young Irish band. Wy and I had read in various interviews like *Rolling Stone* that they were fans of our music, and our camps had been sending messages back and forth. Now, lead singer Bono motioned for us to come out of the audience and join him on stage. Wy obligingly played guitar and sang with Bono as he lay his head on her shoulder during "People Get Ready." Ashley and I sat cheering, exhausted from the Cuban trip.

That holiday week our *Christmastime with the Judds* album came out, and during our December shows, we incorporated a few of the carols from it. While we were singing "Santa Claus Is Coming to Town," I'd ask the children in the audience to come in front of the stage. Gaylon, our bus driver, dressed up like Santa Claus, would pass out treats to them. We'd taped an hour-long radio special with our good friends Lee Arnold and Kevin Delaney, and on Christmas Day I was sitting in Mom's kitchen listening to the old radio on top of the refrigerator when the program came on. I felt as if I was in a time warp as I listened to Wy remembering her childhood Christmases.

When we began our 1988 tour, Wy and I met another of our favorite entertainers when comedian Jay Leno opened for us in Las Vegas at Caesar's. As funny offstage as he is on, we appreciated his refusal to stoop to obscenity. Hanging out in the dressing room, "The Stallion of Stand-Up" as Wy calls him, and I lamented the "olden days when there were unmentionables."

Wynonna and I found ourselves surrounded by real-live clowns when we were ringmasters for Ringling Brothers, Barnum and Bailey Circus for a CBS special. The kid and I got to dress up like clowns and do slapstick in a skit with them. As she watched me covered with goo, slipping and sliding around the ring, Wy dubbed me "The Lucille Ball of Country Music." She and I watched lion tamers working, played with monkeys, held boa constrictors, and danced with real Zulu warriors. The elephant handler told us how the pachyderm had recently used its trunk to take a $100 bill from his pocket and had eaten it. The trainer sent the elephant dung in a shoe box to the U.S. Treasury and received a new bill.

Wy, the animal and nature lover, bought a beautiful farm with a house registered with the Historical Society outside of Franklin. Ken gave her a horse for Christmas and her menagerie now included six dogs and almost thirty cats. She was the vet's best customer, since she has all animals neutered and meticulously cared for. Constantly picking up strays, she works with the animal shelter. Her "cuddle buddy," Loretta Lynn, who travels on the road and flies in the first-class cabin on planes, is the world's most pampered dog. Our road manager concluded, "If there's such a thing as reincarnation, I'd like to come back as a Judd pet!"

In addition to being the biggest animal lover I know, simply put, Wynonna Ellen Judd is the funniest human being I've ever known in my whole life. She makes me laugh so hard I snort (very attractive!), and I can make her laugh so hard she has to do two puffs on her medihaler. (My impromptu "Big Butt Dance" gets her every time.)

It was when she was about four or five, that I began to notice how funny she is. When Wy started kindergarten I sat her down and patiently warned her about accepting gifts and rides from strangers. Satisfied I'd done a thorough job, I stood up to leave with a parting question: "Okay now, what would you do if a strange man offered you a piece of candy?"

"First," she began, as she held up her small finger, "I'd find out what *kind* of candy . . ."

Wynonna doesn't try to be funny. She just is! She doesn't tell jokes, she says and does hilarious stuff without meaning to. Crossing the Canadian border, a custom's official inquired if she knew anything about their beautiful countryside. "Nope," she chirped. "I wasn't into gynecology in school but I bet I see some up here!"

When I corrected, "I believe you must mean 'geography,' dear," she turned pale as I fell off my chair laughing. When a reporter asked her where she was born, Wynonna seriously answered: "I was born in Ashland, Kentucky, so I could be near Mom."

It's like she takes reality by surprise. If I'm the "Lucille Ball of Country Music" as she claims, then I'll call Wy the "Gary Larsen" (the cartoonist who created *The Farside*). After a show in Minnesota, our fans Andy and Carron brought us adult PJs with feet in them. Wearing hers on the bus before bedtime, Wy had her hair done up in a ponytail coming out of the top of her head, like Pebbles on *The Flintstones*. As she finished off the last of some cookies and the dregs of the milk carton, she nonchalantly smashed the plastic milk jug against her forehead, let out a resounding belch, and then disappeared into her room.

Wy does muscle man poses in her underwear. The "crab" sends me to the moon! Childlike, spontaneous, and irreverent, she doesn't let very many people see this side of her. When she and Ashley and I are alone, we are totally uninhibited as we let our hair down and emit wolf-child howls.

The two most common comments we hear after people get to know us are that we're down to earth and funny.

Our wicked sense of humor takes most people by surprise. Wy and I joke and kid about anything and everything. But one thing we don't joke about is our responsibility as artists. We take it seriously and gave it our all every night on stage. It was of tremendous satisfaction to us that another frequent comment we got was that we sound just like or even better than our records.

It seemed hard to believe when RCA called saying the time had come for our first "greatest hits" album, and because "Change of Heart" had been on the obscure first mini-album, they were rereleasing it as the single. Larry and I were together later when we heard over the radio that this torch song I'd written for him so long ago had now just become the number one song in America. Larry was now truly the man he'd longed to be. Devoted, faithful, and happy— except for one thing.

"I love you more than anything in this world," he began. "Would you be buried with my people?" He laughed nervously and then exhaled audibly before turning serious. "I want to spend the rest of my life with you so I'm asking you to marry me. If you say no again, I'm moving out. Living together is wrong."

With that he pressed a small velvet box into my palm and wrapped my fingers closed around it. It was as if he were undressing his heart and laying it timidly at my feet.

"I guess now forever has a golden ring to it," I murmured.

"Better write that down," Larry said smiling, "sounds like a song title!"

The sweetness of his kiss melted in my mouth and drifted down inside me. I pulled away so he could see my face and said: "If you ever leave me again, this time I'm coming with you!"

Things were not going so well for the other man in my life. Ken struggled to arrange a fair royalty deal with RCA, now that our first option was up. While Ken had suffered his first heart attack in 1983 I'd signed us to a ridiculous contract. We'd turned out to be quite a cash cow. When an uncompromising New York lawyer refused a more equitable agreement, Ken had no choice but to accept an offer from MCA. Wy and I felt sad about leaving RCA. I called this lawyer "a heartless homewrecker" to his face, and telling him we felt as if we'd been dragged through a painful divorce.

The Curb MCA contract proved to be a real bugger to negotiate because there were two labels involved, in addition to all Ken's other demanding responsibilities. The Stilts family, along with Wy and I were terribly alarmed about Ken's health and the very real prospect of another heart attack. Under pressure from all sides, Ken showed up at my house with Wynonna to resign as our manager.

There was no way. Instead, the three of us dissolved into tears, layering our hands on top of one another at the center of my kitchen table vowing "Till death do us part." Ken also pledged to quit smoking and take more time off for his family.

Down through his years of dealing with Nashville's music community, Ken had established himself as one of the most scrupulously honest, fair-minded men our industry has ever seen. Besides his genius business sense, Wy and I were always confident and proud to know Ken is respected as a man of his word. It's my definition that "character is what you stand for and reputation is what you fall for!" Ken Stilts has a great reputation 'cause he doesn't fall for anything! Wy claims "Daddy Ken" has BS detectors in his ears, 'cause she can never get away with anything.

Bigger than life, "Mr. Big" has a hearty appetite for living. Wy, Ashley, and I hired a video crew to make a *This Is Your Life, Ken Stilts* film. Using dozens of people significant to him, Ken's life is documented in ribald stories, parodies, and touching testimonials. Since I'm the "Queen of Everything" and Wynonna's the "Princess of Quite a Lot" we felt Ken needed a royal title too. We had a luxurious red velvet robe with gold satin lining custom-made for him with "The King of Think" embroidered across the back. In a mock coronation, we placed a golden crown encrusted with fake jewels on his head, then presented him a royal scepter with a microphone in it so he can loudly broadcast his proclamations to his loyal subjects. The throne we gave him is a large electric vibrating massage recliner, fit for a king to relax in, or perhaps do some more thinking!

Once upon a time Wynonna met a young man who was a real King. The Queen of Everything's Prince Charming (Larry), introduced The Princess of Quite a Lot to Tony King, who became known as A Prince of a King. The four of us would double date all over the kingdom of Nashville. We'd go out to eat and see movies or drive through Taco Bell in the royal truck on our way to redneck bowling lanes.

Tony is a wonderful guy possessed with a great sense of humor, and everyone else fell in love with him too. He was our comrade and Vince Gill's lead guitar player and harmony singer in addition to being a hit songwriter.

Clint Black was working some with us now, and I'd known from the moment I'd watched him from the wings the very first night that he was going to be a major star. Just out of the chute, he had all the markings of a champion. Clint, Wy, and I would try to eat crew meals together 'cause we got along famously.

Eddie Bayers, our session drummer, phoned me at home one night with a hot tip on another rising star. "Mamaw, I just did a session on a good lookin' new guy in town who blows my mind! You and Wy should nab him!" I alerted Ken, and he and Pro Tours put lanky Alan Jackson on some shows.

Rough-and-ready honky tonker Travis Tritt had just arrived on the scene and joined us for some festival dates. Another newcomer who impressed us was personable Lionel Cartwright. Sans cowboy hat, this sweet, handsome fella with soap opera star looks, is also an intelligent songwriter.

I was just pulling up at Wy's to hang out with her on a day off when she came running up crying, "Mommy, somebody called to tell us Keith Whitley's just been found dead!" The tragic news of our friend's accidental death broke our hearts. We'd just finished the tour with him. In the morning we walked our dogs together after we woke up in our buses that were parked side by side. Keith named his black cocker spaniel "Lefty" after his hero Lefty Frizzell. As Lefty and Banjo took their morning constitutionals, Keith would brag about his and Lorrie's baby. I was aware he'd once had a drinking problem, but he seemed to be recovering and had so much to live for.

Wy and I finally got to meet one of our songwriting heroes, the incomparable Roger Miller. Every bit as witty and charming as we'd expected, as badly as I wanted to, I felt unworthy to ask if I could write with him someday.

• • •

Songwriting is weird. I don't know how I write songs. Couldn't tell you. Never had anyone even give me a single tip on how it's done. It just started coming out of me when I was alone on the mountaintop back in Morrill, Kentucky. It's sort of like giving birth. It begins with trying to re-create life and comes out of my being, but interaction with someone else is what plants the seed. Each song has a name and a personality, and I sent them out into the world.

The only song I've ever written that wasn't for the Judds to sing is "The Ballad of Mr. Big," which Larry and I produced in the studio for Ken's personal theme song. Wy and I had given him a gorgeous Wurlitzer jukebox with this comical recording on it. That's when I got the idea to use it as the soundtrack for yet another video about him.

Using the same computer graphics, and format of the questionable tabloid TV show *Current Affair,* Wy and I pose as reporters "Ms. Out-to Getcha" and "Ima Snoop" for our warped parody, "Currently Unfair." This segment titled, *The Secret Life of Mr. Big* is the exposé sequel to our serious original, *This Is Your Life, Ken Stilts.* This time around we hired an actor, who strongly resembles Ken, and with the help of the Stilts family, dressed the actor in Ken's own clothes and used a professional crew to film this look-alike doing outrageous, undignified things the real Ken wouldn't be caught dead doing. It provoked belly laughs and guffaws when we premiered it at our "We Aim to Sleaze You" party.

Some Los Angeles TV guys felt they should make a documentary of Wy and Ashley and me. Enterprising producer Tony Eaton convinced CBS that our real lives were better than fiction and needed to be captured *à la cinema verité.*

Tony introduced us to an imaginative young director with whom Wy, Ken, and I felt an instantaneous rapport. Bud Schaetzle, an irreverent whiz-kid film director, brought along a talented crew who would go on to become the film-making branch of the Judd organization family tree. In this first of many important projects together, Bud, Martin Fischer, Doug Forbes, Bret Wolcott, Mike Salomon, Candy Gonzales, Allen Branton, and Forrest Brakeman became our constant cohorts on an exhausting, but wonderful, six-week filmed excursion *Across the Heartland* of America.

This one-hour special introduces Ashley, now a college sophomore, who plays herself as an amateur filmmaker spending her summer vacation chronicling her singing mother and sister as they do what they do naturally every day, traveling on a bus up and down life's highways. Ashley sums up the home-movie peek behind the scenes as "meet the real Judds," and in her own words describes our success story "as equal parts Mom's imagination and Wynonna's soul." Ashley was so at ease whenever Bud turned the camera on her, that it prompted speculation about her promising potential as an actress. While Wy and I were on stage singing at night, Ken and Bud and the TV crew were encouraging Ashley seriously to consider becoming an actress.

Viewers and critics decided her presence on the show transformed us into "a close-knit everyfamily." We were proud of our first TV special and were grateful to be actually given a chance to demonstrate that we are three distinct individuals. As Wy noted, "We would like for America to see that not only is our music genuine but we're real people too, and we're all three dream chasers."

Our hopes were also realized when *Nashville Banner* reporter Clark Parsons said he felt like he'd "had a visit—not just a show." Reviews like the *Denver Post,* which rated it "a twelve on a one-to-ten scale," and rave comments in *Variety* and the rest of the trades made Ken decide to make it available on home video.

We lifted footage from the special to put together a video for our next blues-drenched release, "Give a Little Love." The song went straight to number one, and the video was voted Video of the Year by *Cable Guide.* The prime-time special also helped broaden our demographics.

One of our favorite comments came from folks confessing, "I never liked country music before you guys came along." For instance, after our first show in New Jersey, critic Lori Hoffman said, "You may now consider this Easterner hogtied to the Judd bandwagon!" We'd long noticed and appreciated the diversity of people at our concerts. There were kids in mohawks wearing T-shirts bearing anti-establishment slogans. The heavy-metal group Ratt showed up at a concert in Fargo and complimented us on our "earthy, rustic sound." Seated next to them was a family who'd brought along the grandparents.

They all came to see us and sat side by side. The teacher and the drop-out, the poor and the privileged, the have-nots and the congenitally wealthy. We met the sick and the healthy, the highbrow and the lowbrow, the oblivious and the aware. We believe in what country music has to offer and sensed its popularity increasing with each passing year. We were hearing and reading comments like Mike Weatherford's from Kansas City that we were helping create "an emerging unprecedented popularity in country music." Wy remarked, "All I can say is, the rising tide lifts all boats!" A guy named Russell Smith in Dallas called us "the most influential country act of this decade."

While the acclaim we were receiving was wonderfully encouraging and helped build our confidence to continue following our instincts, I decided the whole thing was analogous to making a pay phone call. First, Wy and I earn a quarter (practice and find songs). Second, we put the quarter in the phone (make a record). Third, we deliver our message (Judd music gets played). And finally and unexpectedly, after we hang up the quarter comes back in a stroke of luck (good reviews come out)! The musical payoff for us is that folks like and understand our efforts. A favorable review means we got through to one more person.

That spring when Brent and Don called for us to start a new album, the studio machine broke and Wy and I found ourselves with a beautiful day off. I jumped into my '53 Cadillac (Music) and turned up Bonnie Raitt while cruising Main Street in Franklin. Who should I pass in her '57 red Chevy (Redhot) listening to Aretha?! I immediately started writing a combined self-referential 1950s-style rockabilly tune called "Cadillac Red." Craig Bickhardt and John Jarvis helped put music to my playful metaphors:

> She's washed and polished
> And full of high octane
> Ridin' with the top down, cruisin' in the fast lane

> Her red hair's blowin bright as a flame
> Cadillac Red's her name!

When I'd introduce Wy onstage to sing it, I'd declare "this girl can sing the chrome off my '53 Caddy!"

As I was showing my prolific songwriter friend Don Schlitz around my house, he inquired about an old photo from the late 1800s taken of the Judd clan at their original homestead in Louisa, Kentucky.

I began, "A hundred-year-old photograph stares out from its frame, and if you look real close you'll see, our eyes are all the same. Their lives revolved around three things: hard work, family, and faith. Although they died before I was even born, I feel a bond with them. Now they're my guardian angels!" Don's eyes got real big, and he exclaimed "Quick! Write all this down!"

With echoes of the past, this canonical song relates the story of my great-great-grandparents, Elijah and Fanny Judd. As I sang it to Wy and Ashley, it stirred an interest in them to want to know more about their ancestors, so I had our family tree done. I felt as if I'd repaid a blood debt. When she heard it, my aunt Mariolive generously gave me Fanny's cream pitcher, Elijah's Civil War papers, and the handwritten deed to the Louisa homestead dated 1877. Mark and I made a trip with our aunt Evelyn Watseka to the weed-choked Judd cemetery and had our senior aunt tell us anecdotes about our ancestors.

We got to hang out with eccentric Mark Knopfler of Dire Straits after he played on our version of his Carribean-flavored "Water of Love." Having been favorably compared with the Everly Brothers for years now, we decided to pay tribute to them by doing their "Sleepless Nights." Throwing in a Dixieland oddity called "Not My Baby" we even used a clarinet. With our new album, we communicated traditional themes of universal love through a full range of styles.

We really broke Judd Rule Number 3 (acoustic guitars only) when we asked our "uncle" Carl Perkins to introduce electric guitar on his foot-stompin' "Let Me Tell You About Love." A close family friend, he'd been our favorite act to work with in Vegas and on tour.

This living legend would join us onstage in the middle of our show to zap his song with hillbilly mojo and elevate it to the show's highlight.

One of Carl's cowriters on "Let Me Tell You About Love," Paul Kennerley, seemed to have a songwriter's equivalence of perfect pitch. He gave us three number one singles from this album. Wy sounds smoky, shaded, and seductive, on "One Man Woman," and then turns right around and brings the sultry innocence of a teenage country girl on her first date to "Young Love." As we were working in the studio, Brent, Don, and I constantly marveled at her growing vocal mastery and the unique stylistic interpretations that I labeled "Wynonnaisms." Even though she hadn't yet even had her own heart broken, the girl could wring the livin' daylights out of a ballad. Already famous for her cat-in-heat growl, even I was stunned at how my naive little girl could sing with such hard-bitten emotion. I was reminded of a tape measure I'd had taped to the wall while Wy was growing up, to mark her growth in height each year, as we returned to this studio and saw more gold and platinum albums down the hall marking our musical growth.

On my way home from the studio one evening, I stopped by Radnor Lake to meditate about this as yet unnamed album. Asking not just to be creative and free spirited, I prayed to God for spiritual inspiration. I was enjoying the serenity of the placid lake, watching the twilight fade, when suddenly words began to flow through me. It was like an inner, underground stream began bubbling to the surface. My piano-playing buddy, John Jarvis, set my reflective prose to music and I stuck the rough demo in my purse as I headed up to Kentucky for a family gathering for Mother's Day.

After Mark's Sunday morning church service, we sat around the dinner table out on the screened-in porch at his house. I asked all my family what they thought about this new song. I said simply that I'd written "River of Time" about suffering a loss, then admitted it was for Brian. The song was able to thaw years of frozen silence, prompting the first face-to-face conversation our family had ever had about the tragedy that had propelled us out of our home like some centrifugal force. Once again, I saw music opening the door for healing to begin.

Bud, who'd been following us everywhere filming the *Across the Heartland* special, happened to capture this intimate scene. After the TV special aired, Mom received a letter from the retired chief technologist from the Radiation Oncology Division at the Ohio State hospital where Brian had been a patient back in 1963. Ms. Doll Kelch wrote that she'd just happened to see us talking about Brian Judd and remembered treating him and was sorry about his outcome. It meant a lot to Mom and made my brand-new tune special right then and there. Mark disclosed that Brian's death had helped inspire him to become a pastor so he could tell others about eternal life. Of course, I acknowledged my intolerance for watching Brian's suffering as the motivation for my becoming an RN.

We titled this album *River of Time.* Wy and I were down in Florida dressing to go onstage to debut the new material, when Gaylon brought a letter back to my room. I told him I'd have to read it later 'cause I was groping to find an appropriate introduction before singing "River of Time." "Then you really need to read this now!" he urged.

When the letter began "Dear Diana," I knew it was from someone from Ashland. "The last time I saw you I was a pallbearer at Brian's funeral." It was from one of my brother's best buddies, a nice boy who'd carried Brian's homework to him while he'd been in the hospital. Jimmy Lett went on to say the experience helped him decide to become a doctor.

When time for the song came in our show, I looked out at the smiling, handsome physician sitting in the audience and realized that sometimes if you were there you don't need to explain it. If you weren't, no words can explain it. All I said was; "Music is a healer. I believe it expresses emotions words cannot define."

A doctor, a pastor, a nurse, a kind letter from a stranger letting a mother know her dead son had not been forgotten even after twenty-five years: "River of Time" was like finding a box within a box within a box . . .

Love Is Alive

*O*UR ABILITY TO express deep emotion was perhaps rivaled only by our ability to have fun. Smooth as a five speed, we could shift from tears to laughter. Disc jockeys visiting with us on the bus after concerts would remind us nightly that they count on Judd music for up tempos, adding that we "put life into country music." Calling ourselves "Redheaded Boogie-Woogie Babes from Rural Mars," our stage show was a lalapalooza! Wynonna charged toward the audience like a storm trooper and I came prancing out, sashaying across the stage like a filly let loose in a field of clover.

Wynonna and I would playfully interact with the band, who were by now "tight as too small shoes." I'd refer to them as "Foot Soldiers of Country Music—dedicated to bringing the good news of country music to your town." Their individual intros were zany. "He's the best keyboard player in his price range in the business! Our guitar player said he'd give his right arm to be able to play with us! You know 'em, you love 'em, now you can't live without 'em—the Fabulous Judd Boys!" Being a natural exhibitionist, I'd spontaneously insert a joke or a sight gag, and some nights the Judd Boys would throw in a surprise for me.

Wy and I always tried to make people feel as welcome and comfortable as if they'd come to our house for a party on Saturday night. We thrived on the give and take of audience involvement. Talking right to the folks, we'd make eye contact, sometimes even responding to remarks from the crowd. Our desire was to get to know the people we were entertaining and to be open enough to let them get to know us. Every fan who came to the stage was afforded a nod of attention or thanks. When the crowd shook the rafters and became particularly boisterous Wynonna would holler, "Hey! Who's entertaining who?" Acknowledging those fans farthest from the stage and up in the "nosebleed section" of the bleachers, our goal was to turn concrete and steel arenas into the feeling of a family reunion. Our concerts were full of telling details and insights into our personalities and our relationship.

We love to laugh. I'd cajole Wynonna, "Laughter is like internal jogging," and she'd heartily respond, "Well, Mama, we ought to be in great shape!"

Our new road manager, Mike McGrath, quickly got the hang of our bizarre sense of humor. If he didn't take kindly to our request, Mike would raise the pitch of his voice to sound like a cranky old lady and squeak, "Fine! And you?" feigning deafness. When curious people asked him what he did, he'd reply "I'm an astronaut." Wynonna publicly introduced him as our "body bouncer." We all had alter egos, Mike's being "Aqua Boy," a supernatural crime fighter who dissolves into water to escape imminent danger.

Before his first month with us was even over, he'd already caught on to our road code, and interpreted all our hand signals (these are Top Secret). Mike had no trouble finding his harmony for the "Bus Song," our ribald theme song. In crowded elevators he'd lean over to Wy or me, pull up his sleeve as if showing us something and ask: "Excuse me, ma'am, does this look infected to you?"

When we were all seated together in a restaurant, if the waiter announced they were out of anything, we'd all grumble and jump to our feet at exactly the same time, throwing our napkins down on the table as if ready for a mass exodus. Another restaurant gag involved the waiter's description of the dessert selection. The instant we hear the word *chocolate,* in choreographed precision we run our palms up across our faces, messing up our hair, moaning in ecstasy. No restaurant is too fancy to be spared our irreverence. In fact, it makes it more fun.

. . .

It was becoming more difficult to smile, and my year-long bout with CMV seemed to be worsening instead of resolving. I arrived at Caesar's Palace for our biannual appearance disadvantaged by an already sore throat. The extremely arid climate reeks havoc on entertainers' throats, creating what's known among singers as "Vegas throat." Feeling as if all the moisture in my throat had been sucked out, I asked Mike to bring four humidifiers to my room. The next morning I awakened to a mist-filled room. The ceiling mirror over my bed was completely fogged over, and there was a strong peculiar odor. The humidifiers had steamed all the wallpaper off the walls! I rubbed my eyes in disbelief as I recognized the smell as wallpaper paste! Wynonna thought it was a hoot, and wasted no time in telling everyone, "Mom trashed her room!"

But it was no laughing matter when I had to call Ken down to my room to cancel our show for Super Bowl Sunday that weekend. It just so happens to be the biggest event of the whole year for Las Vegas gamblers. I had weaned myself off prednisone and occasionally visited doctors in towns where we were performing, trying to get through our concert that night, hoping to figure out what was really wrong.

A throat specialist in Salt Lake City, Utah, volunteered to give me a medical excuse to cancel our show at the Centrum that January 27. I refused, and Wy and I even did a midnight interview afterward with *Entertainment Tonight*'s Los Angeles correspondent Rob Weller. Larry had accompanied me on the road to do my speaking so I could rest my voice during the day. When Rob inquired who Larry was, I let it slip that we were going to be married.

Rob immediately questioned me about how this would affect my career, and I nonchalantly answered, "Why it won't have any effect, my inamorato and I have already been together for ten years."

Wynonna chimed in, "Larry is our biggest supporter, nothing will change except that Mom and Larry will be happier than ever!"

I assured Rob, "I'm certainly not going to get off the road, if that's what you're getting at. It's in my blood!"

"Yeah," Wynonna said laughing, "Mom will probably be out there wearing colored support hose, glitter in her hair net and rhinestones on her walker!"

Unfortunately, Rob Weller distorted our interview for sensationalism. The lead story on *Entertainment Tonight* erroneously reported, "Naomi Judd is quitting the road to be married." When Ken petitioned the tape from *Entertainment Tonight*, it was clear that Weller had misrepresented our interview. *Entertainment Tonight* is a quality program and took responsibility for Weller's actions. They sincerely apologized to us and immediately ran a retraction on the show. Shortly thereafter, Weller was no longer on the show.

Meanwhile, the news wreaked complete havoc in our office. Promoters panicked, thinking they were being shafted. The media wanted to know why we hadn't called a press conference. Hysterical fans flooded the fan club phone lines. Ken gently scolded me for divulging my wedding plans in the manner in which I did. "*When* are you going to realize you're a star and something like this is a major news story?" he asked with a mixture of amazement and exasperation.

The next morning, in keeping with the Judd slogan, "Give us a guitar and comfortable shoes, and we'll go anywhere!" we set off for Europe and Ireland. Transporting luggage for thirty people, musical instruments, and gear and going through customs and immigration into different countries every few days would wear down a healthy person. In my compromised condition, I didn't stand a chance. Before our show at the air force base in Wiesbaden, Germany, I approached a stagehand to teach me another native phrase with which to greet our audience. "Please tell me to say, 'If each of you will give us just one deutsche mark, we can lease the Concorde home?'" I felt a tap on my left shoulder and as I turned around there stood Ken glowering.

The German audience was attentive and enthusiastic, and Wy kept poking me between songs wondering, "What the heck does *'Ich liebe dich'* mean?" We were relieved to find out it's German for "I love you."

When we flew into Ireland, Wynonna and I felt a wave of sentimentality as we stepped onto the soil of our ancestors' homeland. It was disconcerting to see and hear bomb squads and armed soldiers in the streets of Belfast. Although now elevated to superstar stature in America and England, we found ourselves playing to a few thousand people in an old boxing hall with low ceilings in Dublin. Aside from the poor acoustics and the funky smell, Wynonna and I didn't mind a bit. Actually, we enjoyed the genuineness and intimacy of the experience. The Irish favorably referred to our songs as, "Wang Dang Music."

Wy and I had gotten word that U2 was coming to see us and were, therefore, nervous during the concert. Afterward, the guys were waiting for us in our dressing room to whisk us away to bassist Adam's house, where they had arranged a surprise party.

I hadn't known quite what to expect from these young disaffected reactionaries. Adam lives in a magnificent aristocratic, elegantly appointed mansion. Taking us on a tour of his estate, Adam reveled in explaining that the reason he purchased the home was because the prep school nearby had denied him admittance as a youth. Larry Mullen, the drummer, and Wynonna paired off and became engaged in conversation. As lead singer, Bono, and I conversed, he confirmed my initial impression from the Murfreesboro concert of an extremely intense, profound artist. He's as startlingly electric as heat lightning on a hot July night. Bono and I lounged at the top of the stairs away from the others talking privately for hours. It was nearing dawn when Larry and Wynonna came to get us for a stroll under a full golden moon. It was ethereal and magical. "Now this is truly Ireland!" I said and sighed into the night air. Wynonna's and my imaginations feasted on wizened leprechauns and elves peeking out from behind rock and flowers. We could have sworn we glimpsed pixied sprites and woodland nymphs dancing around mushrooms and toadstools!

The four of us lingered beneath an ancient tree whose gnarled roots sunk deep into Irish earth and history. Tilting our heads back gazing up at its maze of dark branches silhouetted against the moon's glow, the tangle of limbs resembled a collateralization of veins and arteries. I had a heady sensation that we were standing together at the heart of the earth.

"Naomi, are you aware that you are an angel?" Bono inquired solemnly and reverently. "Do you quite understand that God has put you here on earth to help other people?"

I don't understand what made Bono say this, but I do know

there is something profoundly unique about him, and I'm richer because I can call him my friend.

Wy and I returned to play dates in the States right up until my wedding weekend. Larry and I wanted our ceremony to be a spiritual celebration and were determined that it not turn into some show-biz extravaganza. Since his family comes from North Carolina and my folks are all from Kentucky, it was a first-time meeting for most of them. We tried to give them the royal treatment—nice hotels, flowers, anything to make them feel pampered and loved. Old friends flew in from all over, and in lieu of celebrities, we invited real down-home people like our dentist, Gary Owens, and his staff. After all, these were people we had known since we first moved to Nashville. Folks who'd treated us kindly even before our career.

Jo Stilts threw a wedding shower for me. I'd opened a large box from my sister, Margaret, containing a hair net, knee-length support hose, a pair of cheap house slippers, and a loud muumuu. Of course, I immediately put all this on and modeled it. When the next present turned out to be a wooden quilt rack, I began toddling around the room using the rack as a walker, cackling like a little ol' lady for Wy and Ashley to "mix up my Metamucil!" We all laughed till our sides hurt!

My blush pink, taffeta wedding gown with an overlaid lace bodice and poof sleeve was my fantasy design. Its full skirt featured a bustle with a train cascading down the back. The romantic dress rivaled any of my stage outfits and required thirteen fittings for Dez to create. Vanessa did a great job orchestrating the entire event, ordering all the lovely flowers, the fabulous cake, and hiring the best caterers in town.

Even the wedding rehearsal was special. After a nice dinner at the church, Don Potter pulled out his guitar and we all sat around singing. Ed Enoch, Larry's one-time partner from the Stamps Quartet, offered a spine-tingling rendition of "How Great Thou Art." Sitting next to the Reverend L. H. Hardwick, our senior pastor, I mentioned how it was here at Christ Church in 1979 right after our move to Nashville, I'd first seen Larry and Ed sing gospel music. Brother Hardwick proceeded to tell me how some church members had protested that Stamps concert, knowing that lead singer Ed Enoch was a substance abuser at that time. Being the good man that he is, however, Brother Hardwick had chastised the hypocrites, sternly reminding them, "Only God himself is in any position to look down on someone."

I began to weep as I considered how Brother Ed, after discovering this church through that concert later returned and was completely delivered from his addictions. Not only is he now healthy and happy but Ed counsels others and has such a powerful testimony! Then I looked to the man sitting on my other side, my soon-to-be husband, and realized that our wedding would not be taking place tomorrow had it not been for changes in him that were inspired through this church that he'd also discovered the same night as Brother Ed.

The next glorious spring day, May 6, 1989, Larry and I were married in a fairy tale wedding ceremony. While everyone was listening to live music in the romantic, candlelit church, Ken and I nervously waited in the church vestibule with a female detective assigned to guard me. My mouth was like cotton, and I was shaking all over. As I walked toward the water fountain, Detective Betty Anderson dutifully stepped ahead to push the button. Evidently this particular fountain had not been used in a while, as a two foot geyser gushed up into the air and drenched her. It missed soaking the entire front of my gown moments before the processional began.

We had arranged for Bud Schaetzle and a couple friends from our *Across the Heartland* TV crew to film the wedding. Because the media were denied access to the church and reception, Bud later edited a lovely clip to distribute to the networks. Family friend Robert Oermann was the only journalist invited, and he fed his description of the ceremony to the wire services. I almost forgot to slip into the ladies' room to Velcro a remote microphone around my upper thigh. Alone in the privacy of the ladies' room I spoke aloud my heartfelt prayer that this ceremony I'd waited so long for would not only be something Larry, Wynonna, Ashley, and I would remember the rest of our lives but also be as a blessing to others as well. I completely forgot the microphone strapped to my leg was on and was later told that the whole crew stopped what they were doing to listen in.

As my dearest friend in the world, Ken Stilts, escorted me down the aisle, I cried tears of joy! Slowly looking to my left and right, I saw smiling back at me the three hundred people who mean the most in the world to me. Ken, however, was shaking so badly I became worried about him having another heart attack. "Oh great, I'm going to be doing CPR on the altar!"

My sister, Margaret, was my beautiful maid of honor, my radiant bridesmaids were Ashley and Wynonna; my sister-in-law, Middy; and my niece Erin. Larry looked for all the world like a modern Prince Charming in his white tux with tails and white cowboy boots. His older brother, Don Strickland, served as his best man, and the groomsmen were Reggie Strickland, his younger brother; brother-in-law, Gene Boone; and friends Ed Enoch, Tony King, and Guy Penrod. My brother Mark and Larry's father, Rev. Ralph Strickland, officiated along with our senior pastor, Brother Hardwick, and associate pastor, Brother Dan Scott. Hey, I figured, with four ministers on the job, there was no way anybody could break us asunder!

In her creamy eloquent voice, Ashley read some beautiful scripture. Then Don and Wynonna began singing a moving wedding song titled "It Takes Three." It was a total surprise to Larry and me and I almost completely lost it. While Earl had been doing my hair that morning, a messenger delivered a letter from Wynonna that was so touching I shared it during the ceremony. In essence, she related what it meant to see me finding happiness after the difficulties I'd faced in life, and she welcomed Larry as her stepdad. Larry and I spoke directly to each other as we personalized our wedding vows. Our senior pastor's wife, Montelle Hardwick, said it was the most spiritual of all the hundreds of weddings she's attended.

The gala reception was held at the gorgeous antebellum Redd Mansion. There were tables of delicious food and the bluegrass group the Dillards played their special brand of bluegrass. All those years as Larry and I faithfully watched *Andy Griffith,* he'd teasingly promise, "Someday we're gonna have them play at our wedding!"

The tabloids tried every way in the world to crash the festivities, but our Major George Currey's security team was too smart for them. At one point, a van pulled up at the mansion's gate under the premise of a delivery, but when one of our security guys stuck his head inside the back of the van he discovered a camera man! Toward the end of the evening, the party crashers were so frustrated they literally leapt out of the woods in a mad dash for the house. Intercepted again. These people lack common decency.

Late that night when the white limo finally drove Larry and me home, my Prince Charming swooped me up in his big strong arms to carry across the threshold. I rested my head on his shoulder and whispered tenderly, "Don't let me forget to take this microphone off."

Larry accompanied us to the villa in Lake Tahoe that week while Wynonna and I were performing, causing her to joke: "Mom and I are so bonded, she even took me on her honeymoon!" We were deeply touched by one very special wedding gift. After our show at the Shoreline Amphitheatre in Mt. View, California, a girl who had gone into labor in the middle of our previous year's concert and named the baby after me, presented us with a beautiful handmade Double Wedding Ring quilt. KNEW/KSAN sponsored the effort to make the quilt, composed of ninety-four pieces of fabric having special meaning to their listeners. The station also gave us a scrapbook with those fans' letters identifying the quilt pieces. One of my favorite stories was that of a police officer who contributed a piece of his uniform the night he was shot pursuing a criminal. The man had been medically discharged from the force and sought consolation in our music and wanted to thank us.

Just before the wedding, Larry found our dream farm, which just happened to be a few miles down the road from Wynonna. I teased Wy that the next time she had to fill out a form that asked "nearest living relative" she could say eight miles.

Behavioral scientists tell us we're a combination of heredity and environment. Since Wy and I descended from farmers and spent pleasant childhood hours on farms, we come by this desire to own land naturally! While all my playmates had been playing games entertaining typical fantasies, I dreamed of owning land exactly like our "Peaceful Valley." Standing arm in arm with my new husband in the midst of several hundred of the most gorgeous acreage I've ever seen, I could hear echoes of the old man's voice from *Gone with the Wind:* "Land, Katie Scarlett, 'Tis the only thing in the world that lasts."

Larry remarked, "Nobody really 'owns' land anymore than we could own water, fire, or air. We're just caretakers of this place."

We had the world by the tail. Wynonna hired a trainer to go on the road with us, and shed twenty-five pounds prompting me to say, "They'll call us the duet that weighs the same!" I introduced her as "A streamlined powerhouse of crooning." I remember the night she and Tony King came over to break the news of their engagement. Squealing and hugging her, I couldn't help express both joy and relief, "Most mothers worry about their daughters marrying any ol' Tom, Dick, or Harry, but in your case I worried about you marrying Moe, Larry, or Curly!"

I used to joke that Wynonna Judd was a late bloomer, that she didn't get her birthmark until she was about eight. Now Ashley had waited until she got to college to go through a delayed rebellious stage. "Miss Smarty Pants" thought she knew all the answers, but in reality didn't fully understand the questions. Wy would scowl, "Ashley, you turn answers into riddles, you tell me one thing and out the other. And stop throwing around hundred dollar words!"

Ashley refused to shave her legs or underarms, wore pungent patchouli oil, and mismatched, oversize clothes. Ashley also had her nostril pierced. Larry said she had a "piercing need for individuality."

As soon as she fell asleep that night, I tiptoed into her room and pulled back the covers to search for tattoos with my flashlight.

Right after Wynonna and I were invited to perform at the governor's inaugural ball for our home state, Ashley graced the front page of the paper protesting Governor Wilkerson on the steps of the state capitol in Frankfurt, Kentucky, with the NAACP. As a member of the Student Association for Racial Justice, she instigated and led a protest against a racist remark by an associate of the new governor.

Demonstrating a strong social conscience, Ashley also volunteered once a week in the community soup kitchen, taught French to five-year-olds, and was an officer in her sorority, Kappa Kappa Gamma. She ran the women's radio program on campus, and I was impressed with her delivery.

Ashley's liberalism made for some, shall we say, "lively and interesting" dinner table conversation at our house! Wynonna fumed that Ashley was "full of crap." Unassailable, Ashley's acerbic rebuttal was always, "Wynonna, you're simply uninformed and melodramatic." When their ricocheting dialogue began to get out of hand, Larry and I would ceremoniously dive for cover under the kitchen table to diffuse the tension.

I slipped home to Ashland for a few days for my twenty-fifth high school class reunion that July 1989, feeling nostalgic and fostering a guarded hope that they wouldn't treat me any differently than when they had known me "back when." It was a wonderful occasion and many were intent on sharing with me the exact moment and circumstances when they'd discovered their daydreamy former classmate Diana Judd was also country music's Mama Judd. They turned their own spotlight on me to make me the recipient of two awards: one for having the oldest child and a special award for being the "Class of '64's Favorite Singing Group, the Judds." It pleased me greatly to discover that they were getting a kick out of keeping up with our escapades. In turn I congratulated my old friends on their successful marriages, listened with interest to stories of their lives, and oohed and aahed appreciatively as they whipped out photos of their kids. I left with a continuing sense of friendship unchanged by twenty-five years and was deeply satisfied when those "who knew me when" like Mary Childers Quillen decided, "Well Diana, you haven't changed one bit. Girl, you just have nicer clothes!"

The hometown newspaper noted my attendance at the reunion by interviewing Mom. My heart began racing as if I was about to read a review by the foremost critic in the world. Although I was forty-three years old, Mom still watched me for signs of improvement. She says, "You're never too old to know better." I realized that we can't really begin to stop seeking our parents approval until after we've had some. Mom talked about my "strong individualism even as a child, my dramatic personality, and vivid imagination." She spoke of her "faith in my ability to achieve anything I set my mind on," and that she used to wonder if I wouldn't become a writer or an actress in a soap opera. "Now she and Wynonna live in a soap opera!" she exclaimed. Mom concluded, "But to tell you the truth, they haven't changed a bit. My daughter and granddaughter are just the same as they always were, they just have more money to spend now!"

What Mom was saying is that we haven't been adversely affected by the career, but in reality Wynonna *was* changing—in a positive way. She was beginning to come out of her shell. She'd lived a quarter of a century now and had begun running her own home and farm. Wy drew strength from the rocklike presence of Ken and security from the immutable simpatico relationship between the three of us. I was no longer her "Beloved Enemy," although we did indulge in some verbal fencing now and then (just to keep in practice!).

Instead I began reading in interviews: "I have my Mama on a pedestal, and although I hate to admit it, I'm becoming more like her!" Doing a phoner on her day off at her farm, Wy confided, "Oh no! I just caught myself making lists, putting Post-Its everywhere and folding towels the same as my Mom!" If it was once hard to tell us apart, now it seemed strange seeing us apart. I had a sweatshirt made for those occasions when I would venture out solo that bore this message: "No, I don't know where Wynonna is."

I was wearing it one afternoon when I set out alone with Banjo for a walk around the charming town of Medford, Oregon. Tiring easily nowadays, I stopped to rest on a park bench across from a homeless man stretched out asleep. Staring at him for the longest time, I wondered such things as what happens to him when he needs medical attention or if anyone knows or cares how or even where he is! If sanity is containing or controlling our confusion, perhaps this fella just didn't keep the lid on his confusion well enough to suit those around him. I remembered how perilously close to being on the streets the kids and I had often been. My unanswered questions and the image of that man sleeping out in the open on a park bench in dirty rags haunted me for days.

My sense of helplessness in the face of suffering is at times so overwhelming I have to vent it in some fashion. I had long noticed that when I write, I create an alternative world and give reality to experience. Wynonna and I had witnessed so much of man's inhumanity to man in our odyssey across the United States, but how does one express such things in mere words within the confines of a three-minute song? I can no more make myself write than I can lift my refrigerator. I just waited.

Lying in the dark, being jostled in my bed on the bus the next night, the words showed up, in sudden illuminations like the flickering lights of passing trucks.

"I'd gladly walk across the desert with no shoes upon my feet, to share with you the last bite of bread I had to eat. I would even swim out to save you in your sea of broken dreams; when all your hopes are sinking, let me show you what love means." I was happy with this first verse, 'cause I believe dreams and hopes are as important to our survival as food, water, clothing, and air.

Country/Christian singer/songwriter Paul Overstreet was having supper with Larry and me one night at our home. We were just discussing how imagination springs forth from the fertile womb of the human spirit, when Paul spied a postcard of the Grand Canyon from Ashley on our refrigerator door. Looking at it closely he made the observation that "sometimes the only way we can cross life's great divides is to let love be a bridge." I knew this was the missing piece in my puzzle.

I phoned Paul the next morning to thank him for the idea, and let him know I was giving him equal credit as a cowriter. "I can't accept that," he argued loudly. "Ideas run the world!" I insisted. "They make the difference between war and peace."

The following day I was cooling off at a sidewalk café in Rhode Island. I listened to two guys sitting next to me arguing. The older man's facts were right, but his tone was so brusque his son was obviously shutting him out. I smiled to myself, reflecting on how I'd *finally* come to the realization that the only way I ever got through to Wy and Ashley is when I stayed calm, rational, and loving. Walking back to our motel, the second verse and chorus came to me.

"I would whisper love so loudly every heart could understand, that love and only love can join the tribes of man. I would give my heart's desire if only you could see, the first step is to realize that it all begins with you and me. Love can build a bridge between your heart and mine. Love can build a bridge, don't you think it's time?" With "the first step is to realize, it all begins with you and me," I was suggesting in essence, "It's better to light one small candle than to curse the darkness."

John Jarvis set my prose to music and I begged Ken to do a video in the Grand Canyon like the scene of the postcard. Never one to be outdone, Ken fired back with an even better idea. We would be the first music artists in history to do a 3-D video. (One of Ken's greatest pleasures in life is doing things that people say can't be done!)

Before you could say vertigo, Wynonna and I found ourselves perilously perched several thousand feet above yawning chasms in Sedona, Arizona's Oak Creek Canyon. I discovered how severe my fear of heights really is and was assigned a professional rock climber. Wearing a harness under my clothes, I was attached to Fred as he hung by his fingertips, lurking on the other side of the peaks. Meanwhile, over on solid ground, the crew of eighty people watched nervously. Fearing for our safety, Ken began experiencing chest pains and began popping nitroglycerin pills. That's when I gave him another name: "Chief Big Ideas."

When my vertigo threatened to prevent shooting some of the spectacular scenes we wanted, I phoned my Nashville doctor and described my unusual and difficult predicament. "I'll tell you what you need to do," the doctor replied somewhat seriously. "Find a new manager!"

In spite of dizzying heights, the lack of conveniences out in the middle of nowhere, and the usual rigors of filming, the splendor of the Red Rocks area, the camaraderie, and our belief in the song made the week one of the most memorable experiences of our career. In fact, it was so phenomenal, the week was captured in an hour-long documentary on the making of the song's 3-D video. Wy and I hung out with Native Americans, and in our favorite moment, we stand side by side with Larry and Ashley, and people from all races holding hands on a peak during a rapturous sunset.

As we were singing "Love Can Build a Bridge," Bud Schaetzle and his crew filmed us as they circled in a helicopter. I was filled with joy in every corner of my being. Wy said, "Now this is literally and figuratively 'A Peak Experience!'" The only thing missing was the homeless man.

. . .

From the deserts of Arizona to the shimmering blue-green water of Hawaii, Christmas means hope, Bob Hope that is. He'd invited us to be his guests on a network Christmas special, so we took the family and made yet another minivacation of our hectic work-week. Wy swam with dolphins, and we went deep sea fishing.

Our favorite part was doing a comedy sketch parody called *Steel Petunias* based on the popular movie *Steel Magnolias*. I donned a hairpiece to portray Sally Field, the mother, with Wynonna in an even more outlandish wig for her Julia Roberts role as the daughter. We were about to perform our skit in front of the live Hawaiian audience on the Kona coast of the Big Island, as Bob, Wynonna, and I stood huddled together waiting to go on. In drag for the beauty parlor scene, Bob Hope suddenly began giving comedic pointers, "Now it's obvious you love comedy kiddo, just be sure to pause after your punchlines for laughs. Never cheat yourself out of the audience's response." It was one of those impossibly ridiculous moments, old ski nose himself standing beneath a palm tree in lipstick, eye shadow, and a dress teaching me his craft. Wy and I kept cracking up doing the skit and relished every zany minute of it.

When we returned to Nashville for our well-deserved annual Christmas break, I was counting down the days to December 21, like a child awaiting the arrival of Santa Claus. Ashley, a French major in college, had spent her fall semester studying at the École des Beaux-Arts in LaCoste, France. It had been unnerving for me having my child so far across the ocean, and I'd carried my passport with me day and night the entire four months she'd been gone. Ashley phoned home on December 19, to let us know she'd be spending the night at a youth hostel in Frankfurt, Germany, after doing some sightseeing with some other students before catching her flight early in the morning of December 21. She said it was Pan Am's flight from Frankfurt, connecting at Heathrow in London into New York's La Guardia and then home to Nashville.

I was finishing up the Christmas decorations, while Larry ran to the arts and crafts store to pick up materials to make welcome-home banners to take to the airport. I could hear Mom out in the kitchen baking Ashley's favorite cake with the TV on. Suddenly, Mom appeared in front of me, speaking slowly and distinctly like a kindergarten teacher talking to a five-year-old.

"Honey," she began in a strangely even tone, "where is the piece of paper with Ashley's flight information on it?" I went blank trying to imagine why she needed to know this insignificant piece of information so early in the morning. Then I could hear the familiar voice of evening news TV anchor Peter Jennings, and it dawned on me he was interrupting regular programming for a news bulletin. Without saying a word I ran past Mom into the kitchen. Looking terribly somber, Peter was reporting something about a Pan Am flight that had just exploded in midair over Lockerbie, Scotland. When he suddenly looked right into the camera and announced the flight originated in Frankfurt, Germany, the horror of this statement seized me like a vise.

Although standing in the middle of the warmth and security of my very own kitchen I have never known such terror. "This cannot be happening," I muttered to myself. And yet the live pictures of devastation on the TV screen were undeniable. As Jennings droned on about "there being no survivors," I could feel my heart pounding against my ribs.

Although she was standing at my side steadying me, Mom's voice sounded thin and very far away. "We have to pray that Ashley was not on this flight, we must stay calm." I dashed pell-mell to my bedside table where I had written Ashley's information. My scrawl simply noted that Ashley would depart from Frankfurt on an early Pan Am flight headed for Heathrow with only the pertinent information about the exact time and flight number of the Nashville arrival from New York. I lunged for the phone to call Martha at our office. She knew the moment she heard my voice it was an emergency. "Quick, call our friends at American Airlines," I pleaded. "We've got to get the passenger list for this Pan Am plane crash!" Martha put me on hold to do so just as our associate pastor, Dan Scott, appeared at the door. He was dropping off Talitha and Tiffany, his two young daughters, so they could help us make Ashley's welcome-home banners. Dan was exactly the person I needed to see at this moment! Cutting short their happy holiday greeting, I pointed to the TV.

Grabbing Dan by the shoulders I insisted, "We must pray now." Carefully selective of our words, we asked that Ashley was on a different plane, and prayed for all the passengers and their families. Numb, we stood around in front of the big TV in the living room, switching from channel to channel, hoping to hear more information.

When Larry returned with his arms full of poster board and paints, the sight of us with fear frozen on our faces and the awful scenes on the TV told him everything. Martha reported the phone lines at La Guardia were shut down and the manifest had been seized. There had been lots of students from the University of Syracuse in New York on the flight. They too were flying home for the holiday's after a semester abroad, and their poor families were already at the airport eagerly awaiting their return. By now La Guardia was in complete pandemonium.

I could not tear my eyes away from the TV. The live footage from Lockerbie, Scotland, showed huge jagged pieces of twisted and scorched metal scattered over lovely green fields. It seems incongruous that anything so grotesque could happen in such an idyllic place. The idea that my child's young body might actually be there somewhere was beyond comprehension. It is every parents' worst nightmare. This however was daytime and I was fully awake. For hours, time stood still, there was no past, no future, only the uncertain moment. Montelle Hardwick, our senior pastor's wife, called me with a word of knowledge. "Naomi, you must trust and have faith," Montelle pleaded. "I have the strongest sense that somehow someway Ashley has been spared." Ashley had been baptized months earlier, and Montelle went on to say that she sensed that "the Lord has his hand on Ashley."

I stood with the phone to my ear listening to the soft, comforting words of this dear woman as nightmarish pictures from Scotland flashed upon the TV screen in front of me. When they suddenly began showing hysterical parents collapsing on the floor in La Guardia, I walked slowly and deliberately into my bathroom, shut the door, and got down on my face and prayed like I've never prayed before in my life. Long a believer in hope, I was now learning about faith.

Wynonna arrived and couldn't even speak. She stood looking

out the window, wringing her hands. Although unable to obtain any information whatsoever from the airlines, Ken called to console us and to tell us the arrival time of the only flight from La Guardia to Nashville that evening. "We're going to the airport," I announced, "get everyone together." It was an act of faith after the seven most excruciating hours of my life.

No one talked as twenty of us sat huddled together in the waiting area of the Nashville terminal watching the plane land. As the passengers began disembarking, it felt as if my head was going to explode from tension as I watched people appear one by one in the doorway. No Ashley. That day I had been reliving every event of Ashley's life. Suddenly, like some miraculous apparition, she appeared. Bright, radiant, smiling, completely oblivious to any possibility of doom and disaster. A great cry went up from our group. Everyone began grabbing at her, stroking her hair, kissing her, crying, but I was unable to move. We made instant eye contact through the flailing arms of the huddle, and she squealed, "Hi, Mommy!" I felt faint as if a plug had been pulled and all the tension and panic was being drained away. She was suddenly there hugging me. I was crying so hard I couldn't talk or even think about explaining to her what we had been through.

Ashley's flight had left Frankfurt twenty minutes after flight 103. The airline did its best to protect their passengers from learning of the tragedy. The phone lines were all jammed at the New York airport, and in an effort to take care of the grieving families, the connecting passengers arriving in La Guardia had been marched straight to their connecting flights without being allowed to make any phone calls. Ashley became distraught when she found out what happened, realizing that she'd slept in the same room with some of these students and eaten breakfast with them only hours before their tragic death.

It was the strangest holiday we've ever had. I couldn't have cared less whether we had a tree, a single present. All I did was hug and stare at Ashley. Wy couldn't let Ashley and me out of her sight. I was completely haunted by the crash of Pan Am flight 103. I'd awaken in the middle of the night grieving for the parents and creep into Ashley's room and sit on her bed till dawn watching her while she slept.

When New Year's Eve arrived, I couldn't bring myself to go to Ken's big party. I sent Ashley and Wynonna on while Larry and I settled down in front of our fireplace with our dogs and a pan of popcorn.

I was glad we hadn't booked ourselves to do a New Year's show and was even more relieved not to be working as a nurse. New Year's Eve is historically one of the busiest nights of the year in a hospital. It's associated with blood and pain and the aftermath of drinking and driving, overdoses, and arguments.

Wynonna, Ashley, and Ken called us at midnight to exchange New Year's greetings and let us sing "Auld Lang Syne" with them over the telephone. When I contentedly returned to the warmth of the fireplace and Larry's companionship, something began to stir within me and I began speaking these words from Roy Pearson's *Prayers for All Occasions* out loud.

> Eternal spirit, in the stillness and quietness of this moment, I seek your power, will, and peace. Always beyond us yet ever within us, I acknowledge you as the God of might, the Lord of love, creator of all things, greater than I can imagine, wiser than I can comprehend, patient beyond my deserving and generous beyond anything I could ask or desire.

Then I continued with my own prayer

> I give you praise for touching my life once again with your mercy, and offer this prayer for those who have no knowledge of your love. I intercede for the families who mourn tonight, asking that you would allow them the confident assurance that your thoughts and ways are higher than ours. I beseech you to deliver them from the turbulent storms of sorrow, allow them to find your strength in their weakness, your hope in their bereavement, and some sense of purpose from their deprivation. Grant them the peace that their loved ones have a new life that earth cannot contain and a knowing that they rest safely in the arms of Jesus. I acknowledge all our blessings of 1989, and seek your guidance for the deepest insight and the highest vision for that part yet to be lived. And thanks again God for allowing me to play "Alice in Careerland." Amen.

102 Reasons Why

*J*ANUARY 1, 1990, the winds of change blew hard, irreversible, and bitterly cold. I groggily awakened to the New Year with a bad headache, aching all over. The last two months had been hard. During our filming of the Bob Hope Christmas special in Hawaii, there were times I felt on the verge of collapse. I would whisper to Wynonna, "Please get it right on this take, 'cause I can't shoot this scene over." Over the holidays, exhaustion fell on me like some heavy smothering blanket I couldn't kick off to save my life. I was reduced to napping every afternoon. We were cutting a new album and I dragged myself to the studio to support Wy and to sing harmony on Brent's new song with a funky punch called "Born to Be Blue."

Instead of sitting in my usual chair at the console with Brent and Don while she was laying down her lead vocal, I stretched out on the couch, covering myself with my coat. I so wanted to be there and was sick and tired of being sick and tired!

"Mommy you look terrible," Wy remarked when she plopped down to rub my feet. Shot through with enthusiasm for our new project, Wynonna's live-wire energy was making me feel aware of just how exhausted I was, so I snapped, "Your performance just wrung me out! She's Super Singer! Able to leap high notes in a single bound, conquers octaves and navigates melodic hairpin curves with ease! The Countess of Hip, you are more infinitely cool than all the shades of blue!"

Ashley had come down with a terrible flu after Christmas and although I knew my own immune system was shot, I couldn't resist taking care of her. Since it was time for Ashley to return to the University of Kentucky, I insisted on taking her to our doctor to have her white count checked. If it was lower than it should be, she had no business going out in public because she would be susceptible to germs. It was January 12, Friday, the day after my forty-fourth birthday. While I was waiting in the doctor's office, I petitioned one of the nurses to run some blood work on me. Knowing that Wynonna and I were supposed to embark on our winter tour in four days, I also scheduled an appointment to reevaluate all of her asthma medications. We were to kick it off in the Northeast and severe cold sometimes precipitates asthmatic attacks.

Monday morning I sent Ashley back to college and as Wynonna and I were returning to the doctor's office, Dr. Mitchum crooked his index finger, motioning me to accompany him down the hall to his office. Clearing his throat as he folded his arms across his chest, he began, "Naomi, you're a very sick little girl."

"What's going on?" I heard myself ask.

"You have hepatitis," he announced, pausing to allow time for it to sink in. "Your ALT, the enzyme that indicates damage in the liver, is extremely elevated."

"Why that's absolutely impossible!" I insisted, checking my limited mental file on hepatitis, which included only types A and B.

"In the past few years we've identified many different forms of hepatitis. You tested negative for both A and B," he affirmed. "There's now a test to identify type C, and I'll get one so we can check you for C as soon as possible. You can't have D because you must have B before you can get type D, and your symptoms don't match type E."

Wynonna appeared in his doorway. "What's going on?" she inquired with a worried frown.

Instantly I blurted out, "Am I contagious?" as my mind flashed on all the times Wynonna and I accidently drank out of the same glass of water on stage.

"I doubt that you are," the doctor responded. "Yet we have no way of knowing for sure until we pinpoint your type of hepatitis."

I realized there was a gap in my knowledge of hepatitis because of these recent findings. As Wynonna sunk down into the chair beside me, I could only explain that *-itis* on the end of a word means "inflammation of" and that *hepatic* was the word for liver. "So honey, all this means is that I have an inflammation of my liver, just like sometimes you have bronchitis, inflammation of the bronchus, or tonsillitis, inflammation of your tonsils. I'm sure it's nothing to worry about and I'll just take the necessary medicine and be fine in no time."

Dr. Mitchum slowly shook his head and said he knew of no medication or therapy. "Naomi, you need to come back in a week for a hepatitis C test and to begin monitoring blood work."

"I'm sorry, but we leave early in the morning for our 1990 tour so I'll have to call you after we get back," I responded.

"NAOMI! Listen to me, you're not going anywhere except straight home to bed! You're not gonna feel like putting on panty hose, let alone travel. I've seen the amount of energy you put out on stage, and you're not gonna be able to stand long enough to sing a single song. Besides, haven't you seen today's paper? They're in a blizzard up there!" We discussed Wynonna's medicine and left.

When we were alone in the elevator, I took her hands in mine and insisted, "You will tell no one about this. I'm your mother, and I'm pulling rank on you. Let me handle this one. Just go home and get ready as if nothing's happened. I'll meet you at the airport early in the morning."

No sooner had I started my car when the car phone rang, "Hey girl, it's Barbara Mandrell, I'm putting together a TV special honoring Ralph Emery, and knowing how you and Wy love him, you're one of the first people I'm calling to be involved."

My mind was whirring as I stammered something about calling Ken at the office to see what our itinerary looked like. After some brief chitchat, we signed off so she could call Ken. I was struck by the contrast between Barbara's characteristically bubbly, chipper enthusiasm and my bone weariness. Before I walked into the doctor's office, all I had were symptoms. Now I had a disease.

Arriving home, Vanessa was already waiting with Dez for the final fitting on the "Conehead Dress" to wear when we cohosted the

American Music Awards the following week. Much to my chagrin, I discovered I could barely stand long enough for the fitting. Before they'd even finished, Earl arrived to cut my hair. I had to share the diagnosis with him to begin trying to make some sense out of all this.

"Well Mamaw, I had hepatitis A and remember it's the least serious one. It went away after a couple of months and didn't cause side effects or any more problems. I think I got it from eating shellfish from polluted waters, but it's so contagious it's also spread by person to person contact, not washing hands after using the restroom, and food handlers."

"At least I know I don't have B and I'm relieved 'cause it's a bad one!" I sighed. I told Earl what I remembered about how it's blood borne, so you get it from sexual contact, body fluids, sharing needles, blood transfusions, contaminated surgical instruments, mother to child, bloodsucking insects, organ transplants, that sort of thing. You can even get it from sharing a toothbrush or razor of an infected person. Hepatitis B is far more contagious than AIDS and has over three hundred million carriers worldwide. At least 300,000 new cases are diagnosed in America a year. It turns chronic in ten percent of those cases and twenty-five percent go on to get cirrhosis or liver cancer, which is almost always fatal. I'd just discovered some startling new information: liver disease is the fourth killer in this country after deaths related to heart disease, cancer, and deaths related to drugs or alcohol. That's almost unbelievable.

When Larry came home that night I asked him to help me pack. Being such a "I'll do it myself person," the unusual nature of this request prompted Larry to set me down in a face-off. "Naomi, you're like some alabaster box with secrets locked tightly inside. Fess up!"

"I have hepatitis, Larry," I blurted out, feeling some relief at the release of my confession.

"But you don't look yellow!" he observed staring down at my hands held loosely in his. As he was getting my suitcases out, I explained that the liver is the most misunderstood and overworked organ in the human body, and in medicine we call it "the factory," because it performs such a multiplicity of functions. About five hundred functions in fact! If it's being attacked it can't perform the vital tasks our bodies depend on it to do every day. Sometimes when it's in trouble, the liver can't remove bilirubin (a waste product from the destruction of worn out red blood cells) from the blood anymore so the yellowish bilirubin pigment stains the skin, causing jaundice. *Jaundice* is derived from a word that means "yellow."

Larry had been building a horse barn at our farm and was exhausted, so I insisted he turn in while I took my bath. Wrapped in a towel, as I stepped into the dark stillness of our bedroom, I stooped to turn on the night-light so I could finish packing. My shoulders and the back of my neck ached worst of all. I seemed to be moving in slow motion. I laid down beside the open suitcase, curled up to rest for just a moment and lapsed into fitful sleep.

The next morning, with considerable dread, I reached for the phone to call Ken and cancel our tour. Ken came on the line sounding upbeat. "I was just sitting here looking through the annual *Billboard* 'Year End Compilation' issue," he started right in. "The Judds are still at the very top of country music's aristocracy! You're listed in the top five artists for the year 1989, along with Alabama, Randy Travis, Kenny Rogers, and Dolly Parton. Congratulations!"

"Yeah, that's just great!" I said with a sigh. "But I've also made another list—the list of people who have liver disease. Ken, I have non-A, non-B hepatitis and I'm so sorry I can't make it to the airport today for our tour."

Ken and I had long ago established a shorthand of empathic communication. Ken knows me well enough to appreciate that I fully grasped the seriousness of canceling a week's worth of shows on a moment's notice like this.

The following Monday, January 22, 1990, we were slated to cohost the American Music Awards in Los Angeles with Gloria Estefan, Anita Baker, and Alice Cooper. "I am determined to represent country music on that show," I stated adamantly. "Not only is it a coup for a country artist even to be asked to emcee the three-hour prime-time special but I feel strongly about standing up for middle America in what sometimes becomes a vulgar display of egos, excesses, and plain ol' poor taste.

"Listen Ken, if I can just stay in bed for a week to regain my strength, I know I can do it!" Malleable Ken agreed to call our friend Gene Weed, with Dick Clark Productions, who even suggested arranging for me to have my own Winnebago to retreat to during our full day of rehearsals before the actual show.

Although I wasn't able to even get out of my pajamas that week, I was besieged with guilt about canceling our road shows. Each day I'd look at my itinerary to see where we should have been. "What I wouldn't give to feel normal again and be there singing in Normal, Illinois!" I declared ruefully to my dogs.

Turning on CNN, I watched reports of the blizzard in the Great Lakes area where we'd canceled. Then flipping the remote, I caught the upcoming AMA promos of footage of Wynonna and me, exuding energy and healthful radiance. I clicked the off button and stared at the remote in my hand, muttering under my breath, "I don't feel remotely in control of my life anymore."

The next week, Wynonna and I sat in front of Randy Travis on the flight out to Los Angeles for the AMAs. As we were filing off the plane, Randy commented, "Naomi, are you upset about something? You sure don't seem like yourself these days!"

Dick Clark set up a small "quick change" tent in the wings for me to sit in during the breaks of the rehearsal. Pert Gloria Estefan stuck her head in to introduce herself, and I patted the empty folding chair beside me, inviting her inside to chat. Being a fitness buff, Gloria began explaining her regimen and conviction that we must really take care of ourselves to keep up with the rigors our careers demand. I wholeheartedly concurred as I considered the irony of our conversation.

Wynonna was like a friendly puppy, running around chatting and visiting with everyone. She and I hit it off instantly with Anita Baker, so much so that I confided to Anita my hepatitis diagnosis so she wouldn't think I was always this slow and lackluster. Being the gracious lady she is, Anita sent me a bouquet that night.

Wy and I made it through the show with Martha Taylor literally following me around carrying a folding chair. Dwight Yoakam, who's like a distant relative and knows us well, picked up on something being amiss. He'd been telling me a long-winded story that I couldn't retain. "With your iron will, you'll be able to 'will' it away!" Dwight offered encouragingly. I even pulled off my pledge not to meet Alice

Cooper. Unapproving of the message he sends out to our youths, I simply had no desire to be around him.

The day after the AMAs, I consulted a gastrointestinal specialist in Los Angeles. That doctor checked everything but my prostate! He explained in detail how the enzymes ALT (alanine aminotransferase) and AST (aspartate aminotransferase) spell out densely coded messages about damage or inflammation going on within the liver. Reviewing his findings, the doctor explained: "Naomi, you've got a smoldering fire going on in the cells of your liver. It could erupt into flames at any moment, and there is absolutely nothing we can do about it. It's a virus causing the trouble, and unfortunately, we don't know much about viruses. You already know that it's a virus that causes cancer and AIDS. I also regret having to tell you that non-A, non-B hepatitis tends to go chronic." This last statement knocked the wind out of me. I was already sick and tired of being sick.

Although there must be thousands of physicians in Los Angeles, our old family doctor from the 1970s happened to be in the same building with the specialist. Riding down in the familiar elevator, I was overwhelmed by the drastic differences between then and now. I used to have to wait to take cabs on hot, smoggy street corners to get to this building. I had no medical insurance, no money, but back then I was healthy as a young racehorse. This afternoon I walked slowly out of the building to a waiting chauffeured white limousine parked behind the bus stop. Headed for Sunset Recording Studios, alone in privacy and air-conditioned comfort, I gazed out the tinted windows at Sunset Boulevard as we drove past places I'd once worked for minimum wage. I glanced up as we glided by our old house on Larabee Street.

I'd come up with a tune titled "Rompin', Stompin', Bad News Blues" with Don Schlitz for the new album and Wynonna had sung it to nasty perfection. We were so excited that blues woman Bonnie Raitt had agreed to decorate it with a microtonal palate of her famous slide guitar. Counting on adrenaline to get me through the session, I stiffened up, threw my shoulders back, lifted my chin and burst into the studio, where everyone was waiting to begin. Cheerfully acknowledging Wynonna and Bonnie seated side by side at the console, I laughed, "Well if it ain't Ms. Spunk and Ms. Funk!"

Jumping up to hug me, Bonnie fired right back, "And how are you, Ms. Wits and Glitz?" She turned to introduce me to a nice-looking fellow chatting with Brent and Don over by the tape machine. "Okay," Bonnie began with a disclaiming tone, "I know I've introduced you and Wy to beaux of mine before, but this one is no wastrel. I am in L-O-V-E! Meet actor Michael O'Keefe."

After Bonnie finished enhancing the sexy swagger of the song, Bonnie, Wynonna and I retreated to one of those typical studio rooms equipped with a Mr. Coffee, a water cooler, and a coffee table strewn with industry magazines. Acknowledging Bonnie's recent quadruple Grammy win, Wynonna began, "Bonnie, I was beginning to wonder if people were ever going to catch on to how cool you are!"

"Yeah, sometimes by the time a person makes it, he's had it!" Bonnie sighed. "I'm still pretty bowled over by the whole thing."

Extremely humble, Bonnie quickly shifted the subject to Wynonna. "Wy baby, I've been noticing you belting it out like some leather-clad rock siren lately." I suddenly felt like a fly on the wall watching with glee as Wynonna was being lavished with compliments from her long-time idol.

"How'd you learn to sing like this so young?" Bonnie queried. "You're no eye-fluttering innocent, but you haven't even had your heart stomped on real good yet! Your Mom's helped spare you the years of sex, drugs, booze, and fending off the unwanted affections and uninvited advances of cretenoid males in seedy nightclubs."

Wynonna didn't answer, so I responded, "Yeah, the kid here may sing like she knows what she's talking about, but there's Muslim women that's got more street smarts than Wynonna Ellen Judd!" With that, Wynonna shot me a slightly bemused dismissive look.

I continued on, "As insecure as Wynonna is, I think the reason she is able to sing with such powerful conviction is because as you know, Bonnie, when you're really busy singing you don't have time to watch yourself or become self-conscious. When Wy's acknowledging that basic holy and sacred emotion, she's able to sing with a religious-tinged fire. As a result, both of you are not just tough, but strong; not just smart, but wise; not just sexy, but sensual. Each of you exhibit a compelling openness. Geez, I sound like the moderator in a forum on characteristics and personal philosophies of great twentieth-century killer redheaded singers!''

Wy commented, "Bonnie, as I was just watching you play, I was remembering how much courage it took for me to call and invite you to our first Los Angeles concert. You just don't know what it means to us to have you on one of our songs.''

With that Bonnie took on the air of a loving older aunt encouraging Wynonna to take a lesson from her own notorious bacchanal years. Now that she finally had her life in order, Bonnie shared with us the irony of her current song, "Nick of Time." Like the girl she sings about, Bonnie was also beginning to wonder if she did wind up marrying Michael, whether she'd have children. I consoled, "Bonnie, time's just nature's way of keeping everything from happening at once.''

The three of us went on about everything from Bonnie's social consciousness and political activism to staying sane while living in Hollywood. Wy and I were relieved to hear Bonnie describing a home she was renting in Marin County as a respite from Los Angeles.

"Being out here is like going down the sewer in a glass-bottom boat," I scowled.

Wy jumped in, "Yeah, I'm thankful that we lived out here once though, 'cause now when I come out I'm able to keep it in proper perspective. I also know that Mom's lifestyle experiments here—the modeling, the colorful jobs, and meeting all those weirdos—and being on her own in a big city without money and having to be resourceful really contributed to her self-reliance and sense of style. It stoked the engine to drive her great American dream machine.''

I went on, "Although Wy and I are unashamedly working class and you're from show-biz Beverly Hills upper crust, Bonnie, all three of us have been battered by disappointments and buoyed by music. It's helped us beat the devil and share common ground. None of us has a yearning for those great symbols of California life: country clubs, poodles, or heart-shaped swimming pools!''

Just then, a giggly, wiggly, pneumatic blond in fishnet and spandex popped in to get a cup of coffee for her rock musician boyfriend. As soon as she was out of sight an exasperated Wynonna yelped, "Man, everybody here looks like they just stepped out of an MTV video!" With that the three of us reverted to catty talk about the male infantile obsession with large breasts, spike heels, and trashy lingerie. We let out a loud Meow!, high-fived, and hugged good-bye.

Wy and I returned home to Nashville in a fog of uncertainty. Unable even to get out of bed the next couple of days, I had to cancel shows again. Wynonna plowed on laying down lead vocals in the studio, calling to check on me, and playing her takes over the phone. There once was a time when we were like spontaneous combustion, but now I was becoming more and more aware of how sensitive and considerate she is to me.

In addition to building a big horse barn, Larry was busy remodeling an older home out at Peaceful Valley in hopes that we could move into it within a year. He'd come to me with another wonderful suggestion. "Honey, since we have so many blessings, I feel like we should share them. There's lots of single working moms that go to our church, I'm going to find a young boy who could use a little companionship and guidance."

Very naturally, seven-year-old Casey Robertson entered our lives. His struggling mom, Donna, worked in a warehouse, barely able to keep them in a low-rent housing project. Irresistibly cute, Casey reminded me of Elliot, the boy in *E.T.* He made straight A's at school, was unusually bright, and showed artist talents. Casey began spending weekend's, summer vacations, and holidays with us, becoming like a member of our family, and we all reaped the rewards of Larry's great idea.

More blood work indicated that my liver enzyme was fluctuating, and Dr. Mitchum explained this was characteristic of the disease.

Then I was relieved when he informed me that I tested negative for hepatitis C, but I hated to hear that virtually all of the 150,000 new cases of type C reported each year go chronic. I now felt a huge question mark hanging over my head. "We may never know the etiology of your disease," the doctor continued, "but I think it's a fair guess that you may have gotten infected from a needle stick while working in the intensive care unit. The only good news I can tell you, is that you aren't contagious."

Wy and I both exclaimed "Whew!" and she interjected, "Mom, you have a designer disease." Driving home, I promised her and myself, "I'm going to beat this thing by becoming involved in healing myself!"

Dr. Mitchum's a good doctor, but like most doctors, he never even mentioned nutrition. After a session with a Nashville nutritionist, I begrudgingly gave up caffeine (coffee, tea, soft drinks, and chocolate), fried foods, sugar, and junk food. I cut down red meat to once or twice a month and began eating fish, chicken, and turkey instead. I'd quit drinking soft drinks years ago because they're so bad for you, but cutting back on morning coffee was hard. I began using flavored blends in a one-half decaf and one-half regular ratio instead, and never even missed straight coffee.

As I began studying nutritional therapy, I found scientific proof supporting the benefits of vitamin and mineral supplements. Ninety-one-year-old scientist Linus Pauling, two-time winner of the Nobel Prize, convinced me to start taking one thousand milligrams of vitamin C three times a day with a potent multivitamin at supper.

I slept off and on around the clock for the next couple of weeks. When the body's fighting anything, it's imperative to sleep as much as possible to allow it to do what it needs to do.

I was desperately determined to do our show in Austin, Texas, at the Frank Erwin Center with Ricky Van Shelton the next month. I wanted to prove to myself I was still in the game. The Friday-night concert had been sold out for a long time. Having so little energy, I petitioned Mike McGrath to fly with me into Austin Thursday night so I could get a good night's rest. As usual, Wy would ride the bus with the rest of the entourage. During our layover at DFW in Dallas, I discovered I'd made a huge mistake. When fans approached for autographs, I had to sit even to sign my name. I slipped into a stall in the ladies' room to be alone so I could decide whether to go on. Sometimes wisdom is simply knowing what to do next.

When we did arrive in Austin, I stepped around the corner from the luggage carousel and sat down on the floor. A salesman glanced at me as he walked by, then after a few steps, turned and stared.

Cocking his head he wondered aloud, "Hey, aren't you Naomi Judd?"

"Yep, it's me," I responded wearily. "I'm just a little tired."

"Well," he gushed, "I want you to know I came in off the road just so I can take my family to yours and Wynonna's concert tomorrow night."

As I obliged him an autograph, I looked up and added, "Thanks mister. Now I know I made the right decision."

As planned, I stayed in bed all day the next day. Pops Webber came and walked Banjo for me. I finally had to take the phone off the hook after all the Judd Boys and crew kept calling to see "how their Mamaw was." I asked Gaylon to come get me a few minutes early so I could prepare him. "This is the new drill," I started out. "Please stand on my side at stage right and keep your eyes on me during the set. If I pull on my right earlobe it means I'm going down, come get me." Living on the road, Gaylon and I spent almost as much time together as Larry and I, and I knew I could level with him. He looked as if the sun had suddenly stopped shining.

On the bus that evening, Wynonna and I locked ourselves in her room and put out our "Do Not Disturb" sign. "Listen to me sweetheart," as I wrapped my arm around her and she laid her head on my shoulder. "Okay, so maybe I'm not Iron Woman, some elemental force. IF . . . I should have to leave the stage at anytime during the show, you MUST carry on."

Jumping straight into the air like she'd been shot from a cannon, Wynonna began shaking her head violently from side to side and thrashing her arms, "No way, José! If *you* leave, *I* leave! It is not even open for discussion."

"All right already," I backed off, familiar with this strong reaction. "If push comes to shove I'll sit on a darn stool and sing."

When Mark Thompson came on the bus for vocal warm-ups, I instructed him to figure out some band instrumental in case I needed a break. This tune became known as "The Stall Song."

Yet when the lights came up and I saw the sea of ten thousand fans spread out before us, I reacted with unexpected reservoirs of strength. Going on stage for me is like throwing some wondrous ignition switch.

As soon as the show was over, Ricky Van Shelton appeared at the bus door to check on me. Aware of all our uncharacteristic cancellations the last month, Ricky asserted in a surprised tone, "Naomi, if there's something wrong with you, you sure aren't letting on, girl. You just demonstrated emotional security, intellectual alertness, and megawatt energy!"

As our friend Ricky settled into the couch and Wynonna handed him a cold drink, I began, "Ricky, we've been telling the public that our cancellations were due to a virus I'm contending with. That's one hundred percent accurate. But that virus happens to be hepatitis. Don't worry though, I may have hepatitis, but it doesn't have me!"

I slept fifteen straight hours that night. When I awoke, I saw that Gaylon had pulled the bus up smack dab in front of my motel room to save me steps. I lived with a wakeful fatigue. After walking sixty feet or so I had to pause and rest. I've never been much on exercise or sports, but now just being around energetic people like my friend choreographer Twyla Tharp, made me tired. The doctor said I could "exercise as tolerated," which now meant activities of daily living.

Concerned about my sagging shoulders being a giveaway, Wynonna came up with another idea. "Mom, anytime we're in public and you have bad posture I'll give you a cue to straighten up by saying the name Ilene!" Sure enough, leaving for the show that night as we stood signing autographs at the bus door, Wynonna chirped, "Oh yeah, sign one for Ilene Dover."

For that show in Midland, Texas, on February 10, Mike McGrath started using a golf cart to get me back and forth from the bus to the stage steps. At first I balked at the notion, but I really had no choice.

As soon as we returned to Nashville, I met with a new doctor to get a second opinion. "Your enzyme's higher than ever," he reported with all the warmth of a glacier. "The active inflammation going on in your liver is destroying hepatic cells. Now these dead cells will turn into scar tissue called cirrhosis and the damage is irreversible. Cirrhosis usually goes into cancer, but before that, the various functions of the liver will begin shutting down, so it's hard to say which one will actually be your demise."

"How about them Dodgers!" I sarcastically responded. Under ordinary circumstances I would have expressed my shocked dismay at this physician's dangerously negative bedside manner, but I was too physically weakened and disturbed by the conversation to deal with him. Instead, I dressed as quickly as I could, rushing to leave his office. I passed him in the hall on my way out.

"I need to see you back in a week," he muttered in his monotone voice.

"Nope," I responded matter-of-factly. "You just shoved me out of an airplane at thirty-five thousand feet without offering anything to break my fall. I'm going to find a doctor who will give me a parachute. It's called *Hope!*"

I'd remain in bed at home until time to go out on the road for a few weekend dates. We pulled out of Nashville on Friday night, February 23, about midnight and ran into a severe snowstorm on our way to Indianapolis.

I guess I'd been asleep a couple of hours when suddenly I awoke with a start. I had a sense something terrible was happening! Sitting up on my knees in the middle of my bed on the bus, I felt my heart racing and I couldn't breath. I felt cold yet I was perspiring and I was hysterical. I grabbed at my throat struggling for air. At first I wasn't sure if I was awake or just having a nightmare about being in a coffin. The claustrophobia and terror were so intense I was moaning out loud, "What's happening to me, am I dying, going crazy or am I having a heart attack?"

I threw open the door to Wynonna's room where she and my Mom, who'd come on the road to help me, were sound asleep. I sat down on the foot of my bed and began trying to be aware of and control my breathing. Desperate to see lights and human beings, I jerked open my curtains, only to discover the window was frosted over. I ripped open my pajama top and pressed my entire chest against the thin layer of ice to melt it. The shock of the cold made me gasp for air. I put my face down against the floor-board register to breath in the warm air. My initial urge was to run up front to be with Gaylon, but I knew I'd awaken Wynonna and Mom while passing through their room. I couldn't let anybody see me like this! I picked up my intercom phone and talked to Gaylon. Since my voice was about an octave higher than normal, he immediately demanded to know what was wrong. "I'm just having a bad dream, that's all," I answered. It was the beginning of my journey into fear. My first panic attack.

Disturbed by the news of my illness, brother Mark and my sister-in-law, Middy, had come to Indianapolis to see us. Mark seemed uncomfortable. Although he's an intelligent man and a minister who's always there to support his parishioners, I sensed that it was déjà vu of Brian's Hodgkin's disease for him. Middy and I have always been extremely close, so much so that she's actually more like a sister. Since Middy is a professor of nursing at a college in Kentucky, I began pumping her for information about liver disease. Mark went into the parlor of my hotel suite to watch TV. "Middy," I began in a confidential tone, "I know we all have a breaking point, but this is the last thing I ever expected to have happen to someone as centered as I am. How come I had a panic attack?"

"Naomi, you're caught in a crisis, and with what you've been through, I'm not surprised! First of all, having felt like you've had the flu for so many months on end has made you feel trapped, a prisoner within your own body. You're also experiencing a loss of control—something highly unusual for you! That unfortunate visit to the doctor who told you the disease is terminal and there's nothing they can do, must have given you a feeling of helplessness and impending doom. I know, that you feel responsible for the livelihood of so many people, it's a tremendous burden of pressure not knowing whether you're going to be well enough to do a show tonight or not."

She went on to tell me some facts about panic attacks, the psychological term for anxiety that's so frighteningly severe it goes far beyond ordinary fear. "The condition is apparently common, but it's diagnosed much more commonly in women. This disorder often begins in late adolescence or early adult life, and may initially show up in mid-adult life too. It may be limited to a single brief period of intense stress or life crisis and never happen again, or may reoccur several times, or in the worst instance, becomes chronic." I found a 1-800-64-PANIC number to call for additional information on panic attacks as well as a 1-900-737-3400 number.

I realized the choking, smothering sensations and feeling of unreality, depersonalization, and fear of dying did come from my intense fear of being trapped. Then it dawned on me that some passing trucker might have seen me pressing my bare breasts against the window. Middy and I cackled as she exclaimed: "Don't you know he'd have a story to tell his buddies!"

That night on stage in front of 22,500 fans, the old Naomi came to life. Wynonna was so thrilled to see me kicking up my heels as my usual self, it turned out to be a fabulous show. On the bus that night, Wynonna rubbed my feet, made me take my vitamins and generally bossed me around. When we stopped at a truck stop on our way to Battle Creek, Michigan, she inquired with her famous crooked smile, "Hey Mom, want me to bring you anything, maybe some Carter's Little Liver Pills?"

Instead she returned with a ballpoint pen featuring a real photograph of a man wearing only shorts. When I tilted the pen upside down, his pants disappeared. "I thought that might perk you up!" she quipped.

It was Sunday, February 25, in an attempt to alleviate the fears of our road organization, we called a meeting in our dressing room immediately after the show. I leveled with the guys, then asked if they had any prayer requests. As we went around the circle, just about everyone there expressed a need. "We're the United Confederacy of Life's Highway!" Wynonna announced. An apt description I thought.

As we were returning to the motel, a Michigan fan named Colleen Casey removed her glove to reveal a tiny gold guardian angel nestled in her palm. "I saw this and somehow thought of you," she smiled, unaware of the significance. Trusting Colleen, and remembering she was in nursing school, she was the first fan I shared my diagnosis with as I was pinning her little angel on my shoulder.

I'd missed the fans so much. The interaction between us had become such an important part of my life. There had been times I'd wanted to pick up the phone and call some of them in my loneliness, but I couldn't stand the thought of their worrying about me.

Wy called me "the pin cushion," because I got stuck for blood work at least once a week now. She often accompanied me to the doctor's office. She observed the phlebotomist, and admiring bluish veins through my translucent skin, Wy told the doctor, "Mom says she used to hide on IV test days during nursing school, 'cause she was such an easy target everyone wanted to start one on her! I think she should go naked as a road map on Halloween. What do you think?"

Ashley came home from the University of Kentucky to check on me and liven things up. She and Wynonna would lie in bed with me, picking on each other while reading magazines.

"Ooh, gross. Make Wynonna stop it," Ashley suddenly yelped.

"I didn't do anything, that's just my stomach growling," Wynonna retorted.

"Well that's an *internal* fart," Ashley retaliated.

With that Wynonna dumped a glass of ice down Ashley's blouse. Then she pinned Ashley to the bed and noisily licked her ear. Ashley *really* hates that.

The Houston Livestock and Rodeo at the Astrodome is one of our favorite events. Wynonna and I had long established a bus rule that road trips longer than ten hours automatically call for air travel instead, but now all the rules were out the window. Walking through airports and dealing with the public had simply become too tiresome for me so we rode the bus. After we checked into our hotel room, I could hear Wynonna laughing through the wall. She pounded twice, a road code signal to turn on the TV. "*Love Connection* is hilarious today," she yelled.

When I flipped on the TV I got a local news bulletin about a child named Stormy who'd just passed away from complications of her liver transplant. Slowly I sat down on the foot of the bed and wept for this beautiful little girl and her family. Stormy had hepatitis and had endured many severe complications. Suddenly the phone startled me, it was Dr. Mitchum with the most recent test results. "Naomi, you need to come straight home," he admonished me. "Your ALT is at an all-time high. We've got to do a liver biopsy and I insist you go on complete bed rest." It was a preposterous moment. Wynonna laughing raucously in the next room, images on the TV screen in front of me of grieving parents with a ragged hole in their hearts, and the insistent authoritative voice of my doctor coming through the telephone at my ear. "What the heck am I going to do, Dr.

Mitchum?" I cried, reaching into the bedside table drawer with my free hand to take out the Gideon Bible.

"Let go and let God," came his reply.

Somehow uncertainty had wormed its way into my fairy tale life and permeated everything. Seated at my makeup mirror on the bus preparing for the show that night, I made a decision that this would be my last concert for a while. I dare not even consider the remote possibility that it might be my last. I was intent on pulling out all the stops for this performance.

Forty-four thousand Texans roared approval when I shouted through my microphone, "Hey ya'll, is it true that Texas invented country music?" As Wynonna and I released emotions and passions unmistakably born of real-life experiences through our songs and interactions, the applause rolled over us like some thunderous surf submerging us in love and understanding.

Spontaneously, I grabbed my microphone from its stand and stalked toward the video camera man. Video projectors arranged around the arena flashed our pictures to even the most remote part of the grandstands affording each and every person a "magnified close-up of our nose hairs," as Wynonna loved to say.

"All right Lone Star State," I commanded, "everybody stand up." The vast audience rose to their feet in unison. In my periphery, I was aware that Wynonna and the band members were scurrying futilely to check their set list to find out where I might be headed.

"Now everybody . . . put your right foot out," and they did! Meanwhile, Wynonna sidled over next to me, and when I nodded down to her right foot, even she complied with my order. "Now . . . put your right foot in," and they all did! Then I began singing lustily, "You do the hokeypokey and you turn yourself around, that's what it's all about!!"

The crowd went wild as they rocked the Astrodome. I linked my arm through Wynonna's and twirled her around as if we were partners at some old-fashioned hoedown. As we came offstage, as is the tradition, the kid and I were seated up on the back of an open convertible for our ride around the arena. I just happened to be wearing my gold lamé "Ms. America" dress, and Wynonna and I waved like homecoming queens till all the blood ran from our arms.

Just when I thought things couldn't get any worse . . . they did! I went down for the full count this time. The symptoms of hepatitis are fever, weakness, nausea, vomiting, muscle aches, lethargy, headaches, and abdominal discomfort. I was so terribly sick, I could barely get out of bed. It was depressing to feel as bad when I awoke each morning as I had when I went to sleep. Alone all day in our bedroom, I depended on the dogs to bark their greeting to Larry, signaling me he was coming in the back door. I'd lock myself in the bathroom to change nightgowns, brush my teeth and hair so I didn't completely freak him out. We were a study in contrast; Larry had been working outdoors at physical labor, so he was getting healthier and radiated energy. Although I'd tried to hide how bad it actually was, one night I was disoriented and walked into a wall. He called Ken.

C. S. Lewis called friendship "the most mature of all loves." Ken informed me he was canceling our week at Vegas with Clint Black.

"But, Ken!" I argued weakly.

"Save your breath young lady, I'm pulling the plug. Not only am I canceling this week in Vegas, but I'm canceling the following week's worth of shows in Lake Tahoe."

I had long known that both weeks were sellouts and that canceling at this late date would mean millions in losses for the hotels, because they wouldn't be able to scrounge up a comparable draw at this late date. Not only did this make me feel as bad mentally as I already felt physically but there was the awful realization that Wynonna and I personally support a lot of people. As Wynonna says, "If the Judd girls don't sing, the boys don't eat!"

Ken, who has the uncanny ability to read my mind started right in, "And Naomi, don't you worry about the organization. I'm calling a meeting to assure everyone that payroll will go on as usual until you're well enough to return."

The next morning a huge basket of fragrant, colorful flowers arrived from Holmes Hendrickson, the entertainment director of

Harrah's at Lake Tahoe. The card read, "We'll miss seeing you and Wy, but we care about your health most of all. Take care and know we all love you. Holmes and staff." I was touched not only by the kindness of this generous spirited man who proved that you *can* combine business with pleasure, but his permission to rest was like a soothing balm on my conscience.

As I lay there in the unnatural hush of my darkened room, I carried on internal monologues as the weeks dragged agonizingly by. "I'm trying to make a comeback and nobody even knows I'm gone." It was like I was an outsider, cut off from everything I knew and loved. I felt so dreadful, I was unable to sleep for more than a few hours at a time. The headache kept me from reading so I flipped on the TV. There was a desperate Susan Hayward, whom I've been told I resemble, behind prison bars on her way to the gas chamber in the 1958 movie *I Want to Live!* "No thanks!" I scowled, quickly changing to another channel.

CNN flashed a news bulletin about Gloria Estefan's horrible bus crash in Pennsylvania. Wide-eyed with disbelief, I watched the live footage of her being transported in a neck brace on a stretcher from her bus into the ambulance. My mind flashed back on my new friend's conversation backstage at the AMAs on the blessings of health.

The news switched to the scandal of Donald Trump's divorce from Ivana. The interest in their excessive lives seemed so irrelevant, I decided that "a celebrity is someone who is famous for being famous." We don't have a royal family in America, so we've made celebrities our aristocracy. Fame creates its own etiquette, allowing famous people to be themselves in a way no one else is allowed to be.

Now I knew that Ken was going to have to make a public statement of my diagnosis to explain another month's worth of major cancellations. We quickly discovered that the public is as uninformed about liver disease as I had been.

It is shocking that there's so little education or prevention of this fourth largest killer of Americans! I called the American Liver Foundation in Cedar Grove, New Jersey, at 1-800-223-0179 and spoke with Thelma Thiel, who became its leader when her child died from liver disease.

It seemed so incongruous that this could be happening when we'd just had the greatest year of our entire lives, not only professionally but personally as well! Wy and I had healed our relationship. Larry and I were finally married, happier than we'd ever expected, and had even found our dream farm. And blossoming Ashley was spared the tragic plane disaster.

Having felt as if I had the world's worst case of flu for months now, every minute dripped like water torture on my head. I dreaded the nights, shuddering as claustrophobic darkness closed in. There were more hallucinogenic, smothering panic attacks. I felt submerged by a terrifying flood of murky black waters, sucked down into a swirling vortex.

I hardly knew myself anymore. There were two Naomi's now. The one I'd been before, and the stranger to which I found myself chained. I had our lawyer draw up my will and selected a spot in Peaceful Valley for a family cemetery. I wrote out instructions that I was not to be embalmed and stated I wanted to be buried in a simple pine box.

A friend from church, Janet Vaughn, who'd been helping with errands and cleaning for years had now also begun cooking for us. "Saint Janet," as I call her, prayed with me and lovingly watched over me. One afternoon I sent her to the bookstore to get the latest medical journals on hepatitis.

The further I got into the chapter on liver disease in *Luckman's and Sorensen's Medical-Surgical Nursing,* the scarier it became. It was as if the book were saying my name. It gave one of the causes of chronic active hepatitis as CMV infection in immunocompromised hosts. Wait a minute, I never thought about the fact that I could have gotten hepatitis from CMV while I was on all that prednisone that obliterated my immune system for a year!

Then I came on a reference in another book that said I may have as little as three years to live. There it was in black and white. I knocked this book out of my lap like it was on fire and got down on my face on the rug beside my bed.

"Father, by whom all things are made," I cried out, "I love medicine, but realize I've been treating these books as if they were a bible and looking to doctors as if they were gods. I'm asking to join into a partnership with you so that I may be cocreator with you in my healing. I know your desire is for me to be well and happy. I realize you're a supernatural being and that the universe runs on spiritual laws, I'm stickin' with you!"

With that, I put all those books back in Ashley's bedroom and haven't looked at them since. I'd been fact finding, now it was time for fact facing.

I called Dr. Mitchum at once to discuss this scary new information, and he immediately urged me to get to the Mayo Clinic in Rochester, Minnesota. My fingers couldn't dial the phone fast enough to hear Ken's take-charge voice. He began making arrangements. My sister, Margaret, and I know each other so well and can tell each other anything, so I phoned her next. As family, we collaborate to root each other in a shared belonging to a dimension greater than our individual lives. To support my optimism, Margaret began singing the song from *The King and I:* "Whenever I feel afraid, I hold my head erect and whistle a happy tune so no one will suspect, I'm afraid. The result of this deception is very strange to tell, for when I fool the people I meet, I fool myself as well!"

I couldn't bring myself to tell Larry, so instead I found a psychologist who deals with terminally ill patients and their families. I knew I would need help in telling Larry that there is a chance I might die.

Larry thought we were going to see this guy because I needed help in dealing with my constant pain and this nightmarish uncertainty that was ruling our lives. We hadn't been there five minutes before the psychologist asked me to tell him the exact diagnosis and prognosis. Staring straight ahead at the doctor, I repeated verbatim what I'd read. The instant Larry got the gist of what I was saying, out of my periphery I saw his whole body jerk. The psychologist spun around, touched his finger to Larry's knee and asked, "Excuse me Mr. Strickland, but are you hearing this for the first time?" For the next couple of hours we dealt with the brutal truth. The doctor pointed out that we were at a turning point in our marriage. This was a chance for Larry to become my warrior and protector. A time to learn that marriage not only multiplies joy, but divides sorrow.

Our pals Jack and Jerry Calhoun, who make buses, sent their private plane to fly me up to Rochester, Minnesota. Flying commercially was, of course, out of the question since I was too ill to make even the long bus ride. Sweet Janet drove us to the airport and cried and hugged us as Larry carried me from the car onto the plane.

Being sick is not my style, and I hated being in public in this weakened condition, so I instinctively relied on my sense of humor. When we arrived at the world-famous Mayo Clinic and were told to go to the admitting office I retorted: "Hey, I ain't admittin' to nothin'!" The night before I was to meet my doctor and begin tests, I was praying in my room that God would send me a physician like Jesus, the Great Physician, who went about healing not only diseases but also the people who have those diseases. I needed a doctor who would be a friend and understand my faith.

Larry turned on *The 700 Club*, and there was actress Ann Jillian. Ann had just waged a successful battle against breast cancer and was sharing her personal story of how she incorporated God's love with modern medicine to heal her mind and body. Then show host Pat Robertson stared right into the camera and said, "There's someone who needs to know it's all right to ask strangers in the hospital to pray with them and talk openly about their beliefs."

My first answered prayer came early the next morning as soon as I met Dr. Dalton. Kind, brilliant, and experienced, he'd trained under my brother Brian's hemotologist, Dr. Charles Doan. We were instantly friends.

The Mayo Clinic is a utopian fantasy of what a medical clinic should be for a nurse-turned-patient like me. As I went from department to department, having all the tests done, I patted each caring person with whom I came in contact on the back. It was tough on my ego being in a wheelchair. At one point, another patient came over and inquired, "Excuse me, but aren't you Naomi Judd? What are you doing here? Were you hurt in a skiing accident in Aspen or something?"

Everything is metabolized through the liver, which detoxifies poisons and inactivates drugs. Since my liver was in too much turmoil to be subjected to medication, I was given only a pinch of the topical anesthetic lidocaine at the injection site for the liver biopsy. I inhaled a deep breath so they could inject a needle under my ribs into the liver and aspirate tissue through a large hypodermic syringe.

I was not prepared for the pathology report the following day. Dr. Dalton revealed that the inflammation in my liver had probably been going on since 1986. The first thought that crossed my muddled consciousness was that my three-year death sentence had just been whittled down to perhaps a few months, maybe even days. I wasn't paying attention to the next part of what Dr. Dalton said and had to ask him to repeat it. It was something about interferon, a naturally occurring defense mechanism produced in blood cells and tissues to fight foreign invaders within the body.

Interferon is also manufactured as an antiviral drug used to help boost the body's own immune system. It's not a cure, because it can't kill the virus, it just keeps the virus from replicating. "We need to start you on interferon therapy immediately," he insisted. "I'm going to send you down to the chemotherapy lab for your first injection, but before you go, I'll send in our interferon nurse to explain the protocol to you."

A kindly, middle-aged lady began explaining to us that I'd have to inject myself three times a week and to expect some pretty uncomfortable side effects, because interferon launches a war inside the body while fighting the virus.

I interrupted her. "Do you believe in God?"

"Of course I do!" Betty Steiner replied. I'd had four days of excellent medical, surgical, pharmacological, information, now I needed to talk about what was *really* going to make the difference in healing me. Betty, Larry, and I had a wonderful conversation about the power of faith, and I could feel some of the tension floating away. When it was time to go for chemo, this guardian angel hugged me in the doorway and added, "I'm so glad I happened to be here today. The regular interferon nurse, who's not a believer, called in sick. Naomi, just remember this," she said squeezing my hand, "Isaiah 26:3: 'Thou wilt keep him in perfect peace, whose mind is stayed on thee.' "

Having worked oncology as an RN myself, there was no way I was going to let Larry go down there with me, so I sent him to the cafeteria. As my dear friend and companion Martha Taylor, who'd accompanied us on the whole trip, pushed my wheelchair, I told her how much I loved her. "Have I ever told you that you're twenty-four karat, Ms. Taylor?"

I've always believed in telling my loved ones how I feel, but it was especially important these days.

If I had had any inclination for self-pity, it would have been completely abolished by the sight of the folks semireclining in lounge chairs hooked up to their chemotherapy IVs. As the nurse swabbed my leg with alcohol before giving me my first injection of interferon, I gently held Sue Barnes's wrist and asked if she, Martha, and I could have a prayer. This was the second time in my life that I had ever petitioned strangers to pray with me. The first time had been as I lay on the OR table earlier that day before the liver biopsy. Somewhat embarrassed and timid, I inquired if the masked doctors and nurses minded. I was pleased to discover that not only did they not mind but they appreciated my praying for them as well!

That evening back in our room I suffered one of the worst nights of my entire life. Already polluted by unrelenting misery, my body's reaction to the introductory interferon shot exaggerated my discomfort almost beyond my ability to withstand. The only analgesic I was allowed was one regular Tylenol, when what I wanted was one hundred milligrams of morphine in an IV! Larry never left my side and my greatest comfort came from him rubbing my back as we listened to our church choir tapes. The instant I'd turn my tape recorder on, I'd hear Assistant Pastor Dan Scott triumphantly sing, "I got a feeling everything's gonna be all right!"

It was not helpful talking to Wynonna long distance, because she was already a basket case, and I was so worried about her, it made me feel even worse. For this reason, I had dissuaded her from accompanying us to the Mayo Clinic. It was so unnerving and scary for her to see me—whom she'd never seen have a cold—this debilitated. "Mommy, I miss you and I've missed being on the *Dreamchaser* together. I'm starting to wear my stage clothes around the house. Today I drove down to Music Row and waved at fans, just to see if they'd recognize me and wave back," she joked, trying to make me laugh, but I could hear her sniffling in between the pauses.

I was glad she had Tony for comfort and support. Ashley remained oblivious to the actual extent of my condition. A senior at the University of Kentucky, she was preoccupied with preparing for spring finals and I hadn't wanted to worry and distract her.

Then the headache from hell completely took over. Anyone who's ever had a migraine or a severe headache that lasts more than forty-eight hours can appreciate how it begins to wear on one's nerves! Larry would bundle me up and take me for a drive around the lake. He drove me out to Peaceful Valley whenever I was strong enough to make the trip. I thought about how during the war fifteen-year-old Anne Frank, writing in her diary during her two-year hideout in "The Secret Annex," had said that when we're sad, lonely, sick, etc., going outdoors is one of the greatest things we can do.

Larry and I sat on the lovely bridge we'd just finished building across a creek in the valley. Its stones are the color of rain and engraved in the middle are the words: *Love, Faith,* and *Courage.* I'd taken these words from Brian's tombstone, and now I needed them to see me through my own ordeal. It suddenly dawned on me since Larry and I had built this bridge, I'd begun writing "Love Can Build a Bridge!" Instead of wedding presents, family and friends planted flowering trees around the bridge to remind us that marriage is also a living, growing thing. Looking around at the wild roses, dogwoods, redbuds, and weeping willows, the last words for the song came: "When we stand together, it's our finest hour. We can do anything, ANYTHING if we keep believing in the power."

My Mom came to take care of me, and her wonderful sense of humor and strength kept me from going completely crazy. Finally, even allowing for my high threshold for pain, the unrelenting headache was more than I could bear. Larry called Wynonna, who came straight over in the middle of the night in her pajamas and climbed into bed with me. He alerted my liver specialist at Nashville's Vanderbilt Hospital, a sharp young woman physician who'd actually trained under Dr. Dalton in Rochester and acts as my local liaison with the Mayo Clinic. She urged, "Come to Vanderbilt right away. We need to draw blood." The results on the stat blood work were unbelievable!

"Naomi," the elated doctor began, "we've had a discussion

about you and thought we were going to have to pull you off interferon because of the unusual severity of your side effects, but your ALT has nose-dived down within the normal range! We only know of one other patient to exhibit such a marked improvement! Tomorrow you must give yourself another injection of interferon and proceed with the protocol."

It was as if mercy had been holding her breath and suddenly gave forth with a loud audible exhale.

Although I didn't feel physically any the better, the early morning light brought hope. Stiffly and slowly, I shoved the bottoms of my pajama pants down into my boots, threw on a coat, and drove myself to our church. I had dragged myself here before to ask for a miracle, now like a happy, grateful child I came with no other intent except to give thanks and praise to my Heavenly Father.

Unpleasant side effects from interferon lessen with time. During the next month I was able to sing harmony in the studio. Working on the new album had been the only thing to keep Wynonna from feeling swept away like some uprooted growth down the currents of life. I arrived at the studio while she was imprinting her lush vocal tones on a haunting song called "Calling in the Wind." It felt great to be there after so long an absence and I shook my head acknowledging Wy's words. "You said I could call on you if ever I was lonely, you swore you'd always be my friend. And now my heart is tired and oh my soul is hungry. I need to talk to you again. I can hear love calling in the wind. Open up my heart and let it in. Love's calling in the wind. You said I may not see you standing there beside me, but you would be there just the same. Your hand upon my shoulder, always there to guide me. All I had to do was call your name."

Wynonna and I were in such demand we'd been booked at least a year in advance, so Ken had been canceling on a month-to-month basis. Against the advice of my doctors, I decided to go back on the road the end of April. The interferon was working, and I missed Wy, the road, and fans too much. I had to get back inside my life!

With tremendous anticipation and relief we arrived at Billings, Montana. Although I still felt as if I had a mild case of the flu, the excitement helped distract me. The show was a bit ragged and everyone acted a little giddy. That night on our drive to Great Falls,

Montana, we were all sitting around the front of the bus in our bathrobes with our hands folded in our laps looking around grinning at each other, so happy to be together again. Without any warning I threw my head back and began belting out the words to the song "People": "People, people who need people are the luckiest people in the world!"

That night, to prove "I was back," when Mike McGrath had his back turned, I slipped into the front bathroom. Knowing Mike's routine well, I waited patiently five minutes until he went to step into the tiny bathroom to brush his teeth. The instant he opened the door, I lunged at him with a blood curdling scream. Mike fell back on the floor clutching his heart dramatically and Wynonna pounced on him, tickling him unmercifully.

Wy seemed more vulnerable than ever before and made sure we always had adjoining hotel rooms. Ken had a refrigerator installed in the bus in which to keep my interferon. Interferon is a human protein that must be refrigerated within a very specific temperature range. It's like milk, in that it spoils easily. If Wynonna and I flew and had to be away from our bus, I carried the expensive interferon vials packed in ice in a small Igloo cooler. I kept hypodermic syringes in my purse. It was unnerving when airport security guards wanted to check the cooler and shake the vials. Calmly as I could, I'd try to explain to them that my life depended on this fragile stuff.

Excited about being back in the familiar territory of our life on the road, I wrote the words to a rollicking upbeat number called "This Country's Rockin'," while Keith Sykes and Robert Johnson did the music. Its double entendre suggests that not only is America a mighty cool place, but that Wynonna and I were back full steam ahead with our brand of country music! I was aware now of a super heightened sense of intuition. Wynonna claimed she could almost see radar antennae coming out of my head. "I've noticed one unusual side affect of hepatitis," I confided to her. "I've got amazing peripheral vision now, 'cause I can see things all around me now better than ever!"

I think we can learn from any situation we're involved in and once again noticed a habit I'd developed long ago in response to chaos. In an effort to make some kind of sense out of problems, I try to see if something good can come from them. Ashley calls it making lemonade from lemons. Believing that conflicts are an everyday part of life presenting us with an opportunity to grow, Wynonna and I started having heart-to-heart talks every afternoon before sound check. She'd heard it said that "the best things in life aren't things," and now this point was dramatically driven home with the realization that all our money in the bank, all our platinum albums and awards could not take away my life-threatening virus.

Since we'd never been able to, it had been great fun to waltz into a store for the first time and feel the rush of power and momentary thrill of being able to buy whatever struck our fancy. Soon as they'd see us coming through the door, store managers would almost trip over themselves to get to us, offering us something to drink, etc. If they were playing rap or heavy-metal music, they'd automatically turn it off because they figured out Wy and I wouldn't stay long enough to buy anything. But we soon realized that you can't buy everything. As Wy says, "Where would you put it?"

Referring to having enough to pay for necessities, I explained to her, "Money can't buy happiness, it just calms your nerves!" Wynonna and I had discovered for ourselves the old axiom of Acts 20:35 is actually true. It really is more blessed to give than to receive.

Everytime that Wynonna and I tried to do something for someone else it had a strange boomerang affect. The Sanskrit word *karma* literally means "come back." We always got more out of being chairmen of the United Way, raising money for charities, doing benefits, sponsoring the LPGA's Skins Game for Vanderbilt's Children's Hospital than the effort we put into it.

For instance, we'd done a benefit in 1989 to help defray the medical costs for our friend Heather Farr, a pro golfer with the LPGA, who was diagnosed with advanced breast cancer at twenty-four. Now Wynonna and I turned to them as we observed firsthand how Heather and her devoted mother, Sharon, handled her chemo, radiation, surgery, and bone marrow transplants. Their courage and optimism set an inspiring example for Wy and me and the Judds and the Farrs became very close.

Also, country music gave us opportunities to meet and observe firsthand women and men who were literally helping to change the world. People like Marian Wright Edelman, winner of the Albert Schweitzer Humanitarian Award, founder and president of the Children's Defense Fund, the nation's most powerful force for children. Marian shows all of us that there's immeasurable joy in living our lives in less selfish and more purposeful ways. Marian told us, "Every life matters, and we're responsible for each other."

Wy and I had the priviledge of broadening our horizons by getting to hang out and become friends with some big-time scientists like Henry Kendall, Ph.D., professor of physics at the Massachusetts Institute of Technology, winner of the Nobel Prize in Physics and founder of the Union of Concerned Scientists. Henry taught us we're also responsible for our earth and all the things in it. Although Wynonna didn't know what a quark was, Henry was able to make her understand that our entire world is in very serious trouble because of the "destructive pressure we're thoughtlessly putting on our fragile global environment." Henry explained that American culture's loss of connection to the earth leaves us feeling disconnected to life itself. Wy and I began recycling at home, became more aware of conserving resources, and changed to earth-friendly products.

I'd also discovered there's scientific proof of how such altruism stimulates the bodies own immune system. Even watching altruism has a strong effect. When scientists showed a group a documentary on Mother Teresa working with street people in Calcutta and then measured the participants' saliva for germ-fighting antibodies, they discovered the salivary antibodies had increased dramatically! Helping others is not only good mentally, emotionally, and spiritually but even physically.

Larry and I were discovering new things about each other, although we'd been together for a decade. Oh, I already thought I knew everything (he hates pineapple and loves crossword puzzles), but now I saw a brand-new side of him. When the going gets tough, the tough get tender. Larry emerged to take his place as the head of our family. Wy and Ashley looked to him for strength and guidance. I began fully to appreciate how difficult it must be to be married to a female celebrity. It requires a strong sense of self-knowledge and an intact, secure ego. Stand by your manhood!

About this time Larry and Reba McEntire's husband, Narvel

Blackstock, became friends. Besides having common backgrounds, Larry and Narvel share the unusual characteristic of being married to hard-headed, famous women. The four of us began spending time together and enjoy a uniquely special comradery. When we go over to their house for supper, Reba and I don't wear makeup or dress up. Larry always wants to see their horses, and he and Narvel talk about cars, motorcycles, golf, and politics. Reba and I play with their little boy Shelby and gab about what's going on with our friends, our careers, and generally the kind of stuff all women talk about.

Wy and I were doing dates trying to carry on normally. The last week of June 1990, we even took Ashley and Casey with us on the bus as we were working our way toward Florida. On days off, I stayed in bed, while they all went to enjoy Walt Disney World in Orlando.

As we were headed north once again, I began feeling worse. I'd been on interferon shots for three months and knew the side effects should be minimal by now, so I became alarmed as the nagging old symptoms began to rear their ugly heads. Our writer friend Neil Pond of *Country America Magazine* was riding on the bus with us doing a full-length interview on the way to a gig at Knoxville, Tennessee. I began having trouble finishing my sentences and had to really concentrate during our outdoor concert that night.

Before I knew it, we were in Evansville, Indiana, preparing for a Sunday-evening show. As Ashley and I were leaving our bus to go to the stage, I brushed a mosquito off my chest right at the scoop neckline of my dress, and felt a good-size lump. Ashley witnessed this, and I caught the look of panic in her eyes, so I quickly put my finger to my lips and muttered, "Not a word to anyone." Then I had to rush out onto the stage and smile and entertain the crowd.

At midnight after the show, Wynonna, Ashley, and I were excitedly headed to Kentucky to see Mark and Middy's brand-new baby boy Brian Judd. "Ashley, nothing is going to spoil this family day! Don't worry, I'll call my doctor from Mark's house and set up a biopsy." As our family gathered to celebrate this long-awaited precious new life, I was grateful for a glimpse into the miracle of creation and its reminder that life is constantly beginning again.

At six A.M. the very next morning July 10, 1990, Ashley, Larry, and I arrived at a Nashville hospital for my breast biopsy. Wynonna was already so distraught, I'd made the decision not to tell her until afterward when we knew the results.

After a consultation long distance with my Mayo Clinic doctor, my Nashville surgeon decided my liver couldn't tolerate any anesthesia except for a pinch of topical lidocaine at the operable sight. The pre-op blood work showed my ALT had indeed gone back up. The interferon wasn't working as well anymore, so they instructed me to double my dosage. This bad news added to the mounting tension.

I foreswore anything to even make me drowsy for the biopsy procedure. It was unnerving for the OR staff to have a patient fully alert, let alone someone who's also a nurse. But I was cool as a cucumber, and my blood pressure was normal as we began.

As soon as the surgeon opened me up, all the monitor's alarms went off. I looked up and saw on the readout that my blood pressure was seventy over forty and nose-diving. I knew I was headed into cardiac arrest. As the head nurse requested the "crash cart," with resuscitation equipment, our eyes met. It was totally nerve-wracking for all of us because we all knew I was fully aware of the danger I was in.

An anesthesiologist came flying into the room gowning and masking as the surgeon hollered, "The epinephrine in the lidocaine has pooled in the beta receptors of her legs and pulled her blood pressure down!" Although I was beginning to feel warm, fuzzy, and drowsy as I started to lose consciousness, I fought back with everything I had. I wasn't about to have Larry and Ashley go out to Wy's farm and tell her, "Sorry, your Mom died during a breast biopsy." I began praying the entire 121st Psalm out loud, "I will lift up mine eyes into the hills from whence cometh my help. My help cometh from the Lord, which made heaven and earth. . . ."

They were able to stabilize me to complete the surgery, and thankfully the lump was found to be benign. When Larry called Wynonna to tell her, while I was in the recovery room, she went all to pieces. She demanded to hear my voice and I said, "Sweetheart, guess this just ain't my year!"

Wynonna had been having slice-and-dice nightmares, depression, and more episodes of asthma attacks so I found a family therapist for us. The therapist had thirty-five years of experience as a licensed clinical-care social worker. She was recommended by a mutual friend (which is the best way to find a therapist) and was like a spiritual, wise, loving grandmother. Wy and I needed help desperately, and both agreed that she was perfect for us. Our commitment to work together was an initiation from death to a new life. *Education* means to "lead out," and the therapist would walk with Wy and me on our journey out of darkness into light. We sensed the experience was going to change us forever.

Wynonna and I believe that at sometime in everyone's life, during a life-changing circumstance, he or she can benefit from therapy. Our spirituality was already healthy, and even pioneering psychoanalysist Carl Jung declared that spirituality is central to healing and growth in people. But you can't separate spirituality and psychology. Self-awareness and contemplation are all avenues to finding and living truthfully. It requires imagination and openness, and I knew Wynonna and I were capable of that!

Among the first things the therapist taught us is that "peace is not just the absence of conflict, but the ability to deal with it." She began helping us to pause and reflect and live fully in the moment. She would say, "All we really have is this moment and if we stay aware and grounded in it, we can't get crazy over worrying about stuff that might or might not happen." The therapist taught us to be conscious of our breath and to control our breathing. She reminded us to pay attention to our five senses. It sounds simple and obvious, but most people aren't aware of how important and valuable it is.

I so wanted Wynonna to become dedicated to reality. I wanted her to start considering what I'd learned from Scott Peck's *The Road Less Traveled*, that "glaciers come and glaciers go, the world is constantly changing, therefore, we must all keep revising our maps." I hoped that soon she would be able to welcome challenges to her maps of reality, because to heal the spirit we must be open to the challenges of life's realities. I began challenging her to become who she really is. If something were to happen to me, I wanted Wy to be able to handle it.

I was dealing with another brand-new reality. A month earlier Ashley had left the University of Kentucky to choose from a multiple career choice: (A) She'd been accepted in the Peace Corps and could go to Africa; (B) She could go for her anthropology degree at the University of Arizona to become a cultural anthropologist; or (C) She could go to Hollywood and try to make it as an actress. Pretty diverse options wouldn't you say? She chose C.

A few days after my breast biopsy, Ashley packed up her stuff, hooked a U-Haul onto the back of her car and headed off for California. I admit I saw myself in her, the gypsy, drawn like a moth to the flame of adventure—and Oh, no! Not another U-Haul!

There was an internal battle going on within me. Although Ashley had been right beside me at the hospital, I was careful not to let her know that my interferon therapy was failing. Selfishly, I wanted to scream, "No you can't go to Hollywood and be on the other side of the country away from me when I need you, I may be dying! If you love me, you'll stay!" But the mother in me knew that more than anything, I wanted Ashley to realize her potential and become self-actualized. I stroked her hair as I held her close and whispered, "Take care of yourself my little giraffe."

"Why do you call me little giraffe, Mommy?" she wondered.

"Because you're always sticking your neck out," I lovingly replied.

I wasn't feeling very strong physically, but I maintained my cool until Ashley actually pulled out of the driveway. I stood motionless after the U-Haul disappeared out of view, then I broke down. Larry and Wynonna were upset that I hadn't told Ashley the truth and made her stay, but I explained, "I just couldn't do that! That would be emotional blackmail."

I went inside and listened to our song "Dreamchaser," which was written about Wy and me, and marveled at the irony of how it now also applied to Ashley's new adventure.

> I'm gonna pack my bags and drive all night
> I'll be in the mountains by mornin' light
> Drive the roads I traveled years ago
> As a young girl leavin' home.
> With dreams as big
> As the trees were tall
> I knew I'd have nothing

Or I'd have it all,
And you all know what happens
When the bright lights call,
You're either gonna make it
Or you're gonna fall.
I'm a dreamchaser, a star gazer
That's what I am
But I've always known
I'd come back home
When I found my rainbow's end.

The next morning Wynonna and I flew all day to get to Canada to perform at the Calgary Stampede Rodeo. Exhausted, I walked into my hotel room that night on the twenty-seventh floor of an inner-city hotel whose windows did not open. I immediately felt claustrophobic, and the panicky thoughts of Ashley being so far away from me made it even worse. Our bus with the refrigerator hadn't caught up with us, so I wound up staying up all night trekking out to the ice machine to keep refilling the ice in my small Igloo cooler to maintain the viability of my interferon. The next day, Mike McGrath and I went to a walk-in clinic down the street to have my ALT checked. As I suspected, it was now quadruple the norm. I was back in serious trouble.

Fortunately, we'd scheduled two days of rest and I insisted on going to Banff, Canada, because I knew I needed to saturate myself with the majesty of the outdoors to do some thinking. *God* stands for "Great Out Doors." I felt as if I'd taken a lot of people out on a withering limb, being out on the road this last year. If I were in trouble, the Judds were in trouble. It was a huge domino effect. Now that the interferon wasn't doing what we'd hoped, I had to consider what might happen. I couldn't stand the thought of passing out onstage in front of people or being hospitalized in some strange town. Most of all, I had to think of what was best for my partner.

Alone, I walked down to the breathtakingly gorgeous lake. Sitting by an evergreen at the emerald water's edge, I began praying for a sign that the momentous life-changing, far-reaching decision I knew that only I could make would be the right one. I believe, as

Scott Peck does, that sudden insights, premonitions, and dreams are gifts of grace from the invisible hand and unimaginable wisdom of God that guide us through our spiritual journey.

Suddenly I saw a shooting star. The shooting star was myself. A life illuminated by flash bulbs, Klieg lights, and footlights, lighting up the heavens, in one brief instant vanished. I felt a mortal chill upon my heart, a lingering tremor along my nerves. I don't know how long I sat alone, disowning my fate, until I realized the lateness of the hour and the piercing night chill. I rose and inhaled a long, deep breath, then pitched a stone out into the lake as if to punctuate the finality of my decision.

Walking back to the hotel I passed by the bus. I slipped inside the spooky quietness and sat in the middle of my bed and let the atmosphere of my wonderful life envelope me. I opened the closet and took out my favorite stage dress. A lovely memory lurked in every fold. I was haunted by nightmares that night. I dreamed I lived alone in a dingy, shabby apartment, ruled by penury, starved for companionship, existing on sacrifices and self-denial.

The next day, Monday, July 17, knowing that Ken would be busy at his office in Nashville, I called to tell him that I was going to resign from the music industry. "Ken," I began haltingly in a quivering voice, "you and I need to talk. I've come to a decision . . ." But before I could even complete the sentence Ken abruptly stopped me.

"Don't say another word. I'm coming there, we'll talk."

Ken was waiting for us down in Los Angeles where we were scheduled to do *The Arsenio Hall Show*. As he walked into my hotel room, I could barely look at him. "Ken, you know as well as anyone, I feel as if the career were my life. It's as if I were born to do this, yet I can't go on pretending I'm not ill, living from show to show, keeping Wynonna in emotional turmoil. We've got to come up with a plan to wrap this up."

In his wonderfully caring way, Ken first expressed his grief. He cried as he acknowledged that he'd known this dreaded conversation was coming.

"Ken, I'm sorry to have to ask you this," I began, "but I'm gonna have to ask you the biggest favor I've ever asked of you in my life. There's absolutely no way I can tell Wynonna, so you must. I simply can't say the words *It's over*. It's the hardest thing I've ever had to do in my whole life, and I cannot bring myself to do it."

The next day I avoided Wynonna. Ken and I tried not to be in the same room with her because the three of us have never kept anything from each other. Even while we were singing or talking to our pal Arsenio that night, all I could think about as I looked at Wynonna was, how in the world are we gonna tell this child that I'm abandoning her? The next day, after *The Arsenio Hall Show*, was a day off in San Francisco, and we decided that would be the time.

I'll never forget that day as long as I live. Ken came in my room, and I propped myself up in bed. His eyes were clouded with sadness, and he said little. When he opened the door for Wynonna, she stood motionless out in the hallway, hesitant even to enter. He had to take her by the hand and lead her in. I think she knew by the inherited habits of thoughts and feelings.

"Wy honey, sit down please," Ken asked imploringly. She eased into a chair between my bedside and the window, looking out over foggy San Francisco Bay, but watching me out of the corner of her eye. The only thing I remember Ken saying was the first words: "Sweetheart, you're Mom's very sick, and she doesn't seem to be getting any better."

I was only vaguely aware that he was still speaking after that. I could only look at Wynonna's face.

She forced a swallow and her eyelids lowered, and she seemed very far away. I've never seen such naked sorrow in anyone. The tears were streaming down her face, but Wy sat motionless with her head rested back against the chair. The three of us said nothing for the next hour. It was as if all the molecules of the world had suddenly rearranged themselves.

Sometimes the worst pain is watching someone else in it. I knew that to Wynonna, the end of our partnership meant not just the end of my life, but the end of her life as well. Finally I spoke, "My darling child, this decision is my 'Sophie's Choice.' I'm afraid there are no safe options. Although I can't even imagine ending our career together, I've begun to pray that we will both have a spiritual awakening from this confusion, that this awakening will lead to wholeness and integration. Maybe our wounds can be doorways to our souls. You and I must now give over our willing and trust in our higher power."

Wynonna hadn't moved in the longest time, and she slowly drew her shoulders up as if protecting herself from some sudden gust of cold wind. She never stopped crying. Then Ken spoke, "Wy, you can't push the river, it's time we all face the truth and went with the flow. The main thing is for your Mom to survive this illness. She's got to retire and concentrate on taking care of herself. I'm afraid it's her only chance."

"I feel like I'm dying," Wynonna finally uttered. A shadow moved across her face, and she closed her eyes. "Then I quit too," she said in a soft flat voice. "I'm outta here. I'm gonna move in with Mom, 'cause all I care about is being with her."

"I've always believed that I appreciated this career more than you Wynonna, but the reality is that you need it more than me," I spoke up. "You need to sing like you need to breathe. I've crawled over broken glass to get us here, so don't you dare think for one instant that you're gonna throw it all away young lady! You're gonna carry on the family business. God gave you your talent, and it's your destiny to use it. I'm not going to allow you to let our organization and fans down. Together, we're gonna work through this. The first thing you need to do whenever you find yourself in a hole is to stop digging!"

When we returned to Nashville, Wynonna and I were numb and went straight to our therapist. We began by talking about the unusual depth of our relationship. The therapist asserted we were going to have to cut that psychological umbilical cord that was still attached. Like everyone else who knows us, she acknowledged that she'd never before seen such a bond between a parent and child. Perhaps it was because from the instant Wynonna was conceived, I had to fight for her. I always felt as if she were mine and mine alone, just the two of us against the cruel unpredictable world. I was willing to claw and scratch and fight for her. As a single parent, I was constantly shielding her from those who didn't understand her extreme vulnerability and artistic temperament. I'd carried her on my back into adulthood. I realize now, I did her no favor by trying to do everything for her. Even after she hitched her wagon to my star, I held the reins. It was time to turn them over to her.

Human beings live about 80 percent in their subconscious mind and only about 20 percent in their consciousness. This is scary, because it means we act mostly out of old impulses; without even being aware of what we're doing. It prevents us from being all we can be.

Wynonna began opening herself up, becoming a detective in her own life. "Mom and I had a love-hate relationship," she informed the therapist. "Now when I look back, I'm starting to see what I did, and I'm mortified. I was tormenting her when I was threatening not to go onstage and refusing to sing. I can see that I did that because I know how much I depend on, need, and love her. I resented my complete dependence on her, so I would do things like show up late on purpose, I mean show up late for a TV show and embarrass her in front of crews. I don't do drugs and stuff, and never was into that mess, but my rebellion was in making her wait on me, because I'm the lead singer."

As we discussed Wy's overwhelming concern of losing me, the therapist explained Elisabeth Kübler-Ross's study, that there are certain stages of grieving that everyone must go through when suffering a loss, whether it's loss of dreams, a life plan, a life, a love affair, a friendship, a limb, a pet, etc. There's denial with shock and numbness, anger with searching and yearning, disorientation and bargaining disorganization, depression, and it is hoped, acceptance through resolution and reorganization.

She declared that fear is the most evil thing on earth. Since fear and peace or love are the exact opposites, you cannot experience love and fear in the same moment. The therapist suggested we work on trying to replace fear with love. C. S. Lewis calls God "the love that loves all loving," so we saw that fear is definitely of the devil.

Wynonna and I would go back out on the road and each afternoon in the motel room we'd discuss the life-saving lessons we were learning. The rest of the day, Wynonna reminded me of Tom Hanks's character in the movie *Big*, because she was like a child trapped in an adult's body trying to pretend she was okay and going about her business.

Although I'd doubled my dosage of interferon, my ALT still remained way too high. It was do a show, take a shot. One night

Wynonna came into my bedroom on the bus to kiss me good night just in time to see me injecting myself. She began to cry in frustration and asked, "Mommy, why do you even bother since the inflammation is still going on?"

I answered matter-of-factly, " 'Cause honey, who knows what I would be like if I didn't give myself the shots."

Early the next morning, September 1, as the bus dropped us off for a couple of days at home, I noticed on my calendar that I was off the interferon program. The Mayo Clinic's program began July 1988, and because it was still in the experimental stages, patients are only allowed to be on the medicine for six months. If they relapse, they're later allowed to take it a second time.

There was another significant event happening that day. Ken had wanted to provide Wynonna and me with a beautiful new bus for our last days together on the road, so as Gaylon pulled up in my driveway he reminded me, "Mamaw, since this is the last time you'll ever see the *Dreamchaser,* you need to get all of your things off."

As I stuffed all my personal affects into big Hefty bags and dragged them up through the bus, Wynonna and Gaylon looked so pitiful as they sat there watching me. "I've always said that my room was my 'womb' and now I feel like I'm having a hysterectomy," I squalled half-laughing, half-crying.

Yet as I stood in my kitchen doorway watching this bus that had been our home and represented our career and life together pull away out of sight, fear set in. There was no more interferon, no more *Dreamchaser* and soon there would be no more music. I called out to Larry, but found a note on the counter saying that he was out at the farm bush hogging. Sitting at my kitchen table having my cup of special coffee, I started imagining that I might not live to see Wynonna and Ashley get married and would, therefore, never know my grandchildren. Such paranoid thoughts were too painful.

I jumped in my car and drove straight down to Main Street in Franklin to a store called Magic Memories to buy lace christening gowns, handmade baby blankets, and Beatrix Potter dishes for these future grandchildren. I thought of what I wanted to say to them in a letter to be packed away in a chest with all their heirlooms.

Out of nowhere, as I was walking around the store, I realized that this fear and darkness was from Satan himself, the author of doubt and despair. God doesn't send sickness and trials, Satan does! The devil was trying to make me give up. Knowing the Bible gives us scriptural authority to rebuke Satan and command him to flee from us, I began doing just that, and out loud too!

I was experiencing a very valuable lesson. There is evil in the world and in our heart, and if we don't acknowledge it, our naïveté can lead to serious trouble! The angel of belief and the devil no doubt can both play roles in a well-rounded faith. I told my friend Gloria, the store owner, what was going on, and we discussed how truth has a stopping point and insists on defense and 100 percent commitment, but insight has many layers. It involves imagination and awareness and invites reflection and further exploration. I used her phone to call Wynonna, Tony, Larry, and three of the Elders of our church to arrange for a prayer healing that very night.

Called "The Four J's," Jim Enoch, Jack Hughes, and John Saucier (along with Jesus), these three wonderful older men are amazing prayer warriors on a first-name basis with the Lord. They anointed me with oil, and that night I claimed my healing. I stepped out in faith, just I had that disturbing night on the porch at Charles Bidderman's house back in 1979 after we'd just moved to Nashville and found ourselves penniless, jobless, and homeless. That earnest prayer had been answered with a miraculously successful career. Now once again against seemingly impossible odds, I was asking for another miracle. I prayed that I might live and that Wynonna and I would rise from the ashes of our loss as whole and happy women.

I decided that all my physical symptoms were temporary and focused on the restoration of my health.

Hope is a gift we give ourselves and remains when all else is gone. It propels us beyond doubt and keeps us from sinking in our fears. It helps us picture the way we want things to be so we can bring them about. From that night on, hope was my constant companion.

Let Me Tell You About Love

*L*IFE IS HARD. Wynonna and I had begun open-heart surgery on our relationship. We knew we'd have to learn how to live all over again. Because Wy was experiencing very strange nightmares, I began sleeping with the door open between our rooms in the bus. I'd be awakened in the middle of the night hearing her hollering out and thrashing around. She dreamed she could breathe under water.

For the next month our life was an untidy sprawl of events; our only anchor was doing the shows at night. Then came October 8, 1990, time for the CMA Awards Show. Wynonna, Ashley, Larry, Ken, Martha, and I were still the only ones who knew that my ride was coming to an end. Although it was our seventh CMA, Wynonna and I were as nervous as if it had been our first. After having always revealed so much about ourselves, it was difficult to contain this secret, yet I didn't want to spoil the award show. We'd decided to wait until a week afterward to make a public statement of my retirement.

At the rehearsal for our performance, some of the stagehands commented to Wynonna that she seemed unusually uptight. She flashed me a panicky "what am I gonna tell 'em?" look. I winked and smiled at her, then Wynonna rallied with, "Let's just say, till you've walked a mile in a man's moccasins, you can't imagine the smell!"

When we were finished, I sat on the edge of the fabled Grand Ole Opry stage soaking up the behind-the-scenes excitement. There now were so many newcomers I dubbed them "The Youth Brigade." We met Mark Collie, Joe Diffie, Mark Chestnut, Diamond Rio, Brooks and Dunn, Hal Ketchum, Shenandoah, Sammy Kershaw, Lee Roy Parnell, Aaron Tippin, Collin Raye, and Tracy Lawrence.

Beginning to feel like an old-timer, I got up and sauntered back into the Opry House to Roy Acuff's room to hang out with him. As usual, I found him straddling a chair in his doorway. Roy hugged me and invited me to "sit and visit a spell."

"Mr. Roy," I began, "I was thinking about you the other night as I was reading something interesting on the bus. Scientists have figured out four things that exist in people who live to be very old."

"Well do tell!" Roy exclaimed. "I want to live another eighty-seven years!"

I listed them for him: "Optimism, keeping busy, activity and mobility, and ability to adapt to loss."

"Yep, I'll go along with that," he laughed knowingly. "The Grand Ole Opry has helped me stay in touch with all four of those."

When I told Roy that for the first time in history by the year 2000 older folks would outnumber the young, he wistfully remarked, "I'm not sure I'll be around to see that happen."

Our conversation got around to our shared belief that country music is important to America, because it speaks of morals, wisdom, truth, and righteous lifestyles for people. "It was incubated in the homes, small towns, factories, and churches," Roy elaborated.

"Well I guess you could call us musician-aries!" I quipped, as I got up to hug him good-bye.

As I strolled back out to the *Dreamchaser* to get dressed for the show, I stopped in to visit artist friends on their buses parked side by side. I petted Nancy and George Jones's little dog, as George told me about how worried he'd been about some health problems Nancy was having. I kept my secret to myself. Newcomer Garth Brooks was passing a football with his sound engineer. "I see we're booked on a bunch of dates to open for you and Wy, and we're looking forward to it," Garth called to me as he was completing a pass.

Wynonna and I always enjoy the award shows because all the artists come together, and we perceive the whole event as a celebration. Unaware I had hepatitis, in my acceptance speech the year before, I'd said, "One of the most important scriptures is 'And this too shall pass.'" It seemed so ironic now. We had had a family Bible study at the Strickland reunion and Larry's dad, Ralph, had brought this passage to my attention saying, "Realizing this truth helps us to relish our fleeting peak experiences and offers comfort that the hard times don't last forever either."

Unfortunately, for some, the award shows aren't much more than exalted games and personality contests. We all know competition can be destructive. Preferring teamwork, I've never been much for competition. In fact, I find it quite enough of a challenge living up to the expectations I have for myself! I remember being aware of this even as a child playing musical chairs, when I'd watched disappointed children's faces as they were systematically excluded, until only one smug little boy remained.

Now don't get me wrong. Wy and I *love* the validation of being acknowledged for our efforts. And being honored is actually a double thrill, because not only do I enjoy the pat on the back but I want it for my daughter as well. When we share and celebrate this joy together, it's compounded!

While putting on our makeup, Wynonna and I began discussing the fact that success and excellence are often competing ideals. "Why do you say that being successful doesn't necessarily mean you're excellent?" Wynonna wondered.

"Success is achieving or attaining goals that will elevate your importance in society, whereas excellence is striving for quality in your personal work, regardless of whether the culture recognizes it or not," I answered. "It seems to me that success is only after money, fame, and power, but excellence is knowing in your heart that you've done your absolute best."

Wy and I feel so fortunate to know so many artists who understand the difference, like our friends Christopher Parkening, one of the greatest guitarists in the world, and Kathleen Battle, a beautiful soprano for the Metropolitan Opera.

As that old Mayberry philosopher Gomer Pyle says: "Surprise! surprise! surprise!" We won Duo of the Year for the seventh time in a row. Our acceptance speeches were a hormonal convergence. Wy said, "I want to thank you guys for allowing me to realize that I've

got the coolest Mom in the universe!" I stated my grateful acknowl-
edgment of "my first-born child and my heavenly Father, from whom
all blessings flow." Then I faltered, stopping abruptly to stammer,
"I'm sorry, words aren't enough."

The moment we came offstage, instead of allowing us to be
whisked away to the press tent, a pale Chuck Thompson escorted us
straight to the bus. "Ken has had another heart attack," Chuck began
in a somber tone. "He made me swear to wait until you'd won your
award to take you to him at the hospital." Ken's sense of helplessness
at not being able to intervene in my health crisis, the added stress of
this award show, and our upcoming retirement press conference
created stress leading to excruciating angina. As he had for seven
straight years, Ken had been determined to escort us to the wings for
our performance. Then he was rushed to the hospital.

We found the entire Stilts family nervously pacing the waiting
room of the cardiac care unit. The head nurse came in to tell us Ken
had refused to be sedated until he saw Wy and me. Just as she was
leading us into the unit, a code was called over the loudspeaker and
the nurse turned on her heels and fled. We all feared that Ken had
had a cardiac arrest, and his devoted wife, Jo, broke down. I hurriedly
gathered everyone in a circle. In our fancy gowns and tuxedos, we all
joined hands to pray that Ken might be spared.

Suddenly I looked up at Jo and her children, Tina, Steve, and
K.J., and informed them I'd had a premonition that Ken had turned
the corner and was now out of danger. It was a mighty bold statement to make, but I'd never been so sure of anything. Just then the
nurse returned to the waiting room and said, "He's all right now."

At Ken's bedside, Wynonna and I each took one of his hands
and smiling through tears Wynonna teased him, "What are you trying
to do, upstage Mom?" When Ken was later sent to the Mayo Clinic
to replace his occluded right carotid artery, I suggested he ask if we
weren't eligible for a family discount.

Wy and I went to Caesar's in Vegas for a week, and Ken
reminded us we needed to tell our organization about my retirement
before announcing it to the public. As he called everyone together in
his suite, once again I was concerned about the effect from all this
stress on him. Ashley flew in from California. She, Wy, and I stood

together holding hands in the hall waiting for Ken to get everyone assembled and quieted down. Wynonna seemed like a lost child.

"Are you okay sweetheart?" I asked her.

"My skin is closer than it seems," she answered matter-of-factly.

After my daughters and I were seated, I looked around at our extended family and declared, "The time has come, the walrus said, to speak of many things." The look that passed between us all was more telling than the words that followed.

Completely unable to fathom my doing anything other than this career, Pops Webber blurted out with choked emotion, "Mamaw! What on earth will you do?" Assuming my Mamaw personality I responded, "Maybe I'll turn my carport into a beauty shop!"

Ken, Martha, Wynonna, Ashley, and I returned to my room where I then had to call and inform Brent and Don back home in Nashville. They couldn't believe it. Our *Love Can Build a Bridge* album would be our last studio album together. We returned to Nashville to face the dreaded press conference.

I was not physically well, Wynonna was a basket case, so everything was left to poor Ken—as usual. "Girls, although RCA has moved to a new site, I thought you might want to do your press conference in the old room where it all began when you were signed to RCA after your live audition. I also figured you'd like to compile the list of press people to be in attendance." This was such an intimate occasion, I personally selected the media representatives.

When the limousine came to our home to take Wynonna, Ashley, Larry, and me down to Music Row, everyone acted as if we were on our way to a funeral. As the limo pulled up behind the old RCA building next to the Dumpster where we used to throw our bags of ripe garbage, I smiled over at Wy and commented, "The more things change, the more they stay the same."

Once again, Wynonna and I were like those two lost, scared little girls back in '83.

The four of us had been holding hands and as we saw Ken approaching to get us out of the car. I looked up at Wy, Ashley, and Larry and whispered, "I just want you to know that in all this darkness you are the light I see by."

As Ken led us into the familiar building he paused for a moment and apologized. "Girls, I hadn't expected it to be so depressing in here. There's no carpet on the floors, just dingy drywall and bare dirty windows. Everybody's sitting on metal folding chairs and there's no heat. I'm afraid it looks pretty desolate." Indeed the grayness of the concrete and the dreary darkness of that rainy October day reflected our moods.

All eyes were on me as we entered the room. A week earlier at the award show, there had been much speculation after Wy had unwittingly held on to me to help me to the stage, where we delivered our emotional acceptance speeches. Rumors were flying that something serious was going on with my health. Wrong as usual, the tabloids insisted I had cancer.

The president of RCA, Jack Weston, rose to his feet, and gave me a lingering hug before beginning to address the room. Jack's voice quivered as he spoke of RCA's love for us. My mind flashed back to my unplanned wedding at age seventeen when I'd also had no choice but to stand by helplessly as a kind official solemnly presided over another ceremony that changed my life.

Then it was my turn to speak, but for almost a minute nothing would come out. Finally, I declared, "Today is pretty much the most difficult day of my life. I have to resign. I must retire from the music industry I love so much." I began grasping for words as tears flowed. "There is simply no way to tell you what these seven years have meant to me. It has been the adventure of a lifetime."

I thought I heard the sound of breaking glass. There! The painful words were out. Ken was visibly shaking, and Wynonna was weeping openly. Ken announced that Wynonna would continue on, and that the next year she would release her first solo effort on the new label, MCA.

Our multimedia, music journalist friend Robert Oermann, with concern written across his face, raised his hand to ask the first question. "Can you have a liver transplant, Naomi?"

"Yes," I responded, "but only as a last resort. It has the highest mortality rate of any surgery, requiring twelve hours on the operating table. It creates ongoing medical problems, and the recipient must be on antirejection drugs the rest of his or her life. But the first problem is in finding a donor. One out of every three candidates for a liver transplant dies before a liver is available."

There were other questions and many people simply wanted to express their concern and best wishes for my health and for Wynonna's future.

Unexpectedly, Wynonna announced that she was postponing her impending marriage to Tony King to devote all of her time to me. I was hearing this for the first time along with everyone else. "Always a bridesmaid, never a bride," I thought to myself. I felt guilty about interrupting Wy's life and considered the irony that I'd always figured the only reason we'd ever stop touring would be so she could have a family.

Before we rose to leave, I vowed to survive. I thanked our media friends for coming, for their support and friendship throughout the years. "You've allowed me to have more incredible experiences in my forty-four years of life than a hundred people have in full lifetimes. This is not the end, but just a continuing chapter in the saga of the Judds."

Once out in the privacy of the hall, Wynonna, Ashley, Larry, Ken, Martha, and I stared at each other in tearful disbelief. Now the world knew.

To prevent the distraction of TV crews, as we had done with our wedding, Ken had Bud Schaetzle singlehandedly film the press conference. Bud gave us quick hugs, called me "Wonder Woman," and departed to the editing booth to get the footage distributed to television. Everyone in our organization was going to Ken's house to watch the onslaught of media coverage we knew was imminent. Wynonna, Ashley, Larry, and I were so numb we didn't know what we wanted to do. Wy was holding my hand so tightly she almost cut off the circulation. "I think we'll just go on home," I muttered in a thin, faraway voice.

We didn't want anything to do with the limo once we got back home, because it was too show biz. All of us had been too nervous to eat anything that day. Larry and I got into our truck, and Wynonna and Ashley followed us in Wy's old Ford pickup to Dotsons Restaurant in Franklin. Just as we pulled up side by side in the parking lot at 4:30 P.M. on October 17, a news bulletin came on radio station WSIX.

"Ladies and gentlemen, today at 3:00 P.M., in the old RCA building, country music superstars Naomi and Wynonna Judd announced to the world that mother Naomi must retire because of a life-threatening liver disease."

I slowly looked over at Wynonna in her truck. Her head was resting against the steering wheel, and she was crying. She turned in my direction and our eyes met. I kissed Larry on the cheek and suggested he go on inside and eat with Ashley. "Wynonna and I need to be together," I said softly.

As I climbed up into the cab of her truck, our sorrow was palpable. The emptiness of renunciation immobilized us and I don't know how long we sat there listening to the radio and the rain. Wy murmured, "I feel like I'm dying, Mommy." Just then the radio station began playing *Love Is Alive*.

Still unaware of the news, Franklin locals coming out of the restaurant smiled and waved at us under their umbrellas. We flipped to WSM, just as our buddy Kevin O'Neal, the program director, came on the air. Kevin had been at home when he'd heard the announcement, and had rushed over to the station. "Folks, I am so upset by this sad news I want to do something! I know that there will have to be, at some point in time, a last concert for the girls. I think we should start a petition to insist they have their final performance here at home in Nashville. I'm going to send our mobile units out onto the streets with petitions to sign, and we'll leave the doors open here at our studio so people can walk in off the street and sign up."

Wynonna and I were touched by Kevin's gesture, but it had not yet crossed our minds that there would have to be a final show. Singing together one last time was too bizarre even to consider.

Visibly upset by this prospect, Wynonna pulled out of the parking lot and began driving aimlessly around the back roads of Williamson County. These were the very same roads we used to drive when we were searching for a home after we moved here in 1979. I realized we were alone together once again in unknown territory. Just then I had a strange premonition that my illness would become a trailhead to hidden paths on a journey to find peace.

As darkness fell, we listened to Judd songs on every country radio station on the dial. People were calling, in disbelief, to verify the report. George Jones came on the air and said, "If you're listening out there, girls, I just want you to know that Nancy and I love you."

When fans began telling stories about how much our music meant to them, Wynonna and I were able to smile through our tears.

We had no idea what time it was, as Wy and I finally drove back to her farm. There were no lights on and it seemed as if we were the only two people in the world. We plopped down side by side on the couch in her TV room. As soon as we flipped on CNN, there was the announcement. It was on TNN and all three networks for the 10 o'clock news. It seemed as if by now the whole world knew. Wynonna said it felt like being in an old *Twilight Zone* episode, because of the eerie sensation of being in limbo. When Wy dropped me off at my home after midnight, she hugged me good night for the longest time and slipped me a card she'd written before leaving to go to RCA that afternoon. I read it just before getting into bed and cried myself to sleep.

Then began a great blizzard of publicity. Wy proclaimed us "The Media Goddesses." The next morning my retirement was on the front page of all the newspapers. I stayed home to rest, packing for another pilgrimage to the Mayo Clinic. Larry was watching one of our favorite shows on TNN, *Crook and Chase*. As Lorianne Crook began announcing my retirement, she broke down and wept, leaving Charlie Chase to fumble with her lines. I wanted to reach out and hug my friend and assure her, "It's okay, don't cry for me. Somehow I'm gonna make it."

Upon my arrival at the Mayo Clinic, I saw the initial concern in Dr. Dalton's face knowing that it had now been three weeks since I'd been off the interferon. I told him, "I have begun studying the relationship between the mind and body. I'm sure that you would agree with me that one of medicine's greatest frontiers is immunology, the study of how the immune system can heal the body. I have lots of questions, and I'm going to follow where they lead me. I'm educating myself so I can heal myself!"

Knowing that today's doctors are overwhelmed by their patient

October 17, 1990
2:15 p.m.

Dearest Mommy –

This morning I sat outside my barn taking in God's creation and listening to the silence eager to hear His voice – He must be the only Master who could possibly grasp all these things that I feel. The words you wrote "silence so deep only my soul can hear" echoed in my head. I truly believe with all my heart that in time you and I will come to understand better why? and what his reasons are for all that is happening to you and I.

This day brings a great sadness in my life. I have come to love you with such an overwhelming and

desparate love that I cannot
grasp the idea of us not
being side by side on the
stage. But there is a small
bit of hope inside me that
deep down within me I know I
must reach for and cling to with
all my might. With the help
of the people around me and
Gods grace and his love for
all of us, I know we will
be alright.
          I love you, I admire
your faith and your strength.
You'll never really know
though how incredibly much
you have touched my life.
          ·ⁿYour oldest Daughter·ⁿ

load and keeping up with new advances in technology, I wasn't surprised that Dr. Dalton hadn't gotten around to investigating psychoneuroimmunology (PNI).

But I had. *Psycho* refers to the mind; *neuro* refers to the body's nervous system, which transmits messages from the mind throughout the body; and *immunology* is the body's innate, natural ability to defend itself. The mind controls the body so it can stimulate the immune system or harm it.

What this means is the power of our thoughts cannot be overestimated! Our emotions and our perceptions of the world cause our brain to send out messages that are then translated into actual bodily reactions. For example, if I embarrass you, you are going to blush, demonstrating how your mind instigates an instant body reaction. The mind is the deepest influence on the body. Asthmatics have been known to sneeze at plastic flowers. People with terminal illnesses who've been given a prognosis of a limited length of time to survive sometimes endure beyond that limit to make it to a significant event like a relative's wedding. Intense rage or fear can precipitate a fatal heart attack.

Our attitudes, beliefs, and emotional states, ranging from love and compassion to fear and anger, can trigger chain reactions that affect our blood chemistry, heart rate, and the activity of every single cell and organ system in the body. A great book written by leading authorities from the nation's top medical centers called *Mind, Body, Medicine* by Daniel Goleman and Joel Gurin is full of indisputable facts from research in many areas. Blair Justice, author of a very accessible book, *Who Gets Sick,* says, "We're in the midst of as dramatic a transformation as has ever occurred in science." Dr. Justice refers to the work of Dr. Candace Perth, a biochemist with the National Institute of Mental Health, which proves that emotions aren't just in the brain, they're in the body. Dr. Perth studies neurotransmitters and neuropeptides, which are the biochemical equivalents of thought.

The placebo effect also shows us how our mind can influence our body. As a nurse, I personally saw this phenomenon. When the doctor prescribed nothing more than a plain sugar pill to a patient, he experienced the desired physical effect, as if the phony pill had actually contained real medicine.

As a nurse and a patient, I found all this revolutionary scientific data to be thrilling. It means that we all have control over our bodies! The recognition of the mind's ability to help the body will inspire a whole new way of thinking about healing. The mind-body connection will lead to the overthrow of obsolete, rigid perceptions and expensive medical practices. Medicine has already proved unsatisfactory and materialistic by not seeing the patient as a whole human being.

As we discussed psychoneuroimmunology, Dr. Dalton acknowledged that through the years he'd definitely observed how important social support, friends, family, optimism, hope, and a sense of control are to a patient's recovery. Dr. David Spiegel at Stanford University School of Medicine has documented how patients with a caring family and a good attitude have a much better chance at recovery. More than a decade ago, attempting to learn how he could help women dying from breast cancer, he began organizing support groups for them. Dr. Spiegel found that women in his support group ultimately lived an average of eighteen months longer than other women with comparable breast cancer and medical care who were not involved in a support system.

Dr. Dalton and I talked about how stress seriously harms the body and undermines its ability to deal with disease. Thirty years ago, before the field of PNI opened up, Dr. Hans Seyle pioneered studies on how stress can break down the body's protective mechanisms. Although he recognized that stress is part of our lives and can't be avoided, he discovered that it's not the stress itself but how you perceive and handle it that determines how it affects the body. I'm under stress daily, but I love my career so I handle it well. Wy says, "We try to coexist peacefully with stress and remind ourselves we're human beings, not human doings!"

Therapists like Jon Kabat-Zinn, head of the Stress Reduction Clinic at the University of Massachusetts Medical Center, uses meditation to control stress, pain, and illness. I personally practice my own form of meditation every morning in my devotional quiet time. Taking afternoon walks when I'm on the road or strolling in my valley at the farm in the evenings are all ways of relaxing, being in the moment, listening to my inner stirrings, and increasing awareness and mindfulness. I tell Wynonna, "When you can't change the way things are, change the way you feel about them!"

When I worked in the cardiac care unit, I came across a medical report that stated that more heart attacks occur on Monday mornings at 9:00 A.M., causing more people to die at that precise time than any other day or time of the week. This statistic alone speaks volumes about how powerful and dangerous stress is! In addition to obvious physical risk factors for heart disease like hypertension, heredity, smoking, being overweight, and stress, the two most important risk factors are a person's self-happiness rating and job dissatisfaction.

I never thought much about the brain and the mind being two different things, but the brain is an organ that actually has matter and the mind is an information process, responsible to the constant communication going on within the body. The mind is what the brain does. Some people consider their body as a lump below their neck that they have to drag around, considering it an accident waiting to happen, programmed to destruction. But that's not so! Every cell in the body is alive and metabolizing. Molecular biologists have proven that every cell in the body changes every six months. My close friend, Dr. Deepak Chopra, one of the pioneers in the mind-body frontier who combines modern science with ancient wisdom, says the body hears and believes everything the mind says. The body is a continually constructive process that wants to heal itself and maintain balance. The body is a miracle!

For a chronically ill person, a miracle is something that occurs suddenly and unexpectedly and not in association with any form of treatment. The medical term doctors use for a miracle is *spontaneous remission*. I was proud to meet Stephen Rosenberg, chief of surgery at the National Cancer Institute, who knows firsthand about medical miracles. A patient of his was miraculously cured of a particularly aggressive type of cancer. This man had fist-size tumors in his stomach, three tumors in the liver, and hardened lymph nodes. Although he should have died within a few months, Mr. D'Angelo had a spontaneous and complete remission of his cancer!

Dr. Rosenberg was so excited and inspired after witnessing this miracle, he began pioneering cancer treatment. In his book *The Transformed Cell*, Rosenberg says, "It is every immunologist's dream to use the immune system to cure cancer." Dr. Rosenberg and his wife, Alice, an R.N., are the sort of brilliant and compassionate healers we need more of. They told me, "People care about how much you know, but they also need to know how much you care."

I personally witnessed a miracle. As soon as I'd returned from my first visit to the Mayo Clinic, my dear friend Assistant Pastor Dan Scott introduced me to a nice-looking young man named Steve Shima. In 1990, Steve was diagnosed with angiofibroma, a tumor the size of an egg that was so advanced it had thirty-three feeding vessels. The tumor was wrapped around his optic nerve and attached to the carotid artery deep in the base of the skull. Although doctors had given up on him, Dr. Robert Cantrell, a surgeon and ophthalmologist at the University of Virginia Hospital at Virginia Beach, chair of the head and neck division, was so impressed by Steve's faith, he believed that Steve possessed the potential to be healed. In an amazingly complicated surgery, the surgeons took out Steve's left eyeball to gain access deep into his skull.

There was no trace of cancer anywhere! An audible gasp went up in the operating theater, because many of the surgeons and nurses immediately feared they'd operated on the wrong patient. Dr. Cantrell pointed to the x-rays, CAT scans, and MRI scans taken only days earlier to identify Steve. This case is a documented medical miracle.

Steve and I have become very close and feel as if we're members of some special club. I call it the Plank Club because we've walked out to the edge of the plank. You cannot come this close to death and not have a life-changing experience! Steve's now an ordained minister and remains cancer-free.

Every doctor with whom I've talked has stories about miracles they've witnessed. I joined the Institute of Noetic Sciences in Sausalito, California, which promotes research and education on mind-body medicine. The founder, Edgar Mitchell, received his doctorate from MIT. As an *Apollo* astronaut, he was the sixth man to walk on the moon. His institute is a group of our nation's most brilliant doctors, writers, biologists, anthropologists, and other scientists.

The institute has published an encyclopedic volume of more than one thousand cases of medically reported spontaneous remissions. As project director Caryle Hirshberger, a biochemist and cancer researcher, says they hope "it will be useful to doctors and restore hope to patients. Spontaneous remission may be the best evidence for a system of natural self-repair." I was hoping for a spontaneous remission myself, but also knew I needed to work like the dickens at certain things every day to achieve my goal!

I told Dr. Dalton that back home on the days after I'd had blood drawn, my hand would be shaking as I phoned the lab for the results. It seemed as if my very life hinged on that report. One day shortly after my prayer healing, Wynonna and I were leaving Vanderbilt Hospital when we saw a bumper sticker that said "Ask Me About My Grandchildren." Wynonna commented, "Mom, I'm gonna have a bumper sticker made for you that says 'Ask Me About My ALT,' 'cause everyone seems to gauge your future by your blood work!"

Then she said something very revealing: "Mom, I realize now that if such a terrible thing could happen to the Queen of Everything, the world in general is no longer a safe place."

I told her I was no longer afraid to call and find out about my lab results. I'd discovered that security is not in a lab report, CAT scan, x-ray, or biopsy. I wanted her to understand that security comes from within.

Before I left the Mayo Clinic, as always, Dr. Dalton instructed me to go home to rest. He'd been insisting all along that I retire, so when I told him we were embarking on a farewell tour, let's just say he was not pleased. "Then I don't think you should do more than maybe one show a month, Naomi, and only then if you feel up to it."

I told Dr. Dalton we were about to schedule the Farewell Tour, explaining that I needed a year not only to work Wynonna through her grief of losing me as her partner, but also to help her overcome her fears of going solo. I insisted I needed to disengage myself as naturally as I could from a career that meant the world to me. I promised to return for a checkup afterwards to prove to him that PNI works!

Although concerned about me, Dr. Dalton left me with these

parting words: "Naomi, if anybody in the world can pull this off, you can."

Back home, it was time to get down to the nuts and bolts of arranging this Farewell Tour. Ken addressed me in a grave tone: "Naomi, I really want you take some time to consider seriously the commitment you're about to make. First of all, it troubles me that you might be jeopardizing your health, and I'm also concerned about the reputation you and Wy have worked so hard to build up over the years with promoters and fans. What if you have to cancel suddenly?"

"Forget my liver for a minute," I replied. "You know me well enough to know if I had to hang it up right now, I'd flat out die of a broken *heart!* I don't know how long it's going to take, but it's important to me to say thank you and good-bye to fans everywhere. I realize it's very risky, but I'll assume full responsibility for this decision."

They booked us to play in 120 cities across America during a twelve-month period. I had to take a nap after just hearing about it. In our meeting, we tossed around several names for our last tour, and Dwight came up with "Going Out of Business Sale."

Our first concert marking the beginning of the Farewell Tour was at the Sports Arena in Fargo, North Dakota. As our private plane touched down that evening, television crews from the local stations were swarming. Wynonna became quite upset and scowled, "Look at them! Just like people that stop and gawk at a wreck along the highway!"

I admit I had to do a quick attitude adjustment on myself as well. "Look sweetheart, you and I are depending on this tour to work out a lot of critical issues. We're going to have to stay focused on our purpose."

It was a very special show that night. I savored every minute detail of the ritual of preparing for the stage. I took the outpouring of understanding from the audience as a sign. They were telling me I'd made the right decision to do the Farewell Tour.

Wynonna and I were seated side by side on stools, bathed in a beautiful golden light on the darkened, bare stage singing "Guardian Angels." As I looked upon those dear smiling faces, my brave front suddenly cracked. "Tonight is the beginning of the end," I silently admitted to myself as tears filled my eyes. Quickly slipping off my stool, I pretended to go for a glass of water back on the drum riser, but a local newspaper reporter at the side of the stage caught me wiping my tears. The next day he wrote that Wynonna looked suddenly terrified and pained to be left out front alone, a poignant glimpse into the future. As I rejoined her, I spontaneously made a self-fulfilling prophecy to the crowd: "You all are now our guardian angels: The Lord is my doctor and the fans are my medicine." It was the only reference made all night to my illness.

It was imperative that we not mention my retirement. I reminded Wynonna every night before we took the stage that I would have no part of any self-pity. Except for a veiled mention of gratitude to the audience for their support during a "difficult time," our concerts continued to be high-spirited jubilation, appropriately tough, tender, or funny as each song's mood dictated. I reinforced our professionalism to Wynonna by demanding, "Don't you dare get out there and cry or act maudlin. These good people have paid their hard-earned money to be entertained and lifted up. Besides, they have their own problems!"

Our first network television appearance after the retirement announcement undermined all my good intentions. Not only were we intimidated by being in the presence of the venerable Barbara Walters for her prime-time special, but it would be the first time we would speak publicly about the end of our duet.

The very first question Barbara asked me was about Brian's death. Now with our recent news, the last thing in the world Wy and I expected was a question about the past! Unfortunately, my Mom happened to be there at Wynonna's house that afternoon, sitting off camera behind Barbara. I saw the look on Mom's face as she was being reminded she could possibly now lose a second child. I struggled to change the subject, but we lost control of our emotions the minute the interview began.

Next, the first question Barbara asked Wynonna was, "What are you going to do the first time you're onstage alone and you look over and see your Mom's not there?"

No one had brought this up yet, and Wynonna's knee-jerk reaction of pain and fear reflected all over her face on national television. Although we rallied to stress the positive and talk about upbeat things, we were not able to direct her questions. Most people don't realize that an artist has no control whatsoever about the way a show is edited. The same is true for magazine or newspaper interviews. In fact, we don't even get to pick the photographs!

By the time we did the *Donahue* show which is taped live in front of a studio audience, we had sorted out our responses and had a better grip. Responding to a question of my prognosis from a concerned fan, I even assured her, "Don't worry honey, this is not my tombstone, this is just a stepping-stone!"

We appeared on the cover of *T.V. Guide* in what would become the year's best-selling edition. Our hosting segment on *Nashville Now* was their most-watched show of the year.

In all our interviews, I attempted to shed light on the mysteries of liver disease, informing people that hepatitis B vaccine to prevent hepatitis B infection is available. I encouraged everyone who works in health care or is at risk to get this life-saving vaccine. The American Liver Foundation asked me to become their first celebrity spokesperson.

Wynonna and I were more than ready for a break! As we do every Thanksgiving, our entire family converged at Mom's. Wib, who's quite a handy man and has turned the garage into a workplace, made a large sign to stick in the front yard proclaiming, "Please respect family time together: No Visitors."

It was the first time for all of us to be together since my diagnosis. Although we didn't refer to it, everyone seemed unusually affectionate. More grateful than ever for my family, I was capturing mental pictures of our ordinary moments. As usual Margaret's husband, Jamie, Larry, Ashley, and Tony were playing hearts at the table in the sunroom, while Josh and Allison revived old toys from the attic that their mother, Mark, and I had once played with. Wynonna was on the couch reading fan mail to her teenage cousin, Erin, while Margaret set the table, and I helped Mom baste the turkey. Mark was quietly reading the farmer's almanac, looking up occasionally to watch Middy feeding baby Brian.

Reverend Mark gave an eloquent blessing, and as we began passing around Mom's delicious traditional Thanksgiving fare, we began an oral tradition I had instigated some years ago. Beginning with Mom, the original Judd, we proceed around the table and everyone articulates what he or she has to be thankful for that year. Since it was especially poignant this year, Mom seemed a bit overwhelmed as she paused to consider which blessing to single out. "Our health and our senses of humor," she offered with a sigh.

Everyone seemed to be taking it quite seriously, and even all-boy Joshua, waving his turkey drumstick, allowed, "My cool family and all that stuff."

Ashley paid recognition to "the indomitable spirit of the Judd matriarchy."

Overcome with emotion, Wynonna was barely audible as she muttered, "Remission. I think it's the most beautiful word in the world."

When brother Mark's choice was "landmarks," we all understood, because it was little Brian's first Thanksgiving.

I was sitting next to Middy, who after a ten-year wait held her baby close to her breast, overcome with emotion; she could only muster a nod downward at his sleeping little face. I'm always last, and it seemed as if everything had been covered.

I was thankful for this wonderful old house that shelters the collective soul of our family dynasty and still holds us together like psychological glue. Mom has lived here for forty-one years now, having purchased it with Daddy from my Judd grandparents before I was barely four years old. Our budding family of six started out sleeping in this room in which we were now eating, renting out the upstairs and attic. During our childhood, as we grew, we took over the whole house. From then on our family was happily intact, insulated from the outside world by familial security, just as these walls and roof protected us from the seasons.

Then just over decade later, after all our lives fell apart from Brian's death, my pregnancy, and Margaret's elopement, everything turned topsy-turvy. Divorced, alone, and starting over, Mom once again had to live downstairs and rent out the upstairs. When Mom married Wib, her life changed completely. She literally moved the house to a new site around the block. Reunited at last, as we look out from within this same home, we all see a new direction!

The old place is a veritable Judd museum, full of mementos from our earliest beginnings, tokens of our accomplishments, a scrapbook showing our spouses, children, and friends who we are. It's a place where time seems to stand still. As I proudly watched Josh performing his first piano piece, my mind wandered back thirty some years ago when Margaret and I shared that piano bench as we played our duet of "Camel Train." Allison now plays jacks on the kitchen floor in the very same spot that Margaret and I, Wynonna, Ashley, and Erin had. Last night when I opened our worn set of children's books to read a bedtime story to Brian, I smiled at the sight of my own crayon scribblings. As the oldest reading to the youngest, I felt as if I were passing the torch. Soon Brian would discover the cigar box of crayons in the cupboard drawer.

The important sense of security and roots this house allows all of us is perhaps most keenly appreciated by Wy, Ashley, and myself, since we've never lived anywhere longer than five years. Like vagabonds in hotels in a different city each night, Wy and I sometimes feel like curators of a disposable culture. Ashley had really needed the cozy familiar constancy and sense of connectedness to her sister and me while she lived in my old bedroom when we were separated during that first year on the road.

Watching Mom teaching Ashley her recipe for chocolate meringue pie, I realized that Mom also passes along her secrets to life. Her wacky sense of humor peppers all our personalities. It even surfaces in Mark's sermons, and it's no small coincidence her first grandchild, Wynonna Judd, happens to be one of the world's funniest people. That Thanksgiving night, as I stopped in to kiss Wy and Ashley good night, I found Mom sitting on the side of their bed, wearing her bathrobe, slippers, and a Judd ball cap.

That week we were the grand marshals in our hometown's holiday parade. The big day kicked off at the local Kentucky Highlands Museum. Wynonna and I donated two of our favorite stage outfits and platinum albums. Everyone, from my grade-school teachers to piano teachers as well as old neighbors, were our guests at the museum reception.

In a formal ceremony on Winchester Avenue, the main street of Ashland's downtown area, the city leaders proclaimed the area between the Presbyterian church and the First American Bank as Judd Plaza.

Wy and I conducted a press conference inside the bank on the same spot where retired president G. B. Johnson, my oldest friend Piper's stepfather, had granted me my first loan. Piper had flown in all the way from San Francisco and stood beside me dabbing her eyes with a handkerchief.

As Wy, Ashley, and I took our place on the grandstand on the sidewalk in front of the bank to view the parade, Ashley whispered to us, "Man, this whole homecoming day is like something out of a movie!" There were Shriners with their fezzes; bikers on their Harleys; school marching bands; baton twirlers; beauty queens waving from convertibles; fire engines; and hundreds of Brownies, Girl Scouts, and Boy Scouts. The three of us jumped to our feet, stomping, whistling, and applauding as the Ramey Boys Home float passed by. The boys made every bit of it themselves and were the grand prize winners. My Mom's good-natured friend, Martha Compton, slipped up beside us to say thirty thousand folks had turned out for the parade. Wy, Ashley, and I felt a powerful sense of community and were so proud to be natives of this fine American town.

We met a struggling local singer that night about whom Mom had been sending me newspaper and magazine clippings. She knew Billy Ray Cyrus from Flatwoods, Kentucky, and some of his family members. Mom introduced Billy Ray to Wynonna and me at our press conference in the bank, but we were surrounded by people and were far too excited and overwhelmed to pay him much mind. As he passed in front of our grandstand during the Thanksgiving parade, Billy Ray flashed us an "I'll be seeing you" smile and raised his fist in his now-famous gesture.

That Christmas of 1990, everyone came to my house for a quiet, restful holiday. Beginning with our first T-shirt back in 1983, I'd been collecting Judd concessions and souvenirs in trunks for Wy, Ashley, and myself and gave them as part of their Christmas presents. Afterward, our whole family packed up and headed for Lake Tahoe for the Judds' annual week-long engagement and New Year's Eve party.

Dolly Parton was playing at another hotel in Tahoe and arranged for Wy and me to be guests at her first show, which happened to be just after our first one. Visiting in her dressing room afterward, standing there with glittery spangles dripping off her cantilevered frame, Dolly surprised us by announcing she was coming with us back to Harrah's to catch our second show. Dolly's childhood friend and longtime personal assistant, Judy Oglesby, leaned over and whispered, "Now this is a rare occasion!"

Walking into our backstage area, Dolly asked, "What side of the stage is yours Naomi? I'll just sit in a folding chair in the wings." During our show, Wynonna and I would look at each other and giggle as we glanced over at our outrageous friend hidden just out of the audience's sight. As we began the quietly acoustic, intimate part of the show, I turned to Wynonna and asked if she thought she could remember all the words to my favorite song even though we hadn't sung it in many years. A look of surprise flashed across Wy's face but after thinking for just a second she answered, "Yes." Without either of us ever saying the name of the tune, we began singing Dolly's "Coat of Many Colors." It was a richly emotional moment for me, finally getting to sing my Daddy's favorite song just before my singing career came to an end. Later Wy and I told Dolly about her song being one of the first we'd learned back in Morrill, Kentucky. I described how our singing it culminated in one of the few times I ever saw my Daddy cry, as he told us about his own coat of many colors.

Dolly, who loves attention as much as I, hadn't been able to remain hidden during our show and ran out onstage during our finale. Afterward in our dressing room, when she tried to sit on a leather couch in her leather pants, Dolly slid right off onto the floor! We busted out laughing.

A few weeks later at the prestigious Grammys in New York, Wy and I met Bette Midler and Mariah Carey at the rehearsal. Both Bette and Mariah had elaborate set designs and a stage full of backup singers for their numbers. As usual, they sent Wy and me out with nothing but a microphone to perform "Love Can Build a Bridge." Feeling intimidated, not to mention slighted, Wynonna was almost too nervous to perform. When I reminded her it would throw the live three-hour program into pandemonium if we didn't sing, she summoned up her professionalism. When we walked out onto the stage that night, we found ourselves singing to Robert Duvall, Jack Nicholson, Richard Gere, Cindy Crawford, and Bernadette Peters in the front row.

"Love Can Build a Bridge" seemed to reach out to people. We'd been inundated with stories from people who were using this song to help heal their relationships. There were letters from women's shelters, sexual abuse clinics, and church and teaching organizations, informing us they'd chosen it as their theme song. Some troops fighting in Operation Desert Storm wrote that they'd made it their unit's anthem, citing not only its brotherhood theme but also the coincidence of the first line: "I'd gladly walk across the desert with no shoes upon my feet, to share with you the last bit of bread I had to eat." We even received word the song and video were being played in such diverse and unlikely places as Moscow!

The next year, when the song was eligible, Wynonna and I won a grammy for Best Country Performance by a Duo or Group with Vocal for "Love Can Build a Bridge," and it was also chosen Best Country Song. I don't write as well as I want to, but I write as well I can, and sometimes I get real lucky and write better than I'm actually capable. That song was definitely one of those times!

Back home in Nashville, as usual, January meant time to put a new stage show together. Ken, Wynonna, and Chris Dunbar, our choreographer, met at my home. Sitting around my kitchen table, we began to compile our last set list. The harsh realization that this was the last time I'd be singing these songs was too overwhelming, and I felt I was beginning to lose control. The positive side is that Wy was touched by my vulnerability. This was the day she began calling me the "wounded healer."

To keep myself on track, I began studying the works of a man who knows as much about the Bible as anyone I've ever come across. At my prayer healing, elder John Saucer had given me a thin volume called *Releasing the Ability of God* by Charles Capps. A simple statement in it helped change our lives. "Words," Capps wrote, "are the most important thing in the universe."

I remember laying the book down on my lap and staring off into space for a moment trying to imagine if that could be possible! I went into Wy's room to show her. "Look Wy," I said," He quotes John 1:1: 'In the beginning was the Word, and the Word was with God, and the Word was God.' This is one of the most incredible, metaphysical statements in the Bible! God spoke the universe into being, and the entire universe stands in obedience to God's words. Genesis 1:3 says: 'And God *said*, Let there be light: and there was light.' "

Wy and I read on together as Capps explained how God's word never changes, but it changes things. I discovered we have the authority to fight evil forces with the words from our mouths through prayer. Proverbs 18:21 says: "Death and life are in the power of the tongue: and those who love it will eat the fruit thereof." Capps's book says the first thing is to "determine what is the will of God." We already knew faith as a spiritual law designed to unlock unseen treasures, and an element that makes prayer work. Prayer gets its power from faith, and faith works by love.

That night Wynonna and I learned a simple but powerful lesson: Never pray the problem, always pray the answer.

Instead of praying, "Lord, I'm afraid the inflammation of my liver is getting worse and it will get out of control and kill me," I began praying the thing I desired. I began saying, "Heavenly Father, I thank you for healing my disease, for the magnificent experiences coming out of this Farewell Tour, for the unification of my family and for Wynonna's emergence as a whole person."

Wy and I began to bird dog each other about saying only positive things. We even brought Charles Capps and his wife, Peggy, out on the road with us. I thanked him by saying, "A teacher for a day is like a parent for a lifetime!"

Everyday I considered God's promises as I continued to investigate the mind-body link. I have an open belief system and an insatiable curiosity, but I also practice discernment. It helps that I'm an R.N.

I was inundated with information regarding treatments, most of which were well intentioned, some of which were valid, but some of which were foolish. I was becoming a clearinghouse for information on liver disease.

Every night people with liver disease, cancer, AIDS, and so on, showed up at the bus door or sent cards and letters. I saw myself in every one of them. There were times I felt overwhelmed by their suffering. All I could do was talk or write to as many as my strength would allow, telling them what I knew to be true. It became yet another extension of our involvement with the fans.

My talented writer friend Belinda Mason, who contracted the HIV virus from a contaminated blood transfusion during a difficult delivery with her second child, Clayton, passed away. Belinda, a white, heterosexual, middle-class female, was on the National Commission for AIDS and struggled to educate people against the stereotyping of AIDS victims. The last time I saw her, we were visiting in my hotel room, and the last thing she ever said to me was, "The quality of life is not measured by length but by the fullness with which we entered into each present moment."

I still felt tired twenty-four hours a day. After a show in Memphis, I was laid out on top of my bed still wearing my stage dress when Wynonna appeared with a concerned look.

"Mom, you just gotta come up front and talk to this lady. She has metastatic breast cancer and a bunch of kids but her husband can't handle it and has left her."

"Send her back to my room," I agreed wearily. I don't remember if that woman even told me her name, but I sure recognized her pain. She was the first stranger I ever prayed over for a healing. As she was leaving, I reached in my bedside drawer and handed her my own little book by Charles Capps. I felt recharged when she left, and told Wynonna, "Compassion fuels the spirit just as passion fuels the body."

Wynonna was becoming very protective and bossy. If I was on my feet too long talking with a fan, she'd grab me around my waist and sweep me up onto the bus. If I stayed up too late determined to read that last fan letter, she'd come up front and flip the master switch on Gaylon's dashboard, leaving me in darkness. When I gave up and finally went back to my room, she'd have my bed turned down and offer to rub my feet.

Sick children were roughest on us. Before they'd come up on the bus, I'd remind Wynonna, "They get enough sympathy in the hospital and at home, we're going to give them a fantasy, some excitement, so don't you dare cry! You can lock yourself up in your room with a box of Kleenex . . . later."

Wy would dramatically introduce me as the Queen of Everything as I appeared in my full-stage outfit wearing my rhinestone tiara. In our ceremony, I would theatrically wave my magic wand and declare, "Abracadabra, fear be banished!" as I gently touched the rhinestone scepter to the top of their little heads. After asking permission of their parents, Wynonna and I would teach a child to sing "Jesus Loves Me."

One night after this ritual, it occurred to me that my whole life is a ceremony. I'm always trying to bridge the gap between the physical and the spiritual, between myself and all the world around me.

Guardian Angels

*T*HE FAREWELL TOUR was becoming a sacred journey. Every time we could slip home for a few days, we'd go straight to our therapist. With great psychological penetration and insight, she became like the North Star that guides travelers and points them in the right direction. She began to show us how to take care of our souls. According to Thomas Moore's book by the same name, care of the soul doesn't involve solving problems, self-improvement, personalities, and relationships, and its goal is not to make life trouble-free. Rather, care of the soul refers to giving our everyday lives, the depth and value that comes from soulfulness. It has to do with cultivating a richly expressive and meaningful life at home as well as out in society, by paying attention to small details as well as major decisions. It has to do with rediscovering and reclaiming our soul.

Everybody's always saying that Wynonna has soul, so I looked it up in the dictionary. Soul is the part of the human being that thinks, feels, and makes the body act. The spiritual part of a person distinct from the physical, it's also the energy or power of mind or feelings spirit fervor. It can also be the essential part, the essence, the substance of a human being, the quality that stirs emotion or sentiment. Soul also has to do with genuine authenticity and depth. I realized soulful can refer to many different things, like food, music, friends, or memorable experiences that touch the heart.

Soul isn't a tangible thing, but a quality of the dimensions of our life experiences, of really knowing ourselves. It has to do with depth, value, relatedness, heart, and personal substance and doesn't necessarily refer to religious belief or immortality. Because the soul is partly in the present and partly in eternity, it became important for me to remember it when I was feeling badly. The thought of my soul continuing on after my bodily demise was helping me face the concept of my mortality. It was definitely helping me to realize what's really important in life. My illness was allowing me to restore my soulfulness. It was teaching Wy and me so much about character, nature, destiny, and time.

The body is a collection of facts so I'd begun paying attention to the signs and symbols of its suffering and distress. I noticed how close the word *symptom* is to the word *symbol!*

Wynonna and I began talking about honoring the expressions of our souls, by living out the ordinary parts of our everyday existence in such a way that contributed to quality, meaning, integrity, and depth.

We began tending to our immediate surroundings, because the soul feeds on whatever life grows in its immediate environment. I believe you become what you see. When fans brought us flowers we attached a permanent vase on our front table and changed them every night. We paid extra attention to our clothes and jewelry. Wy became very selective about the music she played while we were getting ready on the bus. One night I noticed Wynonna studying her guitar as if she were really awakening to its beauty for the first time.

After a show, as we were leaving town, she and I would sit together and read through the fan mail and take time to appreciate their gifts and tokens of friendship. On a typical night I received a bag of Chinese herbs, a plaque of the poem "Footprints," a bottle of KM (a potassium-mineral supplement), two jars of peach preserves, homemade crafts, a dozen portraits of us, crosses and rosaries, a book of devotionals, and a belt saying "S—— Happens." Radio stations made huge cards and had them signed by listeners. Unable to part with any of these items, I built a fan room at my farm in which to store and display them.

Since both of us have always been hearth keepers, we opened our eyes to a new appreciation of our homes, which are filled with personal treasures from our travels. Now when I look at my two favorite pieces of art, I appreciate the spirits of the two women who created them, Jinni Thomas and Martha Slaymaker, both of Albuquerque, New Mexico. Martha, who's a cancer survivor and one of my heroines, formed a network of fellow artists with terminal illnesses for healing through creativity.

While playing in the Southwest, Wynonna and I began studying the American Indians. We found *The Spirit of Native America—Beauty and Mysticism in American Indian Art* by Anna Lee Walters fascinating. In the hundreds of Native American languages, there is no word that comes even close to our definition of art. These Native North Americans never set out to create art for its own sake. In traditional American Indian thinking, there simply is no separation between art and life or between what is functional and beautiful. Wy remarked, "This is the attitude we have toward our music!"

Wynonna and I shared a belief that music is the language of the spirit. Pastor Dan Scott also calls music "the breath of God and a window to heaven." I'd never intellectualized my ritual of listening to peaceful tapes every morning while getting a massage, but now I found out just how it promotes relaxation and creativity.

In my research I began discovering that every bone, tissue, and organ in our bodies has a specific resonance frequency. Certain frequencies can actually effect healing and promote balance! Entrainment is the phenomenon whereby powerful rhythmic vibrations are used to guide the brain into natural rhythms for healing and deep relaxation states. My R.N. and professor sister-in-law, Middy, told me about Our Lady of Peace hospital in Louisville, Kentucky, a mental hospital since 1951 that combines Christian principles into the philosophy of care. They use music to calm agitated patients. Beginning by playing music that matches the manic level of agitation, like heavy-metal music, they gradually decrease the frenetic type of music until the patient is subdued. Wynonna also found all of this music therapy especially interesting.

When we were studying the American Indians at night on bus trips, Wy discovered there's also no native equivalent to our word for religion. To them the ordinary is sacred and all everyday life is a source of religion, part of the infinitely renewable cycle that defines their cosmology. According to Black Elk, an Oglala Lakota holy man, "Peace . . . comes from within the souls of man when they realize their relationship, their oneness with the universe and all its powers, and when they realize that at the center of the universe dwells Wakan-Tanka and that the center is really everywhere, it is within each of us. Wakan-Tanka translates to the great mysterious."

Our church is a personal, sacred place of healing, and Larry, Wynonna, Ashley, and I enjoy the living traditions of community on Sunday mornings when we are home. In his intriguing book *Who Needs God*, Harold Kushner says, "There is a kind of nourishment our souls need, even as our bodies need the right foods, sunshine, and exercise." It's not naive or simple-minded idealism for us, it's a very valuable symbolic, reflective, emotionally satisfying, and unifying ritual. Sunday is our family day. After church, we go to our favorite restaurant and try to spend the day outdoors, if the weather permits. Peaceful Valley is like a personal temple. It's a place where we're fully in touch with all five senses, get recharged, and feel connected to our life force. Monks seclude themselves in monasteries, some Native Americans go off on their vision quests, ascetics go out into the desert, the Judds go out into the country!

The clamor and rush of our busy schedules causes our souls to be habitually neglected. When the soul is neglected it does not go away. Psychologist Robert Sardello points out that psychological symptoms such as loss of values, depression, emptiness, addiction, alienation, meaninglessness, and a tendency toward violence are indications that our souls are trying to get our attention. These negative expressions are signs that our souls are starving for depth and meaning. I think today our individual souls are hungry and the soul of the world is starving! When we don't deal with issues they become repressed. Under our therapist's expert guidance, Wynonna and I began peeling off layers of our consciousness like layers of an onion.

A soulful life consists of many colors and even shadows, and I was trying to help reveal this to Wy. While trying to explain Jung's theory of shadow to Wynonna, I said, "Okay honey, this woman that you've decided to be automatically creates a dark double—the woman you've decided not to be. The dark double consists of the

As a single mom, Naomi struggled to keep her two high-spirited, teenage girls in line. Here are nineteen-year-old Wy and fifteen-year-old Ashley in the kitchen of the Del Rio Pike home.
(SLICK LAWSON)

Wy meets newborn cousin, Brian Judd, in June 1990, the date before Mom's breast biopsy.

The Judd home was purchased from Naomi's grandparents when she was four. Naomi's mother still lives here, and this is how it looks today.

Ashley, wearing braces, reading to Wy on the bus late at night, on the road to the next show.

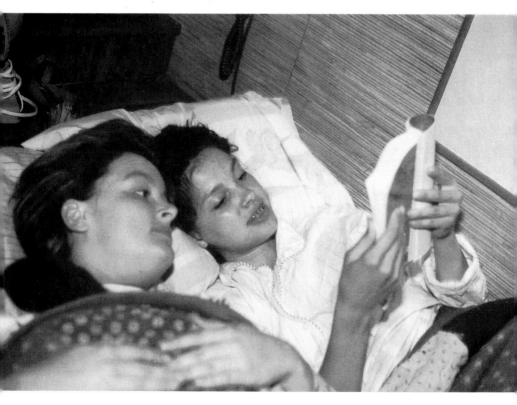

Backstage with godchild Casey Robertson, Larry, and friends Steve and Karen Shima. Naomi and Steve became close after his miraculous recovery from cancer.

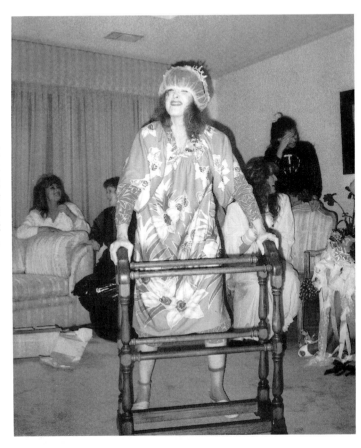

Naomi at her bridal shower imitates an old lady, using a quilt rack as a walker. Wy sits at far left and Ashley stands at right, laughing.

While touring, Naomi and Wy would stop in to visit with family.
Wy loves to play with cousin Joshua Judd Mandell.

In 1992 Ashley
starred in an
independent film,
Ruby in Paradise,
creating a sensation
and winning the
Grand Juror's Prize
at Robert Redford's
prestigious Sundance
Film Festival.
Influential film critic
Roger Ebert said she
should be nominated
for an Academy
Award.
(JULIE DENNIS)

The Dreamchaser, their customized Silver Eagle tour bus, was their traveling home out on life's highways. This is Wy's room, and Naomi's quarters are in back.

Larry, who sang bass for Elvis, gives Naomi, Ken, and his grandson Andy a private tour of Graceland. They're in the Jungle Room, where Larry relaxed with the King.

The Judds transcended country music and had friends all over the world. Rock idols U2 came to see them perform in U2's hometown, Dublin, and threw a party for them afterward.

The girls are congratulated by Minnie Pearl after co-hosting the Academy of Country Music Awards in 1987. The Judds are credited with helping country music become as popular as it is today.
(JASPER DAILY)

In 1991 newcomer Garth Brooks frequently opened for the Judds on the Farewell Tour, and walked them to the stage for their last road concert.

Visiting backstage in Lake Tahoe, girlfriend Dolly Parton admires the hand-made quilt given newlyweds Larry and Naomi by fans. Wy liked to joke, "Mom took the Judd Boys and me along on her honeymoon!"

This is Naomi's favorite picture of Ashley and Wynonna, whom she proudly calls "the jewels in my crown, the joy of my being."

Borrowing their famous vinyl outfits from the Country Music Foundation Hall of Fame, they're backed up by the Jordanaires on "Don't Be Cruel." Naomi, who was determined the Farewell Concert be a celebration of love, laughter, music, and life, told Wynonna, "This isn't my going away party—you're the one who's going places." (MICHAEL CLANCY)

possibilities you rejected because of choices you made consciously."

But Jung taught that the soul can profit by coming to terms with both kinds of shadows.

Our therapist told us that the soul tries to speak to us not only through our body but through our intuitions and dreams. Unfortunately, most of us go through life rejecting, judging, or just ignoring our inner life rather than paying attention to the valuable existential messages hidden there. I was reading Michael Murphy's book *The Future of the Body* from the Esalen Institute in Big Sur, California, when I realized I'd been dreaming about the house in which I grew up several times a week ever since I left home. Our therapist said in her thirty-five-year practice she'd never encountered such an obsessional dream. It was because I'd felt snatched from the bosom of my family at seventeen, torn from the life I loved. Mom was on the road with us so I told her about my panic at being locked out that winter day back in 1964. She went straight to her purse and handed me the front door key. Now I carry it wherever I go as a symbol that I can reclaim my life.

Wy was having a recurring dream that while she was singing onstage alone, the band persisted in laughing and talking among themselves, paying no attention to her. The audience would get up and straggle out. She didn't believe anyone would take her seriously without me there. Her self-confidence was inversely proportional to her talent! We began to address the issue of her lack of self-esteem. I reminded her of what Eleanor Roosevelt said: "No one can make you feel inferior without your consent!"

As we stayed up all night talking on long bus rides, I tried to explain to Wynonna, "Honey, self-esteem, which includes self-appreciation, self-confidence, and acceptance, is what will enable you to confront fear and change. It will give you the ability to go on with your life and to take risks. You must challenge yourself now to become who you really are. My departure can be a rite of passage for you. You must first realize behavior is controlled less by what is true than what you believe to be true!"

I described to her what my genius friend Dr. Marvin Mimsky, professor of physics and cofounder of the Artifical Intelligence Lab,

said: "Perception is more important in dealing with reality than fact."
As in your case, your perception of yourself is a poor representation
of the truth!

Sometimes in the afternoons, Wynonna and I would take walks
or sit on the bed in our motel room discussing her perception of
herself and what she would like to become. I reminded her, "You are
what you imagine yourself to be, so you should be careful about what
you imagine!"

Wynonna was struggling with survivor's guilt. She felt not only
unworthy to carry on but was deeply troubled by the unfairness of my
disease and the loss it was costing me.

One night after she thought I was asleep, I overheard her talking
to Mike, our road manager. "I can't believe it's all turning out this
way! All I've ever done is get up and sing. Mom's the one who
deserves this career. She's worked her butt off for it, while it's just
been dumped in my lap. I feel like I'm getting a battle field promotion!"

Even though our Farewell Tour was just really getting under
way, it was time for Wynonna to start thinking about her first solo
album. Because it takes so long to select songs and prepare to record,
Wynonna had no choice. Ken factored days off on the road for me
to rest and for Wy to fly home to Nashville. Not having any experience putting things together by herself, she'd start to come unhinged
and say: "Putting together an album by myself is like trying to
assemble a jigsaw puzzle without first seeing the picture on the box."

I told her to close her eyes and create that picture in her mind's
eye.

Ken had met with MCA about my diagnosis and retirement
decision before our public press conference at RCA on October 17.
He'd been worried the label might invoke their option to the leaving
member clause and drop me from the new contract. Much to our
relief, MCA left the door open for me to record with Wynonna
anytime she and I chose. They even wrote me a personal letter saying
they would like nothing more.

Wynonna knew that she was gonna have to make lots of drastic
changes to find herself. "To belong or to rebel—*that* is the question!" I teased her.

Preparing to be a soloist, she wanted to step out musically to avoid repeating the Judd sound, and it was time for this natural evolution. Shortly before my diagnosis, I'd felt a creative restlessness. Responding to this urge to expand musically I'd bought a piano and had been taking some refresher lessons. I informed Wy I was going to start playing piano onstage while she took some featured solos in our show. I co-wrote a song with Mike Reid called "My Strongest Weakness" for us, and warned her I was being drawn to write more bluesy, gutsy material. I even confided to our lead guitarist, Steve Sheehan, we would be adding an electric guitar in the future. My expanded musical vision for the Judds would never be realized.

For nostalgic reasons, Wynonna couldn't bear to think of recording with Brent and Don at Creative Recording Studios. Tony Brown, who used to be with RCA and happened to be in the live audition that fateful night in 1983, was now with MCA. Tony has a talent on country's cutting edge and a personality compatible to Wynonna's, so they agreed to work together. She would continue to cling to Don Potter as her coproducer, guitarist, and session leader.

The hard part was telling Brent about the necessary change. Wynonna and I drove out to his lovely farm in Franklin, and the three of us sat out in the gazebo watching his wife, Janel, work their horses. Wy took her first step as a solo artist as she informed Brent of her new direction. Brent Maher is one of the classiest people we've ever known in our lives, and although the news took him by surprise, he expressed complete understanding and offered his best wishes. I thanked him for making it as easy as possible for Wy. As he walked us out to our car, Brent hugged Wynonna, and told her she was the greatest singer anywhere and professed there was no doubt in his mind that she would be a phenomenal success.

We hadn't been back on the road long when on March 17, just as I was waking up that Sunday morning, Vince Gill, who was working with us at the time, came and knocked on the bus door. It startled me because I could see that Vince had been crying. "Seven people in Reba McEntire's band and her tour manager have just been killed in a plane crash in California," he announced solemnly.

Coincidentally, we were in Oklahoma City, near where both Vince and Reba are from. That afternoon at soundcheck, Vince,

Wynonna, his fiddle player, Andrea, and I gathered around one microphone and sang Appalachian gospel songs. Wy and I dedicated "River of Time" in memory of the plane crash victims that night.

Our own keyboard player, Larry Miller, had just been in a devastating car crash and had suffered serious permanent neurological damage. We hired John Glazer as our new keyboardist, partly because of his talent and partly because of his sensitive personality. We were all so emotionally fragile on the Farewell Tour, we needed someone who blended in. Not long after Jon had joined us, as we were getting ready to do the *Tonight Show* for our last time, Jon got word that his mother had been found dead. When I went to him, he insisted on doing the show, and I switched one of our song choices to "Guardian Angels" for his sake.

Ken booked three of his management companies' acts intermittently to share the concert bill with us throughout the Farewell Tour. Raucous, southern-fried country rockers, Pirates of the Mississippi; dreamboat Billy Dean; and our close buddies McBride and the Ride. We were also working a bunch of dates with Garth Brooks as our opening act. It didn't take long to realize that Garth's tenure as an opening act would be short-lived! Everywhere we played, we sold out, and it became almost an every-night occurrence to be called into the building before our concert to have our picture taken as a beaming hall manager presented us with a plaque commemorating the new house record. We had almost twenty-five thousand people in San Diego and even sold out the huge Tacoma Dome with more than thirty thousand in attendance.

When I noticed we were booked for our final stop at the Astro Dome in Houston, I was looking forward to meeting Blair Justice, author of that first book I'd read on psychoneuroimmunology called *Who Gets Sick*. I called Dr. Justice, who's professor of psychology at the University of Texas, to arrange for him to come out to the show. Over the phone, he thought I was calling myself "the judge," and had absolutely no idea who we were. I found this quite refreshing. Dr. Justice declined my offer until I casually mentioned I had chronic active hepatitis. "Hang on there just a minute! You're trying to tell me you have chronic active hepatitis and you're able to do a show at the Astro Dome?" he asked.

It was enough to get him to change his plans, and when he and his therapist wife, Rita, came back to the bus after our performance, Blair shook his finger at me teasingly and said, "You little stinker! I know exactly what you're doing on this farewell tour. You're stimulating your body's own self-healing mechanisms with all this love and support!"

"I'm teaching myself PNI under the spotlight. Hepatitis threatened to turn off the spotlight, but I'm using my career to heal myself. The fans are literally and figuratively 'wishing me well!' " I admitted. "Your book is helping save my life, and now I want to tell others. I believe we teach what we want to learn. You may not believe what you discover, and you may discover what you believe!"

Blair wholeheartedly agreed with me, adding, "Yes, whether sick or healthy we must continue to broaden our horizons. The more things we're interested in, the more we enjoy life altogether!"

Laughter is good medicine, says Proverbs 17:22: "A merry heart doeth good, like a medicine." Much research has been done on the therapeutic effects of laughter. Norman Cousins, editor of the *Saturday Review* and faculty member of UCLA, wrote about it extensively. When we laugh, the brain releases endorphins, opiate-like painkillers. Laughter causes us to breathe deeper and faster and take in more oxygen. It lowers the blood pressure and the heart rate, stimulates the immune system, and helps us relax in stressful situations. He who laughs lasts!

I listened to Dr. Annette Goodheart, a psychologist researching the positive power of humor, who said that although the average four-year-old laughs five hundred times a day, the average adult laughs only fifteen times a day. Wy blurted out, "Well Mom, we're definitely not average adults!"

To which I responded, "We don't laugh because we're happy, we're happy because we laugh!"

A sense of humor has to do with intellect, but what Wy and I prefer about laughter is that it's illogical.

I personally love to laugh at embarrassing moments. Those awkward situations when we get caught in our own pretense. An ironic self-knowledge lies at the core of my own sense of humor. One night after a show in Canada, as I was going through the hotel lobby on my way up to my room to bathe, I saw Wy and the Judd Boys with McBride and the Ride's guys playing darts in the lounge. When I came back down, I stopped just around the corner and left my long coat on a chair. Wearing my flannel pajamas, house slippers, and my hair back in a ponytail, I marched into the noisy bar and with a straight face clapped my hands and announced: "All right! Lights out, everybody brush your teeth and get in your bunks!"

The stunned patrons, some of whom had been at the concert, were speechless as Wy and all the guys fell in behind me. The bartender laughingly hollered good night and called out: "Hey Naomi, you're a goofball!"

Without turning around I replied: "Yes, but I'm a professional—that's *Miss* Goofball to you!"

Sometimes when Wynonna and I were having one of our particularly heavy conversations, to derail us with absurdity I'd begin singing a ridiculous song I'd made up called "My Liver's Gone Bad and Boy Am I Mad." Wynonna would take her boot off and throw it at me, but still couldn't keep from laughing.

Victor Borge said, "Laughter is the shortest difference between two people." How else in the world could you explain some of my friendships? Dr. Leon Lederman, a tall genius with an Einsteinian mop of wavy white hair who grins like a leprechaun with a mischievous twinkle in his eye, won a Nobel Prize in physics. Leon, who wrote a brilliant book on the evolution of physics called *The God Particle,* helped create the world's first major super-conducting accelerator, is trying to revitalize the Chicago city schools, and is chairman of the board of the American Association for the Advancement of Science.

Now I don't know a muon neutrino or an upsilon particle (both of which he discovered) from my big toe, yet Leon and I hit it off the moment we met. Why? Because of a sense of humor! Sometimes he takes a break from writing his current book on the super-conducting super-collider he's building in Waxahachie, Texas, to call me and laugh for an hour long distance. Actually, Judd music and his passion for science do have some things in common: truth, beauty, and nature. Leon rewrote the lyrics to "Grandpa (Tell Me 'Bout the Good Old Days)" to "Grandpa, tell me once more . . . about when this country dared to explore where no one had ever gone before . . ."

Likewise, Ed Morris, a Nashville music writer and my favorite curmudgeon, is a skeptic, an agnostic, and a devout pessimist. Although he and I would definitely seem to be like oil and water, we enjoy a wonderful friendship. Wy and I've discovered through the years that you can tell a lot about a person by their reaction to the Judds.

We were halfway through the Farewell Tour when Ed, who writes for *Billboard* magazine, dedicated his September 28, 1991, column to a benevolent piece titled "Roses for Mama."

Our office faxed me the article on the road and as I read on, I detected that Ed was not only paying tribute but also seemed to be defending me. After checking this out with Ken, I was shocked to discover that some industry people who didn't know us actually suspected the Farewell Tour might be some Machiavellian scheme for Wy and me to get rid of each other and make a pile of money.

I was outraged! I wanted to find out who these people were and make them read the pathology report on my liver biopsy. I wanted to bring them on the bus with Wynonna and me to observe the psychic ferment we were knee-deep in.

We were in beautiful Monterey, California, to perform that night so I walked down to the ocean and sat alone at the water's edge for the next few hours. I realized that, as Wynonna puts it, "most people just don't get it." Eventually I was able to release my anger, accepting Wynonna's theory.

The truth of the matter is, I'm a terrible business woman. I think money is like manure, it's only good if it's spread around. I also think that stars need to take long breaks and reconnect with real life. Fame is very seductive and dangerous. It encourages vanity and self-absorption because of the public's constant adoration and because you are featured in the spot light as the center of attention. A celebrity becomes accustomed to talking about himself or herself incessantly during interviews.

Fame also leads to excesses of every imaginable kind. Artists are prone to forget to pay attention to their families and nourish relationships. I've watched them get completely out of touch with reality and become more demanding than a whiny invalid. So far, Wynonna and I had been strengthened, not strangled, by fame. I was adamant in reminding her that life *is* more important than show business.

Lord knows I've learned that fame, power, and money do not make you bulletproof! A talented writer named Sharon McCrum was observing Wynonna and me during the Farewell Tour for inclusion in her novel *The Hangman's Beautiful Daughter*. Referring to my plight she wrote, "Nothing can save you when your time's come. Not fame, nor optimism, nor wealth, nor physical fitness, nor other people's love." We are but brief guests of this earth.

As I sat watching the sunset over the ocean that evening in Monterey, I considered how that at the end of our lives it doesn't matter a flip what kind of car we drive, how many toys we have, what kind of house we live in, who we know, what kind of job we have, or how much money we make. What matters is what we've done for others.

Wynonna gave me a sweet surprise. We'd had a rough long haul to Missoula, Montana, and blew a bus tire. By the time I got to my motel room, there was no room service, just the restaurant's Sunday buffet, crammed with families getting mom out of the kitchen.

I was on the phone long distance to Paris talking with Ashley, who called to say happy Mother's Day in French, when someone brought me the morning paper. There was a photo and story that immediately grabbed my attention! The AP ran a picture of a large man wearing nothing but a diaper, cowboy boots, and cowboy hat directing traffic at a busy intersection. Someone at businessman Joe Murphy's office entered him in a contest at KBOW to win tickets to our sold-out concert that night in Missoula by doing "something outrageous." Murphy allowed, "It was embarrassing as hell, but if I didn't do it my kids told me I might as well move out of the house!" Then I saw the *USA Weekend* supplement, and on the cover was a photo of Wy and me with the title: "Mother's Day Surprise—This story is Wynonna Judd's secret gift to her Mom, who will read it today for the first time. Wynonna tells us what she has learned from gutsy Naomi's reaction to a career-ending illness."

In the lengthy article, Wy refers to how I taught her by example to "work hard, dream big, take risks, and love family and God."

She said, "Mom's never been a stage mother—far from it! To be honest, she's always been more worried about me personally than professionally. Music was my whole world and Mom knew I was safe once I got onstage with my guitar. She worried about stuff like me being lazy, being late or disrespectful, or not having a life. She doesn't want me to wake up on a bus to nowhere someday unhealthy and unhappy. I'm thankful she raised me with Christian beliefs and stuck by the ways in which she was raised back in Kentucky. Even when the day comes when she won't be with me onstage, she'll be there in spirit. A part of her will always sing through me when I'm singing alone. She's given me what I'll need to carry on. Happy Mother's Day Mom. I love you."

Wy and I seemed to be living in the past, present, and future all at the same time. We were constantly reminiscing about the great times we'd had, savoring each day on the road and the experiences the show that night brought, yet with the future hanging over us like Damocles' sword. Our therapist had given us a small, smooth stone, shaped like a heart, and when things got tough and we didn't know what to say, we'd simply pass it back and forth.

Wy and I frequently wrote each other cards and letters. Sometimes facing each other with our emotions became too overwhelming, so we thought it best to write instead to keep from losing it altogether.

When time came on May 29, for her first track date on her solo album, I wrote her a card comparing her to being a little seed planted in darkness. I told her she would be restless, scared, and alone; that she would have to struggle toward the light; and that her growth to stretch up into that light might be a painful struggle, but that she would finally burst with joy and bear fruit. I reminded her that from this toil, seeds would be released and scattered in the cycle of the seasons to come. Never able to be serious for too long though, I signed it "Yours in sickness and in health, Mommy."

That first day she started in the studio, I stayed away, because I felt she should be completely in charge and wanted her to enjoy the experience. I was afraid my presence would make her feel uncomfortable or guilty. But the next day, May 30, was her twenty-seventh

November 9, 1991

Dearest Mommy—
　　　So many thoughts in my head lately. How in the world have you and I managed to find ourselves in the midst of all this madness, yet become not only stronger but closer than ever?
　　　I feel a love for you that goes beyond this world. Perhaps it is because you have not only won my respect for your incredible spirit, but because you are my hero. I shall spend many years proudly becoming more and more like you.
　　　Remember always,

that whatever becomes of the two of us, we shall always have each other. No matter, where I am or what I'm doing, your sweet spirit will always be with me and I will remember all the things you've told me. I know sometimes you must feel as though you are alone, but when you do look down into the palm of your hand. I'll be looking up at you with a smile.

You are loved by so many. I'm proud to be your Princess of Quite a lot. We've shared so many wonderful times. I love you.

birthday and she demanded I come by. It was my only time to celebrate with her, so I pulled up to a back door loaded down with a cake and presents. After having her birthday at Creative Studio with Brent and the Judds' session players for eight straight years, it was really strange walking into a different studio. Never before had a birthday symbolized such a year of growth and change!

As I wandered around looking for my daughter, I met all the new musicians, who told me she was nervously watching for me by the main door to show me around. By the time I found her, I'd met everyone and knew my way. Tony Brown, who was warm and friendly and makes us feel comfortable, was very understanding of Wy's fragile moods. Gentleman Bruce Hinton, head of MCA Records, released a statement proclaiming, "We do not perceive Wynonna as a new act. With the release of her solo debut album in 1992, she will take her place in our industry as a Superstar."

Spring meant time for the ACMs, where we had been asked to sing "Love Can Build a Bridge" in the finale with the International Children's Choir. The finality of doing this show turned out to be a real test for me, and I was balking. Ken had to come down to my room before rehearsal and straighten me out. He knew just what to say, "Naomi, Wynonna's gotta hit such power notes on this song, if you're emotional, there's no way she'll be able to pull this off. Once more, you've got to be strong for her."

He was absolutely right. Wynonna, who often mirrors my emotions, looked as if she was about to flee any second while doing the runthrough of the song. As much for her sake as mine, I called a quick break. "Sweetheart, you know I believe the three most important words in the world are *love, faith,* and *hope.* This song is already about love, but it's important to me that the last word I say at the end of this show is the word *hope.* Why don't you take my hand after we've sung the last note and step down off the riser. As we walk out toward the audience I'd like to conclude with: 'And I believe there's always hope.' "

Since we were encircled by the children's choir, Wy realized we needed to practice it with them. As soon as we'd walked out to the lip of the stage, I looked down into the beautiful face of the little German girl whose hand I was holding, and asked, "And what might your name be?" The child smiled up at me and answered with one word: "Faith." Wy and I stared at her in disbelief.

Interaction with fans had never been more important. In every town we were saying good-bye and thanks to special friends who'd followed us for years. One girl from Colorado, whom we thought we knew pretty well, slipped us a confidential letter. We were shocked to discover that she had been dealing with an issue of sexual abuse by her brother-in-law by becoming associated with us and our music. One of our favorite fans was Libby McKinney, a grade-school teacher from Kernersville, North Carolina, who frequently incorporated her personal association with us into her job. For instance, she tries to instill tolerance and fair-mindedness in her class by teaching them "Love Can Build a Bridge." And then there was Lynn, our friend from Vermont who has forty-six personalities (at last count).

Multiple personality disorder is a creative survival mechanism of children who are sexually or physically abused or traumatized before the age of eight. The abuse is so heinous that the child can't begin to comprehend or deal with it so instead, since all children pretend, they splinter off into various personalities to diffuse the pain and confusion.

Lynn had discovered Judd music while locked up in a sanitarium after one of her personalities tried to kill her. She told us, "There was something so primal about the blending of your voices, in addition to the lyrics, the melodies, and the rhythms. I fell in love with Judd music before I even knew that you two were mother and daughter, or anything about your personalities and backgrounds. I also have a redheaded daughter, Jamie, who's very sensitive and creative like Wy. Coincidentally, I also lost a brother named Brian to Hodgkin's disease."

I slipped up to the Mayo Clinic for my checkup and this time I was actually looking forward to getting my blood chemistry checked. When Dr. Dalton entered the examining room I told him I had something very interesting to share with him. I knew that the thymus gland at the base of the neck is the immune control central for the young body and that after the age of twenty this small gland begins to shrivel up, so that by the age of fifty it's completely atrophied. Thus I had begun taking thymus-replacement supplements, made from calves' thymus glands with a multivitamin and mineral supplement to assist my body's beleaguered attempts to fight off this tenacious virus. Physicians recommend replacement therapy when other glands or parts of the body fail, so this made perfect sense. Estrogen and progesterone replacement are prescribed for women in menopause or who've had hysterectomies, and insulin is given when the islet of Langerhans isn't functioning adequately. If the thyroid gland flags, a patient takes a synthetic thyroid supplement. Dr. Dalton wanted to know how I heard of this thymus supplement.

I learned about the supplement through Dr. Carson Burgstiner, a prominent board-certified obstetrician and gynecologist physician who is past president of the Medical Association of Georgia and vice chairman of the delegation to the American Medical Association from Savannah, Georgia. He was ill with hepatitis B for seven years when he realized that he should literally and figuratively do as the Bible says, "Physician, heal thyself." Seeking to replace his thymus gland, Dr. Burgstiner discovered his local health food store offered this immune-system booster. Within three weeks after taking this thymus supplement with a multivitamin, his liver studies became normal! He sent his blood work to the Centers for Disease Control and Prevention in Atlanta, Georgia; to the Harvard Medical Center; and to the Scripps Institute in California for confirmation. Dr. Burgstiner has not only healed himself, but he's now back in full practice and trying to tell others: "The impact of thymic-hormonal replacement has enormous potential in immune-system diseases, from allergies and hay fever to rheumatoid arthritis, lupus, cancer, and AIDS. This simple glandular hormone could answer a lot of prayers."

There are various research trials on injectable thymosin being conducted, but I've been following Dr. Milton G. Mutchnick's study at Wayne State University, School of Medicine in Detroit. I learned about him when one of his own doctors, Dr. David Green, called me after Wy and I were on the cover of *People* magazine, which interviewed me about my hepatitis. By the conclusion of their one-year study, 86 percent of the thymosin-treated patients cleared the hepatitis B virus from their DNA! Clinical, biochemical, and serological improvement in patients responding to thymosin were sustained, and they have no side effects!

"Now, Dr. Dalton, I began thymic supplements last month. Have you gotten the results of *my* blood work today?"

"Yes, Naomi," he announced proudly. "We are surprised and delighted that your ALT has dropped to the near-normal range!"

"Told you so!" I squealed. "Just call me *The Body of Evidence!*"

I'd started to feel better and actually began to have days that I felt normal. What a wonderful luxury that was!

While we were touring out on the West Coast, Wy flew back east to attend Bonnie Raitt's wedding to Michael O'Keefe, the actor she'd introduced us to at Sunset Studio. Bonnie had a relatively celebrity-free wedding, inviting just a few other artists like Jackson Browne and Darryl Hanna.

I used this rest period for Ashley and me to rent a car and drive up to our old stomping grounds in Marin County. Rancho Nacasio, the western-style restaurant with the live country band where I'd worked ten years ago to put myself through nursing school, had reopened. When Ashley and I slipped inside in the middle of the afternoon, there were only a few locals at the mahogany bar having a cold one. The young female bartender recognized me even with my hat and dark glasses, saying she hoped to see our concert the next day at the San Rafael Civic Center. Just then "Lazy Country Evening," a song I'd written when we lived down the road, began playing on the jukebox. It was a unique feeling of closure for me. I put my arm around Ashley reminding her how, although it seemed preposterous at the time, I'd vowed that someday we'd be on that very jukebox. Quick-thinking Ashley turned my pep talk around: "Yeah, well then, Mom, you just remember this moment if ever you have any doubts about overcoming your illness!"

Judge William Webster, head of the CIA, came to our show at Wolftrap Amphitheatre in Vienna, Virginia. Knowing that Judge Webster had been under unbelievable pressure, I inflated my whoopie cushion and placed it under a cushion on the bus where he always sat. Wynonna and Mike said they'd seen me do some pretty daring things, but they couldn't believe I'd actually go through with this irreverent prank. But I did! The results were explosive, and we all screamed with laughter!

Our good-natured friend Judge Webster invited us to be his

guests at a private awards ceremony at the White House. President Bush was conferring Judge Webster with the highest commendation any American civilian can receive, the Presidential Medal of Freedom. Although I was beginning to feel better, I was still tired and knew that I should hang out in the hotel room, but I insisted that Wynonna fly to Washington.

After the ceremony, President and Mrs. Bush invited the judge, his new wife, Lynda Jo, and Wynonna up to their living quarters within the White House for a casual visit. Wynonna enjoyed the special time and this homey behind-the-scenes look at our country's highest office as she played with Millie, the First Dog. President Bush later described to me that as Wynonna was leaving she shook his and Barbara's hands and exclaimed, "Gee thanks, this is the most swell field trip I've ever been on!"

The Farewell Tour itself had turned into an amazing phenomenon. As the going-away party's hostess, I'd burst onto the stage, joining Wy on the verse from the song "This Country's Rockin' ":

> . . . So crank up the music,
> Turn up the juice
> Just put me in the spotlight
> And turn me loose.
> You better hold on tight
> This country's gonna rock tonight!

I attracted attention like a lightning rod and became aware that Wynonna was beginning to feel left out. Although she was grateful that fans were turning out to say good-bye, I think she was wondering if they were going to come back to support her when she returned alone next year. I reminded her of the line of the song from which she'd gotten her name: "Flagstaff, Arizona, don't forget Winona." She seemed to be curling up within herself and was going into a very real depression. Some days she was like a planet out there governed by her own laws, treating the people around her as satellites.

I'd long since been forced to forgo sound check to stay in my room and rest. Wy complained that the Judd Boys weren't paying attention to her at sound check saying, "They treat me like their kid sister."

I realized she was right and would need to start fresh as a soloist with a new band. There were too many memories associated with me and these guys, just as there were with Brent.

We were now working with Garth Brooks, and sometimes Wy would walk or ride her bicycle with her trainer to sound check. They'd underestimate the amount of time it required and when her sound check ran over, it cut into Garth's time. When I confronted her about this, she became quite testy and picked up another nickname—Godzilla. I think watching Garth's electrifying stage presence caused her to shudder as she realized she'd soon be out there competing against him. Ken showed up on the road to do an attitude adjustment on Godzilla.

Poor Ken, feeling helpless is not his style! For years Wynonna thought he was Superman, now she began to see that he was not some demigod after all. One night she asked, "Mommy, do you remember reading me the story *The Wizard of Oz?* When Dorothy finally arrives at the Emerald City and is about to go before the Wonderful Wizard of Oz, Toto sneaks and pulls down the curtain to reveal that the Wizard of Oz is not some magical omnipotent creature, he's just a normal man. Well now I finally see Ken as a real person."

Ken had an announcement of his own, "Girls, December 4 will be your Farewell Concert." My shoulders went limp and I was speechless. Wynonna clinched her fists and silently pounded the arms of the couch. Ken pressed on, "And I think we should televise the concert live."

"No!" Wynonna and I yelled in unison. "It's too personal and special to do on TV!" Wynonna insisted, turning to me for my reaction. "Ken, I totally agree with Wynonna."

Ken listened patiently to our protestations for a few minutes before continuing, "I think we should make it available on TV because you two have always shared everything with your fans. There's so many people that want to be there for your final performance, but can't. I think you owe it to them. I also think we should show it on cable, because any of the three networks would chop up the concert with dog food and car wax commercials. Your time would be cut down significantly by station breaks and you wouldn't have any creative control. Knowing you, I figured you might want to contribute part of the concert's income to the American Liver Foundation. Why don't you think about it and we'll pick up this conversation in a few days."

The first thing I did was get my calendar and count down how many concerts we had left till December 4. From then on Wynonna really went downhill. She'd stay up all night and then sleep all day till sound check. She refused to meet with me in the afternoons.

On September 28, we had a show in San Bernardino, California, with Merle Haggard. We pulled our bus up next to the stage and turned out all the lights so as not be a distraction for the audience. Wy and I were sitting up front in the dark in our bathrobes with the sunroof open listening to his show. After his last bow, Haggard came straight down the stage steps to our bus door. Mom, who traveled with us quite a bit these last days, invited Haggard on up. Merle, who's not a man with great social skills, seemed even more shy and awkward than usual. After taking his hat off, he sat down beside me on the couch, and kept on staring down at his hands while twisting the brim of his Stetson. He seemed to be struggling to find words to express himself. Finally he spoke. "Naomi, I just came to tell you, kid, that I think you're getting a mighty raw deal." I reached over and gently patted his hand. Haggard added, "I also want you to know that I did what you suggested and quit cigarettes!"

He looked straight across at Wynonna and told her, "Now girl, there's an awful lot of mighty fine singers coming up these days, in fact I've never seen the likes of it. But I gotta tell you that you're the greatest girl singer I've ever heard."

Wynonna didn't know what to say. After thanking him, she introduced Haggard to my Mom. Merle mumbled something about his own mother's recent passing, and asked Mom if she was familiar with his song about mansions. When Mom said she wasn't sure, Haggard told her the song had been his momma's favorite and began singing it. Mom, Wynonna, and I were entranced sitting there together in the dark listening to Merle Haggard singing his mother's favorite song to my Mom.

Early the next morning we flew back to Nashville for our last awards program. On the way to the Country Music Association show I stopped by Vanderbilt to have my blood drawn and got my real reward. My ALT continued to be right at the top of the normal range! My thymus supplement, daily practice of PNI, plus God's grace were working! Ken, Wynonna, and our organization were terribly disappointed and upset that the CMA didn't deem it appropriate to acknowledge the end of the Judds on this show. Fans and media people took note of the CMA's oversight, however, with critics like Robert Oermann expressing their outrage. The umbrage affected me the least.

We went out in style as we accepted our eighth straight and final award for duo to a standing ovation. It meant the Judds were undefeated at all three major country music award shows for eight consecutive years! We'd won six Grammys and a vast collection of other awards, including international honors, making us the most awarded and successful duet in country music history. The Judds were Country Music's top-grossing act of 1991, according to Amusement Business. Year-end box office grosses from Pollstar showed us as the number three top touring act of the year in any form of music.

I fully appreciated that this last network TV appearance was my parting chance to speak to country music fans. I shared with them that when we'd moved to Nashville, I didn't have much to show for my life, but that their belief in us had forever changed us. I noted that one of the greatest things that's happened during our career was that I've become a better mother and cheerfully added: "and for that, Wynonna and Ashley Judd are eternally grateful!" I closed by saying, "When I am alone at my farm in the years to come, the memory of you will be that of some invisible choir singing to me the most beautiful love song of all."

Back in the press tent I hugged my dear friend, Sandy Lovejoy, good-bye. Sandy, a whiz journalist from Phoenix, Arizona, who's written about us down through the years with the most piercing insight, insisted, "Naomi, you've gotta write your life story."

I told her, "We're signing with Villard Books of Random House in New York and we picked them because of the editor Diane Reverand. Diane 'gets it,' just like you, Sandy. Our perceptions of the past are often distorted through the lens of time, but thanks to reporters like you, the Judds' career is one of the most written about and best documented ever!

Because I need to rest as much as possible, Ken has asked Bud Schaetzle, who's already out here filming us on the road, to help me start researching and just get going."

"During the Farewell Tour, just as he's captured other important episodes of our life, Bud has been busy shooting behind-the-scenes footage. This documentary of our last days together will be available as a home video. Bud stops by my room sometimes in the afternoons and tapes me going through my old journals to begin getting personal events in chronological order. After the Farewell Concert I plan to hole up at the farm and write the book myself in longhand. I want it to be about our genesis; from old testaments to new revelations! I'm willing to tell the stupid stuff I've done in hopes that somebody out there might learn from my mistakes. Experience lets you recognize a mistake the second time you make it, and I've got lots of experience! I'll tell you one thing, girlfriend, Eve was the only woman without a past!"

Speaking of our past, Wynonna and I were scheduled to perform in Omaha, Nebraska, at Aks-Ar-Ben, the venue where we'd made our first public concert appearance back in 1984. As soon as we walked in the backstage area, the stage manager met us saying, "I'll never forget that night that you opened for the Statler Brothers! After they'd played their opener tape, 'The Star Spangled Banner,' and someone began introducing you, I was watching in the wings and saw the expressions of panic on your faces as you looked toward the sides of the stage for an exit. I hollered to a couple of the stagehands to bar the door, that you were fixing to leave! We've rooted you on, as you've climbed the ladder to the top in country music. It's great to have you back, although tonight is bittersweet."

During the show, acknowledging that Wy and I had now come full circle, I declared, "The end contains the beginning."

Next, when we performed in Raleigh, North Carolina, Larry's

family saw us performing as a duet for the last time. In Pennsylvania, my sister, Margaret, and her family did so as well. It seemed as if something special took place at every show.

At our concert in Indianapolis, Indiana, our American Indian friend Red Crow, who'd just played the elder chief Ten Bears in the movie *Dances with Wolves,* visited with us on the bus, suggesting natural herbal remedies for me.

We headed for the Far East—New Jersey that is! While we were performing for the weekend at Trump's Castle in Atlantic City, I was involved in an elaborate scheme to trick Wynonna for a TV show called *Super Bloopers and New Practical Jokes.* Hosted by Dick Clark and Ed McMahon, it featured celebrity flubs, miscues, and pranks. I told Wy we needed to indulge The Donald by granting an interview with his aspiring journalist nephew. We hired a gooberish actor, and I made up the list of off-the-wall questions.

A crew had built a room of two-way mirrors for the TV cameras to hide behind. As Wynonna and I entered the room, I set her up by whispering: "Honey, I'm worn out after our performance, so you'll have to answer most of the questions." The nerdish guy asked Wynonna stupid things like: "Since you and your boyfriend are both singers, when you're alone and feeling romantic, do you sing love songs to each other?" "How old were you when you recorded 'Delta Dawn' [a song by Tanya Tucker]?" "Do you get your stage clothes from the Home Shopping Network?" "How much money do you make?"

Incredulous, but trying to be polite, Wy struggled to maintain her cool, but kept looking to me as if to beg, "Mom, get me outta here!"

Donald and Marla burst in, revealing the joke and the show ended with Wynonna vowing to get even with me. I've been watching my back ever since.

Although Wy had to postpone a show in Orlando after she injured her back horseback riding at my farm, I never had to cancel. While we were playing the Great Lakes area, I awakened one morning in Saginaw, Michigan, to find a note on the bus's door, saying Bruce Johnson, our stage manager, had been rushed to the hospital, but was holding off an emergency appendectomy till I could get there. I raced into the motel lobby telling the desk clerk, "Quick! Call me a cab for the hospital!" News travels fast, and within an hour the word was out that "Naomi Judd's dying in a Saginaw hospital."

Each night we'd hire a local policeman to be our bodyguard. Wynonna called him "the cop du jour." For our last show in Green Bay, Wisconsin, we were assigned a female hostage negotiator named Dawn. When Wynonna asked her what her greatest fear was, Dawn replied, "Being taken hostage."

Wynonna exclaimed, "How interesting! Mom's an R.N. and has always been afraid of being physically incapacitated. Me, I've never done anything on my own, so my greatest fear is abandonment. But I guess a certain amount of freedom comes even realizing and facing your fears!"

It was November now, just a few dates left. Every night as we were starting up the buses and trucks to head for the next town, Mike McGrath and I would acknowledge the countdown. Then I'd give the signal: "The dog barks and the caravan moves on." The press followed us incessantly. We were on the cover of all the magazines, even twice in one year for popular *People* magazine. Inside the nucleus of our bus, we hovered together for support.

By now Wynonna refused even to get off the bus except to do the shows. It worried me, because there are no windows in her room and because she slept all day, she never saw sunlight anymore.

I'd gone out several times that Saturday afternoon in Biloxi, Mississippi, to check on her. The cold winter air was motionless and the water was absolutely still. As I stepped up on the bus, I found Wynonna sitting silently with Loretta in her lap up front. She was still in her pajamas although it was almost time to leave for the show. I sat across from her for a long time without saying anything, then looking out over the water I commented, "The water must be perfectly calm before it can reflect the heavens." Still no response, so I cautiously inquired, "And what color is your mood ring today?"

Wy began ranting and raving, "I can't take it anymore!" she screamed. "I broke up with Tony today for good, because I know that sooner or later he'll abandon me too! For twenty-seven years now you've been the first person I see when I wake up in the morning, the last person I see at night when I go to bed. We even sleep six feet apart. How can you leave me?"

With that she ran into her room. When I followed to try and soothe her, she insisted I leave. Her tantrum was really self-flagellation.

I sat on my bed back in my room trembling, wondering if we'd have a show that night. Eventually, Mike and our bus driver came out and drove us to the gig. Mike buzzed me on the intercom saying, "Mamaw, there's a preacher here at the bus door says he's from Slidell, Louisiana, and has driven a long way to give you 'a word of knowledge.' The guy sure seems sincere and he doesn't even want an autographed photo, tickets for the show, or anything! Claims he just wants to talk to you personally for five minutes. What do you think?"

"Bring him on up, I'll see him," I answered.

When I passed through Wy's room she snarled, "You can do your own hair tonight!"

The pastor made no attempt at small talk, getting right to the point: "I'm not here because you're a celebrity, Naomi. I'm here because I feel you're about to be put to an awful test and I came to remind you that you're God's child and He's faithful to those who live according to his will. I read an interview today in which you commented that it's not only December 4 that you're worried about, it's the unknown December 5. I bring you a message: 'Jesus is love and was sent to get us over and across difficult things in this life.' When you sing 'Love Can Build a Bridge' for the last time on December 4, in your mind substitute Jesus for love."

He took both my hands in his, said a brief prayer over me, and vanished. I had Mike chase after him, but he'd already gotten into a car and driven off into the night.

"Wow, what do you make of that?" Mike asked. "He was helping me with my gepyrophobia, fear of crossing bridges," I smiled. "I've had it ever since I was a child. December 4 will be the ultimate bridge to cross." Suddenly I was reminded of a scripture from Hebrews 13:2: "Be not forgetful to entertain strangers: for thereby some have entertained angels unawares."

I burst into Wynonna's room to tell her what had just transpired and she broke down and apologized. During the show I referred to her as "Hurricane Wynonna," declaring, "Folks, you can't control the weather and you can't control tempestuous Hurricane Wynonna!"

As she and I ascended to the highest platform on our stage to be seated on benches beside each other to sing "Guardian Angels," one of the most amazing things that's ever happened onstage occurred.

Streams of haze from the smoke machine behind the stage swirled within shafts of subdued lights projected around us on the darkened stage. Just as Wynonna sang a line from "Guardian Angels" ("And if you look real close you'll see our eyes are just the same") the image of an old man's face was formed by moving vapors. He had a beard just like Elijah, my great-great-grandfather, about whom I wrote the song. It's a good thing I don't sing on that line, as I twitched and blinked my eyes.

Instantly, Wynonna gave me a stare, acknowledging that she saw it too! Then as if encouraging us onward during this last leg of our journey together, as Wynonna and I harmonized on the words we'd sung so many times before, we felt surrounded by our very own ancestral messengers of love and comfort: "Sometimes when I'm tired I feel Elijah take my arm, he says, 'Keep agoing, hard work never did a body harm,' and when I'm really troubled and I don't know what to do, Fanny whispers, 'Just do your best, we're awful proud of you.' They're my guardian angels and I know that they can see, every step I take they're watching over me. I might not know where I'm going, but I'm sure where I come from. They're my guardian angels, and I'm their special one."

Our eyes locked, Wynonna and I felt as if we were the only two people in the world in spite of the sold-out arena. We knew that we'd been visited by guardian angels ministering to us as emotional and inward creatures of God. After the show, we rushed back to the privacy of the bus to try to fathom this splendid mystery. Some of the band members and crew even came over to ask what had transpired, as even they had sensed something.

The meet and greets were lengthy that night and Wynonna and I were emotionally wrung out, when Mike reminded us we'd also promised to see a young lady with Down's syndrome. Uncharacteristically, I spoke up. "Mike, I'm not sure I'm up to seeing anybody else tonight!"

"But she says she has a special message for you Mamaw," he continued. Having already received two special visits in one night, I dared not send this one away!

Introducing herself as Holly, the girl began to prophesize to us with childlike sincerity. "I was born with a tender heart," she began. "Naomi, I came to tell you that Jesus died on the cross that you might be healed. Wynonna, I came to tell you not to be sad when your mother's no longer by your side. The uplifting memory of her faith in you will carry you through your difficult times."

For a moment Wynonna and I could not even speak. As they got up to leave, Holly's mother turned to us. "I had Holly when I was older than I should have been, but now she is the joy of my life and I believe she is an angel."

Wy and I agreed.

No sooner had Holly left, when Ernie Stuart, our band bus driver and head of transportation for our organization, stepped up on the bus white as a sheet and perspiring. I immediately panicked because Ernie has hepatitis B. He'd been diagnosed several years ago and had been in and out of the hospital. He'd even spent last Christmas in the hospital. I'd taken him presents and decorated his hospital room as best I could. Ernie, who calls me his "liver buddy," cried: "I'm passing blood and I feel dreadful." We put him on a plane home to Vanderbilt Hospital.

Ashley joined us on the road for our last week of the Farewell Tour. This past year she'd been moving in and out between the layers of our lives as her busy schedule allowed. She was working as a hostess at our favorite restaurant in Los Angeles, The Ivy, and had gotten signed for representation by the prestigious Triad Agency, later acquired by the William Morris Agency. The day she got her braces off, to celebrate, she'd gone for her first movie audition. Lo and behold, they were so impressed, they offered her a small part in the movie *Kuffs*! I told Ashley it was in keeping with the now-famous Judd tradition of getting signed on the spot.

Next, Ashley landed the female lead on a *Star Trek* episode! We watched it five or six times in a row till Wynonna and I could pantomime all of Ashley's lines. I may be the only person in history who's ever cried through an entire *Star Trek—The Next Generation* episode. We were stunned at her extraordinarily natural acting ability! It was the first time we'd ever seen her act in anything. Ashley was never even in a high school drama. She'd been attending Robert Carnegie's Playhouse West in North Hollywood. Considered one of the best acting coaches, I'd been greatly impressed by Robert's integrity and passion for his work. He and his wife, Maxine, and I became friends, and I was relieved Ashley was in such good hands.

After sitting in on Ashley's classes, I changed my impression of acting. I once thought it was convincing pretending, until Robert straightened me out, saying, "Acting is living truthfully under imaginary circumstances."

A very cautious man, Robert nonetheless told me, "I believe Ashley has a rare gift."

She had just been given a juicy role in NBC's hit series *Sisters,* as Swoosie Kurtz's rebellious daughter. Every Saturday night, while we were onstage singing, Wynonna and I taped Ashley's show. We gave Ashley her royal title: "Queen of the Screen."

Lying on my bed, the three of us discussed a book Ashley had given me called *Hollywood vs. America* in which respected film critic Michael Medved describes how out of touch Tinseltown is with real people. Medved notes the big studios lose money because they create poor representations of what people really wish to see, and he describes how the film capital undermines America's strength by ridiculing morals, values, and decency.

I suggested Ashley could be like the woman Esther in the Bible. The Book of Esther is unique because it's the only book in the Bible that doesn't say the word *God,* anywhere. Yet Esther is important because she represents morals, respect, and decency by her lifestyle. Wy agreed adding, "The entertainment field needs many Esthers," and took a new road code name for herself, Polly Esther!

When Wynonna, Ashley, and I get together we're usually three high-spirited horses, but these days our mood was quietly attentive toward each other. Together the three of us have an exponential strength. Ashley was born with open hands. Wynonna was born with clinched fists. I was born with working hands.

That night of November 21, on the drive to our next to last show in Cincinnati, Ohio, the three of us again stayed up all night talking. With Wynonna on one side and Ashley on the other, we sat huddled together on the front couch under an afghan a fan had just given us, discussing the different directions our lives were taking us. I said, "Right now I feel like a mother bird with her two babies in a wisp of a nest hanging out over the edge of a rocky cliff, trying to get you ready to leave the nest."

Ashley calmly predicted: "Mom, you will reinvent yourself in the mythic goddess tradition of death and rebirth." She also noted, "Wy will set new records in country music and that America will eventually experience Wynonnamania!"

For the first time since she'd been working on her new album, Wynonna actually wanted to play us a song. She couldn't even look at me as she sang:

> I was raised on *love's* foundation
> The Rock of Ages goes unshaken.
> The *faith* and *hope* that was given to me
> Is stronger than the blackjack tree.
> My mama taught me how to stand alone
> She let me go, but she still holds on
> And I can still feel all that love from here.

Love, faith, and *hope.* There's those three words again! In this moment I realized that it was not merely a mother's pride I was feeling; indeed I had two extraordinary young women for daughters.

Upon our arrival in Cincinnati, we had a reception for the Ramey Home boys from Ashland, Kentucky. We'd brought them down on a chartered bus to treat them to a special outing. Wynonna, Ashley, and I hung out with these fine young men, trying personally to encourage them to do something constructive with their lives.

Snipper, our former bodyguard, was in a hospital in Cincinnati, where he spent a year and two months recuperating from a liver transplant. He'd left our organization several years ago because of alcoholism. Good-natured Snip once said, "Mamaw, I don't have a drinking problem, I have a quitting problem!"

Since liquor is metabolized through the liver, people who drink too much for too long develop cirrhosis, which leads to liver failure and death.

Following our show, Wynonna, Ashley, Ken, and I went on our bus to the hospital, and a security guard sneaked us up the back steps to Snip's room at 2:00 A.M.

We barely recognized our old friend, who was unable to speak because of tubes in his nose and mouth. His mother, Maria, told us how Snip would sometimes call out for Wy and me in his hallucinations. I leaned over and kissed Snip's forehead to tell him good-bye and whispered: "Tomorrow's our last road concert. I wish you could be there with us." He blinked his eyes real hard and stared straight at me to let me know he understood. Then he started to cry.

Still dressed in complete stage wear, I tiptoed up and down the liver transplant ward visiting with patients who were unable to sleep. I must have been a startling sight, and a woman gasped, "Either I'm dreaming or you're a magical apparition."

When I stopped at one man's bedside for a chat he said, "You're gonna be okay, 'cause you're Naomi Judd!"

"No, no!" I corrected him, "Hey! God isn't healing me because I'm great—he's healing me because he's great!"

I was exhausted from the emotional toll the night had taken, and as I prepared for bed as usual, it seemed impossible this could be the last time to sleep in my little bed on the *Dreamchaser*. As I pulled back the covers and turned to the window to pull the drapes, I saw we were just pulling out of town and all the neon signs seemed to be flashing "Good-bye. Good-bye."

I sat there on the side of my bed staring out the windows for some time, resisting sleep, dreading to awaken to my last day on the road. Then, suddenly, there were no more city lights, just inky blackness as if some great switch had been flipped to turn off all the electricity. The whole world seemed to be asleep, and I felt so alone. The Farewell Tour had been like driving the bus at night. In darkness we had only been able to see what lay just in front of us in the headlights, but eventually we came to the end of our journey.

The Last Song

CHANGE IS THE true nature of this world. Change is the one thing we can be sure of. But I didn't want change. I had the most wonderful life of anyone I knew!

As I began waking up slowly that morning of our last road concert on November 23, I was attacked by terrible thoughts and began tossing fitfully in bed. With hepatitis, waking up was always difficult, rather like trying to start a car on a cold morning. Drifting somewhere in that state between half-awake and half-asleep, I began to imagine that I was losing my footing, falling from the height of our career. I jerked violently and startled myself wide awake.

Opening my curtains I saw through the pouring rain that we were at the Hyatt hotel in downtown Lexington, Kentucky, where we'd stayed every previous year for concerts at Rupp Arena. We weren't far from the seventy-five-dollar-a-month project apartment complex we'd lived in when Wynonna was a baby. I sat there mesmerized by raindrops on the window, considering my strange clock. Married with a child at eighteen, scrubbing floors in that awful apartment, cutting out coupons to buy necessities while my friends were away at universities and dating. Already divorced and struggling alone to raise children during my twenties, while peers were just getting married. Putting myself through college in my thirties and moving around the country while my settled counterparts were sending their children off to college. Now retired at forty-five, wondering what in the world would happen next!

I was in such a negative mood, I slipped right back into bed. Banjo snuggled up against the curve of my neck. I realized that the end was drawing dangerously close. I knew I was still too young and adventurous to live on a meager diet of memories. I wanted to continue traveling the world, not just pace the inner world of reminiscence. I was actively at war with myself, negotiating internal conflicts, when I spotted a message I'd scribbled on a hotel notepad and taped onto my makeup mirror. It was a quote from the Suttapitaka: "Though he should conquer a thousand men in a battlefield a thousand times, yet he indeed who would conquer himself is the noblest victor." I knew I must practice some dynamic centering before I got off the bus.

I should have known it was not going to be a normal sound check. When Wy and I arrived at the venue, we were greeted by knowing smiles and tender hugs from all the band and crew wives and children. We were so pleased to see all of them, as they reminded Wy and me that we were not alone but connected by a vast network of precious friendships. I motioned Wynonna and the band up to the stage, where we sat cross-legged in a circle. Emotions were sky high, and I realized this was the right time for our guys to be allowed to express themselves and release their sadness.

"Does anyone have anything they'd like to say?" I inquired.

"Today I realize happiness is not at the end of the road, it's all along the way," George, our drummer, replied sheepishly as he quoted my favorite expression.

Odell, our young pedal steel guitar player, spoke up with his dry humor: "Someday they should do a mini-series on you girls. Please get Tom Cruise to play me."

Lead guitarist Steve Sheehan added: "No outsider could ever understand what we've all been through together."

I flashed back to the night Steve showed up in the doorway of my room on the bus to confide that his wife had just left him for his best friend, his one-year-old son's godfather. I remembered the lunches we had together on the road as he poured his heart out while trying to cope like a gentleman with his messy divorce. As with Steve, I was usually the first to hear the bad news and the good news. Mark Thompson was holding his beautiful daughter, Katie, Wynonna's godchild, in his lap, and I recalled the day she was born. His wife, Mello, now holding newborn Erin, was seated in the front row beside the other wives, and they were lined up like a portrait gallery of mothers with their children.

Pops Webber was uncharacteristically quiet. Attempting to draw him out of his shell, I gave a nod in his direction: "Pops, you old jazz man you, you and I have lived our whole lives like jazz. Always improvising to life's rhythm!"

Removing his glasses to wipe away tears, Pops could only shake his head and mutter: "Nobody will ever know, Mamaw! Nobody will ever know!"

Perhaps he was referring to the time his fourteen-year-old daughter got hooked on drugs and ran off with a guy in the carnival, and how he clung to all of us for his sanity.

"Well, you guys have been like my brothers," Wy declared. Then with her crooked grin she tagged it with: "Brothers I never wanted, that is!"

Our monitor man, Brooks Thomas, was pointing to his watch, his silent signal that we needed to go to work. As we rose to our feet, I concluded by saying: "We are a tribe, a group of people with similar feelings and loyalties who live and work together, united by customs, a community. Whatever happens, I know that we'll be friends for life. As your tribal elder, I declare that of this moment you're being promoted. You are no longer 'The Fabulous Judd Boys.' Wynonna and I now proclaim you *'The Fabulous Judd Men!'* "

It was also my last official act as the reigning Queen of Everything in Juddom, and in a mock ceremony I passed my scepter and tiara on to Wynonna, "The Princess of Quite a Lot."

Tonight as I went through my ritual of getting ready back in my room on the *Dreamchaser,* I opened my drapes and turned off the lights so I could sit on the side of my bed and observe the human parade streaming into the coliseum. I caught myself muttering, "Thank you. Thank you." A reporter once asked me the best gift I'd ever gotten from a fan. He was expecting me to say a painting or a handmade craft, yet my immediate response was: "That they see me as their friend."

To go out in front of people, you must have a sense that you know what you're doing and enough self-assurance to be able to do your thing, but I never see myself as different from others. My strength comes from feeling like one who's representing them, urging them on. I see myself in their circumstances and hope they can imagine themselves in mine.

One night, as Wynonna and I were harmonizing on "Grandpa," I was struck by what a paradox we are. While we were singing "do daddies really never go away?" I had to acknowledge that Wynonna and Ashley were children of divorce. We represent family, yet our extensive touring separated us from our loved ones. We sing about home while living in a traveling bus. We allude to permanence, but were rarely in one spot more than a day. Our kitchen table had been the coffee shop at any one of a million Holiday Inns. Our neighbors were the truckers in the truck stops, the room service personnel, local stagehands, the fans. We were down-home, yet sometimes found ourselves in the company of presidents, celebrities, movie stars, sports heroes, and various and sundry living legends. It's an incredibly difficult and exhausting lifestyle with pressures and stress that sometimes reach inhuman proportions.

Many times since my diagnosis, I'd considered an ominous question: If I had indeed acquired this non-A, non-B, virulent hepatitis from a needlestick while working as an R.N., what would life be like if we hadn't gotten signed at RCA? I would have no medical insurance, no savings account, no job, no husband, and no support system. Wynonna and I might not even be in each other's lives. Tonight I was made aware of all the things country music had given me: self-confidence, validation, and financial security, allowing me to feel welcome and at home wherever I go in the world. It got our family back together, helped Wynonna and me to heal our relationship, and now the Farewell Tour saved my life. My immune system was stimulated enough to control the hepatitis virus.

To me the stage is symbolic of life. I'm never more alive or more fully myself than when I'm onstage. It's a wondrous place where kindness, beauty, loyalty, and laughter are played out. Wy and I can sing about heartbreak and pain, while the sting is removed. All facets of my personality are released: I can be a coquettish flirt or the girl next door, a comedian, a team member, and a proud mother. I'm a cheerleader urging the crowd to smile and enjoy themselves, a hostess inviting our guests to join in fellowship, relax, and forget about the nagging concerns of their everyday lives. Through the years the stage had become our home, church, playground, workplace—the center of all our needs.

Onstage Wynonna and I express how we feel about each other, demonstrating mutual admiration and unconditional love.

If watching our interaction was enjoyable, observers always noted that our contrasts, the differences between the two of us, made for mighty interesting viewing as well. I was the feminine fun-loving foil for Wynonna's ambitious hard-belting seriousness. We had such a good time on stage together and quickly discovered that fun is infectious. There are ideas in melodies, a musical intelligence. The stage allows a chemistry of thoughts and feelings, an inexplicable bond of kinship. Singing expresses the human experience, and our role was to say what others are unable to say.

"The Infinity Tour," as Wy called it, had become finite and Ken and Jo Stilts, Martha Taylor, and Larry waited nervously in the front of the bus while Wynonna and I were back in our rooms putting on our makeup. Seated at our lighted makeup vanities, Wy and I conversed through our open bedroom door as Ashley sat watching quietly on my bed.

Wy and I chatted about one of our first shows at the Gore Community Center, a cinder block barn in the Georgia piney woods a block from a worm farm. Gary Gordon, the man who'd booked the show, had taken all of us to his home afterward to have supper. His schoolteacher wife kept saying, "I'm telling you, you two gals are gonna be huge someday!"

Wynonna and I were so blissfully happy to be starting out on the road singing together, we couldn't imagine feeling any more fulfilled than we were that very moment.

Tonight I told Wy, "I surely enjoy success now, but I still don't quite believe it. Every time I get in my nice car and open the sunroof, I think about those old clunkers we had all our lives."

Wynonna sighed and said, "Momma, face it, we've become hooked on the road. We have addictions—we're diesel sniffers!"

When I grew wistful and silent, Wynonna laid down her mascara and leaned over to look through the doorway at me. "What is it Mommy?" she asked.

"Oh, I was just considering that I'm gonna have to go cold turkey on December fifth," I answered. "There's no detox center I can go to that will help get me over my dependency on this lifestyle with you."

The reminiscing had turned painful so Wynonna began rummaging through her tape box. Suddenly, Amy Grant's poignantly beautiful song "Got My Hopes Set High" replaced the awkward silence with our friend's message of faith-filled expectations.

Then came that dreaded knock at the door, and for the last time Mike McGrath announced: "It's showtime!"

Ken appeared with a solemn expression and said in his stately cadence: "I want you both to know how much I love you and that these last eight years have been the greatest, most enjoyable part of my life."

As the three of us stood there holding hands in Wynonna's room, I told her: "Sweetheart, when Ken and I were considering titles to begin planning this farewell tour, I suggested we call it 'The Sunset Tour,' because although I may be sort of like the evening star, you are like the golden sun that rises the next morning."

Ken walked us up to the front of the bus where Larry led us, Ashley, Jo, and Martha in a prayer.

Garth Brooks, who had been touring with us for the previous six weeks, came knocking on the bus door, asking if he could escort Wynonna and me to the stage. Larry was already on my left, Ashley in between Wynonna and me, with Ken on her arm, but gentleman Garth joined our little group as we headed toward the backstage area. Wynonna and I thanked him for sharing these last tour days with us, and I predicted: "This is my last road concert, and it's also the last concert you'll be an opening act!"

As we paused for a traditional team huddle with the band, I had my Mom, who'd brought two busloads of people from Ashland, mark the occasion with a picture of our road family.

At the bottom of the stage steps Wynonna looked as if she were about to burst into tears and I had to scold her. "Do it!" I commanded.

"Do what?" she wondered, seemingly oblivious to what I meant.

"You know—Ferdinand!"

Every night for eight years before she ran up the steps, Wynonna would paw the ground like Ferdinand the Bull as I hollered, "Go get 'em." Just then Tim Rogers, our production manager, came over the walkie-talkie: "We're waiting on you Mamaw, ain't nobody doing nothing till we hear you say it!"

It was my turn to perform the little ritual I had started years ago to signify closing night of a long spell out on the road. "Okay boys, this is it. 'Tonight we really are rounding third and headed home!' "

It was a wonderful show, but Wynonna and I were aware every second that it was the dress rehearsal for the upcoming televised Farewell Concert the following week. Knowing that John David Sisler, the boy I had my first crush on, was out in the audience of eighteen thousand, I took advantage of my last chance for revenge and prissily announced that "choosing Sandy Blankenship over me in the seventh grade had been a bad move!"

Wy shot me one of her familiar "I can't believe you said that" looks.

As Wynonna and I left the stage after the finale, Bud's camera crew was following us filming for the Farewell Tour documentary. Once I got past the point where people backstage could see me, I lost control and ducked behind a pillar.

Wynonna and I spent some time alone on the bus before heading into the big reception with all the busloads of family and friends from Ashland. As Wynonna, Ashley, Larry, and I stepped into that large room, it was like being in a hall of mirrors. All these people who'd known us all our lives were standing there looking at us, reflecting our past back at us.

Aunt Faith, Daddy's youngest sister, died during the Farewell Tour. Hope was there with her family, as well as all the other Judd aunts and cousins. Ashley calls them, "our gene pool!"

Aunts Evelyn Watseka, Marioline, and Ramona had written to me faithfully since my illness, just as Aunt Pauline had sent get-well letters to Brian. As they hugged me, how I wished my Daddy were there too.

Our long-time family physician, Dr. Wayne Franz, who had diagnosed Brian and had done my pregnancy test, smiled as he said: "I'm proud of you, Diana."

"You'll never know what hearing that means to me!" I replied.

Dr. Franz didn't remember that autumn evening back in 1963 when I disappointed him by informing him that I thought I was pregnant, but I'd never forgotten it. As I stood in between him and Wynonna, introducing them for the first time, I considered how no one has a crystal ball in this life. We don't know what good we're creating when we simply try to do what's right.

My early life as Diana Ellen Judd from Ashland, Kentucky, was there in front of me that night, and next week, my recent life as Naomi Judd of the Judds would reach a conclusion. Who would I be next? Perhaps we are all three people: the way we see ourselves, the way others see us, and the way we really are.

The *Dreamchaser* arrived at our farm gate in Franklin, Tennessee. I moved out of my beloved traveling house. Standing on our front porch at 4:00 AM surrounded by all my belongings, Wy and I stood silent and motionless for a few moments staring at the *Dreamchaser* waiting down at the gate. I nodded for Larry to go on in and gave him a goodnight kiss on the cheek. Without a word, Wy and I walked back down and went to bed in our beloved clubhouse. We figured it would be easier to let go in the morning light.

December 4 was about a week away. I knew I must be ready to flow with change, so the moment I exited that stage I could let go gracefully. I still had a fear of collapsing into a sobbing heap, clutching the base of my microphone stand as they tried to pry me loose.

A therapist specializing in biofeedback came out to the farm to teach me guided imagery. If a picture is worth a thousand words, imagery is even more dense with information! In fact, words are slower than imagery to affect the relaxation process. Long before I began researching PNI, I was using imagery to facilitate control and mastery over stressful or difficult situations.

For instance, if Wynonna and I were singing live at the Grammy's, during rehearsals and whenever the stage was not being used, I'd walk out and imagine just how I wanted the performance to go. At our sound checks every afternoon I would roam the stage and sometimes even the arena, visualizing how I wanted to express myself. Imagery and biofeedback have proven to be of great therapeutic value in bringing about physiological changes, providing psychological insight, and enhancing emotional awareness.

I was not only concerned about controlling my emotions in public during the most stressful night of my life but I was determined that the trauma not compromise my fragile health. A Nashville-area specialist in biofeedback, Dr. Bob, began by helping me learn about progressive muscle relaxation. When Dr. Bob asked me to go back in memory to a place where I'd experienced unconditional love and a stress-free atmosphere, the first thing that came to mind was our front porch when I was a child. He helped me get in touch with associations from all five senses and encouraged me to return to that place not only on December 4 but anytime I felt myself in tough situations.

Our farewell concert was set for Murfreesboro, Tennessee, near Nashville at the Middle Tennessee State University's twelve-thousand-seat Murphy Center, the largest indoor venue in our area. When tickets went on sale they sold out in a record seventeen minutes. It was now bitter cold winter. Having learned that people from all fifty states had been camping out for days to be in line, I sent the folks who help us at our farm over to Murfreesboro with coffee, hot chocolate, donuts, autographed photos, etc. Dorthey, our housekeeper; her husband, Steve, our farm foreman; and her sister-in-law, Peggy, our personal secretary, returned with messages and stories about conversations with these hardy, loyal fans. In many instances I knew exactly who they were referring to as soon as they described a person.

Wynonna showed up at the farm one evening to take a walk in the valley, saying: "Mom, I feel like a bird with a broken wing."

As we headed down the valley hand in hand, I corrected Wynonna. "You're not a sparrow with a broken wing, you're an eagle! An eagle is the only bird that won't seek shelter in a storm. Instead it faces into it, spreads its wings, and allows the turbulence to carry it to even greater heights."

I confided to her I was counting on grace to get us through that last song together. Grace, that divine influence on our hearts, is more than God's favor on us, it's an unrepayable kindness.

Wynonna exclaimed, "Oh, I think I get it. You mean kind of like I take one step and God takes ten!"

That Friday night Larry and Ashley fell terribly ill. A particularly nasty strain of flu, the Beijing variety, was blitzing Nashville and waylaid them. They spiked fevers, were sick to their stomachs, and ached all over. I knew I had no choice but to move to a hotel and pray that I didn't succumb to it as well. There was just too much riding on this pay-per-view concert.

To me the most important thing was that Wynonna get through our last show to prove to herself that she could do it. She said, "Mom if I survive it, then I know I can do anything! I also want you to go out as heavyweight champ."

Wynonna, Ken, and I had invested a small fortune to produce this Viewers Choice cable TV special. The enormity of the event was beginning to hit us. Not only had fans come in from all over the country, but crew people everywhere had been calling Bud and Ken asking if they could be part of the history-making show. Guys like Jim Yockey, who'd been the camera man at WSM for Ralph Emery's early morning show back in the 1980s. Sometimes it seemed a bit like orchestrating my own funeral, but I was bound and determined that December 4 be a celebration and that I say good-bye with class, style, and dignity.

It was raining cats and dogs Saturday morning, November 30, as I left the farm to move into a modest motel in Murfreesboro near the venue. I'd been counting heavily on taking walks in Peaceful Valley with Wynonna, Ashley, and Larry on these days before the concert. As I began unpacking in the drab motel room, I felt so isolated from my loved ones. Sitting on my bed looking around the bare room, I felt a separation from the whole outside world. Did this symbolize my future, cut off from everything I knew and loved?

My fears suddenly began multiplying. To keep myself from having a panic attack, I began to control my breathing and reached for the Gideon Bible in the drawer. I opened right to Romans 8:38–39: "For I am persuaded, that neither death, nor life, nor angels, nor principalities, nor powers, nor things present, nor things to come, nor height, nor depth, nor any other creature shall be able to separate us from the love of God, which is in Christ Jesus our Lord." I looked up from these pages and felt that it wasn't Ashley and Larry who were quarantined; God was sequestering *me* so he could deal with me alone!

When we arrived at the coliseum that afternoon for our first production meeting with the huge crew, Wynonna and I were overwhelmed by the magnitude of this project. We snagged a much sought after director, Lou Horvitz, who'd filmed Diana Ross's concert in Central Park. Indeed it seemed that everyone involved was the best in his or her field. Wy and I found it a little scary that we were to have a brand-new stage, new lighting, etc. I noticed right away that she didn't seem to feel well, and her first hello told me that she had a sore throat and her voice was tired.

After all of our introductions we were shown around the coliseum to acclimate ourselves. Vanessa had created a quick-change tent off stage right for our three costume changes. Huge video screens would show highlights of our career during the two-minute wardrobe breaks. For sentimental reasons, we'd decided that instead of having new outfits made, we'd pull out dresses from the past.

Vanessa had an idea. "Naomi, you keep referring to this as your 'going away party,' so you've got to wear the ultimate party dress! We need to borrow your Red Vinyl and Wynonna's Black Vinyl from the Country Music Hall of Fame. I suggest the midnight blue Claudette Cobert for the middle acoustic segment and your gold velvet Miss America dress to say good night to America."

Wynonna, Ken, and I sat on the empty stage with Bud Schaetzle, discussing the format for the show. As Wynonna and I looked over the set list, it was frustrating not being able to do more tunes. We felt enormously proud of the music we'd created. Wynonna said: "It's durable! We put heart in our art."

I had an inspiration! "You guys, speaking of heart, we've got to have Brent and Don be part of this. Let's have them come out onstage and do the very first song we ever learned. We need to go out like we came in."

Wynonna seemed exhausted and asked if she could leave early

to go back to her farm to rest. As I was leaving, Martha slipped me a present. "This is to remind you that although you're by yourself in that motel we're all still with you in spirit."

It was a beautiful guardian angel statue holding a lighted candle, her wings gently moving.

When we returned for rehearsal the next afternoon on Sunday, everyone was very anxious to do a runthrough since Wynonna had begged off the day before. The moment I heard her speak, I knew she was worse, not better!

"How ya doing my little diva with the deviated septum?" I asked as I gave her a squeeze.

She whispered hoarsely, "Mommy, I can't sing again today, I think I should save my voice. Let's just ask Mark Thompson to sing my part and you sing harmony on him, so that they can check the set list for camera placements, lights, and technicalities."

Ken, Bud, Lou, and Allen Branton, our lighting guy, suddenly appeared lined up in formation in front of us looking very concerned. I told Wynonna I was going to fix her some hot herbal tea, but slipped into the production office to call our family doctor. He agreed to put Wynonna on prednisone and some other oral medications. Since it was the Sunday night after Thanksgiving, I had trouble finding a pharmacy that was even open. Rehearsal turned into a disaster, and Wy left early again.

In my hotel room that night, I realized that everything that could possibly go wrong had. I felt alone on the grim edge of disaster. Not only was Wynonna getting worse as the clock was ticking away but it now occurred to me that since her resistance was so low, she was susceptible to the flu that had now begun making its rounds among members of our crew. When I called the farm hoping to hear some comforting words, Larry and Ashley were so ill they couldn't talk for more than four or five minutes. I paced my motel room singing the chorus from *Cinderella*: "No matter how your heart is grieving, if you'll keep believing—the dream that you wish really will come true."

As soon as we arrived at rehearsal Monday afternoon, I knew from the pinched look on Wynonna's face we were in serious trouble even before she pointed to her lips and shook her head no, indicating that she had no voice. Just as various crew members began descending on us, begging answers to very pressing questions, she pulled a child's magic slate out of her purse and scribbled "I'm scared." I stepped in front of Wynonna and announced that I would be doing all the communicating because she needed to conserve her energy. I printed a small sign declaring "Don't Ask Me!" and stuck it in the brim of her hat.

After another unsatisfactory abbreviated rehearsal, Ken, Bud, Wynonna, and I retired to the privacy of our quick-change tent. Ken looked as if he were about to have another heart attack as he finally asked, "Just how bad is your throat?" For the first time all day she opened her mouth and tried to answer him but nothing came out. Not even a squeak. "My God!" we all gasped in unison.

It was now 9:00 on Monday night, forty-eight hours before the live televised farewell concert. Instinctively, I reached for Ken's portable phone, realizing the prednisone prescription from our family doctor hadn't been at all effective. I flashed on the prospect that Larry Gatlin's voice doctor, who'd gotten Larry through his terrible voice crisis, might help us. I quickly phoned Larry's home for the doctor's phone number. As I was dialing the stranger's home, Ken nodded glumly toward his watch as if to say "Fat chance."

"Is this Dr. Ossoff?" I asked, struggling to control my anxiety. "And do you believe in God?" was my second question. When he answered, "Yes I do," I sighed with relief and continued, "Then I hope that you realize that He gave you a talent to heal people! You don't know me, my name is Naomi Judd, but I need you to help my daughter."

Somehow I'd said the right thing. This doctor agreed to not only get dressed immediately and come out in the middle of the frigid night but called his associate and had him open Vanderbilt's voice clinic in Nashville. Ken told his nephew Doug to take Wy, and suggested she spend the night at the nearby Vanderbilt Plaza Hotel, since Dr. Ossoff would need to see her again the next morning on Tuesday. Wynonna and I were panic-stricken at the thought of being separated by the distance, both stuck in hotels. She scribbled on her magic slate, "Mommy, I can't believe all this is happening, I'm so sorry." I hugged her, rocking back and forth as I reassured her everything would be okay, saying, "Let's just pray the answer not the problem!"

They whisked her off into the night and I was left standing alone.

Chuck Thompson, our press agent, called my room reminding me he already had *Good Morning America*, Dave Zimmerman of *USA Today, Entertainment Tonight*, and lots of other important interviews set for early Tuesday morning to let people know about our concert, which was the following night. I had to do them solo, and make excuses for Wy's absence. I psyched myself up and served my homilies and quotes like bacon and eggs. I'd become rather adroit at the sixty-second sound bite, those annoying symptoms of America's short attention span.

On *Good Morning America*, when Joan Lunden asked me what I would be doing after December 5, my answer was, "I'm going to form a post-traumatic stress syndrome support group for redheaded mothers with chronic liver disease who are forced to retire from duets with dynamic singing diva daughters."

All the time I had the uncanny sensation that Wynonna was watching me from her hotel room. When I showed up to do *Entertainment Tonight* with my dear friend Dick Heard, he knew something was wrong, because he'd never seen us apart in all the years he'd been interviewing us. When I confided in him that Wy had no voice, he choked.

After my last interview, I went straight to a phone to get the diagnosis from the voice doctor himself. As I was dialing his number at Vanderbilt, where I called for my own lab report, I had to fight off that awful feeling that goes with a sickening loss of control. It was no coincidence that his receptionist came on the line, congenially asking, "I'm Hope, may I help you?"

With sophisticated technology, they'd been able to visualize Wy's vocal cords, and said her throat was in bad shape. "Naomi, in her extreme agitation and anxiety, Wynonna's not been eating and the gastric juices from her stomach have refluxed and bathed her vocal cords, irritating them. She's also experiencing some upper respiratory tract infection and her tonsils are inflamed, and that's why her lymph glands are swollen and she doesn't feel well. We have her on medication and are giving her treatments here in our office. I'll see her again this afternoon before she comes to your last rehearsal tonight. I need to keep her here in the complex so I can treat her first thing in the morning before she has to get ready for the show. I know what your next question is—will she be able to sing? All I can say is that we're doing the best we can."

How could this be happening? I walked to the window in my motel room, leaned my forehead against the cool glass and stared out for the longest time. The cold rain was turning to sleet and the world seemed to be going about its business, completely oblivious to the fact that we were about to self-destruct. An insight suddenly flashed through my mind, and I began calling our therapist as fast as my fingers would work.

After repeating what the doctor had said, I told our therapist, "Having discovered for myself this past year how our body speaks to us in symbols known as symptoms, I believe Wynonna's inability to speak or sing is a subconscious attempt to keep from having to say good-bye to me. I know she's unaware of what she's doing, but could she be acting out a fear of the last song?"

The therapist agreed with my theory, and said she was shutting down her practice to come be with us. At our last dress rehearsal that Tuesday night, December 3, we all knew we were in desperate straits. Although we had the greatest crew in the country assembled, a gorgeous multitiered stage, and the best lighing, there was no cohesion because everything hinged on us singing a full show runthrough. Our song set list included numbers we hadn't sung in years, songs our new keyboard player had never played. Although we needed badly to rehearse them, we simply couldn't. Since Wy wasn't singing, she also wasn't moving. The lighting guys were left in the dark. Bud would have to instruct the camera operators, "Just follow the girls wherever they go! It's called 'winging it,' guys."

Wy arrived with her magic slate under her arm, dark circles under her eyes. When Bud and Lou came rushing toward us, Wynonna and I glanced over at each other and began laughing hysterically. Bud Schaetzle is short and heavy set, while Lou is tall and thin, reminding us of Bud Abbott and Lou Costello. Bud asked imploringly, "Godzilla, do you have any words of wisdom for us?"

Nodding her head while she was writing something on her magic slate, Wy held it up high above her head for everyone to read. It said "Never put your tongue on a glacier."

Ken and I sneaked off to the quick-change tent so no one could overhear what we were about to say. "Wynonna's just upped the ante again in this high-stakes poker game. What happens if she can't sing tomorrow night?" I nervously questioned him.

"We'd be ruined," he answered flatly. "We've spent all this time and money building this boat with so many people on board. Tomorrow night we launch it and hope it floats. If it doesn't, well . . . all we can do is pray toward heaven and row like hell toward shore!"

"I've been through earthquakes and floods, been fired, kicked in the face, heartbroke, and slam-dunked, but I've never been through anything like this before," I said with a moan.

Just as I'd suspected, Ken confided that he'd been popping nitroglycerin pills. I didn't know if Wy had a voice and I didn't know if Ken was going to have another heart attack! I didn't know whether Ashley and Larry would be able to get out of their sick beds and make it to the concert. Bud was experiencing serious back problems and on medication, postponing surgery. Remarkably, I seemed to be the only healthy one and yet this whole event was because of my illness!

Ken and I sat huddled together seeking comfort from each other, knowing all the while that no one had the answers this time. "Ken, do you remember what I promised you the day Wynonna and I first came out to your office and asked you to manage us?"

He chortled, then replied, "Yes, you promised that if I agreed to take you two girls on that you would be infinitely more interesting than stocks and bonds! This whole thing is part Greek tragedy, part soap opera!"

Just as we were hugging good night, I let out a deep sigh as I realized the next time I saw him would be at showtime, and my skirt fell down. "Freeze and close your eyes!" I ordered as I frantically scooped my skirt back up off the floor.

When I shut my motel door behind me, I realized that after tomorrow night, the nights were going to be toughest on me. What was I to do alone at the farm when the sun went down? I was used to putting on my Judd lips, laughing with Wy as she did my hair, decking myself in rhinestones getting ready to sing my heart out, communicating with thousands of friends. I couldn't worry about the future now, I knew how important it was for me to get a good night's sleep tonight. Although I don't take sleeping pills, tonight I wished I had one.

As I was running my bath, I looked over at my favorite photo of Wynonna and Ashley propped against the Kleenex box on my bedside table. They're smiling at me cheek-to-cheek, big sister Wy with her arm protectively around Ashley. Next to it was the photo of Larry kissing me on our wedding night. I turned out all the lights, lit my scented candles around the bathtub, and soaked. As I crawled into bed in the dark, I lay there watching the soft glow of Martha's guardian angel statue moving her wings till I fell asleep.

I had a strange dream that night. Wynonna was standing alone in the middle of our bridge in Peaceful Valley. She needed to cross over from the past to the future waiting for her on the other side. Time had come for her to make her solo debut and I was supposed to introduce her. Her rapt audience were all critters: deer, raccoons, dogs, cats, birds, red-tailed hawks, skunks, coyotes, rabbits, groundhogs, squirrels, and woodland creatures. Scared and frantic, mournfully she kept crying out, "Mommy, mommy, where are you?"

But she could no longer see or hear me. I had changed forms and now I was the wind. An old protective instinct raged in my bosom and I longed for a voice to say, "Music will carry you across, my daughter of song!" So I summoned all my energy and blew through her hair, rustling the leaves and swirling through the treetops so loudly they made a whistling noise that sounded like: "Sing! Sing!" And Wynonna sang a song no one had ever heard before.

When I awoke it was December 4. Jung believed the number four signifies completeness, wholeness. I gulped as I realized that today all the things I'd learned this past year would be put to the final test. My sustained emotion remained a concern for Wynonna.

Major George Currey knocked at the door to take me to the venue, but just as I was walking out of my room a news bulletin came on TV. America's longest-held hostage, Terry Anderson, was being released from prison. "Today's the happiest day of his life—the saddest of mine," I thought to myself.

In the car I noticed that George didn't look well and asked: "Are you all right?"

Trying to evade the question he simply responded, "Oh, I'll make it." George was so concerned and caught up in the melodrama, he was experiencing severe chest pains. He ended up having a quadruple bypass after the concert.

It was a depressingly ugly day and as we pulled down into the coliseum, a crowd of fans, most of whom I recognized, were shivering in the cold. I immediately called for George to stop the car, rolled down the windows, and sat there chatting with them. A young girl showed me a tattoo on her shoulder of the Judds' logo. Their tender words of comfort made me cry. They said, "You and Wy are like our family and we wanted to be with you." One of them gave me a coffee mug with the words from 1 Corinthians 13:13: "And now abideth faith, hope, and charity, these three; but the greatest of these is charity."

When I walked into the dressing room everyone was there. Larry, Ashley, Mom, our therapist, our pastor and his family, Ken's family, and our friends the "Beauty Team": Vanessa, Earl, and Norma. Ashley pressed a letter in my hand she'd written before leaving the farm.

Ma Mere,

On this sad yet inevitable day, my heart aches for you and I feel the need to remind you of the strong, proud woman I've known you to be for all of my twenty-three years.

I wouldn't trade anything for the way that Wy and I were raised. Not because our lives were always smooth or because I can now safely cherish it as offbeat. It's because our upbringing is a record of you: your craziness and wild dreams, the traveling, the colorful characters you brought into our home, your ethics and the compassion for people you instilled in us, the unconditional love you gave sister and me coupled with the constant reminder "you can do anything you set your heart on!"

You are the single most interesting and inspiring person I know. When I look back on your exploits and trials, I gain a sense of confidence and a pattern for my own future adventures. There is a sacred pact among the three of us, and a special closeness in sharing each other's secrets. Wynonna and I are firmly anchored in this world by your awesome love for us. As much as people can belong to one another, sister and I belong to you.

Tonight as I sit with Nana and Pop, watching with millions of your admirers as you gracefully sing your last note, I will once again be grateful to you for another example how to conquer adversity. Because I know your indomitable spirit better than anyone, I have a sense of security that you'll be all right tomorrow.

I have to get ready now, I'm out of space, and I'm crying.

I love you with all my heart Mom,

Ashley

There was such an eerie calm. The locker room was laden with flowers and everyone was acting so somber, it reminded me of a funeral parlor. There was a knock at the door and Dr. Ossoff and his two assistants walked in carrying instruments in front of them, looking like the three wise men bearing gifts. As they were doing a treatment on Wy, the doctor advised: "You'll have only your middle range, so you can't count on your low register and you won't be able to hit high notes." Just then Dr. Ossoff's pager went off telling him his son had just been in an accident, but he chose to stay for Wynonna.

Wynonna was still whispering and said to us, "I don't know what's going to happen out there. For a long time now I've felt like December 4 was knowing where and when I was going to die, but not knowing how I would act and how it would actually feel. I'm hanging on by my fingernails."

I encouraged her, "If you start to lose your grip, just freefall into love. The fans are our safety net. I trust our fans, I know that they will be there for us. Trust is proof of real love."

I could hardly stand to look at my Mom, for I saw in her face the helplessness and pain she was feeling for me that I was experiencing toward Wynonna. As I hugged her, Larry, and Ashley good-bye, I offered them a brave smile and sighed, "Life is short, but it's wide!"

Side by side, as Wynonna and I began our last walk toward the stage, our footsteps echoed down the corridors. We called each other "Thelma" and "Louise," referring to the recent movie of the same name of two renegade women living out their fantasy on the road, driving toward some unknown destination. At the end of the movie Thelma and Louise hold hands and drive off a cliff into the Grand Canyon, rather than conform to the world that's mistreated them.

Ken, who flanked us, looked like Atlas, who was condemned to carry the world on his shoulders. "Mr. Big, you got style!" Wynonna exclaimed, referring to Hemingway's definition that "style is grace under pressure."

Bud appeared walking backward in front of us, sweating like Albert Brooks in the movie *Broadcast News*.

"Butthead [as we affectionately call him], you look like you're about to break out all over in worry warts!" I teased.

"Are you girls ready for this?" he inquired, seeming desperate to know.

"Yeah, but I'd rather run naked through a teamster meeting," I answered sarcastically.

We came into the backstage area to find the atmosphere positively charged with electricity and tension! The entire crew was dressed all in black for camouflage. Guys wired with headsets snapped orders, and everyone around us seemed to have a walkie-talkie. In eight years I've never seen such an explosive mix of high drama and anticipation!

Suddenly I heard myself talking and looked up to see videos being played on the giant screens around the arena. For the last fifteen minutes, the coliseum audience of twelve thousand fans, friends, and industry insiders had been viewing a brief documentary chronicling our career with tributes from the biggest names in show business. I'd recommended our good friend, country music commentator John Davis, to be the evening's host, and he was doing a wonderful job. Director Lou Horvitz greeted us over a walkie-talkie from his post at command central, announcing that an unprecedented number of homes were tuned into this live concert event.

As Mike McGrath was handing Wynonna her can of gold glitter hairspray, I took it from him and asked, "May I?" For eight years this walk to the stage had been my favorite thing. I'd strut and fluff my colorful petticoats with great aplomb, flashing an enthusiastic smile to backstage crew members and onlookers as they stepped back to clear a path for Wynonna and me. Tonight I felt like a rare flower, some hot-house delicate blossom grown for exhibition.

When we reached the stage steps, Wynonna and I were clinging to each other, yet afraid to allow our eyes to meet. I could feel her shaking violently. Suddenly the drums thundered a familiar down-beat. The vibrating bass boomed, and a signature piano riff mingled with an oh-so-sweet guitar chord. Music, motion, and colors swirled, swelling, building, and ringing truer than anything we'd ever known.

We heard Ken shout, "We're on live TV—go!" Wy gasped for air just as she had when she made her first bungee jump. When it came my call to join her onstage, at the top of the steps I turned and glanced back over my shoulder at Ken. He looked up from his executive producer post with a terrified questioning look across his face, perhaps wondering if I was going to chicken out at this last second. I felt as I had when I was a child going off the high dive for the first time. I'd talked myself into climbing the ladder, but became terrified when I looked down and saw the height. When I turned around to try to go back down, the ladder was full of other kids and there was only one way out. I had to take the plunge.

It was another leap of faith. The moment my feet hit the stage, there was no turning back. Now it was just the kid and me. No matter how much they loved us, Larry, Ashley, Mom, Ken, our therapist, our pastor, my doctor, none of them could come out here. I hit the top of the riser running, and the instant I appeared, thousands of flashbulbs erupted.

Wynonna and I paraded the length of the well-appointed stage drinking in the thunderous applause like water. I opened my arms out toward the audience as if I were ushering them into our parlor and exclaimed: "Tonight is a celebration of love, laughter, music, and life. I am so glad you all are with us for the biggest night of our lives!"

As Wy and I looked out into the smiling sea of faces, we felt a penetrating thrill of exhilaration as we recognized that we were all attached by mysterious bonds of kinship.

After the week-long conspiracy to keep Wynonna and me apart, I didn't want to leave her side. We were walking a tightrope, but we were intertwined now and harmoniously balanced. She was actually singing! Her voice sounded husky and raw. As predetermined, we knew there were no guarantees. We could only take it a song at a time. I'd wanted to make an announcement about her throat ordeal, but there was really no need. There was now such a super-heightened sensitivity, I felt as if we had subconscious access to the audience.

Wynonna and I suspected that some people were expecting a tearful swan song, an emotion-drenched last hurrah. Instead, I strutted the perimeter of the stage and coquettishly inquired: "Did you guys really think somebody who'd wear a party dress like this one would just retire to the farm without throwing a blow-out bash?"

Our entire career passed before us as Wynonna and I sang nineteen of our favorite songs. Through them we were retracing all the concerts, and my mind went back to a Sunday noontime matinee at the Puyallup Fair in Washington State. In my snapshot memory, I saw the diverse crowd spread out before us, the Ferris wheel looming in the background. I could feel the breeze that was blowing in my hair and smell the wares of the food vendors out on the midway next to the stage.

When it was time to perform "River of Time," all I could think of was my first introduction of the song: "Music expresses emotions that words can't define." I thought of how too often we devalue words and intone them with false sincerity or write them without much thought, so they become mere husks of meaning, stripped of all their power, failing to move us. How was I going to explain the complexity, mystery, transcendent feeling of oneness Wynonna and I were experiencing? Before I began trying, I paused for a moment in frustration considering that the most important things are always the hardest to say.

Wynonna was supposed to begin the song standing downstage with me seated upon a riser behind her. For a moment, as I paused to find my words of introduction, she looked as if she feared I was losing it. Before she started up the ramp to rescue me I just spoke my heart: "I think Wynonna and I love country music at this moment more than we ever have. It is real music for real people. I believe that music is the breath of God; I think it's a healer."

For the next moment I was spellbound as Wynonna sang the

words straight to me. Although I'd written these prophetic lyrics, it was as if I were hearing them for the first time: "I'm holding back a flood of tears, just thinking about those happy years. All the good times that are no more, my love is gone, gone, gone for ever more. Silence so deep only my soul can hear says now the past is what I fear. My future isn't what it used to be, only today is all that's promised me. Flow on river of time, wash away the pain and heal my mind. Flow on river of time, carry me away."

My mind flashed to an image of Jesus standing at the shore of the river Jordan, waiting to be baptized before beginning his life's work. This song was Wynonna's baptism by fire. She came over to my side and we sang together: "We're all driven by the winds of change, seems nothing ever stays the same. It's faith that guides me around the bend, life's forever beginning, beginning again." The words rang with a purging, resonating truth.

Then it was time to excuse the band, lower the lights, bring Brent Maher and Don Potter onstage for our favorite segment in the show. Unrehearsed, Brent described sitting around the table with the kerosene lamp on Del Rio Pike. He referred to "our uniqueness and wacky sense of humor." Don recalled how we'd looked in our "little country dresses and war paint." He said that the moment we opened our mouths to begin singing he felt "the pleasure of the Lord." My hand resting gently on Wynonna's knee, we listened to them describing our humble beginnings. It was the alpha and omega, the beginning and the end. I had such an intense longing to prolong, perpetuate that moment, exalting in what the four of us had meant to each other.

As Wynonna and I began the first song we ever learned together after dedicating it to my Mom, "The Sweetest Gift, a Mother's Smile," we were suddenly transported back to that mountaintop in Morrill, Kentucky. Wynonna was twelve years old with combs in her hair, barefoot in overalls.

When we performed our anthem, "Why Not Me," I smiled as I considered how the Great God of Luck had whacked us on the head with his magic wand. I knew that after tonight it would remain in Wy's show as part of the dynamic continuum of what we stand for and achieved.

The Jordanaires joined us onstage to sing harmony on "Don't Be Cruel" as they had with the King back in 1956. Carl Perkins featured his protorock guitar licks on his "Let Me Tell You About Love." We dedicated "Love Is Alive" to Ken, and then it was time for Wynonna and me to face each other.

When she referred to me as the "Queen of Everything," I allowed that "Wynonna and Ashley are the jewels in my crown and I wish that I had my scepter so I could freeze this moment in time." As we joined each other side by side on stools, Wy acknowledged that there almost wasn't a show, referring to her serious throat problems. Wynonna expressed a thought we both felt deeply, "The one thing that's perfect tonight is that you guys are all out there sharing this with us."

I picked it up by saying: "I feel like I've been Cinderella gone to the ball for the last eight years, but the hour is drawing nigh and I'm going home with my Prince Charming. This is not my going away party," I declared looking into Wynonna's sorrowful face. "I'm not going anywhere, you're the one who's going places. I want you to understand that the deepest source of your identity is not being a Judd, or even being my daughter. The deepest source of your identity is the Lord."

As we harmonized on "Grandpa," knowing we'd never do it again, made it sadder than a thousand sad songs. Toward the conclusion, Wynonna needed support from the fans and asked them to sing to us while she took a break, sipping her hot tea laced with honey. As they did, it was an ephemeral, transitory moment, where strangers turn to friends through a shared language.

Wynonna's voice was now on its way out. We knew we were nearing the end and Wynonna was beginning to cry, so I comforted her: "Life is all about embrace and release, embrace and release. Now you must spread your wings and fly my darling, and go toward the light. Go toward the light."

The psychic reverberations created a mesmerizing force that began to carry Wynonna and me. Just as we'd felt ourselves perched precariously on the brink of drowning in a sea of emotions, Wy and I suddenly felt upheld by the underpinning strains of "Love Can Build a Bridge." As the Christ Church Choir began assembling onstage, I realized what our therapist had said about no one being able to go out there with Wynonna and me but the Lord himself. Our own church choir became a symbolic representation of the Holy Spirit standing behind us. I looked over and saw Ashley, Larry, and Mom on my right, Ken on my left, and the fans before us. It seemed as if the stage were being levitated.

As we stood hand in hand, beginning our last song together, I knew this was the bottom of the ninth in the World Series with the bases loaded and Wynonna up to bat. As I joined my dearest companion in harmony for our last time, it was like lucid dreaming. I felt like a dragonfly, suspended in air, with gossamer wings beating very, very fast. As Wynonna hit the impossibly high notes with a church soloist lung power, she looked like a pre-Raphaelite painting. She was so beautiful with her chin tilted upward in soft golden light beaming down like a ray from heaven. Tears, sparkling like diamonds, cascaded down her cheeks. It was a supernatural, sacred moment and nothing will ever outshine its brilliance.

I spoke my final words to America saying: "Wynonna and I feel so blessed to have traveled this great country for the last eight years. You all are what inspired me to write this song. For I believe in the power of love, and I believe that there is always hope."

As we waved our slow-motion good-bye while walking up to the highest point on the multitiered stage, Wynonna and I expected to ascend into heaven. I felt a lofty clear peace, and it was the most complete moment of my life.

I paused for one precious, lingering moment before Wynonna slipped her hand around my waist to lead me away. As our music disappeared into the atmosphere, I realized I was acting out a metaphor for mortality; a brief life lived out onstage, making my last bow before vanishing silently into the darkness.

As Wynonna and I hit the bottom of the steps and touched concrete, she was pulling me along by my right hand. Perhaps she was afraid I'd break loose and bolt for another bow. By the time we were back in the locker room, I was numb. The same group of family and friends came flying in, hugging us while squealing accolades.

"People are still sitting in their seats with their mouths open, they can't believe how stupendous that was. They don't want to get up and leave," Ashley exclaimed. Wynonna was sitting beside me on the couch, both of us staring dead ahead into space. "Okay you oil wells!" Wynonna declared.

"To what does that refer?" Ashley asked.

"I call people who gush with compliments oil wells," Wynonna replied.

Everyone was so relieved and thrilled that Wynonna had been able to sing and I'd maintained my composure, that the atmosphere was more of gladness than sadness. After relaxing a few minutes, we all headed down the hall to a huge reception. On our way, we passed a crowd gathered around an Amish buggy. Getting closer, we realized it was Al Teller, Tony Brown, Bruce Hinton, Zach Horowitz, all the MCA folks who presented me with the buggy as a going away gift.

If the reception after our last road concert in Lexington, Kentucky, had been a hall of mirrors of people who new us from birth, this reception was made up of people who had been there since the dawn of our career. Besides our organization, there were media people, RCA staff, musicians, songwriters, and of course *lots* of celebrities.

When I looked at Ricky Skaggs, I remembered his homecoming at the high school in Louisa, Kentucky, where our folks had seen us perform for the first time back in 1984. There were artists like Restless Heart, Highway 101, and Sawyer Brown, reminding us of all the rodeos, crew dinners, and nights off bowling on the road. Our celebrity girlfriends Reba McEntire, Kathy Mattea, and Emmylou were all there, plus Larry Gatlin, who was breaking up his own family trio. We'd personally sent for some of our fans: schoolteacher Libby McKinney from North Carolina, our friend Lynn with the multiple personalities, and her sweet daughter Jamie.

Before leaving the venue, Wynonna, Ashley and I walked around thanking the staff, the stagehands, and our crew. I gathered up an armload of flowers from the dressing room to dry for a souvenir. We climbed into the *Dreamchaser* for the final ride home. As I waved to fans in the parking lot, I felt ever so much like Cinderella after the ball. I knew that soon my beautiful carriage would turn into a pumpkin.

We had only gone a few miles before we passed by the old

Rutherford County Hospital where I'd worked my last days as an R.N. I told Wy, Ashley, Larry, and Bud the story about driving there for my shift that Sunday afternoon in 1983 and hearing "Had a Dream" on the country countdown over my old car radio. They were dumbfounded by the remarkable coincidence that my nursing career and singing career ended within blocks of each other!

Just as we were approaching the large intersection, I saw the Krystal fast-food restaurant where I used to go at midnight after my shift, *if* I had any money. To celebrate my last night at the hospital, I threw myself a little graduation party. I dug enough change out of the glove compartment to get myself a hamburger and a drink. I didn't have enough to get fries.

Ashley suddenly sprang to her feet screaming: "Stop the bus!" The driver made a screeching left turn and the bus lumbered into the parking lot. The caravan of carloads of fans that stretched almost half a mile behind us followed suit. Still dressed in full stage regalia, Wynonna, Ashley, and I ceremoniously marched arm in arm into Krystal's.

Clerks at the counter froze in mid-motion, staring at us as if we were aliens from outer space. The local patrons seated in booths stopped chewing. As the three of us scanned the overhead menu, throngs of fans came rushing in till there was no more standing room. Since the three of us eschew fast-food fare, we were unsure what to order. Ashley finally decided, "Oh heck, we'll just take one of everything!" I stepped around into the kitchen saying a quick hello and tipping everyone, before we disappeared as miraculously as we'd appeared. It was an ironic twist of fate.

Just as we pulled out to head toward the farm I looked back over my shoulder in the direction of the old Rutherford County Hospital and had a very unnerving thought. Was that where I incurred the needle stick that gave me this hepatitis? Wynonna observed my pensiveness and disappeared into her bedroom. She returned wearing what she calls her "big-butt pajamas," cold cream all over her face, with her hair pulled up into a ponytail coming out of the top of her head. She knew it was my favorite end-of-the-day ritual.

Ashley sat on the couch, her arms folded across her chest

beaming proudly. Wynonna and I slumped in the booth exhausted yet exhilarated at the same time.

The driver told me as he pulled in at the farm gate: "I've been driving all my life, but this trip from your last concert to your farm was the longest drive I've ever had to make." Wy, Ashley, Larry, and I stood together on the front porch and watched the *Dreamchaser*'s taillights fade out of sight down our country road.

We got into our robes, sat around the kitchen table, thrilled to be reunited. Before we knew it the sun came up prompting Wy to holler: "Shew, here comes God with his brights on!"

The most magical day of our lives had slipped away. Wynonna declared: "Mom, all your training paid off, we're awarding you a gold medal."

Taking her face in my hands, I looked into her tired eyes and said, "December 4 was *Juddgment Day*, and your first name is no longer 'Naomi and Wynonna.' Your new name is now just 'Wynonna.' Tonight you made the emotional down payment on your solo career. Now you know that *you can do anything!*"

We all slept till noon and reconvened at the kitchen table, reading the newspaper accounts of the concert, answering all the congratulatory phone calls. The farewell concert on cable TV was the most successful music event in the history of pay-per-view. The next few days, we took walks together in Peaceful Valley and had the family time we'd missed before the concert. We called this period "the ember days," as we basked in the afterglow.

Saturday the 7th, we threw a Glory Party out in Peaceful Valley for the crew before they flew back to the West Coast. After a big dinner, we patted everyone on the back in a mock awards ceremony. We took a hayride to the back of the valley where we built a huge bonfire and roasted marshmallows.

Then it was sort of like after a funeral for me—when all the relatives go home, the flowers wilt, and everyone returns to his normal routines. I'd promised my doctors I'd check into the Mayo Clinic for a post–farewell concert exam and passed all my tests with flying colors.

I was left to install the photos in the scrapbooks, the newspaper clippings in the press books. Newspaper columnist Jack Hurst described the farewell concert as: "Riveting to its core." *Music City News* columnist Kimmy Wix called it: "A perfect show, if that's possible. One of the most memorable country performances of all time." Hard-nosed Bill Bell of the *New York Daily News* called me: "The last of the red-hot mommas."

Pop music critic David Barton said: "Wynonna choked on the first lines of 'Grandpa,' but as the song progressed her voice grew stronger as she forced out the lyrics, tears rolling down her cheeks. As she added her harmony, Naomi watched her daughter with love and care in her eyes, and at that moment the audience, television cameras, platinum records, and acclaim disappeared and her only concern seemed to be in helping her daughter through the emotional experience.

"It was a moment that one doesn't expect from a pay-per-view television special, but it was a deep, painfully real one, and it provided a memorable coda to what has been one of popular music's most dramatic stories."

Perhaps as so many observers have inferred, the Farewell Concert was a metaphorical sacrifice of myself so that Wynonna could find herself. It was a double trajectory. Although we would each graduate to our respective worlds, together we defined family.

Just as a mystical entity arose when Wynonna and I sang in harmony, so our lives and experiences together transcend the actual story you just read to reveal a higher truth. The Judds are a soaring paean to what happens when a fairy tale and grim reality collide.

Wynonna and I are the quintessential rags-to-riches story, tangible examples of the American dream, hope sellers, and living proof that it pays to believe in miracles. In our struggles, tragedies, and triumphs you glimpse the prospect of your own.

EPILOGUE

Every Ending Is a New Beginning

*T*HE LAST SONG divided our lives into a before and an after. That was then and this is now. It's fall of 1993 and enough has happened in the last two years to fill a second book!

At first, I strung together memories like precious pearls on a necklace and wore them proudly. I considered all the events of the past eight years, turning them over and over again in my mind like stones in the palm of my hand.

Then reality set in. The stage was gone. The fountain of life had dried up. I isolated myself at the farm going for days without seeing another living soul. As Henry David Thoreau said: "I had three chairs in my house: one for solitude, two for friendship, three for society." Although solitude is refreshment for the soul, I discovered the hard way that isolation weakens the spirit. Proverbs 18:14 says: "The spirit of a man will sustain his infirmity: but a broken spirit who can bear?"

In this long interlude of reflection, writing this book became a voyage of self-discovery on my journey to wholeness. Sometimes I felt like my displaced namesake, the Naomi of the Bible, who was searching for her homeland. Suffice it to say, I found what I was looking for, too. An old Zen adage says: "Enlightenment that can be described isn't enlightenment."

I do not consider myself an author. Words only exist because of their meaning. Once you've gotten the meaning you can forget about these words. I hope that long after the last page is turned, the message will remain.

The Judd aunts sold our ancestral home in Louisa, Kentucky. Now Wynonna and I, with our adjoining farms in Tennessee, feel it's up to us to become our generation's version of Pauline and Zora. I am deeply disturbed by the unkindness, materialism, and violence in our world. My philosophy is "Slow down, simplify, and be kind." I rarely wear makeup, I raise my own vegetables, and nature is my entertainment. I hang out with folks who ride in limousines only if someone in the family dies.

I have a secret meditation place hidden deep in the woods, where I go to ponder what Don Potter told me: "Sometimes the worst thing that happens to us is also the best." There's an exquisite Italian marble statue of a guardian angel there. We have wonderful visits, and she's the only one who hears me sing these days.

Ernie Stuart, our band bus driver, passed away of liver failure. I talked to him just a few hours before he died. Our lighting director Han Henze's mother, Diana, died of hepatitis C soon after. I promised them and all our other now-deceased friends that I would continue the struggle to find a cure for liver disease. With some of the revenues from the Farewell Concert, I've formed the Naomi Judd Research Fund.

I remain in remission, as the doctors scratch their heads in amazement. Since nothing has been found to kill the virus, I say it's rather like having a monster in the basement. I know it's down there, but I manage to keep it under control. Every day I try to translate my beliefs, visions, and values into physical proof of how the mind can heal the body.

We're at the crossroads where medicine, science, and spirituality are coming together as a new force for healing. Books like *Healing and the Mind* and the PBS series, of the same name by Bill Moyers, showed that we are indeed on the cusp of a medical revolution. Recognition of this long-overdue truth can help solve the health-care crisis America finds itself in today.

Nothing beats love. Love is the greatest healing power there is, nothing else comes close. Not ancient cures, modern medicines and technologies, or all the interesting books we read or the wise things we say and think. Love has a transformational power. It's helped me conquer all the battles in my life. Most recently it has even spared me from the dark night of the soul.

In January of 1992, only a month after the Judds' last song, Wynonna had to "face the music" alone. Scheduled to make her first solo appearance on the American Music Awards in Los Angeles, she was to perform the single "She Is His Only Need," from her debut album *Wynonna*. She was so anxious and fearful the night before the show, I had Wy and Ashley come to my hotel room. I turned out the lights, calmly sat them down on either side of me and played a song from our earliest musical beginnings back in Morrill, Kentucky. It was Ricky Skaggs singing a capella the old-time Appalachian song "Gospel Train."

"Remember who you are. Do not forsake your birthright," I reminded her gently. "God brought us this far. Now we who are the objects of his mercy should be the instruments of his praise."

Wy's album went platinum in just three days, out-selling Bruce Springsteen and Def Leppard's concurrent releases. Her first solo concert came a few months later in April 1992, in Midland, Texas. She was a basket case again. When it came time to go to the stage, as usual, she still couldn't find her left shoe. When I walked her to the steps, she was as nervous as we had been back in Omaha, Nebraska, prompting me to say: "Sweetheart, *life* is like singing in public for the first time!" Then I made her do Ferdinand the Bull. Knowing that she'd be on her own onstage the next seventy minutes, Wy asked if I had any parting words.

I replied: "Aw honey, you've found out the hard way now that Judd women always land on their feet. You'll be great!"

But Wy wasn't satisfied and snapped, "No, c'mon! Give me some *real* advice!"

I turned gravely serious, as if I were about to impart some ageless bit of maternal wisdom. Leaning forward confidentially, I said in solemn tones, *"Never,* never watch sausage being made!" With that I shoved her up the steps. I remained behind, gripping the rail, resisting the urge to follow.

Wynonna was singularly spectacular! She's like the qualities of her singing: powerful, unique, soulful, spontaneous, and unrehearsed. She keeps the audience on the edge of its seat because she exhibits that raw uncertainty of real life. Wy hired three superb backup singers to replace me, and her crack new band is fantastic. When she dedicated "All That Love from Here" to me in a performance that was rhapsodic, I sat spellbound at the side of the stage by the monitor board, watching from behind dark glasses so she couldn't see my tears when she kept looking over for approval.

That night in the Lone Star state, a lone star was born. It was a painful process, but as I told her afterward on the bus: "Birth is messy!" Larry can't get over the uncanny resemblance Wy bears to Elvis. Not only did Wynonna never meet Elvis, she never even listened to his records or saw him perform. Reviewers often refer to her audiences' response as "the second coming of Elvis." Critics compare Wy with Tina Turner, Etta James, and of course, Bonnie Raitt.

I stayed out on the road with Wynonna and held her hand for her first six shows. I promised, "I'll hold the lantern while you chip the wood." After the sixth concert, unbeknownst to her, I'd arranged to slip on back to Ashland with my mother. When Wy returned to the bus and found my good-bye note on her pillow, she went all to pieces. She paced the bus, tried to sleep in my bed, but couldn't. For the next year she wouldn't change anything in my room, insisting my tiara and scepter remain where I left them, poised on my pillow.

These last two years have been a roller-coaster ride for her as she returned alone to the same venues, the same hotels, the same truck stops. Although triumphantly successful on her own, she's still signing fans' photographs from our Farewell Tour, and answering the ever-present question, "How's your Mom?"

Wy just ordered a new bus. There was nothing wrong with the *Dreamchaser,* she said it was "haunted." It's hard not seeing each other for weeks, but I call almost every day and leave sweet or funny messages on the code-a-phone at her farm. Sometimes I just anonymously hum the melody to "Jesus Loves Me."

As Ashley predicted, America is experiencing Wynonnamania. Her debut album made history as the first studio country album by a female country artist to sell triple platinum, and her second one, *Tell Me Why,* shipped platinum. Recently when she performed in the

Washington, D.C., area, the new head of the CIA, the Honorable James Woolsey, came to her show. When he came up on the bus, she initiated the director of the CIA with my whoopie cushion. Yes, the torch is being passed!

And now I am Wynonna's biggest supporter. From behind her eyes I smile knowingly at the world who adores her. I sit at my kitchen table at the farm and read interviews in which she quotes me. I look up and grin at Larry, exclaiming: "Wow, she heard me after all!"

"The apple doesn't fall far from the tree," he responds.

Larry's now a manager and producer in the music industry and partners with Narvel Blackstock, Reba's husband. When I visit Larry's office, I get to see my friend Reba, whose office is just across the hall. Larry and I are closer than ever, and now it's my turn to support him in the music business.

Ashley is a shining star! During a hiatus from her NBC series, *Sisters,* the summer of 1991, she starred in an independent film, *Ruby in Paradise.* Although this introspective story of a young woman from east Tennessee was Ashley's first movie, it won the highest honor, Grand Jury Prize, at Robert Redford's prestigious Sundance Film Festival. Influential film critic, Roger Ebert, said she deserved to be nominated for an Academy Award for her starring role as Ruby. Ashley has created quite a sensation and become a media darling! She turns in a stunning performance as the lone survivor of a serial killers' massacre in the Oliver Stone movie *Natural Born Killers,* due out the summer of 1994. Ashley now travels the world impressing people with her breezy, articulate banter, gregarious natural charm, and peaceful stillness.

I sometimes sit in stunned amazement at how all this has happened. Because we extend in all directions, I call our family "The Four Winds": Wynonna's a singer, Ashley's an actress, Larry's a producer and a manager, and I'm a writer. I will always be an artist, blending together the colors of life, combining body, mind, and soul as if they're artistic materials to create new forms of power and beauty. I believe 2 Corinthians 5:17: "Therefore, if any man be in Christ, he is a new creature: old things are passed away; behold all things are become new."

In the beginning people knew us as a duo—Naomi and Wynonna. Then there was one—Wynonna. Now folks realize we're a trio—Naomi, Wynonna, and Ashley! I am more proud of my family as people than I am of their successes. Ashley rolls her eyes when I tell her, "I think it's great you know how to act up on the screen, but it's more important that you know how to act in real life!" I know that someday I'll be sitting in the front row at the Oscars, bursting with pride, as she makes her acceptance speech for Best Actress. In my mind, I'll be seeing my beautiful, bright, imaginative, and curious child tugging at my skirt hem asking: "Mommy, tell me another because!"

As Wynonna continues to break records and set new standards in country music, I am the first to proclaim: "Told you so!" And yet when I look at Hurricane Wynonna, the Countess of Hip, I see my funny kid who was always trying to hide her peas in her glass of milk. The world may idolize them, but to me they'll always be two laughing little sisters with black rings around their necks, hanging their heads out the window of the U-Haul making noises like a siren.

Ashley is the picture, Wynonna is the voice, I am the silence. And now the world hears the sound of one voice singing. Yet every night, sometimes around 8:00 P.M., in an empty auditorium in my mind, Wynonna and Naomi dance onto the stage. They share with me their love, laughter, life experiences, and music. For in my heart's quiet home, the Judds will live forever.